A MEDITATOR'S REFUGE

A Vipassana Insight Reference Guide
To Awaken Consciousness and Exit Samsara

ALAN CLEMENTS

———⊦⊦———

With selected teachings from
VENERABLE MAHASI SAYADAW of BURMA
and **VENERABLE SAYADAW U PANDITA**

Foreword **INGRID JORDT**
Assisted by **MARTINA HLAVCOVA**

WORLD DHARMA PUBLICATIONS

Published in 2024 by World Dharma Publications & Buddha Sasana Foundation
Copyright © Buddha Sasana Foundation (US registered non-profit 501 (c) (3))

Buddha Sasana Foundation (BSF) has asserted the right to be identified as the creator/caretaker of this Work in accordance with the Copyright, Designs and Patents Act 1988.

All rights reserved. No part of this publication may be reproduced, stored in a retrieval system, or transmitted in any form or by any means, electronic, mechanical, photocopying, recording or otherwise, without the prior written permission of the copyright creator/caretaker/owner.

Cover design by World Dharma Publications
Typography by World Dharma Publications

Library of Congress Cataloging-in-Publication Data

p. cm.

First printing: January 11, 2024

ISBN 978-1-953508-32-4

World Dharma Publications
www.WorldDharma.com

FOREWORD

In 2021, Alan was diagnosed with a terminal heart condition. Not a fuzzy prognosis that presages death like some distant inevitability, but a diagnosis of the immediate. Now. Death at any second.

What a gift.

Alan has used the time since his diagnosis to meditate on death and suffering, love and forgiveness, grieving and repair. In Hawaii he applied for the right to die by medically assisted release, thinking to consciously choose his own exit. He rethought this approach. Rather than opting for a path of certainty and self-command he entered the "most sacred conversation" he's ever had, choosing to be present in the realization that every moment is a moment closer to death. "Death will come at any second if you don't do anything."

In these past two years, Alan has been more productive than ever: three books, numerous talks, performances, films and retreats. "I wrote for my daughter, the children and people on this earth. I have this deep feeling of the embryo in life, the children, the birds, the trees, the ecosystem of this... feeling this deep integrated largeness. For me, my reason to be has been cultivating something from my own process alone on the road to a more inclusive dharma... Desmond Tutu... your freedom and mine are interconnected. It's one thing to do your own life. Co-relating to the multi-relationality called totality... it's not just about death alone but rebirthing. Aspire to the things you want to be known for in your memorial."

Upon first reading *A Meditator's Refuge – A Vipassana Insight Reference Guide To Awaken Consciousness and Exit Samsara*, I was filled with excitement and energy. The words elevated, recalibrated, and returned me to feeling the urgent necessity to practice "as though my head were on fire" and to freshen my mind in the wonder, reverence and awe of the Buddha's teachings.

Alan was one of my first Dhamma teachers, guiding me in the practice of vipassana when I was first introduced to it at 23. He recommended that I travel to Burma, where I would meet our teacher, U Pandita Sayadaw, the successor of Mahasi Sayadaw, Alan's preceptor when he was known as the monk, U Aggacāra. In the four decades that have elapsed since, Alan and I have aspired to be exemplary spiritual friends to one another, having resolved to support each other's practices until we reach nibbana. If you are lucky enough to have a spiritual friend, a noble friend, you have in that person a Dhamma refuge. For as the Buddha proclaimed, "Spiritual friendship is not half of the holy life, but the whole of the holy life."

True-hearted friendship is established upon mutual rejoicing in the Dhamma and the goal of awakening by effecting moral virtue, mental concentration, and wisdom. A spiritual friend serves as a virtuous exemplar, inspires and nurtures meditation and mental cultivation and motivates the aspiration for spiritual liberation. Imagine, therefore, a life bereft of spiritual friends who inspire, guide, encourage and help nurture for you the progress of Dhamma development and insight. Imagine, further, an interruption to the succession of wise practitioners of the Buddha's teachings, for the learning not to be passed down. Or for the teachings to be distorted to conform to present historical circumstances and its local preoccupations with power, politics, economy, society or psychic curiosity and wellbeing.

Yet, this inevitably is the way *samsara* unfolds. We are all ensnared in an infinite cycle of entangled mutual delusion. The dispensation of a Buddha's teachings (*sāsana*) is finite and exquisitely rare. It arises like a great blaze and then, through increasingly feeble efforts and spiritual capacity directed at keeping the blaze burning from one generation to the next, the *sāsana* slowly dies down, before extinguishing altogether.

Buddham saranam gacchami ~ I go for refuge to the Buddha;
Dhammam saranam gacchami ~ I go for refuge to the Dhamma;
Sangham saranam gacchami ~ I go for refuge to the Sangha.

Taking refuge in the Buddha (the fully enlightened teacher), the Dhamma (the Truth of cosmic law and order), and the Sangha (the monastic order that preserves and perpetuates the teachings in scriptures and practice) establishes a yogi's conscious sincerity of aim to commit to the practices of the teachings. And for such an aim to be fulfilled, there must be suitable circumstances for practice.

Alan and I had the opportunity to practice in Burma at a unique (and very brief) window in the country's history, and the history of the Buddha Sāsana. U Nu, Burma's first Prime Minister, had endeavored to promote the Buddha's teachings universally. With government support and the generosity of lay donors (such as Mahasi Sasana Yeiktha founder, Sir U Thwin, and many, many donors and supporters, as well as the Mahasi Sasana Yeiktha Nuggaha committee, and most especially the monks at Mahasi Yeiktha), all foreign yogis who sincerely desired to practice Vipassana meditation were provided with all the necessary requisites, that they might strive to realize the teachings of the Buddha *in this very life*.

Alan and I have often commented on how fleeting a moment that was, as we have watched Burma over the decades oscillate between periods of relative, if repressive, calm, and periodic descents into paroxysms of military violence and political destruction. During times of political unrest, or in seemingly arbitrary moments of relative calm, the military government would suddenly show up at the meditation center with a notice that foreigners must leave the country. Even during tranquil periods, we might be required to travel temporarily out of the country to renew a visa process that permitted only a few months stay at a time.

Tragically we have watched as our teachers departed this world one by one, extinguishing the living presence of Dhamma knowledge and wisdom of which they were luminous exemplars. The place of our spiritual refuge – Burma – seemed to us to have become the burning end of a world epoch in which Dhamma was practiced as a full and rich tradition, but which was now descending into chaos, much like the end of the World Age predicted in the texts.

We watched and witnessed: Alan writing about the fledgling

democracy movement and the military's resurgent attempts to subdue the citizens of the country, and I myself writing about the Mass Lay Meditation Movement and the military's efforts to subdue Buddhism in its conquest of the lifeworld in Burma.

Around the turn of the new century, we also witnessed novel transformations in Dhamma practice in the hands of a new generation of practitioners. These could be traced to the rare Dhamma missions that had brought the teachings of mindfulness practice – especially as codified by Mahasi Sayadaw – to America and the West. Bridging cultural and historical worlds, the Dhamma has been taken up with new significance, and ways of accommodating the life worlds of new practitioners. This is to be expected and welcomed. However, there are also teachings that have become mislaid, and can be recovered only with the efforts of learning, deep practice and monastic discipline. A monastic, meditative and scholarly tradition has a richness that cannot be conveyed by an app or a weekend retreat. It is in recognition of this deficit that Alan's anthology of Dhamma teachings and meditation practice is here offered as a *Meditator's Refuge*. As Alan related to me when approaching me to write this foreword, "Engage in *satipatthana* and you have a *kalyāṇamitta* [spiritual friend] here."

Aware of the shortness of time left to him, the *Meditator's Refuge* is Alan's mostly unedited handwritten entries into a notebook he kept for more than forty years. It is the teachings of the Buddha as handed down through canonical texts, commentary and practical discourses on meditation by Sri Lankan and Burman elders *(thera)* in the Theravada line.

Alan kept copious notes, hundreds of pages, relating to the right conditions for undertaking Satipatthana practice. At one time portions of his notes were confiscated by military authorities as he left the country, on one of the expulsions ordered by the *Tatmadaw* [trans. *Royal Armed Forces*, but really just Burmese military]. I recall how deeply he felt the loss of those handwritten notes of his meditations. Before the age of the internet and the immediately downloadable, living as a monk in a turbulent country meant rarity of access to a Buddhist library (with its white ant-eaten books). One needed to depend on one's own handwritten notes and memory to carry around the teachings.

As a monk, U Aggacara was frequently expelled from Burma, interrupting his meditation and training. In 1980, after having been given 24 hours to leave Burma, U Aggacara left for the famed Island Hermitage in Sri Lanka, one of the few places that afforded a refuge for foreign monks. There he spent a year in 1980-81 making ample use of the library, where he undertook painstaking efforts to transcribe key aspects of the Pali Canon and its commentaries. The notebooks were intended as a compendium to the practice in the event that he would no longer have access to the refuge of the teachers and the teachings of Burma. "I intuitively put together the book I would want to have as a compendium if I didn't have a teacher. It was desire driven by an intensive period of meditation. This book would refer me so that I could not get stuck in any particular *nyana* (insight level) and to navigate that. If I needed a *kalyāṇamitta* this book would serve it. I documented everything I could find that would support me to navigate the intensive meditation approach to consciousness. I included Abhidhamma and The Progress of Insight. I drew from what books were available at the time, which were Buddhaghosa, and Mahasi, then put in handwritten notes from a two-and-a-half-month retreat (where I took a lot of notes on how to approach intensive meditation)."

A Meditator's Refuge is an abridged compilation of sources reflecting the preoccupations of a yogi and a pure expression of *saṃvega* (spiritual urgency) in the context of uncertain access to teachers and teachings. Alan's impulse to carry away in a private notebook the most essential teachings that might lead to liberation continues the tradition of transmission.

The work is not over-edited. Nor is it intended to be comprehensive in the way that Burmese *Tipitika* (the definitive canonical collection of scripture of Theravada Buddhism) scholars or Buddhist academic scholars might attend to the meaning of every Pali word. There are other books for that. This is a notebook from personal experience, a streamlined version of what you need to know if you find yourself suddenly forced on a journey without access to the entire library of sources. In other words, it is a personal notebook for liberation when the unbearable weight of samsara and one's position in it (either as a wish for rebirth or a wish for death) can no longer be abided. It is a primer for release from the Conditioned.

Alan has been a teacher of Satipatthana meditation in the Burmese Mahasi tradition, and this has been the guiding force in his life.

Overview of Chapters

Chapter One begins with explanation of the *Dhammacakkappavattana Sutta*, the Four Noble Truths (the central insight leading to release from the cycle of rebirths through enlightenment) as expounded in the *Samyutta Nikāya* of the *Tipitika* Canon.

The second chapter provides an explanation of *Paticcasamuppāda* (Dependent Origination) and describes the causes of suffering.

Chapter Three elaborates upon the Fifty-Two mental factors (*Cetasika*) from the 5th c Buddhist scholar Buddhaghosa's commentary (*Atthasālinī*) found in his great treatise, the *Visuddhimagga* (The Path to Purification). Here Buddhaghosa expounds upon the *Dhammasangani*, the first book of the *Abhidhamma Pitaka*, which enumerates all mental and material phenomena and the four ultimate realities. Mahasi Sayadaw expands upon the Abhidhamma commentary to reiterate that ultimate, personally experienced phenomena is called an "ultimate reality," that "what truly exists."

The chapter on *cetasika* (mental factors which accompany consciousness) establishes the conditions of ultimate reality and of conventional reality (as these are based on conceptual illusions). It is a pivotal chapter in that it can be read as a kind of meditative reflection on kinds of wholesome, unwholesome and delusional or deceptive impressions of mental phenomena that we experience. And it establishes the grounds upon which the path of purification may be undertaken toward the goal of nibbana by "seeing things as they truly are."

Chapter Four is a treatise on Ultimate Realities (*paramattha*).

Chapters Five and Six enumerate the Requisites of Enlightenment and the 62 wrong views.

Chapters Seven and Eight itemize the concentrative meditations and the Knowledge of Supernormal Powers.

Chapters Nine through Seventeen concern how to undertake

satipatthana Vipassana practice. They explain how to practice and how to report the Stages of Insight and the explanation of these, including emotional reactions to Stages of Insight and experiences of insight, including the *Meditation Teacher's Diary* (Mahasi Sayadaw's compilation of thousands of yogis' experiences for pedagogical training purposes).

Chapter Eighteen, *A Meditator's Refuge – A Vipassana Insight Reference Guide To Awaken Consciousness and Exit Samsara*, is Alan's own extremely detailed and careful advice for undertaking practice based on his years of leading meditation retreats. Western yogis new to the practice will find this section particularly valuable as Alan deftly introduces the new yogi to intensive vipassana practice and comportment, as well as outlining the potential pitfalls to be avoided. These are written in the form of 274 aphorisms, admonishments and encouragements for practice.

The final chapters concern *kamma* as Action and Volition (based on the Pali Canon and commentaries by Ledi Sayadaw) and Death and Rebirth (as outlined in the *Visudhimagga*.)

The Passing Away of the Venerable Mahasi Sayadaw of Burma, written by Alan (Bhikkhu U Aggacara) in 1982, forms the concluding chapter. In it he relates the death of his teacher, preceptor and one of the great Buddhist saints of the 20th century. It is a fitting final chapter, reminding us that spiritual friends, mentors and teachers also pass on, and it is upon us to transmit what we have gained from them to future generations. *A Meditator's Refuge* is such a compendium, given to us by a life-long yogi and nibbana-striver. It is a wisdom capsule for those who might find themselves expelled from the places where Dhamma has long been established, and those who seek refuge in truth and dhamma striving.

May all beings be happy and free from suffering.

Ingrid Jordt
January 1, 2024
Berkeley, California

INTRODUCTION

In 2021, I was confronted with a revelation – a terminal heart condition, an immediate sentence to the embrace of death. Not a vague premonition of mortality, but an unequivocal diagnosis that whispered, "Now. Death is at your doorstep, poised to knock at any second."

Strangely enough, after the initial shock and tumultuous reflection, I welcomed it. What a gift it proved to be.

Since that fateful moment, most days transformed into a meditation on mortality, suffering, forgiveness, transcendence and love. Amidst the beauty of Hawaii, I found myself contemplating the delicate equilibrium between life and release, pondering whether to choreograph my own exit with a medically assisted final act. Yet, an alternate path beckoned – a path leading me into the depths of the most sacred discourse I've ever encountered: A dialogue with Death itself.

I opted for presence over command, yielding to the awareness that each fleeting moment propelled me closer to the inevitable end. "Death," I whispered to myself, "will arrive in a heartbeat if I remain stagnant."

In these fleeting two years, an unforeseen wave of vitality seized me, propelling me into creative artistry. Three books materialized, their pages a testament to my enduring love for my daughter, for Earth's progeny, for every living entity gracing this planet. A profound connection to life's essence took root within me – from delicate embryos to majestic trees, tender birdsongs to intricate ecosystems. My purpose crystallized into nurturing a more inclusive *Dharma*, weaving its threads into existence's expansive tapestry. Desmond Tutu's wisdom reverberated within – your freedom and mine, inseparable strands in the interconnected web. This voyage wasn't solely about embracing death; it was about (re-)birthing a new, aspiring to a living *Dhamma* - bringing freedom itself onto the world's memory in ways both human and profound.

The pages of *A Meditator's Refuge – A Vipassana Insight Reference Guide To Awaken Consciousness and Exit Samsara* stand witness to this odyssey. As I immersed myself in its assembly, along with the support of my *Dhamma* friend Martina Hlavcova, a heightened energy coursed through me, rekindling the passion of a lifelong pursuit. The words, akin to ancient Suttas, reignited the flame of urgency within, reminding me to practice "as though my head were ablaze." The teachings of Buddha, meticulously inscribed in this tome, reignited the awe, reverence, and wonder that have guided me since my first encounter with the Buddha's Four Noble Truths.

My *Dhamma* journey, interwoven with my beloved teachers and closest of allies, stands as a testament to the transformative power of noble friendship. In the realm of *Dhamma*, a true spiritual friend is a refuge, a guiding star that illuminates the path. For in the words of the Buddha, "Spiritual friendship is not half of the holy life, but the whole of the holy life." Such friendships are crafted from shared rejoicing in the *Dhamma*, a mutual dedication to moral virtue, mental clarity, and wisdom. It is a bond that nurtures meditation, kindles the flames of aspiration, and fuels the yearning for true liberation – freedom from defilements.

Time, that slippery magician, granted me a fleeting moment to immerse myself in the profound embrace of Burma (presently Myanmar), a sacred space where *Dhamma* flourished against the tapestry of shifting political currents. U Nu's vision – Burma's first Prime Minister – supported by benevolent visionaries and compassionate hearts, created Mahasi Sasana Yeiktha Meditation Center – an oasis where the wisdom of Mindfulness Meditation could bloom. But like whispers in the wind, those days of uninterrupted practice vanished, often disrupted by the unpredictable tides of political turmoil.

Amidst these tumultuous currents, my cherished teachers departed, one by one, carrying with them irreplaceable reservoirs of *Dhamma* wisdom. The once-bright torch of tradition began to flicker, threatened by the encroaching darkness of dictatorship, distortion and neglect. The cycle of *samsara*, with its veils of delusion, spun its relentless web, ensnaring the country in its illusions.

Yet, amidst this ebb and flow, my dedication to the *Dhamma* endured, unyielding. Over the years, I penned words that bore witness to Burma's struggle, documenting the dance between democracy and military might. Meanwhile, my long-time colleague Fergus Harlow and I chronicled the four-volume set, *'Burma's Voices of Freedom'*, recording the eternal struggle between freedom and forces that sought to subdue it. Together we watched and bore witness to the undulating currents that shape existence.

As the new period dawned, winds of change carried the teachings of mindfulness practice across continents and cultures. The *Dhamma*, like a skilled weaver, adapted and wove its threads into new tapestries, embracing diverse minds and hearts. Yet within this vibrant transformation, some threads risked fraying, and certain teachings threatened to slip through the cracks of time. In a world enamored with instant gratification, a monastic tradition's meditative richness, steeped in contemplation and scholarship, couldn't be encapsulated in an app or condensed into a weekend retreat.

It was this recognition, this yearning to preserve the essence of *Dhamma*, that birthed *'A Meditator's Refuge'*, an anthology of both personal notes and key teachings of my *Dhamma* teachers: not over-edited, but raw and personal, a whispered promise to fellow seekers who might one day find themselves journeying through the labyrinth of life without access to a wealth of teachings. This guide, a distillation of decades of handwritten notes and my teachers' key teachings on meditation and the progress if insight, serves as a companion for those who seek liberation when the weight of existence becomes unbearable.

My life as a meditator, a practitioner of Satipatthana in the Mahasi tradition, has culminated in this anthology. It opens with the Buddha's Four Noble Truths, the bedrock of wisdom that leads to Enlightenment, and delves into *Paticcasamuppāda*, unraveling the intricate tapestry of suffering. Chapters flow as humble rivulets of wisdom, exploring mental factors and ultimate realities, illuminating the path of intensive insight meditation practice. From concentrative meditations to insights into *Kamma*, death, and rebirth, these pages form a roadmap to liberation, a whispered promise to future seekers.

The urgency of these teachings is underscored by their source — a notebook and the most sacred teachings of my teachers, cherished and safeguarded even in the face of global turbulence. It all began in the hallowed sanctuary of the Island Hermitage in Sri Lanka in 1980, where I painstakingly transcribed key sections of Buddhist Canon and commentaries, preserving wisdom that might otherwise slip into oblivion. The notebook, a repository of insights, became a compass, guiding me through the intricate labyrinth of consciousness.

Today, as I offer *A Meditator's Refuge – A Vipassana Insight Reference Guide To Awaken Consciousness and Exit Samsara* to you, I reflect on the impermanence of it all. The fleeting moments, the elusive seconds, the rhythm of existence. Just as my dear teachers, Mahasi Sayadaw, Sayadaw U Pandita, Sayadaw U Javana, and Sayadaw U Sujata departed this realm, leaving behind a legacy of wisdom, so too shall we pass. But like the flame passed from candle to candle, the light of *Dhamma* endures, carried by those who have tasted its sweet nectar.

May this guidebook be your lantern in the darkness, illuminating your path of practice. May it be a bridge that spans generations, connecting seekers across time. In every page, in every word, may you find solace, guidance, and the unwavering assurance that the *Dhamma*, like a river of compassion, flows through eternity.

With metta,
Alan Clements
January 7, 2024
Ubud, Bali

TABLE OF CONTENTS

A Brief Introduction To Mahasi Sayadaw 15

1. **The Four Noble Truths** 17
   A. The Noble Truth of Suffering 17
   B. The Noble Truth of the Cause of Suffering 17
   C. The Noble Truth of the Cessation of Suffering 18
   D. The Noble Truth of the Path Leading to the Cessation
      of Suffering 18
      1. Right understanding/view 19
      2. Right thought 21
      3. Right speech 22
      4. Right action 23
      5. Right livelihood 23
      6. Right effort 24
      7. Right mindfulness 25
      8. Right concentration 25

2. **Dependent Origination** (PATICCA SAMUPPĀDA) 29
   A. The Arising of the Wheel of Existence (BHAVACAKRA) 29
   B. The Cessation of the Wheel of Existence 30

3. **The Fifty-Two Mental Factors** (CETASIKA) 39
   A. The Seven Universals (SABBA-CITTAKA) 41
   B. The Six Particulars (PAKINNAKĀ CETASIKAS) 49
   C. Explanation of the 14 AKUSALA CETASIKAS 58
   D. Explanation of the 25 KUSALA CETASIKAS 75

E. Relationship of the Mental Factors 83

4. Ultimate Realities (PARAMATTHA DHAMMAS) 87
A. Ultimate Reality 88
    1. Conceptual illusions.. 89
    2. Hearsay and such.. 92
    3. Description vs. experience.. 94
    4. The correct definition of ultimate reality............................. 97
    5. Transience 98
B. The Two Meanings of Activity... 101
    1. The meaning that ordinary people know 102
    2. The meaning that insight meditators know 102
C. Categories and Classification of Consciousness (CITTA) 104
D. All Types of Consciousness Classified 105
    1. Consciousness pertaining to the sense sphere
       (KĀMĀVACARA-CITTĀNI) 105
    2. 18 types of rootless consciousness (AHETUKA — CITTĀNI).... 107
    3. 24 types of beautiful (SOBHANA) CITTAS of the sensuous
       sphere (SOBHANA CITTĀNI) 108
    4. 15 types of form sphere consciousness of the JHĀNAS............. 111
    5. 12 types of formless sphere JHĀNA consciousness 112
    6. 8 types of supramundane consciousness (LOKUTTARA —
       CITTĀNI) 113
    7. Summary of consciousness classifications 114

5. Requisites of Enlightenment (BODHIPAKKHIYA — DHAMMA) 117
A. SATIPATTHANA ~ 4 Foundations of Mindfulness....................... 117
    1. KAYA — NUPASSANĀ — SATIPATTHANA............................... 117
    2. VEDĀNA — NUPASSANĀ — SATIPATTHANA........................... 120
    3. CITTA — NUPASSANĀ — SATIPATTHANA 121
    4. DHAMMA — NUPASSANĀ — SATIPATTHANA......................... 121
B. Explanation of the Four Right Efforts (SAMMAPPADHĀNA) 123
C. The Four Bases of Success (IDDHIPĀDA) 124
D. The Five Controlling Faculties (INDRIYA)................................ 125
E. The Five Mental Powers (BALA) 125

INTRODUCTION

   F. The Seven Factors of Enlightenment (BOJJHĀNGA) 126
   G. The Eight Path Factors 127

6. Enumeration of Sixty-Two Wrong Views 129
   A. Speculations about the Past (PUBBANTAKAPPIKA):
      ~ 18 Views 129
      1. Eternalism (SASSATAVĀDA): Views 1-4 129
      2. Partial – eternalism (EKACCASASSATAVĀDA):
          Views 5-8 130
      3. Doctrines of the finitude and infinity of the world
          (EKACCASASSATAVĀDA): Views 9-12 132
      4. Doctrines of endless equivocation (eel-wriggling):
          Views 13-16 133
      5. Doctrines of fortuitous (by chance) origination:
          Views 17-18 134
   B. Speculations about the Future (APARANTAKAPPIKA)
      ~ 44 Views 135
      1. Doctrines of percipient immortality (SAÑÑIVĀDA)
          ~ (Doctrines of conscious survival): Views 19-34 135
      2. Doctrines of non-percipient immortality (ASAÑÑIVĀDA)
          ~ (Doctrines of non-conscious survival): Views 35-42 135
      3. Doctrines of neither percipient nor non-percipient
          immortality (N'EVASAÑÑI NĀSAÑÑIVĀDA): Views 43-50 136
      4. Annihilationism (UCCHEVĀDA): Views 51-57 136
      5. Doctrines of NIBBĀNA here and now
          (DITTHADHAMMANIBBĀNAVĀDA): Views 58-62 137
   C. Summary of the 62 Views 139

7. Concentration 145
   A. Explanation of the earth KASINA (PATHAUT – KASINA
      – NIDDESA) 151
   B. Detailed Instructions for the Development of the Earth
      KASINA 152
   C. The First JHĀNA Explained 159
   D. Recollections (ANUSSATIS) 164
      1. Recollection of the attributes of the BUDDHA 164

    2. Recollection of the DHAMMA 169
    3. Recollection of the SANGHA 170
    4. Recollection of one's SĪLA (virtue) 171
    5. Recollection of one's CĀGA (generosity) 172
    6. Recollection of one's SADDHA (faith) 173
    7. Recollection of death (MARANA ANNUSATI) 174
    8. Contemplation on the 32 parts of the body 181
    9. Mindfulness of breathing 186
    10. Contemplation on the special qualities of NIBBĀNA 198
 E. The Four Divine Abidings (BRAHMA – VIHĀRAS) 199
    1. METTĀ (loving-kindness) 199
    2. KARUNĀ (compassion) 207
    3. MUDITĀ (sympathetic joy) 209
    4. UPEKKHĀ (equanimity) 210
   F. Reflection on Repulsiveness in Food – Nutriment 212
   G. Analysis of the Elements 218
   H. The Benefits of Developing Concentration 225

**8. Description of Direct Knowledge
– The Supernormal Powers 227**
A. The Five Kinds of Direct Knowledge 227
B. Method of Development (Brief) 228

9. The Meaning of SATIPATTHANA 231

10. Instructions to Insight Meditation 241

11. Practical Insight Meditation Basic Practice 253
A. Basic Practice Preparatory Stage 253
B. Basic Exercise I 255
C. Basic Exercise II 256
D. Basic Exercise III 257
E. Advancement in Contemplation 263
F. Basic Exercise IV 264
G. Summary 265

12. Five Benefits of Walking Meditation 267

INTRODUCTION

13. Guidance For The Meditator During the Interview Session 277

14. The Progress of Insight Through the Stages of Purification 325
  A. Purification of Conduct (SĪLA — VISUDDHI) 326
    1. Morality by Means of Abandonment 327
    2. Morality by Means of Abstinence 328
    3. Morality by Means of Mental Volition 328
    4. Morality by Means of Restraint 329
    5. Morality by Means of Non-Transgression 329
    6. Morality as Remote and Immediate Conditions for Concentration and Knowledges 330
    7. The Practice of Morality is Essential 331
  B. Purification of Mind (CITTA — VISUDDHI) 332
  C. Purification of View (DITTHI — VISUDDHI) 333
    1. Analytical knowledge of mind and body (NĀMA — RŪPA — PARICCHEDA — ÑĀNA) 333
  D. Purification by Overcoming Doubt (KANKHĀ — VITARANA — VISUDDHI) 336
    2. Knowledge by discerning conditionality (PACCAYA — PARIGGAHA — ÑĀNA) 336
    3. Knowledge by comprehension (SAMMASANAÑĀNA) 342
    4. Knowledge of arising and passing away (UDAYABBAYA — ÑĀNA) 350
  E. Purification by Knowledge and Vision of What Is Path and Not Path (MAGGĀMAGGA- ÑĀNADASSANA — VISUDDHI) 359
  F. Purification by Knowledge and Vision of the Course of Practice (PATIPADĀ — ÑĀNADASSANA — VISUDDHI) 360
    5. Knowledge of dissolution or passing away (BHANGA — ÑĀNA) 363
    6. Knowledge of fearfulness (BHAYA — ÑĀNA) 367
    7. Knowledge of misery (ĀDĪNAVA — ÑĀNA) 369
    8. Knowledge of disgust (NIBBIDĀ — ÑĀNA) 371
    9. Knowledge of desire for deliverance (MUÑCITU — KAMYATĀ — ÑĀNA) 373

      10. Knowledge of re-observation (PATISANKHĀ – ÑĀNA) 375
      11. Knowledge of equanimity about formations
          (SANKHĀRUPEKKHĀ – ÑĀNA) 381
      12. Insight leading to emergence (VUTTHĀNAGĀMINĪ
          – VIPASSANĀ – ÑĀNA) 391
      13. Knowledge of adaptation (ANULOMA – ÑĀNA) 396
      14. Maturity knowledge or "Change-of-lineage"
          (GOTRABHŪ – ÑĀNA) 398
  G. Purification by Knowledge and Vision (ÑĀNADASSANA –
     VISUDDHI) 401
     15. Path knowledge (MAGGA – ÑĀNA) 401
     16. Fruition knowledge (PHALA – ÑĀNA) 401
     17. Knowledge of reviewing (PACCAVEKKHANĀ – ÑĀNA) 404
  H. The Fetters and Their Eradication at the Various Stages
     of Enlightenment 408
  I. Seven Principles of Self – Examination Regarding the
     SOTĀPANNA Attainment (MAHĀPACCAVEKKHANĀ) 408

15. The Eighteen Great Insight Knowledges 419
A. The Seven Main Contemplations 420
    1. Contemplation of impermanence 420
    2. Contemplation of unsatisfactoriness 442
    3. Contemplation of not-self 445
    4. Contemplation of disenchantment 455
    5. Contemplation of dispassion 456
    6. Contemplation of cessation 458
    7. Contemplation of relinquishment 460
B. The Remaining Contemplations 466
    1. Contemplation of destruction 466
    2. Contemplation of fall 467
    3. Contemplation of change 468
    4. Contemplation of the signless 471
    5. Contemplation of the desireless 474
    6. Contemplation of emptiness 474
    7. Insight into phenomena that is higher wisdom 475
    8. Knowledge and vision of things as they really are 475

    9. Contemplation of danger 476
    10. Contemplation of reflection 477
    11. Contemplation of turning away 480

16. Insight **483**
  A. Mind and Body 483
  B. Cause and Effect 484
  C. Effects of Concentration 487
  D. Seeing the Three Characteristics 488
  E. Distractions from the Path 491
  F. Disappearance 493
  G. Disillusionment 495
  H. Looking for Relief 497
  I. Equanimity 498

17. Nibbāna **503**
  A. The Experience of NIBBĀNA 503
  B. Entering Fruition 506
  C. Clarifying the Insight Knowledges 508
  D. Practicing for Higher Paths and Fruitions 509
  E. A Note on PĀRAMĪ 512
  F. Definitions of NIBBĀNA 513
  G. Two types of NIBBĀNA 518
  H. Experiencing NIBBĀNA 522

18. Meditation Teacher's Record Book **527**
  A. Three Types of Yogis 532
  B. NĀMA-RŪPA-PARICCHEDA-ÑĀNA (The Knowledge That
     Distinguishes Between Mind and Matter) 533
  C. PACCAYA PARIGGAHA ÑĀNA (The Knowledge That
     Distinguishes Between Cause and Effect) 547
  D. SAMMASANA ÑĀNA (Investigation Knowledge) 554
  E. UDAYABBAYA ÑĀNA (The Knowledge Aware of the Arising
     and Passing Away Phenomena) 565
  F. BHANGA ÑĀNA (The Knowledge That Was Aware of
     Dissolution) 588

G. BHAYA ÑĀNA (The Knowledge of Awareness of Fearfulness) 595
H. ĀDĪNAVA ÑĀNA (Knowledge of Misery) 596
I. NIBBIDĀ ÑĀNA (The Knowledge of Wearisomeness or Disgust) 597
J. MUÑCITU KAMYATĀ ÑĀNA (Knowledge of the Desire for Deliverance) 600
K. PATISANKHĀ ÑĀNA (Knowledge of Re-observation) 602
L. SANKHĀRUPEKKHĀ ÑĀNA (The Knowledge that Can View Psycho-Physical Phenomena With Equanimity) 606
M. ANULOMA ÑĀNA (The Linkage) 613
N. GOTRABHU ÑĀNA 616
O. MAGGA ÑĀNA 616
P. PHALA ÑĀNA 616
Q. ARIYA BHUMI 620
R. Summary 627

19. A Meditator's Guide to Intensive Practice 633

20. Kamma 719
Definition of KAMMA/CETANĀ ~ Action ~ Volition 719
A. VIPĀKA – Fruit or Result 721
B. KAMMA/VIPĀKA (ABHIDHAMMA Classification) 723
C. The Cause of KAMMA 724
D. The Doer of KAMMA/ Who Reaps the Result 724
E. Where is KAMMA? 724
F. The Results of KAMMA are Unthinkable 725
G. Is Everything Due to KAMMA? 725
H. The Five-fold Cosmic Order (NIYĀMA-DIPANI) 726
I. The Six Roots of KAMMA 730
J. The Cause of Inequality, Variation and Diversity Among Beings 733
K. The Ten Ways of Action (10 AKUSALA, 10 KUSALA) 736
L. Ten Ways of Moral Action (KUSALA KAMMA) 741
M. The Sense-Door Thought Process (CITTAVĪTHI) 743
N. Classification of KAMMA 758
O. Classification of KAMMA With Reference to Its Time of Operation 760

INTRODUCTION

P. Classification of KAMMA According to Its Function (KICCA) 762
Q. Classification of KAMMA According to the Order
   That KAMMA Takes to Come to Fruition 764
R. The Nature of KAMMA 767
S. Concluding Points About KAMMA 771
Z. KAMMA Quotations, Examples, Illustrating Points 772

21. Death and Rebirth **775**
A. Definition of Death 775
B. Causes of Death According to Dependent Origination 777
C. Death Signs Appearing at the Dying Moments 780
D. How the Thought-Process at Death Functions 781
   1. CUTI − CITTA (death consciousness) ~ PATISANDHI
      − CITTA (rebirth consciousness) 783
E. Planes of Existence 785
F. Explanation of the Various Planes of Existence 788
   1. Time in relationship to existence 794

**22. The Passing Away of the Venerable Mahasi Sayadaw
   of Burma** **797**

A BRIEF INTRODUCTION TO MAHASI SAYADAW

THE VENERABLE MAHĀSI SAYADAW, one of the foremost Burmese monks of the twentieth century, played a critical role in disseminating the liberation teachings of early Buddhism. He was a rare example of someone who combined the most extensive and thorough knowledge of the Pali texts with the wisdom that comes from the deepest realizations of meditation. The range of both his theoretical and practical understanding was acknowledged when he was asked to be the chief questioner at the Sixth Buddhist Council, held in Yangon in 1954.

In his teaching role Mahāsi Sayadaw was largely responsible for the widespread practice of Vipassanā, or Insight Meditation. In Burma he established hundreds of meditation centers around the country where ordinary lay practitioners, as well as monastics, could come and receive instruction and guidance in Satipaṭṭhāna meditation, the practice of the Four Foundations of Mindfulness, which the Buddha declared to be the direct path to liberation. In these centers and those in other Asian countries, hundreds of thousands of people were introduced to this meditation practice. Through his disciples these teachings were later brought to the world.

Chapter One: An explanation of the *Dhammacakkappavattana Sutta*, the Four Noble Truths (the central insight leading to release from the cycle of rebirths through enlightenment) as expounded in the *Samyutta Nikāya* of the *Tipitika* Canon.

DUKKHA is usually translated as suffering ~ but suffering does not convey the subtle extension of meaning which DUKKHA has. Some things are DUKKHA but not suffering: A pleasant feeling is not suffering but is DUKKHA because it is ANICCA.

1.
THE FOUR NOBLE TRUTHS

A. The Noble Truth of Suffering

A – Births is suffering ~ first appearance of 1 or more KHANDAS
B – Old age is suffering ~ decay of beings
C – Death is suffering ~ disappearance of KHANDAS, breaking-up
D – Sorrow is suffering ~ mental distress, inward woe
E – Lamentation is suffering ~ mourning for the loss of loved ones, etc.
F – Pain is suffering ~ the painful and unpleasant produced by bodily contact
G – Grief is suffering ~ the painful and unpleasant produced by mental contact
H – Despair is suffering ~ intense mental suffering
I – Association with the undesired is suffering
J – Separation from the desired / loved is suffering
K – Not to get what one wants is suffering
L – In short, the five aggregates of grasping are suffering

B. The Noble Truth of the Cause of Suffering

A – It is craving / desiring / thirsting / wanting which gives rise to fresh rebirth
    1- Sensual craving
    2- Craving for existence
    3- Craving for self-annihilation
B – Bound up with pleasure and lust

C – Taking delight in sights, sounds, smells, flavors, bodily sensations and mental formations

D – Through craving / grasping / clinging, attachment arises, of which there are four kinds:
  1- Attachment to sense pleasures
  2- Attachment to wrong views, opinions and preconceptions
  3- Attachment to rites and rituals / wrong paths and practices
  4- Attachment to the belief in a self or individual entity

C. The Noble Truth of the Cessation of Suffering

This, BHIKKHUS, is the noble truth of the cessation of suffering:
IDAM KHO PANA, BHIKKHAVE, DUKKHANIRODHAṂ ARIYASACCAṂ

The complete cessation / giving up / abandonment of that craving, complete release from that craving and complete detachment from it:
YO TASSĀ Y'EVA TANHĀYA ASESA ~ VIRĀGANIRODHO, CĀGO, PATINISSAGGO, MUTTI, ANĀLAYO

For through the total fading away and cessation of craving, clinging / grasping / attachment (rooted in greed, hatred, delusion) ceases; through the cessation of rebirth, decay and death / sorrow / lamentation / pain / grief / despair cease: Thus, comes about the complete cessation of this whole mass of suffering. (Sam. Nik. XII)]

D. The Noble Truth of the Path Leading to the Cessation of Suffering

A – This, BHIKKHUS, is the noble truth of the path leading to the cessation of suffering:

IDAM KHO PANA, BHIKKHAVE, DUKKHANIRODHAGĀ-MINT PATIPADĀ ARIYASACCAṂ

It is the noble eightfold path, namely:
  1- Right understanding SAMMĀ DITTH
  2- Right thought SAMMĀ SAṄKAPPA
  3- Right speech SAMMĀ VĀCĀ

4- Right action SAMMĀ KAMMANTA
5- Right livelihood SAMMĀ ĀJĪVA
6- Right effort SAMMĀ VĀYĀMA
7- Right mindfulness SAMMĀ SATI
8- Right concentration SAMMĀ SAMĀDHI

Truly, BHIKKHUS, this middle way understood by the TATHĀGATA produces vision, produces knowledge, and leads to calm, penetration, enlightenment, NIBBĀNA:

AYAṂ KHO SĀ, BHIKKHAVE, MAJJHIMĀ PATIPADĀ
TATHĀGATENA ABHISAMBUDDHĀ CAKKHUKARANĪ,
ÑĀNAKARANĪ, UPASAMĀYA, ABHIÑÑĀYA, SAMBODHĀYA,
NIBBĀNĀYA SAṂVATTATI

1. Right understanding/view

There are three kinds:
1. A. All beings are the owners of their KAMMAS (the wholesome and the unwholesome KAMMAS done by beings belong to them and always accompany them on their wanderings in SAMSARA.) KAMMA cannot be taken from the doer or destroyed for it is imprinted on his mental continuity and will fruit when conditions permit. KAMMAS are mental, verbal and bodily volitional actions.
    B. All beings are the heirs to their KAMMAS (wholesome and unwholesome KAMMAS done by beings are their inherited properties that always accompany them wherever they may wander in this SAMSARA.) KAMMA is the only property inherited by beings during their future rebirths.
    C. All beings are born of their KAMMAS (only the wholesome and unwholesome KAMMAS made by beings are the cause of their continued rebirths in SAMSARA).
    D. All beings are related to their KAMMAS (only one's own bodily, verbal and mental KAMMAS are constant companions who accompany one and result in happiness and prosperity or unhappiness / misery / poverty in one's future lives).

E. All beings are supported by their KAMMAS (wholesome and unwholesome KAMMAS made by beings are their real support wherever they may wander through many lives and world-cycles.) They are supported by their KAMMAS: This means they can be relied upon. If wholesome they can take shelter in and give protection against physical and mental affliction ~ for long life, available food, drink, medicines, etc. One relies on present KAMMA to assist one in obtaining favorable conditions thus giving alms, cultivating SILA and practicing BHĀVANĀ is one's work. Therefore, these actions will be one's support. One can take refuge in four things: BUDDHA, DHAMMA, SANGHA ~ and one's wholesome KAMMAS.

These 5 first statements refer to past KAMMA which fruits in the present time.

The following statement concerns present KAMMA which will fruit in the future.

F. Whatever KAMMAS beings shall do – whether wholesome or unwholesome – of that they will be the heirs. Whether bodily, verbal or mental KAMMAS that have been made, those beings who individually made them will receive the fruits of them, even after many lives or eons.

~ End of the first characteristic of right understanding ~

2. Having a correct understanding and right view of the ten subjects
   1) There is (moral significance in) almsgiving / generosity.
   2) There is (moral significance in) large offerings.
   3) There is (moral significance in) small gifts.
   4) There is the result of wholesome and unwholesome KAMMAS. (This means the right view that unwholesome bodily, verbal and mental volitions done in previous lives yield painful results in future lives, while refraining from such unwholesome KAMMAS and cultivating wholesome KAMMAS subsequently bears the fruit of happiness.)

5) & 6) There is moral significance in what is done to one's mother and father.
7) There are beings of instantaneous rebirth (due to the force of their previous KAMMA. These beings are born ~ at approximately age 16 ~ complete with limbs and other organs of the body which need not develop further but remain as they are ~ DEVAS and BRAHMAS: These are usually invisible to humans.)
8) There is this world.
9) There is another world. ('This world' means this world system with its human plane, the 4 lower worlds, 6 DEVA worlds and 20 BRAHMA planes, while in all directions from this world system there are an infinite number of other world systems which are called 'the other worlds').
10) There are beings in the world who, having realized by their own power of concentration, insight and ABHIÑÑA the truth regarding this world and other worlds, make it known to others (i.e., Enlightened beings).

~ End of the SECOND characteristic of right understanding ~

3. Having a correct understanding and right view of the Four Noble Truths
   1) Knowledge of real DUKKHA
   2) Knowledge of the true causal arising of DUKKHA
   3) Knowledge of the cessation of DUKKHA
   4) Knowledge of the right path leading to the cessation of DUKKHA

~ End explanation of right understanding ~

2. Right thought

This is explained under three headings:
1. Thoughts of renunciation (i.e. Generosity) NEKKHAMMA SAṄKAPPA: the mental state where there is absence of greed and

ability therefore to renounce the five sense pleasures ~ i.e., pleasant sight, sound, smell, taste, touch ~ to renounce attachment to the 5 aggregates ~ renunciation of mind and body. Renunciation is interior renunciation, the ability to loosen one's greed and attachment to things, so it is possible to become generous in giving to others.)
2. Thoughts of harmlessness (METTĀ) or good-will ~ ABYĀPĀDA SAṄKAPPA: The mind or heart which wishes the happiness, peace and freedom for all sentient beings without distinction.
3. Thoughts of non-violence and compassion (KARUNĀ AVIHIMM-SA SAṄKAPPA: Touching the DUKKHA of all sentient beings with compassion.

~ End explanation of right thought ~

3. Right speech
There are four types of right speech:
1. Abstinence from falsehood ~ (MUSĀVĀDAVIRATI) ~ This means abstaining from speaking untruth so as to make it appear as truth, and speaking of truth as though it were untruth.
2. Abstinence from back-biting ~ (PISUNAVĀCĀVIRATI) ~ This means abstaining from the kind of speech which makes two friends lose confidence in, and regard for, each other; speech which creates dissension between two people. This includes tale bearing.
3. Abstinence from offensive, abusive and harsh words ~ (PHA-RUSAVĀCĀVIRATI).
4. Abstinence from frivolous talk or useless chatter ~ (SAMPHAP-PALĀPAVIRATI) ~ This means abstaining from speech which contains no:
    a) words relating to worthy goals i.e., long life, health, proper livelihood, etc.
    b) words relating to DHAMMA i.e., words that relate to ways and means for attainment of beneficial results
    c) words relating to good conduct (i.e., words that instruct one for the removal of greed, hatred and delusion for the betterment

of those who listen to them: As opposed to words meant only for the sheer entertainment of the listeners (i.e., novels, plays, some music and movies included): Simply, words that inspire DHAMMA and words that don't.

4. Right action
This is threefold:
1. Restraint from intentionally taking the life of any living creatures by physical action or verbal incitement i.e., causing abortion, killing eggs, etc.
2. Restraint from 'taking that which is not given' with the intention of stealing any property in the possession of the owner, without the knowledge of the owner, either by physical exertion or verbal incitement.
3. Restraint from sexual misconduct (abstention from causing suffering to other beings out of one's greed, craving or desire for pleasant sensations ~ sexual as well as pleasures of the other senses. Included here also is the abstention from the ingestion of intoxicating substances, and gambling).
    ***Note regarding the use of intoxicants: the Middle Way is not meant as 'drinking in moderation' ~ i.e., avoiding the extremes of drunkenness and total abstention. A comparative example: not wholesale murder or total abstention from it, just 'killing in moderation'! (This is a tricky and sensitive point).

~ End explanation of right action ~

5. Right livelihood
There are four kinds:
1. Restraint from livelihood based on wrong conduct ~ (DUCCA-RITAMICCHĀJĪVA VIRATI). Wrong conduct means either the threefold unwholesome bodily action beginning with killing living creatures, or the fourfold unwholesome verbal actions. ~ Any livelihood gained in this way will be wrong. So will be making a living by

the sale of the 5 kinds of merchandise: a) weapons b) living beings c) meat d) intoxicants e) poisons. When one abstains from such wrong conduct in livelihood, right livelihood is practiced.

2. Restraint from livelihood based on improper means ~ (ANESANAMICCHĀJĪVA VIRATI). This refers to the ways of wrong livelihood not to be practiced by the BHIKKHUS and Anagarikas: 21 kinds of wrong livelihood for BHIKKHUS called ANESANA, such as giving fruit and flowers to families, or medical preparations, or flattering them in some way, or acting as a messenger ~ with the hopes of increasing one's gains.

3. Restraint from livelihood based on deception of others ~ (KUHANĀDIMICCHĀJĪVA VIRATI). There are five sorts of deception:
   - KUHANA (deception by working wonders; fraudulently obtaining gifts by making people think that one possesses extraordinary qualities such as high virtue, JHĀNAS, or the Noble Paths and fruits, causing people to have a high opinion of oneself, deceptively acquired.)
   - LAPANA (shameless talk which pleases donors so that they make a gift.)
   - NIMITTA (making hints and gestures to invite offerings)
   - NIPPESANA (harassing with words so that one is obliged to give gifts)
   - LĀBHENA LĀBHA NUIGISANA (giving a small gift to get a bigger one). Abstinence of such wrongful and deceptive means of livelihood is Right Livelihood.

4. Restraint from livelihood based on low worldly knowledge ~ (TIRACCHĀNAVĪJA MICCHĀJĪVA VIRATI). This is a livelihood based on the predictive arts ~ palmistry, interpreting bodily marks, astrology, etc.

6. Right effort
This can be analyzed into four components:
1. Avoiding (to practice the 8-fold path with the intention to avoid unwholesome conduct in its 10 modes, from arising in this life or following existences).
2. Overcoming (to practice the 8-fold path with the intention to prevent AKUSALA ~ which has not yet arisen, but is liable to arise in the future ~ from arising at all until ARAHATTA is attained).
3. Developing (to make an effort in developing unrisen higher mental purities).
4. Maintaining (to make an effort to maintain one's SĪLA ~ SAMĀDHI ~ PAÑÑĀ until ARAHATTA). Effort is only one DHAMMA factor; above are its various functions.

~ End of explanation of right effort ~

7. Right mindfulness
There are four SATIPATTHĀNAS:
1. Mindfulness of the body (KĀYĀNUPASSANĀ SATIPATTHĀNA)
2. Mindfulness of feeling (VEDANĀNUPASSANĀ SATIPATTHĀNA)
3. Mindfulness of consciousness (CITTĀNUPASSANĀ SATIPATTHĀNA)
4. Mindfulness of mental objects / DHAMMAS (DHAMMĀNUPASSANĀ SATIPATTHĀNA)

8. Right concentration
This is developed by means of three stages:
1. PARIKAMMA ~ BHĀVANĀ ~ Preparatory work on development.
2. UPACĀRA ~ BHĀVANĀ ~ Access concentration and its development.
3. APPANĀ ~ BHĀVANĀ JHĀNA: Attainment of concentration and its development via the 25 meditation subjects ~ KAMMATTHĀNA

that lead one to the attainment of at least the first JHĀNA (40 subjects total)
- 10 KASINAS ~ 4 colors ~ 4 elements ~ space and light
- 10 ASUBHAS ~ repulsiveness of the body
- 1 contemplation on the 32 body parts
- 1 ANAPANĀ SATI
- 3 BRAHMA VIHARAS ~ METTĀ, KARUNĀ, MUDITĀ

~ End explanation of the Four Noble Truths ~

The second chapter provides an explanation of *Paticcasamuppāda* (Dependent Origination) and describes the causes of suffering.

2.
DEPENDENT ORIGINATION
(PATICCA SAMUPPĀDA)

A. The Arising of the Wheel of Existence (BHAVACAKRA)

A – Dependent on ignorance (AVIJJA) arises volitional formations. (SANKHĀRA)

B – Dependent on volitional formations arises rebirth consciousness. (VIÑÑĀNA)

C – Dependent on consciousness arises mental and physical phenomena. (NĀMA~RŪPA)

D – Dependent on mental and physical phenomena arise the six-sense bases. (SALĀYATANA)

E – Dependent on the six-sense bases arises contact. (PHASSA)

F – Dependent on contact arises feeling. (VEDANĀ)

G – Dependent on feeling arises craving. (TANHĀ)

H – Dependent on craving arises clinging / grasping / attachment. (UPĀDĀNA)

I – Dependent on clinging arises becoming / volitional actions. (BHAVO)

J – Dependent on becoming arises rebirth. (JĀTI)

K – Dependent on rebirth arises old age (JĀRA), death (MARANAM), sorrow (SOKA), lamentation (PARIDEVA), pain (DUKKHA), grief (DOMANASSA) and despair (UPĀYĀSA).

~ Thus, there is the arising of the whole mass of suffering ~

B. The Cessation of the Wheel of Existence

A – Through the entire cessation of ignorance, volitional formations cease.
B – Through the cessation of volitional formations, rebirth consciousness ceases.
C – Through the cessation of rebirth consciousness, NĀMA~RŪPA ceases.
D – Through the cessation of NĀMA~RŪPA, the six-sense bases cease.
E – Through the cessation of the six-sense bases, contact ceases.
F – Through the cessation of contact, feeling ceases.
G – Through the cessation of feeling, craving ceases.
H – Through the cessation of craving, clinging / attachment ceases.
I – Through the cessation of clinging, becoming / volitional actions ceases.
J – Through the cessation of becoming, birth ceases.
K – Through the cessation of birth, old age, death, sorrow, lamentation, pain, grief and despair cease.

~ Thus, there is the complete cessation of this whole mass of suffering

Complete explanation of above factors:

A – Through ignorance, volitional formations arise. (AVIJJA PACCAYĀ SAṄKHĀRA)
  i) What is meant by 'ignorance':
     a. Not knowing the Noble Truth of DUKKHA
     b. Not knowing the Noble Truth of the Origin of DUKKHA
     c. Not knowing the Noble Truth of the Cessation of DUKKHA
     d. Not knowing the Noble Truth of the Path leading to the Cessation of DUKKHA
  ii) What is meant by 'through ignorance, volitional formations arise':

There are six kinds of Volitional / KAMMA formations:
  a. Formations of merit (PUNNABHISAṄKHĀRĀ): ~ Wholesome volitions in the sensuous sphere (KĀMĀVACARA) and the form sphere (RŪPAVACARA), culminating in generosity (DĀNA), morality (SĪLA) and mental development (BHĀVANĀ).

2. DEPENDENT ORIGINATION (PATICCA SAMUPPĀDA)

    b. Formations of demerit (APUNNABHISAṄKHĀRĀ): ~ Unwholesome volitional activities motivated by any form of anger (DOSA), greed (LOBHA), and delusion (MOHA).
    c. Formations of the imperturbable (ĀNEÑUABHISANKHĀRĀ): ~ Wholesome actions (CETANA) in practicing JHĀNIC (APPANA) concentration in the formless sphere.
    d. Bodily formations (KĀYASANKHĀRĀ): ~ Volitions connected with physical action.
    e. Verbal formations (VACĪSANKHĀRĀ): ~ Volitions connected with speech.
    f. Mental formations (CITTASANKHĀRĀ): ~ Volitions that arise in the mind – not connected with body or speech.

B – Through volitional / KAMMA formations, consciousness arises. Six types of consciousness arise through volitional formations:
    1. Eye consciousness (CAKKHU – VIÑÑĀNAM)
    2. Ear consciousness (SOTA – VIÑÑĀNAM)
    3. Nose consciousness (GHĀNA – VIÑÑĀNAM)
    4. Tongue consciousness (JIVHA – VIÑÑĀNAM)
    5. Body consciousness (KĀYA – VIÑÑĀNAM)
    6. Mind consciousness (MANO – VIÑÑĀNAM)

C – Through consciousness, mental and physical phenomena arise: (VIÑÑĀNA PACCAYĀ NAMARŪPAṂ)
    i) Mental phenomena are 4 in number
        a. Feeling aggregate (VEDANAKKHANDHA) ~ Three kinds:
        * Pleasant Feeling
        * Unpleasant Feeling
        * Neither Pleasant nor Unpleasant Feeling.
        b. Perception aggregate (SAÑÑAKKHANDHA)
        c. Mental volitional formations aggregate (SANKHĀRAKKHANDHA) ~ The remaining 50 CETASIKAS excluding the above two
        d. Consciousness aggregate (VIÑÑĀNAKKHANDHA)
    ii) Physical phenomena are 28 in number: 4 primary elements and 24 secondary.

a. The four great primary elements (MAHA- BHŪTA)
   1. Earth element ~ of extension (PATHAVI DHATU).
   2. Water element ~ of cohesion (APO DHATU).
   3. Fire element ~ of temperature (TEJO DHATU).
   4. Air element ~ of support / motion (VAYO DHATU).
b. The 24 secondary elements which are derived from and dependent on the 4 great primary elements (UPĀDAYA RŪPANI):
   1. Eye base (CAKKHĀYATANAṂ)
   2. Ear base (SOTĀYATANAṂ)
   3. Nose base (GHĀNĀYATANAṂ)
   4. Tongue base (JIVHĀYATANAṂ)
   5. Body base (KĀYAYATANAṂ)
   6. Heart base (HADAYA VATHU)
   7. Male sex (PUM BHĀVA)
   8. Female sex (ITTHI BHĀVA)
   9. Vital force (JIVITA)
   10. Nutrition (AHĀRA RŪPA)
   11. Visible form (RŪPA)
   12. Sound (SADDA)
   13. Odor (GANDHA)
   14. Taste (RASA)
   15. Element of space (AKASA DHĀTU)
   16. Intimation through body (KĀYA VIÑÑĀTTI)
   17. Intimation through speech (VACĪ VIÑÑĀTTI)
   18. Lightness (LAHUTĀ ~ (VIKĀRA RŪPA)
   19. Pliancy (MUDUTĀ)
   20. Adaptability (KAMMAÑÑATĀ)
   21. Growth of corporeality (UPACAYA RŪPA)
   22. Continuance (SANTATI RŪPA)
   23. Decay (JARATĀ)
   24. Impermanence (ANICCATĀ)

D – Through mental and physical phenomena, the six-sense bases arise: (NĀMARŪPA PACCAYĀ SALĀYATANAṂ).
There are six bases:

2. DEPENDENT ORIGINATION (PATICCA SAMUPPĀDA)

1. Eye base
2. Ear base
3. Nose base
4. Tongue base
5. Body base
6. Mind base

E – Through the six-sense bases, contact arises (SALĀYATANA PACCAYĀ PHASSO).
 There are six kinds of contact:
 1. Eye contact (CAKKHU- SAMPHASSO)
 2. Ear contact (SOTA- SAMPHASSO)
 3. Nose contact (GHĀNA- SAMPHASSO)
 4. Tongue Contact (JIVHĀ- SAMPHASSO)
 5. Body Contact (KĀYA- SAMPHASSO)
 6. Mind Contact (MANO- SAMPHASSO)

F – Through contact, feeling arises (PHASSA PACCAYĀ VEDANĀ).
 Feelings (Pleasant ~ Unpleasant ~ Neutral) arise, caused by:
 1. Eye contact (CAKKHU SAMPHASSAJĀ VEDANĀ)
 2. Ear contact (SOTA SAMPHASSAJĀ VEDANĀ)
 3. Nose contact (GHĀNA SAMPHASSAJĀ VEDANĀ)
 4. Tongue contact (JIVHĀ SAMPHASSAJĀ VEDANĀ)
 5. Bodily contact (KĀYA SAMPHASSAJĀ VEDANĀ)
 6. Mind contact (MANO SAMPHASSAJĀ VEDANĀ)

G – Through feeling, craving arises (VEDANĀ PACCAYĀ TANHĀ).
 There are six kinds of cravings:
 1. Craving for visible objects (RŪPA TANHĀ)
 2. Craving for sounds (SADDA TANHĀ)
 3. Craving for smells (GHĀNA TANHĀ)
 4. Craving for tastes (RASA TANHĀ)
 5. Craving for bodily Contact (PHOTTABBA TANHĀ)
 6. Craving for mental Objects (DHAMMA TANHĀ)

H – Through craving, clinging / grasping /attachment arises (TANHĀ PACCAYĀ UPĀDĀNAM)

There are four types of clinging/attachment:
1. Clinging to sensual pleasures (KĀMUPĀDĀNAM)
2. Clinging to wrong views (DITTHUPĀDĀNAM)
3. Clinging to rites/ rituals/ wrong practices (SĪLABBATUPĀDĀNAM)
4. Clinging to a personality belief (ATTAVĀDUPĀDĀNAM)

I – Through clinging, volitional action and further existence arises: (UPĀDĀNA PACCAYĀ BHAVO)

There are two kinds of becoming (BHAVA):
1. Volitional action which leads to future existence (KAMMA BHAVA)
   There are three kinds:
   a. PUÑÑĀBHI SAṄKHĀRA ~ The sensuous sphere, such as DĀNA AND SĪLA, will ordinarily lead to existence as a human or DEVA in that sphere, and cause consciousness to arise there.
   b. APUÑÑĀBHI SAṄKHĀRA ~ Such unwholesome actions as violating the 5 precepts will ordinarily lead to the lower form of KAMMA BHAVA ~ i.e., to the 4 APAYA- LOKAS.
   c. ĀNEÑJABHI SAṄKHĀRA ~ JHĀNIC attainments will lead to existence as a BRAHMA in the formless spheres, and cause consciousness to arise there (UPAPATTI BHAVA).
2. The three major divisions of existence ~ rebirth after death
   The three divisions are:
   a. KĀMA BHAVA ~ existence in sense sphere
   b. RŪPA BHAVA ~ existence in form sphere
   c. ARŪPA BHAVA ~ existence in formless sphere
   Some planes are without perception ~ Others are very subtle. ~ Others are classified according to KHANDHAS:
   d. SAÑÑĀ BHAVA ~ existence in spheres with perception
   e. ASAÑÑA BHAVA ~ existence in spheres without perception
   f. NEVA-SAÑÑĀ-NĀ-SAÑÑĀ- BHAVA ~ existence in sphere of neither-perception nor non-perception
   g. EKAVOKĀRA BHAVA ~ existence where there is only 1 aggregate
   h. CATUVOKĀRA BHAVA ~ existence where there are 4 aggregates

2. DEPENDENT ORIGINATION (PATICCA SAMUPPĀDA)

    i. PAÑCAVOKĀRA BHAVA ~ existence where there are all 5 aggregates

J – Through volitional action and further existence, rebirth arises ~ (BHAVA PACCAYĀ JĀTI)

JĀTI or 'rebirth of beings belonging to this or that realm of existence' means:
1. the first appearance of one or more KHANDHAS (JĀTI).
2. their first appearance simultaneously with all the sense organs (SAÑJATI).
3. entering the womb or shell of an egg at the time of conception (OKKANTI).
4. spontaneous appearance of fully developed being DEVA/BRAHMA (ABHINIBBATI).
5. arising of KHANDHAS (KHANDHĀNAṂ PĀTUBHĀVO).
6. appearance of sense organs (ĀYATANĀNAṂ PATILĀBHO).

K – Through rebirth, there arise old age, death, sorrow, lamentation, pain, grief and despair ~ (JĀTI PACCAYĀ JARĀ MARANAṂ).
1. Old age (JĀRA), decay
   a. means the decay of beings in existence.
   b. their becoming aged (JIRANATĀ).
   c. becoming toothless (KHANDICCAṂ).
   d. becoming gray-haired (PALICCAṂ).
   e. becoming wrinkled (VALITTACATĀ).
   f. decrease in vigor (AYUNOSAṂHANI).
   g. decrepitude of their sense bases (INDRIYĀNAṂ PARIPĀKO).
2. Death (MARANAṂ)
   a. passing away (CUTI)
   b. the state of passing away (CAVANATĀ)
   c. breaking up (BHEDO)
   d. disappearance of the aggregates (ANTARADHANAṂ)
   e. the end of this life (KĀLAKIRIYĀ)
   f. dissolution of the aggregates (KHANDHĀNAṂ BHEDO)
   g. discarding of the body (KALEBARASSANIKKHEPO)

h. the cessation of life or vital energy (JĪVITINDRIYASSA UPACCHEDO)
3. Sorrow (SOKA)
    a. sorrowfulness (SACANĀ)
    b. inward sorrow (ANTO SOKO)
    c. inward woe (ANTO PARISOKO)
    d. inward burning sorrow (CETASO PARIJJHĀYAM)
    e. mental distress (DOMANASSA)
    f. the pang of sorrow (SOKA SALLA)
4. Lamentation (PARIDEVA)
    a. wailing, mentioning their respective names and qualities (PARIDEVO)
    b. state of such mourning (ADEVANĀ)
    c. state of such wailing (PARIDEVANĀ)
    d. state of being a mourning / mourner (ADEVITATTAM)
    e. state of being such as mourner / wailer (PARIDEVITATTAM)
    f. talking vainly (VĀCĀPALĀPO)
    g. talking incoherently (VIPPALĀPO)
    h. repeated grumbling (LĀLĀPPO)
    i. state of repeated grumbling (LĀLĀPPITATTAM)
5. Pain (DUKKHA): The painful and the unpleasant as the result of bodily contact: ~ This is what is known as 'pain'.
6. Grief (DOMANASSA): The painful and the unpleasant as the result of mental contact: ~ This is what is known as 'grief'
7. Despair (UPĀYĀSA)
    Mental suffering, sorrow, lamentation and despair arise through
    a. loss of relatives
    b. loss of property
    c. loss of health
    d. loss of virtue
    e. loss of right views
    f. others' loss or gain
    g. any other suffering

Thus, the entire mass of suffering arises, so the vicious circle of existence is complete and the process of volitional activities (arising through Ignorance and what follows) continues ad-infinitum ~ or until the attainment of NIBBĀNA.

~ End explanation of Dependent Origination ~

2A. DIAGRAM OF DEPENDENT ORIGINATION SHOWING THE THREE PERIODS OF TIME

Three time periods	Twelve factors or NIDĀNAS	Four groups of five modes each	
PAST	1. Ignorance 2. KAMMA formations	KAMMA process 5 KAMMIC causes Factors 1, 2, 8, 9, 10	5 causes in the past
PRESENT	3. Consciousness 4. Mind and Matter 5. Six sense-bases 6. Contact 7. Feeling 8. Craving 9. Clinging 10. Becoming	Rebirth process 5 KAMMIC results Factors 3, 4, 5, 6, 7 KAMMA process 5 KAMMIC causes Factors 1, 2, 8, 9, 10	And now a 5-fold fruit 5 causes now
FUTURE	11. Rebirth 12. Decay / Death and all Suffering	Rebirth process 5 KAMMIC results Factors 3, 4, 5, 6, 7	And yet to come a 5-fold fruit These make up the 20 modes

Chapter Three elaborates upon the Fifty-Two mental factors (*Cetasika*) from the 5th c Buddhist scholar Buddhaghosa's commentary (*Atthasālinī*) found in his great treatise, the *Visuddhimagga* (The Path to Purification). Here Buddhaghosa expounds upon the *Dhammasangani,* the first book of the *Abhidhamma Pitaka,* which enumerates all mental and material phenomena and the four ultimate realities. Mahasi Sayadaw expands upon the Abhidhamma commentary to reiterate that ultimate, personally experienced phenomena is called an "ultimate reality," that "what truly exists."

3.
THE FIFTY-TWO MENTAL FACTORS (CETASIKA)

I. Listed in six categories
   A. 7 Universals (SABBA-CITTAKA)
   B. 6 Particulars (PAKINNAKA)
   C. 14 Immorals (PĀPA-JATI)
   D. 26 Morals (KALAYĀNAJATIKA)
   E. 2 Illimitables are within the 25 morals (APPAMAÑÑĀ)
   F. 4 Abstinences are within the 25 morals (VIRATIYO)

II. Complete list of all 53 Mental Factors
   A. Seven Universals
      1. Contact (PHASSA)
      2. Feeling (VEDANĀ)
      3. Perception (SAÑÑĀ)
      4. Volition (CETANĀ)
      5. Concentration (EKAGGATA)
      6. Psychic Life (JIVITA)
      7. Attention (MANASIKĀRA)
   B. Six Particulars
      1. Initial Application (VITAKKA)
      2. Sustained Application (VICĀRA)
      3. Effort (VIRIYA)
      4. Joy (PITI)
      5. Desire-to-do (CHANDA)
      6. Deciding (ADHIMOKKHA)

C. Fourteen Immorals
   1. Greed (LOBHA)
   2. Hatred (DOSA)
   3. Delusion (MOHA)
   4. Wrong View (DITTHI)
   5. Conceit (MĀNA)
   6. Envy (ISSĀ)
   7. Selfishness (MACCHARIYA)
   8. Worry (KUKKUCCA)
   9. Shamelessness (AHIRIKA)
   10. Fearlessness (ANOTTAPA)
   11. Restlessness (UDDHACCA)
   12. Sloth (THINA)
   13. Torpor (MIDDHA)
   14. Perplexity / Doubt (VICIKICCHĀ)
D. Twenty-five Morals
   1. Non-Attachment (ALOBHA)
   2. Good will (ADOSĀ)
   3. Confident trust (SADDHĀ)
   4. Mindfulness (SATI)
   5. Moral shame (HĪRI)
   6. Moral dread / discretion (OTTOPPA)
   7. Balance of mind (TATRAMAJJHATTATĀ)
   8. Composure of mental properties (KĀYAPASSADDHI)
   9. Composure of mind (CITTAPASSADDHI)
   10. Buoyancy of mental properties (KĀYALAHUTĀ)
   11. Buoyancy of mind (CITTALAHUTĀ)
   12. Pliancy of mental properties (KĀYAMUDUTĀ)
   13. Pliancy of mind (CITTAMUDUTĀ)
   14. Adaptability of mental properties (KĀYAKAMMAÑÑATĀ)
   15. Adaptability of Mind (CITTAKAMMAÑÑATĀ)
   16. Proficiency of Mental Properties (KĀYAPAGUÑÑATĀ)
   17. Proficiency of Mind (CITTAPAGUÑÑATĀ)
   18. Rectitude of Mental Properties (KAYUJUKATO)
   19. Rectitude of Mind (CITTUJUKATO)

D₁. Two Illimitables
　20. Sympathetic Joy (MUDITĀ)
　21. Compassion (KARUNĀ)
D₂. Four Abstinences
　22. Right Speech (SAMMĀVĀCĀ)
　23. Right Action (SAMMĀKAMMANTA)
　24. Right Livelihood (SAMMĀ ĀJIVA)
　25. Non-Delusion / Wisdom (AMOHA / PAÑÑĀ)

3A. Mental factors individually explained

A. The Seven Universals (SABBA-CITTAKA)

~ (These have to arise with every moment of consciousness) ~

1. Contact ~ (PHASSA)
    When an object presents itself to the Consciousness through one of the six-sense doors, the Mental State Contact arises. When the eye-organ ~ forms/ colors ~ attention ~ light~ is all present, Seeing Consciousness arises. Similarly with the ear-organ / sound / attention / air, Hearing Consciousness arises; and so on with the nose and odors, tongue and tastes, body and sensations, mind and mental objects. When the various components arise together, it is their coincidence that is known as Mental Contact. Contact means "it touches": Like a pillar which acts as a strong support to the rest of the structure, even so is Contact to the co-existent mental concomitants. According to PATICCA~SAMUPPĀDA, contact leads to Feeling, but in actuality all these mental states are coexistent. For states arisen in one conscious moment, it is not valid to say that "This arises first", and "That afterwards". Contact is mentioned first in order of teaching. One could also say there are Feeling and Contact, Consciousness and Contact, Perception and Contact, Volition and Contact.

2. Feeling ~ (VEDANĀ)
    Like contact, VEDANĀ arises with every moment of consciousness:
    ~ With AKUSALA CITTAS, KUSALA CITTAS, VIPĀKA

CITTAS and KIRIYĀ CITTAS. It arises with all CITTAS in all planes of existence: APAYA LOKAS, Human Plane, DEVA LOKAS, RŪPA BRAHMA LOKAS, and ARŪPA BRAHMA LOKAS, with all RŪPA and ARŪPA JHANA CITTAS, and with LOKUTTARA CITTAS (which experience NIBBĀNA). VEDANĀ is of three kinds: ~ pleasurable feeling (SUKHA), painful feeling (DUKKHA) or neither pleasurable or painful feeling (ADUKKAM ASUKA). Strictly speaking, it is VEDANĀ that experiences an object when it comes in contact with any of the senses. It is VEDANĀ that experiences the pleasurable or non-pleasurable effects of a bodily, verbal or mental action (KAMMA), done in this life or in a previous existence. VEDANĀ will arise with every moment of visual contact, hearing contact, smelling, etc. There is no power or force that can prevent the arising of VEDANĀ. The characteristic of VEDANĀ is experiencing, tasting the object.

3. Perception ~ (SAÑÑĀ)

    The chief characteristic of SAÑÑĀ is the cognition of an object by way of a mark (as 'blue', etc.). It is SAÑÑĀ that enables one to recognize an object that has once been perceived by the mind through the senses. Its procedure is likened to that of the wild animal when discerning the scarecrow, the work of man. Perception is the apprehension of ordinary sense objects, such as trees, houses, chairs, etc. On the occasion of sensory stimulation, SAÑÑĀ means the awareness of the marks, real or imaginary, by which an object whether of sense or thought is, or may hereafter be, recognized. Memory is related to SAÑÑĀ. SAÑÑĀ, VIÑÑĀNA and PAÑÑĀ should be differentiated from one another. SAÑÑĀ is like the mere perception of a rupee coin by a child. Because of its whiteness, roundness and size, the child merely recognizes the coin as a rupee, utterly ignorant of its monetary value. A man, for instance, discerns its value and utility, but is not aware of its chemical composition. VIÑÑĀNA is comparable to the ordinary man's knowledge of the rupee. PAÑÑĀ is like the analytical knowledge of the chemist who knows all its chemical properties in every detail. SAÑÑĀ cannot bring about the penetration of the characteristics of an object as

ANICCA, ANATTA and DUKKHA. This is the function of PAÑÑĀ. When CITTA experiences a mental concept, SAÑÑĀ also perceives that concept and performs its function of marking or remembering accordingly. SAÑÑĀ arises with every CITTA and perceives objects through the six-sense doors. When one is reading, speaking or being spoken to, it is SAÑÑĀ that recognizes the letters, the concepts and meaning of the letters and spoken sentences. SAÑÑĀ functions by allowing the remembrance of one's thoughts, so that we can reason about a subject.

SAÑÑĀ can be AKUSALA, KUSALA, VIPĀKA and KIRIYA (CITTAS of the four JĀTIS). There can be Wrong Perception / Remembrance and Right Perception Remembrance. When SAÑÑĀ arises with DITTHI (Wrong View), there is Wrong Remembrance ~ one takes recognizing for self, and takes that recognition for something which 'exists', i.e., recognizing people and things. There are only PARAMATTHA DHAMMAS that are ANICCA, ANATTA and DUKKHA. Aryans also think of concepts but have eradicated Wrong View ~ when they look at a flower, for example, they do not take the recognition for self or as 'lasting'.

There are four perversities of SAÑÑĀ ~ SAÑÑĀ VIPALLASA (Ang. NIK. IV, 4, 9) ~ four perversions of Perception. To hold the view that in the permanent, there is Permanence, is a perversion of Perception, Thought and View. To hold that in DUKKHA there is Not-DUKKHA is a perversion of Perception, Thought and View.

To hold that in the Not-Self, there is Self is a perversion of Perception, Thought and View. To hold that 'In the foul, there is the fair' is a perversion of Perception, Thought and View. These are the four perversions of SAÑÑĀ. Perceptions are of six kinds, classified according to the sense door through which it arises (for example, Perception of visible objects through the eye, etc.)

4. Volition ~ (CETANĀ)
CETANĀ is the factor of determining the activities of the accompanying mental concomitants so as to bring them into harmony. This CETANĀ is what is known as KAMMA

(Volitional Action of Body, Speech and Mind). Where there is no CETANĀ, there is no KAMMA. (VIS.MAGGA ~ CETANĀ (p. 21) ~ "It wills; thus, it is Volition, 'it collects or coordinates' is the meaning: Its characteristic is the state of 'willing'. Its function is 'to accumulate'. It is manifested as 'coordinating'." It coordinates the other DHAMMAS it accompanies on the object. CITTA cognizes the object, it is the leader in knowing the object. The CETASIKAS which accompany CITTA share the same object, but they each have their own task to fulfill. PHASSA contacts the object, VEDANĀ experiences the taste of the object and SAÑÑĀ remembers the object. KAMMA sees to it that the other DHAMMAS it accompanies fulfill their tasks with regard to the object which they all share. ~ The KAMMA (CETANĀ) which accompanies VIPĀKACITTA and KIRIYACITTA merely coordinates the tasks of the other DHAMMAS it accompanies: it does not 'will' KUSALA and AKUSALA and it does not motivate wholesome or unwholesome deeds. When CETANĀ is energetic enough, "It wills KUSALA and AKUSALA and when it has such an intensity that it motivates a deed through Body, Speech or Mind, it is capable of producing the result of that deed, later on."

5. Concentration ~ (EKAGGATĀ)

The characteristic of CITTA is cognizing an object and thus, every CITTA which arises must have an object. There is no CITTA without an object, but it can know only one object at a time. EKAGGATĀ is the CETASIKA which causes CITTA to focus on that one object. EKAGGATĀ causes Hearing Consciousness to focus on sound. Hearing Consciousness can only know sound, and likewise with each other Sense Consciousness and its object. EKAGGATĀ can accompany all JĀTIS. When it accompanies an AKUSALA CITTA, it is called MICHA SAMĀDHI. When EKAGGATĀ accompanies an AKUSALA CITTA, it is not strong. (Commentary to ATTHASĀLINI: "...yet it is called Steadfastness, not because of its strength, but because it is intent on one action, for instance murder, until that is accomplished.") In Wrong Concentration, ATTHASĀLINI, "the one-pointedness of mind is

3. THE FIFTY-TWO MENTAL FACTORS (CETASIKA)

the steadiness of Mind free from distraction when taking life, etc. Being well concentrated, one can steal others' property; with a mind governed by a single function, they fall into wrong behavior. So, there is one-pointedness of mind in the occurrence of immorality."

EKAGGATĀ which accompanies a KUSALACITTA is called SAMMĀ SAMĀDHI or right concentration. ~ VIS.MAGGA (p. 22) ~ "It puts consciousness evenly on the object, or it puts it rightly on it, or it is just the mere collecting of the mind: Thus, it is concentration. Its characteristic is non-wandering, or non-distraction. Its function is to conglomerate canescent states as water does bath powder. It is manifested as peace. Usually, its proximate cause is SUKHA ~ pleasant feeling. It should be regarded as steadiness of the mind, like the steadiness of the flame of a lamp in a windless place.

When SAMMĀ SAMĀDHI accompanies LOKUTTARA CITTA, SAMMĀ SAMĀDHI is also LOKUTTARA and it makes the CITTA focus on NIBBĀNA.

Then SAMMĀ SAMĀDHI is a factor of the Supramundane Eightfold Path (LOKUTTARA MAGGA). When there is Right Mindfulness of whatever NĀMA or RŪPA appears, with SATI there is also Right Concentration at that moment. Thus, development of both takes place.

6. JĪVITINDRIYA: ~ (Life- faculty ~ vitality ~ psychic life)
As with all 7 of the universal CETASIKAS, this one being one of them arises with every CITTA and it sustains the 'life' of the other DHAMMAS with which it arises. It is of two kinds: there is RŪPA JĪVITINDRIYA and NĀMA JĪVITINDRIYA.

RŪPA JĪVITINDRIYA is a kind of RŪPA produced by KAMMA, which maintains the other RŪPAS with which it arises. It occurs only in living bodies ~ VIS.MAGGA~ "RŪPA JĪVITINDRIYA only maintains canescent kinds of RŪPA, only at the moment of Presence and not after the moment they fall away. It does not prolong Presence at the moment of dissolution because it is itself dissolving... each RŪPA lasts only as long as its moment of CITTA; it arises and falls away together with the other RŪPAS it accompanies."

NĀMA JĪVITINDRIYA ~ VIS.MAGGA~ "Its characteristic should be understood in the way stated under material life, for that is life of material things and this is life of immaterial things. This is the only difference here. ~ ATTHASĀLINI: "Life is that by which associated states live. It exercises government over associated states by the characteristic of 'ceaseless watching'; hence it is a controlling faculty (INDRIYA) and gives the compound life faculty (JĪVITINDRIYA). It is the dominant influence over continuity in (organic) processes. It has the ceaseless watching over states undivided from itself as its 'characteristic'; the processes of such states or co-existent states as 'function'; the establishing them as 'manifestation'; states that have kept going as 'proximate cause'."

The function of NĀMA JĪVITINDRIYA is to make the CITTA and its accompanying CETASIKAS occur: It maintains their lives and keeps them going until the moment they fall away. Since JĪVITINDRIYA arises and falls away together with the CITTA, it performs its function only for a short while. Every CITTA which arises lasts actually for three extremely short moments. 1- Arising moment (UPPĀDA) 2- Static moment (THITI) 3- Cessation moment (BHAṄGA) JĪVITINDRIYA ~ and the other DHAMMAS which arise together are as bound up with one another like "the boatman and the boat". The CITTA and the CETASIKAS cannot occur without JĪVITINDRIYA, and JĪVITINDRIYA cannot arise without CITTA and the accompanying CETASIKAS. When these fall away, those have to fall away as well. When, for example, 'seeing' arises, JĪVITINDRIYA has to arise together with seeing, otherwise seeing could not arise. Seeing needs JĪVITINDRIYA in order to subsist during that very short moment of its life. When seeing consciousness falls away, JĪVITINDRIYA also falls away. Then another CITTA arises and this CITTA is accompanied by another JĪVITINDRIYA which maintains CITTA and the other CETASIKAS. JĪVITINDRIYA has to arise with every CITTA in order to vitalize CITTA and its accompanying CETASIKAS. As lotuses are sustained by water, and an infant is sustained by a nurse, so are mental and physical states. "By JĪVITINDRIYA, both types of JĪVITINDRIYA arise at the moment of conception. They simultaneously perish at the moment of death. Hence death is regarded as the destruction of this JĪVITINDRIYA, only to immediately arise again (unless ARHATTA) due to KAMMA at the moment of rebirth consciousness of the next existence.

7. Attention ~ (MANASIKĀRA)

The function of MANASIKĀRA is to bring the desired object into view of Consciousness, or turning the mind toward the object. It is like the rudder of a ship, which is indispensable to take her directly to her destination. Mind without MANASIKĀRA is like a rudderless ship. The selective or coordinating activity of attention may be aroused from within or from without ~ spontaneously (i.e., without volitional effort on one's own part or on the part of another), or from without by the object itself; and it is directed to this one object. MANASIKĀRA should be distinguished from VITAKKA (initial application). The former directs its concomitants to the object, while the latter applies or throws them on the object. VITTAKA is like a favorite courtier that introduces a villager (mind) into the presence of a king (object). In MANASIKĀRA, there is no peculiar vividness or clarity. This vividness to some extent may be attributed to SAÑÑA.

There are three kinds of MANASIKĀRA: Two kinds are CITTAS and one is the CETASIKA MANASIKĀRA (see above). The two MANASIKĀRAs as CITTA ATTHASĀLINI are "the PAÑCA DVĀRAVAJJANA CITTA, the 5-sense door adverting consciousness, and the MANO DVĀRAVAJJANA CITTA, the mind-door adverting consciousness. The PAÑCA DVĀRAVAJJANA CITTA succeeds the BHAVANGA PACCHEDA, arrest BHAVANGA. The stream of BHAVANGA CITTAS is arrested when the PAÑCA DVĀRAVAJJANA CITTA, the first CITTA of the sense-door process, adverts to the object which impinges on one of the sense doors. According to the commentaries, the MANASIKĀRA which is the PAÑCA DVĀRAVAJJANA CITTA is the 'controller of the sense-door process'. The MANO DVĀRAVAJJANA CITTA adverts to the object through the mind door and it is succeeded by the JAVANA CITTAS. According to the commentaries, the MANASIKĀRA which is the MANO DVĀRAVAJJANA CITTA is the 'controller of the JAVANAS'. When the MANO DVĀRAVAJJANA CITTA is succeeded by KUSALA CITTAS, there is 'Wise Attention', and when the MANO DVĀRAVAJJANA CITTA is succeeded by AKUSALA CITTASA, there is 'Unwise Attention'." Thus, the two kinds of MANASIKĀRA which are CITTA PARAMATTHA are the controller of the sense-door process and the controller of the JAVANAS.

~ Summarizing the seven 'Universal' CETASIKAS

All the Universals arise with every CITTA for all beings with CITTA in all planes of existence. They arise and fall away with the CITTA and they share the same object with the CITTA. They are of the same JĀTI as the CITTA they accompany and of the same plane of consciousness. In the planes of existence where there are both NĀMA and RŪPA, CETASIKAS arise at the same 'base' (VATTHU) as the CITTA they accompany, and thus they may arise at the eye-base, ear-base, heart-base, etc. CETASIKAS never arise by themselves; they always accompany CITTA and other CETASIKAS. When an AKUSALA CITTA arises, all the accompanying CETASIKAS, the Universals included, are AKUSALA as well. If KUSALA, they all become KUSALA. If SOBHANA, this conditions the Universals to be quite different from the UNIVERSALS that, for example, accompany AKUSALA CITTAS. There are ten types of CITTAS which are accompanied only by the Universals with no other CETASIKAS present. They are the DVIPAÑCA VIÑÑĀNA (five pairs) ~ seeing consciousness, hearing consciousness, tasting consciousness, smelling consciousness and body consciousness. These CITTAS are VIPĀKA CITTAS and they can be either KUSALA or AKUSALA ~ thus five pairs. All other CITTAS which are not (accompanied) DVI PAÑCĀ VIÑÑĀNA are accompanied by other CETASIKAS besides the Universals.

(For a more detailed analysis of the Universals as a whole, as well as a full explanation of the above mentioned (five pairs), refer to Nina van Gorkom's CETASIKA Study, Part 1 The Universals, Chapter 8, pp 4-8.)

3B. Explanation of the mental factors

B. The Six Particulars (PAKINNAKĀ CETASIKAS)

1. Initial application or applied thinking (VITAKKA)
   The Particulars are of the same JĀTI as the CITTA they accompany. When they accompany KUSALA, they are also KUSALA ~ likewise for AKUSALA, VIPĀKACITTAS and KIRIYACITTAS. However, the Particulars do not always arise with every CITTA, like the Universals. Since both the Universals and the Particulars arise with CITTAS of the four JĀTIS, they are classified as one group (CAÑÑASAMĀNA CETASIKAS).

   VITAKKA is the CETASIKA which 'thinks' of the object the CITTA cognizes. Its function is to direct the mind towards the object of cognition. Directing the accompanying CETASIKAS towards the object, just as someone ascends to the King's palace depending on the King's favorite relative or friend, so consciousness ascends to the object depending on VITAKKA. (VITAKKA is the application of the mental concomitants on the object; MANASIKĀRA is the directing of the concomitants to the object). Ordinary VITAKKA simply throws the mind to the surface of the object. When it is developed, it becomes the foremost factor of the first JHĀNA ~ ATTHASĀLINĪ ~ "VITAKKA has the function of impinging. By initial application of mind, the individual is said to 'strike at and around the object'. Its manifestation is 'bringing the mind near the object'. VITAKKA should not be confused with PHASSA contact. PHASSA has to arise with every CITTA: It contacts the object so that CITTA can cognize it. VITAKKA does not arise with every CITTA. When it arises, it brings the mind near the object." ~ VIS.MAGGA. ~ "Hitting upon is what is meant by VITAKKA ~ applied thinking. Its characteristic is directing the mind onto an object ('mounting the mind onto the object'). Its function is to 'strike and thresh' at the object. Threshed and struck by applied thought, when the meditator concentrates on the meditation subject (SAMATHA YOGI), VITAKKA 'strikes' the object again and again." VITAKKA arises in the sense-door process as well as in the mind-door process. The function of VITAKKA remains the same: It 'lifts' the CITTA onto the object, whether it is a visible-object, hearing-object, etc. VITAKKA arises with all KĀMĀ VACARA CITTAS, except the DVI PANCA VINNANAS 5 pairs: seeing, hearing, smelling, taste and bodily sense. (For complete details of the realm of VITAKKA, refer to Nina Van Gorkom's The Particulars, chapter 9, pp 3-8). VITAKKA is a conditioned DHAMMA (SAṄKHARA DHAMMA) which arises together with CITTA. It arises and dissolves with the CITTA it accompanies. How does VITAKKA perform its function when one is engaged in a conversation or thinking of a story? In reality, there are many VITTAKAS arising / passing with the CITTAS which succeed one another. It is because of SAÑÑA, Perception-Remembrance, which arises with every CITTA, that one can remember the previous thought and that there is a connection in our thoughts.

When VITAKKA accompanies an AKUSALA CITTA, VITAKKA is also AKUSALA: ~ Likewise with other JATIS. There are three kinds of AKUSALA VITAKKA:

1- Thought of sense pleasures (KAMA VITAKKA);

2- Thought of malevolence (VYAPĀDA VITAKKA;

3- Thought of harming (VIHIṂSA VITAKKA)

(Mij. Nik. 1, no. 19, p. 148)

Buddha as a bodhisattva said he considered both AKUSALA and KUSALA as VITAKKA, thus AKUSALA VITAKKA conduces to 'self-hurt', to the hurt of others and to the hurt of both; it is destructive of intuitive wisdom, associated with distress, not conducive to NIBBĀNA.

There are three kinds of KUSALA VITAKKA:

1- Thought of renunciation (NEKKHAMMA);

2- Thought of non-malevolence (AVYĀPADA);

3- Thought of non-harming (AVIHIṂSA).

3. THE FIFTY-TWO MENTAL FACTORS (CETASIKA)

These KUSALA VITAKKAS lead neither to self-hurt, nor to the hurt of others, nor to the hurt of both; but they are for growth of intuitive wisdom. They are not associated with distress; they are conducive to NIBBĀNA.

VITAKKA is one of the factors of the eightfold path, and under this aspect it is called SAMMĀ SANKAPPA, Right Thought. SAMMĀ SANKAPPA has to arise together with SAMMĀ DITTHI, Right Understanding, in order to be a factor of the eightfold path. SAMMĀ SANKAPPA directs the CITTA towards the NĀMA or RŪPA, which is object of SATI at that moment, and SAMMĀ DITTHI realizes its characteristic as it is. When there is SAMMĀ SANKAPPA, there is no AKUSALA VITAKKA, no thought of sense-pleasures, or of malice, or of harming.

2. Sustained application, sustained thinking, discursive thinking (VICĀRA)

    VIS. MAGGA. ~ "Its characteristic is one of continued pressure on (occupation with) the object. Its function is to keep connascent [simultaneously growing, like heat and flame of an oil lamp] mental states occupied with that. It is manifested as keeping consciousness anchored on that object. VICĀRA is the continued exercise of the mind on the object. Like a bee alighting on a flower is VITAKKA, like its gyrating around the flower is VICĀRA. Like the beating of a drum or the ringing of a bell is VITAKKA, the reverberation is like VICĀRA." Both CETASIKAS arise in the first JHĀNA. VITAKKA hits the meditation object again and again. It directs the CITTA towards it. VICĀRA keeps the CITTA anchored on the meditation subject. In the second JHĀNA, VITAKKA is not present as it is no longer needed, indeed an obstacle to its attainment. As the CITTA no longer needs to be directed towards the meditation subject, VICĀRA still arises. In the subsequent stages of JHĀNA which are more tranquil and more refined, VICĀRA is no longer needed." (More details/ particulars by N.V. GORKOM, Ch. 9, p. 9 - 10).

    1- Effort ~ Energy (VĪRIYA)

    VIS. MAGGA. ~ "VĪRIYA is the state of one who is vigorous

(VIRA). Its characteristic is marshalling or driving; its function is to consolidate connascent states. It is manifested as 'non-collapse'. Because of the words bestirred, he strives wisely. Its proximate cause is a sense of urgency, or its proximate cause is grounds for the initiation of energy. When rightly initiated, it should be regarded as the root of all attainments. (Rightly initiated = Right Effort accompanying KUSALA CITTA). "Some CETASIKAS are INDRIYAS. Controlling faculties, they control their opposites. VĪRIYA controls indolence or laziness. When there is VĪRIYA, there cannot be indolence at the same time. It overcomes idleness in the sense of predominance. VĪRIYA does not allow associated states to recede, to retreat. It uplifts and supports them. As an old house is supported by new pillars, even so concomitants [things associated] are aided and supported by VĪRIYA."

"VĪRIYA accompanies all AKUSALA and all KUSALA CITTAS, but it does not arise with all VIPĀKA or KIRIYA CITTAS."

"Right Effort arises together with the CITTA which is mindful of ANĀMA or RŪPA appearing now. The only way to be free from birth, old age, sickness and death is to be mindful of any ANĀMA and RŪPA. As it becomes evident as continuously as possible, moment after moment, this is Right Effort. Right Effort develops from Right Mindfulness (the four SATIPATTHANAS)."

"VĪRIYA is also an INDRIYA when developed. INDRIYAS need to be balanced in order to achieve the attainments of JHANAS and NIBBANA. VĪRIYA and SAMADHI need to be balanced. If one is strong in SAMADHI but weak in VĪRIYA, there will be idleness, a sinking mind. If strong in energy and weak in concentration, there will be agitation, since energy favors such mind states. So, these two INDRIYAS should be balanced, for attainments are only possible when they are in balance."

"Right Effort of the eightfold paths is explained as the four 'Right Endeavors' (SAMMAPPADHĀNAS).

1- The effort to avoid AKUSALA which has not yet arisen.

2- The effort to overcome AKUSALA which has arisen.

3- The effort to develop KUSALA which has not yet arisen.

4- The effort to maintain and bring to maturity the KUSALA which has arisen.

"Right Effort of the eightfold path (four aspects above) is accompanied by SAMMA-DITTHI and SAMMA~SATI. Thus, to develop SAMMĀ~VAYĀMA ~ Right Effort ~ one should be mindful of NAMA~RŪPA as it appears at any of the six-sense doors. This is the way to develop the four Right Efforts. (For complete details / particulars, see N.V. GORKOM, Ch. 11, p. 1 & p. 10).

4. Pleasurable interest ~ Joy ~ Enthusiasm ~ Zest ~ Delight (PĪTI)

VIS. MAGGA. ~ "PĪTI refreshes, gladdens, satisfies, thus it is Happiness. It has the characteristic of satisfaction. Its function is to refresh the body and mind; or its function is to pervade (thrill with rapture). It is manifested as Elation." ~

ATTHASĀLINĪ ~ "PĪTI takes an interest in the object which CITTA cognizes and which is also experienced by the accompanying CETASIKAS. It is satisfied, delighted with that object..." ~ VIS. MAGGA ~ (Difference between the 2 DHANA factors, SUKHA (Bliss) and PĪTI (Happiness).

~ The English editions of the ATTHASĀLINĪ and the Vis. Mag. translate the same Pali terms differently) "...and wherever the two are associated, Happiness (PĪTI) is the contentedness at getting a desirable object, and Bliss (SUKHA) is the actual experiencing of it. Where there is Happiness, there is Bliss; but where there is Bliss, there is not necessarily PĪTI. (4th JHANA has SUKHA but PĪTI has been abandoned at the 3d JHANA).

PĪTI is included in the SAṄKHĀRAKKHANDA: SUKHA is included in the VEDANĀKKANDA (Feeling Aggregate). If a man exhausted in a desert saw or heard about a pond on the edge of the wood, he would have Happiness (PĪTI); if he went into the wood's shade and used the water, he would have Bliss (SUKHA, Feeling, Taste of the object).

PĪTI has five different types of intensity ~ VIS. MAGGA. ~ 5 kinds of PĪTI

1. Minor happiness (KHUDDAKA PĪTI) ~ the thrill of joy

that causes the flesh to creep or it raises the hair on one's body.
2. Momentary happiness (KHANIKA PĪTI) ~ like flashes of lightning at different moments; a type of instantaneous joy like that of lightning.
3. Showering happiness (OKKANTIKA PĪTI) breaks over the body again and again, like waves on the seashore.
4. Uplifting happiness (UBBEGA PĪTI) ~ can be powerful enough to levitate the body, floating in the air like a lump of cotton carried by the wind.
5. Pervading ~ rapturous happiness or suffusing joy (PHARANA PĪTI); the entire body becomes enveloped / engulfed in an all-pervading flood of joy, like a flood that overflows small ponds. This type of PĪTI is developed in JHĀNA. It is the 'Root of Absorption' and comes by growth into association with JHĀNA: ~ In the case of the KĀMAVACARA CITTAS ~ PĪTI arises with the CITTAS which are accompanied by pleasant feelings. Whenever there is interest in the object and delight with it, there is also a pleasant feeling; in such cases, there cannot be an indifferent feeling or unpleasant feeling.

~ PĪTI does not arise with the two types of DOSA MŪLA CITTAS or with the two types of MOHA MŪLE CITTA. It does arise with the four types of LOBHA MŪLE CITTA which are accompanied by pleasant feelings. In such case, the LOBHA is more intense due to the pleasant feeling than the LOBHA MŪLE CITTAS accompanied by a neutral feeling (four types also). PĪTI does not arise with PĪTI these CITTAS.

~ PĪTI is the precursor of SUKHA.
~ PĪTI is an Enlightenment factor.

5. Wish or desire-to-do (CHANDA)
CHANDA is not the same as LOBHA. CHANDA can be KUSALA, AKUSALA, VIPĀKA or KIRIYA ~ VIS. MAGGA. ~ "CHANDA ~ zeal ~ (desire) is a term for 'Desire-to-act'. CHANDA has the characteristic of the desire to act. Its function is scanning for

an object. It is manifested as need for an object. That same object is its proximate cause. It should be regarded as the (mental) extending of a hand in the apprehending of an object."~ ATTHASĀLINĪ ~
"CHANDA searches, looks for the object which CITTA cognizes. It needs that object. The object it needs is also its proximate cause."

CHANDA arises with the eight LOBHA~ MŪLA~ CITTAS. When CHANDA arises with LOBHA, it looks for the desirable object. LOBHA has the characteristic of grasping, and is always AKUSALA. CHANDA also has a different characteristic and becomes the same JĀTI it arises with.

"CHANDA also arises with the two types of DOSA~MŪLA ~CITTA. CHANDA looks for the object the DOSA~MŪLA ~CITTA dislikes. It needs the undesirable object. CHANDA is quite different from LOBHA, which is attached to an object and which can never accompany a DOSA~MŪLA~CITTA.

"There are three types of CHANDA"
1. KĀMACCHANDA ~ sensual craving – immoral
2. DHAMMACCHANDA ~ righteous wish
3. KATTUKAMYATĀ CHANDA ~ the mere wish-to-do – unmoral

"CHANDA does not accompany the two types of MOHA~MŪLA~CITTA. One type is accompanied with Doubt (VICIKICCHĀ). When there is MOHA, which is ignorant of the true nature of realities and when there is Doubt, which has 'wavering' as function ~ and which is not sure about the object ~ there cannot be at the same time CHANDA, which searches for the object and desires it.

The second type of MOHA ~ MŪLA~ CITTA accompanied by distraction (UDDHACCA or Restlessness) cannot be accompanied by CHANDA either. This type of CITTA also lacks decision (ADHIMOKKHA), which is sure about the object. CHANDA always accompanies KĀMAVACARA~SOBHANA~CITTAS. KUSALA CITTA with CHANDA desires to act in the KUSANA way (i.e., DĀNA, SILA and BHĀVANĀ).

KUSALA CETANA is different than KUSALA CHANDA.

The KUSALA CETANA wills KUSALA. It is the wholesome intentional volition which is able to produce a pleasant result in the future. All 24 SOHANA CITTAS are accompanied by CHANDA. CHANDA is a necessary factor for all kinds of KUSALA KAMMA. It assists the CITTA in carrying out its work. In order to develop a meditation subject (SAMATHA), the Will-to-Do is necessary. Without this wholesome desire, one would not want to develop it. "The Will-to-Do is the beginning in the development of the meditation subject; the discarding of the hindrances is the middle; JHANA is the end."

CHANDA accompanies RŪPA VACARA and the ARŪPAVACARA CITTAS. CHANDA is very different according to the different types of CITTAS, of different planes of CITTA, it accompanies.

The LOKUTTARA CITTAS are accompanied by CHANDA, which 'desires' ~ CHANDA NIBBĀNA. When there is Right Mindfulness, there is at the same time wholesome desire, KUSALA CHANDA. KUSALA CHANDA is a SANKHĀRA DHAMMA. It arises when there are the appropriate conditions.

6. Determination ~ Resolution ~ Deciding (ADHIMOKKHA)
VIS. MAGGA. ~ "It is the act of resolving, of resolution. Its function is not to grope. It is manifested as 'decisiveness'. Its proximate cause is a thing to be convinced about. It should be regarded as like a boundary post, owing to its immovableness with regard to the object." ~ ADHIMOKKHA presupposes a certain amount of hesitancy on the part of the mind, whether it shall attend or not to a particular object out of many presented. Literally, it means to release the mind onto the object. It is the freedom from the wavering state of mind between two courses open to it. It is the property by which the mind decides, or chooses to attend to 'this rather than that' in the field of presentation (finally making the conclusion, 'just this one'). It isn't judgment.

ADHIMOKKHA is opposed to VICIKICCHĀ ~ Doubt or Indecision. It is compared to a judge who finally settles a case. It is compared to a steady pillar owing to its unwavering state. It is intended to connote the unwavering state of mind between the courses open to it. ADHIMOKKHA does not arise with the five pairs ~ DVI PAÑCA VIÑÑANAS which are only accompanied by the Universals ~ nor does it arise with the type of MOHA MŪLA CITTA accompanied by Doubt. When Doubt is present, there cannot be at the same time the CETASIKA (ADHIMOKKHA) which 'does not grope' and is 'convinced' about the object. ADHIMOKKHA accompanies all the other CITTAS. ADHIMOKKHA is one among the many CETASIKAS which assists CITTA in cognizing the object. When, for example, the eye-door adverting Consciousness adverts to visible object, in this case the eye-door adverting Consciousness adverts to visible object and not to any other object. ADHIMOKKHA is convinced as to the object, so that the CITTA can cognize that object. ADHIMOKKHA which is 'sure' ~ convinced ~ about the object, should not be confused with PAÑÑA, which has 'illuminating' and 'understanding' as characteristics. PAÑÑA is sure about the true nature of realities.

~ Summarizing the Six-Particulars ~

The Six-Particulars do not arise with every CITTA, but they arise with CITTAS of the four JĀTIS ~ The Universals and the Particulars arise with CITTAS of the 4 JĀTIS and these 13 CETASIKAS are classified as one group: the AÑÑASAMĀNĀ CETASIKAS. When the AÑÑASAMĀNĀ CETASIKAS arise with AKUSALA CITTA, they are all AKUSALA; they assist the AKUSALA CITTA in carrying out its work in the AKUSALA way, with the KUSALA CITTA being accompanied to it. They are all KUSALA. They assist the KUSALA CITTA in carrying out its work in the KUSALA way. CETASIKAS are conditioned by the CITTA and the other CETASIKAS they accompany, and they are of an entirely different quality according to when they accompany AKUSALA, KUSALA, VIPĀKA, or KIRIYA CITTAS.

When KĀMĀVACARA KUSALA CITTA arises, it is accompanied by the Universals, the Particulars, which are VITAKKA,

VICĀRA, VIRIYA, CHANDA and ADHIMOKKHA. PĪTI arises only when the VEDANĀ is a pleasant feeling. All are KUSALA in this case ~ CETANĀ wills KUSALA; VITAKKA thinks of the object in a wholesome way; ADHIMOKKHA is convinced about the object (in the wholesome way) of KUSALA CITTA; VIRIYA supports the CITTA and the accompanying CETASIKAS in the wholesome way; PĪTI, if it arises, takes interest in the object and refreshes CITTA and the other CETASIKAS; CHANDA desires to act in the wholesome way.

3C. Explanation of the mental factors

C. Explanation of the 14 AKUSALA CETASIKAS

1. Greed ~ Attachment ~ (LOBHA)
   AKUSALA DHAMMAS are impure and dangerous. They lead to all kinds of DUKKHA. LOBHA does not arise with every AKUSALA CITTA. It can only arise with the 8 LOBHA-MŪLA~CITTAS. These CITTAS have both MOHA and LOBHA as their roots. ~VIS.MAG. ~ Greed has the characteristic of grasping an object 'like glue'. Its function is 'sticking', like meat placed into a hot pan; it is manifested as 'not giving up', like dye on a cloth. Its proximate cause is seeing enjoyment in things that lead to bondage. Swelling with the current of craving, it should be regarded as taking beings with it to states of loss, as a swift-flowing river does to the ocean.

   At the moment of LOBHA we enjoy the object of clinging and we do not see that LOBHA makes us enslaved; we do not see the danger of LOBHA.

   ~ LOBHA is attached to many different kinds of objects, and it has many degrees. Different names designate the LOBHA CETASIKA, KĀMA-lust, RĀGA-greed, TANAA-craving, ABHIJJHĀ (covetousness) ~ When LOBHA is coursing it motivates AKUSALA-KAMMA-PATHA (unwholesome course of action) through body, speech or mind. ~ There is LOBHA, not only when we want something, but very often when one 'enjoys' pleasant sights, sounds, smells, tastes, tangible objects and mind objects. (e.g., Liking sitting on something soft; aversion to sitting on hard floor).

LOBHA can be accompanied by a pleasant feeling, or by an indifferent feeling. LOBHA w/SUHKA VEDANĀ is accompanied by PĪTI. One becomes delighted with pleasant feelings and one becomes attached to them, however one thinks the sense object is intrinsically pleasant, MOHA. ~ When there is LOBHA, there are MOHA, AHIRIKA, ANOTAPPA and UDDHACCA as well. MOHA does not see the true nature of the object of clinging; it does not see that it is only a conditioned DHAMMA which is ANICCA, ANATTA and DUKKHA. AHIRIKA is not ashamed of AKUSALA, and ANOTAPPA does not see the danger in it. UDDHACCA is confused, it prevents the CITTA from KUSALA.

~ LOBHA may be accompanied by an indifferent or neutral feeling; it is not as intense as with a pleasant feeling. All degrees of LOBHA, subtle to gross, are dangerous.

~ LOBHA actions that hurt others are an obvious danger, LOBHA as enjoyment of sense objects is subtle. It makes one enslaved. In that moment the object is clung to and taken for happiness (it's ANICCA, ANATTA and DUKKHA). Unpleasant object = aversion usually, thus samsara.

~ LOBHA to KUSALA. Coming out of JHANACITTA~ defilements of VIPASSANĀ; tranquility, joy, concentration, etc. Attachment to SATI, wanting more of it or wanting it to last. ~ TANHĀ-craving, also designates LOBHA.

3 classifications of TANHĀ ~

1. ~ KĀMA-TANHĀ: sensuous craving, objects through the 6 doors, also the sense-sphere CITTA. One wants to see and hear ("Live life!"), wants to go on seeing and hearing in the future. Indeed, for eternity.

2. ~ BHAVA-TANHĀ – craving for becoming~ eternity belief of DITTHI, self that goes on forever.

3. ~ VIBHAVA~TANHĀ: craving for non-existence- annihilation belief. DITTHI is present, 'a self that ends at death'.

~ TANHĀ classified another way ~
1. KĀMA-TANHĀ is craving for the sensuous objects and also for the KĀMAVACARA CITTAS and their accompanying CETASIKAS.
2. RŪPA- TANHĀ- craving for RŪPAVACARA CITTAS and their accompanying CETASIKAS.
3. ARŪPA- TANHĀ- craving for ARŪPAVACARA CITTAS and their accompanying CETASIKAS.

~ So long as there is TANHĀ there will be birth, old age, disease and death. ~ TANHĀ is a conditioned DHAMMA. ~ Craving is a link in PATICCA-SAMUPADA-MOHA and TANHĀ are the roots of the existence wheel. "The KAMMA which produces rebirth is symbolized by the building of a hut. Whoever still has the desire to 'build' will be reborn."

2. Hatred~ Anger ~ Aversion ~ (DOSA)
Dosa arises with 2 types of CITTA, the DOSA-MŪLA-CITTAS; when the CITTA does not like the object it experiences there is aversion. When there is DOSA, the VEDANĀ which accompanies the CITTA is always an unpleasant feeling. There always seem to be numerous causes for DOSA, and they can be mistaken as a cause which is external to oneself. Of course, the real cause is one's inner DOSA accumulation, and it can always find an object. (Another person's actions, speech, etc. "Too hot/cold/windy" etc.)

~ There are many degrees of DOSA ~ from slight dislike, irritation, moodiness, fear, anger, revengeful hatred, strong DOSA can motivate heinous crimes ~ (ANANTARIKA KAMMA) which produce an unhappy rebirth (after the life during which one committed the crime has ended.)

~ 1. ~ Kills one's mother
~ 2. ~ Kills one's father.
~ 3. ~ Kills an ARAHAT
~ 4. ~ With evil thought draws blood from a Buddha.
~ 5 ~ By his intent creates a schism in the SANGHA.

VIS. MAGGA. ~ "The characteristic of anger (DOSA) is 'flying into anger like an enraged snake'. When one hits a snake, he is likely to become fierce and attack. DOSA is aggressive, just like a snake which has been hit. The function of DOSA is spreading of itself or writhing as when poison takes effect. When poison has been taken it affects the whole body and it causes pain. DOSA likewise has an ill effect and it is dangerous, like poison. The function of DOSA is also compared to a jungle-fire which burns that on which it depends. DOSA is destructive like the jungle-fire which consumes the whole forest. DOSA is harmful for the mind and body.

When there is DOSA there cannot be any happiness. ~ When DOSA is present there is patience or METTĀ. Recognizing this, one can easily see the disadvantage of having DOSA."

ATTHASĀLINĪ ~ 'Hatred as offending': that which offends or hates is DOSA. Hating is the act or mode of offending. Hatred is the state of the offending mind or person. Offense in the sense of 'forsaking nature' is disorderliness ~ 'disordered temper'. Upsetting is the actor mode of such offending. That which opposes is opposition. That which opposes repeatedly is hostility. ~ The mind of the hostile person is rough, hard-hearted. On account of this fault not a word is well-chosen, but is ill-spoken, not completed: this is abruptness. In anger there is no finished speech, or even if speech during anger is so, it is without measure.

DOSA can harm oneself and others. ~ The proximate cause for DOSA is 'grounds for annoyance' like (the sight, smell or perception of) urine mixed with poison. ~ "Even so, BHIKKHUS, some BHIKKHU here is very gentle, very meek, very tranquil – so long as disagreeable ways of speech do not assail him. But when disagreeable ways of speech assail the BHIKKHU, it is then that he is to be/needs to be/should be called 'gentle,' is to be called 'meek,' is to be called 'tranquil'..."

The ANĀGĀMĪ stage uproots DOSA from the mind. All forms of it will never arise again. DOSA can arise on account of any object experienced through any of the 6 doors.

The Buddha compared someone who angers very easily with an open sore. An open sore is painful at the slightest touch, is unpleasant to look at, and is foul.

~ DOSA only arises in the 11 sensuous planes of existence. It doesn't arise in the RŪPA and ARŪPA- BRAHMA planes, due to it being suppressed or uprooted by the power of SAMADHI or enlightenment. LOBHA and MOHA arise in 30 planes of existence.
~ DOSA motivates AKUSALA KAMMA through body, speech and mind. MOHA always accompanies DOSA. Ignorance blinds one to the true nature of realities. SATI of DOSA is the true means of eradication. At the moment of SATI there can be no DOSA.

3. Delusion ~ Ignorance ~ Bewilderment ~ (MOHA)
AKUSALA HETUS (roots) are AKUSALA CETASIKAS, which are the foundation or root of the AKUSALA CITTA. Only three types of AKUSALA CETASIKAS are AKUSALA HETUS: LOBHA, DOSA and MOHA. There are, apart from the HETUS, several other AKUSALA CETASIKAS which can accompany AKUSALA CITTA. But there are four types of AKUSALA CETASIKAS which arise with every AKUSALA CITTA. These CETASIKAS are:

1. ~ MOHA ~ delusion ~
2. ~ AHIRIKA (shamelessness) ~
3. ~ ANOTAPPA (recklessness),
4. ~ UDDHACCA (restlessness)

~ VIS.MAGGA ~ "MOHA delusion has the characteristic of 'blindness', or that of 'unknowing'. Its function is 'non penetration' or that of' concealing the true nature of an individual object'. It is manifested as 'the absence of right practice', or it is manifested as 'darkness'. Its proximate cause is 'unwise attention'. It should be regarded as the root of all that is unprofitable."

~ When there is MOHA there is darkness. MOHA does not see that the object which is experienced is only a conditioned reality (SANKHARA DHAMMA). It does not see the object as ANICCA, ANATTĀ or DUKKHA.

~ There are two types of MOHA – MŪLA-CITTA, one accompanied by restlessness, one by doubt. When one it attached to something, this LOBHA- MŪLA-CITTA with MOHA does not see the true nature of the object clearly, it is not self, satisfactory or static. It does not see that attachment is sorrowful and it is DUKKHA.

~ With DOSA- MŪLA-CITTA there is MOHA as well. (One doesn't see the object in light of the TI-LAKKHANA). Thus, when LOBHA and DOSA are present, the individual accumulates MOHA as well. MOHA simply does not see that conditioned realities are ANICCA, ANATTĀ and DUKKHA.

~ Delusion is not understanding the 4 noble truths, one is confused regarding KAMMA and VIPĀKA. One doesn't recognize that actions have results ~ such as SILA, DANA, BHĀVANĀ.

~ MOHA conditions birth (wrong view). MOHA is different from DITTHI, MOHA does not know the true nature of realities, and DITTI has wrong view about them. When one takes realities for self or SUKHA, there is DITTHI. Whenever DITTHI arises, MOHA will always be present. When one commits AKUSALA KAMMA through body, speech or mind, there is always MOHA. MOHA doesn't know that "KAMMA brings an unpleasant result, and can produce an unhappy rebirth."

~ Ignorance is called 'the greatest taint'. Ignorance is like gloom, since it covers up the truth, it conceals the arising and passing away of conditioned realities.

4. Wrong view ~ (DITTHI)

Wrong view is a distorted view of reality. Because of the wrong view one takes the impermanent for permanent. What is DUKKHA for happiness, what is ANATTA for ATTA? With wrong view one does not see phenomena (NĀMA- RŪPA) as they really are. MOHA covers up the true nature of reality and DITTHI sees them wrongly.

~ DITTHI does not arise with every CITTA. DITTHI is a kind of clinging, it arises only with LOBHA- MŪLA-CITTA. DITTHI arises with 4 of the 6 LOBHA- MŪLA-CITTAS. 2 types of LOBHA- MŪLA-CITTA with DITTHI are accompanied by pleasant feelings, and 2 types are with indifferent feelings.

~ ATTHASĀLINĪ ~ DITTHI is untrue view, from being 'held amiss. A false view is a wrong view. A view found unskillful by the wise as bringing disadvantage is also a wrong view. Further, by it associated states see wrongly, or itself sees wrongly; or it is the mere act of wrong seeing. Thus, it is wrong view. It has unwise conviction as its characteristic; perversion as function; wrong conviction as manifestation; the desire not to see the noble minded (ARIYANS) as proximate cause. It should be regarded as the highest fault.

~ Unwise conviction means unwise clinging or unwise adhering. With DITTHI, one clings to a false view of reality. DITTHI has perversion as function, meaning the deviation from what is right, from the right path. DITTHI passes over the intrinsic nature of phenomena; it considers them perversely, or with distortion, or as permanent, etc. DITTHI is vile and brings disadvantage because it makes one follow the wrong path/practice which does not lead to the goal: The eradication of defilements.

~ The manifestation of DITTHI is wrong conviction. When there is clinging to a wrong opinion, it is a manifestation of DITTHI. e.g., Believing that there are no KUSALA or AKUSALA KAMMAS, and that they bring results accordingly.

~ The origin of this wrong view called DITTHIGATA is due to
1. ~ Hearing an unprofitable/evil doctrine,
2. ~ Unwholesome friendship,
3. ~ The desire not to see noble minded people,
4. ~ Unsystematic thought.

~ If one does not listen to the DHAMMA explained correctly, there are no conditions for the development of the right view. Wrong views are the highest fault because when they arise, they pierce right views and counter them. Wrong view is dangerous and fearsome, because it can lead to many kinds of AKUSALA KAMMA.

There are 62 kinds of DITTHI, BRAHMA- JĀLA- SUTTA- DIGHA: There are 3 main ones: eternalistic, annihilistic, semi-eternalistic ~ One holds that some phenomena are permanent while others are not. Belief in a self is "SAKKAYA- DITTHI". ~ (For detailed explanation of the 3 main wrong views, see page 24-25. AKUSALA CETASIKAS notebooks. N. V. Gorkam).

1. ~ There is no result in a moral act (NATTHIKA DITTHI).
2. ~ There are no causes for defilements, for purification, for energy, all is without causes (AHETUKA DITTHI).

3. ~ There is no such thing as moral action or immoral action (KUSALA and AKUSALA KAMMAS) (no merit) (AKIRIYA-DITTHI).
   ~ Only these 3 kinds of DITTHI are AKUSALA KAMMA PATHA (a completed course of unwholesome action). These three DITTHIS should be regarded as dangerous, evil deeds which spring from such DITTHI. ~ All kinds of DITTHI, subtle or gross, arise because of not seeing the five KHANDAS (NĀMA and RŪPA) according to their actuality. ~ Buddha has compared DITTHI to a seed from which a plant with a bitter taste grows. ~ Right view is compared to a seed from which a plant with a sweet taste grows. ~ A SOTĀPANNA has eradicated DITTHI completely.

5. Conceit ~ (MĀNA)
   ATTHASĀLINĪ ~ "Conceit is fancying (deeming, vain imagining); it has haughtiness as characteristic, self-praise as function, desire to (advertise self like) a banner as manifestation, greed, attachment, dissociated from wrong view as proximate cause." Should be regarded as a form of lunacy. ~ Conceit, overweening and conceitedness signify mode and state. Loftiness is in the sense of rising upwards or of springing over others. Haughtiness, i.e., In whom conceit arises, he it lifts up, and keeps upraised, 'flaunting a flag' in the sense of 'swelling above' others. Conceit favors the mind all round. Conceit arising repeatedly is like a banner. The banner flies above all other flags. Desire for self-advertisement. ~ An upholding of oneself, one compares oneself with another ~ which constitutes the 3 forms of conceit ~
   1. ~ I am better than... (superior to) others ~
   2. ~ I am equal to... (the 'no difference' attitude) ~
   3. ~ I am worse than... (inferiority complex if sustained) ~

   These 3 ways of comparing may occur in someone who is actually superior, actually equal and in someone who is actually inferior. Under this aspect there are 9 kinds of conceit.
   Conceit arises only with the 4 types of LOBHA-MŪLA-CITTA, which are not accompanied by DITTHI. MĀNA and DITTHI do not arise at the same time. Neither does MĀNA arise

every time a LOBHA-MŪLA-CITTA that is without DITTHI. MĀNA is haughtiness, arrogance, vanity, pride, comparing one's own qualities with those of another ~ to one's own advantage. MĀNA is only eradicated upon the attainment of ARAHATSHIP.

Conceit can arise on account of each of the objects which are experienced through the senses. "I received such a pleasant object (6 senses). How unfortunate that a person lives without such things." ~ The upholding of oneself.

Experience of pleasant objects through the senses is only VIPĀKA, conditioned by KAMMA (ANATTA). ~ One can be proud of one's knowledge, one's birth, rank, position, race, caste, religion, skin color, teeth, hair, their wealth, their particular skill or inadequacy if related to as inferior. It can be any comparison of one's work, beauty, ugliness, one's look compared to another. Conceit may arise due to the 8 LOKA DHAMMAS ~ praise, pleasure, fame, gain; and also, their opposites. Competition, competitive mentality: "I know more DHAMMA than..." "My experience is broader..." "He's much wiser than me..." etc. ("Things are the way they are" ~ UPEKKHA) ~ "Prejudices about certain people." When there is SATI, there cannot be MĀNA ~ METTĀ is the opposite of conceit. It is thoughts of love to all, free of distinction, with oneself no better or less than anyone else. MĀNA is the comparing mind, the absurdity to think of one's NĀMA- RŪPA as better, equal or less than someone else's!

6. Envy ~ (ISSA)

Envy ~ Selfishness (MACCHPIRIYA) ~ and worry (KUKKUCCA) can arise with the 2 types of DOSA-MŪLA-CITTA, which are always accompanied by an unpleasant feeling. Our attachment to a pleasant feeling that accompanies sight, sounds, etc. conditions DOSA. When someone else receives a pleasant object, one may be jealous or envious: "Why does he receive it (i.e., an object, praise, fame, recognition, attention, etc.) and I don't?" ~ ISSA. Rooted in DOSA. ~ "Bitter or longing contemplation of another's better fortune, circumstances or qualities" ~ Oxford Dictionary

Lack of appreciation or absence of inclination to congratulate others upon their success in life. Envying others' success and prosperity shows and produces dissatisfaction with one's own condition. When there is ISSA, there is aversion towards the object.

~ ATTHASĀLINĪ ~ ISSA has the characteristic of envying, of not enduring the prosperity of others, the function of taking no delight in such prosperity. The proximate cause being such prosperity. Jealousy is synonymous with envy; envy is opposed to MUDITA. ~ "Appreciative joy."

~ According to ABHIDHAMMA classification (not SUTTAS though) ISSA is considered a fetter (SAMYOJANA) ~ A SOTĀPANNA has eradicated ISSA completely. One should develop SATI and MUDITA to overcome ISSA: ~ Learn to rejoice in others' happiness.

7. Selfishness ~ Stinginess ~ Avarice (greed for personal gain) ~ (MACCHARIYA)

~ Selfishness only arises with a DOSA-MŪLA-CITTA; not with every DOSA however. It can't arise with a LOBHA-MŪLA-CITTA or exclusively with a MOHA-MŪLA-CITTA, as when MACCHARIYA arises there is also aversion towards the object of experience.

~ MACCHARIYA = the want of generosity of heart ~ Five kinds of stinginess regarding dwelling, family, gifts, reputation and doctrine.

DHAMMASANGANĪ ~ 'Stinginess' is the expression of meanness. 'Avariciousness' is the act or mode of being mean. 'Mean spirit' is the state of one endowed with stinginess." Let it be for me only, and not for another." ~ Thus, wishing not to diffuse all one's own acquisitions. One is 'closed' with avarice; this state of being is a synonym for 'soft meanness'. Such a mind state as this hinders generosity.

Stinginess is 'spoon feeding', for when the pot is full to the brim, one takes food from it by a spoon with the edge bent on all sides: It is not possible to get a spoonful. So too the mind of a selfish, stingy person is bent in. When it is bent in, the body is also bent in (as one 'contracts'), it recedes and is not diffused. ~ Thus, stinginess is said to be niggardliness; a mind that is shut and gripped; a mind that shrinks from opening, making gifts; in doing service to others, one does not easily stretch out beyond one's self interest. The MACCHARIYA state makes the individual recede from giving to others what belongs to himself; it also wishes to take that which belongs to another. It has the characteristic of 'hiding' or 'seizing' ~ thinking "May it be for me and not for another." One's own property is the proximate cause. One can't endure the thought of sharing in common with others; it should be regarded as mental ugliness. ~ VIS.MAG.

~ Avarice ~ The 'stain of avarice' is one of the dark states that corrupt 'the natural transparency of consciousness'. The proximate cause of envy is someone else's property, or what they are about to acquire.

There are five kinds of stinginess:

~ Dwelling: all aspects of: a room, a house, a chair, a pillow, etc. Any place we are comfortable can give rise to MACCHARIYA.

~ Family~ e.g A BHIKKHU doesn't want to share with another BHIKKHU the family he is used to visiting, not wanting to introduce friends to other friends.

~ Stinginess about 'gains'~ includes robes, clothing, alms food, food, lodging, one's home and medicines, any belongings in general.

~ Stinginess regarding words of praise ~ or 'reputation'. Reputation refers to personal beauty as well as praise of merits. Here the person who is mean as to the beauty of the body, wishes not to hear it said that another is worthy of faith, and beautiful. One who is mean or selfish as to praise of merits does not wish to have another's praises sung, on account of his virtue, ascetic practice, progressor behavior, etc. ~ One usually likes and wants praise, fame, gain and pleasure, and does not want others to have the same. (No understanding of AKUSALA-KUSALA KAMMA & VIPĀKA).

~ One can be stingy as to DHAMMA. Perhaps one does not want to share DHAMMA with others because one is afraid or fearful that others will have the same knowledge, or more knowledge than oneself. (Both book DHAMMA and experience of reality.) Of course, there are times that one doesn't teach, out of consideration for the DHAMMA or out of consideration for other people ~ The MAHANIDDESA & CULA-NIDDESA of the 'KHUDDAKA NIKAYA" explain how one can be stingy with regard to the 5 KHANDAS, and the (12) AYATANAS ~ (Bases: 6 internal & 6 external) ~ All ways of classifying NĀMA- RŪPA. Ex. PAÑÑA is a SANKHARAKKHANDHA ~ When one is stingy with regard to PAÑÑA CETASIKA one does not want to help others to develop PAÑÑA, etc. with other CETASIKAS.

Stinginess is foolish; one cannot keep PARAMATTHA DHAMMAS. Stinginess is "I-ness", the opposite of ANATTA. With AKUSALA CITTA there is MOHA which keeps the TI-LAKKHANA hidden. Thus AKUSALA-KAMMA is produced, the SOTAPANNA has eradicated all forms of stinginess ~ MACCHARIYA.

~ When MACCHARIYA is present in the concealment of one's own property, the necessity to hide something because one is afraid to share it, lest they themselves be without: hungry, thirsty, without proper clothing or shelter. The VIPĀKA of this MACCHARIYA is just those conditions including PETA and lower births. Because of MOHA one is blinded to the real laws of existence, thus they do that which leads to one's own harm and causes harm to others. ~ MACCHARIYA is a miser. This state should be understood as extremely dangerous.

8. Worry ~ Regret ~ (KUKKUCCA)
Anxiety or undue anxiousness for what has been done wrongly, or for right actions that have been left undone ~ DHAMMASANGANĪ ~ Consciousness of what is lawful in something that is unlawful; consciousness of what is unlawful in something that is lawful; consciousness of what is moral in something that is immoral; and consciousness of something immoral in something that is moral ~ All this sort of worry, fidgeting, overscrupulousness, remorse of conscience, mental scarifying ~ this is what is called 'worry.'

By this imagining an improper thing to be proper when transgression is committed, when offense against something is done, in one who recollecting it regrets: "I have done badly, wrongly", worry arises by way of after-regret.

~ ATTHASĀLINĪ ~ "A contemptible act is 'KUKATA"; the state of a displeased mind, produced by making such an act its object is KUKKUCCA ~ worry. It has repentance as characteristic; sorrow at deeds of commission and omission as function; regret as manifestation; deeds of commission and omission as proximate cause. It should be regarded as a state of bondage (mental slavery).

~ KUKKUCCA can only arise with DOSA-MŪLA-CITTA, when there is worry or regret, there is also aversion towards the object which is experienced at that moment. DUKKHA VEDANĀ always accompanies KUKKUCCA.

~ Misconduct in act, word and thought, including all AKUSALA CITTAS conduce to remorse. ~ Worry is not exactly the meaning of KUKKUCCA, one could say they are worried about the future. However, KUKKUCCA pertains to the past. (An approximate cause is unskillful deeds performed, and skillful deeds left undone (e.g. saving the life of an insect you see drowning.) Remorse is equal to mental burning. ~ KUKKUCCA arises when there is no purity of SĪLA, when there is no watchfulness as to the six-doors, or immoderation in eating, when there is no vigilance, no SATI-SAMPAJAÑÑA (clear comprehension of NĀMA and RŪPA) and no cultivation of the four applications of mindfulness. ~ The person who clings to the sense experience of their bodies, who have omitted KUSALA acts and committed AKUSALA acts will be afraid and fearful of death. One trembles at the thought of death. ~ The opposite will lead to peace at death.

~ KUKKUCCA is a 'hindrance' coupled with restlessness, NĪVARANAS are AKUSALA CETASIKAS which hinder the performing of KUSALA. It is not necessary to worry about the past. ~ NĀMA- RŪPA observation now. ~ The SOTAPANNA has eradicated gross KUKKUCCA, subtle KUKKUCCA goes upon attainment of ANĀGĀMI (and all DOSA goes then). Of course, KUKKUCCA is a SANKHARA DHAMMA, which arises due to causes. The SOTAPANNA has not uprooted the 'NĪVARANA

KUKKUCCA', but only the KUKKUCCA; which is a kind of worry which is actually scruples with respect to VINAYA (SĪLA).

9. and 10. Shamelessness ~ (AHIRIKA) ~ Recklessness ~ Fearlessness ~ (ANOTTAPPA)

These two CETASIKAS along with MOHA and UDDHACCA ~ restlessness ~ arise with every AKUSALA CITTA. ~ VIS. MAGGA.

~ "AHIRIKA (Consciencelessness) has no conscious scruples, thus it is consciencelessness; it is unashamed; thus, it is shamelessness. ANOTAPPA (recklessness) is non-dread, the inability to perceive the consequences of one's actions. AHIRIKA has the characteristic of absence of disgust at bodily (speech and thought) misconduct, or it has the characteristic of immodesty. When an unwholesome act is about to be committed, there's no feeling of shame, such as: "I will be corrupted if I do this", or "Some humans and devas may know this of me". One is unable to see the worthiness inherent in KUSALA and the unskillfulness of AKUSALA. ANOTAPPA has the characteristic of non-dread, absence of dread on their account, or the absence of anxiety about them. It's the lack of anguish over the performance of AKUSALA, resulting in subsequent discomfort. Lack of scruples (Oxford dictionary- feeling of doubt about the morality of something, one's actions, hesitation so caused) ~" PARAMATTHA MAÑJŪSĀ ~ commentary to VIS.MAGGA.

~ Doing evil without being ashamed of it is the function of AHIRIKA; doing evil without dreading it is the function of ANOTAPPA. AHIRIKA manifests as "not shrinking from evil because it is not ashamed of it and does not loathe it". ANOTAPPA manifests as "not shrinking from evil because it does not see the danger of it, and does not fear its consequences". The proximate cause of AHIRIKA is no respect for oneself. The proximate cause of ANOTTAPPA is no respect for someone else.

AHIRIKA is compared to a domestic pig which does not abhor filth ~ KILESAS are unclean and impure. AHIRIKA does not abhor KILESAS; does not loathe it; is not ashamed of it, no matter whether it is LOBHA, DOSA or MOHA, avarice, conceit, jealousy — or any other AKUSALA DHAMMA.

ANOTAPPA is compared to a moth which is attracted to the fire although the fire is dangerous for it. LOBHA, DOSA and MOHA, all AKUSALA DHAMMAS are dangerous. But ANOTAPPA does not fear (a repulsion born of insightful understanding) the danger of AKUSALA (unhappiness now and such consequences as an unhappy rebirth). The reckless mind.

AHIRIKA and ANOTTAPPA always arise together with MOHA. MOHA does not know the true nature of realities, and does not know that AKUSALA KAMMA produces AKUSALA-VIPĀKA. Ignorance of the truth conditions AHIRIKA, which is not ashamed of AKUSALA, and ANOTTAPPA, which does not dread the danger of AKUSALA. ~ The origin of AHIRIKA is within oneself and the origin of ANOTTAPPA is outside oneself. (Their opposites are HIRI ~ moral shame ~ and OTTAPPA ~ fear of blame).

(HIRI sees that AKUSALA is impure and revolting, OTTAPPA sees the danger and consequences of AKUSALA. These two states should be regarded as the guardians of the world). ~ When one sees the true nature of AKUSALA one wants to develop wisdom, which can eradicate them. Upon the attainment of ARAHATTA, AHIRIKA, ANOTTAPPA, UDDHACCA and MOHA vanish for good.

11. Restlessness ~ (UDDHACCA)

Restlessness arises with every AKUSALA CITTA. VIS. MAGGA ~ It has the characteristic of disquiet, 'like water whipped by the wind'. Its function is unsteadiness, like a flag or a banner whipped by the wind. It is manifested as turmoil, like ashes flung with stones. Its proximate cause is 'unwise attention to mental disquiet'. It should be regarded as a distraction of consciousness ~ agitated or unquiet, unsteady, dispersed state of mind ~ mental turmoil. Restlessness even arises with LOBHA-MŪLA-CITTAS accompanied by a pleasant feeling. If one is attached to a quiet place, even though one thinks of themselves as being calm, there is restlessness, a mental disquiet. UDDHACCA is one of the hindrances; it forms a pair with worry. The ARAHAT has eradicated UDDHACCA.

12. Sloth ~ Stolidity ~ (THĪNA)

13. Torpor ~ Languor ~ (MIDDHA)

These two AKUSALA CETASIKAS always arise together; when present in the mind one does not have the energy for KUSALA. ~ THĪNA is that which is indisposed. Indisposition of the adhering and cohering; clinging, cleaving to, stickiness; stolidity, a stiffening, a rigidity of the mind ~ this is called stolidity ~ inertness ~ adhering is the mode of hanging downwards. The consciousness, namely, when unable to strengthen the postures, hangs downwards. THĪNA is like a lump of butter which is too stiff for spreading. ~ Dimness of the mind's consciousness of an object, sloth is opposed to VIRIYA-energy, lack of vitality or motivating force. ~ ATTHASĀLINĪ ~ "Sloth has the absence of, or opposition to striving as characteristic, destruction of energy as function, sinking of associated states as manifestation; the proximate cause is unsystematic thought in not arousing oneself from discontent and laziness (or indulgence).

AKUSALA CITTA is accompanied by VIRIYA, but it is AKUSALA VIRIYA, wrong effort: this is quite different from KUSALA VIRIYA, right effort. When there are THĪNA and MIDDHA, there is no energy for the performing of DĀNA, SĪLA, listening or practicing DHAMMA. All the accompanying CETASIKAS that arise with THĪNA- MIDDHA begin to sink or wilt.

MIDDHA ~ torpor ~ is that which is in the disposition and unwieldiness of CETASIKAS, or one's mental body. A shrouding, enveloping, barricading within: torpor that is sleep, drowsiness, slumbering. There is no courage for KUSALA. A morbid state of the mental factors, unwieldiness of intellect, perception is impaired. ~ Torpor has unwieldiness as characteristic, closing the doors of consciousness as function, shrinking in taking the object, or drowsiness as manifestation; proximate cause is unsystematic thought in not arousing oneself from discontent and laziness (or indulgence). (Unsystematic thought = unwise attention = no SATI). Mental heaviness ~ THĪNA- MIDDHA form a pair and become one of the five hindrances. Sloth and torpor are eradicated upon ARAHATSHIP. (In ARAHAT sleep ~ there is a lapse into

BHAYANSA CITTA in physical fatigue owing to the weakness of the sentient body in ARAHATS. When this arises unmixed with thought-process they sleep (due to bodily tiredness not THĪNA-MIDDHA ~ they are uprooted). Thus sleep-rest is called slumber (Oxford dictionary: Peaceful, tranquil rest) ~ The 2 types of MOHA-MŪLA-CITTA cannot be accompanied by THĪNA- MIDDHA. ~ THĪNA- MIDDHA should be considered dangerous as they hinder and prevent the performing of DĀNA, SĪLA and BHĀVANĀ. ~ Overindulgence in food and sleep give rise to THĪNA- MIDDHA. ~ The Buddha said moderation in food prolongs life and one ages softly~ thus urgency of SATI ~ wisdom ~ freedom.

14. Doubt ~ Perplexity ~ (VICIKICCHĀ)

Doubt can only accompany one type of CITTA: the type of MOHA-MŪLA-CITTA which is MOHA-MŪLA-CITTA VICIKICCHĀ SAMPAYUTTAM (CITTA rooted in ignorance accompanied by doubt). ~ VICIKICCHĀ is not conventional doubt, it is doubt about realities, about NĀMA-RŪPA, about KAMMA and VIPĀKA, about the four noble truths, about their dependent origination.

DHAMMASANGANĪ ~ VICIKICCHĀ ~ "Doubt is the hesitating, the dubiety, (doubtfulness) which on that occasion is puzzlement, perplexity, distraction, standing at crossroads, collapse, uncertainty of grasp, evasion, hesitation, incapacity to grasping thoroughly, stiffness of mind, mental scarifying; such is perplexity." ~ Doubt means exclusion from the cure of knowledge. Fluctuation is the inability to establish anything in any one mode, thus "Is this state permanent or is it impermanent?" Because of the inability to comprehend, there is uncertainty of grasp. Doubt has 'shifting about' as characteristic, 'mental wavering' as function, 'indecision or uncertainty in grasp' as manifestation, 'unwise attention' as proximate cause; it should be regarded as danger to attainment." ~ One can have doubts about the BUDDHA, DHAMMA & SANGHA, or about the past or future or both, or whether there is enlightenment, NIBBĀNA. Doubt is one of the 5 hindrances; it hinders one in the development of DĀNA, SĪLA, BHĀVANĀ.

The SOTAPANNA has eradicated doubt and wrong views; they

know that the 8-fold path is the only way to achieve liberation from KILESAS.

~ Summarizing the 14 AKUSALA CETASIKAS ~

1. MOHA ~ (ignorance)
2. AHIRIKA ~ (shamelessness) arising with every unwholesome
3. ANOTAPPA ~ (fearlessness of blame)   mind state (AKUSALA CITTA).
4. UDDHACCA ~ (restlessness)
5. LOBHA ~ (greed) arising with 8 types of CITTA – the LOBHA-MŪLA-CITTAS
6. DITTHI ~ (wrong view) arising with four types of LOBHA-MŪLA-CITTAS
7. MĀNA ~ (conceit) arising with the four types of LOBHA-MŪLA-CITTAS which are without DITTHI; it may or may not arise with these CITTAS, but only these if it does.
8. DOSA ~ (aversion) arising with 2 types of CITTA ~ DOSA-MŪLA-CITTAS
9. ISSA ~ (envy) may or may not arise with the two types
10. MACCHARIYA ~ (selfishness)   of DOSA- MŪLA- CITTA, but they
11. KUKKUCCA ~ (worry) never all arise together.
12. THĪNA ~ (sloth) may or may not arise with four types of
13. MIDDHA ~ (torpor) LOBHA-MŪLA-CITTA which are SASAN KHARIKA, and with one type DOSA- MŪLA-CITTA which is SASAN KHARIKA. They always arise together.
14. VICIKICCHĀ ~ (doubt) arises with one type of MOHA-MŪLA-CITTA

D. Explanation of the 25 KUSALA CETASIKAS

1. Non-greed ~ non-attachment ~ (ALOBHA)
   By its means one is not greedy. It has the characteristic of the mind's lack of desire for an object, or it has the characteristic of non-adherence, 'like a water drop on a lotus leaf'. Its function is not

to lay hold like a liberated BHIKKHU. It is manifested as a state of not treating as a shelter, like that of a man who has fallen into filth. ~ Can be absence of greed or active generosity (DĀNA) ~ non grasping ~ renunciation of object restrains one from attachment to objects. Is one of the three wholesome roots.

2. Non-hate ~ Goodwill ~ (ADOSA)
By its means one is not angry. It has the characteristic of 'lack of savagery', or the characteristic of 'non-opposing', like a gentle sandalwood does. It is manifested as 'agreeableness, like the full moon'. ~ ADOSA is opposed to DOSA. It is not the mere absence of hatred or aversion, but is a positive quality: virtue. ADOSA is one of the three roots of skillfulness in action, speech and thought. Absence of coarseness is also a characteristic. It is called (also) ABYĀPĀDA (peace of mind) ~ ADOSA is synonymous with METTĀ.

3. Trustful confidence ~ Faith ~ (SADDHA)
Its characteristic is having faith, or the characteristic of trusting. Its function is to clarify, or to enter into, like setting out to cross a flood. Its manifestation is non-fogginess, or it is manifested as resolution. Its proximate cause is something to have faith in, or its proximate cause is the things beginning with hearing the noble DHAMMA that constitute the four factors of the stream-entry ~

~ 1. ~ waiting on good men
~ 2. ~ hearing DHAMMA
~ 3. ~ wise attention
~ 4. ~ and practice in accordance with the DHAMMA

Also, in 1. ~ absolute confidence in BUDDHA DHAMMA and SANGHA and possession of noble virtue). It should be regarded as that because it takes hold of profitable things.

4. SATI ~ (Mindfulness)
By its means one remembers. It has the characteristic of not wobbling. (APILĀPANA= not wobbling = is the steadying of an object, the remembering and not forgetting it; keeping it as immovable as a stone instead of letting it go bobbing about 'like a pumpkin in water'

(pm.482)). Its function is not to forget. It is manifested as guarding, or as the state confronting the objective field. Its proximate cause is strong perception, or its proximate cause is the foundations of mindfulness; it should be regarded as 'like a pillar' because it is firmly founded, or like a doorkeeper because it guards the eye-door, and so on. ~ It can become an INDIRIYA, and when strong an enlightenment factor. It is the continuous noticing of an object in successive moments of perception. It does not allow the object to float away.

~ SATI is the opposite of superficiality and of obliviousness.

5. Moral shame ~ (HIRI)
Has conscientious scruples about bodily misconduct, speech and thought. It is a term for 'intelligent modesty'. It is ashamed of performing the unskillful or leaving undone the skillful. It has the characteristic of disgust at evil. It has the function of not doing evil; it is manifested as the shrinking from evil. Its proximate cause is self-respect ~ inner conscience which creates an abhorrence for evil. It is different from worry or remorse in that it acts in the present moment to prevent any evil from arising. Hesitation in doing unwholesome acts, speech and thought through shame of being known and censored by the noble and wise. HIRI is not shyness; it arises from within.

~ Shame of AKUSALA has nothing to do with DOSA. HIRI sees that AKUSALA is ugly and impure.

6. Moral dread of evil ~ Discretion ~ (OTTAPPA)
Has the characteristic of dread of the consequences of unskillful bodily actions, speech and thought. It has the function of abstaining from the unskillful, and that in the mode of dread. It is manifested as shrinking from evil. Its proximate cause is respect for others. Anguish, abstinence over wrong-doing out of respect for others. Reflection on the fearsomeness of error.

HIRI and OTTAPPA are regarded as the two dominant factors that rule the world. No civilized society can exist without them.
~ Fear of AKUSALA ~ sees the danger of AKUSALA and its

consequences. ~ OTTAPPA has an external origin. One refrains from evil because one does not want to behave in such a way as to be blamed by someone else ~ or the world.

6. Balance of mind ~ Specific neutrality ~ (TATRA-MAJJHATTATA) This is neutrality, equanimity in regard to those states of consciousness and consciousness concomitants arisen in association with it. It has the characteristic of conveying consciousness and accompanying concomitants evenly (i.e., evenness of mental factors in execution of their respective functions). Its function is to prevent deficiency and excess, or its function is to inhibit partiality (i.e., Impartial view of the object). It is manifested as neutrality; it should be regarded as like a driver who looks on with equanimity on thoroughbreds progressing evenly. This is sometimes synonymous with UPEKKHA (a factor of enlightenment).

7. Composure of mental properties ~ (KĀYA-PASSADHI)

8. Composure of consciousness ~ (CITTA- PASSADHI)
#8 means composure of the 3 mental bodies (aggregates). Feeling, perception and SANKHĀRA (volitional formations, calmness, quiet, composure, serenity of mental properties and CITTA, smooth and even functioning). They have the characteristic of quieting disturbance of mental properties and CITTA. Their function is to crush disturbance of the mental properties and CITTA. They are manifested as inactivity and coolness of mental properties and CITTA. Their proximate cause is the mental (body) and consciousness. Both groups are set at rest, and cool. It is 'like the cool shade of a tree to a person affected by the sun's heat'. They should be regarded as opposed to the defilements of agitation, worry, restlessness and excitement, which causes turbulence and lack of peacefulness in the mental body and in consciousness. When sufficiently developed this factor, PASSADHI (tranquility) becomes a factor of enlightenment.

9. Buoyancy/Lightness of mental properties ~ (VEDANĀ KHADHA, SAÑÑA & SANKHĀRA) (KĀYA – LAHUTĀ)

10. Buoyancy/Lightness of consciousness ~ (CITTA – LAHUTA)
   Agility, lightness, fluidity, mobility, swiftness of function of mental properties and CITTA. (The capacity to act and reply quickly). It is like the laying down of a heavy burden. They are manifested as non-sluggishness of the mental properties and CITTA. They are opposed to THĪNA (stiffness) and MIDDHA~ sloth and torpor which cause heaviness and rigidity in the mental factors and consciousness.

11. Pliancy/ malleability of mental properties (3 KHANDHAS) ~ (KĀYA-MUDUTĀ)

12. Pliancy/ malleability of consciousness ~ (CITTA- MUDUTĀ)
   They have the characteristic of 'quieting rigidity' in the mental properties and consciousness. Their function is to overcome stiffening in mental properties and CITTA. They are manifested as 'non-resistance'. Their proximate cause is the mental properties and consciousness. They are opposed to the defilements of DITTHI and MĀNA, which cause stiffness of mind and concomitants.
   ~ Both mean susceptibility, elasticity, resilience of mental factors and consciousness.

14. Adaptability/wieldiness of mental properties ~ (KĀYA-KAMMAÑÑATĀ)

15. Adaptability/wieldiness of consciousness ~ (CITTA – KAMMAÑÑATĀ)
   They are the wieldy state of mental factors and consciousness. They have the characteristic of 'quieting unwieldiness' (of unserviceableness or unworkableness of mental properties and CITTA). Their function is to crush unwieldiness in the mental properties of CITTA. They are manifested as success in making something an object of the mental properties and consciousness. Their proximate cause is the mental properties, and CITTA, as bringing trust in things that should be trusted in, and as bringing susceptibility of application to beneficial acts. (It is like heated metal made fit for use; like the refining of gold.) They are opposed to the remaining hindrances.

16. Proficiency of mental properties ~ (KĀYA- PUGUÑÑATA)

17. Proficiency of consciousness ~ (CITTA- PUGUÑÑATA)
    The proficient state of mental factors and consciousness have the characteristics of healthiness of the mental properties and CITTA. (Fitness, competence, skillfulness of function, opposed to sickness or incompetence ~ opposed to faithlessness). Their function is to crush unhealthiness of mental properties and mind. They are manifested as absence of disability; proximate cause is mental properties and CITTA.

18. Rectitude of mental properties ~ (KĀYUJUKATĀ)

19. Rectitude of consciousness ~ (CITTUJUKATĀ)
    The straight state of mental properties and CITTA. Straightness, honesty, lack of insincerity or hidden selfish motives. Characteristics of uprightness of mental properties and CITTA. Function is to crush tortuousness in the mental properties and CITTA. Manifested as non-crookedness. Proximate cause is mental properties and CITTA. Opposed to deceit, fraud, deception, craftiness which cause tortuousness to the mental properties and consciousness.

    ~ All these 19 concomitants are common to all types of moral (KUSALA) consciousness unlike the AKUSALA CETASIKAS, which do not arise in an AKUSALA CITTA in total. No AKUSALA CITTA arises without all 19 factors. Along with this SOBHANA group, additional KUSALA CETASIKAS may arise according to the type of consciousness.

    ~ Two Illimitables ~ (APPANAÑÑĀ) ~

20. Sympathetic joy ~ (MUDITĀ)
    Feeling the gladness of others, sharing their good fortune. Rejoicing in another's happiness. Appreciation of, or congratulating another upon their success, their delight. MUDITA is characterized as gladdening (produced by others' success); its function resides in not being envious. It is manifested as the elimination of aversion-boredom. Proximate cause is seeing beings succeed. It succeeds when it makes aversion subside; it fails when it produces merriment.

~ MUDITA has joy based on home life as its near enemy, since both share in seeing success. ~ Explanation ~ When a man either regards as gain "the obtaining of visible objects cognizable by the eye that are sought and associated with worldliness, or recalls those formerly obtained that are past, ceased and changed, then joy arises in him. Such joy as this is called joy based on home life; and aversion (boredom) which is dissimilar to the similar joy, is its fair enemy."

21. Compassion ~ (KARUNĀ)
    This is characterized as promoting the aspect of allaying suffering. (The wish for the removal of DUKKHA of others.) "That which makes the hearts of the good quiver when others are afflicted with sorrow." It is manifested as 'non-cruelty'. Its proximate cause is to see helplessness in those overwhelmed by DUKKHA. It succeeds when it makes cruelty subside, and it fails when it produces sorrow.
    ~ KARUNA has grief as its near enemy, since both share in seeing failure. (This grief comes from sense objects that are desired that are not obtained, or objects obtained that were cherished that pass.) Cruelty ~ wickedness (HIMSĀ) is its far enemy, for it is not possible to practice compassion and be cruel to breathing beings simultaneously.
    ~ MUDITĀ and KARUNĀ are Illimitables because they exist without limit among living beings. ~ Boundless, measureless states. They take as their object an infinite number of beings. Their detailed description can be found in VIS. MAGGA. CH. IV.P .321 ~ The 4-divine abiding. METTĀ and UPEKKHA are not included here since they are synonymous with ADOSA and balance of mind. #7 ~ Respectively, they can also be cultivated without limit also.

    ~ Three abstinences (VIRATIYO) ~

22. Right action ~ (SAMMĀ-KAMMANTA ~ or abstinence from bodily misconduct) ~ Abstinence from taking life ~ taking that which is not given with intention to steal ~ and sexual misconduct ~ (adultery ~ sensuous actions that cause unnecessary DUKKHA).

23. Right speech ~ (SAMMĀVĀCĀ ~ or abstinence from wrong speech) ~

1.~Abstinence from saying that which is not true with the intention to deceive.

2.~ slandering words that separate friendships.

3.~ harsh speech

4.~ frivolous talk

24. Right livelihood ~ (SAMMĀ ĀJĪVA) ~ Refraining from trade in poisons, intoxicants, weapons, slaves and animals for slaughter.

    These three have the characteristic of non-transgression in the respective fields of bodily conduct, speech and livelihood. Function is to draw back from such behavior, speech, etc. They manifest as the non-doing of the things that ought not to be done. Proximate causes are the special qualities of PATTI, HIRI, OTTAPPA, finesse of wish. Should be regarded as the mind's averseness from evil-doing.

~ Summary of the three abstinences ~

~ Right action, speech and livelihood are also 3 CETASIKAS and not merely statements after the fact. They are mental tendencies bent on avoiding action, speech and livelihood motivated by any of the AKUSALA CETASIKAS, or the three AKUSALA MŪLA-CITTAS. Strictly speaking these three factors collectively arise only in the supramundane CITTA~ (LOKUTTARA CITTA). In other cases, they arise separately because there are three volitions of mind. When all three are present in the LOKUTTARA CITTA they are regarded as factors of the path (MAGGANGA) and they constitute SĪLA.

25. Wisdom ~ non-delusion ~ (PAÑÑĀ) ~ Has the characteristic of penetrating things according to their individual essences, or it has the characteristic of sure penetration. Its function is to illuminate the objective field, like a lamp. It is manifested as 'non-bewilderment, like a guide in a forest'. It is one of the three roots, ADOSA & ALOBHA, of all that is profitable. ~ PAÑÑĀ literally means right knowing. One with it understands reality as it really is. Seeing phenomena as they truly are in the light of ANICCA, ANATTA and DUKKHA. Connotes not only the absence of delusion, but the presence of wisdom. The culmination of PAÑÑĀ is the mind of a wisdom-BUDDHA.

E. Relationship of the Mental Factors

The 7 common or universal factors are always present in all states of consciousness. The 6 particulars arise occasionally with either wholesome or unwholesome factors (Immorals), and the 19 wholesome CETASIKAS must always arise together (the remaining 6 function differently). No KUSALA factors may arise when any AKUSALA factors are present, and vice versa; each are mutually exclusive.

~ MOHA is present in all AKUSALA CITTAS. MOHA is always accompanied in all AKUSALA CETASIKAS by AHIRIKA, ANOTTAPPA and UDDHACCA in varying degrees. No other AKUSALA CETASIKAS are necessarily present in all AKUSALA CITTAS. ~ When LOBHA arises with MOHA, DOSA cannot be present since the former grasps at an object, while the latter pushes it away. DITTHI and MĀNA are rooted in MOHA and always accompanied by LOBHA-MŪLA-CITTA. They are subject to the same laws that govern greed; MĀNA and DITTHI cannot exist in the same CITTA, like two lions that cannot live together in the same cave. ~ DOSA may accompany MOHA when DOSA is not present, and envy, avarice and worry can arise only when DOSA is present. Only doubt and sloth are torpor (the latter 2 are always found together) and are not dependent on any root cause, arising either separately from, or together with, LOBHA, DOSA and MOHA. The more that these unwholesome factors are present in consciousness, in whatever combinations, the more intense and pervasive these root factors become. Firmly established in one moment, their presence causes a propensity for their future arousal. They can become habitual constituents of an individual's mental states. (The first states to arise in response to an object arising at the six-doors).

Wholesome factors ~ relationship ~ KUSALA CETASIKAS are not governed by a specific set of rules as are the AKUSALA CETASIKAS. ~ Except for PAÑÑĀ ~ non-delusion or wisdom, which must be cultivated especially, and the 3 abstinences and 2 Illimitables, which function only in unique states usually associated with great BHĀVANĀ development. The remaining 19 KUSALA CETASIKAS all arise together, each CITTA differs because of the variance in development of each CETASIKA in its particular strength and dominance in a given moment. ~ The 6 particulars arise independently or together in various combinations whenever their particular intensifying functions are called upon. In either KUSALA, AKUSALA CITTAS they become the same as the root, either KUSALA or AKUSALA. With various JHANA states all six can arise together. ~ Rapture, one of the particulars, cannot arise unless SUKHA VEDANA is present; SUKHA can arise without rapture but the opposite cannot occur. The presence of joy and rapture also enlivens the factor of vitality in a way likened to the vigor which results from an old person suddenly discovering a new reason to live. Faith increases the perceptual acuteness of concentration and SATI. Confidence in a practice facilitates the development of the practice. ~ Both SATI and SAMĀDHI are fed by joy and rapture since these two factors are instrumental in the development of SADDHA. ~ DOSA is always accompanied by an unpleasant feeling; all associated states rooted in DOSA also have DUKKHA VEDANĀ arising with them. 'Displeasing' is the nature of DUKKHA VEDANĀ (to ordinary minds), thus aversion for the object can arise. It can never arise with a pleasant feeling. ~ Just as sloth and torpor arise inseparably so are the 6 pairs of tranquility, buoyancy, pliancy, adaptability, proficiency and decisiveness. (These six pairs offer a cool suppleness to the consciousness).

~ End explanation of the 52 CETASIKAS ~

Chapter Four is a treatise on Ultimate Realities (*paramattha*).

4.
ULTIMATE REALITIES
(PARAMATTHA DHAMMAS)

1. Firstly, they are divided into two:
   1. NĀMA ~ (mentality) ~ has the function of experiencing
   2. RŪPA ~ (materiality) ~ cannot experience anything

   ~ NĀMA has the function of experiencing something, while RŪPA cannot experience anything. NĀMA can experience both mental phenomena and material phenomena.

2. The PARAMATTHA DHAMMAS can be further divided in four ways:
   1. CITTA ~ (consciousness) or (a moment of experience)
   2. CETASIKA ~ (mental factors accompanying consciousness)
   3. RŪPA ~ (material phenomena)
   4. NIBBĀNA ~ (the unconditioned reality)

   ~ CITTA, CETASIKA and RŪPA are PARAMATTHA DHAMMAS that are conditioned realities. They all arise from causes; they are all conditioned by other occurrences. The fourth type, NIBBĀNA, is the unconditioned reality. It is not caused by any other thing. It does not arise and it does not cease. All other realities are ANICCA, ANATTA and DUKKHA.

3. The PARAMATTHA DHAMMAS can be further divided by way of the five types or aggregates or groups into which they fall. (PAÑCA-KHANDHAS)

(All types ~ All conditioned NĀMAS and RŪPAS can be classified under the five KHANDAS)
1. RŪPA - KHANDHA ~ (4 great primary elements and the 24 secondary elements ~ details p.13 ~ 3B and 3 II.) All aspects of the body are included under RŪPA
2. VEDANĀ – KHANDHA ~ (is a CETASIKA ~ threefold ~ pleasant feeling, unpleasant feeling, and neutral feeling ~ details p.14 #7 and p.20 #2)
3. SAÑÑĀ – KHANDHA ~ (is a CETASIKA ~ perception ~ it marks the object so that it can be recognized now and in the future. ~ Details p.20 #3)
4. SANKHĀRA – KHANDHA ~ (this comprises the other 50 CETASIKAS which arise in various combinations with CITTA ~ Details pp. 19 – 42.)
5. VIÑÑĀNA -KHANDHA ~ (consciousness ~ CITTA ~ all types of CITTA are classified under this KHANDHA)

A. Ultimate Reality

(Manual of Insight – Mahasi Sayadaw, Chapter 3, pp. 93- 106)

We cannot say that conditional, relative realities are 'ultimate.' Only timeless, immutable realities should be accepted as 'ultimate.' Ultimate reality (PARAMATTHA) consists only of the following elements, because they are absolute and immutable facts of experience: mind, mental factors, matter, and NIBBĀNA.

An ultimate, irreducible phenomenon is called an 'ultimate reality.'

What we learn from others is also not necessarily true, so it should not be considered ultimate reality. On the other hand, what we empirically experience ourselves is never false but always true. Therefore, mind and mental factors, matter, and NIBBĀNA are called "ultimate reality," because they can be empirically experienced.

As the ABHIDHAMMA commentary says:

An ultimate, personally experienced phenomenon is called "an ultimate reality." The expression "empirically experienced" (SACCIKATTHA) refers to ultimate realities, not to illusions like magic and mirages that should not be accepted. The words "ultimate reality" refers to an ultimate reality that should not be accepted by hearsay, and so on.

Phenomena that we can personally experience are called "empirically experienced," "what truly exists," as well as "ultimate truth." There are fifty-seven of these ultimately real phenomena: the five aggregates, the twelve sense bases, the eighteen elements, and the twenty-two mental faculties.

According to the commentary these fifty-seven classes of phenomena are called "empirically experienced" or "ultimate reality." They can be summarized into the four ultimate realities of mind, mental factors, matter, and NIBBĀNA or mind and matter, in brief. For simplicity's sake, I will refer to them here as 'mind and matter'.

1. Conceptual illusions

When a magician conjures gold, silver, or gems out of a brick, a piece of paper, or a stone, people are under the illusion that these are genuinely gold, silver, or gems. Such imaginary things are said to be "not genuinely existing" (ABHŪTATTHA) or "not personally experienced" (ASACCIKATTHA), since they are mistaken for something genuine, just as a thirsty deer mistakes a mirage for water from a distance. Concepts such as woman, man, hand, foot, and so on have this kind of illusory nature. On the other hand, mind and matter can be experienced as they really are, so they are said to be "ultimate reality," "personally experienced," and "genuinely existing" (BHŪTATTHA).

For example, when people see a visible form with their eyes they know, "I see a visible form" or "The visible form that is seen exists." This visible form is what really exists and what is genuinely known at the moment of seeing; it is not an illusion like the gold, silver, or gems created by a magician or a mirage mistaken for water. Seeing would not be possible without a visible form. Therefore, a visible form that can be seen with the eyes is called a reality that genuinely exists or that is personally experienced. If a form is personally experienced, it is also called 'an ultimate reality'.

The experience of seeing a visible form is followed by a mental process that investigates and determines it to be of a certain shape: tall or short, spherical or flat, square or round, woman or man, face or arm, and so on. This mental process of investigation can only be experienced in an obvious way when one encounters an especially novel object, since the investigation of new objects takes time. This type of investigation is not usually apparent, since it doesn't take much time to investigate an object that one has seen before and is familiar with. Thus, ordinary people are under the illusion that they actually see the forms or shapes that they imagine, because they cannot distinguish between prior and subsequent processes of seeing and investigation.

According to the ABHIDHAMMA sub-commentary:

> The function of eye-consciousness is only to see visible forms, not to ascertain physical gestures or movements. However, succeeding mental processes follow so quickly that ordinary people think that they see, as if with their real eyes, the movement known by the succeeding mental process of investigation.
>
> For example, when we see a hand moving, our eye-consciousness sees only the visible form. It is not able to know that it is a hand or that it is moving. The mind is very fast, however, so the movement that the succeeding mind of investigation knows is taken to have been seen with the eyes. Ordinary people cannot distinguish between preceding and succeeding mental processes. On the other hand, a meditator who has practiced insight proficiently can recognize the mental process of seeing visible form as distinct from the subsequent mental processes that know it as a hand, and movement.
>
> The Pāli texts give the example of a swinging torch to clarify this point. If a lit torch is twirled in the darkness, it will appear as 'a solid ring of fire' to anyone watching. If it is swung in a linear or triangular pattern, then it will appear as a line or triangle. In reality, there is no circular, linear, or triangular shape to the fire, only the red visible form that can be seen moving from place to place where the fire passes. In reality, it is the succeeding mental processes that merge the visible forms that appear in different places and interpret them as a circle of fire and so on. This is the actual example from Pāli texts.
>
> Another example of this is found in people who cannot read well.

4. ULTIMATE REALITIES (PARAMATTHA DHAMMAS)

They must read slowly to comprehend a piece of writing from the context, carefully reading word by word. The mental process of investigation is apparent to them because it proceeds so slowly. On the other hand, for those who read well, the mental process of investigation is much faster and therefore cannot be clearly detected. It seems as if they can read just by seeing the words. Similarly, when we see a novel object, we can experience the processes of seeing and investigating separately because they proceed more slowly. On the other hand, when we see a familiar object, the mental process of investigation goes unnoticed because it occurs so quickly.

So, it seems to us as if we know a familiar woman or man as soon as we see them. But in reality, after we see them, investigation immediately follows. It is only due to this investigation that we can determine whether it is a woman, a man, and so on.

Thus, as with the circle of fire, woman and man are not considered to be absolute realities, realities that genuinely exist, are personally experienced, or are ultimately true; but are instead merely conventional realities (SAMMUTIPAÑÑĀTI) consisting of concepts. We can understand this by thinking thusly: "If we subtract all of the clearly visible forms or shapes from the matter or substance that we take to be a woman, a man, and so on, no such woman or man would be left to be seen. What we actually see is only visible form, and not a woman, a man, and such. We see only a collection of visible forms; we cannot see a woman, man, and such. The seeing of a woman, man, and such is a concept; it does not truly exist as imagined."

You may ask, "Can't we touch a woman or man, even though they lack any visible phenomena by which they can be seen?" In this case too, what we touch is not a woman or man but simply phenomena that can be experienced by touch. One can only touch a tangible object (PHOTTHABBA); there is not any woman or man we can touch. If we subtract all the tangible phenomena that we can clearly touch, there would be no woman or man to be touched. Therefore, the concepts of woman, man, and so on are called "realities that do not genuinely exist" and "are not personally experienced." The woman or man that we think we see or touch is not what really exists. Because it is not personally experienced it is not ultimately real, meaning that it is not an ultimate reality.

What really exists is referred to as "eye-sensitivity" (CAKKHUPASĀDA). Eye-consciousness occurs because eye-sensitivity sees visible forms. We could not see visible forms if there was no eye-sensitivity. How could we see then? For example, if a mirror is clear, we can see reflections of form in it. If the mirror were not clear, we could not see reflections of form in it, because the reflections would not appear. Therefore, in order for there to be seeing, there must be eye-sensitivity; and there must be visible forms that really exist, are realities that genuinely exist, are personally experienced, and are ultimate reality. Thus, seeing really exists. And thanks to its existence we can see a great variety of forms. If seeing did not exist, we could not know what we see, let alone say what it is. Therefore, eye-consciousness is also called "a reality that genuinely exists," is "personally experienced," and "ultimate reality." The same is true of sound, ear-sensitivity, and ear-consciousness in the case of hearing, and likewise for the other senses.

2. Hearsay and such

Things learned through hearsay and such may be true or false. So, such truths are not regarded as higher reality (UTTAMATTHA) or ultimate reality (PARAMATTHA). On the other hand, what can be empirically experienced really exists and is regarded as higher reality and ultimate reality. The term 'and such' in the phrase "hearsay and such" refers to realities that are accepted on the basis of tradition, scripture, logic, method, reason, or personal opinion. Realities that are accepted on the basis of these, rather than through personal experience, cannot be regarded as ultimately real.

What is handed down through tradition by our teachers and forefathers (PARAMPARĀ), as well as what we receive through hearsay (ITIKIRĀ), are sometimes true and sometimes not. So, they should not be considered ultimate realities. Also, the validity of what is considered to be in accord with scripture (PITAKASAMPADĀ) depends on the quality of the scripture. Even when a scripture is reliable, it is still necessary to correctly interpret it in order to extract genuine truth from it. So, such truths are not yet considered ultimate realities. Ideas arrived at through logic (TAKKAHETU) are not always true, and therefore they should not be considered to be ultimate realities. Ideas that are arrived at methodically (NAYAHETU) may be true or not, depending on the rationality of the method, and so they should not be considered to be ultimate realities. Ideas that are accepted based on reason (ĀKĀRAPARIVITAKKA) or personal opinion (DITTHINIJJHĀNAKHANTI) are also not always true, and thus they cannot be considered to be ultimate realities.

For all these reasons, in the KĀLĀMA SUTTA and elsewhere the BUDDHA discouraged us from holding views based on hearsay, tradition, and so on. A truth accepted by any of these means is not reliable. Instead, he instructed us to experience the truth empirically for ourselves, through practice. It is only through empirical knowledge that we can experience mental and physical phenomena.

A person who is born blind cannot, by any means, know the colors white, red, yellow, or blue, no matter how others may describe those colors. He or she is simply not able to comprehend the experience of 'seeing'. Similarly, someone with a deficient sense of smell cannot know the difference between fragrant and putrid odors, regardless of how others may explain them. One cannot truly know the flavor of a food that one has never tasted, no matter how it is described. And one cannot understand the pain of a headache, toothache, or stomachache if one has never had them.

Likewise, one cannot really know insight knowledge, JHĀNA, or the path and fruition if one has not yet attained them, regardless of how they may be explained in accordance with scripture. We cannot say that understanding an object by means of hearsay, tradition (ANUSSAVA), or inference (ANUMĀNA) is to know its ultimate truth. Real, empirical knowledge belongs only to insight meditators, those who achieve JHĀNA, and noble ones. Therefore, whatever is known through hearsay and such is merely conceptual and not a real, ultimately existing mental or physical phenomenon.

Since we can see visible objects, they can be empirically known. And since it is obvious that the continuum of life possesses eye-sensitivity and eye-consciousness, they too can be empirically known. The same is true for the mental and physical phenomena of sound, ear-sensitivity and ear-consciousness, and similarly for the other senses of smell, taste, touch, and thought. We can clearly experience these mental and physical phenomena by means of 'insight' knowledge, 'path' knowledge, 'fruition' knowledge, and 'reviewing' knowledge (PACCAVEKKHANAÑĀNA). Because we can empirically know them, these truly existing mental and physical phenomena are called empirical reality, higher reality, and ultimate reality.

Because we know that these phenomena truly exist through personal experience, they are real. And because they are not accepted through hearsay or on the basis of scripture, they cannot be incorrect realities. Therefore, they are also said to genuinely exist and are empirically experienced.

3. Description vs. experience

Sub-commentaries on the ABHIDHAMMA say:

Knowledge that is based on hearsay and such may or may not be true, so it is not ultimate reality. Only empirical facts are ultimate realities. To communicate this point, it is said that "They cannot be experienced by hearsay; they are higher realities (UTTAMATTHO)." Being ultimate, genuine realities are called "ultimate realities." Mental and physical phenomena that can be empirically known are phenomena that cannot be pointed out. Therefore, they are called "higher realities." Because genuinely existing mental and physical phenomena are irreducible, they are ultimately real and are therefore called "ultimate realities." Insight knowledge of re-observation, insight knowledge, and so on clearly experiences these ultimate realities, but these realities cannot be pointed out on the basis of having heard about them from somebody else. They are the intrinsic characteristics (SABHĀVALAKKHANĀ) of mental and physical phenomena.

The phrases "cannot be experienced by hearsay" (ANUSSAVĀDIVASENAGAHETABBO) and "cannot be pointed out" (ANIDDISITABBASABHĀVO) that the ABHIDHAMMA commentary and sub- commentary use above have essentially the same meaning. The commentary says that ultimate realities cannot be experienced by means of hearsay and such, while the sub-commentary further explains that descriptions of ultimate realities cannot help others understand them. Both phrases, however, refer to the fact that one can only know ultimate reality through empirical knowledge.

Since it may be difficult to understand why ultimate reality "cannot be pointed out," I will explain it further. I will begin by asking, "Why are true phenomena said to be indescribable?" It is certainly possible to describe the true characteristics of phenomena. For example, the earth element has the characteristic of hardness, mind has the characteristic of cognizing the object, contact has the characteristic of touching the object, and so on. So why are the intrinsic characteristics of mental and physical phenomena said to be 'indescribable'?

It is true that we can describe mental and physical phenomena in terms of their characteristics: This is why Pāḷi texts, commentaries, and sub-commentaries provide descriptions of them. However, what we understand by recourse to scriptural descriptions is not ultimate reality, but simply names and concepts – like earth element (PATHAVĪDHĀTU), mind (CITTA), and contact (PHASSA). These names do refer to ultimate realities, and thus they are called "concepts that refer to what ultimately exists" (VIJJAMĀNAPAÑÑATTI) or "concepts that refer to ultimate reality" (TAJJĀPAÑÑATTI). But if their manner is learned – that is, the way the earth feels hard, the way the mind cognizes objects, the way that mental contact connects with objects, and so on – then what is known is simply concepts about the manner (ĀKĀRAPAÑÑATTI) of these phenomena. If one knows them as solid forms or powder, then what one knows are concepts of form or shape (SANTHĀNAPAÑÑATTI).

A learned person knows the descriptions of the path, its fruition, and NIBBĀNA from the Pāḷi texts, and can also talk about them. However, unenlightened persons can never take the genuine path and fruition as objects; they can never experience them. And before attaining knowledge of change-of-lineage (GOTRABHŪ) they can never take NIBBĀNA as their object; they can never experience it. Therefore, unenlightened persons do not understand path, fruition, and NIBBĀNA through personal experience, and so these are not yet ultimate realities for them. Since they know these realities only through oral tradition, lineage, or in accordance with the scripture and reasoning, they only have a conceptual understanding of them. Such understanding is either a concept of name (NĀMAPAÑÑATTI), a concept about the manner, or a concept of form or shape.

In fact, even the mundane phenomena that we believe we understand are still only conceptually known unless personally experienced. Ordinary people can experience the mental and physical phenomena that belong to the domain of the senses (KĀMĀVACARA), since they obviously occur in the continuum of life. They can also experience phenomena when they appear at the six sense doors, and by practicing insight. Those who have achieved JHĀNA can experience JHĀNIC phenomena as well. We can realize that such-and-such is called "the earth element," such-and-such is called "consciousness," and such-and-such is called "mental contact" by checking our own experience against Pāḷi texts and DHAMMA talks.

For example, a person who has never eaten grapes doesn't yet know the actual taste of grapes, although he or she has learned about it from somebody else. Only when he or she actually eats them does he or she know how grapes really taste. People usually think that supramundane phenomena are so profound that ordinary people cannot understand them, but that anyone can understand mundane phenomena. I have already mentioned the example of a person who is born blind and cannot know forms.

To explain the fact that the intrinsic characteristics of mind and body cannot be described, the ABHIDHAMMA sub-commentary says:

"Phenomena cannot be described in an ultimate sense. This means that we cannot understand the intrinsic characteristics of mental and physical phenomena based on descriptions but only based on our own experience. Only what we experience personally is ultimate reality. How profound that is! Reflect on this repeatedly until you understand it."

4. The correct definition of Ultimate Reality

In the ABHIDHAMMATTHAVIBHĀVINĪ, ultimate reality (PARAMATTHA) is defined in accordance with the ANUTĪKĀ as "the highest" (UTTAMA), "not false" (AVIPARĪTA), "truth" (ATTHA). "Highest" and "ultimate " have the same literal meaning, while "not false" is a synonym of ultimate. Other synonyms for ultimate include: "existence" (BHŪTA), "real existence," or "things as they are" (YATHĀBHŪTA), "true" (TATHA), "real" (TACCHA), and "not untrue" (AVITATHA).

Following the explanations given in the commentaries and sub-commentaries, we should correctly understand ultimate reality in this way: the four realities—mind, mental factors, matter, and NIBBĀNA—that can be personally experienced, are immutable, and really existing are called "ultimate realities." We should always keep this correct definition of ultimate reality in mind.

There is a misapprehension that ultimate realities are eternal and unchanging while conventional realities (PAÑÑATTI) are transitory and changing. Accordingly, it is explained that ultimate realities are eternal in several ways: in terms of characteristics or with regard to consequences. Matter (RŪPA), for instance, is defined as malleable or transformable and subject to alteration by cold, heat, and so on. However, it is also said that it is characteristically perpetual. This contradiction is actually rooted in confusing the words AVIPARĪTA (not false) and AVIPARINANĀTA (unchanging), thinking that they have the same meaning.

The word AVIPARINANĀTA is composed of the root √namu with the pre-fixes vi- and pari-: The literal meaning of this word is "unchanging." By extension it can be read as "enduring" or "perpetual." On the other hand, the word AVIPARĪTA is composed of the root √i with the same prefixes, vi- and pari-. The literal meaning of this word is "not false," or, in other words, "true." The sub-commentary to the PARAMATTHAVIBHĀVINĪ) defines ultimate reality as "not false (AVIPARĪTA); truth (ATTHA)." This explanation should resolve the confusion mentioned above. Keep these correct definitions in mind to better understand what is meant by the term "ultimate reality."

5. Transience

The notion that concepts are transitory is completely wrong. In fact, concepts do not appear, exist, or disappear at all. Since they do not have any real existence in an ultimate sense, it is impossible to say that they arise or pass away. It is impossible for conventional truths to arise, exist, and pass away, because they are not what really exists, but are merely imaginary constructs.

Take a person's name, for example. When does that name come into existence? Where does it exist: in one's head, or body, or somewhere else? When does it pass away? Actually, a name cannot be said to come into being, to exist anywhere, or to disappear. It is purely imaginary, isn't it? It seems to disappear when people forget it or no longer use it, but it is impossible for it to vanish. That is why today we still know the name of the hermit SUMEDHĀ, who lived four incalculable eons and a hundred thousand world-cycles ago. The same is true of names like 'woman,' 'man,' 'pot,' 'sarong,' and so on.

All conceptual designations, like 'woman,' 'man,' 'pot,' and 'sarong,' are like a person's name; they do not arise, exist, or disappear. Ultimately, such persons or things do not exist anywhere.

Instead, the collection of visible forms that one sees, all the sounds that one hears, all the tangible objects that one touches (and so on) are considered to be the solid substance of a woman, man, etc., and we think that they really exist. As explained before, such conceptual ideas are formed by the failure to distinguish between the preceding mental processes of seeing, hearing, touching, and so on – and the succeeding mental processes that imagine solid forms. Just as we cannot find a cart that exists apart from its component parts, such as wheels, axles, etc., so we also cannot find a man or a woman that exists apart from mental and physical phenomena.

Here are some examples that the Pāḷi texts mention to illustrate this point:

A Line of Termites

From a distance, a line of moving termites looks like a continuous line. However, there is no line apart from the individual termites that comprise it. In the same way, there is no person or solid substance apart from the mental and physical phenomena that comprise him or her.

A Sand Bag
When a sand bag is hung up and punctured, a constant stream of sand flows out of it. When the bag is pushed back and forth, the stream of sand seems to move back and forth. We conceive of the stream of falling sand as something that flows down. In fact, there is neither a stream nor its movement but only successive grains of falling sand. When the hole in the bag is sealed, or all of the sand has emptied out, the stream no longer appears to exist or to move. But we cannot say that the stream disappears, because there wasn't actually any inherently existing stream apart from the individual grains of sand. In reality, to say that the stream no longer exists means that the grains of sand are no longer falling in succession. In the same way, there is no person apart from mental and physical phenomena, and there is no moving hand or foot apart from the physical phenomena that arise in successive movements. There is also no death of a person apart from the absence of new mental and physical phenomena arising.

A Rope
A rope appears to be a solid entity. However, there is no rope apart from the individual strings that comprise it. The thickness or length of a rope depends on the number and length of the strings that comprise it. A long rope does not inherently exist. In the same manner, there is no inherently existing form of a person apart from mental and physical phenomena that have no solid substance. There is no inherently existing person who lives for one hour, one day, one month, one year, and so on apart from mental and physical phenomena that don't even last for the blink of an eye.

A River
A river seems to flow continuously because the water that flows downstream is constantly being replaced with new water. However, if

one gazes at the river in one spot, one will find that the water that one sees at present is different from the water one saw only a moment ago. In the same way, a man or a woman seems to be the same person all the time because passing phenomena are continuously replaced with new ones. This is a concept of continuity (SANTATIPAÑÑATTI).

A Tree

A tree is composed of its parts: the trunk, branches, twigs, leaves, and so on. Actually, there is no inherently existing form of a tree apart from these parts. Some kinds of evergreen trees never appear to shed their leaves, because the leaves they shed are continuously replaced with new ones. This gives the impression that these trees are always green and lush. However, by observing the old leaves that are shed and new buds that sprout, we can know their impermanence. This example shows that solidity (SAMŪHA PAÑÑATTI), form or shape, and unending processes exist only in a conceptual sense, not in an ultimate sense.

By repeatedly reflecting on these examples, we can all come to realize that the conceptual realities of woman, man, and so on are like a person's name: They do not appear and disappear, and they do not exist anywhere. They are only objects of our imaginations. We can conclude that conceptual realities do not change.

Among the ultimate realities, NIBBĀNA is called an unconditioned reality (ASANKHATAPARAMATTHA). It is subject to nothing and does not arise and disappear, and so it is said to be permanent (NICCA) and stable (DHUVA). All the other ultimate realities are conditioned realities (SANKHATAPARAMATTHA). Being subject to relevant conditions, they actually appear and disappear, and so they are said to be impermanent (ANICCA) and unstable (ADHUVA). These conditioned ultimate realities, internal or external, are what really exist in the present, really happened in the past, and will come into existence in the future. Aside from conditioned phenomena and unconditioned NIBBĀNA, all other objects that we imagine in our mind are conceptual things.

Names or words, for example, are concepts of name. The persons or things indicated by these words are concepts of things

(ATTHAPAÑÑATTI). Names or words, such as the Pāli word RŪPĀMMANĀ, which means "(visible) form object" in English, are all imaginary things. They do not arise in the present, have not arisen in the past, and will not arise in the future internally or externally. They cannot be experienced anywhere. Thus, they are regarded as concepts of name, and not as ultimate realities.

On the other hand, the phenomenon indicated by the words "visible object" is a genuinely visible object that can be experienced the moment that one sees it, or reflects upon it later. What one experiences in this way is ultimate reality, while the things that one does not really see or experience are only imaginary visible objects. They may be concepts of names or words, concepts of gesture or manner, or concepts of solid forms.

They are not real ultimate realities because they do not exist, have never existed, and will never exist as objects, neither internally nor externally. And because they do not exist anywhere, they cannot be experienced. We can compare these imaginary objects to ghosts that timid people imagine, or to objects that appear in dreams. All such objects seem real, but they do not actually exist; they merely appear in our imagination. Thus, all of the objects that the mind creates are conventional realities.

The same is true with regard to all other aspects of our other senses: eye-sensitivity, eye-consciousness, sound, ear-sensitivity, ear-consciousness, and so on. These names or words are conventional realities, while the objects that we can empirically experience are genuine ultimate realities (NIBBATTHITAPARAMATTHA).

B. The Two Meanings of Activity

Verbs such as 'going,' 'standing,' 'sitting,' 'sleeping,' 'bending,' 'stretching,' and so on are all concepts. Since these words indicate real actions and intentions, they are called "concepts that refer to what ultimately exists" (VIJJAMĀNAPAÑÑATTI) or "concepts that refer to ultimately real phenomena" (TAJJĀPAÑÑATTI). Recall that the actions indicated by these verbs are ultimately constituted of mind, mental factors, and matter. The meaning that concepts indicate is twofold: the meaning that ordinary people know and the meaning that insight meditators know.

1. The meaning that ordinary people know

When ordinary people move, stand, sit, sleep, bend, and so on, their experience of doing so is mingled with notions of 'I,' 'hand,' 'foot,' and 'bodily shape.' Their experience is actually a concept of person (PUGGALAPAÑÑATTI), or a concept of form or shape. Their experience is not an ultimate reality, because there is no inherently existing personal identity or form apart from the intention to move, the physical process of moving, and so on. So, knowledge and so on cannot find them.

You may ask, "Why shouldn't the realities indicated by concepts that refer to things with actual existence be considered ultimate realities?" It is because what we understand depends on how we think. For example, prior to the BUDDHA'S appearance, words like 'matter,' 'feeling' (VEDANĀ), 'earth '(PATHAVĪ), and so on were used without any empirical knowledge of their meaning. What was understood when using those words at that time was not ultimate reality but merely concepts of form, feeling, the earth element, and so on. Even today, due to how they think, some learned Buddhists still only know the concepts of form and so on that these words indicate. It is not necessarily the case that we will know ultimate reality just because words refer to empirical facts.

2. The meaning that insight meditators know

When a meditator's insight knowledge matures by constantly observing mind and body, he or she becomes aware of both the intention to move and the subsequent gradual process of movement. A meditator also perceives that as soon as preceding phenomena disappear; subsequent ones replace them. Thus, he or she realizes that there is no self that moves, as the sentence "I move" would suggest. Through his or her own insight knowledge, a meditator knows that what really occurs is the intention to move, followed by the gradual physical process of movement. When standing, a meditator can experience the intention to stand and the resulting sequence of moments of stiffness that support the standing posture.

Insight meditators comprehend that the phenomena involved in the process of standing appear and disappear from moment to moment and that the sentence "I stand" is merely a concept. In actuality, they know through their own insight knowledge that there is no self who stands but only the sequential processes of intention and stiffness.

In the same way, we can see bending as a process caused by the intention to bend, followed by an inward movement that progresses in separate little movements. We can see that the phenomena involved in bending arise and pass away moment by moment. So, the sentences, "The arm is bending," "The leg is bending," or "I am bending" are just words; there is no arm, leg, or person that bends. Meditators know through their own insight knowledge that there is only the intention to bend and the gradual movement of bending. The processes of sitting, lying down, stretching, and so on should be understood in the same way. The realities that one knows in this way are regarded as ultimately real phenomena because these are realities that can be known as they really are by means of empirically observed insight knowledge. This is how to distinguish between conventional and ultimate realities.

English words such as 'woman,' 'man,' 'hand,' 'foot,' 'pot,' 'sarong,' and so on are all concepts of name. They refer to forms or entities that cannot be directly experienced because they do not exist in an ultimate sense. As explained previously, what one regards as a man or woman is only an interpretation of mental and physical processes. There is no person, only the processes of mind and body. The moment we see something or someone, what we truly see is only visible form. The moment we hear something, what we truly hear is only sound. The same is true for smell and taste. The moment we touch something, what we truly touch is the earth element (PATHAVĪDHĀTU), characterized by softness or hardness, the fire element (TEJODHĀTU), characterized by warmth, heat, or coldness, or the air element (VĀYODHĀTU), characterized by tension, tightness, or looseness.

We touch no man or woman apart from these bodily sensations. We cannot empirically know the form or shape of a woman or man.

When eye-consciousness of a woman has ceased, for example, we can only know the woman by means of the subsequent, third mental process (VĪTHI) of investigation. Although we know her, our knowledge is not an empirical knowledge, but only a conclusion based on previous encounters. So, we can empirically know, in ourselves, what is arising and what has arisen by reflecting about it through thoughtful reconsideration (PATISANKHĀNAÑĀNA). We can also empirically know this through insight knowledge. With thoughtful reconsideration and insight knowledge, we can determine that these conventional realities do not clearly exist, because we cannot empirically find a 'woman.' We cannot empirically experience a 'person' through insight knowledge. When our insight knowledge grows sharp and mature enough, however, we are able to experience the genuine phenomena that underlie such concepts. As the saying goes:

"As ultimate reality emerges, concepts submerge. This means that we simultaneously know the real, ultimate realities of mind and body, as well as the illusory nature of concepts. It is the opposite however for those who have not yet attained any insight knowledge.

As concepts emerge, ultimate reality submerges."

This means that only concepts clearly arise, whereas the ultimate realities of mind and body submerge. So, for ordinary people, the conceptual form and shape of a so-called 'man' or 'woman' prevail, while mental and physical phenomena such as colors, sounds, and so on become apparent only when they are deliberately considered. This is because ordinary people cannot distinguish between preceding and succeeding processes of mind. This is how to differentiate ultimate reality from concepts.

C. Categories and Classification of Consciousness (CITTA)

~ They are divided in four ways according to whether it is: ~
1. KĀMĀVACARA CITTA ~ consciousness pertaining to the sense sphere
2. RŪPAVACARA CITTA ~ consciousness pertaining to the form sphere

3. ARŪPAVACARA CITTA ~ consciousness pertaining to the formless sphere
4. LOKUTTARA CITTA ~ supramundane consciousness

~ The four categories of CITTA are classified according to whether they are: ~
  1. Wholesome or skillful ~ KUSALA CITTA ~
  2. Unwholesome or unskillful ~ AKUSALA CITTA ~
  3. The result of KAMMA (past) ~ VIPĀKA CITTA ~
  4. Neutral consciousness (no effect) ~ KIRIYA CITTA ~

~ There are:
  1. In the sensuous sphere ~ 54 types of consciousness
  2. In the form sphere ~ 15 types of consciousness
  3. In the formless sphere ~ 12 types of consciousness
  4. In the supramundane ~ 8 types of consciousness

This totals 89 types of consciousness in all ~ CITTA can also be classified as 121 types ~

4A 1. Definitions ~
1. KUSALA = ^{A}KU = BAD = √SAL, to shake, to tremble, to destroy, thank, which shakes off evil or contemptible things is KUSALA.
^{B}KUSA = √LU = to cut = KUSALA is that which cuts off vice.
~ That which cuts off evil by wisdom = KUSALA
~ Productive of happy results = KUSALA
~ General rendering = wholesome, skillful

2. AKUSALA = opposite of KUSALA

~ KĀMĀVACARA-CITTĀNI ~

D. All Types of Consciousness Classified

1. Consciousness pertaining to the sense sphere (KĀMĀVACARA-CITTĀNI)
~ In the sensuous sphere there are 12 types of AKUSALA CITTAS

(unwholesome consciousness) that have roots: ~

A. CITTAS rooted in attachment ~ (LOBHA-MŪLA-CITTAS) ~ Greed
  5. CITTA, *₁ unprompted, accompanied by * pleasure, connected with DITTHI
  6. CITTA, *₂ prompted, accompanied by pleasure, connected with DITTHI
  7. CITTA, unprompted, accompanied by pleasure, disconnected with DITTHI
  8. CITTA, prompted, accompanied by pleasure, disconnected with DITTHI
  9. CITTA, unprompted, accompanied by neutral feeling, with DITTHI
  10. CITTA, prompted, accompanied by neutral feeling, with DITTHI
  11. CITTA, unprompted, accompanied by neutral feeling, no DITTHI
  12. CITTA, prompted, accompanied by neutral feeling, no DITTHI
     * Pleasant feeling

B. CITTAS rooted in aversion ~ (DOSA-MŪLA-CITTAS) ~ Ill-will
  13. CITTA, unprompted, accompanied by unpleasant feeling, with aversion
  14. CITTA, prompted, accompanied by unpleasant feeling, with aversion

C. CITTAS rooted in delusion ~ (MOHA -MŪLA-CITTAS) ~ Ignorance
  15. CITTA, accompanied by neutral feeling, with doubt
  16. CITTA, accompanied by neutral feeling, with restlessness

8 types are rooted in greed, 2 in aversion, 2 in delusion ~ thus 12 types of AKUSALA CITTAS

   *₁ ASANKHĀRIKA = unprompted = done spontaneously without external or internal inducement

*₂ SA- SANKHĀRIKA = prompted = instigated, deliberation, induced by oneself or another

~ Examples for the 12 types of AKUSALA CITTAS ~
A. LOBHA-MŪLA-CITTAS
1. With joy a boy instantly steals an apple, viewing no evil thereby.
2. Prompted by a friend, a boy joyfully steals an apple, viewing no evil thereby.
3. ~ 4. ~ The same illustration serves for the 3rd and 4th types of consciousness with the difference that the stealing is done without any false view.
5. ~ 6. ~ 7. ~ 8. ~ Same as above, except that the stealing is done with a neutral feeling

B. DOSA-MŪLA-CITTAS
9. With anger one murders without any premeditation (with DUKKHA VEDANA)
10. With anger one murders another after reflection (with DUKKHA VEDANA)

3. DOSA-MŪLA-CITTAS
11. A person doubts the existence of the BUDDHA, or the efficacy of the DHAMMA, owing to his delusion.
12. A person is distracted in mind, unable to concentrate on an object.
13. ~ AHETUKA-CITTĀNI ~

4B.2 ~ (Cont'd) ~ Consciousness classified

2. 8 types of rootless consciousness (AHETUKA – CITTĀNI)
A. CITTAS which are unwholesome results. (AKUSALA VIPĀKA CITTĀNI)
4. Eye – consciousness, accompanied by a neutral feeling
5. Ear – consciousness, accompanied by a neutral feeling
6. Nose – consciousness, accompanied by a neutral feeling
7. Tongue – consciousness, accompanied by a neutral feeling

8. Body- consciousness, accompanied by an unpleasant feeling
9. Receiving – consciousness, accompanied by a neutral feeling
10. Investigating – consciousness, accompanied by a neutral feeling

B. CITTAS which are wholesome results without roots (KUSALA VIPĀK'AHETUKA CITTĀNI)
   11. Eye – consciousness, accompanied by a neutral feeling
   12. Ear – consciousness, accompanied by a neutral feeling
   13. Nose – consciousness, accompanied by a neutral feeling
   14. Tongue – consciousness, accompanied by a neutral feeling
   15. Body – consciousness, accompanied by a pleasant feeling
   16. Receiving – consciousness, accompanied by a neutral feeling
   17. Investigating – consciousness, accompanied by a pleasant feeling
   18. Investigating – consciousness, accompanied by a neutral feeling

C. Functional (KIRIYA) CITTAS without roots ~ (AHETUKA KIRIYA CITTĀNI)
   19. Five sense – door adverting consciousness accompanied by a neutral feeling
   20. Mind – door adverting consciousness accompanied by a neutral feeling
   21. Smile – producing consciousness (of an ARAHANT) accompanied by a pleasant feeling

7 AKUSALA VIPĀKA CITTAS ~ 8 KUSALA VIPĀKA CITTAS – 3 KIRIYA AHETUKA CITTAS ~ Thus 18 types of rootless consciousness

~ SOBHANA-CITTĀNI ~

4B.3 ~ (Cont'd)~ Consciousness classified

3. 24 types of beautiful (SOBHANA) CITTAS of the sensuous sphere (SOBHANA CITTĀNI)
A. CITTAS which are KUSALA ~ (KĀMĀVACCARA KUSALA CITTĀNI)
   1. CITTA ~ unprompted ~ accompanied by pleasant feeling ~ associated with wisdom

4. ULTIMATE REALITIES (PARAMATTHA DHAMMAS)

    2. CITTA ~ prompted ~ accompanied by pleasant feeling ~ associated with wisdom
    3. CITTA ~ unprompted ~ accompanied by pleasant feeling ~ associated without wisdom
    4. CITTA ~ prompted ~ accompanied by pleasant feeling ~ associated with wisdom
    5. CITTA ~ unprompted ~ accompanied by neutral feeling ~ associated with wisdom
    6. CITTA ~ prompted ~ accompanied by neutral feeling ~ associated with wisdom
    7. CITTA ~ unprompted ~ accompanied by neutral feeling ~ associated without wisdom
    8. CITTA ~ prompted ~ accompanied by neutral feeling ~ associated without wisdom

B. CITTAS which are wholesome result (KUSALA VIPĀKA)
    1. CITTA ~ unprompted ~ accompanied by pleasant feeling ~ with wisdom
    2. CITTA ~ prompted ~ accompanied by pleasant feeling ~ with wisdom
    3. CITTA ~ unprompted ~ accompanied by pleasant feeling ~ without wisdom
    4. CITTA ~ prompted ~ accompanied by pleasant feeling ~ without wisdom
    5. CITTA ~ unprompted ~ accompanied by neutral feeling ~ with wisdom
    6. CITTA ~ prompted ~ accompanied by neutral feeling ~ with wisdom
    7. CITTA ~ unprompted ~ accompanied by neutral feeling ~ without wisdom
    8. CITTA ~ prompted ~ accompanied by neutral feeling ~ without wisdom

C. CITTAS which are functional or neutral (KĀMĀVĀCCARA KIRIYA CITTĀNI)

1. CITTA ~ unprompted ~ accompanied by pleasant feeling ~ with wisdom
2. CITTA ~ prompted ~ accompanied by pleasant feeling ~ with wisdom
3. CITTA ~ unprompted ~ accompanied by pleasant feeling ~ without wisdom
4. CITTA ~ prompted ~ accompanied by pleasant feeling ~ without wisdom
5. CITTA ~ unprompted ~ accompanied by neutral feeling ~ with wisdom
6. CITTA ~ prompted ~ accompanied by neutral feeling ~ with wisdom
7. CITTA ~ unprompted ~ accompanied by neutral feeling ~ without wisdom
8. CITTA ~ prompted ~ accompanied by neutral feeling ~ without wisdom

~ 8 KUSALA CITTAS ~ 8 KUSALA VIPĀKA CITTAS ~ 8 KIRIYA CITTAS ~ Thus there are 24 types of SOBHANA CITTAS of the sensuous sphere.

~ Summary ~ Sensuous sphere CITTAS types: ~

12 AKUSALA CITTAS ~ 18 AHETUKA CITTAS ~ 24 SOBHANA CITTAS ~ Thus there are 54 types of sensuous sphere consciousness, of which 23 types are VIPĀKA CITTAS ~ 20 types are KUSALA and AKUSALA ~ 11 types are KIRIYA CITTAS ~ Thus 54 types in all.

~ End ~ KĀMĀVACARA-CITTA classification ~

~ RŪPĀVACARA – CITTĀNI ~

4B.4 ~ (Cont'd) ~ Consciousness classified

4. 15 types of form sphere consciousness of the JHĀNAS

A. (RŪPĀVACARA KUSALA CITTĀNI) ~ CITTAS which are KUSALA ~
   1. First JHĀNA CITTA with initial application (VITAKKA), sustained application (VICĀRA), joy (PĪTI), happiness (SUKHA) and one-pointedness (EKAGGATĀ)
   2. Second JHĀNA CITTA ~ with VICĀRA ~ PĪTI ~ SUKHA ~ and EKAGGATĀ.
   3. Third JHĀNA CITTA ~ with PĪTI ~ SUKHA ~ and EKAGGATĀ.
   4. Fourth JHĀNA CITTA ~ with SUKHA ~ and EKAGGATĀ.
   5. Fifth JHĀNA CITTA ~ with equanimity and one-pointedness

B. CITTAS which are VIPĀKA ~
   6. First JHĀNA VIPĀKA with VITAKKA ~ VICĀRA ~ PĪTI ~ SUKHA ~ and EKAGGATĀ
   7. Second JHĀNA VIPĀKA CITTA with VICĀRA ~ PĪTI ~ SUKHA ~ and EKAGGATĀ
   8. Third JHĀNA VIPĀKA CITTA with PĪTI ~ SUKHA ~ and EKAGGATĀ
   9. Fourth JHĀNA VIPĀKA CITTA with SUKHA ~ and EKAGGATĀ
   10. Fifth JHĀNA VIPĀKA CITTA with equanimity and one-pointedness

C. CITTAS which are neutral (KIRIYA) ~
   11. First JHĀNA KIRIYA CITTA with VITAKKA ~ VICĀRA ~ PĪTI ~ SUKHA ~ and EKAGGATĀ
   12. Second JHĀNA KIRIYA CITTA with VICĀRA ~ PĪTI ~ SUKHA ~ and EKAGGATĀ
   13. Third JHĀNA KIRIYA CITTA with PĪTI ~ SUKHA ~ and EKAGGATĀ
   14. Fourth JHĀNA KIRIYA CITTA with SUKHA ~ and EKAGGATĀ
   15. Fifth JHĀNA KIRIYA CITTA with equanimity and one-pointedness

5 types of KUSALA RŪPA JHĀNA CITTAS ~ 5 types of VIPĀKA RŪPA JHANNA CITTAS and 5 types of KIRIYA RŪPA JHĀNA CITTAS

~ Thus, there are 15 types of RŪPĀVĀCARA JHĀNA CITTAS ~

Definition ~ JHĀNA ~ derived from the root "JHE" = to think, BUDDHAGHOSA explains JHĀNA ~ "JHĀNA is so called because it thinks closely of an object or because it burns those adverse things" (NIVARANAS = hindrances) ~ JHĀNA= willful concentration on an object.

~ End ~ RŪPĀVĀCARA JHĀNA CITTA classification ~

~ ARŪPĀVĀCARA – CITTĀNI ~

4B.5 ~ (Cont'd) ~ Consciousness classified

5. 12 types of formless sphere JHĀNA consciousness

A. KUSALA JHĀNA (ARŪPĀ) CITTAS ~
   1. JHĀNA CITTA dwelling on "infinity of space" ~ (ĀKĀSĀNAÑCĀYATANA)
   2. JHĀNA CITTA dwelling on the "infinity of consciousness" ~ (VIÑÑĀNAÑCĀYATANA)
   3. JHĀNA CITTA dwelling on "nothingness" ~ (ĀKIÑCAÑÑĀYATANA)
   4. JHĀNA CITTA dwelling on "neither perception nor non-perception" ~ (NEVASAÑÑA- N'ĀSAÑÑĀYATANA)

B. CITTAS which are JHĀNA (ARŪPĀ) VIPĀKA CITTAS ~
   5. VIPĀKA JHĀNA CITTA dwelling on "infinity of space"
   6. VIPĀKA JHĀNA CITTA dwelling on the "infinity of consciousness"
   7. VIPĀKA JHĀNA CITTA dwelling on "nothingness"
   8. VIPĀKA JHĀNA CITTA dwelling on "neither perception nor non-perception"

C. CITTAS which are functional ~ neutral (ARŪPĀ) KIRIYA JHĀNA CITTAS
   9. KIRIYA JHĀNA CITTA dwelling on "infinity of space"
   10. KIRIYA JHĀNA CITTA dwelling on the "infinity of consciousness"
   11. KIRIYA JHĀNA CITTA dwelling on "nothingness"
   12. KIRIYA JHĀNA CITTA dwelling on "neither perception nor non-perception"

~ 5 types KUSALA ARŪPĀ JHĀNA CITTAS ~ 5 types VIPAKA ARŪPĀ JHĀNA CITTAS and 5 types of KIRIYA ARŪPĀ JHĀNA CITTAS ~ Thus there are 15 types of ARŪPĀ JHĀNA CITTAS

~ End classification of ARŪPĀ JHĀNA CITTAS ~

~ LOKUTTARA – CITTĀNI ~

4B.6 ~ (Cont'd) ~ Consciousness classified

6. 8 types of supramundane consciousness (LOKUTTARA – CITTĀNI)

~ These are CITTAS ~ experiencing NIBBĀNA ~ unconditioned PARAMATTHA DHAMMA

A. CITTAS which are LOKUTTARA MAGGACITTA ~ (4)
   1. SOTĀPANNA MAGsGA CITTA
   2. SAKADĀGĀMI MAGGA CITTA
   3. ANĀGĀMI MAGGA CITTA
   4. ARAHATTA MAGGA CITTA

B. CITTAS which are resultant supramundane consciousness (LOKUTTARA PHALACITTA)
   1. SOTĀPANNA (fruit) PHALA CITTA
   2. SAKADĀGĀMI PHALA CITTA
   3. ANĀGĀMI PHALA CITTA
   4. ARAHATTA PHALA CITTA

~ 4 types LOKUTTARA MAGGA CITTA ~ and 4 types

LOKUTTARA PHALA CITTA ~ Thus there are 8 LOKUTTARA CITTAS (associated with NIBBĀNA)

~ End classification of LOKUTTARA CITTAS ~

7. Summary of consciousness classifications

Thus, there are 89 different types of CITTA which can be experienced. 12 AKUSALA CITTAS ~ 21 KUSALA CITTAS ~ 36 VIPĀKA CITTAS ~ 20 KIRIYA CITTAS ~ in the sensuous sphere there are 54 types of CITTA ~ form sphere (RŪPA JHĀNA) 15 types ~ and in the ARŪPA JHĀNA sphere 12 types ~ and 8 types of LOKUTTARA CITTAS.

These different classes of CITTAS can also be divided into 121 types according to whether the CITTAS of the path and fruit (MAGGA-PHALA) of the 4 ARIYAN CITTAS are accompanied by the JHĀNA factors of the 1st, 2nd, 3rd, 4th and 5th JHĀNA, thus there are 16 additional types of MAGGA CITTA and 16 additional types of PHALA CITTA. (Thus, the LOKUTTARA CITTA types become 40 instead of 8.) Equaling 121 types.

~ End classification of CITTA types ~

Chapters Five and Six enumerate the Requisites of
Enlightenment and the 62 wrong views.

5.
REQUISITES OF ENLIGHTENMENT (BODHIPAKKHIYA-DHAMMA)

~ 37 in number ~

~ The BODHIPAKKHIYA-DHAMMAS consist of 7 groups~

1. SATIPATTHANA, foundations of mindfulness (4 factors) (p.53-55)
2. SAMMAPPADHĀNA, right efforts, (4 factors) (p.56)
3. IDDHIPĀDA, bases of success, (4 factors) (p.57)
4. INDRIYA, controlling faculties, (5 factors) (p.58)
5. BALA, mental powers, (5 factors) (p.59)
6. BOJJHAṄGA, factors of enlightenment, (7 factors) (p.60)
7. MAGGAṄGA, path factors, (8 factors) (p.60)

1. KAYA – NUPASSANĀ – SATIPATTHANA
2. VEDĀNA – NUPASSANĀ – SATIPATTHANA
3. CITTA – NUPASSANĀ – SATIPATTHANA
4. DHAMMA – NUPASSANĀ – SATIPATTHANA

A. SATIPATTHANA ~ 4 Foundations of Mindfulness

1. KAYA – NUPASSANĀ – SATIPATTHANA
(Application of mindfulness to insight into the functioning of the body)

   1. **Mindfulness on breathing (ĀNĀPĀNA-SATI)**

   2. **Mindfulness on the postures of the body** ~ (walking, standing, sitting, lying, bending, stretching, turning, reclining ~ all moments as well as times of being stationary)

3. **Clear comprehension** ~ 4 types (CATU- SAMPAJAÑÑA)
   = the discerning of things rightly, entirely and equally is clear comprehension = produces non-delusion.
   1. Clear comprehension of purpose (SĀTTHAKA- SAMPAJAÑÑA)
   2. Clear comprehension of what is suitable, fit, to oneself ~ suitability (SAPPĀYA- SAMPAJAÑÑA)
   3. Clear comprehension of resort (GOCARA- SAMPAJAÑÑA) = one's meditation subject
   4. Clear comprehension of non-delusion (ASAMMOHA- SAMPAJAÑÑA) = clearness

   Extending these 4 comprehensions in times of such bodily action at:
   1. Clear comprehension in going forwards and backwards.
   2. Clear comprehension in looking straight on or around (all directions.)
   3. Clear comprehension in the bending and stretching of limbs.
   4. Clear comprehension in wearing robes (clothes), carrying bowl
   5. Clear comprehension in the partaking of food and drink.
   6. Clear comprehension of cleansing the body (bathing, washing, defecating, urinating).
   7. Clear comprehension in walking, standing, sitting, lying, going to sleep, upon awakening, speaking. keeping silent

   (For complete details ~32 parts ~ VIS.MAGGA.p.26B)

4. **Reflection on repulsiveness of the parts of the body:** ~ **32 body parts**
   1. Head hairs ~
   2. Body hairs ~
   3. Nails ~ (20)
   4. Teeth ~ (32)
   5. Skin ~ (inner & outer)
   6. Flesh ~ (900 pieces)
   7. Sinews ~ (900 ~ bind body together)
   8. Bones ~ (300 total)
   9. Bone marrow
   10. Kidney ~ (2)
   11. Heart
   12. Liver
   13. Midriff (conceals heart & kidneys)
   14. Spleen

5. REQUISITES OF ENLIGHTENMENT (BODHIPAKKHIYA-DHAMMA)

15. Lights (above heart)
16. Bowel
17. Entrail
18. Gorge (food in stomach)
19. Dung (excrement)
20. Brain
21. Bile
22. Phlegm
23. Pus
24. Blood
25. Sweat
26. Fat
27. Tears
28. Grease
29. Spittle
30. Snot (trickles from brain)
31. Oil of joints
32. Urine

24 secondary elements, also 28 total

5. Reflection on the four great elements: ~ (MAHĀBHŪTAS)
1. Earth element of extension ~ (PATHANI DHATU) = hardness, softness.
2. Water element of cohesion ~ (APO-DHATU) = what keeps form as a mass.
3. Fire element of temperature ~ (TEJO-DHATU) = heat, cold, warmth.
4. Air element of support/motion ~ (VAYO-DHATU) = wind, resisting, conveying, vibration.

6. The nine cemetery contemplations: ~ (One thinks of his own body thus)
1. Contemplation of a dead body 1,2, or 3 days after; swollen, blue, festering.
2. Contemplation of a dead body being eaten by crows, hanks, vultures, dogs, jackals, or worms.
3. Contemplation of a dead body reduced to a skeleton together with some flesh and blood held in by tendons.
4. Contemplation of a dead body reduced to a blood besmeared skeleton without flesh but held in by tendons.
5. Contemplation of a dead body reduced to a skeleton held in by tendons but without flesh and not besmeared with blood.
6. Contemplation of a dead body reduced to bones gone loose and scattered.

7. Contemplation of a dead body reduced to bones, white in color.
8. Contemplation of a dead body reduced to bones more than a year old heaped together.
9. Contemplation of a dead body reduced to bones gone rotten and become dust.

~ End explanation of KAYA- NUPASSANĀ- SATIPATTHANA ~

5A2. (CONT'D) EXPLANATION OF SATIPATTHANA

2. VEDĀNA – NUPASSANĀ – SATIPATTHANA
(Application of mindfulness to insight into the functioning of the feelings)

~ Three types of feeling ~
1. Pleasant feeling ~ (SUKHA VEDĀNA)
2. Unpleasant feeling ~ (DUKKHA VEDĀNA)
3. Neutral feeling ~ neither pleasant nor unpleasant

~ There are 6 kinds as to their arising:
1. Feelings arising from eye-contact
2. Feelings arising from ear-contact
3. Feelings arising from nose-contact
4. Feelings arising from tongue-contact
5. Feelings arising from body-contact
6. Feelings arising from mind-contact

~ Owing to contact ~ feeling arises ~

~ End explanation of VEDĀNA – NUPASSANĀ-SATIPATTHANA ~

5A3. (CONT'D) EXPLANATION OF SATIPATTHANA

3. CITTA – NUPASSANĀ – SATIPATTHANA

~ Contemplation on the state of mind ~

(Application of mindfulness to insight into mental activities or consciousness)

Knowing one's mental activities as they occur ~ thinking associated with lust, greed, aversion, generosity, delusion, non-delusion, if one is reflecting, planning, remembering, rejoicing, excited, concentrated, lazy, happy, disgusted, are all included here. Mindfulness of the knowing faculty, knowing, or consciousness, etc.

5A4. (CONT'D) EXPLANATION OF SATIPATTHANA

4. DHAMMA – NUPASSANĀ – SATIPATTHANA

~ Contemplation of mental objects ~

1. **Mindfulness of the five mental hindrances ~ (NIVARANAS)**
   1. Dense desire
   2. Anger
   3. Sloth and torpor
   4. Restlessness and worry
   5. Doubt

2. **Mindfulness of the 5 aggregates ~ (PAÑCA-KHANDHAS) ~ explained p.43**
   1. Materiality ~ RŪPA – KHANDHA
   2. Feelings ~ VEDĀNA – KHANDHA
   3. Perception ~ SAÑÑA – KHANDHA
   4. Mental volitional activities ~ remaining 50 CETASIKAS ~ (SANKHARA – KHANDHA)

5. Consciousness ~ (VIÑÑA – KHANDHA)

3. **Mindfulness of the six internal and six external sense bases (AYATANAS)**
    A. Internal
       1. Eye, 2. Ear, 3. Nose, 4. Tongue, 5. Body, 6. Mind base
    B. External
       1. Color, 2. Sound, 3. Odors, 4. Tastes, 5. Tactile objects, 6. Mental objects

4. **Mindfulness of the factors of enlightenment (BOJJHANGAS)**
    1. Mindfulness
    2. Investigation
    3. Energy
    4. Joy
    5. Tranquility
    6. Concentration
    7. Equanimity

5. **Mindfulness contemplation/understanding of the four truths**
    1. This is suffering according to reality.
    2. The case of craving is understood according to reality.
    3. One understands the non-occurrence of both suffering and its origin according to nature, as NIBBĀNA.
    4. One understands the real path which penetrates suffering and realizes cessation.

~ End explanation of DHAMMA – NUPASSANĀ-SATIPATTHANA ~ and the section on the 4 SATIPATTHANAS ~

B. Explanation of the Four Right Efforts (SAMMAPPADHĀNA)

1. Effort to overcome or reject unskillful acts, words, thoughts that have arisen or are in the course of arising: (Rejecting ~ LOBHA, DOSA, MOHA)
2. Effort to avoid (in this life and future lives) the arising or unskillful acts, words and thoughts that have not yet arisen: (all AKUSALA KAMMAS is what is meant here)
3. Effort to arouse the arising of skillful (KUSALA) acts, words and thoughts that have not yet arisen: (Cultivating ALOBHA, ADOSA and AMOHA)
4. Effort to increase and to perpetuate the KUSALA KAMMAS that have arisen or are in the course of arising (Perpetuating ~ ALOBHA, ADOSA, MOHA ~ DĀNA, SILA, BHĀVANĀ)

SAMMAPPADHĀNA = is a proper/right/correct effort carried out intensively with resolve, power, determination, without wavering. It has no element of unwillingness or holding back, zealous.

This effort is characterized in ANG.NIK.DUKA NIPĀTA:
1. Let the skin remain
2. Let the sinews remain
3. Let the bones remain
4. Let the flesh and blood dry up ~ I shall not permit the course of my effort to stop until I win that which may be won by human ability, human effort and human exertion. ~ "If the end is attainable by human effort, I shall not rest or relax until it is attained, until the end is grasped and reached."

- ~ Ven. PHUSSADEVA TUERA ~ ARAHANT only after 19 years, strenuous effort ~ sit, walk
- ~ Ven. MAHANAGA ~ ARAHANT only ~ 7 years, only standing and walking + 16 following years of diligent practice
- ~ Ven. MAHĀSIVA ~ ARAHANT only after 30 years of daily striving ~ sit, walk, etc.

C. The Four Bases of Success (IDDHIPĀDA)

1. CHANDA = The zeal or desire to obtain, to reach, to accomplish, in this case CHANDA means that there is nothing within or without that will obstruct that driving inner quest. "If I do not attain this accomplishment in this life, I shall not rest content, better to die in a battle than live on in defeat."

2. VIRIYA = Untiring resolve and determined, unshakeable energy to accomplish the task at hand ~ uproot the KILESAS from the mind. (See p.56, 4 Right efforts).

3. CITTA = Conscious ~ mental devotion to inner development, so one-pointed that one could easily forget to eat and sleep ~ in order to acquire, or come to complete knowledge of the 5 IDDHIS = signified the fact of having perfected ~
   1. Full knowledge of NĀMA-RŪPA
   2. Full knowledge of DUKKHA SACCA ~ first noble truth
   3. Full knowledge of SAMUDAYA SACCA ~ second noble truth
   4. Full knowledge of NIRODHA SACCA ~ third noble truth
   5. Full knowledge of & development of MAGGA SACCA ~ fourth noble truth

   (These are the five essential IDDHIS of the BUDDHA SASANA.)

4. VIMAMSĀ = investigation = knowledge of or wisdom that can clearly perceive.
   1. The greatest of DUKKHA involved in *samsaric* existence.
   2. The advantages/necessities of the IDDHIS.
   3. The subtle DHAMMAS and their nature.
   4. A person who possesses such knowledge can no longer find pleasure in any worldly pursuit except the development and perfection of the IDDHIS. He finds gratification only in the acquisition of deep and profound IDDHIS. The deeper the DHAMMAS, the greater is his resolve to attain them.

Those who do not possess any one of the 4 bases of success cannot differentiate between the shallowness and profoundness of life, superficiality and depth of the DHAMMA.

D. The Five Controlling Faculties (INDRIYA)

INDRIYA signifies the act of ruling or of controlling. = the control or rule that one exercises over one's mind.

1. SADDHĀ or SADDHINDRIYA = confident trust, faith.

Two kinds of faith ~ 1. PAKATI-SADDHĀ = ordinary path that led one to perform acts of DĀNA, SĪLA and BHĀVANĀ. 2 ~ BHĀVANĀ -SADDHA ~ unwavering confidence developed or matured through BHĀVANĀ. (This is what is meant by SADDHA INDRIYA ~ not an ordinary path). ~ It is perfected upon attainment of SOTA PANNA MAGGA.

2. VĪRIYINDRIYA = 2 kinds ~ 1. PAKATI-VĪRIYA = ordinary worldly energy, 2.   BHĀVANĀ- VĪRIYA = non fatiguing energy cultivated through BHĀVANĀ. ~ Both mental energy and bodily energy ~ untiring awareness of NĀMA- RŪPA as it becomes evident at each of the 6 sense doors.

3. SATINDRIYA = the firm establishment of mindfulness of NĀMA- RŪPA. Until NIBBĀNA is reached = LOKUTTARA-SAMMĀ-SATI. ~ 4 foundations of mindfulness

4. SAMĀDHINDRIYA = the firm establishment of concentration until NIBBĀNA is reached = LOKUTTARA- SAMMĀ-SAMĀDHI = NIBBĀNA concentration ~ 8 JHANAS.

5. PAÑÑA- INDRIYA = firm establishment of wisdom which dispels uncertainty and confusion regarding NĀMA- RŪPA = last five of the 7 purifications

E. The Five Mental Powers (BALA)

~ The mental powers (BALĀNI) are called this because they overpower opposing mental states. ~ They are powerful in the sense of being unshaken by opposition. ~

1. SADDHĀ- BALA = power of confidence developed through SATIPATTHANA that has the answer to put an end to craving ~ wanting.
2. VĪRIYA- BALA = power to dispel all forms of condolence. ~ Content with little food ~ sleep ~ one shelter. ~ Being fearless ~

bold and firm in living alone ~ dedicated to mind development. ~ This power comes through BHĀVANĀ.
3. SATI- BALA = power to dispel confusion through BHĀVANĀ efforts
4. SAMĀDHI – BALA = power to dispel distraction ~ wandering mind ~ BHĀVANĀ.
5. PAÑÑĀ- BALA = power to dispel delusion

~ The 5 opposites of the BALAS are 1. ~ Craving, 2. ~ Laziness, 3. ~ Absent mindedness, 4. ~ Distraction, 5. ~ Delusion

F. The Seven Factors of Enlightenment (BOJJHĀNGA)

~ 7 constituents of supramundane path knowledge
1. SATI- SAMBOJJHĀNGA = SATI CETASIKA ~ SATTIPATTHANA ~ SATINDRIYA ~ SATI -BALA ~ SAMMĀ-SATI- MAGGANGA = the enlightenment factor 'Mindfulness.'
2. DHAMMAVICAYA- SAMBOJJHĀANGA = PAÑÑĀ- CETASIKA ~ VĪMAMSIDDHIPĀDA ~ PAÑÑĀ-INDRIYA ~ PAÑÑĀ-BALA ~ SAMMĀ-DITTHI MAGGANGA = the enlightenment factor of 'Investigation of DHAMMA.' (= 5 purifications, 10 insight knowledges, ANICCA, ANATTA, DUKKHA)
3. VĪRIYA- SAMBOJJHĀNGA = VĪRIYA- CETASIKA ~ SAMMAPPADHĀNA ~ VIRIYIDDHIPĀDA ~ VĪRIYINDRIYA ~ VĪRIYA- BALA ~ SAMMĀ- VĀYĀMA- MAGGANGA = the enlightenment factor of 'Energy'.
4. PĪTI- SAMBOJJHĀNGA = the joy and happiness (PĪTI- CETASIKA) that appears when insight appears and develops by the practice of SATIPATTHANA = the enlightenment factor of 'Joy.'
5. PASSADDHI- SAMBOJJHĀNGA = PASSADHI (KĀYA + CITTA) – CETASIKA = the access of becoming calm and tranquil in both body and mind = the enlightenment factor of 'Tranquility.'

5A4. (CONT'D) EXPLANATION OF SATIPATTHANA

6. SAMĀDHI – SAMBOJJHĀNGA = EKAGGATA- CETASIKA = SAMĀDHINDRIYA, SAMĀDHI- BALA ~ SAMMĀ – SAMĀDHI MAGGANGA = the enlightenment factor of 'Concentration.'
7. UPEKKHĀ – SAMBOJJHĀNGA = TATRAMAJJHATTATĀ – CETASIKA ~ The mental factor of refined balance of mind of equipoise. ~ Equanimity which is free from anxieties and efforts for mindfulness = the enlightenment factor of 'Equanimity.'

(MAGGANGA) ~ Details pp. 2 -10 ~

G. The Eight Path Factors

1. Right view (SAMMĀ – DITTHI)   ⎫ Wisdom group
2. Right thought (SAMMĀ – SANKAPPA) ⎬ (PAÑÑA)

3. Right speech (SAMMĀ – VĀCĀ)
4. Right action (SAMMĀ – KAMMANTA) ⎬ (SILA) group ~ Morality
5. Right livelihood (SAMMĀ – ĀJIVA)

6. Right effort (SAMMĀ – VĀYĀMA)
7. Right mindfulness (SAMMĀ – SATI) ⎬ Concentration group (SAMĀDHI or Meditation group)
8. Right concentration (SAMMĀ – SAMĀDHI)

~ End explanation of 37 requisites of enlightenment ~

6.
ENUMERATION OF SIXTY-TWO WRONG VIEWS

(AS EXPLAINED IN THE BRAHMAJALA SUTTA ~ DIG. NIK. 1)

"There are, BHIKKHUS, some recluses and brahmins who are eternalists, and who on four grounds proclaim the self and the world to be eternal. And owing to what, with reference to what, do these honorable recluses and brahmins proclaim their views?"

A. Speculations about the Past (PUBBANTAKAPPIKA) ~ 18 Views

1. Eternalism (SASSATAVĀDA): views 1- 4

1. ~ An individual through diligent effort attains to such a degree of SAMĀDHI that he has the ability to recollect numerous past lives: as many as hundreds or thousands of births; could recall his name, his appearance, clan, pleasurable and painful experiences, life span, etc. "Passing away there, I arose..." and so on.

He speaks thus: ~ "The self and the world are eternal barren, steadfast as a mountain peak, standing firm like a pillar and through these beings roam and wander (through the round of existence) pass away and re-arise, yet the self and the world remain the same just like eternity itself." ~ (One believes this because of JHANNA-ABIÑÑĀ ability to recollect past lives. ~ Conviction based on (limited) personal experience).

2. ~ An individual... has the ability to recollect numerous past lives: "Throughout 2, 3, 4, 5 or 10 eons of world contraction and expansion (SAMVATTA – VIVATTA)" (These are the two primary divisions of the great Aeon ~ MAHĀKAPPA). He can recall his name. etc.

He speaks thus: "...just like eternity itself." (Based on JHĀNA-ABIÑÑĀ ability to recollect past lives ~ conviction thus founded on personal limited experience).

3. ~ (Same as above except for the extent of time recollected.)
"Up to 40 eons of world contraction and expansion"

4. ~ (Same as above except for the extent of time recollected.)

~ Herein, BHIKKHUS, some recluse or brahmin is a rationalist, an investigator, he declares his view thus, hammered out by reason, deduced from his investigations, following his own flight of thoughts, thus: "Thus the self and the world are eternal... (same as above) ... the same just like eternity itself."

(~ BRAHMAJĀLA SUTTA ~ 62 DITTHIS)

2. Partial – Eternalism (EKACCASASSATAVĀDA): Views 5-8

5. "There are BHIKKHUS, some recluses and brahmins who are eternalists in regard to some things, and non-externalists in regard to other things, and who on four grounds proclaim the self and the world to be partly eternal and partly non-eternal."

~ World lapses-contracts-disintegrates after long period of time. ~ While contracting beings for the most part reborn in ABHASSARA BRAHMA-LOKA (6th of the RUPA-LOKAS). ~ There they live mind-made, feeding on rapture, for a long period. ~ After a long period ~ the world begins to expand once again. ~ While world is expanding, an empty palace of BRAHMA appears. ~ Certain beings due to the exhaustion of merit pass from ABHASSARA- LOKA and re-arise in an empty palace. There he lives mind-made feeding on rapture. ~ As a result of dwelling alone for so long, dissatisfaction arises, and he yearns for other beings to come to this place. ~ Just at that moment ~ due to the exhaustion of their life-span of merit ~ certain other beings pass from ABHASSARA-LOKA and re-arise in the palace of BRAHMA.

~ Thereupon this being who re-arose there first thinks to himself: ~ "I am Brahma, the Lord, the maker and creator, the Supreme Being, the Almighty, the Father of all that are and are to be. ~ And these beings have been created by me. ~ What is the reason? ~ Because first I made the wish: That other beings might come to this place. ~ Now beings have come." ~ And the beings who re-arose there after him also think: ~ "This must be Brahma. the Lord, the Creator, etc. ~ and we have been created by him. ~ Because we see that he was here first ~ and we appeared after him. The being who arose first ~ possesses longer life, greater beauty and greater authority than the beings who arose after him. ~ Now, after a long period, a certain being after passing from that plane, takes rebirth in this world ~ He then attains mental concentration and recollects his immediately preceding life." ~ He speaks thus: ~ "We were created by him, by Brahma, the Lord, the Creator, etc. ~ He is permanent, stable, eternal, not subject to change, and he will remain the same just like eternity itself. But we, who have been created by him and have come to this world, ~ we are impermanent, unstable, short-lived, doomed to perish."

6. ~ Certain gods called 'Corrupted by play' ~ These gods spend an excessive time indulging in the delights of laughter and play, and as a consequence they become forgetful; and when they become forgetful, they pass away from that place ~ and take rebirth in this world. ~ They attain SAMĀDHI ~ recollect previous birth (though none other). He speaks thus: "Those gods not given to play and laughter do not become forgetful ~ then they do not pass from that plane. ~ Those gods are permanent, stable, eternal, and will remain the same just like eternity itself. ~ But we were gods corrupted by play ~ who spent excessive time indulging in the delights of laughter and play ~ and became forgetful ~so passed therefore from that plane ~ coming to this world. ~ Now we are short-lived, unstable, impermanent, etc."

7. ~ Certain gods called 'Corrupted by play' ~ They contemplate each other, with envy, anger arises in their mind towards one another ~ thus their minds and bodies become exhausted. Consequently, they pass from that plane ~ and are reborn to this world. ~ (Same as #6, except they see that those who do not pass do not contemplate others with envy.)

8. ~ Herein, BHIKKHUS, some recluse or brahmin is a rationalist, an investigator; he declares his view, hammered out by reason, deduced from his investigations, following his own flight of thought thus: "That which is called 'the eye', 'the ear', 'the nose', 'the tongue' and 'the body' ~ that self is impermanent, unstable, non-eternal, subject to change. But that which is called 'mind', or 'mentality', or 'consciousness', that self is permanent, stable, eternal, not subject to change; ~ and will remain the same, just like eternity itself.

(~ BRAHMAJĀLA SUTTA ~ 62 DITTHIS) (ANTĀNANTAVĀDA)

3. Doctrines of the Finitude and Infinity of the World (EKACCASASSATAVĀDA): Views 9-12

9. ~ Individual develops SAMĀDHI ~ thus concentrated he abides perceiving the world as finite and bounded.

10. ~ Individual develops SAMĀDHI ~ thus concentrated he abides perceiving the world as infinite and boundless.

11. ~ Individual develops SAMĀDHI ~ thus concentrated he abides perceiving the world as finite in the upward and downward directions, but as infinite across. He thus contradicts those who declare the world as finite or those who declare it to be infinite. The world is both finite and infinite.

12. Herein, BHIKKHUS, one is a rationalist and investigator, declares his view hammered out by reason, deduced from his investigations. ~ The world is neither finite nor infinite. To speak that it is 'infinite' is false; ~ 'finite' is false; ~'; both finite and infinite' are false. ~ "The world is neither infinite nor finite" is alone correct.

(AMARĀNIKKITEPAVADA)

4. Doctrines of Endless Equivocation ("eel-wriggling"): Views 13-16

"Some recluses and brahmins are evasive when questioned"

13. ~ An individual knows he doesn't understand what is 'wholesome' and what is 'unwholesome.' Therefore, out of fear of making a false

B. Speculations about the Future (APARANTAKAPPIKA) ~ 44 Views

1. Doctrines of Percipient Immortality (SAÑÑIVĀDA) ~ (Doctrines of conscious survival): Views 19-34

A. 19. Material
   20. Immaterial
   21. Both material and immaterial
   22. Neither material nor immaterial
B. 23. Finite
   24. Infinite
   25. Both finite and infinite
   26. Neither finite nor infinite
C. 27. Of uniform perception
   28. Of diversified perception
   29. Of limited perception
   30. Of boundless perception
D. 31. Exclusively happy
   32. Exclusively miserable
   33. Both happy and miserable
   34. Neither happy nor miserable

~ outside of these are none ~

2. Doctrines of Non-Percipient Immortality (ASAÑÑIVĀDA) ~ (Doctrines of non-conscious survival): Views 35-42

"Individuals on 8 grounds proclaim the self to survive non-percipient after death." They proclaim the self is immutable (unchanging) after death, non-percipient and:

A. 35. Material
   36. Immaterial
   37. Both material and immaterial
   38. Neither material nor immaterial
B. 39. Finite
   40. Infinite

41. Both finite and infinite
42. Neither finite nor infinite

~ outside of these are none ~

3. Doctrines of Neither Percipient nor Non-Percipient Immortality (N'EVASAÑÑI NĀSAÑÑIVĀDA): Views 43-50

"Individuals on 8 grounds proclaim the self to survive neither per nor non – percipient after death"

They proclaim: "The self is immutable after death, neither percipient nor non-percipient, and ~

A. 43. Material
44. Immaterial
45. Both material and immaterial
46. Neither material nor immaterial
B. 47. Finite
48. Infinite
49. Both finite and infinite
50. Neither finite nor infinite"

~ Outside of these there are none ~

4. Annihilationism (UCCHEVĀDA): Views 51-57

51. ~ Individuals assert ~ "The self has material form ~ comprised of 4 primary elements ~ originates from father and mother ~ self is then destroyed upon breakup of the body."

52. ~ "Self is not completely annihilated at death. ~ Another self ~ Divine ~ having material form pertaining to the sense sphere ~ feeding on edible nutriment ~ you neither know nor see, but I know and see it. (Talking to an individual #51). Since this self is annihilated and destroyed with the breakup of the body and does not exist after death, at this point the self is completely annihilated."

53. ~ Another agrees with #52, "But it is not at the point you say that the self is annihilated. For there is another self ~ divine ~ material form ~ mind-made ~ complete in all its limbs and organs, not destitute

...ns about the Future (APARANTAKAPPIKA)

... of Percipient Immortality (SAÑÑIVĀDA) ~
(Doctrines of conscious survival): Views 19-34

A. 19. Material
   20. Immaterial
   21. Both material and immaterial
   22. Neither material nor immaterial
B. 23. Finite
   24. Infinite
   25. Both finite and infinite
   26. Neither finite nor infinite
C. 27. Of uniform perception
   28. Of diversified perception
   29. Of limited perception
   30. Of boundless perception
D. 31. Exclusively happy
   32. Exclusively miserable
   33. Both happy and miserable
   34. Neither happy nor miserable

~ outside of these are none ~

2. Doctrines of Non-Percipient Immortality (ASAÑÑIVĀDA) ~
(Doctrines of non-conscious survival): Views 35-42

"Individuals on 8 grounds proclaim the self to survive non-percipient after death." They proclaim the self is immutable (unchanging) after death, non-percipient and:

A. 35. Material
   36. Immaterial
   37. Both material and immaterial
   38. Neither material nor immaterial
B. 39. Finite
   40. Infinite

41. Both finite and infinite
42. Neither finite nor infinite

~ outside of these are none ~

3. Doctrines of Neither Percipient nor Non-Percipient Immortality (N'EVASAÑÑI NĀSAÑÑIVĀDA): Views 43-50

"Individuals on 8 grounds proclaim the self to survive neither per nor non – percipient after death"

They proclaim: "The self is immutable after death, neither percipient nor non-percipient, and ~

A. 43. Material
    44. Immaterial
    45. Both material and immaterial
    46. Neither material nor immaterial
B. 47. Finite
    48. Infinite
    49. Both finite and infinite
    50. Neither finite nor infinite"

~ Outside of these there are none ~

4. Annihilationism (UCCHEVĀDA): Views 51-57

51. ~ Individuals assert ~ "The self has material form ~ comprised of 4 primary elements ~ originates from father and mother ~ self is then destroyed upon breakup of the body."

52. ~ "Self is not completely annihilated at death. ~ Another self ~ Divine ~ having material form pertaining to the sense sphere ~ feeding on edible nutriment ~ you neither know nor see, but I know and see it. (Talking to an individual #51). Since this self is annihilated and destroyed with the breakup of the body and does not exist after death, at this point the self is completely annihilated."

53. ~ Another agrees with #52, "But it is not at the point you say that the self is annihilated. For there is another self ~ divine ~ material form ~ mind-made ~ complete in all its limbs and organs, not destitute

of any faculties ~ but you neither know or can see it." ~ Telling #52. "But I know and see it. ~ It's destroyed also at the breakup of the body."

54. ~ Another agrees with #53 ~ "All the same ~ except that there is another self – reached by the attainment of infinite space ~ reached by surmounting perception of material form. ~ You don't know or see it, but I do ~ destroyed at death also."

55. ~ Same ~ "but self-belonging to infinite consciousness, surmounting infinite space" ~ (same)

56. ~ Same ~ "but self-belonging to base of nothingness, surmounting infinite consciousness" ~ (same)

57. ~ Same ~ "but self-belonging to neither perception nor non-perception, surmounting infinite nothingness" ~ (same)

~ Outside of these are none ~

5. Doctrines of NIBBĀNA here and now (DITTHADHAMMANIBBĀNAVĀDA): Views 58-62

"Individuals maintain a doctrine of NIBBĀNA here and now, on 5 grounds proclaim for an existent being NIBBĀNA here and now." ~

58. ~ "When this self, furnished and supplied with the 5 strands of sense pleasures, revels in them ~ at this point the self attains supreme NIBBĀNA here and now."

59. ~ Individual agrees with #58, "…but it is not at that point that the self attains supreme NIBBĀNA here and now" ~ What is the reason #59 states? ~ "…because, sense pleasures are impermanent, suffering, subject to change, and by their change, sorrow, lamentation, pain, grief and despair arise. But when the self, quite secluded from sense pleasures, secluded from unwholesome states, enters and abides in the first JHĀNA ~ at this point the self attains supreme NIBBĀNA, here and now."

60. ~ Same ~ but self in second JHĀNA (lists CETASIKAS) = supreme NIBBĀNA here and now.

61. ~ Same ~ but self in third JHĀNA = supreme NIBBĀNA here and now.

61. ~ Same ~ but self in fourth JHĀNA= supreme NIBBĀNA here and now.

~ Outside of these are none ~

- This concludes 44 grounds of those who hold speculations about the future. ~

- There are no other speculations of the past, future and the past and future together ~

- Total DITTHIS 62. ~ Outside of these there is none. ~

This, BHIKKUS, the TATHAGĀTA understands. And he understands that "These standpoints, thus assumed and thus misapprehended, lead to such a future destination, to such a state in the world beyond. He understands as well what transcends this, yet even that understanding he does not misapprehend; and because he is free from misapprehension, he has realized within himself the state of perfect peace. Having understood as they really are the origin and passing away of feelings, their satisfaction, unsatisfactoriness, and the escape from them, the TATHAGĀTA, BHIKKHUS, is liberated through non-clinging.

~ End explanation of BRAHMAJĀLA SUTTA ~ 62 DITTHIS ~

Those who hold these 62 speculations regarding the past, future and the past and future together ~ that is the feeling of those who do not see: That is only the agitation and vacillation of those who are immersed in craving. "These 63 conceptual theorems ~ that too is conditioned by contact. That they can experience feeling without contact ~ such a case is impossible." ~ BUDDHA then states that these feelings (of Brahmins and recluses) arise only because of contacts through the 6-bases of contact, with feeling as condition arises in them: Craving ~ craving ~ clinging, etc.

C. Summary of the 62 Views

A. Speculations about the past (18 views)

1. Eternalism (SASSATAVĀDA)
1. Based on recollection of up to 100 000 past lives ~

6. ENUMERATION OF SIXTY-TWO WRONG VIEWS

2. Based on recollection of up to ten eons of world contraction and expansion ~
3. Based on recollection of up to forty such eons ~
4. Based on reasoning ~

2. **Partial Eternalism (EKACCASASSATAVĀDA)**
   5. Theism ~
   6. Polytheism held by beings who were gods corrupted by play ~
   7. Polytheism held by beings who were gods corrupted by mind ~
   8. Rationalist dualism of an impermanent body and an eternal mind ~

3. **Extensionism (ANTĀNANTAVĀDA)**
   9. View that the world is finite ~
   10. View that the world is infinite ~
   11. View that the world is finite in vertical direction but infinite across ~
   12. View that the world is neither finite nor infinite ~

4. **Doctrines of endless equivocation (AMARĀNIKKITEPAVADA)**
   13. Held by one fearful of making a wrong statement ~
   14. Held by one fearful of clinging ~
   15. Held by one fearful of being cross-examined ~
   16. Held by one who is dull and stupid ~

5. **Doctrines of fortuitous origination (ADHICCASAMUPPANNAVADA)**
   17. Based on recollection of the arising of perception after passing away from the plane of non-percipient beings. ~
   18. Based on reasoning. ~

B. Speculations about the future (44 views)
1. Doctrines of percipient immortality (SAÑÑIVĀDA). The self is immutable after death, percipient, and ~
   19. Material
   20. Immaterial
   21. Both material and immaterial

22. Neither material nor immaterial
23. Finite
24. Infinite
25. Both finite and infinite
26. Of uniform perception
27. Of diversified perception
28. Of limited perception
29. Of boundless perception
30. Exclusively happy
31. Exclusively miserable
32. Both happy and miserable
33. Neither happy nor miserable
34. Neither finite nor infinite

2. Doctrines of non-percipient immortality (ASAÑÑIVĀDA). The self is immutable after death, non-percipient, and ~
    35. Neither finite nor infinite ~
    36. Immaterial ~
    37. Both material and immaterial ~
    38. Neither material nor immaterial ~
    39. Finite ~
    40. Infinite ~
    41. Both finite and infinite ~
    42. Neither finite nor infinite ~

3. Doctrines of neither percipient nor non-percipient immortality (N'EVASAÑÑI NĀSAÑÑIVĀDA). The self is immutable after death, neither percipient nor non-percipient, and ~
    43. Material ~
    44. Immaterial ~
    45. Both material and immaterial ~
    46. Neither material nor immaterial ~
    47. Finite ~
    48. Infinite ~
    49. Both finite and infinite ~
    50. Neither finite nor infinite ~

6. ENUMERATION OF SIXTY-TWO WRONG VIEWS

4. Annihilationism (UCCHEVĀDA)
   51. Annihilation of self-imposed of 4 elements ~
   52. Annihilation of a divine sense sphere self ~
   53. Annihilation of a divine fine-material sphere self ~
   54. Annihilation of the self-belonging to the base of infinite space ~
   55. Annihilation of the self-belonging to the base of consciousness ~
   56. Annihilation of self-belonging to the base of nothingness ~
   57. Annihilation of the self-belonging to the base of neither perception nor non-perception ~

5. Doctrines of NIBBĀNA here and now (DITTHADHAMMANIBBĀNAVĀDA)
   58. NIBBĀNA here and now in the enjoyment of the five strands of sense pleasures ~
   59. NIBBĀNA here and now in the first JHĀNA ~
   60. NIBBĀNA here and now in the second JHĀNA ~
   61. NIBBĀNA here and now in the third JHĀNA ~
   62. NIBBĀNA here and now in the fourth JHĀNA ~

~ Summary of BRAHMAJĀLA SUTTA ~ 62 views concluded ~

Chapters Seven and Eight itemize the concentrative meditations and the Knowledge of Supernormal Powers.

7.
CONCENTRATION

(According to VISUDDHI MAGGA ~ Ch. III ~ pp. 84 ~ 478)

~ Taking a meditation subject ~

1. What is concentration? ~ Unification of mind ~ EKAGGATA = SAMĀDHI

2. Its characteristic, function, manifestation and proximate cause: ~ Concentration has non-distraction as its characteristic. ~ Its function is to eliminate distraction. ~ It is manifested as non-wavering. ~ Because of the words being blissful, his mind becomes concentrated. ~ Its proximate cause is bliss.

3. How many kinds of concentration are there? ~ (16 different classifications ~ p.85 V.M.) One of the 16 is: ~ It is of two kinds as access – UPACARA and absorption – APANNĀ.

4. How should it be developed? ~
A. The 10 impediments (p.91. V.M. ~ V29)
    1. A dwelling ~ (overly concerned about)
    2. Family ~ relatives, supports ~ if attached to or too much associated with (p.93)
    3. Gain ~ receiving requisites ~ too occupied with donors (p.94)
    4. Class ~ if in school, groups, classes ~ must sever (p.95)
    5. Building ~ if supervising the construction of something ~ (p.95)

6. Travel ~ if unfinished business, including a journey ~ complete it ~ then begin practice. (p.95)
7. Kin ~ Equals one's teacher, preceptor, pupils, friends, etc. If sick ~ as it is time consuming ~ cure and nurse them ~ then begin practice. (p.96)
8. Affliction ~ any kind of illness ~ impediment ~ cure ~ then begin. (p.96)
9. Books ~ too occupied with reading/study ~ put aside during practice. (p.96)
10. Supernormal powers ~ are an impediment only for insight ~ not for SAMĀDHI. ~ #1-9 are impediments for SAMĀDHI ~ #10 is attained by concentration (p.98)

B. Next ~ approach the good friend, (KALYANA MITTA) the giver of a meditation subject. ~ (p.98)
~ Student should first develop loving kindness towards all members of the community.

C. One takes up meditation subject that suits his temperament ~ 6 types ~ (pp.102 – 111)
1. Greedy temperament
2. Hating temperament
3. Deluded temperament
4. Faithful temperament
5. Intelligent temperament
6. Speculative temperament

~ Faithful temperament is parallel to greedy temperament.
~ Intelligent temperament is parallel to hating temperament.
~ Speculative temperament is parallel to deluded temperament.

("Some would have 14 types ~ taking these 6 single ones together with the four made up of the 3 double combinations and one triple combination with the greed triad and likewise with the faith triad. ~ But if this classification is admitted, there are many more kinds of temperament possible by combining greed etc. with faith etc. ~ Thus it should be understood as 6 types – listed above.")

7. CONCENTRATION

Temperament can be known by observation ~
1. Posture
2. Actions
3. Eating
4. Seeing ~ so on ~ by kind of states occurring.

5. **40 subjects of meditation ~ p.112**
   1. 10 KASINAS (Contemplation devices)
   2. 10 ASUBHAS (Impurities)
   3. 10 ANUSSATIS (Reflections)
   4. 4 BRAHMA-VIHARAS (Sublime states)
   5. 4 ĀRUPAS (Stages of ĀRUPA-JHANA – Formless states)
   6. ĀHĀRE-PATIKŪLA-SAÑÑĀ (Reflection on loathsomeness of food) ~ access – SAMĀDHI – V.M. CH. XI p.372 V.I
   7. CATU-DHĀTU-VAVATTHĀNA (Analysis of the 4 elements) ~ p.380, v.27 ~ v.126

A. 10 KASINAS ~ (Detailed explanation V.M. CH IV ~ p.122)
   1. Earth – KASINA (V.M. p.122)
   2. Water – KASINA (p.177)
   3. Fire – KASINA (p.178)
   4. Air – KASINA (p.179)
   5. Blue – KASINA (p.179)
   6. Yellow – KASINA (p.180)
   7. Blood red – KASINA (p.180)
   8. White – KASINA (p.181)
   9. Light – KASINA (p.181)
   10. Bounded space – KASINA (p.181)

B. 10 ASUBHAS ~ (Detailed explanation V.M. CH VI p.185)
   1. A bloated corpse (p.186)
   2. A livid corpse (p.197)
   3. A festering corpse (p.197)
   4. A corpse cut in the middle (p.197)
   5. A gnawed corpse (p.197)
   6. A scattered corpse (p.197)

7. A hacked and scattered corpse (p.197)
8. A bleeding corpse (p.198)
9. A worm-infested corpse (p.198)
10. A skeleton (p.198)

C. 4 BRAHMA – VIHARAS ~
1. METTĀ ~ loving-kindness
2. KARUNĀ ~ compassion (p.340)
3. MUDITĀ ~ altruistic joy (p.341)
4. UPEKKHĀ ~ equanimity (p.342)

D. 10 ANUSSATIS ~ (See for explanation: V.M.CH VII, p. 204)
1. Reflection on the attributes of the BUDDHA (p.206)
2. Reflection on the attributes of DHAMMA (p.230)
3. Reflection on the attributes of SANGHA (p.336)
4. Reflection on the attributes of one's own SĪLA ~ virtue (p.240)
5. Reflection on the attributes of one's own CĀGA ~ liberality (p.241)
6. Reflection on one's own possession of SADDHĀ ~ trust, SĪLA – SUTA ~ learning, CĀGA and PAÑÑĀ ~ (which are attributes leading to rebirth as DEVAS) (p.245)
7. Reflection on NIBBĀNA
8. Contemplation on the inevitability of death (p.247)
9. Contemplation on the 32 parts of the body (p.259)
10. ĀNĀPĀNA-SATI- KAMMATHĀNA (p.285)

E. 4 ARŪPAS ~ (See for explanation: V.M. CH X p.354)
1. ĀKĀSĀNAÑCĀYATANA ~ dwelling on the contemplation of infinity of space ~
2. VIÑÑĀNAÑCĀYATANA ~ dwelling on the contemplation of infinity of consciousness ~
3. ĀKIÑCAÑÑĀYATANA ~ dwelling on the contemplation of the realm of nothingness ~
4. NEVASAÑÑA- N'ĀSAÑÑĀYATANA ~ dwelling on neither perception nor non-perception ~

F & G (6 and 7 ~ listed above)

7. CONCENTRATION

6. The exposition of the meditation subject ~ ten ways ~

1. As to enumeration ~ (see preceding page) ~ (p.112)
2. Which brings access ~ which bring JHĀNA ~ the 8 recollections, excepting ĀNĀPĀNA SATI & loathsomeness of food; four elements = these 10 only bring access ~ the others bring absorption ~ (p.113)
3. As to the kind of JHĀNA ~ 10 KASINAS + ĀNĀPĀNA SATI = all 4 JHĀNAS 10 ASUBHAS + SATI occupied w/ the body = bring only first JHĀNA
   First 3 BRAHMA VIHARAS = bring first 3 JHĀNAS
4. UPEKKHĀ – BRAHMA VIHARA + ARŪPAS = bring 4th JHĀNAS (p.113)
5. As to surmounting ~ (p.113)
6. As to extension and non-extension ~ (p.114)
7. As to object ~ (p.116)
8. As to plane ~ (p.117)
9. As to apprehending ~ (p.117)
10. As to condition ~ (p.117)
11. As to suitability of temperament ~ (p.117)
    - ~ 10 ASUBHAS + mindfulness of body = 11 subjects suitable for one of greedy temperament
    - ~ 4 BRAHMA-VIHARAS + 4 color KASINAS = 8 subjects suitable for one of hating temperament
    - ~ ĀNĀPĀNA-SATI = for one of deluded temperament
    - ~ First 6 ANUSATIS = for faithful temperament
    - ~ Mindfulness of death + recollection of peace + 4 elements + loathsomeness of food = intelligent temperament
    - ~ remaining KASINAS + ARŪPAS = suitable for all kinds of temperaments
    - ~ any one of the KASINAS = speculative temperament ~ measureless = for deluded temperament

7. Next ~ student should dedicate himself to the BUDDHA and his good friends ~ (p.118)

- ~ one will gain strength and determination in difficult moments with this sincere dedication
- ~ relinquish your person to them

8. Meditator's inclination, dedication, and sincere resolution should be sincere in 6 modes (p.119)

> ~ for it is one of such sincere inclination who arrives at enlightenment ~

1. With inclination to non-greed ~ BODHISATTVAS see fault in greed
2. With inclination to non-hate ~ BODHISATTVAS see fault in hate
3. With inclination to non-delusion ~ BODHISATTVAS see fault in delusion
4. With inclination to renunciation ~ BODHISATTVAS see fault in house life
5. With inclination to seclusion ~ BODHISATTVAS see fault in society
6. With inclination to relinquishment ~ BODHISATTVAS see fault in all kinds of becoming & destiny

9. Meditator should be wholeheartedly resolved upon concentration ~ respect concentration, incline to concentration; ~ be resolved upon NIBBĀNA ~ respect NIBBĀNA ~ incline to NIBBĀNA (p.120)

- ~ Meditator should now receive subject according to one's temperament ~
- ~ See p. 120 v 130 ~ Questions good friend, asks student to determine his temperament ~

7A. CONCENTRATION ~

A. Explanation of the earth KASINA (PATHAUT – KASINA – NIDDESA)

(CHAPT. IV ~ VIS. MAGGA. Pp 122-176)

~ Meditator should avoid a monastery unfavorable to the development of concentration, and go to live in one that is favorable ~

1. The 18 faults of a monastery ~ (It is unfavorable if it has any of the 18) (p.122-125)

1. Large monastery ~ many people gather in such places with varying aims ~ conflict with each other ~ duties left undone: ~ If otherwise it's ok.
2. New monastery ~ much new building construction.
3. Dilapidated monastery ~ much that needs repair ~ meditation practice suffers.
4. Nearby road ~ disturbances by the many visitors.
5. Pond ~ many people come there for drinking.
6. Edible leaves ~ women come and gather such things ~ sing ~ talk ~ the noise disturbs practice.
7. Flowering shrubs ~ same danger as #6.
8. Fruits ~ such fruit trees nearby ~ people come and ask for them ~ disturbance.
9. Famous ~ such monasteries are busy, many devotees come to pay homage.
10. Nearby city ~ many women come into focus ~ important people come also ~ inconvenience.
11. Nearby timber trees ~ cutters come ~ noise ~ etc.
12. Nearby arable lands ~ villagers use monastery grounds as place of work ~ dump trash ~ to dry things.
13. Presence of incompatible persons ~ hostility if a disturbance.
14. Nearby port of entry ~ people constantly arriving ~ crowding, etc.
15. Near the border countries ~ people have no trust in BUDDHA,

DHAMMA, SANGHA, etc. there.
16. Near the frontier of a kingdom: ~ Fear of king's attacks, ~ suspect BHIKKHU of spying.
17. Unsuitability ~ risk of encountering visible data ~ of the opposite sex ~ or to haunting by spirits
18. Lack of good friends ~ teacher ~ preceptor. ~ This is a serious fault.

2. The 5 factors of suitable monastery (resting place) (p.125)
1. A lodging is not too far, not too near (alms village) and has a path for going and coming.
2. Little frequented by day ~ little sound ~ few voices at night.
3. Little contact with gadflies, flies, winds, burning sun and creeping things.
4. Requisites are easily obtainable ~ robes, food, medicine, lodging.
5. Elder BHIKKUS are near ~ observers of the DHAMMA ~ VINAYA ~ skilled in removing doubt.

3. Lesser impediments ~ next ~ these should be severed: ~ (p.126)
1. Cut long head hair ~ nails ~ and body hair.
2. Mend robes. ~ If stained ~ dye them.
3. Repair bowl if necessary.
4. Bed, chair, room, etc. should be cleaned.

B. Detailed Instructions for the Development of the Earth KASINA

A. Nine aspects should be explained ~
1. ~ The four faults of the KASINA
2. ~ The making of a KASINA
3. ~ The method of development for one who has made it. ~
4. ~ The two kinds of signs
5. ~ The two kinds of concentration
6. ~ The seven kinds of suitable and unsuitable
7. ~ Evenness of energy
8. ~ The directions for absorption

B. The earth KASINA ~ (p.126) ~ One who is learning the earth KASINA apprehends the sign in earth that is either made up (KASINA device) or not made up (a sloughed field). He anchors his mind to that object.

1. **Making an earth KASINA ~ (p.128)**

    Making the KASINA from clay~ guarding against the 4 faults: ~ They are due to the intrusion of blue, yellow, red or white. (Do not use clay of such colors). Use clay the color of dawn. ~ Can make a portable one or a fixed one ~ clay should be very clean, make it round. The size of a saucer (4 finger breadths) ~ bigger is also ok ~ should be smooth and even ~ one should then bath and clean room ~ then begin practice ~

    ~ sit 2 to 5 cubits from disc ~ (2.5 times elbow to fingertip ~ KASINA will not appear plainly if further away. ~ If closer, faults in the KASINA appear. ~)

2. **Starting contemplation ~ (p.128) ~ after sitting.**
    1. Review dangers in sense desires (gives little enjoyment, etc.) and arouse longing for escape from DUKKHA.
    2. Next ~ arouse joy of happiness by recollecting specific qualities of the BUDDHA, DHAMMA, SANGHA.
    3. Then open eyes ~ (slightly) ~ gaze at disc ~ apprehend the sign (= apprehend by the mind the sign apprehended by the eye in the earth KASINA) ~ NIMITTA ~
    4. Color of the disc should not be reviewed. ~ Ignore it.
    5. Attention should be given by setting the mind on the name-concept as the most outstanding mental datum ~ relegating the color to the position of a property of its physical support. That conceptual state can be called by any one the meditator likes among the names for earth ~ PATHAVĪ ~ the Great One ~ MAHĪ ~ the friendly one (MEDINĪ) ~ ground (BHŪMI) ~ the provider of wealth ~ VASŪDITĀ.
    6. Continually gazing at it ~ saying mentally: ~ "Earth...earth..." ~ thousands of times ~ until the sign appears.
    7. Thus, developing in this way ~ the disc appears in mind with

eyes closed, as if eyes were open and looking at it = learning sign.

8. After the learning sign is produced, one should not continue to look at the external disc. ~ If doing so, the counterpart sign would not appear. ~ Instead, keeping eyes closed the yogi unremittingly strikes the object in mind with VITAKKA and VICARA. (If the learning sign becomes lost ~ eyes open on disc ~ earth. (Counterpart sign ~ equals UPACARA SAMĀDHI).
9. No hindrances in mind ~ difference is between learning sign ~ and counterpart sign. ~ In learning sign any fault in the KASINA is apparent ~ the moon's disc ~ but it has neither color nor shape ~ for if it had it would be cognizable by the eye, gross and stamped with the TI-LAKKHANA., ~ But it is not like that ~ for it is born of perception in one who has obtained SAMĀDHI. UPACARA SAMĀDHI = abandonment of hindrances ~APPANA = JHĀNA ~ presence of JHĀNA factors.

3. Guarding the sign ~ (p.132)

The arising of the counterpart sign is very difficult. ~ Therefore, if you can enter JHĀNA in that same session by extending the sign, do so. This is good. ~ If not, then you must guard the sign diligently, as if it were the embryo of a wheel-turning monarch. ~
A. There are 7 ways of guarding it. ~ (p.132)
   1. Abode ~ Does SAMĀDHI come and stay ~ mindfulness ~ effort, etc.? ~ If so, it is suitable. ~ If not, one can try different dwellings within the monastery.
   2. Alms resort must be close. ~ (Walk slowly ~ eat carefully ~ moderately).
   3. Speech ~ 32 types of aimless talk is unsuitable. ~ It leads to the disappearance of the sign. Even DHAMMA talk should be minimized.
   4. Persons ~ neighboring company ~ noble ~ kind individuals ~ opposite is detriment. By acquaintanceship the unconcentrated mind becomes concentrated at best.
   5. Food ~ having likable food that suits one's taste: ~ Some like sweet, some like sour.

7A.CONCENTRATION ~

6. Climate ~ must find suitable climate: ~ One likes cool, one likes warm.
7. Postures: ~ Walking suits one ~ sitting another ~ standing ~ lying, etc. So, he should try them for 3 days each ~ and that posture is suitable in which the concentrated mind becomes more so.
8. (If avoiding the unsuitable and cultivating the suitable ~ diligently cultivating the sign ~ JHĀNA will soon follow.)

4. 10 skills in absorption ~ (p.134) ~ (If JHĀNA doesn't occur while practicing in this way ~ the yogi should have recourse in the following ways)
   1. Making the basis clean: Cleansing the internal and external basis.
      ~ Cutting long head hairs, nails and body hairs, or if sweaty ~ bathe = cleansing internal basis.
      ~ Smelly dirty robes ~ unclean dwelling = unclean external basis.
      ~ Must wash and clean = impure light from dirty fuel, glass or wick of lamp.
      ~ The opposite is pure light or basis. (p.134)
   2. Maintaining balanced faculties: ~ Equalizing the 5 controlling faculties (energy, SAMĀDHI, SATI, faith, wisdom) (p.135)
   3. Skill in the sign ~ skill in producing the unproduced sign of unification of mind through the earth KASINA, etc. ~ Skill in developing sign when produced ~ and skill in protecting the sign once developed. (Last skill is what is intended by #3) (p.135)
   4. Exert the mind on an occasion when it should be exerted. ~ Developing energy (investigation of DHAMMA, SAMBOJJANGHA and joy SAMBOJJANGHA) ~ 3 arousing factors of enlightenment when mind is slack, or over-lax. ~ One should arouse these factors by the appropriate means when necessary ~ by wise attention. (p.136)

~ #4 continued ~ exerting the mind when it should be exerted ~

A. 7 things that lead to the arising of the investigation of DHAMMA – enlightenment (p.136):
   1. Asking questions
   2. Making the basis clean
   3. Balancing the faculties
   4. Avoidance of persons without understanding
   5. Cultivation of persons with understanding
   6. Reviewing the field for the exercise of profound knowledge
   7. Resoluteness upon the investigation of states

B. 11 things that lead to the arising of the energy enlightenment factor ~ (p.136):
   1. Reviewing the fearfulness of the states of loss
   2. Seeing benefit in obtaining ~ the mundane and supra mundane distinctions via energy
   3. Reviewing the practice path ~ taken by BUDDHA ~ PACCEKAS ~ great disciples ~ etc. ~ It cannot be taken by an idler ~ I must have the journey.
   4. Being a credit to the alms food by producing great fruit for the givers.
   5. Reviewing
   6. Reviewing the greatness of the heritage ~ of DHAMMA to be acquired by me, it cannot be acquired by an idler.
   7. Removing sloth and torpor by perception of light ~ changing posture ~ open air etc.
   8. Avoidance of idle persons
   9. Cultivation of energetic persons
   10. Reviewing the right endeavors
   11. Resoluteness upon that energy

C. 11 things that lead to the arising of the PĪTI-SAMBOJJANGHA (p.138)
   1. Recollection of BUDDHA
   2. Recollection of DHAMMA

3. Recollection of SANGHA
4. Recollection of SĪLA (one's own)
5. Recollection of generosity (one's own)
6. Recollection of deities
7. Recollection of peace
8. Avoidance of rough/coarse persons
9. Cultivation of refined persons
10. Reviewing encouraging discourses
11. Resoluteness upon that happiness

(A, B & C ~ This is how the yogi exerts the mind on occasion when it should be exerted.)

~ end #4

5. **Restrain the mind on an occasion when it should be restrained.** ~ When the yogi's mind is agitated through excess energy, then instead of developing the 3 arousing enlightenment factors, he should develop the 3 calming factors: Tranquility ~ Concentration ~ and Equanimity: SAMBOJJHANGA (p.138)

   A. 7 things that lead to the arising of tranquility enlightenment factor ~ (p.139)
   1. Using superior/suitable food
   2. Living in good/suitable climate
   3. Maintaining a pleasant/suitable posture
   4. Keeping to the middle
   5. Avoidance of violent persons
   6. Cultivation of persons tranquil in body
   7. Resoluteness upon that tranquility

   B. 11 things that lead to the arising of the concentration enlightenment factor ~ (p.139)
   1. Making the basis clean
   2. Skill in the sign
   3. Balancing the faculties
   4. Restraining the mind on occasion

5. Exerting the mind on occasion
   6. Encouraging the listless mind by means of faith and a sense of urgency
   7. Looking on with equanimity at what is occurring rightly
   8. Avoidance of unconcentrated persons
   9. Cultivation of concentrated persons
   10. Reviewing of the JHANAs and liberations
   11. Resoluteness upon that concentration

C. 5 things that lead to the arising of the equanimity enlightenment factor ~ (p.139)
   1. Maintenance of neutrality towards living beings ~
   2. Maintenance of neutrality towards formations ~
   3. Avoidance of persons who show favoritism towards being and formations ~
   4. Cultivation of persons who show neutrality towards being and formations ~
   5. Resoluteness upon that equanimity ~

(A, B & C ~ this is how the yogi exerts the mind on an occasion ~ to restrain it when it should be restrained) ~ end #5

6. **Encourage the mind on occasion when it should be encouraged. ~ The yogi should stimulate his mind thus. (p.139)**
   A. Review the 8 grounds for a sense of urgency ~
      1. Birth
      2. Aging
      3. Sickness
      4. Death
      5. DUKKHA of lower birth
      6. DUKKHA in the past wanderings
      7. DUKKHA in the future wanderings
      8. DUKKHA now as the result of search for food

~ Also, yogi creates confidence by recollecting the special qualities of the: ~

1. ~ BUDDHA
2. ~ DHAMMA
3. ~ SANGHA

7. **Look upon the mind with equanimity on an occasion when it should be looked upon with equanimity. (p.140)**
    ~ When the mind occurs evenly on the object ~ is unagitated and not listless. At such times the yogi is not interested to exert or restrain or encourage it ~ thus the occasion for equanimity.

8. **Avoidance of unconcentrated persons ~ (p.140) ~ People who are not concerned with renunciation ~ with distracted hearts ~ immersed in worldly affairs**

9. **Cultivation of concentrated persons ~ (p.140)**
    ~ Approaching periodically those who have chosen the way of renunciation and obtained concentration.

10. **Resoluteness upon that ~ (p.140)**
    ~ Resolute upon concentration ~ giving it utmost meaning and importance
    ~ not too lax ~ not too tense ~ balanced effort reaches absorption ~

C. The First JHĀNA Explained

(p.133 VIS.MAGGA, Verse 79-126)

~ At this point the yogi ~ quite secluded from sense desires, secluded from unprofitable things ~ enters union and dwells in the first JHĀNA. ~

~ Five mental factors of first JHĀNA ~
1. ~ Applied thought – VITAKKA
2. ~ Sustained thought – VICĀRA
3. ~ Happiness – SUKHA
4. ~ Bliss – PĪTI
5. ~ Unification ~ SAMĀDHI

~ First JHĀNA abandons (p.144 v.79)
1. ~ Five factors ~ the 5 hindrances p.152 v.104
2. ~ Possesses five factors ~ the 5 JHĀNA factors p.152 v.105-106
3. ~ Is good in 3 ways ~ explained below #3 ~ p.153 v.110
4. ~ Possesses 10 characteristics

(p.145 v.81)
~ Sense desires are incompatible with JHĀNA. ~ When they exist, JHĀNA does not occur.
 ~ The hindrances are the opposites of the JHĀNA factor. ~ When they exist ~ JHĀNA does not occur.

(p.152 v.103)
#3 Is good in 3 ways ~
 1. ~ Purification of the way is "good in the beginning".
 2. ~ Intensification of equanimity is "the middle".
 3. ~ Satisfaction is "the end".

#4 Possesses 10 characteristics ~
 the beginning has 3 characteristics
 the middle has 3 characteristics
 the end has 4 characteristics = 10 (p.153, v.111-113)

(p.152 v.103)
~ The Yogi who enters JHĀNA through dwelling in a posture favorable to that JHĀNA ~
 1. ~ He produces a posture ~ remembers it
 2. ~ A procedure
 3. ~ A keeping
 4. ~ An enduring
 5. ~ A lasting
 6. ~ A behavior
 7. ~ A dwelling

(p.156, v.120-123)
~ When the yogi has attained in such a way ~ the mode of its attainment must be discerned ever so carefully. ~ He recaptures such modes ~ and

all aspects ~ with great skill. ~ "I attained this after eating such a type of food ~ quantity ~ in such a posture ~ in such a lodging" ~ etc. Thus, if the JHĀNA is lost ~ the yogi can recapture it. ~ ~The time of day of attainment ~ the yogi must be hair splitting in his discernment. ~ JHĀNA will only last when it is absolutely purified from states that obstruct unification.

~ This is the procedure to remains in that JHĀNA for a long time. ~

1. Extension of the sign ~ (p.158) ~ Extending the counterpart sign by successive delimitations (knowing beforehand to what extent each successive delimitation will be ~ 5" ~ 5", etc.) ~ The room ~ the monastery ~ the country ~ the world sphere and beyond ~ once attained to the first JHĀNA the yogi should enter upon it frequently, without reviewing it much (as the first JHĀNA factors will appear crudely if reviewed, and yogi will seek the second JHĀNA ~ prematurely) ~ in such cases. Yogi strives for the unfamiliar JHĀNA and falls from the first without being able to attain to the second. ~ Such a one is said to have "fallen in between." ~ Instead, the yogi should acquire first JHĀNA mastery in 5 ways before going onto the second.

~ 2nd ~ 3rd ~ 4th JHĀNA listed ~
~ CONCENTRATION ~ first JHĀNA explained ~

(p.160, v.131)
2. Mastery of JHĀNA in 5 ways ~
 ~1. Mastery in adverting ~ adverting to various JHĀNA factors. ~ Applied thought ~ sustained thought ~ with ability to prolong his conscious process uninterruptedly with 5 JHĀNA factors, then his mastery of adverting is successful. ~ BUDDHA's twin miracle is perfection of adverting mastery (p.160, v. 132)
 ~2. Mastery in attaining ~ ability to enter upon JHĀNA quickly ~ (p.160, v.133)
 ~3. Mastery in resolving ~ ability to remain in JHĀNA for a moment consisting of exactly a finger-snap or exactly 10 finger-snaps (steadying the duration). (p.160, v.134)
 ~4. Mastery in emerging ~ to emerge quickly in the same way. (p.160, V.134)

~3. Mastery in reviewing ~ described in same way as # ~ reviewing impulsions (p.160, v.136)

~ Once the yogi has mastered the first JHĀNA in these five ways ~ upon emerging from that JHĀNA he can regard its flaws ~
1. This attainment is threatened by the nearness of hindrances.
2. Its factors are weakened by the grossness of applied and sustained thought.

(p.161, v.136) ~ The second JHĀNA is quieter ~ so he sets about doing what is needed to attain it.

3. Second JHĀNA (p.161, v.139) ~ 3 factors
   ~ rapture-bliss ~ PĪTI
   ~ happy feeling ~ SUKHA
   ~ concentrated unification – SAMĀDHI
4. Third JHĀNA (p.165, v.153)
   ~ 2 factors
   ~ happy feeling ~ SUKHA
   ~ concentrated unification – SAMĀDHI
5. Fourth JHĀNA (p.171, v.163) ~ 2 factors
   ~ equanimity ~ UPEKKHĀ
   ~ unification ~ SAMĀDHI

   A. 10 types of equanimity ~ (p.166, v.156 – 176)
   1. Six factored equanimity
   2. Equanimity as a divine abiding
   3. Equanimity as an enlightenment factor
   4. Equanimity of energy
   5. Equanimity about formations
   6. Equanimity as a feeling
   7. Equanimity about insight
   8. Equanimity as specific neutrality
   9. Equanimity of JHĀNA
   10. Equanimity of purification

~ End VIS. MAGGA Chapter 4 ~ explanation of earth KASINA ~ etc. ~

7C1.
GENERAL 10 KASINAS

~ SUPERNORMAL POWERS DERIVED FROM
~ (VIS. MAGGA P.182, V. 26-37)

1. Earth KASINA ~ Basis for such powers as ~ creating duplicate bodies of oneself ~ stepping standing or sitting on space or water ~ by creating earth.
2. Water KASINA ~ basis for ~ diving in and out of the earth ~ causing rain storms ~ creating rivers and seas ~ creating earthquakes.
3. Fire KASINA ~ basis for such powers as ~ smoking, flaming, causing shower of sparks ~ countering fire with fire ~ ability to burn only what one wants to burn ~ casting light to see visible objects with the divine eye. ~ Burning up body at time of attaining NIBBĀNA like VEN. ANANDA'S PARINIBBĀNA above the middle of the river.
4. Air KASINA ~ traveling with the speed of wind ~ causing wind storms.
5. Blue KASINA ~ ability to create black forms ~ causing darkness.
6. Yellow KASINA ~ ability to create yellow forms ~ making something gold through resolve.
7. Red KASINA ~ creating red forms.
8. White KASINA ~ creating white forms ~ dispelling darkness ~ causing light for the purpose of seeing visible objects with divine eye ~ banishing stiffness and torpor.
9. Light KASINA ~ creating luminous forms ~ same as #8
10. 10. Limited space KASINA ~ revealing the hidden ~ maintaining postures inside the earth and rocks by creating space in them ~ traveling unobstructed through walls, etc.

~ VIS.MAGGA Chapter VII. p.204 ~

D. Recollections (ANUSSATIS)

~ Reflections on recollection of ~
1. BUDDHA ~ p.206 ~ only UPĀCARA SAMĀDHI
2. DHAMMA ~ p.230 ~ only UPĀCARA SAMĀDHI
3. SANGHA ~ p.236 ~ only UPĀCARA SAMĀDHI
4. One's SĪLA ~ p.240 ~ only UPĀCARA SAMĀDHI
5. One's generosity ~ CĀGA ~ p.241 ~ only UPĀCARA SAMĀDHI
6. One's SADDHA ~ SĪLA ~ SUTA ~ CĀGA ~ PAÑÑĀ ~ p.243 ~ only UPĀCARA SAMĀDHI
7. NIBBĀNA ~ p.317 ~ only UPĀCARA SAMĀDHI
8. Death ~ p.247 ~ only UPĀCARA SAMĀDHI
9. 32 parts of the body ~ p.259-285 ~ can attain up to first JHĀNA only
10. ĀNĀPĀNA-SATI ~ reflection on in and out breathing ~ p.285-317 ~ fourth JHĀNA

1. Recollection of the attributes of the BUDDHA

~ This reflection comes to success in the yogi who possesses "absolute confidence" afforded by the first path (SOTAPANNA) ~ not in any other.

A. Attributes of the BUDDHA. He Is:
   1. Accomplished ~ ARAHANTA (p.206-210)
   2. Fully enlightened ~ (p.206-212)
   3. Endowed with clear vision ~ (p.213-215)
   4. Endowed with virtuous conduct ~ (p.213-215)
   5. Sublime ~ (p.215-216)
   6. Knower of the worlds ~ (p.217-221)
   7. The incomparable leader or men to be tamed ~ (p.221-222)
   8. The teacher of gods and men, enlightened and blessed ~ (1m.1-37), (p.223-230)

Method of reflection ~ that Blessed One is such since he is accomplished, he is such since he is fully enlightened ~ he is (so) for (such and such) reasons. ~

A1. ~ Accomplished ~ BUDDHA is accomplished for these reasons: ~
   1. Because of remoteness ~ stands utterly remote from all KILESA ~ no trace of defilement remains ~ thus he is accomplished. (p.206 v.5)
   2. Because of his enemies ~ the defilements or enemies are destroyed ~ thus accomplished (p.206 v.6)
   3. The spokes have been destroyed ~ the wheel of the round of rebirths ~ with MOHA as the hub ~ because it is the root ~ with the rim of aging and death ~ the remaining 10 states of dependent origination are the spokes ~ thus all of the wheels' spokes have been destroyed upon enlightenment ~ thus accomplished. (p.207 v.7)
   4. He is worthy ~ BUDDHA is the worthiest to receive the requisites. ~ Because of the worthiness of requisites ~ he is accomplished. (p.210 v.23)
   5. Because of the absence of secret ~ is incapable of evil ~ or to do anything in secret for fear of getting a blemished name ~ thus accomplished. (P.2110 v.24)

A2. ~ Fully enlightened ~ (SĀMMĀSAMBUDDHA) is such because he discovered (BUDDHA) all things rightly (SAMMĀ) and by himself (SĀMAM). (p.210 v.26)
   1. What must be directly known is known. ~ Learning the 4 Noble Truths.
   2. Of things to be fully understood is understood. ~ Penetration of DUKKHA ~
   3. Of things to be abandoned they are abandoned. ~ Penetration of the origin of DUKKHA. ~ Abandoning both DUKKHA and its cause ~ TANHA rooted in MOHA.
   4. Of things to be realized they are realized. ~ Penetration of the cessation of DUKKHA.
   5. Of things to be developed they are developed. ~ Penetration of path

A3. and A4. ~ Endowed with clear vision and virtuous conduct ~ (p.213 v.30)

1. Clear vision is of 3 ends (see BHAYABHERAVA SUTTA ~ m.1.) and of 8 kinds (see AMBATTHA SUTTA (d.1-106). ~ There 8 kinds of clear vision are stated ~ made up of the 6 kinds of direct knowledge ~ together with insight and the supernormal power of the mind-made (body).
2. Virtuous conduct (15 things) (p.214, v.31)
    3. ~ Restrain by virtue
    4. ~ Guarding the sense doors
    5. ~ Knowledge of proper amount in eating
    6. ~ Devotion to wakefulness
    7. ~ Possessor of the 7 good states
        A ~ SADOHA   12 ~ first JHĀNA
        B ~ HIRI   13 ~ second JHĀNA
        C ~ OTTAPPA   14 ~ third JHĀNA
        D ~ SUTA   15 ~ fourth JHĀNA
        E ~ VIRIYA
        F ~ SATI
        G ~ PAÑÑĀ

~ Through clear vision (full understanding of all DHAMMAS) he knows what is good and harmful for all beings ~ and through virtuous conduct (Great Compassion) he warns them of harm and exhorts them to do good. (P.214 v.32 ~ Expansive footnote #9, p.215)

A5. ~ Sublime ~ (SUGATA) ~ The BUDDHA is called sublime ~ (p.215, v.33)
  1. Because of a manner of going that is good ~ meaning ~ he has gone (GATA) or purified by the noble path ~ gone without attachment in the direction of safety ~ thus he is sublime. (p.215)
  2. Because of being gone to an excellent place ~ meaning ~ he has gone to the deathless ~ NIBBĀNA ~ thus he is sublime. (p.216 v 34)
  3. Because of having gone rightly ~ meaning ~ he can never return to the defilement because of his attainment of the 4 paths (MAGGA) ~ thus he is sublime. (P.216 v.34)
  4. Because of enunciating rightly ~ he speaks only fitting speech, in the fitting place, at the proper time. (Details explained ~ BUDDHA'S speech) (p.216 v.35)

A6. ~ Knower of worlds ~ This is said because the BUDDHA has known the world in all ways as to its individual essence: Its arising, its cessation and the means to its cessation. (p.217 v.36)

~ There are three worlds
1. ~ World of formations ~ all DHAMMAS of NĀMA-RŪPA (p.217 v.38)
2. ~ World of beings ~ knows all beings' habits, temperaments (p.218 v.39)
3. ~ World of location ~ knows infinite number of worlds' systems

~ He has penetrated each fully ~ (p.218 v.40)

~ So, the world spheres (CAKKAVĀLA) are infinite in number, the world elements are infinite and the blessed one has experiences, and known and penetrated them with the infinite knowledge of the Enlightened One.

~ So, he is a "knower of worlds" because he has seen the world in all ways ~

A7. ~ Incomparable leader of men to be tamed

There is no one (except preceding BUDDHAS) in the world comparable to a BUDDHA'S special qualities ~ of virtue ~ SAMĀDHI ~ PAÑÑĀ, deliverance and knowledge and vision of deliverance. ~ He guides and leads individuals to ultimate freedom ~ even in a single session they may go fully ~ ARAHANTA. (P.223, v.49)

A8. ~ Teacher of gods and men

The BUDDHA teaches by means of here and now ~ of the life to come ~ and of the ultimate goal ~ according to proper case. = Thus, he is a teacher. ~ He is a caravan leader ~ he gets them across a wilderness ~ across the wilderness of birth. ~ He teaches those who are capable of progress ~ animals ~ humans ~ DEVAS ~ BRAHMINS. (p.223, v. 50-51)

A9. ~ Enlightened

He has discovered everything that can be known (=BUDDHA). He is a discoverer of the truths (BUJJHITAR). (p.224, v.52)

A10. ~ Blessed

This is a term signifying the respect and veneration accorded him as the highest of all beings, and distinguished by his special qualities. (p.224-230)
1. He has abolished greed, hatred, delusion, views, TANHA, KILESA ~ thus he is blessed.
2. He divided, analyzed, classified ~ the DHAMMA ~ thus he is blessed.
3. He has made an end to "becoming" ~ thus he is blessed.
4. He has developed virtue and understanding ~ thus he is blessed.
5. He is a frequenter of remote places ~ thus he is blessed.
6. He has tasted the meaning of the law, deliverance, higher virtue, higher consciousness and higher understanding ~ thus blessed.
7. Is a partaker of the 4 JHANAS ~ 4 BRAHMA VIHARAS ~ 4 ARŪPA JHANAS ~ thus blessed.
8. Is a partaker of the 8 liberations ~ 8 bases of mastery ~ thus blessed.
9. Has developed all KAMMATHANAS.
10. Has developed all 37 enlightenment factors.
11. Has developed the 4 SATIPATTHANAS.
12. Has developed the 10 powers of a perfect one ~ 4 kinds of perfect
13. confidence, etc. Thus, he is blessed ~ (many additional details listed in VIS.MAG).

~ The yogi who reflects thus attains fullness of faith ~ SATI ~ understanding and merit ~ He has great happiness and gladness ~ he conquers fear and dread ~ is able to endure pain ~ feels as if he were living in the BUDDHA'S presence ~ etc. If he penetrates no higher, he is at least headed for a happy destiny. (p.230, v.67)

~ End explanation ~ recollection of BUDDHA ~

~ Concentration ~ ANNUSATIS ~ explained

2. Recollection of the DHAMMA
~ UPĀCARA SAMADHI only (p.236, v.81) ~

~ In a solitary place one should recollect the special qualities of both the DHAMMA of the scriptures and the ninefold supramundane DHAMMA ~ as follows: ~ "The DHAMMA is well proclaimed by the blessed one, visible here and now, not delayed (timeless), inviting of inspection, onward leading and directly experienceable by the wise" (p.230, v.69)

~ DHAMMA is well proclaimed (in scriptures) ~ because it is good in the beginning, middle and end, and because it announces the life of purity that is utterly perfect and pure with meaning and with detail.

(p.231, v.70) ~ is good in the beginning with virtue as one's own well-being ~ middle ~ with calm and insight and with path and fruition ~ good in the end with NIBBĀNA.

~ The BUDDHA teaches the DHAMMA with "perfection of meaning" ~ speaks words declaring its meaning ~ with perfection of detail ~ by pronouncing, clarifying, revealing, expounding and explaining it. ~ It is with detail because it has perfection of syllables, words, details, style, language and description. ~ This DHAMMA inspires confidence. ~ Its intention is profound. ~ It is experienceable by the wise ~ a fit object of faith for the worldly. ~ It is utterly perfect due to the absence of anything that can be added. ~ It is pure with immaculateness due to absence of anything to be subtracted. ~ It is pure because it has no imperfection, because it exists for the purpose of crossing over the round of rebirths ~ well proclaimed with no perversion of meaning. ~ The supramundane DHAMMA (p.233, v.74) has been well proclaimed because the way leading to NIBBĀNA has been properly declared. It is 'the noble path' because it does not approach either extreme, but the middle way ~ NIBBĀNA~ is well proclaimed as the deathless, the refuge, the shelter.

~ Visible here and now ~ "Firstly the noble path is 'visible here and now' since it can be seen by a noble person himself, when he has done anything with greed, etc. ~ When a man is infused with greed and is overwhelmed, and his mind is obsessed by greed, then he thinks for his own affliction, he thinks for others' affliction, he thinks for the affliction of both – and he experiences mental suffering and grief. When greed has been abandoned, he neither thinks for his own affliction, nor thinks of others' affliction, nor thinks for the affliction of both; and he does not experience mental suffering and grief." ~ This is how the DHAMMA is visible here and now. (A.1,15)

~ Furthermore, the 9-fold supra mundane DHAMMA is also visible here and now, since anyone has attained it. It is visible to him through reviewing knowledge without his having to rely on faith in another (p.233, v.77).

~ Not delayed (v.80) ~ It has no delay in the matter of giving its own fruit ~ its fruit is immediate next to its own occurrence.

~ Inviting of inspection (v.82) ~ It is worthy of an invitation to come and inspect ~ "come and see". This DHAMMA ~ Why? ~ Because the DHAMMA is real and utterly pure ~ "thus come and see it." ~ The DHAMMA is as pure as the full moon disc in a cloudless sky, as the gem of pure water on bleached cloth.

~ Onward leading (v.83) ~ Inducing realization of the DHAMMA in one's own mind.

~ Thus, it is onward leading ~ onward by the path to NIBBĀNA.

~ It is directly experienceable by the wise (v.85). ~ The DHAMMA is visible in one's own mind ~ another's NIBBĀNA doesn't enlighten others. ~ Thus, the DHAMMA is directly experienceable by the wise.

~ Benefits ~ same as Recollection of BUDDHA ~ p. 236, v.87,88)

3. Recollection of the SANGHA
~ (p.236, v.89) ~

~ One should recollect the special qualities of the community of noble ones as follows: ~ (p.236, v.89)

"The community of the blessed one's disciples has entered on the good way, thus have entered on the straight way, have entered on the true way, they have entered upon the proper way; that is to say, the four pairs of men, the eight persons. This community of the blessed one's disciples is fit for gifts, fit for hospitality, fit for offerings, fit for reverential salutation, as an incomparable field of merit for the world." ~ (AND 111.286)

1. Entered on the good way etc. (p.237, v.90) Have entered on the right way ~ the way that is in conformity with truth ~ the way that is regulated by DHAMMA. ~ The straightway ~ unbent way ~ uncooked, unwrapped ~ noble and true way. ~ Those who stand on the path or have attained ARIYA status can be considered to have entered the good way ~ the straightway ~ because it is the way of avoiding extremes. ~ Entered the middle way ~ entered on the way of abandonment of the bodily and verbal faults ~ entered the true way because NIBBĀNA is what is called true ~ the proper way because one has entered on the way of those who are worthy of proper acts (of veneration).

2. The 4 pairs of men ~ the eight persons ~ 4 pairs = 1 who stands on the first path and the one who stands in the first fruition = one pair ~ and so on~ SAKADAGAMI ~ etc. ~ The 8 persons ~ taking each of the 4 MAGGAS ~ 4 PHALAS as separate persons = 8. (P.237, v.93)

3. The community of the Blessed One's disciples is fit for gifts ~ these 4 pairs of 8 persons ~ they are fit for gifts of the requisites ~ because the community makes the fight bear great fruit.

4. Fit for hospitality, fit for offerings, fit for reverential salutation, as an incomparable field of merit. ~ (Self-explanatory ~ details ~ reflects V.M.p.236, v.96-98)

~ Benefits same as recollection of BUDDHA ~ DHAMMA ~
UPĀCARA SAMADHI only ~ (p.239, v.99)

4. Recollection of one's SĪLA (virtue)
~ (p.246, v.101-v.106) ~

~ One should recollect his own different kinds of virtue as follows: ~ "Indeed, my various kinds of virtue are uptown, unsent, unbleached, unmottled, liberating, praised by the wise, not adhered to, and conducive to concentration" ~ (AND 111-286)

~ If layman or lay woman ~ reflect on your subsequent type of

SĪLA ~ a BHIKKHU or SĀMANERA also reflect according to the proper code.

~ Virtues are liberating since they liberate by freeing from the slavery of craving. (This section in VIS.MAG. is very short ~)

5. Recollection of one's CĀGA (generosity)
~ (p.241, v.107 – v.114) ~

One who wants to develop the recollection of generosity should be naturally devoted to generosity, and the constant practice of giving and sharing. Or alternatively, if he is one who is starting the development of it, he should make the resolution: "From now on, when there is anyone present to receive, I shall not eat even a single mouthful without having given a gift". And that very day he should give a gift by sharing according to his means and his ability with those who have distinguished qualities.

One should reflect on his own generosity as follows: ~

~ "It is a gain for me, it is a great gain for me, that in a generation obsessed by the stain of avarice, I abide with my heart free from stain by avarice, and am freely generous and open handed, that I delight in relinquishment, expect to be asked, and rejoice in giving and sharing." (ANG 111-287)

1. (p.242) "It is gain for me, it is a great gain for me ~ my advantage ~ because now who gives life by giving food shall have life either divine or human. ~ A giver is loved and frequented by many. ~ It is great gain for me that the DHAMMA has been heard ~ and the human state has been attained." ~ Such a person lives with their heart free ~ free of greed and hatred states that darken the natural transparency of consciousness. ~ Becoming freely generous ~ delighting in giving up ~ relinquishing ~ constant devotion to relinquishing ~ giving what others ask for ~ expect to be asked. ~ "I give gifts and I share what is to be used by myself, and I rejoice in both. ~ Recollecting one's own special qualities of generosity of freedom from avarice. Thus, one's mind, obsessed by greed, hatred or delusion, is being inspired by generosity.

Benefits are ~ 1. ~ Becomes ever more intent on generosity
                2. ~ His preference is for non-greed

3. ~ He acts in conformity with METTA
4. ~ Is fearless
5. ~ Has much happiness and gladness
6. ~ If penetrates no higher ~ then at least is headed for a happy destiny.

6. Recollection of one's SADDHA (faith)

~ and SĪLA~ SUTA ~ CĀGA and PAÑÑĀ ~ with deities standing as witness

(p.245, v.115) ~ One who wants to develop the recollection of one's SADDHA should possess the special quality of path evoked by means of the noble path ~ should retreat and reflect on one's own special qualities of faith, etc. with deities standing as witnesses.

~ Such a reflector becomes dearly loved by deities ~ obtains even deeper faith.

~ General ~ the six recollections ~ (p.244, v.199-128)

(p.245, v.121) ~ The 6 recollections succeed only in noble disciples (ARIYAS) ~ for the special qualities of the BUDDHA, DHAMMA, etc. are evident to them.

~ In the MAHĀNĀMA SUTTA (ANG 111-285). The 6 recollections are expounded in detail by the BUDDHA. (v.122)

~ In the GEDHA SUTTA they are expounded in order that a noble disciple should purify his consciousness by means of the recollections, and so to attain higher purifications. (MAGGA-AHALAS) (v.123)

(p.246 v.127) ~ Yet VIS.MAGGA states: ~ Still, these recollections can be brought to mind by an ordinary man too, if he possesses the qualities of purified virtue, and the rest. For when he's recollecting the special qualities of the BUDDHA, etc., [even only] according to what he says, his consciousness settles down. Hindrances are suppressed ~ gladness arises ~ insight is initiated ~ he can even attain ARAHANTSHIP ~ like the elder PHUSSADEVA who saw a BUDDHA figure created by MĀRA. We thought, "How good this appears!" ~ reflecting on how good the BUDDHA must have been. ~ Acquired joy with Blessed One as object ~ insight ~ ARAHANTSHIP!"

~ End VIS.MAG. Chapter VII ~ Description of the six recollections. ~

7. Recollection of Death (MARANA ANNUSATI)
~ (p.247, v.1) ~

Death ~ is the interruption of the life (force) faculty included within (the limits) of a single becoming (existence). ~ Momentary death is not what is meant here. (The momentary dissolution of formations.)

(V.2) 'Death' intended here is of 2 kinds ~

1. ~ Timely death = comes about with the exhaustion of merit, or with the exhaustion of a life span, or with both.
2. ~ Untimely death = comes about through KAMMA that interrupts (other, life-producing) KAMMA ~ attack by a weapon, etc.

So mindfulness of death is the remembering of death ~ the interruption of the life faculty ~

~ Development ~ (p.248, v.5)

~ One should go into solitary retreat and exercise attention wisely in this way:
- ~ Death will take place
- ~ Life faculty will be interrupted
- ~ Or ~ death ~ death.
- ~ If attention is exercised unwisely in recollecting the possible death of an agreeable person ~ sorrow arises.
- ~ If unwisely placed on a disagreeable person ~ gladness arises.
- ~ Recollecting death of neutral people ~ no sense of urgency arises (as happens in a corpse-burning, on seeing a dead body.)
- ~ Recollecting one's own death ~ anxiety arises (as if seeing a murderer with a poised dagger).

~ In all such cases there is neither SATI, nor sense of urgency, nor knowledge.

(p.248, v.6) So the yogi should look here and there at beings that have been killed or have died, and advert to the death of beings already dead but formerly seen enjoying good things. ~ The yogi doing so with mindfulness, with a sense of urgency and with knowledge, after which he can exercise his attention in the way stated above: "Death will take place" etc.

~ By doing so ~ the yogi exercises it wisely ~ by the right means.
~ In time ~ the hindrances become suppressed ~ SATI becomes established with death as the object ~ access concentration is reached.

(p.248, v.8) ~ But one who doesn't succeed in this way should do his recollecting of death in eight ways: ~
1. As having the appearance of a murderer
2. As the ruin of success
3. By comparison
4. As to sharing the body with many
5. As to the frailty of life
6. As sign-less
7. As to the limitedness of the extend
8. As to the shortness of the moment

~ explanation of each is as follows ~

1. Death as having the appearance of a murderer (p.248, v.9)

Recollect thus: ~
1. Just as a murderer appears with a sword, thinking, "I shall cut this man's head off" ~ and applies it to his neck, so death appears. ~ Why? Because it comes with birth and takes away life.
2. Just as a budding toadstool always comes up, lifting dust on its top; so too beings are born, along with aging and death.
3. Rebirth linking-consciousness reaches aging immediately next to its arising.
4. Momentary death comes along with birth.

5. Death is inevitable for what is born.
6. Just as the risen sun moves on towards its setting, and never turns back.
7. Just as the mountain torrent sweeps by with rapid current, ever flowing and rushing on.
8. So too living beings travel on towards death from the time of being born, never turning back, even for a little while.
9. From the very moment of conception in the womb, one cannot but go on and on, nor going can he turn back.
10. Death is as near to one as drying up is to rivulets in the summer heat.
11. Death is as near to one as falling is to fruits of trees when the sap reaches their stems in the morning.
12. Death is as near to one as breaking is to clay pots tapped by a mallet.
13. Death is as near to one's vanishing as dew drops touched by the sun's rays.

~ So, this death, which comes along with birth, is like a murderer with a poised sword. And like the murderer who applies the sword to the neck, it carries off life and never returns to bring it back. ~ Thus, death should be recollected as having the appearance of a murderer.

2. Death as the ruin of success (p.250, v.19)
Recollect thus: ~
1. Success shines as long as failure does not overcome it.
2. Any success that might endure out of reach of failure does not exist.
3. All health ends in sickness ~ all youth ends in aging ~ all life ends in death.
4. All worldly existence is procured by birth ~ haunted by aging ~ surprised by sickness ~ and struck down by death.

~ This is how death should be recollected as the "ruin of success" ~ by defining it as 'death's final ruining of life's successes.' ~

3. Death recollection by comparison (p.250, v.16)
~ By comparing oneself to others. Death should be recollected by comparison in seven ways ~

1. With those of great fame ~ individuals who were greatly famous and had a great following, and had amassed enormous wealth ~ yet death took them. ~ So how shall it not at length overtake me? (v.17)
2. With those of great merit ~ same as stated. ~ So how shall death not overtake me? (v.18)
3. With those of great strength ~ same as stated. ~ So how shall death not overtake me? (v.19)
4. With those of great supernormal power ~ even MAHA-MOGGALĀNA ~ foremost in miraculous power: Death overcame him too ~ so how should it not overtake me? (v.20)
5. With those of great understanding ~ even Ven. SĀRIPUTTA ~ chief in wisdom next to the BUDDHA: ~ He fell into death's power too. ~ So how should it not overtake me? (P.251, v.21)
6. With PACCEKA BUDDHAS ~ who conquered all defilements by themselves ~ are self-perfected ~ stood alone like the rhinoceros: ~ They were still not free from death ~ so how should I be free from it? (p.252, v.22)
7. With fully enlightened BUDDHAS ~ a pure being in every respect ~ with no equal~ even he was suddenly quenched by the downpour of death's rain, as a great mass of fire is quenched by the downfall of a rain of water. ~ So how shall I be free from it? (v.23)

~ Recollecting ~ death will come to me even as it did to those distinguished beings ~

4. Death recollected as to the sharing of the body with many (p.253, v.25)

Recollect thus: ~
1. This body is shared by many.
2. It is shared by the 80 families of worms ~ creatures that live in dependence on the various parts of the body ~ flesh ~ inner and outer skin~ etc. These creatures are born, grow old and die, evacuate and make water: and the body is their maternity home, their hospital, their charnel ground, their privy and their urinal.
3. The body is also shared by several hundred internal diseases.

4. Death can occur also by such external causes as snakes, scorpions, centipedes and what not.
5. Death can occur by all types of accidents that befall the body ~ stumble and fall.
6. In many ways I can risk death ~ bodily imbalance ~ upset by improper food.

5. Death recollected as to the frailty of life ~ (p.253, v.27)
Recollect thus: ~
1. This life is fragile and frail. ~ (All aspects below must occur evenly or death will occur).
2. This life of beings is bound up with breathing ~ bound up with the postures ~ it is bound up with cold and heat ~ bound up with the primary elements ~ and bound up with nutriment.
3. Life occurs only when the in-breaths and out-breaths occur evenly, but when the wind in the nostrils that has gone outside does not go into the person, or when that which has gone inside does not come out, then a being is reckoned to be dead.

6. Death recollected as sign-less ~ (p.254, v.29)
~ As indefinable or unpredictable
Recollect thus in five ways:
1. The span ~ has no sign ~ no fixed amount. ~ So much has gone ~ so much remains. ~ for beings die in all stages of the embryo ~ coming out of the womb ~ first minute, 2nd, 1 week, 1 month, etc. And after that most are consumed this side or the other side of a century. (p.254, v.29)
2. The sickness ~ has no sign because beings die of many different diseases, not just one. Always the uncertainty of life continuing with contact with any disease. (v.31)
3. The time ~ has no sign, since death can occur at any time, not just at noon, etc. (v.32)
4. Where the body will be laid down ~ has no sign, since there is no special spot that death can only occur ~ anywhere it can occur ~ and there the body will be laid down. (p.255, v.33)

5. The destiny ~ unless in the abode of the ARIYAS ~ there is no definition that one who dies there must be reborn here, or vice-versa. ~ This uncertainty in destiny and the world whirls on and on. (v.34)

7. Death recollected as to the limitedness of the extent. (p.255, v.35)

Recollect thus: ~
1. The extent of human life now is short ~ there is no dying for the born.
2. "Oh let me live as long as it takes to chew and swallow 4 or 5 mouthfuls, that I may attend to the Blessed One's teaching, surely much could be done by me!" ~ This is called a BHIKKHU who dwells in negligence and slackly develops mindfulness of death for the destruction of defilements ~ "Oh let me live…to chew a single mouthful." ~ "Oh, let me live… to take an inbreath and out breath ~ or breath in and breath out ~ attending to the teaching, surely much could be done by me." ~ These are called BHIKKHUS who dwell in diligence and keenly develop mindfulness of death for the destruction of KILESAS. (ANG. III ~ 305-6)

So short in fact is the extent of life that it is not certain even for as long as it takes to chew and swallow four or five mouthfuls, or to breathe in or to breathe out. (v.38)

8. Death recollected as to the shortness of the moment ~ (p.256, v.39)

Recollect thus: ~
1. In the ultimate sense the life-moment of living beings is extremely short ~ only a single conscious mind-moment ~ 13 trillion in a blink of an eye.
2. When this momentary consciousness ceases ~ the aging is said to have ceased.
3. Life, person, pleasure, pain ~ just these alone join in 1 conscious moment that flicks by. ~ Gone moment by moment, never to return.

4. When consciousness dissolves, the world is dead.

~ Conclusion ~ (p.257, v.40-41)

~ Recollection of death reaches only UPĀCARA SAMADHI. (Interesting explanation top of p.248)
~ Benefits ~ if mindfully recollected with diligence:

1. The yogi acquires perception of disenchantment with all kinds of becoming (existence).
2. He conquers attachment to life.
3. He avoids excessing and storing.
4. He has no strain of avarice about requisites.
5. Perception of impermanence grows in him. ~ Following on will be the perception of DUKKHA & ANATTA.
6. If recollection of death is not cultivated the being can fall victim to fear, horror and confusion at the time of death, as though suddenly seized by wild beasts, robbers, snakes or murderers.
7. The death contemplated dies undecided and fearless, without falling into such states.
8. And if the yogi doesn't attain the deathless here and now, he is at least headed for a happy destiny on the breakup of the body.

~ Thus, the wise make recollection of death their constant task ~
~ Blessed with such mighty potency
~ With this recollection one becomes diligent ~ urgency grows ~ disenchantment regarding all kinds of existence. ~ Attachment to life dissolves. ~ He condemns evil. ~ One avoids accumulation, lives contented easily.

~ Greed for objects falls away ~ knowledge of impermanence grows ~ ANATTA and DUKKHA follow. ~ Beings who have not developed mindfulness of death fall victims to fear, horror and confusion at the time of death, as though suddenly seized by wild beasts, spirits, snakes, robbers or murderers. ~ He dies undeluded and fearless without falling into any such state.

And if he does not attain the deathless here and now, he is at least headed for a happy destiny on the break-up of the body.

Additional reflections regarding death:
1. Law of KAMMA
2. 5 aggregates ~ ANATTA
3. Law of ANICCA
4. Law of dependent origination

~ **End explanation ~ Recollection of death ~**

~ Concentration ~ 4 additional ANNUSATIS explained ~

8. Contemplation on the 32 parts of the body
~ (p.259, v.42) ~

~ This contemplation in its entirety is never set forth except after the arising of a BUDDHA. And it is outside the scope of any sectarians. ~ The BUDDHA has said of its value:

1. When ONE thing is developed and repeatedly practiced, it leads to a supreme sense of urgency.
2. To supreme benefit.
3. To supreme release from bondage.
4. To supreme mindfulness and full-awareness.
5. To acquisition of knowledge and vision.
6. To a happy life here and now.
7. To realization of the fruit of clear vision and deliverance.

~ That ONE thing is mindfulness of the body.

~ Text ~ This meditation subject is taught as 'The Direction of Attention to Repulsiveness.' (p.260, v.44)

~ Contemplate thus: ~

"A BHIKKHU reviews this body, up from the soles of the feet and down from the top of the hair and contained in the skin as full of many kinds of filth thus:

In this body there are:
1. Head hairs ~ p.266, v.83
2. Body hairs ~ p.269, v.90
3. Nails ~ p.270, v.91
4. Teeth ~ v.92
5. Skin ~ v.93
6. Flesh ~ p.271, v.97
7. Sinews ~ p.272, v.99
8. Bones ~ p.273, v.101
9. Bone marrow ~ p.274, v.109
10. Kidney ~ p.275, v.110
11. Heart ~ v.111
12. Liver ~ v.114
13. Midriff ~ p.276, v.115
14. Spleen ~ v.116
15. Lights ~ v.117
16. Bowels ~ v.118
17. Entrails ~ p.277, v.119
18. Gorge ~ v.120
19. Dung ~ p.278, v.123
20. Bile ~ p.279, v.129
21. Brain ~ p.279, v.126
22. Phlegm ~ p.280, v.128
23. Pus ~ v.129
24. Blood ~ v.130
25. Sweat ~ v.131
26. Fat ~ p.281, v.132
27. Tears ~ v.133
28. Grease ~ p.282, v.134
29. Spittle ~ v.135
30. Snot ~ v.136
31. Oil of the joints ~ p.283, v.137
32. Urine ~ v.138

"No one who searches throughout the whole of this fathom-long carcass, starting upward from the soles of the feet, starting downward from the top of the head, and starting from the skin all round, ever finds even the minutest atom at all beautiful in it, such as a pearl, or a gem, or any kind of precious stone, or saffron, or camphor, or talcum powder: On the contrary, he finds nothing but the various very malodorous, offensive, disgusting sort of filth, consisting of the head hairs, body hairs…and urine." (P.261, v.47)"

To define all the other 31 body parts by: (p.268, v.82)
1. Color
2. Shape
3. Direction
4. Location and delimitation

He should then define repulsiveness in 5 ways ~ (p.268, v.82), by:
1. Color
2. Shape
3. Odor
4. Habitat
5. Location

~ All 5 points are explained in detail under each part. ~ See page and verse.

~ All 32 parts are repulsive in 5 ways. ~ (See V.M. p.269, v.84-89)

1. Color ~ seeing color of head hair in one's food. ~ It is repulsive.
2. Shape ~ to see hair shaped items in food. ~ It is repulsive.
3. Odor ~ burn hair, or other parts and smell. ~ Or do not bathe.
4. Habitat ~ hairs grow on this head of the other 3 parts, like fungus on a dunghill. Head hairs grow on the sewage of pus, blood, urine, etc. ~ thus repulsive.
5. Location ~ like vegetables growing on a charnel ground ~ hairs, etc. grow on and in the filth of this body with its 32 parts.

~ All 32 parts are repulsive in these 5 ways described ~

~ The arising of absorption with this practice ~

Benefits ~
1. Yogi conquers boredom and delight.
2. Yogi conquers fear and dread.
3. He endures cold and heat.
4. He endures unpleasant bodily feelings that arise.

~ End explanation of SATI of the 32 body parts. ~

~ Concentration ~ 4 additional ANNUSATIS explained ~

~ Development of contemplation on the 32 parts of the body ~ (p.261, v.46)

One should know ~
1. ~ The seven-fold skill in learning ~ and
2. ~ The ten-fold skill in giving attention ~

A. 7-fold skill in learning: ~
1. As verbal recitation ~ (p.261, v.49) ~ One should recite forwards and backwards the various divisions of the 32 parts. ~ (6 divisions ~ when repeating backwards always include the previous division ~ but when forward ~ start with the 32 body parts of that division. ~ Divisions are: body parts (1-5), (6-10), (11-15), (16-20), (21-26), (27-32), (5 parts +5+5+5+6+6=32) ~ This recitation should be done thousands of times ~ for it is through verbal recitation that the meditation subject becomes familiar ~ the mind settles ~ the parts become evident.
2. Mental recitation ~ (p.262, v.57) ~ Verbal recitation is a condition for the mental recitation, and vice versa. Should be done as explained under verbal recitation ~ mental recitation is a condition for the penetration of foulness ~ repulsiveness.
3. As to color ~ (v.56) ~ the color of the head hairs, etc. should be defined.
4. As to shape ~ (v.56) ~ their shape should be defined too.

5. As to direction ~ (v.56) ~ in this body ~ upwards from the navel is the upward direction ~ and downwards from it is the downwards direction = Thus defining the parts in their directions.
6. As to location ~ (v.56) ~ the location of this or that part should be defined thus: This part is established in this location.
7. As to delimitation ~ (p.263, v.59) ~ 2 kinds of delimitation of the similar and dissimilar. This part is delimited above and below and around by this ~ dissimilar = head hairs are not body hairs, etc.

~ This meditation subject has been explained from 2 angles: One from that of repulsiveness of the 32 parts (this is a SAMATHA practice); ~ the second way is from the point of view of just elements that comprise this body (this is Insight practice).

~ Thus, this explanation deals only with the SAMATHA practice ~

B. The ten-fold skill in giving attention ~ (p.263, v.61)
1. As to following the order: ~ Follow the serial order without skipping ~ the mind becomes exhausted otherwise (v.62).
2. Not too quickly: ~ If too quickly~ parts will not be clear ~ thus no result (v.63).
3. Not too slowly: ~ If done so, the yogi will not get to the end ~ thus no results (p.264, v.64).
4. As to warding off distraction: ~ The yogi should ward of temptation to give up practice (v.65).
5. As to surmounting the concept: ~ Concept of parts must be overcome ~ consciousness established just on repulsiveness ~ the aspect of... (v.66).
6. As to successive learning: ~ Eventually the yogi should leave out parts that do not appear to him. ~ As practice continues, same parts appear to him, others do not. The Yogi should work on those that have appeared till one out of any two appears to be the clearer. Yogi should arouse absorption on that one clear part. (Many details) (v.67).
7. Re Absorption: ~ It can be brought about in each one of the parts. (p.266, v.72).

8. Balancing factors: ~ SAMĀDHI, energy and equanimity (see p.77-78 of this book), (v.73-74).
9. Balancing factors: ~ Include 3 other factors (p.267, v.77).
10. Skill in enlightenment factors ~ (v.78).

~ Directions should be thoroughly apprehended ~ find suitable abode ~ sever minor impediments ~ and begin preliminary work for giving attention to repulsiveness. ~ Firstly, should apprehend the learning sign in head hairs (V.M. says to look at 1 or 2 palms of hands) and with all of the division parts. ~ Having apprehensive information sources ~ VIS. MAG. CH VIII ~ p.317, v 244 and from 'The Light of DHAMMA' ~ vol V #3 ~ pp.6 -17 ~ ĀNĀPĀNA-SATI instruction by Ven. MAHASI SAYADAW ~ in his words.

~ Concentration ~ ĀNĀPĀNA-SATI-KAMMATHĀNA for the attainment of JHĀNA then, to use as base to develop VIPASSANĀ, to attain NIBBĀANA.

9. Mindfulness of breathing
~ (p.285, v.145) ~

BUDDHA: "BHIKKHUS, this is SAMĀDHI through mindfulness of breathing, when developed and much-practiced, it is both peaceful and sublime, it is an unadulterated blissful abiding, and it banishes at once and stills evil unprofitable thoughts, as soon as they arise." (SAM.NIK. v.32)

~ BUDDHA has said that ĀNĀPĀNA-SATI has 16 bases: ~ (9 kinds of sitting abode) (v.145)

1. The forest, 2. The root of a tree, 3. A rock, 4. A hill, 5. A cliff, 6. A mountain cave, 7. A charnel ground, 8. A jungle hut, 9. An open space, 10. A heap of straw

    (1 & 2 combined =9) (MN. NIK. 1-191)

"A BHIKKHU goes to the forest or to the root of a tree or to an empty (quiet) place. Sits down, folding his legs crosswise (in any convenient manner so as to enable him to sit for a long time), sets his body erect, establishes mindfulness in front of him. Ever mindful, he breathes in; mindfully he breathes out." (Yogi keeps his mind fixed on the aperture of the nose. He will then come to know in a distinct manner the feeling of touch-sensation at the tip of the nose or at the edge of the upper lip, which is caused by the constant flow of in and out breathing). (p.288, v.153- Interesting!)

(This flow should be watched at the point of its touching and contemplated by saying mentally, "coming, going, coming, going" ~ or ~ "in, out, in, out" ~ on every act of in-breathing and out-breathing respectively. The mind should not go along with the flow either on the inward or outward journey, but it should remain at the point of touching.)

~ The 16 bases of training ~

1. Breathing in long, or out long: ~ He knows ~ "I breathe in long" (p.291, v.163 ~ 292, v.168) "I breathe out long". (Long and short breaths are clearly noticed).
2. Breathing in short or out short ~ he knows ~ "I breathe in short; I breathe out short" (p.299, v.169-170).
3. He trains thus ~ "I shall breathe in experiencing the whole body ~ I shall breathe out experiencing the whole body" (p.294 v.171; p.245, v.174).
4. He trains thus ~ "I shall breathe in, tranquilizing the whole body ~ I shall breathe out, tranquilizing the whole body" (p.296, v.175).

Beginning proclamations not capable of JHĀNA
~ After one has already attained JHĀNA see p.299, v.186

5. He trains thus
   ~ I shall breathe in, experiencing happiness (p.309, v.226- p.316, v.228)
   ~ I shall breathe out, experiencing happiness
6. He trains thus
   ~ I shall breathe in, experiencing bliss (p.310, v.299)
   ~ I shall breathe out, experiencing bliss
7. He trains thus
   ~ I shall breathe in, experiencing mental formation (p.310, v.299)

~ I shall breathe out, experiencing mental formation
8. He trains thus
   ~ I shall breathe in, tranquilizing the mental formation (p.310, v.299)
   ~ I shall breathe out, tranquilizing the mental formation
9. He trains thus
   ~ I shall breathe in, experiencing consciousness (p.311, v.231)
   ~ I shall breathe out, experiencing consciousness
10. He trains thus
    ~ I shall breathe in, gladdening the consciousness (p.311, v.231)
    ~ I shall breathe out, gladdening the consciousness
11. He trains thus
    ~ I shall breathe in, concentrating the consciousness (p.311, v.232)
    ~ I shall breathe out, concentrating the consciousness
12. He trains thus
    ~ I shall breathe in, liberating the consciousness (p.312, v.233)
    ~ I shall breathe out, liberating the consciousness
13. He trains thus
    ~ I shall breathe in, contemplating ANICCA (p.313, v.234)
    ~ I shall breathe out, contemplating ANICCA
14. He trains thus
    ~ I shall breathe in, contemplating fading away (p.314, v.235)
    ~ I shall breathe out, contemplating fading away
15. He trains thus
    ~ I shall breathe in, contemplating cessation (p.314, v.235)
    ~ I shall breathe out, contemplating cessation
16. He trains thus
    ~ I shall breathe in, contemplating relinquishment (p.314, v.236
    ~ I shall breathe out, contemplating relinquishment (SAM. NIK. V.321-2)

~ All 16 bases are only found and explained after the arising of a BUDDHA. ~ Sectarians ~ who know mindfulness of breathing ~ only know the first FOUR modes. (PARAMATTHA- MAÑŪSA ~ VIS. M. ATTHAKATHĀ), p.257

~ ĀNĀPĀNA-SATI is not easy to develop in a noisy environment ~ "Noise is a thorn to JHANA" (V.M.p.289 v.155 ~ ANG.NIK v.135) ~ Explains benefit of correct sitting posture ~ p.290, v.160 ~ "Implying pain is a thorn to JHANA"

~ Mahasi Sayadaw

"During this contemplation there will be many hindrances with which the mind wanders. These hindrances should not be followed any longer, but attention should be brought back to the point of touching and contemplation carried on, as "in ~ out", etc.

~ By this means of continuously watching the point of touching and crying on the contemplation:

1. The long in-breathing and out-breathing are clearly noticed when they are long.
2. The short in-breathing and out-breathing are clearly noticed when they are short.
3. Each course of soft in-breathing and out-breathing with its beginning, middle and end is clearly noticed from its touching the tip of the nose to where it leaves the nose. And
4. The gradual change from the strong to the gentler form of in-breathing and out-breathing is clearly noticed.
5. As the in and out breathing become more and more gentle, it appears that they have vanished altogether. In such cases time is generally wasted trying to look for the objects of in-breathing and out-breathing, by trying to investigate the cause of vanishing, and finally by remaining idle without carrying on the contemplation. There is, however, no need to waste time in this manner: If the mind is fixed attentively either on the tip of the nose or upper lip, the gentle form of flow in and out breathing will again appear, and will be distinctly perceptible.

Note 1. By thus proceeding with the continued contemplation of in and out-breathing, it will be visualized in some peculiar forms or shape. (The following are mentioned in the VIS.MAG.)

To some, the in and out breathing appears like a star or a cluster of gems of heart wood, to others like a long, braided string, or a wreath of flowers or a puff of smoke; to others like a stretched-out cobweb or a film of cloud or a lotus flower of a chariot wheel or the Moon's disc or the Sun's disc. It is said that the variety in the forms or objects is due to the differences in SAÑÑĀ (perception) of the individuals. These signs (any one of them) are known as (PATIBHĀGA-NIMITTA). This level of SAMĀDHI which is then developed with the PATIBHĀGA-NIMITTA is called UPACĀRA-SAMĀDHI. On continuing the contemplation with the aid of UPACĀRA-SAMĀDHI then the stage of APPANĀ-SAMĀDHI of the 4 RŪPA-JHĀNAS is developed.

This is the brief description of the preliminary practice for SAMATHA by a SAMATHA-YĀNIKA, who chooses SAMATHA-KAMMATTHĀMA as the basis for realizing NIBBĀNA.

Those who desire to practice VIPASSANĀ should in the first place be equipped with an adequate knowledge of the facts that living beings consist of the TWO sole constituents of NĀMA and RŪPA, that the body and mind are formed due to cause and effect, and that they are in a constant state of ANICCA, DUKKHA and ANATTA.

Description of practice (VIPASSANĀ) for one who possesses JHĀNA ability: ~

"A yogi with the proper knowledge mentioned above should firstly induce the JHĀNIC state which he has already attained, and then contemplate on it. He should then proceed by contemplating continuously the experiences that occur at the 6-sense doors (including knowing mind). If the yogi feels tired or exhausted by having to carry on continually the contemplation of these various objects, he should again induce the JHĀNIC state by making a strong determination that the JHĀNIC state may remain for 14 or 30 minutes. When the JHĀNIC state passes away he should then immediately contemplate on that JHĀNIC state, and afterwards proceed by contemplating continuously the experiences as they occur at any of the six-sense doors. This alternate procedure of inducing JHĀNIC state and then proceeding with the six-sense door contemplation should be carried out repeatedly. When the VIPASSANĀ-SAMĀDHI is sufficiently strong the yogi will be able to carry on the contemplation continuously – day and night –

without feeling any strain. ~ With the full development of the factual knowledge of ANICCA, ANATTA and DUKKHA, MAGGA and PHALA is reached. ~ THIS IS THE VIPASANNĀ PRACTISE OF A SAMATHA-VĀNIKA.

(p.299 v.186 – p.309 v.225)

Method of development ~ ĀNĀPĀNA-SATI according to the VISUDDHI MAGGA

~ Yogi wishing to develop distinction with this KAMMATTHANA should first of all do all the work connected with the purification of virtue (thus no remorse of flurry), ~ after which he should learn the meditation subject in ~ five senses ~ from the KALYANA-MITTA.

(v.181)
The 5 stages are:
1. Learning ~ is learning the meditation subject.
2. Questioning ~ is questioning about the meditation subject.
3. Establish ~ is establishing the meditation subject.
4. Absorption ~ is the absorption of the meditation subject.
5. Characteristic ~ is the characteristic of the meditation subject.

(v.188)
~ Learning the subject in this way he neither tires himself nor worries the teacher.
~ The yogi should then sever the minor impediments (p.74 #3).
~ Getting rid of fatigue: The yogi should seat himself comfortably.
~ Then make sure he is not confused about even a single one of the instructions.
~ The yogi should then gladden his mind by recollecting the qualities of the triple gem (pp.83-87).

~ The 8 stages in giving attention to the meditation subject ~ (p.300 v.189)

1. Counting ~ (v.190) ~ Yogi should first give attention to the meditation subject by counting. ~ Not to stop short of 5 or go beyond 10 or make any breaks in the series. ~ By stopping short of 5 his thoughts get excited in the cramped space, like a herd of cattle shut in a cramped pen. ~ Going beyond ten his thoughts take the number rather than the breaths for their support. ~ Making breaks creates confusion.

(v.191) When counting, do so slowly (that is, late) ~ take in or out breath ~ that which is most clear and begin with ~ "in ~1 ~in ~ 2" ~ "1~ out ~2~ out" ~ etc. ~ whatever way is most suitable to the yogi.

(v.192) When in and out breaths become evident ~ count along with the actual in- breath at the same time: ~ Unlike before, after it was completed. ~ Continuity of observation develops more quickly.

(p.301, v.193) Do not direct one's SATI either inside or outside the body ~ but only at the place of sensation at the nose tip (or upper lip).

(p.301, v.194) Meditation subject has become apparent as an uninterrupted process ~ continue minute awareness (but) remembering not to discern the wind either inside (it will feel like a balloon) or outside the body (one gets distracted outside by the multiplicity of objects) ~ just at the point of contact only.

(v.195) How long does the yogi go on counting? ~ Until, without counting, mindfulness remains settled on the in- and out-breaths as its objects. ~ Counting is just a device for establishing SATI, by cutting off the external wandering of applied thoughts.

2. Connection ~ (p.301, v.196) ~ is the uninterrupted awareness of the in- and out- breaths after counting has been given up (following the successive arising of each breath. ~ Not just one breath, but a multitude of DHAMMAS arising and vanishing).

(v.197) The yogi does not follow the entire breathing process from the beginning at the navel ~ to the middle in the heart region ~ to the end ~ nostril area (only the nose-tip sensation) ~ Why? ~ The yogi's mind becomes distracted internally ~ becomes disquieted, perturbed and shakes ~ same if followed externally.

3 & 4. Touching and by fixing ~ (p.302, v.197-198) ~ When the yogi directs his mindfulness to the subject as described by connection, he should not do so by the beginning, middle and end (as explained above), but rather by touching and fixing. ~ There is no attention to be given to it by 'touching separate from (connection)' fixing as there is by 'counting separate from connection', but when the yogi is counting the breaths in the place touched by each, he is giving attention to them by 'counting' and 'touching'. When he has given up counting and is connecting them by means of mindfulness in that same place, and fixing consciousness by means of absorption, then he is said to be giving his attention to them by connection, touching and fixing.

This can be understood by 3 similes:

(v.199) ~ Simile of the man who cannot walk ~ who is rocking a swing for the amusement of his children. He sits at the foot of the swing post and sees all, both ends and the middle of the swing plank, but yet he does not move. ~ So too with the touch point at the nostrils or upper lip ...SATI just there.

(v.200) ~ Simile of the saw ~ cutting a plank of wood ~ just the saw's teeth touch the plank and this is where one's attention should be placed, without giving attention to the saw's teeth as they approach and recede ~ though they are not unknown to him as they do so. ~ So too the yogi sits with SATI at the touch point; giving attention to the in and out breaths as they approach and recede, though they are not unknown to him as they do so; and he manifests effort, carries out a task and actions an effect.

(v.200) ~ Simile of the gatekeeper ~ Just as a gatekeeper does not examine people inside and outside the wall, asking, "Who are you?" ~ "Where have you come from?" ~ "Where are you going? What have you got in your hand?" ~ for those people are not his concern. ~ But he does examine each man as he arrives at the gate. ~ So too, ~ the incoming breaths that have gone inside and the outgoing breaths that have gone outside are not this BHIKKHUS concern. But they are his concern each time they arrive at the nostrils gate itself.

(v.205) ~ In gradual time based on energetic effort ~ bodily disturbances become stilled by the gradual cessation of gross in- and out- breaths. ~ Then both body and mind become light: the physical body becomes as though it was ready to leap up into the air.

(v.206) ~ When gross in- and out- breaths have ceased ~ consciousness occurs with the sign of the subtle in- and out- breaths as object. And when that has ceased, it goes on occurring with the successively subtler signs as its object.

(v.207) ~ How does this happen? ~ Example ~ As when striking a large bronze gong ~ first awareness of the loud sound ~ and then progressively subtler sound ~ and the awareness thereof.

(v.208) ~ For while other meditation subjects become cleared at each higher state, SATI of breathing does not. ~ In fact, as it is developed more and more, it becomes more subtle for him at each higher stage, even coming to the point at which it is no longer manifest.

What to do at this point? ~ Yogi should not get up from his posture and disturb SAMĀDHI. Otherwise, the meditation subject has to be started anew. ~ Yogi should go on sitting, ever mindful of the place normally touched for the actual breaths (sensation of) as the object of awareness. (Carry on observing the tip of the nose where they normally touch, till they become apparent again.)

(p.305, v.209) ~ The yogi should not panic or become concerned about why the breaths have vanished, or if they will return, or "What is going to happen to me? Will I die?" etc. But yogi should realize that the in- and out- breaths are actually existent in you, only you are not able to discern them, because your understanding is dull.

(v.210) ~ So the yogi fixes his attention on the place normally touched by the breaths, and mindfully remains there.

(v.210) ~ BUDDHA ~ "BHIKKHUS, I do not say of one who is forgetful, who is not fully aware, that (he practices) development of mindfulness of breathing." (MIJ. NIK. III _84)

(v.211) ~ Although any meditation subject (no matter what) is successful in one who is mindful and fully aware, yet any meditation subject (other than this one) gets more evident as he goes on giving it his attention. But this mindfulness of breathing is difficult, and difficult to develop: It's a field in which only the minds of BUDDHAS, PACCEKA BUDDHAS, and BUDDHA's sons are at home. It is no trivial matter, nor can it be cultivated by trivial persons. In proportion ~ as continued attention is given ~ it becomes more perceptual and more subtle ~ so strong mindfulness and understanding are necessary here.

(p.306, v.212) ~ Stresses that the yogi must look for the in- and out- breaths nowhere else than the place normally touched by them. ~ Gives simile to indicate the subtlety of this meditation subject ~ that of "doing needle work on a piece of fine cloth": ~ a fine needle is needed and a still finer instrument for boring the needle's eye.

(p.307, v.214) ~ When the yogi proceeds thus ~ the sign (the learning sign and counterpart sign – both are stated here together) soon appears to the yogi. But it does not appear to be the same to all.

(v.215) ~ (See page 96, this text ~ note #1 ~ explain NIMITTA in detail).

(v.217) ~ And here, the consciousness that has in-breath as its object is one; the consciousness that has out-breath as its object is another; and the consciousness that has sin as its object is another. For the meditation subject reaches neither absorption nor even access in one who has not got these three things (clear). ~ Only by one who does know these 3 things can SAMĀDHI ~ and access and JHĀNA ~ be obtained. (PATISAMBHINDĀMAGGA ~ 1 ~170)

(v.218) ~ When the sign appears to the yogi, go then and tell the teacher ~ "Ven. SIR, the sign has appeared to me." (Also explains how teacher should neither confirm nor deny the yogi's statement, but only encourage him to continue careful observation. Another group says that the yogi should be told "This is the sign friend, well done. Keep giving attention to it, again and again."

(p.308, v.219) ~ The yogi should fix his mind on that same sign ~ and so from now on, his development proceeds by way of fixing. "The clever man anchors his mind upon breathing in and out".

(v.220) ~ As soon as the sign appears, the hindrances are suppressed; ~ his defilements subside, his mindfulness is established, and his consciousness is concentrated in UPACĀRA- SAMĀDHI.

(v.221) ~ Yogi should not give attention to the sign as to its color, or review it as to his (specific) characteristic. He should guard it carefully ~ according to the 7 ways (see p.76 #3A). ~ He should then make it grow and improve with repeated attention, and practice the 10-fold skill in absorption (see p.76 #4) and bring about even energy. ~ (See pages 77 & 78)

(p.308, v.222) ~ As the yogi strives thus ~ 4-fold and 5-fold JHĀNA is achieved by him on that same sign in the same way as described under the earth KASINA. (See pp.80, 81)

~ practice after attainment of JHĀNA ~

5. 6. 7. 8. Observing ~ turning away ~ purification ~ and looking back ~

(v.222) ~ After the yogi has achieved the 4 JHĀNAS (RŪPA JHANAS) and wants to develop/reach purity (ARAHATSHIP) by developing the meditation subject ~ through observing #5 and through #6 turning away he should make that JHĀNA familiar to him by attaining mastery in the 5 ways; (see pp.81 & 82) and then embark upon VIPASSANĀ by defining NĀMA- RŪPA.

~ How?

(p. 308 v 223) ~ On emerging from the attainment (JHĀNA), the yogi sees that the in- and out- breaths have the physical body and the mind as their origin; ~ just as when a blacksmith's bellows are being blown, the wind moves owing to the bag and to the man's appropriate effort, so too, in-breaths and out-breaths are due to the body and the mind. ~ He knows the in- and out- breaths to be RŪPA, also knowing the body to be RŪPA ~ and the consciousness ~ and the states associated with the consciousness ~ as the mind (NĀMA).

(v.224) ~ Having defined NĀMA and RŪPA the yogi progressively passes through the VIPASSANĀ-ÑANAS. Understanding ANICCA, ANATTA and DUKKHA #7 purification takes place, the yogi is liberated (progressively by the 4 noble paths) from LOBHA, DOSA and MOHA ~ and becomes an ARAHAT. After he has reached the fruition of ARAHATSHIP, he attains to the 19 kinds of reviewing knowledge, which is known as 'looking back' #8. ~

The remaining three tetrads [groups of four] apply only to the yogi who has already attained JHĀNA.

(p.309, v.226) ~ Word commentary on second tetrad. He trains thus: "I shall breathe in ... I shall breathe out, experiencing happiness."

(p.311, v.230) ~ He trains thus: "I shall breathe in ... I shall breathe out, tranquilizing mental formations."

(p.311, v.231) ~ Word commentary on third tetrad ~ He trains thus: "I shall breathe in ... I shall breathe out experiencing the consciousness."

(p.312, v.233) ~ He trains thus: "I shall breathe in... I shall breathe out, liberating the consciousness."

(p.313, v.234) ~ Word commentary on fourth tetrad ~ He trains thus: "I shall breathe in... I shall breathe out, contemplating ANICCA."

(p.314, v.236) ~ He trains thus: "I shall breathe in ...I shall breathe out, contemplating relinquishment."

(p.315, v.236-v.244) ~ Conclusion ~ ĀNĀPĀNA-SATI KAMMATTHANA ~

(v.239)

~ This practice brings great peacefulness ~ a blissful abiding.
~ It cuts off the wandering mind of applied thoughts.
~ It is the root condition for the perfecting of clear vision and deliverance.
~ When developed and much practiced it perfects the 4 foundations of mindfulness
~ Which in turn perfect the 7 enlightenment factors which perfect clear vision and deliverance.
~ Is of great benefit also in that the final 'in and out' breath before death is known as they come.
~ If one has attained ARAHATSHIP by ĀNĀPĀNA-SATI with its 16 bases ~ the yogi can always define his life term.

(v.243)

~ He knows my vital formations will continue now for so long and no more.

(v.244)

~ To illustrate the point ~ like the elders who were brothers and lived at the CITTALAPABBATA-VIHARA. One of them calculated his own vital formations in the midst of the community of BHIKKHUS. ~ He asked the others ~ "In what way have you seen BHIKKHUS attain NIBBĀNA?" ~ They replied ~ "Till now we have seen them attain while sitting in their seats ~ sitting cross legged in the air." ~ The elder said ~ "I will show you one attaining NIBBĀNA while walk-ins." ~ He then drew a line on the walk, saying, "I shall go from the end of the walk to the other end and return. ~ When I reach this line, I will attain NIBBĀNA." Saying this, he stepped onto the walk and went to the far end. On his return he attained NIBBĀNA in the same moment in which he stepped on the line.

So let a man ~ if he is wise ~ untiringly devote his days to mindfulness of breathing, which rewards him always in these ways.

~ Conclude explanation in detail dealing with ĀNĀPĀNA-SATI ~

Concentration ~ The 10th ANNUSATI explained:

10. Contemplation on the special qualities of NIBBĀNA
~ (p.317-245) ~

Recollect thus: ~
"BHIKKHUS, insofar as there are DHAMMAS, whether formed or unformed, fading away is pronounced by the best of them. That is to say, the disillusionment of vanity, the elimination of thirst, the abolition of reliance, the termination of the round, the destruction of craving, fading away, cessation, NIBBĀNA. (ANG.NIK III ~34)

(p.319-320, v.246) ~ Also recollect the other special qualities of NIBBĀNA ~ stated by the BUDDHA. "BHIKKHUS, I shall teach you:
The unformed
The truth
The other shore
The hard-to-see
The undecaying
The lasting
The undiversified
The deathless
The auspicious
The safe
The marvelous
The intact
The unaffiliated
The purity
The island
The shelter

(SAM.NIK. IV ~ 360-372)

~ Word commentary of this contemplation is short-and-to-the-point ~ Approx.3 pages. (See VIS.MAG. for complete explanation)

(p.320, v.244) ~ Owing to the profundity of the special qualities of NIBBĀNA (peace), or owing to the yogi's preoccupation in recollecting special qualities of various kinds, he only reaches UPACĀRA-SAMĀDHI and is unable to attain (i.e., does not reach) absorption.

(v.251) ~ Benefits ~ Sleeps in bliss and wakes in bliss
~ His faculties are peaceful
~ His mind is peaceful
~ He has HIRI and OTTAPPA
~ He is confident
~ He is resolved to attain the superior state
~ He is respected and honored by his fellows in the ife of purity
… And if he penetrates no other ~ he is at least headed for a happy destiny

~ Conclude explanation of contemplation of NIBBĀNA ~

E. The Four Divine Abidings (BRAHMA – VIHĀRAS)
~ METTĀ, KARUNĀ, MUDITĀ, UPEKKHĀ
(VIS.MAG. (CH IX p.321.VI ~ 353, v.124)

1. METTĀ (Loving-Kindness)
~ (p.321, v.1)
~ The meditator who wants to develop METTĀ should: ~
1. Learn the meditation subject carefully
2. Sever the lesser impediments
3. Get rid of fatigue and dizziness
4. Sit comfortably in a secluded place

~ To start the meditator should review the danger in hatred-anger-resentment and the advantage of patience.

Why is this to be done? (v.2)

~ Because hatred has to be abandoned and patience attained in the development of this meditation subject, and the yogi cannot abandon unseen dangers and attain unknown advantages.

    (Disadvantages of DOSA ~ one kills living things) ANG.NIK. 1-216

    (Advantage of KHANTI ~ no greater thing exists than patience) SAM.NIK. 1-222

~ (v.3) Thereupon the yogi should embark upon the development of METTĀ for the purpose of secluding the mind from DOSA (seen as danger) and introducing it to KHANTI (known as an advantage).

(p.321, v.4) METTĀ should be developed towards certain kinds of persons and not to certain other kinds at first. ~

~ 4 types of persons that METTĀ should not be developed at first towards. ~ Why? (p.322, v.5)

1. An antipathetic person: ~ to put such a person in a dear one's place is fatiguing.
2. A very dearly loved friend: ~ to put such a person in a neutral place is fatiguing. Easy to weep if they are hurt.
3. A neutral person: ~ to put such a person in a respected one's or dear one's place is fatiguing.
4. A hostile person: ~ anger springs up if such a person is recollected.

Also, it should not be developed specifically towards: ~ 1. The opposite sex, 2. A dead person ~ Why? (p.322, v. 6&7)

    ~ If developed towards opposite sex: ~ lust inspired by that person arises

    ~ If developed towards a dead person: ~ yogi can't achieve access or absorption

A. First of all, METTĀ should be developed only towards oneself.

Repeating mentally to oneself [any suitable formula] (v.8):

E.g., ~ "May I be happy and peaceful" ~ "May I live with love and compassion" ~ "May I be free from pain, sorrow and fear" ~ "May I be liberated"

~ This initial development towards oneself refers to making oneself an example.

~ For even if a yogi developed METTĀ for a 100- or 1000-years in this way ~ "May I be happy" and so on ~ absorption would never arise. But if he develops it thus: ~ "Just as I want to be happy and dread pain, as I want to live and not die ~ so do other beings too" ~ making himself the example ~ then desire for other beings' welfare and happiness arises in him. (p.323, v.10)

B. Next ~ develop METTA towards a teacher or his equivalent or a preceptor or his equivalent. (p.323, v.11)

In order to proceed easily develop METTĀ towards the above. ~ the yogi can recollect such gifts, kind words, etc. as inspire love and endearment, or such virtue, learning, etc. that inspire respect and reverence met within a teacher or his equivalent, etc.

Mentally repeating the formula:
~ "May this good man be happy and peaceful" etc. (Keeping this person clearly in mind as the object of your thoughts of METTĀ). ~ Keep this going continually ~ while sitting, walking or any other posture ~ until absorption is reached.

C. Next ~ should develop METTA towards a very dearly loved friend. (p.323, v.12)

D. Then towards a neutral person as a very dearly loved friend.

E. Then towards a hostile person as neutral.

After developing absorption with a teacher as object ~ and the yogi does not rest content with just that much and wants to break down the barriers ~ he should develop METTĀ towards the types of individuals listed above in that order.

But if the yogi has no enemy ~ or he doesn't perceive another as an enemy even when the other does him harm ~ he should not concern himself then, after developing METTĀ towards a neutral person. ~ **E is only meant for one who actually feels another to be an enemy. (v.13)**

~ Ways of removing resentment ~ hatred ~ or aversion ~ (p.324, v.14)

If resentment arises in him when he applies his mind to a hostile person because he remembers wrongs done by that person ~ he should get rid of that resentment by repeatedly entering METTĀ JHANA towards any of the first-mentioned persons ~ and then after he has emerged each time directing METTĀ towards that person.

But if resentment does not cease despite his efforts to overcome it, he should: (v.15)

1. Should reflect on the simile of the 2-handled saw ~ "The angry BHIKKHU is not a disciple of mine". (v.15)
2. When angry ~ one misconducts himself in body, speech and mind ~ and after death such a person appears in a state of loss.
3. Should remember some controlled and purified state in that person which inspired confidence when remembered. If not mentally or verbally good deeds ~ remember his favorable bodily behavior ~ and ignore all others. (p.325, v.16)
4. If no deeds inspire confidence ~ have compassion for such a person. (v.20)
5. He should then review the fact that he himself as well as others are owners of their deeds (KAMMA). ~ All beings are here due to their KAMMA. (p.327, v.23)

   A. "This anger of mine will lead to my own harm."
   B. "This is not the type of deed that will bring one to full enlightenment."

(By doing this you are like a man who wants to hit another and picks up a burning ember or excrement in his hand and so first burns himself or makes himself stink.)

   C. In another ~" He will become the heir of whatever deeds he does." (p.327, v.24)
   D. "This is not the kind of deed that will bring him to full enlightenment."

E. "But rather it is a deed that will make him fall from the dispensation, and will even lead to states of pain."

(By doing this he is like a man who wants to throw dust at another against the wind, and only covers himself with it.)

6. If resentment still persists the yogi should then review the special qualities of the BUDDHA while he was striving for perfection as a BODHISATTVA. (p.328, v.25)

   A. He did not allow anger to corrupt his mind, even when his enemies tried to murder him. (VIS.MAG. goes on to describe 6 JATAKA stories that depict METTA and KHANTI. ~ Inspiring stories) (v.27-35)

7. If resentment continues:

   Since the yogi has long been used to the slavery of defilements then he should review thus ~ "BHIKKHUS, it is not easy to find a being who has not formerly been your mother...your father...brother...sister...son...or your daughter in this beginningless rounds of rebirth. ~ Consequently, the yogi should think about that person thus: "That person was formerly my mother, who cared and nourished me, cleaned my urine and my excrement without disgust. ~ As my father ~ he worked to support me in order that I may eat and be sheltered, etc. As my brother...' etc. ~ '...so it is unbecoming for me to harbor hate for him in my mind'." (p.331, v.36)

8. ~ But if still unable to overcome such angry thoughts ~ the yogi should review the advantages of METTA thus: ~ (v.37)

1B ~ 11 advantages from the absorption development of METTĀ-BHAVA ~ (p.337, v.59)

1. Sleeps in comfort. ~ Instead of sleeping uncomfortably, turning over and snoring, he sleeps comfortably. ~ He falls asleep as though entering upon an attainment. (v.60)

2. Wakes in comfort. ~ Instead of waking uncomfortably, groaning

and yawning and turning over ~ he wakes comfortably, without contortions ~ like a lotus opening. (v.61)

3. Dreams no evil dreams. ~ When he sees dreams, he sees only auspicious ones ~ as though he were giving DĀNA OR HEARING THE DHAMMA ~ not evil dreams ~ [like] being threatened by wild beasts, surrounded by bandits or falling into a chasm. (v.62)
4. He is dear to human beings. ~ He is beloved by human beings ~ as a wreath adorning the head ~ or a necklace. (p.336, v.63)
5. He is dear to non-human beings. ~ (VIS.MAG gives story of terrestrial DEVA being attracted by a BHIKKHU'S power of METTĀ) (v.69)
6. Deities guard him ~ as a mother and father guard their child.
7. Fire, poisons and weapons do not affect him ~ They do not affect or enter into the body of one who abides in METTĀ. (v.71)
8. His mind is easily concentrated; ~ quickly concentrated with no sluggishness about it. (v.73)
9. The expression of his face is serene. (v.74)
10. He dies unconfused. ~ There is no dying deluded for one who abides in METTĀ. He passes away undiluted, as if falling asleep. (v.75)
11. If he penetrates no higher ~ than METTĀ JHĀNA ~ that is onto ARIYAN path and ARAHATSHIP. Then when he dies, he appears in a BRAHMĀ world as one who wakes up from sleep. (v.76)

~ The yogi then reflects ~ "If you do not stop this thought of anger, you will be denied these advantages."

9. ~ If resentment still persists, the yogi should try resolution into elements. How? The yogi should reflect thus: ~ (p.331, v.38)

A. What is it that you are angry with? Is it the head hairs you are angry with? Body hairs? Urine?
B. Or is it the earth elements you are angry with (that comprise the head hairs, etc.) ~ or the water ~ fire ~ or air element?
C. Or is it the feeling aggregate you are angry with? ~ etc. 4 other aggregates.
D. Or is it the eye-base or visual object you are angry with? ~ etc.? Ear, nose, etc.
~ In this way anger will not find a foothold ~ like a painting in the air.

10. If still angry ~ he should try the giving of a gift. ~ "A gift for taming the untamed". (p.332, v.39)

~ Once hostility has been allayed towards the being who is hostile ~ the yogi can focus his METTĀ on that person too ~ just as towards the one who is dear and the neutral person. He should then break down the barriers by practicing METTĀ impartially over and over again towards the 4 persons: Accomplishing mental impartiality towards himself ~ the dear person ~ the neutral person ~ then the hostile person. (The yogi makes not the smallest discriminations among these 4 kinds of people. ~ If bandits wish to kill 1 of the 4 ~ he doesn't think ~ "Let them take me but not these 3" ~ but perfect impartiality to all. He treats all beings in the whole world equally. (p.333 v.41-42)

~ Thus, the sign and access are obtained ~ simultaneously with the breaking down of the barriers. First ~ second ~ and third JHANAS can thus be obtained. ~

~ Concentration ~ 4 BRAHMĀ-VIHARAS ~ METTĀ-BHĀVANĀ

~ Commentary (selected only) to text ~ (p.333, v.44)

~ Now it is by means of one of these JHĀNAS beginning with the first that the yogi:

"Dwells pervading one direction (the first detain, anyone) with his heart (mind) endued with loving-kindness. Likewise, the second direction, likewise the third direction, likewise the fourth direction — and so above, below and around: everywhere (unspecified pervasion in all places) equally (to all beings classed as imperious, medium, superior, friendly, hostile, neutral, etc). ~ Just as to oneself ~ equally with oneself without making the distinction, "This is another being." (Or alternatively equally is with the whole state of the mind: not reserving even a little, is what is meant). He dwells pervading the entire (possessing all beings) world (the world of beings) with his heart endued with loving-kindness, abundant (abundance is pervading), exalted (in place, from the sense sphere to the fine-material-sphere plane) measureless. (Through familiar and through having measureless beings as its object). Free from enmity (through abandonment of ill-will and hostility) and free from affliction (through abandonment of grief, without suffering).

~ This type of versatility comes about only in one whose consciousness has reached absorption in the first JHĀNA, and the rest.

~ When the yogi has reached absorption ~ the mind deliverance of METTĀ is practiced in these various ways described in the PATISAMBHIDĀ. (p.335, v.49)

1. The mind-deliverance of loving-kindness is practiced with unspecified pervasion in 5 ways ~ (v.50), (also p.336, v.55-56)
   1. May all beings... ('Beings' means: 1. who has LOBHA for the aggregates)
   2. May all breathing things...
   3. May all creatures...
   4. May all persons...
   5. May all those who have a personality (a concept derived from the group of aggregates) ...

~ One can cultivate absorption (any of the 4 JHĀNAS on each one of the 5 phrases separately = thus 20 kinds of absorption)

2. The mind – deliverance of loving-kindness is practiced with specified persons in 7 ways: ~ (335, v.51), (also p.337, v.57)
   1. May all women... ⎫
   2. May all men... ⎬ stated according to sex
   3. May all noble ones... ⎫ stated according to noble
   4. May all non-ARIYAS... ⎬ and ordinary persons ones
   5. May all deities... ⎫
   6. May all human beings... ⎬ stated according to the
   7. May all in a state of loss... ⎭ kind of rebirth

~ One can cultivate absorption (any of the 4 JHĀNAS) on each 1 of the 7 phrases separately = the 20 kinds of absorption.

3. The mind-deliverance of loving-kindness is practiced with directional pervasion in ten ways: ~ (p.335, v.52 & p.337, v.58)
   1. May all beings in an eastern direction...
   2. May all beings in a western direction...

3. May all beings in a northern direction...
4. May all beings in a southern direction...
5. May all beings in an eastern intermediate direction...
6. May all beings in a western intermediate direction...
7. May all beings in a northern intermediate direction...
8. May all beings in a southern intermediate direction...
9. May all beings in a downward direction...
10. May all beings in an upward direction...

~ One continues then with: ~ All breathing things (1-10) ~ Then: ~ All creatures (1-10) ... and so on.

~ Then: ~ May all women (1-10) ... and so on.

Conclusion (mentally face   unspecified pervasion = 20 kinds
                            specified pervasion = 28 kinds

$$48 \times 10 \text{ directional}$$
$$= 480 \text{ kinds of absorption}$$

(According to PATISAMBHIDĀ = 528 kinds)

So, when the yogi develops absorption in any one of these ways, he obtains the 11 advantages. (See p.104 #8)

~ **This concludes explanation of METTĀ-BHĀVANĀ** ~

~ Concentration ~ 4 BRAHMĀ-VIHARAS ~ KARUNĀ – BHĀVANĀ

2. KARUNĀ (compassion)
~ (p.340, v.77)

~ The yogi who wants to develop compassion should begin by reviewing the danger in lack of compassion, and the advantage in compassion.

~ Beginning thus, they should first not direct it towards the dear person (one who is near simply retains that position) and so with the rest: A very dear companion, a neutral person, an antipathetic person and a hostile person (all of whom simply retain their respective positions).

~ It should also be avoided towards one of the opposite sex, and a dead person.

~ How does the yogi dwell pervading ONE direction with his heart endued with compassion? ~

Just on seeing ~ just as he would fuel compassion on seeing an unlucky, unfortunate person, so he pervades all beings with compassion.

1. ~ Therefore, first of all, on seeing a wretched man (unlucky, unfortunate, in every way a fit object for compassion, unsightly, reduced to utter misery, with hands and feet cut off, sitting in the shelter for the helpless with a pot placed before him, with a mass of maggots oozing from his arms and legs, and moaning) ~ compassion should be felt for him in this way:

"This being has indeed been reduced to misery: If only he could be freed from his suffering."

2. ~ (v.79) ~ But if one does not encounter such a person ~ then the yogi can arouse compassion for an evil-doing person, even though he is happy, by comparing him to one who is about to be executed. How? ~

~ A robber caught with stolen goods; ~ King commands to execute him. ~ King's men beat him and lead him to the place of execution. ~ People along the way give him chewables ~ garlands ~ perfumes ~ etc. ~ He enjoys these things ~ as though he were happy. ~ Still, no one fancies him or thinks he is well off. They think: ~ "Poor wretch is about to die ~ each step brings him closer to death."

I.e.: The yogi should arouse compassion for an evil-doing person — even if he is happy.

"Though this poor wretch is happy now, cheerful, enjoying his earth, still for what of even ONE good deed done now in any one of the 3 doors (of body, speech, or mind) he can come to experience untold DUKKHA in the states of loss."

Having aroused compassion for that person in that way ~ (p.341, v.80):

3. ~ He should next arouse compassion for a dear person.

4. ~ Next for a neutral person

5. ~ And next for a hostile person (v.81) ~ If resentment arises ~ deal with it according to the 10 ways of removal (see p.103 ~ 1A) ~

~ successively in the same way as stated under #2.

~ The yogi should break down the barrier between himself ~ the dear person ~ the neutral person and the hostile person ~ by recollecting: "Indeed, in reality he is unhappy too ~ because he is not exempt from the DUKKHA of the round of becoming."

~ The yogi should cultivate that sign ~ develop and repeatedly practice it ~ and should cultivate the 4 JHĀNAS.

~ (v.83) ~ After attaining versatility in the absorption consisting in the unspecified pervasion in 6 ways ~ the specified pervasion in 7 ways ~ and the directional pervasion in 18 ways. (See opposite page #1, 2, 3)

~ The yogi attains the 11 advantages ~ (see p.104-18)

~ **Conclude the explanation of the development of compassion** ~

~ **Concentration ~ 4 BRAHMĀ-VIHARAS ~ MUDITĀ-BHĀVANĀ**

3. MUDITĀ (Sympathetic Joy)
~ (p.314, v.84)

~ The yogi should not develop at first to a dear person, neutral or hostile person: For a neutral and hostile ~ the opposite of MUDITĀ merely in virtue of dearness ~ how much less the neutral and hostile ~ the opposite sex and the dead are also not the field for MUDITĀ.

1. However, the very dear companion can be the proximate cause for it ~ for he is constantly glad: He laughs first and speaks afterwards. (v.85)

2. Or on seeing or hearing about a dear person being happy, cheerful and glad ~ MUDITĀ can arise ~ be aroused thus: ~

~ "This being is indeed glad. ~ How good! ~ How excellent!" ~

~ Just as the yogi would feel MUDITĀ on seeing a dear and beloved person, so he pervades all beings with MUDITĀ.

3. Remembering the dear companion's past happiness ~ one can arouse MUDITĀ. ~

4. Apprehending the dear companion's future happiness and success ~ one can arouse MUDITĀ. ~

~ After having thus aroused MUDITĀ with respect to dear companion ~ he can then direct it successively towards a neutral and a hostile person.

~ If resentment arises ~ overcome it by means of the 10 ways of removing it. (p.103-1A)

~ The yogi should then break down the barriers by means of mental impartiality towards the 4 persons: ~ Oneself, dear companions ~ neutral or hostile person.

~ Cultivating the sign ~ repeatedly practicing ~ yogi should attain the first 3 JHĀNAS.

~ Next develop versatility (p.105, #1,2,3)

~ 11 advantages are obtained (p.104-1B)

~ **Conclude explanation of the development of MUDITĀ** ~

4. UPEKKHĀ (equanimity)

~ (p.342, v.86)

~ The yogi who wants to develop UPEKKHĀ-BRAHMĀ-VIHARA must have already obtained the first 3 JHĀNAS in METTĀ ~ KARUNĀ ~ MUDITĀ.

~ Yogi should emerge from the third JHĀNA ~ after he has mastered it.

~ Yogi should see the danger in the former 3 Divine Abidings ~ because they are linked with attention given to beings' enjoyment ~ "May they be happy" ~ etc., ~ because resentment and approval are near ~ and because their association with joy is gross.

~ Yogi should also see the advantage in UPEKKHĀ ~ because it is peaceful.

~ Yogi should then arouse UPEKKHĀ by looking on with equanimity at a person who is normally neutral; ~ and after that ~ a dear person ~ and the rest.

~ Just as a yogi would feel UPEKKHĀ on seeing a person who is neither beloved nor unloved, so he pervades all beings with equanimity.

~ After developing it towards a neutral ~ he should break down the barriers (of partiality) first the dear person ~ the very dear companion ~ the hostile ~ lastly himself.

~ Develop the sign ~ repeatedly practice.

~ The 4th JHĀNA arises (as explained under earth KASINA)

~ If one has attained 3rd JHĀNA with earth KASINA ~ 4th JHĀNA UPEKKHĀ ~ BR.VIH. will not follow ~ it follows only after continuation of 1 ~ 2 ~ 3 JHĀNAS with METTĀ, etc. ~ because the object is similar ~ and dissimilar to earth KASINA.

~ Yogi next develops the versatility (p.105 ~ #1,2,3)

~ 11 advantages are attained ~ (p.104- 1B)

~ Conclude explanation of the development of UPEKKHĀ-BRAHMĀ-VIHARA ~

(p.343, v.91 ~ p.353, v.124)

~ Concentration ~ 4 BRAHMĀ-VIHARAS ~ conclusion

1. Meaning of each ~ METTĀ ~ KARUNĀ ~ MUDITĀ ~ UPEKKHĀ ~ (p.343, v.92)
2. Characteristics of each ~ (p.344, v.93-96)
3. Purpose of each ~ (p.344, v.97)
4. The near and far enemies of each ~ (p.345, v.98-101)
5. The beginning, middle and end of each ~ (p.346, v.102)
6. The order in extension ~ (p.346, v.103)
7. The outcome ~ (p.346, v.104)
8. Four questions ~ (p.347, v.105-110)
9. As producing three JHĀNAS and four JHĀNAS ~ (p.348, v.111-118)
10. The highest limit of each ~ (p.351, v.119-124)

F. Reflection on Repulsiveness in Food – Nutriment

(VIS.MAG.CH.XI ~ p.371, v.1 ~ p. 379, v.26)

1. Reflection on repulsiveness in food ~ (P.372, v.1)

~ Nutriment (that which nourishes) ~ Four kinds ~ (FT.NT. #2, p.371 V.M.)
1. Physical nutriment
2. Nutriment consisting of contact ~ (touching an object)
3. Nutriment consisting of mental volition ~ (collects itself and associates' states on the object)
4. Nutriment consisting of consciousness

(p.371, v.2)

~ Physical nutriment nourishes (brings on) materiality (4 DHATUS and 4 secondaries, one of the secondaries being nutritive essence.)

~ Contact as nutriment nourishes (brings on) the three kinds of feelings.

~ Mental volition as nutriment nourishes (brings on) rebirth-linking consciousness in the three spheres of becoming.

~ Consciousness as nutriment nourishes (brings on) NĀMA- RŪPA at the moment of rebirth-linking.

(p.373, v.3)

~ When there is physical nutriment there is attachment (craving) which brings peril and fear (simile of the child's flesh. SAM.NIK 11-98)

~ When there is nutriment as contact there is approaching which brings peril and fear. (Approaching means meeting, coinciding with unabandoned perversion of perception due to an object being perceived as permanent, etc.) (See simile of the headless cow ~ S.11-94)

~ When there is nutriment as mental volition there is reappearance (rebirth) which brings peril and fear ~ (Simile of the pit of live coals ~ S.11-00)

~ When there is nutriment as consciousness, there is rebirth linking ~ there is greed ~ there is delighting which brings peril and fear. (Simile of the 100 spears~ S.11-100)

~ All that is intended here of these 4 kinds of nutriment is: ~

(P.373, v.4) ~ Physical nutriment is classified as what is: ~
1. Eaten
2. Drunk
3. Chewed,
4. Tasted

The perception arisen as the apprehension of the repulsive aspect in that nutriment is "perception of repulsiveness in nutriment".

A. Yogi should review repulsiveness in ten aspects in the physical nutriment (p.374 ~ top)

(A. What is eaten ~ B. Drunk ~ C. Chewed ~ D. Tasted (that is to say) As to:
1. Going
2. Seeking
3. Using
4. Secretion
5. Receptacle
6. What is uncooked (undigested)
7. What is cooked (digested)
8. Fruit
9. Outflow
10. Smearing

~ 1. As to Going ~ (p.374, v.6)

1. Even the BHIKKHU must leave the seclusion of his forest dwelling ~ take his bowl and robes ~ and he must go to the village and get nutriment ~ as a jackal for the charnel ground.
2. He must tread the way from his dwelling. First the floor is covered with dust and gecko droppings. ~ Then outside is even more repulsive, fouled with rat-crap, and so on. ~ Then the grounds are even more repulsive ~ defiled with old grass ~ leaves ~ crow droppings, etc. ~ urine ~ spittle ~ excrement. ~ And during the rainy season ~ mud ~ water ~ branches, etc. ~ The road to the village with stumps ~ thorns ~ pebbles ~ stones, etc. (car fumes,

etc.) ~ All for the sake of nutriment. ~ Bad smells ~ such as dead carcasses seen ~ and he is also assailed by the smell. ~ He then has to avoid danger in the village. ~ Savage behavior found therein).

3. Thus, the daily burden of having to go in search of nutriment ~ from the dwelling itself into the village ~ and back again.

~ Oh, nutriment is indeed a repulsive thing! ~

~ 2. As to Seeking ~ (p.375, v.11)

1. Having gone into the village ~ he has to wander from house to house.
2. During the rainy season ~ through mud and puddles.
3. During the hot season ~ he becomes sweaty and dirty from dust blown about by the wind.
4. To reach certain houses ~ one sometimes has to tread in gutters and cesspools covered with flies ~ seething with worms ~ mixed with dogs and pigs' excrement ~ food washing and what not.
5. From which flies come and settle on his outer robe.
6. And even then ~ some give ~ and some not. ~ Some treat him kindly ~ others rudely. ~ Others pretend not to see him ~ some avert their faces. ~ Etc.
7. Yet entry into the village and departure from there has to be done for the sake of daily nutriment.

~ Oh, seeking nutriment is indeed a repulsive thing! ~

~ 3. As to Using ~ (p.376, v.14)

1. After going and seeking one's nutriment ~ and sitting in a comfortable place outside the village ~ and so long as he hasn't dipped his hand into the bowl, he would invite a respected **BHIKKHU** to share it. ~ But after having dipped into it out of desire to eat ~ he would be ashamed to say "Take some." ~ Squeezing it with his hand ~ sweat combines with it ~ and the dry food also recovered becomes sodden.
2. Appearance of the food becomes spoiled ~ then once in the mouth it becomes pounded by the teeth ~ tongue and palate ~ spittle smears

onto it. ~ It becomes like a dog's dinner in a trough ~ and food particles are in between the teeth. ~ Etc.
3. At this point from its original condition it is utterly nauseating, like dog's vomit.
4. Yet it is swallowed because it is no longer in range of the eye's focus.

~ This is how repulsiveness should be reviewed as to using. ~

~ 4. As to Secretion ~ (p.377, v.17)

1. Once the food has been chewed and swallowed it becomes besmeared with internal secretions: ~ such as ~ saliva ~ pus ~ phlegm ~ and blood.
2. It becomes utterly nauseating.

~ This is how repulsiveness should be reviewed as to secretion. ~

~ 5. As to Receptacle ~ (p.377, v.18)

1. Once the food is inside the stomach and covered with various secretions ~ the receptacle it is then in is no gold or silver tray or dish.
2. But if one is 10 years old ~ it's like a 10-year-old cesspit ~ unwashed for 10 years ~ and the same for someone 20 years old ~ 30 ~ 50 ~ 80 ~ and 100 years old.

~ This is how repulsiveness should be reviewed as to receptacle. ~

~ 6. As to What is Uncooked (undigested) (p.377, v.19)

1. Once inside the stomach ~ covered with secretions it remains shrouded in darkness ~ tainted by various smells that are utterly loathsome.
2. What has been swallowed that day ~ the day before ~ and the day before yesterday remain together smothered by phlegm and covered with froth and bubbles produced by digestion through being fermented by bodily heat. ~ It becomes quite loathsome.

~ This is how repulsiveness should be reviewed as to what is uncooked. ~

~ 7. As to What is Cooked (digested) (p.377, v.20)

1. When it has been completely cooked by bodily fires it doesn't turn into gold or silver.
2. Instead it turns into excrement and fills the bowels and it turns into urine and fills the bladder.

~ This is how repulsiveness should be reviewed as to what is cooked. ~

~ 8. As to Fruit (p.378, v.21)

1. When the food has been properly prepared it produces the various kinds of bodily constituents consisting of head hairs ~ body hairs, nails, teeth and the rest.
2. If wrongly prepared it produces the 100 diseases beginning with itch, ringworm, leprosy, plague, consumption, coughs, etc.
3. Such is its fruit.

~ This is how repulsiveness should be reviewed as to fruit. ~

~ 9. As to Outflow (p.378, v.22)

1. On being swallowed it enters by one door ~ it flows out by several doors.
2. Eye-dirt from the eye ~ ear-dirt from the ear ~ nose ~ anus ~ genitals ~ 9 doors.
3. On being swallowed it is even done in the company of a large gathering.
4. On flowing out ~ dung and urine ~ it is excreted only in solitude.
5. On the first day one is delighted to eat it, elated, joyful, and full of happiness.
6. On the second day one clogs one's nose to avoid its smell ~ becomes dismayed and disgusted.
7. On the first day one eats lustfully, greedily and gluttonously.
8. But on the second day, after a single night has passed ~ excretes it with distaste, ashamed, humiliated and disgusted.

~ This is how repulsiveness should be reviewed as to outflow. ~

~ 10. As to Smearing (p.378, v.24)

1. At the time of using one smears hands, lips, tongue and palate ~ they become repulsive.
2. Even when washed ~ it requires additional washings to remove the smell completely.
3. Even once eaten and in the stomach to rise up due to the bodily heat cooking it and it pervades the whole body ~ the mouth and tongue ~ through bodily forces ~ spittle, phlegm, excrement and urine ~ ear wax ~ etc. ~ which smear the ear, eye, nose and other bodily passages.
4. One must continue to wash these passages ~ then the hands have to be washed ~ and (even then) the repulsiveness doesn't depart: ~ every day and often several times daily (even more so when sick ~ dysentery ~ vomiting etc.) washing is needed.

~ This is how repulsiveness should be reviewed as to smearing ~

(p.379, v.25) ~ As the meditator reviews repulsiveness in this way in ten aspects and stroked at it with initial and sustained thought ~ physical nutriment becomes evident to him in its repulsive aspect.

~ He cultivates the sign (see p.379, note #18 for details) again and again ~ develops and repeatedly practices it. ~ He reaches access – SAMĀDHI.

(p.379, v.26) Benefits of this practice ~
1. The yogi's mind retreats, retracts, and recoils from craving for flavors.
2. He nourishes himself without vanity ~ and only for the purpose of ARAHANTSHIP ~ as one who seeks to cross over the desert ~ having to rely on eating his own dead son's flesh.
3. Greed for the 5 strains of sense-desire comes to be fully-understood without difficulty.
4. From that he understands the RŪPA-KHANDHA fully.
5. Perfection of this practice comes about through repulsive reflection of "What is uncooked" ~ etc.
6. If not ARAHANTSHIP ~ at least a happy destiny upon death.

~ **Conclude** ~ explanation of repulsiveness in nutriment ~

Also given in brief ~ MAHĀSATIPATTHĀNA SUTTA ~ DIGHA. NIK~

Given in detail ~ MAHĀHATTHIPADŪPAMĀ SUTTA ~ MAJ.NIK ~
~ RĀHULAVĀDA SUTTA ~ MAJ.NIK. ~
~ DIJĀTUVIBHANGA SUTTA ~ MAJ. NIK. ~

G. Analysis of the Elements

1. Analysis of the four elements (p.380, v.27)

~ Given in brief (one with quick understanding ~ MAHA SATI. SUT. ~)

"BHIKKHUS, just as though a skilled butcher or butcher's apprentice had killed a cow and were seated at the cross-roads with it cut up into pieces, so too, BHIKKHUS, a BHIKKHU reviews this body, however placed, however disposed, as consisting of elements: In this body there are the earth element, the water elements, the fire elements and the air element."

~ Meaning ~ (p.381, v.30)

~ Just as the butcher, while feeding the cow, bringing it to the stables ~ keeping it tied up after bringing it there ~ slaughtering it and seeing it slaughtered and dead, does not lose the perception 'cow' ~ so as long as he has not carved it up and divided it into parts: But then he has divided it up and is sitting there, he loses the perception 'cow' ~ and the perception 'meat' occurs: He does not think "I am selling cow" or "They are carrying away cow" ~ but rather he thinks ~ "I am selling meat" or "They are carrying meat away": So too this BHIKKHU, while still a foolish ordinary person ~ both formerly as a layman and as one gone forth into homelessness ~ does not lose the perception 'living being' or 'man' or 'person' so long as he does not, by resolution of the compact into elements, review this body, however placed, however disposed, as consisting of elements. But when he does review it as consisting of elements, he loses his perception 'living being' and his mind established itself upon elements ~ (That is why the first verse has been stated, v.27)

(Details v.33-34)
1. Internal earth element: ~ Whatever that is ~ internal in oneself ~ that is hard and clung to: (acquired through KAMMA) (p.381-82, v.31)
    1. Head hairs
    2. Body hairs
    3. Teeth
    4. Nails
    5. Skin
    6. Flesh
    7. Sinews
    8. Bones
    9. Bone marrow
    10. Kidney
    11. Heart
    12. Liver
    13. Midriff
    14. Spleen
    15. Lights
    16. Bowels
    17. Entrails
    18. Gorge
    19. Dung
    20. Brain

    ~ or whatever else there is internally in oneself that is hard, harsh and clung to ~ that is called the earth element.

2. Internal water elements: ~ Whatever there is ~ internally in oneself ~ that is water, watery and clung to: ~
    1. Bile
    2. Phlegm
    3. Pus
    4. Blood
    5. Sweat

6. Fat
7. Tears
8. Grease
9. Spittle
10. Snot
11. Oil of the joints
12. Urine

~ Or whatever else there is internally in oneself that is water, watery and clung to. ~ (Characteristic of cohesion)

3. Internal fire element: ~ Whatever is internally in oneself that is fire, fiery, clung to, that thereby is warmed, ages, and burns up; and whereby what is eaten, drunk, chewed and tasted gets completely digested ~ or whatever else there is internally in oneself that is fire, fiery and clung to ~ this is called the internal fire element.

4. Internal air elements: ~ Whatever there is internally in oneself that is air, airy and clung to: ~ up-going winds ~ down-going winds, winds in the belly, winds in the bowels, winds through all the limbs (enable one to make or sit up without collapsing) ~ in and out breath. Or whatever else there is internally in oneself that is air, airy and clung to: ~ this is called the internal air element.

~ Concentration ~ analysis of the four elements ~

Developed in four ways ~

1. With constituents in brief ~ (p.386, v.46)
   ~ The yogi defines the bodily constituents (32 parts) in the way described on the opposite page: ~ 1 ~ 2 ~ 3 ~ and 4 ~ again and again reviewing them thus ~ Access-SAMADHI arises.

2. With constituents by analysis ~ (p.386, v.47)
   ~ The yogi should carry out all directions given for the 32-fold aspect in the recollection of repulsiveness of the 32-body parts (see p.93) ~ The only difference is that instead of seeing repulsiveness the mind should be fixed on the elements of each part.

   (VIS.MAG goes on to explain each of the 32 parts in detail

p.386, v.48- p.395, v.83) ~ concluding each description with ~ for example with teeth ~ "Teeth grow in the jaw bones. Herein, just as when posts are placed by builders in stone sockets and fastened with some kind of cement, the dockets do not know, "Posts are placed in us". Nor do the posts know "We are placed in dockets". So too, the jaw bones do not know, "'Teeth grow in us", nor do the teeth know "We grow in jaw bones". These things are devoid of mutual concern and reviewing. So, what are called teeth are a particular component of this body, without thought: ~ Indeterminate, void, not a living being, rigid, earth element.")

1. Head hairs (p.386, v.48)
2. Body hairs (p.387, v.49)
3. Teeth (p.387, v.50)
4. Nails (p.387, v.52)
5. Skin (p.388, v.53)
6. Flesh (p.388, v.54)
7. Sinews (p.388, v.55)
8. Bones (p.389, v.47)
9. Bone marrow (p.389, v.57)
10. Kidney (p.389, v.58)
11. Heart (p.389, v.59)
12. Liver (p.389, v.60)
13. Midriff (p.390, v.6 1)
14. Spleen (p.390, v.62)
15. Lights (p.390, v.63)
16. Bowels (p.390, v.64)
17. Entrails (p.391, v.65)
18. Gorge (p.391, v.66)
19. Dung (p.391, v.67)
20. Brain (p.391, v.68)
21. Bile (p.392, v.69)
22. Phlegm (p.392, v.70)
23. Pus (p.392, v.71)
24. Blood (p.392, v.72)
25. Sweat (p.393, v.73)

26. Fat (p.393, v.74)
27. Tears (p.393, v.75)
28. Grease (p.394, v.76)
29. Spittle (p.394, v.77)
30. Snot (p.394, v.78)
31. Oil of the joints (p.394, v.79)
32. Urine (p.395, v.80)

3. With characteristics in brief ~ (p.396, v.84)
   1. Earth element should be seen as the characteristic of hardness.
   2. Water element should be seen as the characteristic of cohesion.
   3. Fire element ~ as the characteristic of maturing (ripening ~ warmth ~ coldness).
   4. Air element ~ as the characteristic's distention.

4. With characteristic by analysis ~ (p.396, v.85)
   ~ Taking each of the 32 body parts and seeing that each element is present there by taking the element and its characteristic into mind as an aspect of head hairs ~ etc.

~ Concentration ~ analysis of the 4 elements ~

~ A. Additional ways of giving attention to the 4 elements ~

~ 13 additional ways ~

1. As to word meaning ~ (v.87)

2. By groups: ~ Describing each of the 32 parts as mere groups of the 4 primary elements and 4 secondary elements, ~ 43 groups of 8 states each. (v.88)

3. By particles ~ (interesting explanation): ~ Describing how each of the 4 elements operate together. ~ "So, this mechanism of elements carries on like a magic trick ~ deceiving foolish people with the male and female sex", and so on. (p.398, v.89)

4. As to characteristic etc.: ~ One defines each element in terms of characteristic, function and manifestation. (p.399, v.93)

5. As to how originated: ~ Categorizes each of the 32 parts briefly as to how they originated ~ KAMMA ~ consciousness ~ nutriment ~ and temperature. (v.94)

6. As to variety and unity: ~ all 4 have a different variety of characteristics, function, etc. ~ They are unified as "all being great primaries", TI-LAKKHANA, DHAMMAS, etc. (v.95)
   ~ As to #6 ~ the 4 elements are called 'great primaries' for these reasons.
   A ~ Manifestation of greatness ~ See for details (p.400, v.97)
   B ~ Likeness to great creatures: ~ The great primaries can easily deceive one, being lost in the concept of them. ~ Beautiful man, woman, limbs, etc. (v.98, 99, 100)
   C. ~ Great maintenance ~ because they have to be sustained by the 4 great requisites; because they have to be pounded daily ~ or they are great primaries because their maintenance is great. (p.401, v.101)
   D. ~ Great alteration: ~ World systems are dissolved and scattered ~ as will be the body and the traumas that occur due to the 4 elements alteration. ~ Imbalance occurs. (v.102)
   E. ~ Because they are great, ~ and because they are entities, ~ because it requires great effort to discern them ~ they are existent DHAMMAS that are real. (p.402, v.103)

7. As to resolution (separability) and non-resolution (inseparability): ~ They are separable only due to characteristic, but inseparable since they always arise together in every single minimal material group. (p.402, v.105)

8. As to similar and dissimilar: ~ First 2 are similar in heaviness ~ second 2 in lightness. ~ In the same way they (first part and second pair) are dissimilar. (p.403, v.106)

9. As to distinction between internal and external: ~ Internal elements are the material support for consciousness, ~ external elements are the opposite kind. (v.107)

10. As to inclusion ~ (See V.MAG. for details) (v.108)

11. As to condition: ~ Earth element ~ held together by water ~ maintained by fire and distended by air ~ is a condition for the 3 other primaries by acting as their foundation.
    - ~ Water element ~ founded on earth ~ maintained by fire and distended by air ~ is a condition for the other 3 primaries by acting as their cohesion.
    - ~ Fire element ~ founded on earth ~ held together by water ~ and distended by air ~ acts as a condition for the other 3 primaries by acting as their maintaining.
    - ~ Air element ~ is founded on earth held together by water ~ maintained by fire ~ acts as condition for other 3 primaries by acting as their distention. (v.109)

12. As to lack of conscious reception: ~ Earth element does not know "I am earth element, I am a condition for the others by acting as their foundation" ~ etc. and so on (p.402, v.110)

13. As to analysis of conditions: ~ FOUR conditions for the elements ~ KAMMA ~ consciousness ~ nutriment ~ temperature. ~ (Other details V111-115).

(p.405, v.117) Benefits of this practice:

~ Yogi eliminates perception of living beings. ~ He conquers fear and dread ~ conquers delight and aversion ~ is not exhilarated or depressed by agreeable or disagreeable things. ~ Either ends in deathless – or if not, a happy destiny.

~ Concludes explanation of the analysis of the FOUR great elements ~

(p.406, v.120-p.408, v.126)

~ Conclusion ~

H. The Benefits of Developing Concentration

~ The benefits of the development of concentration, are 5-fold as a blissful abiding ~ here and now: ~

1. What is meant ~ is the development of absorption-SAMĀDHI ~ which provides the benefit of a blissful abiding here and now for the ARAHANTS with cankers destroyed who develop SAMĀDHI, thinking: "We shall attain and dwell with a unified mind for a whole day".
2. After emerging they (non-ARAHANTS) can exercise insight with a concentrated mind. ~ Thus, the benefit of absorption-SAMĀDHI can serve as a proximate cause for insight. ~ So too with access-SAMĀDHI.
3. Having already become an ARAHANT ~ absorption-SAMĀDHI provides the benefit of serving as a proximate cause for the arising of the various kinds of direct – knowledge ~ (See next chapter): ~ such as "Having become one, he becomes many," etc.
4. If an ordinary person has not lost his JHĀNA upon death he will be reborn in the various BRAHMA-like realms depending on his JHĀNA capabilities. ~ Even access- SAMĀDHI attainment ensures an improved form of existence in the happy destinies of the sensual sphere.
5. And such noble ones who have already produced the 8 attainments develop SAMĀDHI thinking: "We shall enter upon the attainment of cessation, and by being without consciousness for 7 days we shall abide in bliss here and now by reaching the bliss that is NIBBĀNA." Thus, the development of absorption-SAMĀDHI benefits them by way of providing for cessation.

~ Conclude section on concentration ~

8.
DESCRIPTION OF DIRECT KNOWLEDGE – THE SUPERNORMAL POWERS

(VIS.MAG.CH XII, p.409-p.445)
(VIS.MAG. CH XIII, p.446-p.478)

A. The Five Kinds of Direct Knowledge

(p.409, v.1)
1. IDDHI-VIDHA-ABHIÑÑĀ (supernormal power) (v.2)
    1 ~ Normally one, he adverts to himself as many (manifold) as 100, 1000, 100 000, resolving, "Let me be many." (p.424, v.59)
    2 ~ Having been many, "...the power to become one again." (p.427, v.68)
    3 ~ He has the power to cause appearance and cause vanishing ~ "to reveal what is hidden" ~ etc. (p.427, v.69)
    4 ~ Has the power to go unhindered through walls, enclosures, through mountains, "as though in one space." (p.432, v.87)
    5 ~ Has the power to dive in and out of the earth. (p.433, v.92)
    6 ~ Power to walk on water without sinking "as if it were solid earth." (p.433, v.95)
    7 ~ Power to travel cross-legged through the air "like a winged bird." (p.434, v.98)
    8 ~ Power to touch the sun and the moon with one's hand. (p.435, v.102)

2. DIBBA-SOTA- ABHIÑÑĀ (Divine ear ~ or celestial ear)

~ Power to hear sounds both heavenly and human ~ far or near ~ (CH. XIII, p.336, v.1)

3. CETO-PARIYA-ABHIÑÑĀ (Power to know ~ or ability to penetrate the minds of others (p.448, v.8)
   ~ Has the power to know all types of consciousness ~ affected by greed ~ hatred or delusion ~ or unaffected by them ~ if distracted consciousness ~ if concentration ~ if ARIYA ~ What stage? ~ What JHANAS? ~ if non-ARIYA ~ etc.

4. PUBBE-NIVĀSA-ABHIÑÑĀ (Power to recollect the incidents of one's past lives ~ existences ~ 10, 20, 100, 1000, 100 000, many eons of lives, there I was 'so' names, of 'such' a race, 'such' an appearance, 'such' was my food, 'such' were my pleasures and pains, my lifespan, etc). (p.451, v.13)

5. DIBBA-CAKKHU-ABHIÑÑĀ (Divine eye ~ or celestial eye) (p.464, v.72)
   ~ Power to see all material forms and color whether far off or near, whether great or small.
   ~ Has also the power to see the passing away and reappearance of beings ~ wherever they may take rebirth ~~ pairing on according to their individual KAMMAS.

B. Method of Development (Brief)

~ If a yogi wants to begin performing these various ABHIÑÑĀS, he must achieve the 8 attainments in each of the 8 KASINAS ending with the white KASINA. He must also have complete control of his mind in the following 14 ways:

1. In order of the KASINAS ~ progressing masterly through the 8 KASINAS (p.410, v.3)
2. In the reverse order of the KASINAS ~ attaining them in likewise manner in reserve order. (v.3)
3. In order and reverse order of the KASINAS (v.3)
4. In the order of the JHĀNAS ~ attaining all 8 JHĀNAS progressively. (v.4)

8. DESCRIPTION OF DIRECT KNOWLEDGE – THE SUPERNORMAL POWERS

5. In the reverse order of the JHĀNAS. (v.4)
6. In the order and reverse order of the JHĀNAS. (v.4)
7. Skipping JHĀNAS ~ skips alternate JHĀNAS without skipping the KASINAS ~ such as first JHĀNA in earth KASINA ~ then third JHĀNA in earth. (p.410, v.5)
8. Skipping KASINAS ~ skips alternate KASINAS without skipping JHĀNAS (v.5)
9. Skipping JHĀNAS and KASINAS (v.5)
10. Transposition of factors ~ attaining first JHĀNA in the earth KASINA ~ then attaining the others in that same KASINA. (p.411, v.6)
11. Transposition of object ~ attaining first JHĀNA in the earth KASINA ~ then the same JHĀNA in the water KASINA ... white KASINA. (v.6)
12. Transposition of factors and objects ~ (See text for details) (v.6)
13. Definition of factors ~ defining only the JHĀNA factors ~ first one has 5, second one 3 ~ third – 2, fourth- 2 ~ and so through ARŪPA JHĀNAS. (p.411, v.7)
14. Definition of object ~ "This is the earth KASINA ~ water ~ white KASINA." (v.7)

~ It is not possible for a meditator to begin to accomplish the supernormal powers unless he has previously completed his development by controlling his mind in these 14 ways. (p.411, v.8)

~ Conclude section on ABHIÑÑĀS ~

~ for complete details refer to VIS. MAGGA ~

Chapters Nine through Fifteen concern how to undertake *satipatthana* Vipassana practice. They explain how to practice and how to report the Stages of Insight and the explanation of these, including emotional reactions to Stages of Insight and experiences of insight, including the *Meditation Teacher's Diary*

(Mahasi Sayadaw's compilation of thousands of yogis experiences for pedagogical training purposes).

9.
THE MEANING OF SATIPATTHANA

Sayadaw U Panditabhivamsa

This book is dedicated to the Most Venerable Sayadaw U Panditabhivamsa with gratitude and devotion from the Thai yogis and supporters; October 2002.

Introduction

The Venerable Sayadaw U Pandita talks frequently about the meaning of SATIPATTHANA. He uses etymology to explain the proper way to note and observe the arising physical and mental objects in the practice of meditation.

This detailed and practical exposition of the term SATIPATTHANA goes to the Sayadaw's credit. It is a formula or recipe for success in meditation. If applied meticulously to one's practice, the dhamma will unfold in no time.

The seven benefits of mindfulness

The practice of SATIPATTHANA meditation leads to the purification of the mind, the overcoming of sorrow and lamentation, the complete destruction of physical pain and mental distress, the entering of the right path and the attainment of NIBBĀNA.

The etymology of SATIPATTHANA

The Pali term SATIPATTHANA is generally rendered as the 'Four foundations of mindfulness'. However, its full meaning can be revealed by breaking up the compound word into its parts, and examining these elements both individually and in combination.

SATI + PATTHANA
or
SATI + PA + (T)THANA

The word SATI derives from the root meaning 'to remember' (SAMSARATI), but as a mental factor it signifies 'presence of mind, attentiveness to the present, awareness, wakefulness and heedfulness', rather than the faculty of memory of the past.

PATTHANA means 'close, firm and steadfast establishment, application, setting up'.

Combining these two elements, the meaning of the compound becomes 'close, firm and steadfast establishment of awareness on the object of observation'. This kind of awareness is also called SUPPATITTHITA SATI, 'steadfast mindfulness'.

The four foundations of mindfulness

The four foundations of mindfulness have a single essence – mindful contemplation of natural phenomena. They are differentiated insofar as this mindful contemplation is applied to four objects:

1. The body (KAYA);
2. The feelings (VEDANA);
3. States of consciousness (CITTA); and
4. Mental objects (DHAMMA). The latter comprise such factors as the five hindrances, the five aggregates, the six sense bases and six sense objects; (general activities), the seven factors of enlightenment and the four noble truths.

SATI

'Mindfulness' has come to be the accepted English translation of the term SATI. However, this is an incomplete rendering. 'Observing power' is a more adequate translation. The full scope of its meaning will be explained by examining its various aspects, such as characteristic, function, manifestation, proximate cause and the further distinguishing factors of mindfulness.

Non-superficiality

SATI has the characteristic of "not wobbling"; that is, of not floating away from the object (APILAPANA LAKKHANA). The commentators have given the simile of a dried, hollow pumpkin thrown into water. The cork or pumpkin will pop up and down on the surface of the water. In the same way, the noting and observing mind should not skim over the object in a superficial manner. Instead, the mind should sink or plunge into the object of observation, just as when a stone is thrown into water it will Sink – or plunge to the bottom.

Suppose you are watching your abdomen as the object of your SATIPATTHANA practice. You try to be very firm, focusing your attention on the main object, so that the mind will not skip off. Instead, the mind will sink deeply into the process of rising and falling. As the mind penetrates this process, you can comprehend its true nature: tension, pressure, movement, and so on.

Keeping the object in view

The function of SATI is the absence of confusion, or "non-forgetfulness" (ASAMMOSA RASA). This means that the noting and observing mind should neither lose sight of, nor miss, nor forget, nor allow the object of observation to disappear. To express this aspect positively, the function of SATI is to keep the object always in view. Just as a footballer never loses sight of the football, a badminton player the shuttlecock and a boxer his opponent's movement, so too the yogi never loses sight of the object of mindfulness.

Confrontation and protection

There are two manifestations of SATI, namely: Coming face-to-face with the object; and protection.

- Face-to-face with the object

The chief manifestation of SATI is confrontation – it sets the mind directly, face-to-face, with the object of observation (VISAYABHUMUKHA BHAVA PACCUPATTHANA). SATI manifests as the mind in a state (BHAVA) of confronting face-to-face (ABHIMUKHA) with an object or objective field (VISAYA).

It is said that the human face is the index of character. Therefore, if you want to 'size up' a person, you have to be face-to-face with that person and examine his or her face carefully. Then your judgment will be correct. But if you stand at an angle, behind or far away from that other person, then you will not be able to distinguish the distinctive features of his face.

Similarly, when you are observing the rising movement of your abdomen, if the mind is really face-to-face with the rising movement, you will notice different sensations in the rising, such as tension, pressure, heat, coolness or movement.

- Protection

If the noting and observing mind remains face-to face with the object of observation for a significant period of time, the yogi can discover a great purity of mind due to the absence of KILESAS (mental defilements). This purity is the result of the second manifestation of SATI – guardianship or protection from attack by the KILESAS (ARAKKHA PACCUPATTHANA). With SATI present, mental defilements have no chance to enter the stream of consciousness.

SATI is likened to a doorkeeper because it guards the six sense doors. A doorkeeper does not admit bad and destructive people; he admits only good and useful people. SATI does not admit unwholesomeness (AKUSALA); it admits only wholesomeness (KUSALA). By not accepting AKUSALA, the mind is protected.

The proximate causes of mindfulness

The proximate causes for the arising of SATI are strong perception (THIRASANNA PADATTHANA) and the four foundations of mindfulness (KAYADI SATIPATTHANA PADATTHANA).

- Strong perception

In order to be mindful of an object, strong and firm (THIRA) perception of it is necessary. As much as perception (SAÑÑA) is firm, strong and steadfast, mindfulness will also be firm, strong and steadfast.

The two functions of perception are the recording and the recognition of formations (SANKHARA), irrespective of their wholesome or unwholesome nature. SAÑÑA is compared to the recording of talks with the help of a tape or video recorder. The recording takes place regardless of the content or quality of the talks. A clear, high-quality recording, such as a state-of-the-art digital recording on CD of a classical concert or opera, is the cause for a clear, strong, impressive listening experience (mindfulness) when replaying the recording.
Similarly, in the meditation practice a strong, clear-cut perception (noting or labeling) of the arising objects of observation is very supportive of strong, clear-cut, steadfast mindfulness.

- Four foundations of mindfulness

Another proximate cause for the arising of SATI is the four foundations of mindfulness (KAYADI SATIPATTHANA PADATTHANA). That is, mindfulness itself is the cause of mindfulness. In fact, the development of mindfulness is the result of continuous momentum, one moment of mindfulness causing the next.

This can be compared to the process of acquiring an education, assuming that the student is studious and does his homework respectfully. Lessons learnt in the lower grades are a cause for learning lessons in the higher grade. Primary school education is a cause for high school education, and this in turn serves as a cause for tertiary and university education.

In a nutshell, mindfulness leads to ever greater and stronger mindfulness.

Immediacy

Immediacy in the awareness of an object of observation is very important. Nothing should come between the presently arising object and the noting and observing. The arising object and the noting mind should not be separated in time. The observation of the presently arising object should happen at once, without any delay. It should be instant. As soon as the object of observation arises, it should be noted and observed. If one's noting and observing is delayed, then the object will have already passed by the time one's awareness turns to it. Objects of the past and future cannot be known correctly, and if the attention cannot remain with objects as they arise, then it is no longer VIPASSANĀ practice. It is no longer dwelling in reality.

Concurrence

When two or more processes occur at the same time, it is the phenomenon of 'concurrence'. Concurrence of the noting and observing mind and the object of observation is an important aspect of SATI. For example, when an object arises, the mind falls on the object simultaneously with its arising, synchronically [as if it exists at one time] with it.

Extraordinary mindfulness

The particle 'pa' of SATI-PA-(T)THANA specifies that the mindfulness should be of an extraordinary or outstanding nature (VISITTHA); excessive, intensive and persistent (BHUSATTHA). Ordinary mindfulness is out of place in intensive SATIPATTHANA meditation. It is this nature of the particle pa, and its practical aspects, which we shall now explore.

Rushing (PAKKHANDITVA PAVATTATI)

The particle pa of SATI-PA-(T) THANA can also be interpreted as PA-(K) KHANDANA: rushing, leaping and plunging. As soon as the object of observation arises, the mind has to rush forward towards (and into) the object of observation with great force, with courage. It attacks the object without hesitation, without thinking, reflecting, analyzing, imagining, questioning, considering, speculating or fantasizing. Thus, several aspects are involved in 'rushing':

- Sudden, impetuous, quick and swift movement with violence, speed or great force, strength and dynamism.

Simile: 'like rushing somebody to the hospital'.

- Capturing, catching or arresting by sudden attack; to make a swift attack or assault; to charge.

Simile: The soldiers capture and defeat the enemy troops in a sudden, forceful attack.

- An eager movement of many people to get to a particular place.

Simile: The crowds rush the gates of the football stadium just before the game begins.

- To move urgently, with excessive speed, haste, or hurry.

Simile: a person at work may say, "I'm in a dreadful rush." Or, in accordance with the saying, "Strike while the iron is hot"; one notes and observes the object while it is 'fresh' or 'hot'.

Yogis should not be noting and observing in a stop-and-go manner. The awareness should not be slack, sluggish, or casual; not lagging behind or late; not gazing. It should be without wandering mind, with no room for thoughts. The noting and observing should not be in a cool and hesitating manner; instead, it must be rushing in a systematic and orderly manner.

Firmly grasping or seizing the object (UPAGGANHITVA PAVATTATI)

A rice farmer when harvesting paddy needs to firmly grasp or seize a bushel of rice. Only then will he be able to cut it with a sickle. Similarly, a meditator has to firmly grasp the object of observation so that the mind will neither slip off nor lose the object under observation.

As mindfulness becomes steadfast, the yogi will be able to firmly seize coarse objects. With more practice, attention can hold on to more refined objects and eventually even very subtle objects can be firmly grasped by the mind. Therefore, a yogi should first try to grasp physical objects before attempting to seize the more subtle type of mental objects like intentions, thoughts, etc.

Covering the object completely (PATTHARITVA PAVATTATI)

The noting and observing mind must cover the object of observation completely, spreading over the entire object, enveloping it, grasping it in its entirety. Not just a part of the object must be observed, but the object should be noted and observed from the beginning, through its middle, to its end.

Unbroken continuity (PAVATTATI)

In the practical sense, this aspect means that the noting and observing of the arising objects of observation should be continuous; that is, one moment of mindfulness connected to the next moment of mindfulness, moment after moment. The preceding moment of mindfulness should be connected with the succeeding moment of mindfulness. In brief, mindfulness should be sustained.

Similes:

- If there is a gap between two floor planks, dust and sand may enter. If there is no continuity of mindfulness and there is a gap, defilements may enter.

- In the past one had to start a fire by rubbing two sticks together. If one fails to rub continuously, but instead takes a rest and resumes rubbing later, no fire will start. Similarly, if mindfulness is not continuous, the fire of wisdom will not ignite.

To reaffirm this aspect negatively, the noting and observing, or mindfulness, of the objects should not have gaps but be continuous; it should not proceed in a stop-and-go manner. People who practice in fits and starts, resting occasionally and then starting again, being mindful for a stretch and then stopping to daydream, are known as 'chameleon yogis'.

Non-manipulating

The universal characteristic of 'not-self' (ANATTA) can be applied to the process of noting and observing the arising physical and mental objects.

A meditator must take great care to watch the objects of observation without manipulating, controlling or governing them. He should simply observe what is there – not what he expects or wants to be there.

Conclusion

What can we now say SATIPATTHANA is? SATIPATTHANA is mindfulness of any noted object by rushing to, entering into and spreading over it, so that the mind stays closely and firmly with it. When noting 'rising', the mind enters the noted object; that is, the rising movement of the abdomen. The mindfulness rushes into it and spreads over it so that the mind stays closely and firmly on this object or phenomenon. The process is then repeated when noting 'falling', and so on for all other objects that arise in the body and mind.

Therefore, in conclusion, SATI or mindfulness must be dynamic and confrontational. Mindfulness should leap forward onto the object, covering it completely, penetrating into it and not missing any part of it. If your mindfulness has these qualities, then swift progress in meditation is guaranteed and, with the fulfillment of the practice, seeing NIBBĀNA is assured.

SATIPATTHANA at a glance:
- close and firm establishment;
- non-superficiality;
- keeping the object in view;
- face-to-face with the object;
- protection of the mind from attack by *kilesas*;
- strong perception;
- mindfulness is the cause of mindfulness;
- rushing and plunging;
- firmly grasping the object;
- completely covering, or spreading over the object;
- immediacy;
- continuity;
- concurrence;
- non-manipulating.

References

1. Buddhaghosa, Acarya. *The Path of Purification (Visuddhimagga)*. Nanamoli (tr..). P.T.S. Chapter XIV, pg. 141
2. Sayadaw U Pandita Bhivamsa, Ven. *In This Very*
3. *Life*. Wisdom, 1992.
4. Sayadaw U Pandita Bhivamsa, Ven. *Raindrops in Hot Summer*. M.B.M.C., 1994
5. Bodhi, Bhikkhu, et. al. *Comprehensive Manual of Abhidhamma*. B.P.S.
6. Mahasi Sayadaw, Ven. *VIPASSANĀ Shunyigyan*.
7. (Burmese).
8. Mahagandayou Sayadaw U Janaka Bhivamsa, Yen.
9. *Sahgahabhasa-tika*. (Burmese). 1990
10. Sayadaw U Pandita Bhivamsa, Ven. Various dhamma talks.

10.
INSTRUCTIONS TO INSIGHT MEDITATION

The Venerable Mahasi Sayadaw

The following is a talk by the Venerable Mahasi Sayadaw Agga Maha Pandita U Sobhana given to his disciples on their induction into VIPASSANĀ Meditation at Sasana Yeiktha Meditation Centre, Rangoon, Burma. It was translated from the Burmese by U Nyi Nyi.

The practice of VIPASSANĀ or Insight Meditation is the effort made by the meditator to correctly understand the nature of the psycho-physical phenomena taking place in his own body. Physical phenomena are the things or objects which one clearly perceives around one. The whole of one's body that one clearly perceives constitutes a group of material qualities (RŪPA). Psychical or mental phenomena are acts of consciousness or awareness (NĀMA). These NĀMA-RŪPAS are clearly perceived to be happening whenever they are seen, heard, smelt, tasted, touched, or thought of. We must make ourselves aware of them by observing them and noting thus: 'Seeing, seeing', 'hearing, hearing', 'smelling, smelling', 'tasting, tasting', 'touching, touching', or 'thinking, thinking.' Every time one sees, hears, smells, tastes, touches, or thinks, one should make a note of the fact. But in the beginning of one's practice, one cannot make a note of every one of these happenings. One should, therefore, begin with noting those happenings which are conspicuous and easily perceivable.

With every act of breathing, the abdomen rises and falls, which movement is always evident. This is the material quality known as VAYODHATU (the element of motion). One should begin by noting this movement, which may be done by the mind intently observing the abdomen. You will find the abdomen rising when you breathe in, and falling when you breathe out. The rising should be noted mentally as 'rising', and the falling as 'falling'. If the movement is not evident by just noting it mentally, keep touching the abdomen with the palm of your hand. Do not alter the manner of your breathing. Neither slow it down, nor make it faster. Do not breathe too vigorously, either. You will tire if you change the manner of your breathing. Breathe steadily as usual, and note the rising and falling of the abdomen as they occur. Note it mentally, not verbally.

In VIPASSANĀ meditation, what you name or say doesn't matter. What really matters is to 'know' or 'perceive'. While noting the rising of the abdomen, do so from the beginning to the end of the movement just as if you are seeing it with your eyes. Do the same with the falling movement. Note the rising movement in such a way that your awareness of it is concurrent with the movement itself. The movement and the mental awareness of it should coincide in the same way as a stone thrown hits the target. Similarly with the failing movement.

Your mind may wander elsewhere while you are noting the abdominal movement. This must also be noted by mentally saying 'wandering, wandering'. When this has been noted once or twice, the mind stops wandering, in which case you go back to noting the rising and falling of the abdomen. If the mind reaches somewhere, note as 'reaching, reaching'. Then go back to the rising and falling of the abdomen. If you imagine meeting somebody, note it as 'meeting, meeting'. Then back to the rising and falling. If you imagine meeting and talking to somebody, note it as 'talking, talking'.

In short, whatever thought or reflection occurs should be noted. If you imagine, note it as 'imagining'. If you think, 'thinking'. If you plan, 'planning'. If you perceive, 'perceiving'. If you reflect, 'reflecting'. If you feel happy, 'happy'. If you feel bored, 'bored'. If you feel glad, 'glad'. If you feel disheartened, 'disheartened'. Noting all these acts of consciousness is called CITTANUPASSANA.

Because we fail to note these acts of consciousness, we tend to identify them with a person or individual. We tend to think that it is

'I' who is imagining, thinking, planning, knowing (or perceiving). We think that there is a person who from childhood onwards has been living and thinking. Actually, no such person exists. There are instead only these continuing and successive acts of consciousness. That is why we have to note these acts of consciousness and know them for what they are. That is why we have to note each and every act of consciousness as it arises. When so noted, it tends to disappear. We then go back to noting the rising and falling of the abdomen.

When you have sat meditating for long, sensations of stiffness and heat will arise in your body. These are to be noted carefully too. Similarly with sensations of pain and tiredness. All of these sensations are DUKKHAVEDANA (feeling of unsatisfactoriness) and noting them is VEDANANUPASSANA. Failure or omission to note these sensations makes you think, "I am stiff", "I am feeling hot", "I am in pain", "I was all right a moment ago", "Now I am uneasy with these unpleasant sensations". The identification of these sensations with the ego is mistaken. There is really no 'I' involved, only a succession of one new unpleasant sensation after another.

It is just like a continuous succession of new electrical impulses that light up electric lamps. Every time unpleasant contacts are encountered in the body; unpleasant sensations arise one after another. These sensations should be carefully and intently noted, whether they are sensations of stiffness, of heat or of pain. In the beginning of the yogi's meditational practice, these sensations may tend to increase and lead to a desire to change his posture. This desire should be noted, after which the yogi should go back to noting the sensations of stiffness, heat, etc.

"Patience leads to NIBBĀNA", as the saying goes. This saying is most relevant in meditational effort. One must be patient in meditation. If one shifts or changes one's posture too often because one cannot be patient with the sensation of stiffness or heat that arises, SAMĀDHI (good concentration) cannot develop. If samadhi cannot develop, insight cannot result and there can be no attainment of MAGGA (the path that leads to Nibbana), PHALA (the fruit of that path) and NIBBĀNA. That is why patience is needed in meditation. It is patience mostly with unpleasant sensations in the body like stiffness, sensations of heat and pain, and other sensations that are hard to bear. One should not immediately give up one's meditation on the appearance of such sensations, and change one's meditation posture. One should go on patiently, just noting as 'stiffness, stiffness' or 'hot, hot'. Moderate sensations of these kinds will disappear if one goes on noting them patiently. When concentration is good and strong, even intense sensations tend to disappear. One then reverts to noting the rising and falling of the abdomen.

One will, of course, have to change one's posture if the sensations do not disappear even after one has noted them for a long time, and if on the other hand they become unbearable. One should then begin noting as 'wishing to change, wishing to change'. If the arm rises, note 'rising, rising'. If it moves, note it as 'moving, moving'. This change should be made gently and noted as 'rising, rising', 'moving, moving' and 'touching, touching'. If the body sways, 'swaying, swaying'. If the foot rises, 'rising, rising'. If it moves, 'moving, moving'. If it drops, 'dropping, dropping.' If there is no change, but only static rest, go back to noting the rising and falling of the abdomen. There must be no intermission in between, only contiguity between a preceding act of noting and a succeeding one, between a preceding samadhi (state of concentration) and a succeeding one, between a preceding act of intelligence and a succeeding one. Only then will there be successive and ascending stages of maturity in the yogi's state of intelligence. MAGGA- ÑĀNA and PHALA-ÑĀNA (knowledge of the path and its fruition) are attained only when there is this kind of gathering momentum. The meditative process is like that of producing fire by energetically and unremittingly rubbing two sticks of wood together so as to attain the necessary intensity of heat (when the flame arises).

In the same way, the noting in VIPASSANĀ meditation should be continual and unremitting, without any resting interval between acts of noting whatever phenomena may arise. For instance, if a sensation of itchiness intervenes and the yogi desires to scratch because it is hard to bear, both the sensation and the desire to get rid of it should be noted, without immediately getting rid of the sensation by scratching.

If one goes on perseveringly noting thus, the itchiness generally disappears, in which case one reverts to noting the rising and falling of the abdomen. If the itchiness does not in fact disappear, one has of course to eliminate it by scratching. But first, the desire to do so should be noted. All the movements involved in the process of eliminating this sensation should be noted, especially the touching, pulling and pushing, and scratching movements, with an eventual reversion to noting the rising and falling of the abdomen.

Every time you make a change of posture, you begin with noting your intention or desire to make the change, and go on noting every movement closely, such as rising from the sitting posture, raising the arm, moving and stretching it. You should make the change at the same time as noting the movements involved. As your body sways forward, note it. As you rise, the body becomes light and rises. Concentrating your mind on this, you should gently note as 'rising, rising'.

The yogi should behave as if he were a weak invalid. People in normal health rise easily and quickly or abruptly. Not so with feeble invalids, who do so slowly and gently. The same is the case with people suffering from 'back-ache' who rise gently lest the back hurt and cause pain.

So also, with meditating yogis. They have to make their changes of posture gradually and gently; only then will mindfulness, concentration and insight be good. Begin therefore with gentle and gradual movements. When rising, the yogi must do so gently like an invalid, at the same time noting as 'rising, rising'. Not only this: though the eye sees, the yogi must act as if he does not see. Similarly, when the ear hears. While meditating, the yogi's concern is only to note. What he sees and hears are not his concern. So whatever strange or striking things he may see or hear, he must behave as if he does not see or hear them, merely noting carefully.

When making bodily movements, the yogi should do so gradually as if he were a weak invalid, gently moving the arms and legs, bending or stretching them, bending down the head and bringing it up. All these movements should be made gently. When rising from the sitting posture, he should do so gradually, noting as 'rising, rising' When straightening up and standing, note as 'standing, standing'. When looking here and there, note as 'looking, seeing'. When walking note the steps, whether they are taken with the right or the left foot. You must be aware of all the successive movements involved, from the raising of the foot to the dropping of it. Note each step taken, whether with the right foot or the left foot. This is the manner of noting when one walks fast.

It will be enough if you note thus, when walking fast and walking some distance. When walking slowly or doing the CANKAMA walk (walking up and down), three movements should be noted in each step: when the foot is raised, when it is pushed forward, and when it is dropped. Begin with noting the raising and dropping movements. One must be properly aware of the raising of the foot. Similarly, when the foot is dropped, one should be properly aware of the 'heavy' falling of the foot.

One must walk, noting 'raising, dropping' with each step. This noting will become easier after about two days. Then go on to noting the three movements as described above, as 'raising, pushing forward, dropping'. In the beginning, it will suffice to note one or two movements only, thus 'right step, left step' when walking fast and 'raising, dropping' when walking slowly. If when walking thus, you want to sit down, note as 'wanting to sit down, wanting to sit down.' When actually sitting down, note (concentratedly) the heavy falling of your body.

When you are seated, note the movements involved in arranging your legs and arms. When there are no such movements, but just a stillness (static rest) of the body, note the rising and falling of the abdomen. While noting thus and if stiffness of your limbs and sensation of heat in any part of your body arise, go on to note them. Then back to 'rising, falling'. While noting thus and if a desire to lie down arises, note it and the movements of your legs and arms as you lie down. The raising of the arm, the moving of it, the resting of the elbow on the floor, the swaying of the body, the stretching of legs, the listing [slant] of the body as one slowly prepares to lie down, all these movements should be noted.

To note as you lie down thus is important. In the course of this movement (that is, lying down), you can gain a distinctive knowledge (that is, MAGGA-ÑĀNA and PHALA-ÑĀNA the knowledge of the path and its fruition). When SAMĀDHI (concentration) and ÑĀNA (insight) are strong, the distinctive knowledge can come at any moment.

It can come in a single 'bend' of the arm or in a single 'stretch' of the arm. Thus it was that the Venerable Ananda became an ARAHANT.

The Ven. Ananda was trying strenuously to attain ARAHANTSHIP overnight on the eve of the first Buddhist Council. He practiced the whole night the form of VIPASSANĀ meditation known as KIYAGATASATI, noting his steps, right and left, raising, pushing forward and dropping of the feet; noting, happening by happening, the mental desire to walk and the physical movement involved in walking. Although this went on till it was nearly dawn, he had not yet succeeded in attaining ARAHANTSHIP. Realizing that he had practiced walking meditation to excess and that, in order to balance SAMĀDHI (concentration) and VIRIYA (effort), he should practice meditation in the lying posture for a while, so he entered his chamber. He sat on the couch and then lay himself down. While doing so and noting 'lying, lying' he attained ARAHANTSHIP in an instant.

The Ven. Ananda was only a SOTAPANNA (that is, a stream winner or one who has attained the first stage on the path to NIBBĀNA) before he thus lay himself down. From SOTAPANNAHOOD, he continued to meditate and reached SAKADAGAMIHOOD (that is, the condition of the once-returner or one who has attained the second stage on the path), ANAGAMIHOOD (that is, the state of the non- returner or one who has attained the third stage on the path) and ARAHANTSHIP (that is, the condition of the noble one who has attained the last stage on the path.) Reaching these three successive stages of the higher path took only a little while. Just think of this example of the Ven. Ananda's attainment of ARAHANTSHIP. Such attainment can come at any moment and need not take long.

That is why the yogi should note with diligence all the time. He should not relax in his noting, thinking "This little lapse should not matter much." All movements involved in lying down and arranging the arms and legs should be carefully and unremittingly noted. If there is no movement, but only stillness (of the body), go back to noting the rising and falling of the abdomen. Even when it is getting late and time for sleep, the yogi should not go to sleep yet, dropping his noting. A really serious and energetic yogi should practice mindfulness as if he were forgoing his sleep altogether. He should go on meditating till he falls asleep. If the meditation is good and has the upper hand, he will not fall asleep. If, on the other hand, drowsiness has the upper hand, he will fall asleep. When he feels sleepy, he should note as 'sleepy, sleepy'; if his eyelids droop, 'drooping'; if they become heavy or leaden, 'heavy'; if the eyes become smarting, 'smarting'. Noting thus, the drowsiness may pass and the eyes become 'clear' again.

The yogi should then note as 'clear, clear' and go on to note the rising and falling of the abdomen. However, perseveringly the yogi may go on meditating, if real drowsiness intervenes, he does fall asleep. It is not difficult to fall asleep; in fact, it is easy. If you meditate in the lying posture, you gradually become drowsy and eventually fall asleep. That is why the beginner in meditation should not meditate too much in the lying posture. He should meditate much more in the sitting and walking postures of the body. But as it grows late and becomes time for sleep, he should meditate in the lying position, noting the rising and falling movements of the abdomen. He will then naturally (automatically) fall asleep.

The time he is asleep is the resting time for the yogi. But for the really serious yogi, he should limit his sleeping time to about four hours. This is the 'midnight time' permitted by the BUDDHA. Four hours sleep is quite enough. If the beginner in meditation thinks that four hours sleep is not enough for health, he may extend it to five or six hours. Six hours sleep is clearly enough for health.

When the yogi awakens, he should at once resume noting. The yogi who is really bent on attaining MAGGA-ÑĀNA and PHALA-ÑĀNA, should rest from meditational effort only when he is asleep. At other times, in his waking moments, he should be noting continually and without rest. That is why, as soon as he awakens, he should note the awakening state of his mind as 'awakening, awakening'. If he cannot yet make himself aware of this, he should begin noting the rising and falling of the abdomen.

If he intends to get up from bed, he should note as 'intending to get up, intending to get up.' He should then go on to note the changing movements he makes as he arranges his arms and legs. When he raises his head and rises, note as 'rising, rising.' When he is seated; note as 'sitting, sitting.' If he makes any changing movements as he arranges his arms and legs, all of these movements should also be noted. If there are no such changes, but only a sitting quietly, he should revert to noting the rising and falling movements of the abdomen.

One should also note when one washes one's face and when one takes a bath. As the movements involved in these acts are rather quick, as many of them should be noted as possible. There are then acts of dressing, of tidying up the bed, of opening and closing the door; all these should also be noted as closely as possible.

When the yogi has his meal and looks at the meal-table, he should note as 'looking, seeing, looking, seeing'. When he extends his arm towards the food, touches it, collects and arranges it, handles it and brings it to the mouth, bends his head and puts the morsel of food into his mouth, drops his arm and raises his head again, all these movements should be duly noted.

(This way of noting is in accordance with the Burmese way of taking a meal. Those who use fork and spoon or chopsticks should note the movements in an appropriate manner.)

When he chews the food, he should note as 'chewing, chewing'. When he comes to know the taste of the food, he should note as 'knowing, knowing'. As he relishes the food and swallows it, as the food goes down his throat, he should note all these happenings. This is how the yogi should note as he takes one morsel after another of his food. As he takes his soup, all the movements involved such as extending of the arm, handling of the spoon and scooping with it and so on, all these should be noted. To note thus at meal-time is rather difficult as there are so many things to observe and note. The beginning yogi is likely to miss several things which he should note, but he should resolve to note all. He cannot of course help it if he overlooks and misses some, but as his SAMĀDHI (concentration) becomes strong, he will be able to note closely all these happenings.

Well, I have mentioned so many things for the yogi to note. But to summarize, there are only a few things to note. When walking fast, note as 'right step', 'left step', and as 'raising, dropping' when walking slowly.

When sitting quietly, just note the rising and falling of the abdomen. Note the same when you are lying, if there is nothing particular to note. While noting thus and if the mind wanders, note the acts of consciousness that arise. Then back to the rising and falling of the abdomen. Note also the sensations of stiffness, pain and ache, and itchiness as they arise. Then back to the rising and falling of the abdomen. Note also, as they arise, the bending and stretching and moving of the limbs, bending and raising of the head, swaying and straightening of the body. Then back to the rising and falling of the abdomen.

As the yogi goes on noting thus, he will be able to note more and more of these happenings. In the beginning, as his mind wanders here and there, the yogi may miss noting many things. But he should not be disheartened. Every beginner in meditation encounters the same difficulty, but as he becomes more practiced, he becomes aware of every act of mind-wandering till eventually the mind does not wander any more. The mind is then riveted on the object of its attention, the act of mindfulness becoming almost simultaneous with the object of its attention, such as the rising and falling of the abdomen. (In other words, the rising of the abdomen becomes concurrent with the act of noting it, and similarly with the falling of the abdomen.)

The physical object of attention and the mental act of noting are occurring as a pair. There is in this occurrence no person or individual involved, only this physical object of attention and the mental act of noting occurring as a pair. The yogi will in time actually and personally experience these occurrences. While noting the rising and falling of the abdomen he will come to distinguish the rising of the abdomen as physical phenomenon and the mental act of noting of it as psychical phenomenon; similarly, with the falling of the abdomen. Thus, the yogi will distinctly come to realize the simultaneous occurrence in pairs of these psycho-physical phenomena.

Thus, with every act of noting, the yogi will come to know for himself clearly that there is only this material quality which is the object of awareness or attention, and the mental quality that makes a note of it. This discriminating knowledge is called NĀMA- RŪPA-PARICCEDA-ÑĀNA, the beginning of the VIPASSANĀ-ÑĀNA. It is important to gain this knowledge correctly. This will be succeeded, as the yogi goes on, by the knowledge that distinguishes between the cause and its effect, which knowledge is called PACCAYAPARIGGAHA-ÑĀNA.

As the yogi goes on noting, he will see for himself that what arises passes away after a short while. Ordinary people assume that both the material and mental phenomena go on lasting throughout life; that is, from youth to adulthood. In fact, that is not so. There is no phenomenon that lasts forever. All phenomena arise and pass away so rapidly that they do not last even for the twinkling of an eye. The yogi will come to know this for himself as he goes on noting. He will then become convinced of the impermanence of all such phenomena. Such conviction is called ANICCANUPASSANA-ÑĀNA.

This knowledge will be succeeded by DUKKHANUPASSANA-ÑĀNA, which realizes that all this impermanency is suffering. The yogi is also likely to encounter all kinds of hardship in his body, which is just an aggregate of sufferings. This is also DUKKHANUPASSANA-ÑĀNA. Next, the yogi will become convinced that all these psycho-physical phenomena are occurring of their own accord, following nobody's will and subject to nobody's control. They constitute no individual or ego entity. This realization is ANATTANUPASSANA-ÑĀNA.

When, as he goes on meditating, the yogi comes to realize firmly that all these phenomena are ANICCA, DUKKHA and ANATTA, he will attain NIBBĀNA. All the former BUDDHAS, ARAHANTS and ARYAS realized NIBBĀNA following this very path. All meditating yogis should recognize that they themselves are now on this SATI-PATTHANA path, in fulfillment of their wish for attainment of MAGGA-ÑĀNA (knowledge of the path), PHALA-ÑĀNA (knowledge of the fruition of the path) and NIBBĀNA-DHAMMA, and following the ripening of their PARAMI (perfection of virtue). They should feel glad at this and at the prospect of experiencing the noble kind of SAMĀDHI (tranquility of mind brought about by concentration) and ÑĀNA (supra-mundane knowledge or wisdom) experienced by the BUDDHAS, ARAHANTS and ARYAS and which they themselves have never experienced before.

It will not be long before they will experience for themselves the

MAGGA-ÑĀNA, PHALA-ÑĀNA and NIBBĀNA-DHAMMA experienced by the BUDDHAS, ARAHANTS and ARYAS. As a matter of fact, these may be experienced in the space of a month or of twenty or fifteen days of their meditational practice. Those whose PARAMI is exceptional may experience these DHAMMAS even within seven days.

The yogi should therefore rest content in the faith that he will attain these DHAMMAS in the time specified above, that he will be freed of SAKKAYA-DITTHI (ego-belief) and VICIKICCHA (doubt or uncertainty) and saved from the danger of rebirth in the nether worlds. He should go on with his meditational practice in this faith. May you all be able to practice meditation well and quickly attain that NIBBĀNA which the BUDDHAS, ARAHANTS and ARYAS have experienced! SADHU (well done)! SADHU! SADHU!

11.
PRACTICAL INSIGHT MEDITATION BASIC PRACTICE

By The Venerable Mahasi Sayadaw

A. Basic Practice Preparatory Stage

If you sincerely desire to develop contemplation and attain insight in your present life, you must give up worldly thoughts and actions during the training. This course of action is for the purification of conduct, the essential preliminary step towards the proper development of contemplation. You must also observe the rules of discipline prescribed for laymen, (or for monks, as the case may be) for they are important in gaining insight. For lay people, these rules comprise the eight precepts which Buddhist devotees observe on Sabbath days (UPOSATHA) and during periods of meditation. 1. An additional rule is not to speak with contempt, in jest, or with malice to or about any of the noble ones who have attained states of sanctity. 2. If you have done so, then personally apologize to him or her or make an apology through your meditation instructor. If in the past you have spoken contemptuously to a noble one who is at present unavailable or deceased, confess this offense to your meditation instructor or introspectively to yourself.

The old masters of Buddhist tradition suggest that you entrust yourself to the Enlightened One, the BUDDHA, during the training period, for you may be alarmed if it happens that your own state of mind produces unwholesome or frightening visions during contemplation.

Also place yourself under the guidance of your meditation instructor, for then he can talk to you frankly about your work in contemplation and give you the guidance he thinks necessary. These are the advantages of placing trust in the Enlightened One, the BUDDHA, and practicing under the guidance of your instructor. The aim of this practice and its greatest benefit is release from greed, hatred and delusion, which are the roots of all evil and suffering. This intensive course in insight training can lead you to such a release. So work ardently with this end in view so that your training will be successfully completed. This kind of training in contemplation, based on the foundations of mindfulness (SATIPATTHANA), had been taken by successive BUDDHAS and noble ones who attained release. You are to be congratulated on having the opportunity to take the same kind of training they had undergone.

It is also important for you to begin your training with a brief contemplation on the 'four protections' which the Enlightened One, the BUDDHA, offers you for reflection. It is helpful for your psychological welfare at this stage to reflect on them. The subjects of the four protective reflections are: the BUDDHA himself, loving-kindness, the loathsome aspects of the body, and death. First, devote yourself to the BUDDHA by sincerely appreciating his nine chief qualities in this way:

Truly, the BUDDHA is holy, fully enlightened, perfect in knowledge and conduct, a well-farer, world-knower, the incomparable leader of men to be tamed, teacher of gods and mankind, the awakened one and the exalted one.

Secondly, reflect upon all sentient beings as the receivers of your loving-kindness and identify yourself with all sentient beings without distinction, thus: "May I be free from enmity, disease and grief. As I am, so also may my parents, preceptors, teachers, intimate and indifferent and inimical beings be free from enmity, disease and grief. May they be released from suffering."

Thirdly, reflect upon the repulsive nature of the body to assist you in diminishing the unwholesome attachment that so many people have for the body. Dwell on some of its impurities, such as stomach, intestines, phlegm, pus, blood. Ponder on these impurities so that the absurd fondness for the body may be eliminated.

The fourth protection for your psychological benefit is to reflect on the phenomenon of ever-approaching death. Buddhist teachings stress that life is uncertain, but death is certain; life is precarious but death is sure. Life has death as its goal. There is birth, disease, suffering, old age, and eventually, death. These are all aspects of the process of existence.

To begin training, take the sitting posture with the legs crossed. You might feel more comfortable if the legs are not inter-locked but evenly placed on the ground, without pressing one against the other. If you find that sitting on the floor interferes with contemplation, then obtain a more comfortable way of sitting. Now proceed with each exercise in contemplation as described.

B. Basic Exercise I

Try to keep your mind (but not your eyes) on the abdomen. You will thereby come to know its rising and falling movements. If these movements are not clear to you in the beginning, then place both hands on the abdomen to feel these rising and falling movements. After a short time, the upward movement of exhalation will become clear. Then make a mental note of rising for the upward movement, falling for the downward movement. Your mental note of each movement must be made while it occurs. From this exercise you learn the actual manner of the upward and downward movements of the abdomen. You are not concerned with the form of the abdomen. What you actually perceive is the bodily sensation of pressure caused by the heaving movement of the abdomen. So do not dwell on the form of the abdomen but proceed with the exercise. For the beginner it is a very effective method of developing the faculties of attention, concentration of mind and insight in contemplation. As practice progresses, the manner of the movements will be clearer. The ability to know each successive occurrence of the mental and physical processes at each of the six sense organs is acquired only when insight contemplation is fully developed. Since you are only a beginner whose attentiveness and power of concentration are still weak, you may find it difficult to keep the mind on each successive rising movement and falling movement as it occurs. In view of this difficulty, you may be inclined to think, "I just don't know how to keep my mind on each of these movements." Then simply remember that this is a learning process. The rising and falling movements of the abdomen are always present and therefore there is no need to look for them. Actually, it is easy for a beginner to keep his or her mind on these two simple movements.

Continue with this exercise in full awareness of the abdomen's rising and falling movements. Never verbally repeat the words, 'rising, falling', and do not think of rising and falling as words. Be aware only of the actual process of the rising and falling movements of the abdomen. Avoid deep or rapid breathing for the purpose of making the abdominal movements more distinct, because this procedure causes fatigue that interferes with the practice. Just be totally aware of the movements of rising and falling as they occur in the course of normal breathing.

C. Basic Exercise II

While occupied with the exercise of observing each of the abdominal movements, other mental activities may occur between the noting of each rising and falling. Thoughts or other mental functions, such as intentions, ideas, imaginings, are likely to occur between each mental note of rising and falling. They cannot be disregarded. A mental note must be made of each as it occurs.

If you imagine something, you must know that you have done so and make a mental note, 'imagining'. If you simply think of something, mentally note, 'thinking'. If you reflect, 'reflecting'. If you intend to do something, 'intending'. When the mind wanders from the object of meditation which is the rising and falling of the abdomen, mentally note, 'wandering'. Should you imagine you are going to a certain place, note 'going'. When you arrive, 'arriving'. When, in your thoughts, you meet a person, note 'meeting'. Should you speak to him or her, 'speaking'. If you imaginarily argue with that person, note 'arguing'. If you envision or imagine a light or color, be sure to note 'seeing'. A mental vision must be noted on each occurrence of its appearance until it passes away. After its disappearance, continue with Basic Exercise I, by being fully aware of each movement of the rising and falling abdomen. Proceed carefully, without slackening. If you intend to swallow saliva while thus engaged, make a mental note 'intending'. While in the act of swallowing, 'swallowing'. If you spit, 'spitting'. Then return to the exercise of noting rising and falling.

Suppose you intend to bend the neck, note 'intending'. In the act of bending, 'bending'. When you intend to straighten the neck, 'intending'. In the act of straightening the neck, 'straightening'. The neck movements of bending and straightening must be done slowly. After mentally making a note of each of these actions, proceed in full awareness with noticing the movements of the rising and falling abdomen.

D. Basic Exercise III

Since you must continue contemplating for a long time while in one position, that of sitting or lying down, (and it is not advised that the meditator should use the lying posture except when it is time to sleep) you are likely to experience an intense feeling of fatigue, stiffness in the body or in the arms and legs. Should this happen, simply keep the knowing mind on that part of the body where such feelings occur and carry on the contemplation, noting 'tired', or 'stiff'. Do this naturally; that is, neither too fast nor too slow. These feelings gradually become fainter and finally cease altogether. Should one of these feelings become more intense until the bodily fatigue or stiffness of joints is unbearable, then change your position. However, do not forget to make a mental note of 'intending', before you proceed to change your position. Each movement must be contemplated in its respective order and in detail.

If you intend to lift the hand or leg, make a mental note, 'intending'. In the act of lifting the hand or leg, 'lifting'. Stretching either the hand or the leg, 'stretching'. When you bend it, 'bending'. When putting it down, 'putting'. Should either the hand or leg touch, 'touching'. Perform all of these actions in a slow and deliberate manner. As soon as you are settled in the new position, continue with the contemplation in another position, keeping to the procedure outlined in this paragraph.

Should an itching sensation be felt in any part of the body, keep the mind on that part and make a mental note, 'itching'. Do this in a regulated manner, neither too fast nor too slow. When the itching sensation disappears in the course of full awareness, continue with the exercise of noticing the rising and falling of the abdomen. Should the itching continue and become too strong and you intend to rub the itchy part, be sure to make a mental note, 'intending'. Slowly lift the hand, simultaneously noting the actions of lifting; and touching, when the hand touches the part that itches. Rub slowly in complete awareness of rubbing. When the itching sensation has disappeared and you intend to discontinue rubbing, be mindful by making the usual mental note of 'intending'. Slowly withdraw the hand, concurrently making a mental note of the action, 'withdrawing'. When the hand rests in its usual place touching the leg, 'touching'. Then again devote your time to observing the abdominal movements.

If there is pain or discomfort, keep the knowing mind on that part of the body where the sensation arises. Make a mental note of the specific sensation as it occurs, such as 'painful', 'aching', 'pressing', 'piercing', 'tired', 'giddy'. It must be stressed that the mental note must not be forced nor delayed but made in a calm and natural manner. The pain may eventually cease or increase. Do not be alarmed if it increases. Firmly continue the contemplation. If you do so, you will find that the pain will almost always cease. But if, after a time, the pain has increased and becomes unbearable, you must ignore the pain and continue with the contemplation of 'rising' and 'falling'.

As you progress in mindfulness you may experience sensations of intense pain: stifling or choking sensations, such as pain from the slash of a knife, the thrust of a sharp-pointed instrument, unpleasant sensations of being pricked by sharp needles, or of small insects crawling over the body. You might experience sensations of itching, biting, intense cold. As soon as you discontinue the contemplation you may also feel that these painful sensations cease. When you resume contemplation, you will have them again as soon as you gain in mindfulness. These painful sensations are not to be considered as something wrong. They are not manifestations of disease but are common factors always present in the body, and are usually obscured when the mind is normally occupied with more conspicuous objects. When the mental faculties become keener you are more aware of these sensations. With the continued development of contemplation, the time will come when you can overcome them and they will cease altogether. If you continue contemplation, firm in purpose, you will not come to any harm. Should you lose courage, become irresolute in contemplation and discontinue for some time, you may encounter these unpleasant sensations again and again as your contemplation proceeds. If you continue with determination, you will most likely overcome these painful sensations and may never again experience them in the course of contemplation.

Should you intend to sway the body, then knowingly note 'intending'. While in the act of swaying, 'swaying'. When contemplating you may occasionally discover the body swaying back and forth. Do not be alarmed; neither be pleased nor wish to continue to sway. The swaying will cease if you keep the knowing mind on the action of swaying and continue to note swaying until the action ceases. If swaying increases in spite of you making a mental note of it, then lean against a wall or post or lie down for a while. Thereafter proceed with contemplation. Follow the same procedure if you find yourself shaking or trembling. When contemplation is developed you may sometimes feel a thrill or chill pass through the back or the entire body. This is a symptom of the feeling of intense interest, enthusiasm or rapture. It occurs naturally in the course of good contemplation. When your mind is fixed in contemplation you may be startled at the slightest sound. This takes place because you feel the effect of sensory impression more intensely while in a state of concentration.

If you are thirsty while contemplating, notice the feeling, 'thirsty'. When you intend to stand, 'intending'. Keep the mind intently on the act of standing up, and mentally note 'standing'. When you look forward after standing up straight, note 'looking, seeing'. Should you intend to walk forward, 'intending'. When you begin to step forward, mentally note each step as 'walking, walking', or 'left, right'. It is important for you to be aware of every moment in each step from the beginning to the end when you walk. Adhere to the same procedure when strolling or when taking walking exercise. Try to make a mental note of each step in two sections as follows: 'lifting, putting, lifting, putting'. When you have obtained sufficient practice in this manner of walking, then try to make a mental note of each step in three sections; 'lifting, pushing, putting'; or 'up, forward, down'.

When you look at the tap or water-pot on arriving at the place where you are to take a drink, be sure to make a mental note, 'looking, seeing'.

When you stop walking, 'stopping'.

When you stretch out the hand, 'stretching'.

When you touch the cup, 'touching'.

When you take the cup, 'taking'.

When dipping the cup into the water, 'dipping'.

When bringing the cup to the lips, 'bringing'.

When the cup touches the lips,' touching'.

When you swallow, 'swallowing'.

When returning the cup, 'returning'.

When withdrawing the hand, 'withdrawing'.

When you bring down the hand, 'bringing'.

When the hand touches the side of the body, 'touching'.

If you intend to turn round, 'intending'.

When you turn round, 'turning'.

When you walk forward, 'walking'.

On arriving at the place where you intend to stop, 'intending'. When you stop, 'stopping'.

If you remain standing for some time continue the contemplation of rising and falling. But if you intend to sit down, note 'intending'. When you go to sit down, 'walking'. On arriving at the place where you will sit, 'arriving'. When you turn to sit, 'turning'. While in the act of sitting down, 'sitting'. Sit down slowly, and keep the mind on the downward movement of the body. You must notice every movement in bringing the hands and legs into position. Then resume the practice of contemplating the abdominal movements.

Should you intend to lie down, note 'intending'. Then proceed with the contemplation of every movement in the course of lying down: 'lifting, stretching, putting, touching, lying'. Then take as the object of contemplation every movement in bringing the hands, legs and body into position. Perform these actions slowly. Thereafter, continue with noting 'rising and falling'. Should pain, fatigue, itching, or any other sensation be felt, be sure to notice each of these sensations. Notice all feelings, thoughts, ideas, considerations, reflections; all movements of hands, legs, arms and body. If there is nothing in particular to note, put the mind on the rising and falling of the abdomen. When sleepy, make a mental note, 'sleepy'. After you have gained sufficient concentration in contemplating you will be able to overcome drowsiness and you will feel refreshed as a result. Take up again the usual contemplation of the basic object. If you are unable to overcome the drowsy feeling, you must continue contemplating drowsiness until you fall asleep.

The state of sleep is the continuity of sub-consciousness. It is similar to the first state of rebirth consciousness and the last state of consciousness at the moment of death. This state of consciousness is feeble, and therefore unable to be aware of an object. When you awake, the continuity of sub-consciousness occurs regularly between moments of seeing, hearing, tasting, smelling, touching, and thinking. Because these occurrences are of brief duration, they are not usually clear, and therefore not noticeable. Continuity of sub-consciousness remains during sleep – a fact which becomes obvious when you wake up; for it is in the state of wakefulness that thoughts and sense objects become distinct.

Contemplation should start at the moment you wake up. Since you are a beginner, it may not be possible yet for you to start contemplating at the very first moment of wakefulness. But you should start with it when you remember that you are to contemplate. For example, if on awakening you reflect on something, you should become aware of the fact and begin your contemplation by a mental note, 'reflecting'. Then proceed with the contemplation of rising and falling. When getting up from the bed, mindfulness should be directed to every detail of the body's activity. Each movement of the hands, legs and rump must be performed in complete awareness. Are you thinking of the time of day when awakening? If so, note 'thinking'. Do you intend to get out of bed? If so, note 'intending'. If you prepare to move the body into position for rising, note 'preparing'. As you slowly rise, 'rising'. Should you remain sitting for any length of time, revert to contemplating the abdominal movements.

Perform the acts of washing the face or taking a bath in due order and in complete awareness of every detailed movement; for instance, looking, seeing, stretching, holding, touching, feeling cold, rubbing. In the acts of dressing, making the bed, opening and closing doors and windows, handling objects, be occupied with every detail of these actions in sequence.

You must attend to the contemplation of every detail in the action of eating:

When you look at the food, 'looking, seeing'.

When you arrange the food, 'arranging'.

When you bring the food to the mouth, 'bringing'.

When you bend the neck forwards, 'bending'. When the food touches the mouth, 'touching'. When placing the food in the mouth, 'placing'. When the mouth closes, 'closing'.

When withdrawing the hand, 'withdrawing'.

Should the hand touch the plate, 'touching'.

When straightening the neck, 'straightening'.

When in the act of chewing, 'chewing'.

When you are aware of the taste, 'knowing'.

When swallowing the food, 'swallowing'.

While swallowing the food, should the food be felt touching the sides of the gullet, 'touching'.

Perform contemplation in this manner each time you take a morsel of food until you finish your meal. In the beginning of the practice there will be many omissions. Never mind. Do not waver in your effort. You will make fewer omissions if you persist in your practice. When you reach an advanced stage of the practice you will also be able to notice more details than those mentioned here.

E. Advancement in Contemplation

After having practiced for a day and a night you may find your contemplation considerably improved. You may be able to prolong the basic exercise of noticing the abdominal movements. At this time, you will notice that there is generally a break between the movements of rising and falling. If you are in the sitting posture, fill in this gap with a mental note of the fact of sitting in this way: 'rising, railing, sitting.' When you make a mental note of sitting, keep your mind on the erect position of the upper body. When you are lying down you should proceed with full awareness as follows: 'rising, falling, lying.' If you find this easy, continue with noticing these three sections. Should you notice that a pause occurs at the end of the rising as well as at the end of the falling movement, then continue in this manner: 'rising, sitting, falling, sitting.' Or when lying down: 'rising, lying, falling, lying'. Suppose you no longer find it easy to make a mental note of three or four objects in the above manner. Then revert to the initial procedure of noting only the two sections; 'rising and falling'.

While engaged in the regular practice of contemplating bodily movements you need not be concerned with objects of 'seeing and hearing.' As long as you are able to keep your mind on the abdominal movements of 'rising and falling' it is assumed that the purpose of noticing the acts and objects of seeing is also served. However, you may intentionally look at an object; then simultaneously make a mental note, two or three times, 'seeing.' Then return to the awareness of the abdominal movements. Suppose some person comes into your view. Make a mental note of 'seeing', two or three times and then resume attention to the rising and falling movements of the abdomen. Did you happen to hear the sound of a voice? Did you listen to it? If so, make a mental note of 'hearing, listening' and revert to 'rising and falling'. But suppose you heard loud noises, such as the barking of dogs, loud talking or shouting. If so, immediately make a mental note two or three times, 'hearing', then return to your basic exercise. If you fail to note and dismiss such distinctive sounds as they occur, you may inadvertently fall into reflections about them, instead of proceeding with intense attention to rising and falling, which may then become less distinct and clear. It is by such weakened attention that mind-defiling passions breed and multiply. If such reflections do occur, make a mental note 'reflecting', two or three times, then again take up the contemplation of 'rising' and 'falling'. Should you forget to make a mental note of body, leg or arm movements, then mentally note 'forgetting' and resume your usual contemplation on abdominal movements. You may feel at times that breathing is slow or that the rising and falling movements are not clearly perceived. When this happens, and you are in the sitting position, simply move the attention to 'sitting, touching'; or if you are lying down, to 'lying, touching'. While contemplating touching, your mind should not be kept on the same part of the body but on different parts successively. There are several places of touch and at least six or seven should be contemplated.

F. Basic Exercise IV

Up to this point you have devoted quite some time to the training course. You might begin to feel lazy thinking that you have made inadequate progress. By no means give up. Simply note the fact 'lazy'. Before you gain sufficient strength in attention, concentration and insight, you may doubt the correctness or usefulness of this method of training. In such a circumstance turn to contemplation of the thought, 'doubtful'. Do you anticipate or wish for good results? If so, make such thoughts the subject of your contemplation; 'anticipating', or 'wishing'. Are you attempting to recall the manner in which the training was conducted up to this point? Yes? Then take up contemplation on 'recollecting'. Are there occasions when you examine the object of contemplation in order to determine whether it is mind or matter? If so, then be aware of 'examining'. Do you regret that there is no improvement in your contemplation? If so, attend to the feeling of 'regret'. Conversely, are you happy that your contemplation is improving? If you are, then contemplate the feeling of 'being happy'. This is the way in which you make a mental note of every item of mental behavior as it occurs, and if there are no intervening thoughts or perceptions to note, you should revert to the contemplation of 'rising and falling'. During a strict course of meditation, the time of practice is from the first moment you wake up until the last moment before you fall asleep. To reiterate, you must be constantly occupied either with the basic exercise or with mindful attention throughout the day and during those night hours when you are not asleep. There must be no relaxation. Upon reaching a certain stage of progress with contemplation you will not feel sleepy in spite of these prolonged hours of practice. On the contrary, you will be able to continue the contemplation day and night.

G. Summary

It has been emphasized during this brief outline of the training that you must contemplate on each mental occurrence, good or bad; on each bodily movement large or small; on every sensation (bodily or mental feeling) pleasant or unpleasant; and so on. If, during the course of training, occasions arise when there is nothing special to contemplate upon, be fully occupied with attention to the rising and falling of the abdomen. When you have to attend to any kind of activity that necessitates walking, then, in complete awareness, each step should be briefly noted as 'walking, walking' or 'left, right'. But when you are taking a walking exercise, contemplate on each step in three sections;' up, forward, down'. The student who thus dedicates himself or herself to the training day and night, will be able in not too long a time, to develop concentration to the initial stage of the fourth degree of insight (knowledge of arising and passing away) TARUNA-UDAYABBAYA-ÑĀNA – On the degrees of insight knowledge see 'The Progress of Insight' by the Venerable Mahasi Sayadaw (published by The Forest Heritage, Kandy, Sri Lanka)} and onward to higher stages of insight meditation. (VIPASSANĀ-BHĀVANĀ).

12.
FIVE BENEFITS OF WALKING MEDITATION

U Pandita Sayadaw

Sayadaw would like to talk about the importance of walking meditation and the five benefits that can be derived from doing walking meditation properly.

The method of doing the walking meditation is usually done in three sections here, although there are one or two yogis who are doing six-section walking. Sayadaw, however, will talk about three-section walking meditation today.

As you all know, the three-section walking consists of a lifting section, a pushing section, and the placing section. In each of these respective sections, there occurs both material and mental phenomena in each of these processes. It is obvious that, in the lifting process, there is first the intention to lift, followed by the various material phenomena occurring in the lifting process. This, of course, conventionally is termed 'lifting', but what is important is to penetrate into this conventional concept and understand the true nature of the intention to lift as well as the lifting process, which actually involves many sensations.

The pair of material and mental phenomena occurring with the lifting process can be experienced, if one makes the diligent effort to be mindful in a very precise and accurate way, following very closely behind the very start of the rising of the lifting process until it ends. This diligent effort can be understood as an appropriate effort in the sense that, if this effort is in excess, one will miss the target. One will overshoot the target. And if effort is lacking, one will not be able to hit the target.

So, this effort should be balanced, should be an appropriate effort, and it can be balanced by making use of accuracy of aim. If one's aim is precise and accurate, then effort can be balanced. So, with this appropriate effort and accurate aim, the mind or the mindfulness will fall right on target, following very closely the whole lifting process, right from the beginning until its end. In that way, one has the opportunity to really understand the path of material and mental phenomena that occur successively.

So, this effort that is balanced by accuracy of aim will help the mindfulness that has been activated to be firmly established on the object of mindfulness. It is only with these three factors — of effort, of accuracy and mindfulness — that concentration will develop. Concentration of course, is the collectiveness of the mind, the one-pointedness of the mind. It is characterized by non-dispersal. The mind is not distracted, is not dispersed elsewhere, but is firmly stuck to its object.

Sayadaw was drawing an analogy between the function or the mechanism of accuracy and the seeing of a line of ants, white ants that are crawling in a single file. From afar, one may think that there is just a static line, white line in the distance. But as one gets nearer, one begins to see that it is not static, it is moving, it is vibrating, or it is 'shimmering' to some extent. Still, it is not clear that it is made up of white ants, crawling in single file. As you go closer, you can see very clearly that it is not actually a line, it is just an illusion. What is happening is that there is one ant, after another ant, after another ant.

In exactly the same way, the factors of effort and accuracy and mindfulness help to bring insight, the faculty of mind, the mental factor called 'insight' nearer the object of observation. The nearer the insight is able to penetrate, or the nearer the insight is able to come toward the object of observation, the clearer its true nature can be seen. The true nature, of course, is in the lifting process. One begins to differentiate not intellectually or by reasoning, but in a very intuitive way, the mental and material phenomena occurring in that process. One begins to see a whole succession of intentions and various physical sensations, and one also can appreciate the conditionality that relates the mind to the matter.

As we get even closer, then the insight will be able to distinguish certain characteristics of these mental and material phenomena: characteristics, for example, of impermanence, of how they come and go, from moment to moment, and that they are separate phenomena, coming and going. There is no one behind it. It is an empty process occurring according to its own laws of cause and effect.

Another example could be that of a movie. As you all know, a movie is only actually an illusion. You are looking and directing your attention onto the screen, and then you see a flash of colors moving and you get the impression that there is something happening there, there are really people there, and so forth. But actually, what is happening is that there is a whole strip of film in the projector moving at a very fast speed.

That produces the illusion of movement, of continuity. If you look closer, if you slow down the speed of the projector, then it becomes very apparent that there is a very quick succession of one frame after another.

This also will become very apparent to the diligent yogi in his or her practice, when mindfulness has been developed to such a high degree of penetrative power, that he or she is able to see a myriad or variety of mental and physical phenomena occurring at a fantastic speed from one moment to another, within a single so-called lifting process.

When one is very mindful, being with each moment in a very penetrative and accurate way, then at that very moment five factors of The Eightfold Path are present. There is, for example, the energy, the effort made to direct your mind, direct your attention to watch the lifting process from the beginning until the end. That of course is 'the right effort'.

Secondly, you have this mindfulness, you are actually trying to direct the mindfulness toward the object of observation. If that mindfulness is able to follow very closely that particular moment, that particular occurrence of physical or mental phenomena, then we have the second factor of the Eightfold Noble Path, 'right mindfulness'.

Thirdly, with the mind firmly established in bare awareness, watching or noting the particular mental or physical phenomena occurring, there is also, as we said earlier, the presence of one-pointedness of mind. With mindfulness firmly established on this particular object, the mind is also one-pointed and free from distraction. That of course is SAMĀDHI, 'right concentration'.

In addition to these three factors of The Eightfold Noble Path, there are two more. Right aim is that quality of mind, which is able to accurately fix the mindfulness on the object of observation. So that accuracy, that precision, is called 'right aim' as one factor.

As one continues with the meditation, right at that moment, with all of these four factors present, and one also comes to know, comes to understand in a very intuitive way the distinction between mind and matter or their interrelationship in terms of cause and effect, all of the characteristics of impermanence. "Impermanence" means a momentary coming to be and disappearing. It is the birth of the new and the death of the old, the rebirth and the death, again and again, from moment to moment. That is one manifestation of impermanence, which can be seen happening from moment to moment, providing our mindfulness is powerful enough and accurate enough. That is 'the right view that comes out of bare awareness'.

To recapitulate, we have these five factors of right effort, right mindfulness, right concentration, right aim, and right view, when we are with the moment, fully with the moment throughout the day.

One of the benefits that can be derived from the practice or the activating of these five factors, of traveling this Eightfold Path, when the mind is with the moment, penetrating with mindfulness into the true nature of what is happening at that particular moment, then that mind, that consciousness is completely free from any sort of defilements. The mind is pure, there is purity of mind, from moment to moment, whenever there is mindfulness, concentration, and so forth.

Secondly, as one is able to make use of that purified consciousness to penetrate into the true nature of what is happening there, we see that there is only this, then one can also be free from the delusion or illusion of self, that in fact there is no one there, only bare phenomena, coming and going. Also, if one is able to comprehend intuitively the mechanism of cause and effect, how the mind and matter are related to one another, then that too will be the cause for one to be free from any wrong misconceptions, any misconceptions about the nature of phenomenon.

If we also are able to comprehend the characteristics of impermanence, see how things arise and pass away from moment to moment, then we will also be free from the illusion of permanence, the illusion of continuity. We can see that everything lasts only for a moment. Out of that understanding of impermanence, of seeing how things come and go from moment to moment, and also understanding the underlying unsatisfactoriness of that process, we will be free from the illusion of satisfaction, from the illusion of happiness, from the illusion that our minds and body are not suffering.

When one comes to know the occurrence of just mind and matter, then one is free from the hallucination of wrong perception that there is self-entity behind what is happening.

If one is also able to understand the true nature of what is happening, one is able to see that in the lifting process there is actually a whole succession of separate intentions and physical sensations, then that understanding too will contribute to freedom from pride or conceit, because there is no one to be conceited, there are only all of these things happening by themselves. Seeing the underlying unsatisfactoriness behind what is happening will free us from the grasp of craving. Seeing that there is no one behind what is happening, will free us from the wrong view of self, and so forth.

These three states of 'mind of conceit', 'craving', and 'wrong view' are also called as a group in Pali, PAPAÑCA, which perhaps can be rendered as 'perpetuating' DHAMMAS: they help to perpetuate one's existence in SAMSARA. So, if one is mindful and is able to develop their insight into what is happening at the particular moment, then these perpetuating DHAMMAS of conceit, craving and of wrong view will be shattered for that particular moment.

Sayadaw's explanation with regard to what happens during the lifting process would be quite sufficient for you to understand the benefits of being mindful during the walking meditation. Sayadaw would like to continue the talk about the 'pushing and placing' process, and if again accurate and penetrative mindfulness is activated, to follow as closely as possible the pushing process right from the beginning through the end, and also the placing process from the beginning to the end, then one will similarly come to understand how mind and matter are quite separate phenomena, and understand also that mind can be the cause and matter the product; or the effect or the intention to push can be the cause for various sensations occurring in the pushing process, as well as the intention to place and the various sensations following the placing process.

This mechanism of cause and effect can also be understood. Taking a further step, one can also penetrate into the characteristics of impermanence, and so forth, as one sees how these intentions and physical sensations of pushing, of pulling, of stretching, of heaviness, and so forth, come and go from moment to moment in the whole series of successive occurrences.

One important practical point to note, however, is that during the walking meditation the placing process begins not when the foot or the ball of the feet touches the ground, but it occurs when the foot is lowered. It occurs from the moment the foot is lowered from the pushing process to the ground.

The BUDDHA himself encouraged the practice of walking meditation and outlined five benefits that can be derived from walking meditation.

The first benefit is that one who does walking meditation will have the strength and energy and stamina to go on long journeys. It must be remembered that, during the time of the BUDDHA, the BHIKKHUS, or monks, were not quite so reliant and they did not have the vehicles to convey them from place to place, and they were also wandering mendicants, so that was a good form of exercise perhaps, and it was important for them to have strength and stamina to help them in their wanderings.

All those yogis who are practicing meditation at the moment can also be considered as BHIKKHUS from the SUTTANTA point of view.

The second benefit is that it will bring about a durable stamina for the practice of meditation. This durable stamina for meditation comes about because, during walking meditation, multiple efforts or double effort is needed. Even if one is not mindful and one is taking a walk outside, one has to put in effort to lift the foot, to push it, to place it. But during walking meditation, in addition to the ordinary effort, the normal effort needed to lift the foot, there is also the mental effort which constitutes right effort, a factor in the Eightfold Noble Path.

We need to have that diligence, that mental effort, in order to activate mindfulness from moment to moment, so that it can stay very firmly with the object of observation. This is very clear to all yogis because in the absence of effort, sloth and torpor easily occurs.

Precisely because double effort is needed in walking meditation, it helps to cultivate a very durable sort of stamina that is needed in this demanding task of meditation. It occurs in every section of the walking, in every part of the walking process. There is effort in lifting the foot. That foot in trying to be mindful, trying to make the mindfulness follow the lifting process, from the beginning to the end, without any gaps in between, and there is effort involved in the pushing motion, in the placing motion, and the corresponding mental energy needed to activate an intuitive, accurate, precise and firm mindfulness.

The third benefit is that too much sitting can be the cause of many ailments. That is the American dilemma. Anyway, too much sitting can be the cause of many ailments and therefore, there is an alternate shift in postures from sitting to walking. It helps to stimulate the body muscles as well as provide the opportunity for good blood circulation.

For the one who has a pretty balanced meditation practice – there is balance in the sitting and in the walking – then it will contribute to good health, which again will contribute to progress in meditation. Since you all know that, for the one in ill health, it is not possible to be mindful in a very effective way.

The fourth benefit is that it will be very helpful for digestion, physical digestion. If one eats food, and the food is not properly digested, then it will create a lot of difficulties and discomfort, and again will be a great hindrance to actual practice. Therefore, if walking meditation is not neglected but carried out in order to balance your posture during meditation, then it will help to ensure that you are kept in good health, your food is being properly digested, and that you will be able to carry on your meditation smoothly.

It is especially important to understand that early in the morning when one gets up from bed, it will be very useful to do some walking meditation, some proper walking meditation, so that one may be able to sit and have the opportunity to develop mindfulness more effectively.

If one sits immediately upon waking up from sleep, then very likely one will be assaulted by states of sloth and torpor, sleepiness and nodding, and so forth. Walking meditation also plays an important part in the period after lunch, after your heavy meal before you sit.

As a fourth benefit of walking meditation, it was shown that it will be helpful for digestion. Therefore, after a meal and before sitting one should take a good walking meditation exercise. That too will help to prevent drowsiness and nodding from occurring in the sitting.

The final benefit of walking meditation is that it will help to reduce or develop a very durable concentration, if one is trying to be mindful in each step of walking, with each section of lifting, pushing, placing. And mindfulness together with the concentration that is trying to observe the lifting, the intention to lift, the lifting process, the intention to push, the pushing process, the intention to place, the placing process, if the mindfulness is continuous, unbroken, so too the concentration.

That concentration is being developed from step to step. Every step that you take is very important, because it builds up the concentration. Towards the end of the walking, if your mind has been so concentrated and be accurately mindful, then it would not have any breaks in between, then by the end of the end of the walking, your concentration will be so great that, in the next sitting, it will be a tremendous help, a tremendous foundation for further development during your sitting.

Besides, it is also possible that, even during walking meditation, provided there is strong mindfulness and concentration, one can even penetrate into very profound aspects of the DHAMMA. One can even get enlightened while walking.

Sayadaw likened the yogi who does not do walking meditation before his or her sitting, to a rundown battery in a car. If an automobile is not used very often, the battery will very naturally become very weak, for as you know, it is only when the engine is used constantly that recharging will occur.

So, for a yogi who neglects walking meditation, it will be very difficult to start their engine, it will be very difficult to start to activate good mindfulness and firm concentration during a sitting. But for a yogi who is diligent in doing both walking meditation before the sitting, as well as after the sitting meditation, it will be quite easy to start the engine. The durable concentration that has been started up during walking meditation is automatically carried to the sitting, and acts as a very, very useful and strong foundation for further development in the sitting meditation.

Today Sayadaw has given you a talk on walking meditation and its benefits, which comes from the SUTTA given by the BUDDHA himself with the hope that all of you will be able to appreciate the importance of walking meditation, and that you will be able to note the points that were given during this discourse, and follow instructions very carefully, be with each moment with penetrative, accurate, precise mindfulness — so that you will be able to penetrate into the true nature of reality, how mind and matter constitute all experiences, how they are interrelated by this mechanism of cause and effect, how they manifest, the characteristics of impermanence, of unsatisfactoriness, of non-selfness — and that you may eventually realize NIBBĀNA here and now.

13.
GUIDANCE FOR THE MEDITATOR DURING THE INTERVIEW SESSION

The practice of SATIPATTHANA VIPASSANĀ BHĀVANĀ, or the development of Insight Meditation practice, is best achieved when cultivated in an uninterrupted manner and under the guidance of a competent meditation teacher. During the course of one's meditation practice, it is necessary to meet with the teacher at regular intervals. These short sessions, known as the interview or reporting session, allow a time for the meditator or retreatant to explain their meditation experiences to the teacher. Such an occasion provides an ongoing opportunity for the yogi or meditator to be properly guided in a manner that facilitates their deepening practice experience and the maturing of their DHAMMA understanding. The basis for the interview session is founded on the firm and sincere wish on behalf of the student to be guided during his or her period of meditation practice. From such openness on the part of the meditator, it allows the teacher the greatest ease in fulfilling the duties of their role.

At times, the teacher will find it necessary for the student's continued meditative development, to correct, admonish, and ask detailed questions, which require precise answers, to encourage or offer praise and so on. The interview period is the most important time for the meditator to be further guided. In order to most effectively allow the teacher to give the yogi the necessary guidance, the interview session has been systematically structured. In order to accommodate such a large number of individuals wishing to undertake a period of intensive

VIPASSANĀ practice, and in order to give the necessary and proper personal guidance and support, a reporting method accompanied by a set of simple guidelines has been developed. It is the meditator's duty to learn the proper reporting method and to present their meditational experiences to the teacher according to the method as best as possible. It is also important to do so in accordance with the guidelines that will be set forth.

VIPASSANĀ meditation practice and teacher guidance, as found within this tradition, might be very unfamiliar to meditators who have come requesting DHAMMA guidance and training. In most cases, unless guided, one might be confused, as to how to properly explain their experiences and, of those experiences, which ones should be explained and in which order and manner. Someone with good intention might simply explain random experiences or give unessential information to the teacher, which would give very little usable information to the teacher in order to accurately guide the yogi. Consequently, proper guidance could only come after much further questioning of the yogi. In order to avoid or minimize the yogi's unnecessary explanation of irrelevant information as well as optimizing the short amount of time available to each meditator for personal interviews, the reporting method should be properly understood. As the yogi develops the ability to give concise, comprehensive and systematic reports, it thus provides an ever-greater opportunity for the teacher to accurately understand the yogi's experience and, therefore, offering more precise support of your practice. When reporting your experiences, use only simple and direct terms that reflect as accurately as possible your actual experience. The interview is a time to be open and frank, explaining just the essential facts step-by-step in a precise, clear, and concise manner. Even though the interview should be kept to just ten minutes, the yogi should try to be relaxed and not feel hurried or nervous. It might be helpful to remember that the VIPASSANĀ retreat situation has been designed for one to personally experience the virtues of the DHAMMA and that the teachings are shared to support one's tasting of these dhamma fruits with loving-kindness and compassion. The interview should be a period where one shares their day-to-day DHAMMA truths with a good DHAMMA friend (KALAYANA MITTA).

13. GUIDANCE FOR THE MEDITATOR DURING THE INTERVIEW SESSION

As posted each meditator has been allocated a ten-minute interview period scheduled to begin at an appointed time. It's important to be both punctual in attending the interview on time and careful not to exceed the allotted time given to each person. When you see the yogi who was scheduled before you leaving the interview room, please immediately make your entrance. Should your interview for some reason begin later than the scheduled time, please simply make a note when it actually begins and figure ten minutes from that time it should end. Reaffirming our commitment to punctuality allows for the least amount of time one's fellow meditators have to wait for their interview.

As one waits for their interview to begin, please continue the practice by doing so in a suitable posture. When you enter the interview room, it's important to do so, as if you were not taking a break from the intensive mindfulness practice. In fact, the entire interview session should be an equal aspect of the day to continue one's careful application of mindfulness. When entering and leaving the room, when sitting down and standing up, when changing one's posture, all movements should be attempted to be noted. The interview session is also a wonderful opportunity to integrate a mindfulness practice, while you speak at the time of explaining your experiences. Sitting and speaking in a relaxed manner is important, but try to be controlled in your bodily movements and not excessively move about while you are speaking. Of course, it's also an important occasion to listen attentively, as this is the time to receive further personal meditative guidance.

Often meditators who are beginning a period of intensive meditation practice, inquire as to proper etiquette during one's interview session with the teacher. (This would also apply to group discussions and during dhamma talks or at any other time you find yourself in a similar situation.) In consideration of one's questions regarding proper etiquette, a brief explanation will be given. It is a sign of respect in greeting members of the SANGHA (the Buddhist monastic order) with hands clasped in front of you around chest high. When you take your seat some distance in front of them, it's also a sign of respect to bow three times in their direction. The three bows are done while seated on the floor and are symbolic in showing honor to the Three Gems, as found within the teachings of the BUDDHA, that is: 1) honoring the BUDDHA, or the fully awakened one, as the initial discoverer of the teachings, 2) honoring the DHAMMA, or the true way of life and reality, and 3) honoring the SANGHA, or the community of Buddhist monastic members. When one bows, however, it is most important to do so slowly and mindfully. After bowing, it's most appropriate to sit with your legs either placed underneath you (as if you were sitting on top of them) or with the legs to one side or the other in a way that the feet are pointed behind you. It is a sign of disrespect to point your feet towards a member of the SANGHA or towards a shrine of the BUDDHA.

When addressing the teacher directly, it is most appropriate to use any of the following words that feel suitable to you. All of the words have basically the same meaning, that of venerable teacher or reverend sir (Venerable Sayadaw, Sayadaw, or Bhante). When speaking directly to or with the teacher, it is also a sign of respect to have your hands clasped in front of you around chest high.

Some people have found it helpful to use a small notebook to occasionally write a few very abbreviated reminders regarding their meditational experiences in order to accurately explain them at the interview session. If you choose to do this, please spend only a few minutes a day with it and stay focused on the practice. Still others have found it unnecessary to do this therefore, it is left as an individual choice.

The next step in the interview session is for the yogi to explain their meditational experiences. In order to convey one's most relevant experiences the following simple step-by-step reporting method should be learned and followed. The reporting method will be explained according to the sequence it should be reported during the actual interview session.

1) The first aspect of practice the yogi should report is to say the total amount of hours you practiced the sitting meditation and the total hours of walking meditation during the previous twenty-four-hour period.

FOR EXAMPLE:

"During the last twenty-four hours I did a total of eight hours of sitting and six hours of walking", or in short, "I did eight hours sitting and six hours walking".

13. GUIDANCE FOR THE MEDITATOR DURING THE INTERVIEW SESSION

2) The next reporting step is to have chosen what you considered to be your one best sitting meditation period and the one best walking meditation period that occurred during that 24-hour period. The word 'best' is used to indicate what was the most interesting to you, or the clearest or perhaps the most unusual or most insightful. If no one sitting and/or walking period stands out in these regards, please choose a sitting period and/or a walking period that most generally characterized your previous twenty-four hours of practice.

3) The next reporting step is to explain your sitting meditation practice. Having chosen one sitting period to explain, it should be presented to the teacher in the following systematic way.

FOR EXAMPLE:

"I would now like to explain my one best sitting meditation period" or "I would now like to explain one of my sitting meditation periods that most generally characterized all of them".

4) Next report how long that sitting period was, and when.

FOR EXAMPLE:

"It was a one hour sitting that took place yesterday from six to seven pm".

5) During one's sitting meditation practice one is generally instructed to focus their mindful attention on the primary object of observation, that of the various sensations that arise in the area of the person's abdomen due to one's breathing in and out. In short this is called 'developing mindfulness on the rising and falling of the abdomen'. The rising and falling of the abdomen is the primary object of meditative attention in the sense that in the absence of any other marked or pronounced object of attention, the yogi should be mindfully observing it. The mind should also revert to it when a secondary object of attention (i.e., thoughts, sounds, various mind states etc.) has been mindfully noticed and passed away. As the yogi inhales the abdomen area begins to rise and expand somewhat rapidly, and goes on rising as one continues to inhale. When the yogi ceases to inhale, the rising movement comes to an end and the falling motion occurs. When mindfully observing the rising and falling movements of the abdomen, the entire process should be experienced and known as best as possible.

6) The scriptural texts urge that this should be made a matter of practice (SABBA KAYA PATISAMVDI). What this statement means is that all of the various physical phenomena manifested as experiential sensations involved in the entire rising and falling movements of the abdomen, (the beginning, middle and end phases of these movements) should be noticed as continuously as possible without a break. The observing or noticing mind should fall on and proceed concurrently with the physical movements of the rising and falling abdomen through its three stages – the beginning, middle and end. To be able to observe the primary object with such precise and ongoing continuity of mindfulness requires, in most cases, time, patience, and a diligent and skillfully applied ongoing effort on behalf of the meditator. Through observing the primary object, one ensures the necessary development of mindfulness, concentration and effort; the factors most responsible in their maturity for the clear seeing of the true nature of life and reality.

When the meditator explains their sitting meditation experiences, it's most important, until instructed otherwise, to explain to the teacher regarding certain aspects of your primary object of attention, in this case the rising and falling movements of the abdomen. There are three aspects to the material or physical nature of the rising and falling of the abdomen. They are classified as:

- Form or shape aspect: This is the form or shape of the abdomen on which the yogi's awareness is attentively focused. The whole of the yogi's body is the form or shape of the body. As the abdomen is part of the body, it is also the form or shape aspect of the physical sensations of the rising and falling abdomen.
- Manner or mode aspect: This is the condition or state of the abdomen at any particular moment. Thus: "Is the abdomen in a flat, inflated or deflated state?" Or in another example: "Is the palm closed into a fist, or is it just an open palm?" As still another example: "Is the body in a sitting, standing, walking or lying posture?"
- Essential character or quality aspect: This is the actual physical sensations or physical elements that manifest themselves during the actual rising and falling of the abdomen. It is this third aspect, or the essential character or quality aspect of the rising and falling

of the abdomen, that the yogi must be able to explain during the reporting session. Therefore, the next step in the reporting session is to relate as precisely as possible what one has come to see, by observing the rising and falling of the abdomen.

7) Explain just the rising motion of the abdomen in the following manner and sequence of presentation. (The falling motion of the abdomen is something you will explain later during the interview). During the one best sitting you've chosen to report on, there would have been many rising and falling motions of the abdomen. When reporting, you must try and confine your reporting to just the clearest period of observation during that sitting. If the sitting was predominately similar throughout the period, explain it as such, but you must be prepared to be detailed and precise without generalization or vagueness.

FOR EXAMPLE: "I sat eight hours and walked six hours. I'll report on a one hour sitting from 6-7 last night. That sitting most characterized my day of sitting practice."

NEXT EXPLAIN: Where did you direct your mindfulness upon sitting down, and say how you mentally labeled that which you began observing.

FOR EXAMPLE: "I sat down and directed my mindfulness to the rising and falling of the abdomen and labeled it 'rising' and 'falling'."

NEXT EXPLAIN: What did you actually observe or 'come to see' when you were attentively mindful of the rising motion. (You'll explain the falling motion later).

FOR EXAMPLE: "I sat down directing the mindfulness to the rising and falling, labeling it as rising and falling. I'll explain just the rising motion first. Generally, in this sitting what I observed as the rising motion was a slow and gradual group of tightening bands of hardness; whereas mid-way through it was a broad area of expanding pressure with a slight sense of heat or warmth to it, until near the end of the motion; and until it came to an end, it appeared as a slow type of pulsation."

ANOTHER EXAMPLE:

"I sat for eight hours and walked for six hours. I'll report a one hour sitting from 5-6 this morning, which was the most interesting sitting since my last reporting session. Upon sitting down, I directed the mindfulness to the rising and falling. I labeled it 'rising' and 'falling'. I'll first explain what I experienced while observing the rising motion. In the beginning of the motion, I observed a short series of abrupt stops and starts in the rising, which were very uneven, a sense of being jagged. All this appeared as sharp and thin experiences of hardness. It was as if there were a number of miniature risings and fallings just in the beginning of this one rising. The mindfulness felt as if it were coming closer and closer to these changing sensation experiences, which turned into tiny particles of pressure, or like vibrating pinhead-size dots of hardness. The mindfulness was very rapid, arising and observing at a level of continuity previously not experienced. It was as if I didn't have to do anything to direct or keep the mindfulness so precise and present. Then for most of the next ten minutes or so, I can't say exactly, I actually lost the idea that I was breathing or meditating or that the abdomen was rising or falling. All I was aware of was these miniscule particles of vibration arising and – nearly instantaneously – bursting like rain drops in a puddle; so many bubbles forming and bursting. But then I emerged as it felt (and I felt) myself sitting, and I knew I was breathing. Generally, thereafter, the rising motion felt coarse and gross throughout, like rough grating areas of tension. The breathing was rapid and shallow. That completes my rising motion. I'll now explain the falling motion."

Further explanation of how to report this aspect of yogi's meditation practice:

This phase of reporting is very important, as you are required to explain as precisely as possible that which you experienced while sitting, the first step being the explanation of what you observed while noting the rising movement of the abdomen. In order to present precise information regarding your experiences requires not only an ongoing careful mindfulness but, in addition, a fair amount of training and practice in learning the correct meditation practice method, the correct reporting method and in developing some skill and ease in areas. It's a process of training that requires time, patience and an ongoing inspired effort to learn, grow, and practice; the fruits of which have the power of gradually transforming one's life and relationships, born from the insights of seeing clearly the true nature of experience. The teacher's role is to try and keep the yogi practicing correctly and with the sufficient amount of mindfulness, concentration, and effort. In order to ensure the fulfillment of both the yogi's and teacher's duties, this reporting method was designed. Thus, by first explaining to the teacher the rising and falling motion of the abdomen or the primary object of the meditator's attention, it provides the teacher very quickly with some of the most essential information regarding the yogi's ability to observe phenomena: with what degree of concentrated focus, with what degree of continuity and concurrence the yogi can observe experience, with what degree of aim and accuracy one observes phenomena, and to what degree one makes the proper or right effort in sustaining the practice.

Without this vital information, which only the yogi can provide, the chances of developing an ever-deepening meditation practice might very well be minimized or jeopardized altogether. Of course, with this information, a competent VIPASSANĀ meditation teacher would be able to guide the sincere student quite easily. Considering all the circumstances within the context of the retreat situation, if the yogi learns the method of practice and the method of reporting and attempts in an ongoing manner to do both of them as skillfully as possible, the yogis' DHAMMA understanding will blossom naturally. The reporting session will provide the teacher with the most vital information about the meditator's practice in the clearest and most concise manner, which in turn provides the teacher with the optimum opportunity to give the yogi the most precise and appropriate instructions — as well provide the necessary opportunity for this procedure to be repeated with as many sincere yogis as possible daily.

Occasionally, in the beginning, certain yogis might ask, "Why it is so important to observe the primary object and to report so thoroughly and precisely one's actual experience of it?" It's said that they feel at such a loss to be able to give such detailed explanations of their experience, or that there are so many other things which are much more interesting and seemingly more relevant than the details of the rising and falling of the abdomen. Such things as: The thoughts that are arising; their different types and the issues they bring up or represent; the various emotions that the yogi has been observing or the different mind states that so pervasively influence one's practice; the various insights that have been occurring; other reflective discoveries, regarding one's behavioral patterns in terms of how they relate, speak and act; breakthroughs in terms of one's conditioning or life's direction. Or other things, such as explaining the continuousness of how much the mind wanders, how much sleepiness there is, how pervasive the pain is in one's knee, back or other part of the body; the degree they judge themselves and their practice; or any of the other wide variety of experiences that so frequently arise at certain stages during one's meditation practice. All these experiences are natural to the practice, as well as events that we can further learn and grow from. The process of self-discovery and mental purification found within the teachings of the BUDDHA is a wide yet carefully articulated path; a path founded on the intention of serving to support one in the uncovering of the veils that shroud one's true seeing of the true nature of life and reality for the purpose of removing all forms of conflict from the heart and mind. It must be stressed, however, that as important as many of one's other experiences are, besides that of the rising and falling, all of these 'other experiences' cannot be brought up during the short interview time allotted for each meditator. Many of them, however, are necessary aspects of one's day to day practice that should be carefully described during one's interview session. These 'other experiences' should also be related to the teacher. Which of these experiences, in what sequence, and regarding the proper manner in which they should be presented, will be explained later. It also might be helpful to understand that, for most meditators embarking on a period of full-time intensive VIPASSANĀ practice, it is important, according to this method, for the yogi to begin their initial sitting meditation development by using a reliable, consistent, and clearly apparent primary object found within one's person to establish thereon their mindfulness development. In this tradition of SATIPATTHANA VIPASSANĀ practice that we are following, in accordance with the instructions given by the late Venerable Mahasi Sayadaw of Burma, the primary object we are using during the sitting meditation is the rising and falling motions of the abdomen.

In the beginning of practice, physical phenomena or physical sensations are generally much clearer and more apparent to the yogi, as to their actual moments of occurrence. Even within the field of physical sensations, some sensations are usually more apparent than others. Still other sensations are both apparent and for the most part consistently present in the yogi's person. In the initial stages of a meditator's practice, the rising and falling sensations of the yogi's abdomen become the area where one directs one's primary focus. Since the breathing process is a consistently occurring process, and the sensations that arise in the area of the abdomen due to this breathing process are generally very obvious, the yogi is instructed to focus their mindfulness as continuously as possible on these two processes; namely, the rising and falling motions of the abdomen. Through the development of a continuity of mindful attention to these changing sensations, the focus of mind gradually develops. Through a clear focus of mind, the changing mental and physical phenomena constantly arising and vanishing at the yogi's six sense doors are seen according to their true nature. In the early stages of practice development, it is often much more difficult for meditators to observe clearly the various types of mental phenomena, as to their actual moment of occurrence. It's usually only after some time that the yogi becomes mindful of the mental phenomena as a prominent object of experience. It's not unusual to have meditators report that it's only after a minute or more do they recognize that they are (and have been) thinking or wandering from this and that object, without mindfulness of having done so; or in other cases, being involved in a particular mind state or emotion for quite a bit of time, before recognizing it as such. On the contrary, most meditators find it much easier and less confusing to use the simple and more apparent physical sensations of the abdomen rising and falling to focus their primary attention on.

Of course, it is essential that when other mental and physical phenomena become more prominent than the sensations being observed in the rising and falling motions, that the yogi notices these secondary experiences as concurrent as possible to their actual arising as possible. This is true in the case of thoughts, mind states, consciousness, or the knowing quality of experience: As an example, when a sound is heard, there is the sound, which is a material phenomenon, and there is the hearing of the sound, which is a mental phenomenon. This 'knowing of the sound' can be known also as 'consciousness', or in this example as 'hearing consciousness'. Feelings also should be observed when they become predominant. (Feelings here are defined as the mental quality or texture of any phenomena as to its pleasant, unpleasant, or neutral taste, so to speak.) Similarly, sounds, sights, tastes, odors – as well as other physical sensations – should be observed when they arise and become more predominant in the body. It is important to mindfully observe all of these mental and physical phenomena as near to their moment of arising as possible. It's also important to be prepared to be able to report to the teacher regarding these secondary objects of meditation, as to what the objects were, and what you actually observed when being mindful of them: (Did they disappear or continue? And if so, did they intensify or become less prominent? Etc.) It's essential in the beginning, however, to first explain one's experiences in terms of what one observed while being mindful of the rising and falling of the abdomen.

As the yogi intently observes the rising and falling movements, it is important for the yogi to try and go beyond just seeing the form and shape of the abdomen or its manner or mode, such as whether the abdomen is inflated, deflated, etc. Rather the meditator should focus on seeing the essential character or quality aspect, such as the various sensations of tension, pressure, vibration and so on. It is on this aspect that the yogi must base and present his or her report to the teacher. These physical qualities such as pressure, tension, vibration and so on are known as SABHAVA LAKKHANA or the specific or particular mark or characteristic of any given physical phenomena, as in the preceding examples as well as all mental phenomena. Physical experience can be categorized primarily into four main groups:

1) PATHAVI DHATU, or the element of extension, such as hardness and softness;

2) TEHO DHATU, or the element of temperature, such as heat and cold;

3) APO DHATU, or the element of cohesion and fluidity; and

4) VAYO DHATU, or the element of motion.

Mental phenomena also have their unique characteristic or particular mark that can be experienced that makes the experience distinguishable from another type of mental or physical experience. The mind state of aversion has its unique experiential flavor, as distinguishable from another mind state, say that of joy, or piti. There are a number of other aspects of both physical and mental phenomena, each with their specific characteristics. Along with SABHAVA LAKKHANA, there are two additional LAKKHANAS or characteristics of mental and physical phenomena.

The second is known as SANKHATA LAKKHANA, or the compounded or conditioned characteristic of phenomena understood through seeing that all conditioned phenomena have three phases:

1) UPPADA, or the arising or beginning of any phenomenon;

2) THITI, or the aspect of duration or continuance or the middle phase of a phenomena; and

3) BHANGA, or the dissolution, breaking up or ending of the phenomena that had arisen.

The third mark or characteristic of all psycho-physical phenomena, is called SAMANNA LAKKHANA, or the general or common characteristic that all such phenomena have common to them, namely: ANICCA LAKKHANA; or the characteristic of change, impermanence and flux; DUKKHA LAKKHANA; or the characteristic of unsatisfactoriness; and ANATTA LAKKHANA, or the characteristic of impersonality, egolessness, or the inherent emptiness of phenomena.

Of these three characteristics, the meditation practice is directed towards realization of the SABHAVA characteristic, or the specific mark of mental and physical phenomena. It is towards this specific quality or particular characteristic inherent in any experiential phenomena that the yogi directs their mindful observation. As the real nature of changing and constantly arising phenomena are accurately observed in a continuous manner at their moment of arising, the yogi will gradually begin to see how these mental and physical phenomena behave, or in other words, the additional characteristics of phenomena will be seen and understood. Observable mental and physical objects will be seen to arise, continue and pass away, indicating their conditioned-ness, or SANKHATA LAKKHANA. As the meditator continues their diligent and skillfully applied mindfulness focusing the attention on those mind-body phenomena that can be experienced – such as the physical elements of heat, hardness, vibration, etc. – and those mental phenomena such as thought, feeling, consciousness and mind states – etc. they will realize or come to insightfully know the common or general characteristics of such phenomena or SAMANNA LAKKHANA: the three characteristics of *Anicca*, or impermanence of conditioned experience; *dukkha*, or the unsatisfying nature of conditioned phenomena; and *anatta*, or the inherent emptiness or egolessness of conditioned phenomena. These other characteristics of conditioned mind body phenomena, besides that of SABHAVA (the specific character or property of a phenomena), will be revealed only when the yogi pays mindfully focused and concurrent attention to the changing objects of his meditation practice. That is, through observing SABHAVA characteristics as continuously as possible, without interruption, the yogis' concentrative and focus power of mind will progressively strengthen. By seeing ever more continuously and clearly the real elements that comprise the mind and body, the true nature and behavioral characteristics of these elements will be wisely comprehended. This type of understanding is called "VIPASSANĀ insight", or "seeing things as they really are". From the wisdom of insight, one can live their life with less clinging and fear, allowing for greater compassion, kindness and clarity, as one moves through the world.

7) To summarize the reporting method as explained up to this point: Please explain your meditation practice to the teacher in the following sequence and manner:

- Report the total hours you practiced the sitting meditation and total hours of walking meditation during the previous 24 hours.
- Report your one best sitting meditation period or the one period that comes the closest to characterizing your overall sitting practice of the previous day.
- Report how long that sitting period was and when it occurred.
- Report where you directed your mindfulness when you sat down and report what mental label you used.
- Report just your experience of the rising motion of the abdomen independent from the falling motion.

When you explain your experience of the rising motion, do so by explaining just the specific characteristics of the rising movement as you observed it during just the clearest period of observation during that sitting.

(Note: This aspect of the reporting session is very important as you are required to explain what your actual experience was while sitting. When describing your experience try to use words that most accurately reflect the bare experience as it was observed. It might prove helpful for the yogi to develop a short list of bare phenomena, description words. Such words as 'hardness', 'softness', 'vibration', 'pulsation', 'pressure', 'tightness', 'tingling', 'density', etc. In addition, it might also be useful to include a group of words that indicate behavioral characteristics of phenomena, such as: 'rippling', 'vanishing', 'solidifying', 'piercing' etc. When describing your experiences try to develop a consistency in using the same words to describe the same type of experiences. This will of course, allow the teacher greater ease in understanding more accurately what your experiences are on a day-to-day basis. Please try to be very careful to keep aside interpretive explanations regarding your practice or experience. Just try as best as possible to describe the rising motion of the abdomen according to the specific characteristics you observed.)

8) The next reporting step is to explain the falling motion of the abdomen:

FOR EXAMPLE:

"I would now like to explain my experience of the falling motion."

NEXT EXPLAIN: What specific characteristics of phenomena did you observe or 'come to see' when you were attentively being mindful of the falling motion of the abdomen?

FOR EXAMPLE:

"Now I'll describe the falling motion. My experience of the falling was one of relaxation, as if that which was previously rigid and tight softened. There was a rippling quality to the bands of soft pressure as they collapsed. The falling sensations do not occur smoothly or evenly, and are always most noticeable towards the end of the motion when it seems to halt with a short series of sharp jagged stops and starts, experienced only as a quivering of stiffness. This completes my report on the falling motion."

(Note: As the yogi continues their meditation practice, they will come to experience a wide and diverse range of experiences regarding that which was observed during the time of attending mindfully to the rising and falling of the abdomen. It's not necessary for the yogi to go looking for certain details or particular experiences within the rising and falling motions. At times the mindfulness and concentration will be strong and focused. At those times observable phenomena will be clearly seen. At other times, this will not be the case and consequently the quality of seeing phenomena will reflect the same.)

The development of mindfulness, concentration, effort and insight, is a process which requires a lot of practice. Throughout this process there will be many ups and downs in one's effort and meditative momentum. This is a natural occurrence in most meditator's practice. The yogi's primary duty is to continue (in the most diligent manner) the continual application of mindfulness towards the predominant object that arises at any of the yogis' six-sense doors. Actually, the objects that the yogi observes during practice are secondary to the fact of always trying to arouse mindfulness, to observe that which is present as near to its moment of arising as possible. By following the proper meditation method, and with the ongoing application of mindfulness, insight will naturally occur and develop. During the interview the yogi's duty is just to explain as clearly, concisely and precisely that which actually was observed during their practice. From this the teacher will guide the yogi accordingly.

A SAMPLE REPORTING TO SUMMARIZE ALL THE STEPS UP TO THIS POINT:

"I sat for nine hours and walked for five hours. The sitting I'll describe was one hour long; it occurred this morning from 8 to 9. When I sat down, I directed the mindfulness to the rising motion and labeled it 'rising'. The 'rising' felt like a large blunt area of very soft pressure, like a slowly stretching sheet of tightness. I felt very little difference in the different rising motions throughout the sittings. Actually, a lot of the time, especially towards the end of the sitting, I could hardly notice any sensations at all in that area. All that appeared was either an image or picture in the mind of the abdomen, and at times one of the whole body sitting on the cushion. That completes the rising motion. I'll now explain the falling motion. When I directed the mindfulness to the falling motion, I would label it as 'falling'. My experience of the falling was almost always of a kind of gripping sensation, somewhat like little particles of pressure collapsing in on themselves. The falling motion was usually very short with an abrupt and rigid ending. This was experienced as 'stiffness' and at times the most predominant sensation was one of heat in that area, which would shift from one area to another very quickly. But this too was often displaced by this reappearing image of the body and abdomen. This completes my report on the falling motion."

The next reporting step — after completing one's explanation of the hours sat, hours walked, where the mindfulness was directed, what mental label was used, what specific characteristics of phenomena were observed in the rising motion and what specific characteristics were observed in the falling motion — is to explain the essential 'other experiences' that occurred during that one sitting being reported on, while engaged in the activity of observing the rising and falling motions of the abdomen.

These 'other experiences' include such mind-body objects as thoughts, imagination, feelings, sounds, images, mind states, such as craving, aversion, rapture, calmness, doubt, worry, restlessness, sleepiness, delight, etc., and other prominent sensations that arose in the body, such as in the case of describing painful sensations that arise during the sitting. These additional 'other experiences' need to be included in the yogi's report to the teacher. They should be included in the following manner.

EXPLANATORY NOTE:
In the beginning of practice, the yogi might encounter some difficulty in being able to observe the rising and falling motions of the abdomen during the sitting meditation, for very long periods of time. It would not be uncommon for the beginning meditator during a one hour sitting to only be able to observe the rising and falling for very short periods: Actually, for only a few seconds at a time before the mindfulness were

to slip off, as it were, and go into a range of additional experiences. For example, if the yogi were able to mindfully observe the rising and falling for approximately 15-25 minutes during a one hour sitting, that would leave 35-45 minutes of the sitting where the mind of the yogi was some place other than observing the rising and falling motions of the abdomen. For the mind to be at some other place besides that of the rising and falling, is not to say that such an experience indicates incorrect practice. It simply indicates that the mindfulness was not on the rising and falling motions. If this particular sitting was characteristic of almost all of the yogi's sitting of that day, that would mean that if the yogi had eight one-hour sittings, that would indicate that the yogi's mindfulness was some other place than with the rising and falling of the abdomen, for approximately 4-6 hours during the sitting meditations of the previous day of practice.

This significant amount of time when 'other experiences' are being encountered is very important to explain to the teacher, in order for understanding of the yogi's day to day practice to be properly and accurately understood. Therefore, it's important for the meditator to report these 'other experiences' in the proper manner and sequence. Remembering that it will be just one sitting period that the yogi will explain, it's very important to include in one's explanation about what the mind was doing during the periods when mindfulness was away from observing the primary object of the rising and falling motions. Generally, the mind would either have been engaged in some form of thought, whether it be simple wandering or disconnected random thoughts, or a more formulated and sequential type of thinking, such as planning, judging, comparing, imagining, fantasizing, reflecting, etc.; a particular mind state, such as joy, calmness, desiring, anger, restlessness, confusion, etc.; or sounds, or other more prominent physical sensations whether painful tension, pressure, heat, numbness, aches, etc. In most cases, it will be a quickly changing array of these different categories of experience, all interspersed with moments of observing the rising and falling motion. Of course, this is just a very basic and comprehensive description of a sitting meditation experience, and meant only to assist in clarifying how to sort out the variety of beginning experiences during meditation practice. The next step would be for the yogi to integrate a description of these 'other experiences' to the teacher in a way that provides a fair amount of clarity as to their actual occurrence during the short period of interview time.

HOW TO REPORT THE OTHER OBJECTS OF MEDITATION THAT OCCUR DURING THE COURSE OF PRACTICE:

1) Thoughts, 2) mind states, 3) feelings as pleasant, unpleasant, or neutral, 4) consciousness as the knowing factor of mind, 5) sounds, odors, sights, and flavors, 6) other predominant physical sensations.

(Note: When the yogi explains their meditative experiences regarding the 'other experiences' they encounter, five points should be explained. Remember that these additional categories of experiences are what occur in between the moments of observing the rising and falling motions. Therefore, it's important to explain these other occurrences in relation to the primary object of rising and falling.)

THE FIVE REPORTING POINTS WHEN EXPLAINING THE 'OTHER EXPERIENCES':

1) What was observed?
When the yogi was engaged in observing the rising and falling motions, and then it was noticed that the mindfulness or the mind went elsewhere, the first thing that should be stated is 'to where the mind went'. In other words, what was the next object the yogi became mindful of? Explain what was observed. For example, "Generally, throughout the sitting, I noticed that when I wasn't with the rising and falling, my mind was (state what you observed…" lost in thought", "focused in the area of my lower back observing the pain arising there", etc.)

2) How did you mentally label that which was observed?
Once mindfulness was reestablished after leaving the rising or falling, or whatever the object was of the next series of mindful moments apart from that of the rising and falling, simply state what label you used regarding the object observed. For example, "During this one period in the sitting, being very mindful of the rising and falling, some workers started hammering outside the meditation hall. The mindfulness left

during a rising motion, and stayed just in the area of the ear. (Point #1: What was observed?). I became mindful of sound. (Point #2: How did you label it?). I labeled it as 'hearing'. The mindfulness then went to 'thought'. I labeled it as 'thinking'..."

3) What were the specific characteristics or the actual experience of that which was observed, and the approximate length of time it was observed?

After having established mindfulness of the object and labeled it, the next step would be to explain just the specific characteristics of what was observed. For example, "I became mindful of sound, labeling it as 'hearing-hearing'. The sound came in very pronounced waves, not one long continuous sound. As mindfulness continued, I noticed tiny particles in the area of the ear. I had no sense of where the sound was coming from, or what was making the sound. The mindfulness became very rapid, having no chance to label any experience. The mindfulness seemed to automatically revert back to the rising and falling motion, at which point there was a very effortless noting of... I think I was with the sound for only a few seconds before the mindfulness came back to the primary object. That completes my report on the falling motion. During this sitting, however, actually somewhat near the end of it, a lot of thought started to arise. I labeled it generally as 'thinking-thinking' but at other times, I was more specific with the label, especially since all the mind was doing was judging, I then labeled thought as 'judging-judging'. The thoughts that arose were nearly continuous; it must have been nearly two minutes before I realized I was involved with thought."

4) Once there was mindfulness established on the object, next explain how that object or series of objects behaved or manifested.

When meditative objects, such as thoughts, sounds, feelings, mind states and physical sensations are mindfully observed, one will come to see these mental and physical phenomena just as they are, according to their particular mark or specific characteristic, enabling each object to be distinguished from that of another. Yet, as stated previously, all mind-body experiences have common or general characteristics that govern them, such as ANICCA LAKKHANA, or constant change,

13. GUIDANCE FOR THE MEDITATOR DURING THE INTERVIEW SESSION

DUKKHA LAKKHANA, or their unsatisfactory nature, and ANATTA LAKKHANA, or the selfless quality of experience. When reporting, however, it's better to use simple everyday language when describing how the observed objects behaved and manifested during your practice — and try not to use such broad scriptural words.

5) Continue reporting your experiences until the experience or series of experiences link back to the primary object.

After point #4 has been explained, it's important to not stop there, but to continue by explaining what you next encountered during the sitting. Continue a series of experience explanations until you return to the primary object of rising and falling. For example, "When the mindfulness left the primary object of the rising and falling, it seemed as if it were sharply pulled by a sudden (Point #1: State the object observed) pain in the right shoulder. I then (Point #2: How did you label it?) labeled it as 'pain-pain'. As mindfulness became more established on the pain (Point #3: State the specific characteristics of the observed and approximate length of time observed); "I noticed very intense piercing type of pressure that lasted for a minute or so." (Point #4: Explain how the specific characteristics behaved.). "As this pressure was observed, it severely intensified and became tighter and denser, a very compact or nearly solid wedge-like area of pressure. The more carefully the pain was observed, the more intense it became. I continued to label it as 'pain-pain', observing only a sense of pressure. Then after that first minute of observing the pain (Point #5: State what the mind did after observing what was described), the entire area of pressure began to quickly break up. (Continue the report by following points 1-5 again.) "As the dense pressure began to breakup, I observed (Point #1: State the object observed) very subtle particles. They felt soft and minute in size." (Point #2: State how you labeled it). "At this point, I couldn't label the mindfulness and the objects were changing too quickly. As the mindfulness continued to alertly notice (Point #3: State the specific characteristics of the observed and approximate length of time observed) these particles of pressure, heat also appeared. I stayed with this for several minutes, observing their ever-changing nature. These particles were intensifying then disappearing, then new ones would arise. Occasionally, they would burst and I could feel at the same time bursts of heat. It all appeared as if I was intently engrossed in observing the myriad of stars shimmering in the night sky." (Having explained point #5, stating the behavior of the observed, it's important not to stop there. What happened next needs to be explained.) You could say, "The bell then rang and I got up from the sitting." You could say, "I then decided to return to the primary object, at which point the abdomen was falling and the mindfulness followed that motion." (Since these 'other experiences' are encounters other than ones with the rising and falling motions, it's important to describe a sequence of experiences from the departure from the primary object until the point of linking it back up with the primary object.) For example, continuing observing the myriad of stars shimmering in the night sky. "As the observation continued, a few thoughts started to arise. Still there was no time to label, as they were very quick thoughts. I don't think I have ever been so interested in something in my whole life. I was fascinated. And here it all started by watching pain; and yet now, as I continued the mindfulness, there was nothing unpleasant about it. In fact, pleasure started to arise quickly. It rippled up my body, like a slow warm wave. I had never before felt so joyful. Thoughts flooded in. All that began to happen was more and more thinking. I didn't want to be mindful of them. I was very pleased with the type of thoughts I was having. In fact, I wanted them to continue, as they were thoughts of wanting to continue practice, and to help establish my parents in the practice, and so on. The joy intensified, and I found myself very satisfied with everything: the practice, with my effort, with the results – until I realized what was happening. I was engulfed with joy, satisfaction and thoughts of how wonderful my meditative results were, and I had neglected to be mindful of these experiences. I at once returned to the 'rising, falling' where the mindful momentum increased quickly. The few thoughts that occasionally arose were noticed almost instantaneously upon their arising, as well as the joy in the mind. I just focused on this mental quality, which at first seemed to intensify it. This lasted for a few minutes, at which point it gradually faded out. I then returned to the rising motion."

After completing one's explanation of the additional mind-body experiences that were encountered during the course of the one period of sitting meditation that was chosen to report, the reporting yogi can state "That completes my sitting meditation report".

Sometimes at this point the teacher might ask the meditating yogi a question or two about their explanation or any other point of interest. If questions arise and some form of dialogue with the teacher ensues, it will be important to answer questions in the same straight-to-the-point manner you gave your initial sitting meditation report. If the yogi has a question about their practice or a need for some instructional clarification, the best way to voice this concern is to wait until the teacher's questions have ended. At that point, ask if this is a suitable time to ask a question about your practice. If the yogi does need to ask a question, it's important that the question be confined to the practice, most notably to that of just your own practice experience, or clarification of the practice method. Other types of questions can wait until the yogi has ended their period of intensive practice, and ask that which is of concern at that time.

SUMMARY OF THE REPORTING METHOD FOR THE SITTING MEDITATION PRACTICE:

1) Report total hours sitting, total hours walking in the previous 24 hrs.
2) Report the one best sitting period, or the one that most generally characterized the overall sitting practice of the previous day.
    Report how long that sitting period was, and when it occurred.
3) Report where you directed your mindfulness when you sat down, and state what mental label was used.
4) Report your experience of the rising motion in terms of the specific characteristics of phenomena observed during primarily the clearest period of observation during that one chosen sitting period.
5) Report your experience of the falling motion in the same manner that the rising motions were explained.
6) Report one's 'other' or 'additional' experiences that occurred when the mindfulness or mind was in some other place than observing the primary object (including such objects, as thoughts, mind states, feelings, consciousness, sounds, odors, sights, flavors, and other

predominant physical sensations, each explained according to their specific characteristics that were observed).

NOTE: When explaining or reporting one's 'other' or 'additional' experiences, there are five points that should be sequentially followed.

7:1) Report what object was observed.

7:2) Report what label you used.

7:3) Report what specific characteristics were observed of the object concerned, and approximately the length of time it was observed.

7:4) Report how the object or series of objects that were observed behaved or manifested.

7:5) Report what happened next by continuing to report your experiences until they link back to the primary object.

7) State that your sitting meditation report has concluded.

8) If there exists a necessary practice-oriented question first, ask if this is an appropriate time to ask it, proceeding accordingly or continuing with the next reporting step.

These nine reporting steps conclude the required method of reporting one's sitting meditation practice. Before explaining the next steps in the reporting sequence, those of reporting your walking meditation experiences, a few sample reports that include all nine reporting steps will be given.

FOR EXAMPLE:

"(Step #1: Total practice hours) "I sat for eight hours and walked six hours". (Step #2: Report one best sitting or sitting that most characterized all sittings) "I would like to explain my sitting practice by describing one sitting that I had that most generally characterized all of my sittings yesterday." (Step #3: Length of sitting and when) "It was a one-hour sitting from nine to ten last night." (Step #4: After sitting down, report where the mindfulness was directed and what mental label was used)." I sat down and directed the mindfulness to the primary object of rising and falling. I labeled the rising motion as 'rising' and the falling motion as 'falling'." (Step #5: Report what specific characteristics of phenomena were observed in just the rising motion during the clearest period of observation). "When I observed the rising most of the time sensations in that area were very vague to me. Generally, when the rising began, I experienced expansion and a hardening type of pressure. Towards the end of the rising the movement became a little uneven. There was a fluttering quality to the tension and pressure." (Step #6: Report the falling motion in the same manner) "This completes my experience of the rising. I'll now explain my experience of the falling motion. When I observed the falling motion, it too was not very distinct. I couldn't follow the motion for very long: Only for a few seconds at a time before the mindfulness would slip off. My experience of the falling, however, was a relaxing or collapsing type of soft pressure. The falling was generally very quick and short. It too at times would not fall all in one continuous motion, but in a quick series of pauses and starts. I experienced this as just very subtle gripping bands of tightness as the falling motion would stop, and a softening of the tightness when the motion would start again. This completes my report on the falling motion." (Step #7: Report 'other' or 'additional' experiences that occurred when the mindfulness was observing something other than the primary object, explaining the series of experiences from the time of departure and up to the point of return to the primary object; explaining experiences according to the five sequential points.) "I would now like to explain some additional experiences that occurred during the sitting. Generally, throughout the hour interspersed with these few second periods of watching the rising and falling motions, I frequently found myself (Point #1: State the object observed) wandering in thought. Actually, thinking was the predominant experience throughout the sitting. Wandering in thought was nearly continuous throughout all the sittings." (Point #2: State how it was mentally labeled) "When I noticed that thinking was occurring, it was labeled as 'thinking-thinking' or 'wandering-wandering'." (Point #3: State what specific characteristics were observed and the approximate length of time observed) "My experience of thinking was like that of being surrounded by a very thick jungle of tangled vines. There was no space between them, overlapping and intertwining, and most of the time very discursive. There was no continuity to them in terms of subject. Just a classic state of wandering mind. These periods of wandering would last at least three or four minutes at a stretch before a moment of mindfulness would arise." (Point #4: State how the object of attention behaved or manifested) "When I would become mindful that I was thinking, there would be a very brief attempt at labeling them; but the thoughts would usually continue. At times they would even intensify and become more pronounced. I would, however, almost instantaneously become re-immersed into the series of thoughts, as if my head went back underneath the surface of a quickly moving river of thought." (Point #5: State what happened next) "Every so often when mindfulness would surface, I would label the thought. Eventually, the thoughts would disappear but only slowly, never quickly. I would then return my attention to the primary object. This pattern reoccurred most of the sitting, except towards the end of the sitting, usually the last ten minutes or so, when…" (If there is more information to report in order to provide the teacher with greater clarity regarding your sitting practice, continue the report, being sure to do so systematically following the five points.) (Point #1: State the object observed) "…a quickly arising sharp pain and accompanying numbness would be felt in the lower leg area of the right foot, primarily in the ankle area." (Point #2: State how it was labeled) "As the mindfulness turned to these sensations, I immediately labeled them as 'pain-pain'. (Point #3: State what specific characteristics were observed and the approximate length of time observed) "What I observed in this area, was very tiny prickly sensations with an aching hard dense spot in the middle of it all. This seemed to be directly on the ankle bone. This lasted for five minutes or so." (Point #4: State how the object of attention behaved or manifested) "As I observed this area of painful sensations, everything intensified very quickly. The numbness increased, as if the lower leg was both being inflated and going to sleep. The particles of vibration felt very sharp and jagged. The pain intensified. I continued to label pain." (Point #5: State what happened next) "Thoughts started to also intensify. I couldn't label them. Everything felt too immediate and tight. I didn't like the pain. I wanted it to go away. I started to become restless and angry. I did manage to note it as restlessness and anger. Even occasionally as the thoughts would feed the aversion and dislike for what was going on, I could note them as just 'thought'. I kept revolving very rapidly through these three experiences of painful sensation, thoughts, and anger. I did the best I could to be mindful of them, as they appeared, but they only seem to intensify. Until at the very end, I started to question why I was sitting with all this pain. I wondered whether I was wasting my time. I noted this as 'doubt-doubt'. It passed immediately. At that point the pain was very intense, so I focused all of my attention solely on the aching sensations of hardness. Within another few seconds, I slowly lifted the leg, noting the intention to move, and then changed the posture, sitting there for a few minutes before beginning a period of walking meditation. This completes my report on the sitting meditation." (Step #9: If there exists a practice-oriented question or a need for instruction clarification, ask first if this is the most suitable time to ask it. If it is, please do so in a very simple and succinct manner.) "I have a question regarding the meditation instructions. Is this a suitable time to ask it? When painful sensations become very intense, when should I leave the primary object and remain just observing the painful area of sensations?"

ANOTHER SAMPLE REPORTING THAT INCLUDES ALL THE REPORTING METHOD INSTRUCTIONS GIVEN UP TO THIS POINT:

"I sat eight and one-half hours and walked five and one-half hours. I'll explain my most interesting sitting, an hour and a half sitting that occurred yesterday afternoon from 3:30 to 5. When I sat down, I directed the mindfulness to the rising and falling motions. I labeled them as 'rising' and 'falling'. I'll first report my experience of the rising motion. During this sitting there was one period of time, for approximately fifteen minutes, when the mindfulness felt riveted to the primary object. As soon as the rising would occur through its duration, until it ended, the mindfulness seemed to effortlessly stay precise and concurrent with these different phases. At this time, the rising motion appeared as very subtle yet distinct bands of taut pressure that inevitably would change into tiny soft particles. They appeared clearly for about ten minutes, then during the last five minutes of this 15-minute period, the rising motion became fainter and fainter, and more and more shallow, until there was just the slightest quivering sensation of ultra-soft pressure.

The mindfulness still remained glued to the object, as if the changing experiences of pressure and the mindfulness of these objects kept arising and disappearing together. I had never so clearly been able to notice how the object and the mindfulness had become a pair-wise occurrence. Even though this only lasted for a few minutes, I realized how empty this process is. There was no one meditating, there was no one who was being mindful. There was just this mental noticing and physical phenomena arising and disappearing. It felt like just a small taste of the egolessness of the process. That ends my explanation of the rising."

"I'll now explain the falling motion. During this same fifteen-minute period where I described the rising motion, I'll explain what I observed of the falling motion. During this period the falling was extremely shallow and subtle, just a very quick dropping pressure. The pressure was very thin, like a feather touching the skin. At times, especially towards the end of the period where there was no experience of a falling motion, I would then try to look more carefully and subtly. Then it would appear again, but just as a flickering vibration. That completes my report on the falling motion. Outside of this period during the sitting the rest of the time passed in a rather uneventful manner. Generally, there were very few thoughts. When they did arise, I often became mindful of them within a few seconds, just a few words would be seen in the mind. There were times when the thought was noticed, just as it peeked its head up into consciousness. Perhaps just the first syllable or so. There was no time to label objects. They appeared and disappeared very quickly, after which the mindfulness would almost always automatically revert back to the primary object. There was one additional period of time during the end of the sitting when pain began to arise in the right knee. At first, I just noticed the pain very quickly. I labeled it as 'pain-pain'. It was a small area of tightness. It felt very dense. It began to break up almost immediately upon noticing it. The area did become very hot though. I labeled it as 'burning-burning'. There was nothing unpleasant about the experience. In a couple of more notings, the tension and heat vanished slowly. I then noticed that a sense of joy and satisfaction arose. I quickly became aware of this, labeling it as 'joy-joy' and as 'contentment-contentment'. It too disappeared within a few notings. I then returned to the primary object and continued sitting for another few minutes, before getting up to do the walking meditation. That completes my sitting meditation report."

9) The next reporting step is to explain your walking meditation practice.

10) The yogi should choose just one walking period to report. It should be the period that was your best walking session, or the one that most generally characterized all of the walking periods. Within this one walking period, please report just the clearest sequence of walking movements that occurred. The walking meditation practice should be reported in the following manner:
   FOR EXAMPLE:
"I'll now report my walking practice."

11) Next, report how long the walking period was that is being reported, and when it occurred.
   FOR EXAMPLE:
"I'll explain a one-hour period of walking that occurred last night from eight to nine."

12) Next, report the type of walking that you did; how many aspects or divisions were made in each step, and how each division was mentally labeled.
   FOR EXAMPLE:
"The sequence of movements I will explain occurred when I only made one noting for each step. I labeled the left step as 'left' and the right step as 'right'. Sometimes I simply labeled the steps as 'stepping' or as 'moving', or as 'walking-walking'."
   OR FOR EXAMPLE:
"The walking movements I'll explain came when I was noting two phases to each step of the leg. When the leg was lifted, I labeled it as 'lifting' and when the leg was being lowered, I used the label 'placing'. Sometimes instead of using the label 'placing', I used 'dropping' and occasionally the label 'lowering'."
   OR FOR EXAMPLE:

"I'll explain a short segment of the walking period that appeared to be the clearest. It was about half way through the hour. I was walking quite slowly noting the three-part walking. When the leg was lifted, I noted 'lifting'; when it was moving forward, I noted it as 'moving'; and when the leg was being lowered, I used the label 'lowering'. There were times when I used the shorter labels of 'up', 'forward' and 'down'."

OR IN SHORT:

"When I walked, the movements were divided into three parts, I labeled them 'lifting', 'moving' and 'placing'."

13) Next report the specific characteristics that were observed sequentially in each of the divisions you divided the walking steps into. If you did one-part walking, report what was observed during the left step or the right step. If two-part walking, report what was observed in the lifting and placing. If three parts, explain each segment concurrently, stating what was observed during the time of lifting the leg, then during the moving forward phase; and conclude by explaining the lowering or dropping movement as to just what was observed.

FOR EXAMPLE:

"I would now like to report my walking meditation. I'll explain a one-hour period that occurred last night from eight to nine. During that period, I broke the walking steps into three parts. During the lifting, I labeled it as 'up', the moving as 'forward', and the placing of the foot and leg as 'down'. During the clearest period of this walking session, when I tried to mindfully observe the lifting movement, I observed an immediate group of rope-like strands of tension and tightness. There was also a distinct area of hardness in the foot. As the leg moved forward, the most evident characteristics were the weight and heaviness. There was also a lot of tightness in the area of the knee. I could feel the tightness in different spots more acutely as the leg slowly moved forward. Towards the end of the forward movement the bands of tightness and the heaviness nearly faded, and it changed into very small 'tingling' vibrations. For a moment, or so I lost a sense of walking or 'leg moving'; there was just these rapidly arising vibrations and the noticing of them. In a very short time, actually as soon as I began to lower the leg, an image of the leg reappeared. As I looked more carefully and tried to walk more slowly, what I noticed was heat and weight. When the foot actually began to touch the floor, the hardness and pressure became more distinct, becoming harder and denser, as the weight was placed more solidly on the foot. That completes my report on the walking meditation."

The walking meditation is an essential aspect of the intensive meditator's daily schedule. Alternating a period of sitting meditation with a period of walking meditation serves to keep in balance some of the necessary mental and physical elements required for the maturing of insight. The walking meditation periods should therefore not be neglected or looked upon as something inferior to the sitting practice. Unlike in the sitting practice, the yogi is only required to observe the primary object as continuously as possible, while including other sense door objects as they arise and become predominant. This is primarily the only effort required of the meditator. During the walking meditation, however, the yogi is required to perform the dual effort of both walking and noticing the steps of the leg that is in motion. For this reason, some yogis find the walking practice a bit more difficult in the beginning than the sitting. As the practice unfolds and deepens, both activities become rich sources of understanding the true nature of the mind-body process. In order to use the walking periods in a manner that conduces to the cultivation of VIPASSANĀ insight, the yogi must try to observe as carefully and as accurately the different steps at the actual time, or concurrently with the actual movement as it occurs. Only then will the true nature of the objects be seen according to their specific characteristics as well as their common behavioral characteristics. When the yogi lifts his foot and leg up and off the ground, there should be the ongoing effort on behalf of the meditator, to observe as concurrently as possible each of the predominant physical sensations as they appear. The yogi should keep attempting to go beyond the sight or vision of the foot and leg, as well as the particular mode of the leg being lifted, and try to focus on seeing the particular physical elements according to their specific marks. During the walking meditation periods, it is not necessary for the yogi to include or note other sense door experiences, such as thoughts, sounds, sights, smells, mind states, or other sensations that occur in other parts of the body. In fact, during the walking, these other classes of experience can be ignored, giving as much energy and attention to just the leg that is in motion. However, should other sense door experiences become continual and extremely predominant, it's best at those times to stop your walking very briefly, making a short mental note of the experience, such as with a very loud sound, stopping briefly making the mental note 'hearing-hearing' – and then resume the walking practice, whether or not the sound disappeared or stopped. Otherwise, the yogi should try and continue the walking period in an uninterrupted manner. As with the lifting movement, so too with the moving of the foot and leg forward, as well as with the dropping or placing. These movements should also be observed as and when they occur. Each segment or division of the walking step, whether it be one-, two- or three- part walking, should be observed from its beginning, through its duration, until its end as continuously, accurately, and mindfully as possible. Always try to focus on the changing array of phenomena, according to their specific or unique quality, such as heat, coolness, lightness, heaviness, pressure, hardness, etc. In the beginning of practice, however, the yogi has a limited ability to be able to observe these changing specific physical characteristics in a very continuous manner. It might appear that, even after several days of very diligent practice, the yogi's mind still wanders considerably while engaged in the walking practice. It's as if the mind wants (and is almost always) somewhere else, besides observing the different movements of the walking steps. As with the sitting, so too in the walking, the yogi needs to exercise a great deal of patience, gentleness, yet determination and perseverance, with practice. As the yogi continues their day-to-day involvement with the intensive practice, the delicate skill of practice adjustments and fine tuning will automatically arise, providing the yogi with an ever-increasing greater resource and capability to wisely comprehend a situation and to skillfully work with it. Each step of the practice can be a rich source of learning and growth, even as one deals with difficulties.

14) The next and final step in the reporting session is to explain to the teacher any additional information about your practice that you feel is essential information to present. Basically, this aspect of the reporting

13. GUIDANCE FOR THE MEDITATOR DURING THE INTERVIEW SESSION

can often be included in one's explanation of the sitting or walking practice. If for some reason, this wasn't done, then at this point in the reporting session you should explain whatever is considered to be important and relevant to the meditator. If the yogi has nothing further to explain after the completion of their walking meditation, then it can be stated that "This completes my reporting". If there is something to explain, provided there is still time available to the yogi, it should be asked "…if there is time to briefly explain an additional experience that happened outside of my sitting and walking practice that I think is important to explain." If there is time, of course, the yogi should speak freely and openly about any aspect of what they are encountering in their practice. The guidance given to a yogi primarily depends on their ability to give precise reports, providing information that is as accurate as possible to the actual experience. The yogi is encouraged to give their report as freely and openly as possible, thus providing the teacher the greatest ease in assisting you with (and through) whatever you might be encountering. It's within this step of the reporting that the yogi should feel comfortable, and supported in coming forward with one's heartfelt concern.

FOR EXAMPLE:

"That completes my walking meditation report. I do have one additional aspect of my practice to explain, is there still time to do this? I feel rather new to this practice, so I don't feel that I have much of a context for understanding what types of things one encounters during practice like we're doing. But for the last several nights, especially the last night, I've been having an amazing number of dreams. I don't usually remember my dreams, but these have been extremely lucid and powerful. It's as if the actual scenario is real and taking place. I don't feel particularly frightened or elated by them, actually. There was a time last night that I felt certain that I was automatically being mindful for short segments of the dream. Is this kind of thing common in practice and is there any type of instruction I should get, to more skillfully integrate these occurrences into the practice?'

ANOTHER EXAMPLE:

"That completes my walking meditation report. I do have one

additional aspect of practice to explain. Is it ok? I'm a little concerned that I haven't been able to sleep for two nights now. Both nights after the last scheduled sitting I go to my room and lie down as if I would be going to sleep. Instead of getting tired, I continue observing the rising and falling, and I become filled with energy and vitality. I lie there for some time, then get up and sit, then lie back down again, thinking I should try to sleep lest I feel tired the whole next day. I still can't sleep, so I have just been continuing a sitting and walking practice. Here it is now 2 and a half days without sleep, and I'm still feeling quite alert. I don't feel worried about it. In fact, it's been extremely interesting, seeing the amount of conditioning I have built in and around sleep, health, and personal needs. Should I try to sleep, or just keep at it until I feel tired enough to sleep? Or should I just carry on, as if nothing special or unusual is happening?"

After the yogi completes their explanation of the walking meditation, thus ending their complete practice report, or if something essential was necessary to further report, and upon the completion of that step of the reporting session, the yogi should end the period and leave the interview room. When leaving the room, it's proper to bow in the direction of the teacher three times, slowly getting up and walking backwards about five or six steps with one's hands clasped in front of them around chest-high, as a sign of respect and gratitude to your teacher. Being as mindful as possible with all of one's movements while leaving the room is most important, continuing to integrate all aspects of the day in the mindfulness practice.

COMPLETE SUMMARY OF THE MEDITATION REPORTING METHOD:

1) Report the total hours of sitting meditation practice and the total hours of walking meditation practice during the previous 24 hours.

2) Decide the one best sitting period or the one session that most generally characterized the overall sitting practice of those 24 hours.

3) As to that one sitting report, report how long the period was and when it occurred.

4) Report where the mindfulness was directed upon sitting down, and state what mental label was used to note the observed process.

5) Report the experience of the first aspect of the primary object. In this instance, the rising motion of the abdomen. Report in terms of the specific characteristics of phenomena observed during primarily the clearest or most insightful period of observation during that one chosen sitting period.

6) Report one's experiences of the second aspect of the primary object. In this instance, the falling motion aspect of the abdomen. Report in the same manner that the rising motions were explained.

7) Report one's 'other', 'additional' or 'secondary' experiences that occurred when the mindfulness or mind was some other place than observing the primary object, such as thoughts, feelings, mind states, consciousness and other physical sensations that arise. Explain these categories of experience, according to five sequential points:
   7:1   Report what object was observed.
   7:2   Report what mental label was used to distinguish the object.
   7:3   Report what specific characteristics were observed of the object concerned and approximately the length of time it was observed.
   7:4   Report how the object or series of objects that were observed behaved or manifested.
   7:5   Report what happened next by continuing to report your experiences until they link back to the primary object.

8) State that your sitting meditation report has been completed.

9) If there exists a necessary practice-oriented question, first ask if this is an appropriate time to ask it and proceed accordingly, or continue with the next reporting step.

10) Report the walking meditation practice. State that you will now explain your walking meditation.

11) Having chosen one walking period that was your best session of the previous day of practice or a walking period that most generally

characterized all of the walking periods. Report just the clearest sequence of walking movements observed during that period. Do so by reporting how long the walking period was that is being reported, and when it occurred.

12) Report the type of walking that you did, according to how many aspects or divisions were made in each walking step, and how each segment was labeled.

13) Report the specific characteristics that were observed sequentially in each of the divisions you divided the walking steps into.

14) Report any additional information about your practice that is felt to be necessary or unusual that occurred outside of a sitting or walking period. If there isn't anything further to present after the walking meditation has been explained, the yogi can state that "This concludes my report for today."

13. GUIDANCE FOR THE MEDITATOR DURING THE INTERVIEW SESSION

THE FOLLOWING IS A PARTIAL LIST OF BARE ATTENTION DESCRIPTION WORDS THAT, WHEN APPROPRIATE, CAN BE INTEGRATED INTO ONE'S REPORTING EXPLANATION:

softness	weight	inactive	
hardness	gravity	dim	sparkling
firmness	pulling	dense	flashes
solid	vibration	accelerated	shallow
hardened	vibrate	rapid	hollow
rocklike	fluttering	rushing	empty
rigid	quivering	lightning-like	muffled
stiff	pulsing	speed up	rhythmic
unmalleable	glowing	little	faded
inflexible	shimmering	tiny	fading
unpliable	glittering	slight	creeping
strong	luminous	meager	step-by-step
powerful	radiant	scant	feather-like
forceful	throbbing	superficial	acute
heavy	reverberating	large	vivid
light	trembling	big	lucid
intense	wobbling	substantial	clear
severe	swaying	trivial	jerky
violent	swinging	trifling	dizzy
harsh	oscillating	microscopic	abruptly
rough	undulating	small	instantly
unpleasant	pulsating	infinitesimal	on-the-spot
pleasant	quaking	minute	automatic
disagreeable	shrilling	immense	effortless
distressing	piercing	very little	spontaneous
flexible	jabbing	bit-by-bit	involuntary
pliant	digging	piece-by-piece	nonvolitional
pliable	thrashing	section	mechanical
malleable	listless	group	automated
weak	sluggishly	segmented	stinging
yielding	rippling	divided	pinching
stretching	waving	pieced	cracking
stretched	pounding	sectioned	twitching
tight	beating	bubble-like	uniform
tense	aching	trembling	distinct
tension	soreness	congested	collected
tautness	smarting	lumped	flowing
unyielding	twinge	swollen	
relaxed	pinching	expanding	moving

slack	stinging	densifying	stationary
loose	sharpness	intensifying	unmoving
limp	racking	heat	still
relaxed	soothing	cool	pass
			budge
loosened	gratifying	cold	proceed
straining	agreeable	turbulent	pronounced
stress	chill	excessive	shifting
tugging	flashing	explosive	fluctuating
traction	collapsing	moderate	cutting
pressure	stabbing	unruffled	angular
pulling	slow	even	curled
elastic	rapid	wave-like	spiraling
rigidity	prolonged	swelling	
stiffness	stretched out	fiery	
tightness	drawn out	serene	
compression	dragging	particles	
compacted	sluggish	miniscule	
puffed	blasted	twisted	
coiled	zigzag	uncertain	drop
looped	graze	unclear	tumbling
entwined	slightly	dazed	skipping
rolled	straight-on	nebulous	crashing
twirled	head-on	detailed	toppling
folded	directly	well-defined	plopping
distant	accurately	acute	shrunken
stark	precisely	pointed	crumpling
grating	wavering	razor-like	suddenly
forked	trembling	stopped	lapse
pinned	soaring	taper off	lodged
raking	zoomed	let up	slackening
breaking up	nicked	decrease	chilled
separating	stroke	diminish	contour
dissolving	thick	loosen	periphery
vanishing	compressed	limp	remote
crumbling	transparent	released	outer
disintegrating	sparse	lax	core
extension	scattered	stiffly	adjacent
cohesive	wide	pulled	instantly
fluid	deep	grabbed	fluttering
fluidity	broad	collapse	quaking
element	packed	inflate	jerking
phenomena	large	balloon-like	trembling
object	thick	slip	shaking

13. GUIDANCE FOR THE MEDITATOR DURING THE INTERVIEW SESSION

streaming	thin	oozed	wiggle
gushing	thread-like	lingered	squirm
flaming	rope-like	open	spasm
swift	pin size	streaked	tremor
fleet	bubble-like	swelling	flurry
accelerating	surfacing	bloated	slippery
dissipated	submerging	dilated	twitching
liquid-like	pronounced	punctured	twisting
watery	clotted	distended	spinning
moist	muffled	expansive	whirling
fuzzy	wooden-like	buoyant	rotating
fluffy	concrete-like	hole-like	revolving
wooly	blurred	porous	pivoting
Airy	extreme	upward	snaking
spot	jellify	downward	arc-like
point	muddled	inverted	yanking
contact	darkened	sideways	distorted
occurrence	caked	ascending	contorted
happening	barren	climbing	swerving
unsettled	bare	sloping	tangled
unfixed	stuffed	inclining	knotted
floating	packed	surging	knot-like
cotton-like	jammed	elevating	wrapping
weightless	murky	ballooning	convoluting
flinched	foggy	enlarging	involuting
swayed	faint	sinking	kink
shuddered	obscure	shrinking	gyrating
recoiled	dim	lessening	unravel
cringed	explicit	abating	unknotted
expanded	vapor-like	plunging	untangled
shrink	barely visible	contracting	unrolling
pressed	brittle	fragile	fiber-like
shortened	crisp	tenderness	toughness
lengthened	fragile	nerve-like	burst
snipped	splinter	electrified	plain
condensed	crushing	raw	flimsy
volume	smashing	exposed	refined
crackle	split	sore spot	gross
popped	fine	sore point	pounding
sputtering	delicate	paralyzed	enlarged
sputtered	smooth	dead spot	compressed
sizzling	velvet-like	blunt	deflated
sweltering	texture	biting	inflated
bulk	bruising	stunned	contracted

spreading	powdery	burning	fibrous
scanning	gritty	scalding	intricate
coarseness	grinding	boiling	splintery
roughness	grating	cramping	gentle
tilting	fray	grinding pain	shift
drooping	friction	gnawing pain	ceased
sag	resistance	inflamed	velocity
engulf	resistant	shooting pain	flurry
slump	thawed	throbbing pain	inflexible
lower	melted	twinge	petrified
wane	fume	piercing pain	recede
rise	gaseous	harsh	conglomeration
bore	fuse	tangible	shivering
drill-like	evaporated	grope	quiver
drilling	dampen	pinching	flickering
shocked	saturate	scratching	meticulous
absorbed	drenched	deadened	jumbled
deteriorated	sprinkling	frozen-like	raised
subsided	watery	flame-like	obscure
lowered	sponge-like	stifling	apparent
gave way	dry	melting	wringing
gouged	parched	blazing	flushes
advanced	gelatinous	glowing	singe
fizzle	sticky	smoldering	freezing
dip	mashed	thawed	solidness
lurching	glutinous	biting	mass
scrambling	paste-like	stone-like	block
alight	foam-like	bendable	vibratory
steep	suds-like	elasticity	spiked
level	bubbling	supple	hair's breadth
crooked	boiling	silky	knife edge
bouncing	freezing	pronounced	razor edge
sprung	fleshy	choking	slender
plunge	pulpy	whisper-like	layered
pulsation	itchy	faint	peel
oscillating	creeping	muffled	slicing
convulse	tickling	flat	vein-like
flap	tingling	amplify	thin strand
reel	delicate	increment	wirelike

13. GUIDANCE FOR THE MEDITATOR DURING THE INTERVIEW SESSION

REPORTING REMINDERS:

1. Be concise, precise, fact by fact.

2. Avoid explaining your practice in terms of a personal evaluation, for example, "Today was a very bad day of practice." "My concentration has been exceptionally good." "Another wasted day." "I can really feel how deep practice is getting now." "My effort has been very poor." etc.

3. Whenever the words, sensations, emotions, mind states, and feelings are used, try to always follow with the very specific type of sensations, emotions, etc. that is being referred to. This will save having to ask the question.

4. Try to relate meditational experience as often as possible in terms of the specific characteristics of the mental and physical phenomena observed.

5. When describing phenomena in terms of their common characteristics, try to avoid using the scriptural words of ANICCA, ANATTA, and DUKKHA. Also try to be much more specific than stating that the phenomena 'changed', was 'empty', or 'suffering'. When explaining the behavior of phenomena, use conventionally specific words that explain how the observed phenomena manifested.

6. Try not to explain that you have "good or bad awareness and concentration" of the rising, falling, or lifting, moving, placing, etc. Rather, state specific sensations observed during rising, falling, or lifting, moving, placing, etc.

7. Try to develop increased skill in giving systematic reports, according to the proper sequence of presentation.

8. When a secondary object called the awareness from the primary object, it's essential to report this category of experience step-by-step, which will avoid having to ask questions due to one of the steps being omitted, or necessary information being left out. In short: "To what object did the awareness go?" "How was it labeled?" "What was

observed in specific detail and for approximately how long?" "What happened to the object after becoming aware of it?" and "What was the next object noticed?" Continue the sequence until the awareness comes back to the primary object.

9. It is important to state what happened to mental phenomena when it was observed, such as all mind states and thoughts (which includes happiness, sadness, fear, rapture, imaginations, visions, plans, anger, worry, restlessness, calmness, etc.) Did it intensify? Decrease? Vanish? etc.

10. Try to develop and practice consistent word use when describing certain experiences during the course of practice. Try to use the same words and phrases to indicate the same type of experience.

11. Try to speak as openly as possible about your practice experience, communicating as honestly as possible just the facts of what occurred.

12. If the yogi has a lot of interesting experiences to relate, please edit first to include the more unusual ones.

13. The meditator's ability to give concise, comprehensive, and systematic reports provides the opportunity for the teacher to give more precise and effective instructions and guidance. It also prevents fellow yogis from having to wait long periods for their interview, as well as provides the yogi with a more optimal usage of their allocated interview time.

14. When asking and answering questions, please be very short-and-to-the-point, making sure that the question was asked or answered clearly.

15. At times the yogi might be asked to explain the degree of concurrence between the object and the noticing mind, and to what degree you are able to notice the movement of the abdomen through its successive phases. Please try and avoid such answers as "That's a difficult question" or "I really can't say, it's always changing or different", etc.

16. At times the question may be asked, "How long can you mindfully

observe the rising and falling of the abdomen, before the mind is pulled off to other objects for more than a few seconds?" Or in other words, "How long can the primary object be observed without interruption?"

WORKING WITH THE ASSISTANCE OF A TRANSLATOR:
Most people have had very little, if any, personal experience in working with or through a translator. Perhaps a few clarifying notes and several suggestions might make the DHAMMA talks, discussions and interview sessions a more fruitful experience for the yogi.

1) It's useful at times to remind oneself of the dependency one is faced with in having to rely completely on the services of a translator in order to gain guidance and instruction from the teacher. Without the translator the teacher would be inaccessible. This first reflection on behalf of the yogi can serve to deepen their gratitude and loving-kindness to that person who is voluntarily offering their services out of compassion for the yogi and the ongoing availability of the teachings of the BUDDHA.

2) Indeed, the entire retreat situation is nearly entirely dependent on the translator. It is not an easy task, especially translating very precise information and subtle and profound dhamma concepts. It requires very careful listening skills as well as very precise speaking skills, in order to convey the student's experiences to the teacher and the teacher's instructions to the student. Understanding the complexity of the translator's role often motivates the yogi even more to follow the prescribed reporting and practice methods in a more careful manner, thus making the translator's work that much easier, which results in greater communication, clarity and consequently more precise guidance from the teacher.

3) Often unknowingly, due to one's inexperience in working through a translator, it's easy to bring to the situation a set of communication qualifications and expectations that are considered to be a basic acceptable level or standard of relating. As one finds oneself faced with the dependency and handicap of a translator, it's easy to make comparisons and judgments to one's every day or previous teacher's quality of communication. Of course, in most instances the

communication quality will not be the same. With all parties very aware of the situation, it allows for the optimum amount of mutual cooperation to improve the communication quality as quickly as possible. One way of deepening one's working relationship with the teacher and translator is to periodically ask the translator for a few points on your way or style of reporting that could be sources of improvement, in order to make the translation work more easily and allow for greater clarity of practice experiences.

4) When speaking, try to have very well- and carefully- formulated sentences. Use simple and precise words. Remember to edit your sentences as much as possible, without jeopardizing the essential or essence material. Omit as much irrelevant material as can be recognized. What one does communicate, try and do so concisely and systematically. Try to speak at a medium pace, not too fast, nor excessively slowly. In this way, it also allows the teacher greater direct access to what is being said first -hand. The teacher is in the process of learning English, and by speaking in this manner, one can actively support that undertaking.

5) Try to be thorough in your reporting, so that obvious omissions on the yogi's part are kept to a minimum. This results in less questioning on behalf of the teacher and translator in order to get the necessary meditational facts, and get a sufficiently clear understanding of the yogi's present meditation experience. On the other hand, over-reporting, especially of unessential information, creates the need for a similar type of questioning. Please remember that if the yogi takes the editing responsibility, it removes the added task from the translator.

6) When the yogi is asked questions, it's important to give very concise answers. Answering a question with as few words as possible will often allow for a much broader and dynamic interview session or dialogue with the teacher.

Undertaking a period of SATIPATTHANA VIPASSANĀ meditation practice, is a very rare and precious opportunity to come across in life. Equally true is for one to engage the kind services of a good DHAMMA friend or suitable meditation teacher to guide and instruct one during their period of VIPASSANĀ practice development. For the individual to have the time, interest and health, along with the necessary components of a conducive retreat environment and the guidance of a competent teacher, brings together a situation of great uniqueness, specialness and potential. An opportunity presents itself where the timeless DHAMMA truths can be personally realized and understood, a chance to develop the richness of insight that changes patterns of being that allow for increased peace, kindness, and clarity in one's life and relationships. One also steps into the arena of dealing straight on with the inevitable pains, expectations, fears, and struggles of facing so directly the timeless conditioned mental and physical complexities born from desire, aversion, and delusion. As one develops ever greater skill and courage in dealing with and overcoming such energies as they arise, brings a fearlessness and spiritual stamina to the heart of the yogi that supports strength, understanding, and balance in the face of dealing with the inevitable vicissitudes of life. The teachings of the BUDDHA are aimed at the highest form of freedom and liberation, the complete removal of DUKKHA caused by LOBHA, DOSA, and MOHA. The BUDDHA prescribed the Noble Eightfold Path as the means to fully accomplish the task of overcoming the *kilesas* or mental defilements. The eight constituents of this path — right view, right aim, right speech, right action, right livelihood, right effort, right mindfulness, and right concentration — are all simultaneously cultivated very actively through the intensive development of the SATIPATTHANA VIPASSANĀ meditation practice, or developing insight on the four foundations of mindfulness. It is this very practice of SATIPATTHANA VIPASSANĀ meditation that the BUDDHA proclaimed throughout his forty-five years of DHAMMA teaching after his great enlightenment, and up until his final passing away, that was the way for the purification of the minds of beings: for overcoming sorrow and lamentation, for the complete destruction of pain and distress, for the attainment of the noble path consciousness and for the realization of NIBBĀNA. Namely, the steadfast practice of mindfulness. Thus, the retreat is designed to optimize the uninterrupted cultivation and ongoing guidance of the mindfulness practice for the purpose of further supporting one in their endeavor to understand the true nature of the mind-body process, and the overcoming of the kilesas. All that comes along and develops during this process of DHAMMA growth up until our final and complete enlightenment, can be likened to the flowers on the tree of wisdom. As each new flower blossoms, the fragrance is shared naturally and openly. In the same manner, as the yogi's wisdom opens, it naturally and effortlessly manifests itself in one's thoughts, words, and actions. From the wisdom of insight, one can actively work for the welfare of other beings.

It is hoped that this paper supportively serves the meditator embarking on a period of VIPASSANĀ practice to better understand the practice method, as well as the reporting guidelines that they will be following during their retreat. It will be found that what has been presented is not definitive, complete or precisely accurate to all meditators who undertake a period of practice. The reporting and practice methods explained within are primarily intended to assist the individual who is relatively new to VIPASSANĀ meditation practice as taught and practiced in the tradition of the BUDDHA teaching, as principally explained by the late Ven. Mahasi Sayadaw and Ven. Sayadaw U Pandita. As the practice deepens and unfolds for each person, so too will the instructions and ongoing guidance reflect those persons' individual needs. So too with the reporting method and format: as practice develops, it's very likely that the interview session format alters considerably.

The reporting session during intensive practice is a very important and special time. It becomes a safe and supportive environment, to share the details of your meditative discoveries. It also becomes a place of valuable learning, challenge, growth, and inspiration. Ultimately, no matter how skilled or poorly one reports their meditative experiences, it is quite secondary to the actual application of the VIPASSANĀ practice. The most important component is for the meditator to keep in their heart the ongoing inspiration and energy to (as uninterruptedly as possible) be mindfully aware of whatever arises. From that all else will naturally unfold.

13. GUIDANCE FOR THE MEDITATOR DURING THE INTERVIEW SESSION

> May all beings live happily and peacefully, cultivating the
> path of mental purification, leading ever
> onward towards the overcoming
> of all suffering

Mahasi Thathana Yeiktha
16 Thathana Yeiktha Road
Rangoon, Burma

March 25, 1986

Alan Clements

14.
THE PROGRESS OF INSIGHT THROUGH THE STAGES OF PURIFICATION

Contents:

A. Purification of conduct (SĪLA- VISUDDHI)

B. Purification of mind (CITTA- VISUDDHI)

C. Purification of view (DITTHI- VISUDDHI)
   1. Analytical- knowledge of mind and body ~ (NĀMA- RŪPA- PARICCHEDA- ÑĀNA)

D. Purification by overcoming doubt ~ (KANKHĀ-VITARANA- VISUDDHI)
   2. Knowledge by discerning conditionality ~ (PACCAYA- PARIGGAHA- ÑĀNA)
   3. Knowledge by comprehension ~ (SAMMASANAÑĀNA)
   4. Knowledge of arising and passing away ~ (UDAYABBAYA- ÑĀNA) in its weak stage involving the ten corruptions of insight ~ (VIPASSANUPAKKILESA)

E. Purification by knowledge and vision of what is path and not path ~ (MAGGĀMAGGA- ÑĀNADASSANA- VISUDDHI)

F. Purification by knowledge and vision of the course of practice ~ (PATIPADĀ- ÑĀNADASSANA- VISUDDHI)
   Including ~ the final stage of arising and passing away.
   5. Knowledge of dissolution ~ (BHANGA- ÑĀNA)

6. Knowledge of fearfulness ~ (BHAYA- ÑANA)
7. Knowledge of misery ~ (ĀDĪNAVA- ÑANA)
8. Knowledge of disgust ~ (NIBBIDĀ- ÑANA)
9. Knowledge of desire for deliverance ~ (MUÑCITU-KAMYATĀ-ÑANA)
10. Knowledge of re-observation ~ (PATISANKHĀ- ÑANA)
11. Knowledge of equanimity about formations ~ (SANKHĀRUPEKKHĀ- ÑANA)
12. Insight leading to emergence ~ (VUTTHĀNAGĀMINĪ or ANULOMA-ÑANA)
13. Knowledge of adaptation ~ (ANULOMA- ÑANA ~ explained separately from ÑANA #12)
14. Maturity knowledge ~ (GOTRABHŪ- ÑANA)

G. Purification by knowledge and vision ~ (ÑANADASSANA-VISUDDHI)
15. Path knowledge ~ (MAGGA- ÑANA)
16. Fruition knowledge ~ (PHALA- ÑANA)
17. Knowledge of reviewing ~ (PACCAVEKKHANĀ – ÑANA)

~ The stages of purification ~

A. Purification of Conduct (SĪLA – VISUDDHI)

~ Purification of conduct in the case of laymen and laywomen is the acceptance of the five – eight – or ten precepts ~ and the proper guarding, protecting and observance of them. This will be enough to invest laypersons with SĪLA- VISUDDHI.

~ Purification of conduct for BHIKKHUS is the well-kept purity of the four-fold conduct incumbent upon monks

1. ~ PATIMOKKHA SAMVARA- SĪLA (restraint according to the disciplinary rules for the monks)
2. ~ INDRIYA SAMVARA- SĪLA (morality consisting in sense control)
3. ~ ĀJIVAPARISUDDHI – SĪLA (morality consisting in purity of livelihood)

4. ~ PACCAYA SANNISSITA- SĪLA (morality consisting in the wise use of the monks' requisites)
5. ~ Of the four-fold conduct the restraint according to the PĀTIMOKKHA rules is of most importance, and essentially speaking, it would be necessary for monks to observe this to acquire SĪLA-VISUDDHI. ~ Only when restraint is pure will one be able to accomplish the development of meditation.

(Manual of Insight- Mahasi Sayadaw, Ch.1, pp. 37- 45)

Moral purification is eventually necessary in order to attain the insight knowledge and path knowledge and fruition knowledge. The PATISAMBHIDĀMAGGA gives the following teaching on this subject:

Morality is the abandonment of ignorance through knowledge, and the abandonment of the perception of permanence through contemplation of impermanence; abstinence is morality; volition is morality; restraint is morality; and non-transgression is morality.

All of these kinds of morality lead to a clear conscience, delight (PĀMOJJA), joy (PĪTI), tranquility, and happiness. They all lead to disenchantment, non-attachment, cessation, peacefulness, realization, enlightenment, and NIBBĀNA.

Restraint is the training in higher morality; tranquility is the training in higher mind; seeing is the training in higher wisdom.

1. Morality by Means of Abandonment

Knowledge that discerns mental and physical phenomena (NĀMA- RŪPA- PARICCHEDA- ÑĀNA) abandons the delusion of a 'person' or 'being'.

Knowledge that discerns conditionality abandons the delusion that living beings appear without any cause, or that they are all created by God, Brahma, or other divine authorities. Understanding impermanence abandons the delusion that anything in the mind or body is permanent.

'To abandon' in this context, means 'to leave no place in the mind for those delusions' — just as light leaves no place for darkness within it. As a result, wholesomeness arises instead of delusion. The abandonment of the mental defilements through insight meditation is therefore considered morality, since it is a foundation or basis (UPADHĀRANA) for wholesomeness, and makes that wholesomeness firm and steadfast (SAMĀDHĀNA). This is also true for the following types of meditative morality.

2. Morality by Means of Abstinence

The commentaries and sub-commentaries unanimously state that the mind that arises during insight meditation (VIPASSANĀCITTUPPĀDA) does not include the mental factor of abstinence from evil (VIRATI). On the other hand, the mind that arises during insight meditation is directly opposed to evil behavior and wrong livelihood. It brings about abstinence or morality by temporarily removing evil behavior and wrong livelihood (TADANGA-PPHĀNA), in the same way that path knowledge brings about abstinence from all evil behavior (MAGGAVIRATI) by completely removing evil behavior and wrong livelihood (SAMUCCHEDAPAHĀNA), although path knowledge takes *Nibbāna* as its object.

When insight knowledges arise, such as discerning mental and physical phenomena, they leave no place in the mind for the defilement of attachment to a person or a being, to non-causality, or to the notion of permanence, satisfactoriness, and self. At such times the mental defilements that lie dormant have no chance to become active in the mind. When they are not active in the mind, there are no thoughts about a person or a being, and thus no obsessive defilements arise. And when thoughts that assume that there are persons or beings do not arise, immoral behaviors such as killing, stealing, and so on do not arise either. Since none of the defilements — whether dormant, obsessive, or transgressive — can arise, one abstains from those defilements while experiencing any of the insight knowledges, beginning with knowledge that discerns mental and physical phenomena. This is why it is called 'morality by means of abstinence'.

3. Morality by Means of Mental Volition

Mental volition often stimulates ordinary people who have no restraint to commit evil deeds. For an insight meditator, mental volition stimulates effective awareness of meditative objects. All of one's noting involves mental volition. This mental volition is weak and mostly not obvious when one's faith, will (CHANDA), and energy are weak. Mental volition becomes obvious, however, when one's faith, will, and energy are strong. So mental volition is considered morality for an insight meditator, because it is a foundation or basis for wholesomeness, and makes that wholesomeness firm and steadfast.

4. Morality by Means of Restraint

The five kinds of restraint mentioned above are called 'morality by means of restraint'. They are included in an insight meditator's state of mind with every noting, and they thereby block and restrain the arising of immorality, mindlessness, ignorance, impatience, and idleness. This restraint protects one from self-indulgence. In an ultimate sense, morality by means of restraint includes only mindfulness, insight, forbearance, and effort.

5. Morality by Means of Non-Transgression

The noting mind, governed by mindfulness, leads to non-transgression, since it leaves no room for delusion and other defilements to arise. Volitional killing, for example, is a transgression, while refraining from killing is a non-transgression. In the same way, mindlessness is a transgression since it allows every kind of mental defilement, whether dormant, obsessive, or transgressive, to arise. The noting mind governed by mindfulness, on the other hand, is non-transgressive since it leaves no room for any defilement, whether dormant, obsessive, or transgressive. Thus the noting mind governed by mindfulness is morality by means of non-transgression.

Among these five kinds of morality, we can only directly experience morality by means of mental volition and morality by means of restraint. Morality by means of abandoning defilements is simply an absence of defilements. According to the VISUDDHIMAGGA, morality by means of abstinence and morality by means of non- transgression are both equivalent to the mind that arises during insight meditation. Although these two are the same in an ultimate sense, 'morality by means of abstinence' refers to abstaining from defilements, while 'morality by means of non-transgression' refers to avoiding transgression by not allowing defilements to arise.

6. Morality as Remote and Immediate Conditions for Concentration and Knowledges

Laypersons can use insight meditation to fully purify the four kinds of morality, regardless of whether or not they have practiced morality for a long time beforehand. We may wonder, however, what kind of morality they must develop as a basis for their concentration and insight knowledge, given that BUDDHA has said on many occasions: "A man established on morality, wise, develops the mind and wisdom…"

The answer is that all meditators should develop concentration and insight knowledge based on two kinds of morality: morality that has been purified before meditation (PUBBABHĀGASĪLA) and morality that is purified during meditation (SAHAJĀTASĪLA). Morality that has already been observed for some time before taking up meditation practice serves as a remote condition or prior cause (PAKUTŪPANISSAYA) for the arising of insight concentration and insight wisdom, as well as for path concentration and path wisdom. The morality that accompanied prior insight knowledges and path knowledge and fruition knowledge also serves as the remote condition for later insight concentration and insight wisdom, as well as for path concentration and path wisdom. The pure morality that accompanies each and every moment of insight knowledge and path knowledge is the immediate condition or present cause (SAHAJĀTANISSAYA) for the concentration and wisdom involved in that very moment of consciousness.

If a person has purified his or her morality before taking up meditation, then his or her concentration and wisdom are based on both remote and immediate moral conditions. If, on the other hand, a person purifies his or her morality only through insight meditation, then his or her initial concentration and wisdom are based only on the immediate moral condition, while his or her succeeding insight concentration and insight wisdom, as well as path concentration and path wisdom, are based on both remote and immediate moral conditions.

7. The Practice of Morality is Essential

The purpose in explaining that the practice of meditation alone can purify morality is not to downplay the importance of practicing morality, but to overcome the mistaken notion that meditation should only be taken up after morality has been fulfilled for a long time, and to refute the idea that morality as an immediate condition is not an adequate foundation for meditation. Such notions may prevent you from beginning meditation sooner rather than later. They may also lead you to deprecate those who properly practice meditation.

In fact, morality should be regarded with the greatest honor and respect. Perhaps ninety-nine percent of the time, lower rebirth is the result of moral violations. More than half of those who enjoy human or celestial births may only be able to do so because they have practiced pure morality. Most of those who obtain path and fruition have probably purified their morality in advance.

So, you should protect your morality with great care, just as you would protect your very life. You should not be negligent about your behavior, thinking that you can correct it later. You might die at any time and be immediately reborn in the lower worlds if your morality is deficient. Morality is especially important for those who are practicing meditation. They should even honor and respect it more than their lives, and keep it fully purified.

Therefore, if you wish to practice meditation, you should observe in advance the five precepts or the eight precepts topped with right livelihood in order to strengthen the development of concentration and insight knowledge, even if your morality is already generally pure. If you plan to participate in an intensive meditation retreat, leaving all worldly responsibilities behind, you should observe the eight or ten precepts.

If you purposely and properly purify morality, then you will have a clear conscience every time you reflect about morality during your meditation practice. You will experience joy and delight, tranquility, happiness, and peace. By observing the physical and mental processes every time they arise, you will see things as they really are, and gain further insight knowledge.

B. Purification of Mind (CITTA – VISUDDHI)

~ If a person possessed of SĪLA-VISUDDHI were to engage continuously in SAMATHA elsewhere (tranquility meditation) such as ĀNĀPĀNA-SATI, his mind would not wander elsewhere but would just settle on the object of attention – and he would gain CITTA-VISUDDHI through arising of UPACĀRA- SAMĀDHI and APPANĀ- SAMĀDHI. Purity of mind means freedom through SAMĀDHI from such hindrances (NIVARANAS) as attention to (or concern with) sensuous objects (all 5 hindrances vanish). When the mind is in such a state of purity ~ through the continuous noting of the tranquil CITTA and accompanying mental factors or any other mind-body phenomena which become evident ~ AND WITH THE PROGRESS OF INSIGHT ~ NIBBĀNA can be realized through MAGGA and PHALA- ÑĀNA. This is how NIBBĀNA is attained through VIPASSANĀ meditation based on SAMATHA- concentration. (This type of yogi is known as a SAMATHA- YĀNIKA).

~ The yogi who practices VIPASSANĀ or insight meditation only from the very onset, without engaging in the SAMATHA concentration ~ is called SUDDHA – VIPASSANĀ – YĀNIKA. Such a yogi practices in this way: ~ The one who is possessed of SĪLA-VISUDDHI continually notes whatever becomes evident through the six-sense doors, such as seeing, hearing, thinking, etc. In the beginning of the practice however it will not be possible to note each and every act of seeing, hearing. etc. As long as the yogi's mind is not fully purified, wandering thoughts arise; sometimes the yogi will perceive the occurrence of these wandering thoughts (or other hindrances), and sometimes he will not. Even if the yogi does take notice of them, it will be only after a short time has lapsed after their appearance. For then the momentary SAMĀDHI of his mind is still quite weak. ~ When the momentary concentration strengthens and becomes strong, the yogi is able to be aware of sense objects as they appear. Such as the in- and out- breathing ~ or the rising and falling of the abdomen ~ or bodily sensations while sitting, touching, bending and stretching (material qualities are evident ~ stiffness ~ hardness ~ softness ~ vibration ~ etc.) As well as acts of seeing, hearing, etc. ~ The yogi's awareness now appears as if it is falling upon these objects ~ as if striking at them ~ as if confronting them again and again. Then as a rule, the mind no longer wanders ~ or his mind will no longer go elsewhere, and attention settles on the object of mindfulness. ~ Only occasionally, and in such degree, will wandering mind occur; and even then, the yogi will be able to notice any such stray thought at its very arising (immediately after its actual arising), then that stray thought will subside as soon as it is noticed and will not arise again. Immediately afterwards he will be able to resume continuous noticing of any object as it becomes evident to him. The mind thus, at this point is called 'unhindered' (NIVARANAS are suppressed completely) ~ While thus practicing the exercise of noticing with 'unhindered mind' ~ the noticing mind will get closer and more fixed on whichever object is noticed at any of the 6-sense doors ~ and the actor noticing will proceed without break. (Not always though ~ however noticing is sharp ~ first syllables and first letter of words ~ if any at all ~ are noticed precisely.) This fixedness of mindfulness on the changing objects of experience is called (VIPASSANĀ – KHANIKA- SAMĀDHI) or 'momentary concentration of insight'. (As mentioned at this point the mind is free from KĀMACCHANDA ~ sense- desire, and also lust and other NIVARANAS – and it is therefore on the same level as UPĀCĀRA-SAMĀDHI.)

CITTA-VISUDDHI is gained thereby through KHANIKA-SAMĀDHI. The mind is no longer mixed up with any hindrances that cause the mind to wander, but it is purely composed ~ thus it is called 'purification of mind'.

~ The states of purification ~

C. Purification of View (DITTHI – VISUDDHI)

1. Analytical Knowledge of Mind and Body (NĀMA- RŪPA – PARICCHEDA – ÑĀNA)

~ Endowed with the purification of the mind, the yogi continues diligent mindfulness; they will arrive at 'the knowledge that discerns and distinguished between mind and matter' ~ or mentality and materiality ~ or mind and body ~ or NĀMA and RŪPA; at such time this analytical understanding of NĀMA- RŪPA will arise with very act of noting.

~ Due to the yogi's improved SATI and SAMĀDHI at this stage ~ they will notice the pairwise occurrence of an object and the knowing of it. ~ When observing the rising of the abdomen the yogi is able to distinguish the (sensation of) rising movement as separate from his consciousness of it. The rising movement is one process (actually many); ~ the knowing of the rising movement is another quite separate process. The same regarding the falling movement and the 'knowing' of it. When walking, the yogi is able to distinguish the walking as 'unconscious matter' (just RŪPA) and his awareness of walking (the changing flow of elements) as 'mind' of NĀMA. This distinguishing process of NĀMA and RŪPA and vice versa holds true for all activities ~ such as stretching ~ reaching ~ bending ~ and so on. ~ (Just elements manifesting ~ quite unconscious of themselves ~ with the earners and knowing of those elements as NĀMA).

~ Thus, when seeing a visual object with the eye ~ the yogi can distinguish each factor involved in the seeing process; ~ the eye is one thing (separate component) ~ the visual object is another component. ~ The yogi knows these to be matter. ~ They know that 'seeing' is still same-thing separate ~ and 'knowing' it is another; ~ being able to clearly distinguish their seeing and the awareness of it as mind- NĀMA.

~ When hearing is noted, he distinguishes the ear and the object of hearing ~ sound ~ to be separate components ~ yet both RŪPA ~ and hearing and the awareness of it as separate ~ yet both minds. ~ The same distinguishing ability applied in the case of the other sense functions.

MAHASI continues to say ~ "When he thinks, he distinguishes the thinking and his awareness of it as mind and the 'seat of the mind' as matter. ~ When awareness of RŪPA is noted ~ the yogi distinguishes 'the awareness' as 'mind', and 'the object of awareness' and the 'seat of that awareness' as 'matter').

~ In each act of noticing, the yogi comes to know analytically the mental processes of noticing, and those of thinking and reflecting. ~ The yogi knows they have the nature of going towards an object ~ inclining towards an object ~ cognizing an object. ~ The yogi knows analytically the material processed going on in the entire body ~ such as rising and falling motions ~ in- and out- breathing (the sensation of them) ~ the sitting posture ~ etc. They know them thus: ~ "They have not the nature of going or inclining towards an object ~ or cognizing an object." ~ Such knowledge is called "knowing matter (the body of RŪPA) by its manifestation of non-determining" ~ which means ~ "having no faculty of cognizing an object."

MAHASI ~ "One should know that the more clearly a material object is known or noticed, the clearer becomes the mental process of knowing it" ~ quotes VIS. MAG. to substantiate (p.684, v.15)

~ In essence: the physical phenomena which are (the object of one's awareness) are perceived at every moment of contemplation in separate forms, without being mixed up with the mind contemplating on them, or with other material phenomena. ~ The mental phenomena such as contemplating, thinking, seeing, hearing, etc. also are perceived at every moment of awareness of them to be in separate states, without being mixed up with either material phenomena or other mental phenomena. At every moment of breathing ~ the body, and the mind which knows the body, are perceived distinctly and separately as two. ~ The yogi knows there is only that pair ~ a material process as object ~ and a mental process of knowing it ~ and it is to that pair alone that the terms of conventional usage: being ~ person ~ soul ~ I ~ me ~ you ~ man ~ or woman ~ refer. The yogi knows that apart from this dual process there is no separate being or person ~ 'I' ~ 'man' or 'woman'. ~ (When such reflections occur the yogi must note ~ reflecting ~ reflecting~ and go on observing his primary object ~ abdomen or nostrils ~ etc.)

(The above is when this ÑĀNA has come to maturity)

(The yogi knows that there is no such entity as ATTA or 'in him' or others. ~ With such knowledge the false view that there is a self-entity is perceptibly removed.) ~ This is purity of view ~ DITTHI-VISUDDHI (which means ~ "Here a BHIKKHU sees what is become as become.

Having seen what is become as become, he has entered upon the way to dispassion for it, to the fading away of greed for it, to its cessation; this is how one with eyes sees." ~ V.M.689, v.33)

~ The stages of purification ~

D. Purification by Overcoming Doubt (KANKHĀ – VITARANA – VISUDDHI)

(~ See VIS.MAG. CH. XIX ~ p.693, v.1 ~ p.703, v.27)
(Description of purification by overcoming doubt)

2. Knowledge by Discerning Conditionality (PACCAYA – PARIGGAHA – ÑĀNA)

~ Insight arising from the full comprehension of causes ~

~ On proceeding further with the contemplation, the yogi will perceive that the material and mental phenomena are arising in the body as effects of their respective causes. ~ The yogi understands ~ because of the mind-intending (mental volition of impulse) to bend ~ stretch ~ move ~ or change the posture ~ there arise the (physical) actions of bending ~ stretching ~ moving or changing. The condition necessary for the body and mental processes becomes evident, when moving any part of the body (toes, eye-lids, fingers, walking, reaching, chewing, etc.) ~ The consciousness of 'intending to move' appears first; ~ he next notices 'the act of moving' (whatever body part it is.) Many hundreds of mental intentions will be noticed while lifting the foot ~ moving it forward, etc.: ~ not only one intention ~ but an infinitesimal amount of them to keep a body part moving. ~ In the beginning of practice because of omission to notice an intention ~ the yogi thinks that bodily movement is quicker than the mind knowing it. ~ At the more advanced stages it becomes obvious that mind is the forerunner; ~ the mind knowing a bodily process is quicker than the material process. He experiences directly that a bodily process takes place after a proceeding mental intention. ~ In other words, because of the mental desire to move (which is the cause) ~ a physical movement (which is the effect) ~ takes place. Whenever a bodily movement is made ~ it's recognized and known that the movement is caused by the desire to make it ~ and apart from this impersonal process of cause and effect there is no 'person', 'I', 'Self' or individual who makes the movement. This is the knowledge that distinguishes between cause and effect.

The yogi further reflects: ~ One's body becomes hot or cold because of the element (fire) of heat or cold. ~ Because of the fluctuation in temperature there are always changes in the physical condition either being hot, warm, cool or cold. ~ The body exists in food/nutriment, and with nourishment because of the ingestion of food/nutriment there always arises new physical energy, ~ he perceives. Consciousness arises because there are objects to notice, ~ and because of ear and sound, hearing consciousness arises. With just conditioning factors ~ and because of attention being directed ~ the mind reaches its object. If these conditioning factors are not present, one realizes that sense-door consciousness will not arise.

The yogi knows the condition for the mental process; ~ in the case of consciousness desirous of wandering ~ indulging ~ roaming ~ drifting ~ reacting, etc. ~ There arises first a corresponding consciousness giving initial attention to the distracting object. If that consciousness is not noticed with mindfulness ~ then there arises a consciousness that wanders ~ indulges ~ drifts ~ etc. If noticed with SATI ~ no stray thought or distraction will arise. ~ The same holds true for other mind-door processes: ~ When greed ~ wanting ~ delighting ~ or being angry arises ~ if noticed with SATI ~ indulging, identification takes place. ~ If noticed with SATI ~ no alteration arises. ~ The yogi knows if there is a noticeable or recognizable object ~ then there arises consciousness engaged in noticing or thinking ~ reasoning or understanding ~ as the case may be; ~ otherwise no such consciousness arises. ~ Consciousness arises in accordance with each object that becomes evident. ~ If there is an object ~ there arises consciousness; ~ if there is no object ~ no consciousness arises.

When contemplating regular and spontaneous bodily movements, such as the rising and falling of the abdomen ~ the yogi notices one after another continuously. Sometimes the rising and falling are so faint that the yogi finds nothing to notice. ~ (It occurs that there can be no knowing without an object; ~ be aware of sitting ~ touching ~ one sensation has hardly vanished ~ then another arises ~ the yogi notices them all accordingly). ~ At this time the meditator will generally experience many and various painful feelings arising in his body. ~ While one is being noticed, another feeling will arise elsewhere. ~ And while that is being noticed ~ again another will appear elsewhere. Noticing each one is clear and steady, but the yogi will only perceive their initial phase of 'arising' and not their final phase of 'dissolution'. ~ Sometimes these painful sensations (such as itching, aches, heat, dullness and stiffness) will appear as almost unbearable experiences. If mindful noticing is stopped ~ such sensations will disappear. When noticing is resumed ~ they will reappear. This is just the nature of the sensitive body; ~ if noticed patiently and carefully ~ with energy ~ they fade away gradually.

The yogi sometimes sees images ~ mental pictures ~ visions of various shapes kinds, and constructs: They become so clear that they appear as if they are being seen with his own eyes. They become extremely vivid and multi-dimensional ~ as if you could live and walk through them. E.g. fantastic images of the BUDDHA ~ with golden radiance or crystal like transparencies of images; ~ faces in minute detail; ~ incredible mental creations ~ celestial scenes ~ palaces with inlaid jewels ~ pagodas; ~ monks ~ friends ~ parents ~ loved ones; ~ trees or woods ~ hills or mountains ~ gardens; ~ or face to face with dead ~ bloated ~ pestering ~ mangled ~ corpses ~ skeletons; ~ swelling of one's body ~ expanding as if filling the entire room; ~ seeing one's body covered with blood ~ worms or maggots; ~ seeing in one's body the organs ~ the veins ~ muscles ~ bones ~ as if seeing them with one's open eyes; ~ seeing celestial ~ radiant figures or grotesque ~ contorted blobs of flesh; ~ or faces of pimples and tumors; ~ and so on. All of which are nothing but mental creations of one's own imagination ~ highlighted ~ sharpened~ and becoming vivid due to one's intense SAMĀDHI. ~

(These objects are not substantially real ~ just a mental reality as well as the reality of the mind that sees them. ~ They are similar to what one comes across in dreams. ~ These can come while sitting ~ walking, etc. ~ Of course ~ just bare attention is necessary; ~ no need to welcome ~ enjoy ~ fear ~ or dislike them; ~ only empty phenomena alone roll on). Here too ~ while the yogi is engaged in noticing one of these mental images ~ another will show itself; ~ while still noticing that, another will appear. Following thus ~ the mental images as they arise ('seeing, seeing'), he goes on noticing them. But though he is engaged in noticing them ~ he will perceive only their initial phase ~ not the final phase.

Some yogis do not experience these types of extraordinary objects or feelings. (While contemplating they can easily become lazy. ~ So note: 'lazy, lazy'... ~ and carry on attentively).

Between sequences of noticing ~ the yogi ~ by considering inferentially ~ comes to know ~ "It is due to the presence of such causes and conditions as ignorance (delusion) ~ craving (desire – wanting something other) and KAMMA (actions) that this body and mind continue. In the same way ~ the yogi perceives the fact that ~ because of AVIJJA ~ delusion ~ (which views life as beautiful and satisfying) ~ and of TANHĀ ~ all kinds of deeds are thought of and done. ~ And because of the attachment to those deeds (actions) that have been committed ~ there arise in successive series, the new VIÑÑĀNAS. ~ He perceives that death is nothing but the passing away of the last one in the successive series of this kind ~ dependent on a new sense-door formation.

When this knowledge has come to maturity ~ the yogi will perceive only body and mind processes occurring in strict accordance with their particular and appropriate conditions, and he comes to the conclusion: ~ "Here is only a conditioning body and mind process and a conditioned body and mind process. Apart from these ~ there is no person who performs the various bodily movements~ or who experiences feelings of joy ~ clarity ~ or pain ~ etc." ~ He will see that life in the past was a formation of body and mind which were dependent on their respective causes, and that there will be a similar process of life in the future.
This distinguishing knowledge of dependent origination of cause and effect is "PACCAYA-PARIGGAHA- ÑĀNA ~ 'knowledge of

discerning conditionality' ~ and at the same time this knowledge relates to ~ "purification (of insight) by overcoming doubt."

Before developing the right understanding of the fact that life consists of NĀMA- RŪPA (dependent on their respective causes) ~ the yogi would have had a number of skeptical doubts (uncertainties ~ questions ~ unclarity) regarding ~ "Did I exist in the past?" ~ "Who was I in the past?" ~ Wondering "Did I only come into existence in the present?" ~ or "Will I continue to exist in the future?" (Essentially ~ DITTHI regarding 'self' ~ 'I' ~ 'ego' ~ 'soul' ~ etc.) Now these skeptical doubts or uncertainties cannot arise, as they have been overcome through "Knowledge born of direct personal experience".

~ from VISUDDHI MAGGA ~

Knowledge established by overcoming doubt about the 3 divisions of time (past ~ present ~ future) by means of discerning the conditions of NĀMA- RŪPA is called "purification by overcoming doubt".

(p.693, v.4) ~ The root causes of birth are discerned: ~ ignorance ~ craving ~ clinging; ~ and KAMMA and nutriment is its condition. ~ So, 5 things constitute its cause and condition: ~ the first 3 are a decisive-support for the body ~ then KAMMA begets it ~ and nutriment sustains it.

(p.694, v.5) ~ Having discerned the material body's condition in that way ~ he discerns mentality in this way: "Due to eye and to visible object, eye consciousness etc. arises ~ (with other sense processes.)"

~ Having discerned that the occurrence of NĀMA- RŪPA is due to conditions ~ (by inference) he sees that in the past ~ as now ~ its occurrence was also due to these conditions ~ and in the future too its occurrence will be due to conditions.

(v.6) ~ When he sees in this way ~ all his uncertainty is abandoned. ~ That is to say, ~ the 5 kinds of uncertainty about the past: ~ "Was I in the past?" ~ "Was I not in the past?" ~" What was I in the past?" ~ "How was I in the past?" ~ "Having been that, what was I in the past?" ~ Also, the 5 kinds of uncertainty about the future: (like above) and also the 6 kinds of uncertainty about the present: ~ "Am I?" ~ "Am I not?" ~ "What am I?" ~ "How am I?" ~ "Whence will this being have come?"

~ "Whither will it be bound?" ~

(v.7) ~ Another yogi sees the condition for mentality as 2-fold ~ according to what is common to all and what is not common to all. ~ Thus: ~ The six-sense-doors and the 6-sense-objects are a condition common to all; ~ but attention (wise attention- SATI) is not common to all. ~ He sees that wise attention is a condition for the profitable; ~ unwise attention is a condition for the unprofitable; ~ thus discerning conditions for NĀMA- RŪPA, regarding the 3-time periods.

(p.695, v.11) ~ Another when he has seen that the formations called NĀMA- RŪPA arrive at aging ~ and that those that have aged dissolve ~ discerns NĀMA- RŪPA conditions by means of dependent origination in reverse order: "This is called the aging and death of formations. ~ It comes to be when there is birth ~ and birth when there is becoming: ~ clinging ~ craving ~ feeling ~ contact ~ 6-fold base ~ NĀMA- RŪPA ~ consciousness ~ formations ~ which arise when there is ignorance. ~ With such discernment ~ uncertainty is abandoned according to the 3-time periods.

(p.696, v.13) ~ Another discerns dependent origination in direct order ... 3-time periods.

(p.696, v.13) ~ KAMMA and KAMMA result. ~ Another discerns NĀMA- RŪPA conditions by means of the rounds of KAMMA and the rounds of KAMMA-result in this way: ~

1. ~ In the previous KAMMA-process becoming there is delusion ~ which is ignorance. ~ There is accumulation ~ which is formations. ~ There is attachment which is craving. ~ There is embracing, which is clinging. ~ There is solution, which is becoming. ~ Thus these 5 things in the previous KAMMA- process becoming are conditions for rebirth, here in the present becoming.

2. ~ Here in the present becoming there is rebirth linking ~ which is consciousness. ~ There is descent into the womb ~ which is NĀMA- RŪPA. ~ There is sensitivity ~ which is sense-base. ~ There is what is touched ~ which is contact. ~ There is what is felt ~ which is feeling. ~ Thus these 5 things here in the present rebirth-process becoming have their conditions in KAMMA done in the past.

3. ~ Here in the present becoming with the maturing of the bases

there is delusion ~ which is ignorance. ~ There is accumulation ~ which is formations. ~ There is attachment ~ which is craving. ~ There is embracing ~ which is clinging. ~ There is volition, which is becoming. ~ These 5 things here in the present KAMMA-process becoming are conditions for rebirth-linking in the future.

4. ~ In the future there is rebirth linking ~ which is consciousness. ~ There is descent into the womb ~ which is NĀMA- RŪPA. ~ There is sensitivity ~ which is sense-base. ~ There is what is touched ~ which is contact. ~ There is what is felt ~ which is feeling. ~ These 5 things in the future rebirth-process becoming have their conditions in KAMMA done here in the present becoming.

~ KAMMA result proceeds from KAMMA, ~ result has KAMA for its source, ~ future becoming springs from KAMMA, ~ and this is how the world goes round. ~ When thus discerned all uncertainty is abandoned regarding the 3 periods of time.

(p.700, v.20) ~ There is no 'doer' apart from KAMMA and its result. ~ The yogi sees clearly there is no drover and above the doing ~ no experiences of the result over and above the occurrence of the result. ~ Phenomena alone roll on.

(p.702, v.22) ~ He understands the aggregates produced in the past with KAMMA as a condition ceased there too. But other aggregates are produced in this becoming with past KAMMA as their condition ~ although there is no single thing that has come over from the past becoming to this becoming. And aggregates produced in this becoming with KAMMA as their condition will cease, and in the future becoming other aggregates will be produced, although no single thing will go over from this becoming to the future becoming.

3. Knowledge by Comprehension (SAMMASANAÑĀNA)
This ÑĀNA includes:

~ ANICCA-SAMMASANA-ÑĀNA ~ (Insight into the Impermanence of Phenomena) ~ DUKKHA- SAMMASANA – ÑĀNA ~ (Insight into Suffering)

~ ANATTA- SAMMASANA- ÑĀNA~ (Insight into Non-Self)

At this stage ~ whether or not the meditators come across

extraordinary objects or feelings they will clearly know the initial ~ middle ~ and final phase of any object noticed. At the beginning of practice ~ while noting one object ~ the yogi had to switch onto a different object that arose ~ the disappearance of an object. ~ They notice the new object that arises. ~ The yogi will discern distinctly that ~ only after each earlier process has ceased ~ there arises a subsequent one. ~ For instance, ~ only when the rising movement of the abdomen has come to an end ~ there arises the falling movement. ~ So also, in the case of walking: ~ only when the process of lifting the foot has ended ~ does the moving forward of the root arise ~ and likewise with the placing of the foot.

In the case of painful feelings ~ only after each single feeling occurring at its particular place has ceased ~ will another new feeling (sensation) arise at another place in the body. The yogi will notice that after 2, 3 or more times noticing a painful sensation that it will gradually grow less, and in most cases cease or disappear entirely.

In the case of variously shaped mental images ~ it is only after each single image noticed has vanished ~ that another new object will come into the mind's focus. ~ The yogi will notice that these mental objects of attention become gradually smaller and less distinct ~ until at last they disappear entirely. ~

At this stage when the meditator's SAMADHI and insight-knowledge have grown in strength ~ they perceive in every act of noticing that an object appears suddenly and disappears instantly. They see how each object ~ even while being noticed ~ comes to destruction and disappearance. (One experiences the dissolving or vanishing of both the object of awareness and the awareness itself, while sitting ~ rising ~ falling ~ acts of moving ~ walking ~ folding ~ reaching ~ etc. One experiences the disappearance of the objector awareness and the awareness itself ~ as with hearing and sound ~ seeing ~ etc. In some cases, the yogi experiences the disappearance of the object of knowing ~ the consciousness of the object ~ as well as the awareness of the object; ~ 3 distinct parts.)

So, at this level of the practice ~ the yogis' perception is so clear ~ in every act of noticing ~ that an object appears suddenly and disappears instantly; ~ just physical and mental phenomena are arising and passing away at every moment of contemplation. ~ The yogi reflects ~ "All comes to an end ~ all dissolves ~ vanishes ~ and disappears. ~ Nothing is lasting or permanent; ~ objects and the knowing of them are constantly undergoing destruction." ~ They reflect ~ "Because we have not in the past so observed and noted the mind and body in this mindful way ~ we took phenomena (everything) as existing permanently (or we were not absolutely sure what ANICCA meant). ~ Now we are utterly sure that all (everything) is changing ~ impermanent ~ in flux; ~ not lasting (even for the slightest amount of time). All is just arising and passing away; nonexistence of object, etc. (after having been). ~ Such knowledge is to be known as ANICCA- SAMMASANA- ÑANA ~ the knowledge that observes ~ explores ~ grasps or understand through direct personal experience ~ the fact of impermanence.)

The yogi further reflects ~ "It is through ignorance (not seeing the true nature of NĀMA- RŪPA) that beings think they enjoy life. ~ But in actuality ~ the truth is that there is nothing to enjoy. There is nothing apart from this continual (barrage) of objects arising and disappearing. ~ Such a dreadful situation. ~ NĀMA- RŪPA is continually afflicted by "arising and passing way": ~ this is not a pleasant or secure situation nor reliable. ~ There is nothing worth cherishing or relying on, and therefore, the situation of having objects, and the knowing of them continually arising and vanishing, is suffering ~ and terribly unsatisfying. He reflects ~ "This universal impermanence is truly frightful and oppressive. (Oppression by continual rise and fall.) If experiencing severe pain ~ the yogi reflects: ~ "All is pain."~ He looks on pain as a barb ~ a boil ~ as a dart. ~ This knowledge is DUKKHA- SAMMASANA – ÑĀNA ~ insight into (the universality of) suffering (in conditioned existence).

The yogi further perceives the fact that NĀMA- RŪPA phenomena do not follow the dictates of one's will (no obedience to command), but are arising and passing away in accordance with their own nature and relative conditioning. (This arising and passing away is just unavoidable ~ a worthless mass of suffering. ~ One cannot stop its process. ~ "It is beyond one's power. ~ It takes its natural course.") ~ This knowledge enables one to see the ego-less ~ empty ~ 'non-self'-nature of experience.

It is realized that NĀMA- RŪPA is not ATTA (self). Commentaries: ~ "What is sinful is 'not self'; ~ 'not self' in the sense of having no core; ~ and because there is no exercising power over it. ~ This knowledge is ~ (ANATTA- SAMMASANA- ÑĀNA).

Having thus seen the 3 characteristics by direct experience ~ the yogi ~ by inference from the direct experience of those objects noticed ~ comprehends ~ all bodily and mental processes of part ~ present ~ or future, ~ and the whole world (of other beings) ~ by concluding ~ "They too are in the same way ~ ANICCA ~ DUKKHA ~ and ANATTA." ~ In respect to these objects not personally experienced ~ the yogi knows them to be just NĀMA- RŪPA formations, constituted in the same way as to those objects he has experienced. (The inference is from present direct experience. These same characteristic principles ~ of ANICCA ~ DUKKHA ~ and ANATTA~ that are of his own person ~ constitute other persons as well) ~ This realization is known as ~ 'Knowledge of comprehension by inference'. ~ (Note: ~ This knowledge isn't clear in the yogi with less intellectual capacity or limited knowledge, who pays little to no attention to such reflection ~ but simply goes on noticing objects. But such a comprehension occurs often to one who yields to reflection ~ which in some cases ~ may occur at every act of noticing. ~ Reflection in brief on these facts can be useful ~ but excessive reflection ~ should be guarded against ~ by determined precise awareness, ~ as it is an impediment to the progress of insight. Even if no such reflections occur at this stage ~ comprehension will nevertheless become increasingly clear at the higher stages. ~ Hence ~ (MAHASI) "No attention should be given to reflections ~ while giving more attention to bare noticing objects. ~ The yogi must ~ however ~ also notice these reflections if they occur ~ but he should not dwell on them." ~ Thus, the yogi proceeds on with the meditation, without any further reflection.

(Manual of Insight- MAHASI SAYADAW, Chapter 6, p.329-334)

Comprehension of suffering

It is very difficult to recognize that the mind and body are oppressive when you are young and healthy and only associate with others whose situation and condition are the same as yours. However, when you frequently encounter old people dying from various terminal diseases, or when you become sick yourself, you will reflect that you too must die just as others do. Then you will also easily be able to understand that your body and mind are oppressive.

When one has yet to empirically observe that mental and physical phenomena incessantly arise and disappear, it will be difficult to recognize that mental and physical phenomena are oppressive. However, if you continuously observe arising and disappearing mental and physical phenomena, you will experience that they do not even last for the twinkling of an eye, but incessantly arise and disappear. They are oppressive because of their constant arising and disappearance. They are impermanent and die or pass away all the time. They are oppressive because their constant arising and disappearing is torture. Then you will be easily able to understand that they are detestable, dreadful, and unsatisfactory. If new phenomena did not come into existence to replace old ones, there would be nothing but death. The fact that we can never be sure that we will not die within a certain period of time is also distressing. By experiencing various types of pain and distress, we are able to understand that the mind and body are nothing but a mass of suffering.

By noting the physical phenomena involved in the rise and fall of the abdomen, sitting, bending, stretching, moving, and so on, you can experience that they instantly vanish even as you observe them. Because this incessant arising and disappearing is frightening or dreadful, one understands that mental and physical phenomena are oppressive. They are frightening or dreadful because they vanish or die in one moment. They are dreadful because they are painful or unpleasant. They are all suffering, and unsatisfactory. Having had this experience and understanding, one understands that past and future physical phenomena are the same as present ones. They are constantly oppressive, frightening, dreadful, and unsatisfactory. (For more detail refer to the section above on the comprehension of impermanence.)

Comprehension of 'not-self'

Theories about the self

Ordinary people who have not yet come to a personal, empirical understanding of the true nature of mental and physical phenomena have a very deep-seated, deluded belief that there is a 'self' within the body. Those who hold such beliefs describe the self in various ways in their scriptures. According to these sources, the self is the owner of the body. It possesses the entire body, or certain parts of the body comprised of the five sensory faculties (**BUDDHINDRIYA**: eye, ear, nose, tongue, and skin), the five functional faculties (**KAMMINDRIYA**: mouth, hands, feet, sex organs, and anus), the faculty that is both sensory and functional consciousness (**UBHAYINDRIYA**), and so on.

In order to refute this belief in a self, the BUDDHA explained in discourses such as the ANATTALAKKHANA SUTTA that:

BHIKKHUS, form is 'not-self'. For if form was self, this form would not lead to affliction, and it would be possible to have it of form: "Let my form be thus; let my form not be thus."

In the Hindu text called the VĪMAMSĀ, the so-called self is described as the 'agent' or 'doer'. The text provides the example of using a sword or saw to cut something as an illustration of this: Although one uses a tool such as a sword or a saw to cut something, the actual 'cutter' is a person, oneself. In the same way, when one uses the 'tools' of the eyes, ears, limbs, and so on to perform actions such as seeing, hearing, walking, standing, sitting, sleeping, bending, stretching, and so on, the self is the actual agent or 'doer'. To remove this delusion, the ABHIDHAMMATTHAVIBHĀVINĪ (a sub-commentary on ABHIDHAMMA) and the commentaries say:

"This indicates that there is no doer or agent other than the law of causality of phenomena.

When moving forward, ignorant people delude themselves that it is the self that moves, or that it is the self that accomplishes the movement, or that it is 'I' who moves, or that it is 'I' who accomplishes the movement.

There is no self-inside that looks ahead or looks to the side…There is no self-inside that bends or stretches."

In VĪMAMSĀ and SANKHYĀ texts, the soul is described as 'the agent that feels pleasure and pain'. Thus, they identify feeling itself with the self. To help eliminate this type of delusion, the commentary on the Satipaṭṭhāna Sutta says:

"Who feels? There is not any individual, being, or person who feels. Thus, one realizes that feeling itself is what feels the pleasure associated with pleasant sense objects and so on. We conventionally say with regard to the appearance of feeling, "I feel."

In order to point out that there is no 'doer' apart from actual phenomena, the commentary says that feeling itself is what feels."

They (the VĪMAMSĀ and SANKHYĀ texts) also describe the self as: "a permanent resident (NIVĀSI) that lasts forever, even after the body that is its home is destroyed; a commander (SAYAMVASI) that controls the entire body with its physical organs and faculties; or a superintendent (ADHITTHĀYAKA) that makes all arrangements." Thus, they sometimes identify the self with just one of the five aggregates, sometimes with two, sometimes with three, sometimes with four, and sometimes with all five. SACKKA, a well-known wandering ascetic during the BUDDHA'S time, identified the self with all of the five aggregates.

As he once said to the BUDDHA:

"I assert thus, Master GOTAMA: 'Material form is myself; feeling is myself; perception is myself; mental formations are myself; consciousness is myself.'"

Overcoming the sense of self

When one notes each arising mental and physical phenomenon, what one comes to experience within a short time is that there are only mental and physical phenomena that arise and disappear. There is no self or entity that exercises complete control. Thus, one can clearly ascertain that there is no 'self' but only mental and physical phenomena that constantly arise and pass away. When one clearly experiences the conditioned and instantaneous appearance and disappearance of the physical phenomena involved in rising, falling, sitting, bending, stretching, moving, and so on, one understands that even if one doesn't want these physical phenomena to arise, one cannot prevent them from doing so. They will arise when all the necessary causes and conditions come together. Even if one doesn't want these physical phenomena to disappear, one cannot prevent them from doing so. And they will disappear when it is "their time". There is no entity that possesses any control over these appearing and disappearing physical phenomena; there is no entity that is permanent and everlasting; there is no entity that carries out one's desires. These physical phenomena do not comprise a controlling entity called self, are not a permanent entity, and are not an entity that carries out one's desires. Thus, one correctly understands that there is no control, that the self does not exist, that there is no 'self', and that there is only the nature of 'not-self'.

This understanding might begin to arise when one observes a phenomenon arising against one's will, or when one experiences a physical phenomenon disappearing, although one wishes it to be lasting and stable. One can only clearly experience the appearance and disappearance of mental and physical phenomena when one observes them. Only then will one understand that there is no permanent self that has control or can carry out one's desires; there are only constantly arising and disappearing phenomena. This is a genuine experience of the characteristic of 'not-self', or a genuine contemplation of 'Insight knowledge by comprehension'.

The VISUDDHIMAGGA explains it this way:

Phenomena all are 'not-self' because they are insubstantial. The phrase "They are insubstantial" means that they lack any substantial self that could be called their owner, the permanent resident, the agent, the feeler, or the commander. That which is impermanent and unsatisfying cannot possibly be the owner, the permanent resident, the agent, and so on, simply because it cannot prevent impermanence, or the oppression of arising and passing away.

Because they do not qualify as the owner, permanent resident, agent, feeler, or commander, the five aggregates are empty.

Because they have no owner themselves, they are 'not-self'.

Note that in view of these commentaries it is not possible to develop a true understanding of 'not-self' just by considering it in terms of lack of solid form. One only develops a true understanding of not-self when one realizes that there is no 'self' that could be identified as owner, permanent resident, and so on. Keep in mind that even formless, immaterial deities can still be subject to the wrong view of self.

Having understood present physical phenomena as explained above, one comes to understand past physical phenomena. One clearly understands: "Because they cannot exercise any control, are not everlasting, and cannot carry out one's desires, they are not-self. There are only natural phenomena."

(The other details are the same as for the contemplation of impermanence.)

(See VIS.MAG. CH XX, v.93, p.734-p.744, v.130)

(Knowledge of contemplation of rise and fall)

4. Knowledge of Arising and Passing Away (UDAYABBAYA-ÑĀNA)

(MAHASI SAYADAW, Manual of Insight Ch. 6, pp.357- 358)

At the beginning of practice, when one's knowledge is still weak, one cannot yet see that mental and physical phenomena are impermanent, unsatisfactory, and not-self. Therefore, one takes them to be permanent, satisfactory, and self. As a result of this, attachment can still arise. However, once one realizes their three universal characteristics with mature insight knowledge by comprehension, one will no longer take them to be permanent, satisfactory, and self. Thus desire, attachment, or lust will no longer be able to arise. It is said that this understanding (due to which attachment and lust can no longer arise) also removes the attachment and lust that could have arisen with regard to mental and physical phenomena.

Once one has contemplated the impermanent, unsatisfactory, and 'not- self' nature of the mental and physical phenomena that one has observed, and those that one has not observed, one can ascertain beyond any doubt that these phenomena are impermanent, unsatisfactory, and not-self. Thus one will no longer be concerned about the way things happen. While one observes mental and physical phenomena as they occur, by seeing their beginning and end one develops an equanimity associated with insight knowledge that clearly understands arising and passing away. At this point one begins to develop insight knowledge of arising and passing away (UDAYABBAYA- ÑĀNA). As the PATISAMBHIDĀMAGGA explains:

"Seeing how present phenomena change is knowledge of arising and passing away.

Whenever one practices, one will see the beginning of each phenomenon, appearing as if emerging from somewhere or sticking its head in somewhere. One also will see phenomenon ending, disappearing suddenly like the flame of a candle when it is blown out. Seeing the arising and passing away of phenomena in this way is called 'Insight Knowledge of arising and passing away.' "

Currently arising physical phenomena are called 'Present physical phenomena.' Their initial arising is called 'Arising' (UDAYA), and their changing into something else is called 'Passing away' (VAYA). The knowledge that penetrates arising and passing away is called 'Knowledge of arising and passing away.'

To gain insight into arising and passing away, one should contemplate the present phenomena, process-by-process or moment-by-moment, rather than past or future phenomena. This is why the BUDDHA said, "See changes in present phenomena, and so on."

The term 'arising' refers to phenomena that have come into existence and can be experienced. The term 'present physical phenomena' refers to the physical phenomena that are currently arising and observed in the three stages of arising, presence, and passing away. However, it is difficult to contemplate such present physical phenomena at the beginning of insight knowledge of arising and passing away. Therefore, begin your insight practice by observing the apparent continuity or duration of present phenomena (SANTATIPACCUPPANNA).

According to the sub-commentary, the phrase 'Currently arising physical phenomena' used in the above passage from the PATISAMBHIDĀMAGGA refers to present physical phenomena (KHANACACCUPPANNA). These are present, momentary phenomena that can be observed to have three stages: arising, presence, and passing away. The phrase does not refer to the present in a conventional sense (ADDHĀPACCUPPANNA) or to the continuity of mental and physical processes happening in the present

(SANTATIPACCUPPANNA). During the immature stages of insight knowledge of arising and passing away, it is only possible to observe the arising and passing away of present phenomena as a continuity or process. However, when that insight knowledge matures, one will also be able to observe the arising and passing away of present momentary phenomena.

(MAHASI SAYADAW, Manual of Insight, Ch. 6, pp.362- 363)

The characteristics of Arising and Passing Away
The five characteristics of arising:

With the arising of ignorance, physical phenomena arise. In this way, one sees the causal aspect of the arising of the aggregate of physicality. Similarly, with the arising of craving, volitional actions, and nutrition, physical phenomena arise. In these ways, one sees the causal aspect of the arising of the aggregate of physicality. By seeing the characteristic of arising, one sees the arising of the aggregate of physicality. Therefore, if one sees the arising of the aggregate of physicality, one sees these five characteristics.

From this passage, we see that the five characteristics of the arising of physical phenomena are: the ignorance involved in volitional actions performed in past lives (AVIJJĀ), craving (TANHĀ), volitional actions that one has performed (KAMMA), nutrition from the food one consumes in this life (ĀHĀRA), and the arising of present physical phenomena (NIBBATTI).

The five characteristics of disappearance:
With the cessation of ignorance, there is the cessation of physical phenomena. In this way, one sees the causal aspect of the cessation of the aggregate of physicality. Similarly, with the cessation of craving, volitional actions, or nutrition, there is the cessation of physical phenomena. In these ways, one sees the causal aspect of the disappearance of the aggregate of physicality. By seeing the characteristic of change, one sees the disappearance of the aggregate of physicality. Therefore, if one sees the disappearance of the aggregate of physicality, one sees these five characteristics.

From this passage, we see that the five characteristics of the disappearance of physical phenomena are: The disappearance of ignorance because it is uprooted through the path knowledge of arahantship; the disappearance of craving; the disappearance of volitional actions; the absence of nutrition; and the disappearance of present physical phenomena.

The BUDDHA gave a similar analysis of the five characteristics of appearance and disappearance for the four mental aggregates of feeling, perception, mental formations, and consciousness. The only difference is in regard to the fourth aspect, which is food in the case of the physical aggregate. For the first three mental aggregates – feeling, perception, mental formations, – food is replaced by mental contact, and for the last aggregate – consciousness – it is replaced by mental and physical phenomena.

Weak stage involving the ten corruptions of insight ~ (VIPASSANUPAKKILESA)

~10 corruptions of insight ~ (p.739, v.105)
1. Illumination ~ (p.740, v.107)
2. Knowledge ~ (p.741, v.114)
3. PĪTI ~ (v.115)
4. Tranquility ~ (v.116)
5. Happiness – bliss ~ (p.742, v.117)
6. SADDHA- faith ~ (v.118)
7. Energy ~ (v.119)
8. Mindfulness ~ (v.120)
9. Equanimity ~ (v.121)
10. Attachment ~ (v.122)

Through previously one is said to know the rising and passing of phenomenal processes ~ in reality one was aware only of the arising in the beginning and the passing away in the end of these processes; ~ one thought that the middle occurrence of each formation lasted for an appreciable length of time. ~ One was then not yet aware of the momentary dissolution of the phenomena concerned. One now realizes distinctly and with rapidity ~ that even where phenomena of a similar nature were occurring in continuous succession ~ they were newly arising and vanishing moment by moment. (The beginning of every object of noticing is clearly perceived and the coming to an end of each noticed object is discerned so vividly that it appears as if it were cut off clearly).

Advanced stage of arising and passing: ~ Due to the more refined-balanced INDRIYAS the yogi's mental process of noticing accelerates as if it became uplifted (or catapulted), and the NĀMA- RŪPA processes to be noticed also arise much more rapidly. ~ When observing the rising and falling ~ one sees clearly that it is dividing itself into 2 or 3 more distinct parts. (Each rising is many risings and fallings ~ same with the falling motion, and in and out breathing. ~ It is not just one process ~ but a manifold number ~ this will be obvious). This same multiple division process will also appear clearly in all other activities: ~ walking ~ the lifting ~ moving ~ and placing are a numerous amount of separate and distinct processes. ~ While observing thoughts one finds the thought and the awareness of it disappearing immediately ~ while observing pain (if any ~ it usually vanishes immediately upon 2 or 3 noticing ~ but will reappear if intensity of SAMĀDHI and awareness wane ~ say towards the end of a sitting ~ or if the pain is particularly a strong one). One finds both the pain and the noting of it dividing and dissolving into separate parts with each act of noting. ~ (The same is true with awareness of sounds ~ distinct pieces or waves are experienced ~ not one continuous sound. ~ Some yogis can even discern which ear the sound is entering) ~ Slight movements ~ sensations ~ spread all throughout the body; ~ bodily and mental processes are observed as many times swifter than the blink of an eye or a flash of lightning. (Note: ~ When the yogi goes on noticing these formations, he will be able to fully comprehend them as they occur. ~ Mindfulness will appear as if plunging into an object that arises. ~ The object too seems to be alighting on mindfulness. ~ One comprehends each object clearly and singly. ~ The yogi reflects; ~ bodily and mental processes are incredibly swift ~ as fast as a machine or engine ~ and yet they can all be noticed and comprehended. ~ (Note: ~ The important thing is to notice clearly and comprehend what arises. ~ If one attempts to follow NĀMA- RŪPA in detail at this point one

14. THE PROGRESS OF INSIGHT THROUGH THE STAGES OF PURIFICATION

will grow tired. At this stage the usual contemplation on selected objects (primary object) should be set aside, and mindfulness should open up to include (choicelessly) every object that arises at the 6-sense-doors. ~ Only after or when one notices that observation would improve if the selected object system were again used should one revert to the usual contemplation (primary object).

If the yogi's wisdom is lacking, they will identify with these experiences. ~ Since mindfulness is so strong ~ not missing an object ~ the yogi might think there is nothing more to know, ~ that what is to be known has been known. ~ He believes so because he knows by direct experience what he has not even dreamt of before.

1. ~ At this stage as a result of insist ~ some yogis (not all) will have the mental vision of a brilliant light appear to them (through their mind's eye). ~ To one this type of mental **illumination** will appear like the light of a lamp, ~ to others like a flash of lightning; ~ like the radiance of the moon or like the sun; ~ and so on. (It's easy to enjoy seeing the light.) Sometimes the light is so brilliant that the yogi finds it difficult to make it vanish by the mere act of noticing it mindfully. (Note: ~ Cease noting it ~ observe other sense-door experience.) To some the inner light is physically manifested: ~ one observes a halo around them; ~ or an aura of clear light encompasses their being; ~ their face feels like radiant light is streaming out through the eyes; one feels pure and transparent both mentally and bodily. ~ To others the illumination lights up a dark room ~ still others a larger area (see VIS.MAG.0.740, v.108). ~ With one this brilliance may last just for a moment ~ with others a gradual increase over days.

2. ~ The yogi's **knowledge** born of insight (as the result of energetic mindfulness) will be sharp ~ strong ~ keen ~ and lucid. He will discern easily and clearly and in separate forms all mind and body processes noticed ~ 'as if cutting to pieces a bamboo sprout with a razor-sharp knife'.

3. ~ There arises also **PĪTI – rapturous joy** in its 5 grades (see p.26 #4 of this book). ~ When purification of mind is gained ~ that rapture begins to appear by causing "goosebumps ~ tremor in the limbs ~ feeling of tears" ~ (unimaginable levels of joy ~ making all other

pleasures seem trifling). It produces a sublime feeling of happiness ~ exhilaration and inner contentedness ~ inner well-being. The entire body is pervaded with an exceedingly sweet and subtle thrill. ~ At such a stage the yogi will often say that he "feels like he is floating" ~ "as if walking on air or a cloud" ~ the whole body feels like it has "risen up and remained in the air without touching the ground" ~ "as if he were floating up and down" ~ "as light as a feather" or "like a piece of cotton". (MAHASI ~ "Some yogis even experience a certain degree of levitation".)

4. ~ There arises **tranquility** of mind (which has the characteristic of quieting the disturbances of consciousness and its mental concomitants). ~ Along with this tranquility appears mental agility, when sitting ~ walking ~ lying ~ or standing ~ the yogi feels exceedingly at ease ~ fluid and comfortable, mind and body are soft ~ smooth ~ and agile while functioning at this so swift a pace. ~ They are pliant and wieldy in being able to attend to any object desired ~ and able to attend to any object for a considerable length of time. ~ One is free from stiffness ~ tightness ~ heat or pain. ~ The body is buoyant and light. ~ Insight penetrates objects with straightness ~ directness and with ease. ~ Mind becomes solid ~ sound ~ straight and unified (with a new found feeling of togetherness). At times when there is no apparent object to be noticed ~ the mind remains tranquil for a long time. (VIS.MAG. p.741, v.116 ~ There is no fatigue or heaviness or rigidity or unwieldiness or sickness or crookedness in his body and mind ~ with his body and mind aided by this tranquility. Etc. The yogi experiences at that time superhuman delight because he comprehends the rise and fall of aggregates ~ (DHP.V.373-4) ~ his mind having reached the level of supreme relief ~ in attentive ~ non-active receptivity.

5. ~ There also arises a very sublime feeling of **happiness,** with **bliss** suffusing his entire body. ~ It is exceedingly refined bliss flooding his being. ~ The yogi might think ~ "Now I am happy all the time. ~ I have found the key to true happiness. ~ This is a happiness never felt before." Etc. Most yogis want to immediately share such insights with others, and tell them of his extraordinary experience.

6. ~ Further strong **faith** pertaining to insight arises in the meditator.

Under its influence ~ the yogi's mind ~ when engaged in noticing or thinking ~ is focused, serene and without any disturbance. ~ The yogi begins to delightfully recollect the power ~ beauty ~ and virtues of the BUDDHA ~ DHAMMA ~ and SANGHA (other friends and yogis practicing SATIPATTHANA). ~ The yogi's mind is intoxicated with abundant faithful confidence in the BUDDHA'S SASANA, and one usually desires to proclaim the DHAMMA to others (one is in awe over the profundity and sublimity of the teaching). One feels great inspiration to live a life of a meditation ~ virtue and purity. ~ One wants to avoid all which is unwholesome (a great sense of humility and sensitivity come over one). ~ One wants to advise dear friends and relatives to practice meditation. ~ One feels profound levels of appreciation to those who have given him the meditation and clear DHAMMA instructions. ~ These and many other similar mental processes will occur. (Basically, an extreme sense of DHAMMA confidence arises.)

7. ~ There arises in the yogi **energy** that is neither too lax nor too tense ~ but is vigorous and acts evenly. ~ For formerly his energy was not always balanced and smooth ~ and so he was at times overcome by sloth and torpor ~ hence he could not notice keenly and continuously the objects as they became evident. ~ And his understanding too ~ was not clear. ~ At other times his energy was too tense and tight ~ and so he was overpowered by agitation ~ still not able to discern clearly. ~ But now his energy is obviously smooth and balanced ('like putting a Lincoln on interstate speed cruise-control ~ as smooth as effortless surfing'). ~ A great sense of commitment to the practices is obvious. ("What can I do to deepen the practice?").

8. ~ There also arises in the yogi strong **mindfulness** pertaining to insight. ~ It is obvious to you that your mindfulness is well and firmly established. ~ While noticing objects ~ the yogi comprehends lucidly the TI-LAKKHANA. ~ The yogi feels that there is no body and mind process in which mindfulness fails to engage. ~ SATI level feels immovable ~ powerful and penetrating.

9. ~ There also arises strong **equanimity** associated with insight ~ the mind which is neutral towards all formations. ~ Under its influence the yogi regards with neutrality even his examination of the nature of

these formations with respect to their being ANICCA ~ DUKKHA ~ and ANATTA ~ and he is able to notice keenly and continuously the bodily and mental processes arising at the time. Then his activity of noticing is carried on quite automatically without particular effort, ~ and it proceeds ~ as it is of itself ~ whatever subject of noticing the yogi adverts to. ~ His adverting works as incisively and sharply as a lightning flash ~ with firm equanimity.

10. ~ There arises further a subtle **attachment** of a calm nature that enjoys the insight graced with brilliant inner light, and other such extraordinary experiences here described. ~ This attachment to one's experiences and enjoyable condition is subtle and peaceful in aspect ~ and it relies on clinging to that insight ~ and the yogi is not able to discern that attachment as a defilement ~ or corruption to deeper practice. (Just empty roll on ~ just silent mindfulness of all conditioned NĀMA- RŪPAS).

The yogi doesn't realize that such subtle infatuated attraction to these 9 qualities is a wrong and unskillful attitude (just mindful detachment until they disappear is enough). ~ The yogi's SATI and ÑĀNA are swift and clear ~ arising and disappearance of objects becomes even more distinct due to his continued application of noticing. ~ ANICCA ~ DUKKHA ~ and ANATTA are sound insights at every act of noticing. ~ The yogi feels that he is enjoying perfect mindfulness. ~ The yogi very often believes at this point that they have finished the task of meditation. ~ "Surely I must have attained path and fruit ~ enlightenment or NIBBĀNA." (This type of thinking doesn't always occur ~ but the main flaw is the attachment to the 9 qualities ~ factors. Just the fact of feeling or taking delight in them is off base, this is a corruption of insight. ~ Due to wrong views ~ pride ~ conceit ~ and craving ~ the yogi becomes corrupted to the further development of practice by being tainted in these 3 ways to the corruptions. ~ This equals 30 ways of corruption according to the VIS.MAG. p.743, v.125) ~ The yogi wavers and takes these experiences as "This is mine ~ this is I ~ this is myself" ~ so at this stage a yogi is very likely to become so satisfied with his progress that he pauses and relaxes his quality of effort and mindfulness. (This is actually the time to step up one's efforts ~ and go all out).

Therefore ~ this stage of VIPASSANĀ- ÑĀNA should be known as ~ the early stage ~ or 'weak knowledge of arising and passing away'. ~ This is mistaking what is not the path for the path. ~ For the same reason the meditator is at that time not in a position to discern quite distinctly the arising and passing away of bodily and mental processes (due to the flaw of delight and) compared to the lucidity (when the corruptions are recognized as such).

E. Purification by Knowledge and Vision of What Is Path and Not Path (MAGGĀMAGGA- ÑĀNADASSANA – VISUDDHI)

(VIS.MAG. p.743, v.126-130)

While engaged in noticing, the yogi ~ either by himself or through instruction from someone else ~ comes to the realization and consequent decision that ~ the brilliant light ~ rapturous exhilaration ~ tranquility ~ acute awareness ~ etc. and the other such experiences undergone ~ are nothing more than empty ~ interchanging phenomena. ~ Attachment to them ~ or delight in them ~ is an obstacle ~ hindrance ~ and corruption of my insight; ~ to rely and follow such experiences is not the true path that leads to enlightenment. ~ Delight in them is merely my ignorance ~ a corruption of insight; ~ and the correct method of contemplation to attain enlightenment is only constant mindful observation of whatever arises as it becomes evident. ~ That alone is the way of insight ~ that is the right path: ~ to realize and decide which is the wrong and right path is the realization of this purification knowledge. ~ "I must go on with just the work of noticing." ~ (This point in the practice can be extremely treacherous ~ and it can become difficult to proceed ~ easy to lose interest and give up ~ or carrying on half-heartedly. ~ Coming down from peak level joy and ease (etc.) can be disheartening ~ so give much encouragement and inspiration ~ watch behaviors closely; ~ Yogi must remain finely focused. (Yogi realizes that all corruptions are ANICCA ~ ANATTA ~ and DUKKHA ~ so he gives them up).

F. Purification by Knowledge and Vision of the Course of Practice (PATIPADĀ – ÑĀNADASSANA – VISUDDHI)

Having come to the decision of acknowledging the (UPAKKILESAS) corruptions as impurities, and proceeding further with the contemplation ~ those experiences of mental illumination ~ rapture and so on ~ will gradually decrease, and the perceiving of the various objects becomes clearer and clearer as they become evident at the six-sense doors. (While thus engaged in noticing ~ the yogi completely overcomes the corruptions of insight). ~ The yogi's knowledge remains concerned exclusively with the arising and passing away of the processes noticed, ~ for then ~ at each act of noticing ~ he sees ~ "The noticed object arisen ~ disappears instantly." ~ It's also clear that each object disappears just where it arises ~ and it does not move onto another place. ~ In this way he understands by direct experience how bodily and mental processes arise and break up, from moment to moment. One comes to know distinctly and clearly the division into 2 to 3 or more parts within each arising and each falling movement of the abdomen: The arising and passing away of material phenomena at each movement in the course of a single bending or stretching of the arm of the leg or in the course of a single step (lifting ~ moving ~ placing) ~ fragment by fragment ~ section by section or piece by piece ~ without reaching from one stage of the movement to another stage thereof ~ will then be clearly perceived. This is the final or mature stage of the knowledge of arising and passing away. ~ It is flawless as it is free from the 10 corruptions.

This is also the beginning of Purification by Knowledge and Vision of the Course or Practice", which includes 8 knowledges ~ plus "Knowledge in conformity with truth" or "Adaptation knowledge" (ANULOMAÑĀNA)

1. Knowledge of rise and fall ~ free from corruptions
2. Knowledge of dissolution (BHĀNGA- ÑĀNA)
3. Knowledge of or awareness of fearfulness or terror (BHAYA- ÑĀNA)
4. Knowledge of misery or danger (ĀDĪNAVA- ÑĀNA)
5. Knowledge of disgust or dispassion (NIBIDĀ- ÑĀNA)
6. Knowledge of desire for deliverance (MUÑCITU- KAYATA- ÑĀNA)

7. Knowledge of re-observation or reflection (PATISANKĀ- ÑĀNA)
8. Knowledge of equanimity about formations (SANKHĀRARUPEKKHA- ÑĀNA)
9. Knowledge of adaptation (ANULOMAÑĀNA)

(From VISUDDHI MAGGA ~ CH. XXI ~ p.746 ~ v.3 ~ v.9 ~ including notes #3 & 4)

~ Final notes regarding the mature knowledge of rise and fall ~

"Now the three characteristics fail to become apparent when something is not even given attention to, and so something conceals them. What is that?" ~

Firstly ~ the characteristic of impermanence does not become apparent because ~ when rise and fall are not given attention ~ it is concealed by continuity ~ the characteristic of pain. – DUKKHA does not become apparent because ~ when continuous oppression is not given attention ~ it is concealed by the postures. ~The characteristic of ANATTA does not become apparent because ~ when resolution into the various elements is not given attention ~ it is concealed by compactness.

However ~ when continuity is disrupted by discerning rise and fall (arising and passing away of NĀMA- RŪPA) ~ ANICCA becomes apparent in its true nature. ~ When the postures are exposed by attention to continuous oppression ~ the characteristic of DUKKHA becomes apparent in its true nature. When the resolution of the compactness is affected by resolution into elements ~ the characteristic of ANATTA becomes apparent in its true nature.

(ft. nt.#3) ~ Commentary? to ĀYATANA-VIBHANGA: ~ "ANICCA is obvious ~ as when a saucer falls and breaks. ~ DUKKHA is obvious ~ as when a boil appears in the body. ~ ANATTA is not obvious ~ whether BUDDHAS arise or do not arise the characteristic of ANICCA and DUKKHA are made known. ~ But unless there is the arising of a BUDDHA the characteristic of ANATTA is not made known.")

(Commentary To MAJ.NIK. SUTTA #22 ~ "Having been, ~ it is not; ~ therefore it is impermanent. ~ It is ANICCA for four reasons: ~ 1 ~ In the sense of the state of arising and passing ~ 2 ~ of change ~ 3

~ of temporariness, and ~ 4 ~ of denying permanence. ~ It is painful DUKKHA on account of the mode of oppression. ~ It is DUKKHA for 4 reasons: ~ 1 ~ In the sense of burning, 2 ~ of being hard to bear, 3 ~ of being the basis for pain, 4 ~ and of opposing pleasure. ~ It is ANATTA on account of the mode of insusceptibility to the exercise of power (personal command). ~It is ANATTA for 4 reasons: ~ 1 ~ in the sense of voidness ~ 2 ~ of having no owner-master ~ 3 ~ of having no overlord ~ 4 ~ and of opposing self.)

When the postures are exposed ~ for when pain arises in a posture ~ the next posture adopted removed the pain ~ as it were ~ concealing it; ~ but once it is known how the pain in any posture is shifted by substituting another posture for that one ~ then the concealment of the pain that is in them is exposed, because it has become evident that formations are being incessantly overwhelmed by pain. ~ Explanation of concealed by continuity (ANICCA) and resolution of the compact (ANATTA) is very interesting.

And here the following differences should be understood:

The impermanent and the characteristic of impermanence: ~ The 5 aggregates are impermanent. ~ Why? Because they rise and fall and change ~ and because their non-existence after having been ~ or more of alteration ~ all are the characteristics of ANICCA.

The painful (DUKKHA) and the characteristic of pain ~ those same 5 aggregates are DUKKHA because of the words "What is ANICCA is DUKKHA." ~ Why? ~ Because of continuous oppression ~ the mode of being continuously oppressed (by rise and fall) is the characteristic of DUKKHA.

The non-self (ANATTA) and the characteristic of ANATTA ~ these same 5 aggregates are ANATTA because of the words "What is DUKKHA is ANATTA." ~ Why? ~ Because there is no exercising power over them. The mode of insusceptibility to the exercise of power is the characteristic of ANATTA.

v.9 ~ "The meditator observes all this in its true nature with the knowledge of the contemplation of arising and passing away; ~ in other words ~ with insight from imperfections (corruptions) and steady on its course."

(Refer to VIS. MAG. CH. XXI ~ p.746, v.10 ~ For detailed description of the 'Knowledge of Dissolution' ~ p.753, v.28)

5. Knowledge of Dissolution or Passing Away (BHANGA – ÑĀNA)

When that knowledge of arising and passing away becomes mature ~ keen and strong ~ it will arise easily and proceed uninterruptedly as if borne onwards of itself. ~ Bodily and mental processes will be easily discernible ~ as the yogi continues practice ~ and when insight becomes even more developed ~ the arising or middle phase (called "presence") of these objects is noticed. It is no longer apparent to the meditator ~ he notices only their ceasing ~ the vanishing ~ passing away or dissolution of all bodily and mental processes; ~ while noticing the arising of the abdomen ~ neither the initial nor middle phase is apparent ~ but only the ceasing phase is discerned. ~ He realizes how swiftly all comes to pass as well as seeing the mental process of noticing them also dissolve ~ and so it is with the falling movement of the abdomen. ~ Thus, it will be clearly known to the yogi that both the rising/falling and the noticing of each vanish immediately ~ one after another in quick succession. ~ The same applies in the case of sitting ~ bending ~ reaching ~ stretching of an arm or leg ~ the noticing of an object and the knowledge of its ceasing occur in rapid sequence. (Note: ~ Some yogis who are sharp perceive distinctly three phases ~ noticing an object ~ its ceasing ~ and the passing away of the consciousness that cognizes that ceasing ~ all in rapid succession. However, ~ it is quite sufficient to know ~ in pairwise sequence ~ the dissolution of an object, and the passing away of the consciousness of noticing that dissolution).

When the yogi can clearly notice these pairs uninterruptedly ~ the particular features or forms of one's body ~ head ~ hand ~ leg ~ arm ~ these shapes are no longer apparent to him, and it appears to him that everything is ceasing and vanishing, ~ just the dissolution of NĀMA-RŪPA. ~ Formerly the yogi's consciousness normally took delight in conceptual objects of shapes, ~ of self ~ etc. ~ And even as far as up to UDAYABBAYA- ÑĀNA ~ the idea of formations with their specific features (marks or image) was always apparent to him. ~ But now that the yogi's knowledge has developed in this way ~ no such idea of the formations features or structure ~ appears to him ~ still less any other cruder concept. ~ At this stage the yogi is likely to feel that his practice/ contemplation is lagging or not up to mark. (To the contrary) ~ mind as a rule takes delight in dwelling on the sight of particular features and forms (concepts); ~ because of their absence ~ mind is wanting in satisfaction (just the manifestation of the aggregates of insight); ~ only on repeated reflection ~ features appear again. ~ But if they are not noticed the fact of dissolution reappears to remain. (Note: ~ at first the yogi feels no delight in this dissolving process. ~ After becoming familiar with that stage of the practice ~ his mind will delight in the cessation of the phenomena: ~ Cessation = dissolution/ vanishing. (With such assurance ~ yogi should resume continuous practice).

(Note: ~ Regarding this dissolution ~ each object that is being noticed ~ seems to be entirely absent or to have become non-existent. ~ Consequently, at this stage of knowledge ~ it seems as if one were engaged in noticing something which has already disappeared ~ or non-existent by having vanished. And the consciousness engaged in noticing appears to have lost contact with the object that is being noticed. It is for this reason that the yogi thinks that they have lost the insight or momentum ~ etc. ~

But not so ~ just carry on ~ paying close attention to yourself ~ work for a no-gap day).

When the yogi notices the objects clearly ~ he thinks that his noticings are not close enough. In fact. ~ the insight is so swift and clear that he even comes to know the momentary subconsciousness (BHAVANGA) in between the processes of cognition ~ when bending ~ moving ~ etc. ~ Intentions are clearly noticed which thereby tend to fade away ~ with the result that the yogi cannot bend or move for some time. ~ At such time open the awareness to include all 6-doors (momentum will build). ~ If not ~ revert to primary object (the object and the knowing of it.) ~ When tiredness and restlessness disappear ~ and momentum increases again ~ resume open 6-door observation. (Sit with whole body. ~ All will be seen ~ heard ~ sensed as fading away. ~ What he sees dissolves in broken parts ~ with no continuation between them. (This is reality).

14. THE PROGRESS OF INSIGHT THROUGH THE STAGES OF PURIFICATION

(Note: ~ Some yogis do not see clearly what is happening because the vanishing is so swift that they feel their eyesight is getting poorer, or they are giddy. ~ Not so ~ they are simply lacking the power of cognition to notice what happens before and after ~ with the result that they do not see the features or forms. ~ At such time they should relax and stop contemplating ~ but the bodily and mental processes continue to appear to them, ~ and consciousness ~ of its own accord ~ continues to notice them. ~ The yogi may decide to sleep ~ but he cannot fall asleep ~ yet he remains vibrant and alert. To just continue to be mindful is enough).

Summary ~ when thus engaged ~ the yogi ~ perceives that in each act of noticing there are 2 factors always present: ~ an objective and subjective one; ~ the object noticed and the mental state of knowing it ~ which dissolve and vanish by pairs ~ one pair after the other. In each single instance of a rising movement of the abdomen ~ there is noticed ~ the fact ~ of the numerous physical (separate pieces) processes constituting the rising movement ~ which are seen to dissolve serially ~ like seeing the continuous successive vanishing of a summer mirage moment by moment. ~ Or it is like the quick and continuous bursting of bubbles produced in a heavy shower of rain drops falling on a water surface. ~ Or it is like the quick ~ successive extinction of oil-lamps or candles ~ blown out by the wind. ~ And similar to that appears the dissolving and vanishing ~ moment by moment ~ of the bodily processes noticed ~ and the dissolution of the bodily processes. Also ~ while noticing other bodily processes and other mental processes ~ their dissolution too ~ will be apparent to him in the same manner. ~ Consequently ~ the knowledge will come that whatever path of the whole body is noticed ~ that object ceases first; ~ and after ~ in the consciousness engaged in noticing that object follows in its wake.

It is the perfectly clear understanding of the dissolution of the two things ~ pair by pair: ~ That is ~ 1 ~ of the object appearing at any of the 6-sense doors and ~ 2 ~ of the consciousness noticing that very object. ~ That is to be known as ~ knowledge of dissolution.

~ VISUDDHI MAGGA ~ p.746-753 ~
~ Herein ~ dissolution is the culminating point of ANICCA

~ and so the meditator contemplates (while aware of dissolution) the entire field of formations as impermanent not as permanent. ~ hen because of the DUKKHA of what is ANICCA and because what is DUKKHA that is ANATTA; ~ so he contemplates that some whole fields of formations (bodily and mental) as painful ~ not as pleasant. He contemplates it as 'non-self' ~ not as 'self'. ~ v.16 ~ But what is ANICCA ~ DUKKHA ~ and ANATTA ~ is not something to delight in. ~ And what is not something to delight in is not something to arouse greed for. ~ Consequently ~ when that field of NĀMA- RŪPA formations (5 aggregates) is seen as ANICCA ~ DUKKHA ~ and ANATTA (in accordance with the contemplation of dissolution) ~ then he becomes dispassionate. ~ He does not delight; ~ he causes fading away of greed. ~ He does not inflame it ~ because cessation of greed ~ not its origination ~ he relinquishes; ~ he does not grasp. ~ By seeing the unsatisfactoriness of formations ~ the yogi ~ inclining towards NIBBĀNA ~ which is the opposite of the formed (meaning KAMMA-produced formations).

~ The yogi knows by inference: ~ "By inference from the object seen by actual experience ~ he defines both the seen and the unseen to have a single individual essence thus. ~ The field of formations dissolved in the past ~ and will break up in the future ~ just as it does in the present. ~ (He infers that all formations ~ past and future ~ disappear ~ like dew drops when the morning sun comes up.) ~ Only formations break up. ~ Their break-up is death. ~ There is nothing else at all."

v.24 ~ "Aggregates cease and nothing else exists. Break-up of aggregates is known as death." He watches their destruction steadfastly ~ as one who with drills a gem with a diamond.

v.28 ~ "When he consistently sees that all formations thus break up all of the time ~ then contemplation of isolation grows strong in him ~ bringing eight advantages ~

1. Abandoning of false view of becoming
2. Giving up attachment to life
3. Constant application
4. A purified livelihood
5. No more anxiety
6. Absence of fear

7. Acquisition of patience and gentleness
8. And conquest of aversion (boredom) and sensual delight

("The yogi comprehends formations constantly, seeing their break-up in order to attain the deathless ~ like the sage with a burning turban.")

(Manual of Insight- Mahasi Sayadaw, chapter 6, pp.383- 384)

At the mature level of Insight Knowledge of Dissolution, one can see observed objects (and the mind that observes them) continuously disappearing, like the continuous popping of sesame seeds in a skillet, the patter of bursting bubbles from raindrops striking a pond, or a constantly shifting mirage. The VISUDDHIMAGGA says that the BUDDHA aimed the following verse from the DHAMMAPADA at meditators whose experience is like this:

'If one sees the world as a bubble,
If one sees it as a mirage,
One won't be seen
By the King of Death.'

When with insight knowledge of dissolution, one sees each object disappearing, one won't be subject to ignorance, craving, clinging, KAMMA, rebirth, or the aggregates. Since there are no aggregates for a new life, there is no death. By gradually passing through the stages of insight knowledge, beginning with insight knowledge of dissolution and culminating in knowledge that is the fruit of arahantship, one will absolutely experience no more rebirth and consequently no more death. The line "One won't be seen by the King of Death" refers to this fact.

(See VIS.MAG.CH, XX ~ p.753, v.24 ~ p.754, v.34)
"Knowledge of appearance as terror"

6. Knowledge of Fearfulness (BHAYA – ÑĀNA)

~ or knowledge of appearance of terror ~

When the "knowledge of dissolution" is mature ~ the yogi will notice continuously the dissolution of sense and mind-door objects, and the act of knowing it: ~ just the ever-vanishing in pairs of mind and its objects ~ just by seeing the dissolution of all object-and-subject formations there will gradually arise in the yogi's mind ~ "Awareness of fearfulness" or the "Knowledge realizing the dreadful nature of things" or the "terrifying nature of things". ~ In the wake of observing the constant and rapid dissolution of all phenomena ~ the yogi also understands by inference that in the past ~ too ~ every conditioned formation has broken up in the same way ~ and in the same way they will break up also in the future ~ and at present it dissolves too. ~ And just at the time of noticing any formations that are evident ~ these formations will appear to him in their aspect of fearfulness. (Such reflections ~ "…as for even the blink of an eye or a flash of lightning nothing lasts". One did not realize this before: ~ As it ceased and vanished in the past so will it cease and vanish in the future. ~ One enjoys life not knowing the truth. ~ Now that one knows the truth of continuous dissolution it is truly a fearful condition: ~ At every moment of dissolution one can die. ~ The beginning of this life itself is fearful; ~ so are the endless repetitions of the arising. ~ Terrifying it is to feel that in the absence of real features and forms the arisings appear to be real and substantial, so are the efforts to arrest the changing phenomena for the sake of well-being and happiness. ~ To be reborn is fearful in that it will be a recurrence of objects that are ceasing and vanishing always ~ fearful indeed it is to be old ~ to die ~ to experience sorrow ~ lamentation ~ pain ~ grief ~ and despair.

~ VISUDDHI MAGGA ~

(p.754, v.32) ~ But does the knowledge of appearance as terror itself fear — or does it not fear? ~ It does not fear ~ for it is simply the mere judgment that passed formations have ceased ~ present ones are ceasing ~ and future ones will cease. ~ So the knowledge of appearance as terror does not itself fear ~ it only forms the mere judgment that in the 3 kinds of becoming ~ past formations have ceased ~ present ones are ceasing ~ and future ones will cease. ~ It is called "Awareness of fearfulness" or "Appearance as terror" ~ only because formations in all kind of becoming, generation, destiny, station, or abode ~ are fearful in being bound for destruction ~ and so they appear only as terror.

(v.33-34) ~ "When (the yogi) brings to mind as impermanent ~ the sign (= sign of past ~ present ~ and future formations) appears to him as terror. ~ When he brings to mind as 'not-self' the sign and occurrence appear to him as terror; ~ he sees them as empty ~ vain ~ void ~ without power or guide ~ like an empty village ~ a miracle ~ etc. (Occurrence ~ though ordinarily reckoned as pleasure ~ appears as terror since it is only a state of being continuously oppressed by rise and fall. And in this case ~ a ceaselessly dissolving ~ eroding ~ situation ~ terrifying indeed).

The yogi sees nothing on which to depend, and becomes as it were weakened in mind as well as body. ~ He is sealed with dejection. ~ He is no longer bright and spirited (and has lost the nature of this ÑĀNA ~ reaction to the distorting sense of fearfulness ~ UPEKKHA views formations for what they truly are ~ neutral). Just continue the practice ~ gradually this will subside and disappear. ~ However, ~ if the yogi becomes lax and indulges in reflective contemplation ~ then grief will assert itself and a sense of fear could overcome him. ~ Observe carefully the yogi's behaviors and manifestation: ~ this kind of emotional fear is not associated with insight, and it should be carefully guarded against ~ by careful and energetic mindfulness.

(See VIS.MAG.CH, XX ~ p.755, v.35 ~ p.758, v.42)
"Knowledge of Contemplation of Danger"

7. Knowledge of Misery (ĀDĪNAVA – ÑĀNA)
~ or Insight into unsatisfactory condition or Knowledge of Contemplation of Danger ~

~ When the yogi has rallied the fearfulness of the dissolving formations and keeps on noticing continuously, then the "Knowledge of Misery" will arise before long. ~ When it has arisen all formations everywhere (past ~ present ~ future ~ all realms) ~ whether among the objects noticed ~ or among the states of consciousness engaged in noticing ~ or in any kind of life or existence that is brought to mind ~ will appear insipid ~ without a vitalizing factor: ~ Undesirable DHAMMAs of an inferior ~ unsatisfying and miserable nature ~ just psycho-physical DHAMMAS ~ dissolving rapidly. ~ So, the yogi sees at that time ~ only DUKKHA ~ only unsatisfactoriness ~ only dreadful misery; ~ thus this knowledge of realizing the faults are defects of material and mental phenomena. ~ (NĀMA- RŪPA) is to be known as the Knowledge of Misery or Insight into the Unsatisfactory Condition (of NĀMA- RŪPA).

~ While practicing and engaged in observing evident objects ~ the yogi is likely to find fault in this manner: ~ This body and mind process ~ being ANICCA ~ is indeed a most dreadful horrifying and (at the very least) an unsatisfactory situation. It was not a good thing to have been born ~ indeed a very tragic thing. ~ It is not good either to continue existence: ~ Ugh! ~ Such DUKKHA! ~ Just ultimate realities alone exist; ~ no 'you' ~ no 'me' ~ "nothing worthy in this world" ~ "such a disappointing arrangement" ~ "time to end this tragedy" ~ "let's put an end to this nightmare": ~It is in vain that one makes efforts to seek wellbeing and happiness. ~ "How dreadful this gloom of ignorance." ~ "Birth is a dreadful thought ~ it must be avoided". ~ Growing old and so on is "a monumental absurdity" ~ "enough of this madness". ~" Oh, how miserable the knowing mind is!" ("Reflecting, reflecting". Carry on.)

~ VISUDDHI MAGGA ~

(v.35) ~ As the yogi repeats ~ develops and cultivates this ÑĀNA he finds no asylum ~ no shelter ~ no place to go to ~ no regret in any kind of becoming ~ destiny ~ or abode. There is not a single formation that he can place high hopes in, or hold onto. ~ The 3 kinds of becoming appear like charcoal pits full of glowing coals, the 4 primary elements like hideous poisonous snakes, the 5 aggregates like murderers with raised weapons, the 6 internal bases like an empty village, the 6 external bases like village-raiding robbers; and all formations appear as a huge mass of dangers destitute of satisfaction or substance ~ like a tumor ~ a disease ~ a dart ~ a calamity ~ an affliction.

~ Conclusion: ~ When all formations have appeared as terror/miserable by contemplation of dissolution ~ the meditator sees them as utterly destitute of any core or any satisfaction, and as nothing but danger or misery.

(See VIS.MAG.CH, XXI ~ p.756, v.43 and 44)
"Knowledge of Contemplation of Dispassion"

8. Knowledge of Disgust (NIBBIDĀ – ÑĀNA)

~ or Knowledge of Contemplation of Dispassion or Knowledge consisting in this contemplation of the wearisome condition ~

Seeing thus the misery in conditioned formations ~ the yogi's mind finds no delight in such a horrifying situation ~ and is utterly convinced without the slightest doubt that conditioned existence is a truly disgusting arrangement. ~ At this stage ~ the mind becomes bored, ~ disgusted and listless. One tends to feel that body – and – mind ~ as the object and the consciousness of noticing it ~ are very crude and tiring. ~ "I'm tired and bored with meditating" ~ "plain sick and fed up with noticing this worthless arising and disappearing act" ~ The yogi sometimes sees his own body decaying and decomposing. He looks upon this body as being so fragile and delicate. ~ At this stage the mind-body noticing process is clearly growing more and more into a disgusting situation: ~ "Such a wearisome condition this mind and body." ~ Although the yogi cognizes NĀMA-RŪPA dissolution by a series of clear noticings, he is obviously no longer alert and bright ~ because he is "flat out disgusted with this thing called life". ~ (You feel like you could just stop in your tracks and fall over. ~ Perhaps round the Earth ~ all appears futile ~ the past ~ present ~ and to go on.) ~ It is ever so easy to pack it in, ~ and almost inevitably one becomes lazy to contemplate. ~ "Enough of this meditation!" ~ But even one's happiest recollections of future construction appear desolate ~ meaningless ~ like bubbles or sand castles. ~

"But life goes on and one isn't overwhelmed by such reflections. You still know the way ~ so nevertheless you cannot refrain from continuing the practice." ~ It is like one who feels disgusted at every step when he has to walk on a muddy and dirty path (perhaps more if the smell of decaying flesh is in the air) and yet he cannot stop going: ("You have to eat...") ~ so he cannot help but to go on. ~ The mind begins to increasingly incline towards that state of peace ~ non-arising ~ non-despair ~ non-occurrence. Towards the freedom from formations, NIBBĀNA. ~ The yogi will know ~ "The ceasing of all formations that are dissolving from moment to moment ~ that alone is the only worthy abiding ~ the only true peace and happiness." ~ (One feels disgusted at the thought of rebirth again ~ as a human ~ DEVA ~ BRAHMA ~ God ~ man ~ woman ~ kind ~ multi-millionaire. ~ Whatever your hopes once were ~ they have all realigned with getting off the wheel ~ the only sensible accomplishment. ~ (The unattractive, wearisome condition is not superficial. ~ The yogi's knowledge is burned onto his consciousness. The passion grows towards mind development ~ everything else is void and meaningless).

~ Summary ~

(BHAYA- ÑĀNA) (ĀDĪNAVA- ÑĀNA) (NIBBIDĀ- ÑĀNA)
fearfulness _____misery_____disgust
(MAHASI ~ progress of insight)
terror _____danger _____dispassion
(ÑĀNAMOLI VIS.MAG)

(VIS.MAG. p.759, v.44) ~ "Knowledge of Contemplation or Danger" is the same as the last two kinds of Knowledges (Misery and Disgust) in meaning. ~ Hence the "Knowledge of Appearance as Terror" ~ while one only has three names. ~ It saw all formations as terror ~ thus the name "Appearance as Terror" arose. ~ It aroused the appearance of danger in those same formations, ~ thus the name "Contemplation of Danger" arose. It arose ~ becoming dispassionate towards those same formations ~ thus the name "Contemplation of Dispassion" arose. ~ Also, it is said in the text: ~ Terror ~ Danger ~ Dispassion ~ Fearfulness ~ Misery ~ Disgust: ~ "These Knowledges are one in meaning; only the letters are different." (PATISAMBHIDĀMAGGA ~ II ~ 63)

(MAHASI ~ Progress of Insight ~ first printing 1980 ~ Concise edition ~ p.14)
"BHAYA~ĀDĪNAVA ~ and NIBBIDĀ ~ These three kinds of VIPASSANĀ- ÑĀNA are in their essence said to constitute only one ÑĀNA, according to PALI ATTHAKATHĀ commentaries. That is why some yogis experience only one or two aspects out of three of these knowledges."

(See VIS.MAG.CH, XXI ~ p.759, v.45 and 46)
"Knowledge of Desire for Deliverance"

9. Knowledge of Desire for Deliverance (MUÑCITU – KAMYATĀ – ÑĀNA)

~ or Insight arising from Desire to Escape ~

When it is released that it would be well only if there were no physical and mental phenomena which are constantly coming into being and vanishing ~ moment after moment ~ there arises the knowledge "looking for an escape from suffering" on account of the unsatisfying oppressive nature of these phenomena. ~ This is to be known as the "Knowledge of Desire for Deliverance" or "Insight Arising from Desire to Escape (from 5 aggregates.)"

When the strengthening of NIBBIDĀ- ÑĀNA which sees and knows all psycho-physical phenomena as DUKKHA ~ an urgent desire arises to abandon ~ renounce ~ and go beyond this body-mind complex (entanglement): This is "Knowledge of Desire for Deliverance."

When through this knowledge (previously acquired) he feels disgust with regard to every formation noticed ~ there will arise in him a dire impulse (that grows and matures) to forsake these conditioned ~ repetitive ~ formations or to become delivered from them. The knowledge relating to that desire is "Knowledge of Desire for Deliverance."

Seeing, hearing, touching, reflecting, standing, sitting, bending, noticing, moving ~ all; he wishes to go beyond and relinquish them all in total ~ without the slightest remainder. (The yogi should notice such wanting ~ and pay bare attention to it.) ~ The yogi will experience a growing inner longing for complete liberation from bodily and mental processes.

At the time of this ÑĀNA ~ most yogis will experience a variety of deep painful feelings arising in the body (sharp and torturous at times ~ most difficult to bear or endure) ~ and also an unwillingness to remain long in one particular body posture. (The uncomfortable and fine level inner fidgetiness and restlessness is apparent from the first few minutes of a sitting, and then while walking also. ~ As the onslaught of all these DUKKH-manifestations intensify ~ one's desire to escape there from grows proportionally ~ until 'every molecule of your being' shouts "Enough of this madness!" ~ and ARAHANTSHIP becomes your only thought.) Even if these states do not arise (to that intensity) the comfortless nature of all formations will become more evident than ever. And due to that ~ between moments of noticing ~ the yogi feels a longing thus: ~ "Oh may I soon get free from that. ~ May I reach the state where these formations cease." ~ At this juncture ~ the yogi's consciousness engaged in noticing seems to shrink from the object noticed at each moment of noticing (a sort of cringing effect like when for instance hearing a piece of chalk screech on the chalkboard: ~ The mind recoils back) and consequently the yogi swipes to escape from it.

(MAHASI ~ FR. SATIPATTHANA Med. p.38) ~ 'The yogi longing for liberation ~ reflects "Every time I notice formations ~ I am meeting with repetitions ~ which are all DUKKHA ~ perhaps I should (will) stop noticing them." ~ The yogi should be aware of such a reflection. ~ Some meditators ~ when so reflecting ~ actually stop noticing formations. Although they do so ~ the formations do not stop taking place, ~ namely: ~ rising ~ falling ~ bending ~ stretching ~ intending ~ and so on. ~ They go on as ever ~ noticing of the distinct formations also continues ~ so reflecting thus ~ the yogi feels pleased. "Although I stop noticing the body and the mind ~ formations are taking place all the time." ~ They are arising and consciousness of them is there ~ by itself. ~ So, liberation from them cannot be achieved by mere stopping to notice them; they cannot be forsaken in this way).

~ VISUDDHI MAGGA ~ p.759, v.45 ~

"When owing to this Knowledge of Dispassion or Disgust" ~ the yogi becomes disgusted towards ~ is dissatisfied with ~ takes no delight in ~ any single one of all the manifest formations in any kind of becoming ~ generation ~ destiny ~ station of consciousness ~ or abode of beings. His mind no longer sticks fast ~ cleaves ~ fastens onto them ~ and he becomes desirous of being delivered from the whole field of formations, and to escape from it: ~ Just like a fish in a net ~ a frog in a snake's jaws ~ or a man encircled by enemies; ~ just as these are desirous of being delivered from the whole field of formations and escaping from it. ~ Then when he thus no longer relies on any formations and is desirous of being delivered from the whole field of formations ~ "Knowledge of Desire for Deliverance arises in him." ~

10. Knowledge of Re-Observation (PATISANKHĀ – ÑĀNA)

Being thus desirous of escaping from the formations ~ where the meditator makes stronger effort, and continues the practice of noting these very formations with the single purpose of forsaking them and escaping there from, ~ realizing the only way out of conditioned existence is by further sustained effort and application of mindfulness, ~ and accordingly ~ making that stepped-up breakthrough level effort, ~ should be known as "Knowledge of Re-Observation." So reflecting with delight upon this knowledge, the yogi continues to notice evident bodily and mental phenomena. (In the case of some yogis ~ they must be told and explained regarding the need to carry on in a continuous and determined way. "It's the only way." ~ "To stop is to be content with delusion and obscurity resulting from the waning of SAMĀDHI and SATI levels; ~ momentum is present ~ utilize it.") ~ The term re-observation indicates re-noticing ~ re-contemplation. ~ At this time the nature- characteristic of all foundations will be clearly evident ~ the TI-LAKKHANA will remain continually before your eyes: ~ "And among these three ~ the aspect of suffering will be particularly distinct." ~

At this stage too ~ there will usually arise in the body various kinds of pains which are severe ~ sharp ~ and of growing intensity. Hence, the whole bodily and mental system will seem like an unbearable mass of sickness, or a conglomerate of suffering. ~ A state of restlessness will usually manifest itself ~ making the yogi incapable of keeping to one particular posture for any length of time. ~ It will be extremely difficult to maintain a posture for long (sometimes even for a few minutes). Indeed ~ at times ~ you don't want to sit down ~ now that you are up ~ or to walk now that you are up ~ or to continue to stand ~ where you are ~ or to move: ~ and soon ~ this is a difficult stage. ~ Bathing could wear one out a bit ~ or more casual walking ~ just DUKKHA. ~ (This stage ~ is the "always wanting to be doing something else rather than what you are doing" stage. ~ You can't help but see ~ and so lucidly ~ the unbearable nature of existence ~ the pain in formations.)

~ MAHASI ~ "Though the yogi wants to change his bodily posture (repeatedly) he should not give in easily to that wish ~ but should endeavor to remain motionless for a longer period in the same posture, and continue to carry on the practice of noticing. By doing so he will be able to overcome his restlessness. Once the yogi realizes that the only sensible thing to do is carry on whole-heartedly ~ soon the yogi will gain momentum. (MAHASI ~ "At that time usually various painful feelings arise in some cases. ~ This need not cause despair; it is only the manifestation of the characteristic inherent in this mass of suffering ~ as stated in the commentaries: Seeing the 5 aggregates as painful ~ as a disease ~ as a boil ~ as a dart ~ a calamity ~ an affliction ~ etc." ~ If such painful feelings are not experienced ~ one of the various (40 total) characteristics of ANICCA ~ DUKKHA~ or ANATTA will be apparent at every noticing: ~ Although the yogi is properly noticing he feels that he is not doing well. He thinks that his consciousness that notices and the object noticed are not close enough. ~ This is because he is too eager to comprehend fully the 3 characteristics. ~ Not satisfied with his practice of contemplation he changes his posture often. ~ While sitting ~ he thinks he will do better by walking. ~ While walking he wants to resume sitting. ~ After he has sat down, he changes the position of his limbs; ~ he wants to go to another place ~ he wants to lie down. (He 'wants the other'). Although the yogi makes these changes, he cannot remain long in one particular position. ~ Again, he becomes restless. ~ All this happens because the yogi has come to realize the true nature of the formations. And also, because he has not yet acquired the "Knowledge of Equanimity about Formations": ~ The yogi is doing well and yet he feels otherwise. ~ (He should try to adhere to one posture and he will find that he is comfortable in that posture ~ as comfortable as any other posture. ~ Continuing to notice the formations energetically ~ his mind will gradually become composed and bright ~ and soon the restless feelings will totally disappear.)

~ MAHASI ~ p.20-21, Progress of Insight: ~ "Having now overcome his restlessness ~ the Yogi's insight knowledge is quite strong and lucid, and by virtue of this even his painful feelings will at once cease as soon as they are firmly noticed. ~ Even if a painful feeling does not cease completely, he will perceive that it is dissolving, part by part, from moment to moment. That is to say ~ the ceasing ~ vanishing and disappearing of each single moment of sensation, ~ feeling will become apparent separately in each corresponding act of noticing. ~ In other words, now it will not be as it was at the time of SAMMASANA-ÑĀNA, when the constant flow or continuity of feelings of the same kind was apparent as a single unit; ~ but if ~ without abandoning the practice ~ that feeling of pain is firmly and continuously noticed ~ it will entirely cease before long. ~ When it ceases in that way ~ it does so for good and will not arise again ~ though in that way the insight knowledge may have become strong and perfectly lucid. ~ Till he is not satisfied with that much ~ he will even think ~ "My insight knowledge is not clear." (Dismiss such thoughts ~ while carrying on continuous mindfulness.) ~ If the yogi perseveres thus ~ his noticing will become more and more clear as the time passes in minutes ~ hours and days. ~ He will then overcome the painful feelings and the restlessness in being able to remain long in any one posture ~ and also the idea that his insight knowledge is not clear enough. ~ His noticing will then function rapidly ~ and at every moment of noticing, he will understand quite clearly any of the TI-LAKKHANA.

"This understanding of any of the 3 characteristics of ANICCA ~ DUKKHA ~ and ANATTA through the act of noticing which functions with promptness in quick succession ~ is called "strong Knowledge of Re-Observation" ~

(PATISANKHĀ- ÑĀNA) ~ continued

~ VISUDDHI MAGGA p. 760, v. 47

~ "Being thus desirous of deliverance from all the manifold formations in any kind of becoming etc. ~ in order to be delivered from the entire field of formations ~ he again discerns those same formations ~ attributing to them the three characteristics by knowledge of re-observation."

v.46 ~ 1. ~ The yogi sees all formations as ANICCA for the following reasons: ~ Because they are non-continuous ~ temporary ~ limited by rise and fall ~ disintegrating ~ fickle ~ perishable ~ unenduring ~ subject to change ~ careless ~ due to be annihilated ~ formed subject to date ~ and so on.

v.46 ~ 2. ~ The yogi sees all formations as DUKKHA for the

following reasons: ~ Because they are continuously oppressed ~ hard to bear ~ the basis of pain ~ a disease ~ a tumor ~ a dart ~ a calamity ~ an affliction ~ a plague ~ a disaster ~a terror ~ a menace ~ no protection ~ no shelter ~ no refuge ~ a danger ~ the root of calamity ~ murderous ~ subject to cankers ~ MĀRA'S bait ~ subject to birth ~ subject to aging ~ subject to illness ~ subject to sorrow ~ subject to lamentation ~ subject to despair ~ subject to defilement ~ and so on. ~ They are considered foul also ~ because they are objectionable stinking ~ disgusting ~ repulsive ~ unaffected by disguise ~ hideous ~ loathsome ~ and so on.

V.46 ~ 3 ~ The yogi sees all formations as ANATTA for the following reasons: ~ Because they are alien ~ empty ~ void ~ ownerless ~ with no overlord ~ with none to wield power over them ~ and so on.

(~ "For this is said in the PATISAMBHIDĀ (i ~5f) in 'The description of what is to be directly known'.")

1. The states that occur in the doors (of consciousness) together with the doors and the object: (Eye is to be directly known ~ visible objects … ~ eye-consciousness~ …eye-contact…feeling pleasant or painful or neutral that arises due to eye-contact …ear/nose/tongue/body/mind…feeling)
2. The 5 aggregates ~ materiality is to be known directly ~ (feeling/perception/SANKHARAS/VIÑÑĀNA…)
3. The 6 doors ~ eye is to be known directly ~ ear …mind
4. The 6 objects ~ visible objects are to be known directly ~ mind-objects…
5. The 6 kinds of consciousness ~ eye-consciousness …etc.
6. The 6 kinds of contact ~ eye-contact…etc.
7. The 6 kinds of feeling ~ eye-contact born feeling …etc.
8. The 6 kinds of perception ~ perception of visible-objects …etc.
9. The 6 kinds of volition ~ volition regarding visible objects …etc.
10. The 6 kinds of craving ~ craving for visible objects
11. The 6 kinds of applied thought ~ applied thought about visible objects… etc.
12. The 6 kinds of sustained thought ~ sustained thought about visible objects …etc.

14. THE PROGRESS OF INSIGHT THROUGH THE STAGES OF PURIFICATION

13. The 6 elements: ~ the earth element is to be known directly ~ fire/water/air/space/consciousness…
14. The 10 KASINAS ~ the earth KASINA … the limited-space KASINA…
15. The 32 bodily parts ~ head hairs…urine
16. The 12 bases ~ the eye base…the visible object ~ mind base ~ the mental object base
17. The 18 elements ~ the eye-element …the mind-consciousness element
18. The 22 faculties ~ the eye faculty …the final knower faculty) investigate further!
19. The 3 elements ~ the sense-desire element ~ the five materials…~ the immaterial…
20. The 9 kinds of becoming: ~ sense-desire becoming ~ fine-material ~ immaterial …percipient ~ non-percipient neither percipient nor non-percipient ~ one-aggregate becoming ~ four aggregates …five aggregates becoming.
21. The 4 JHĀNAS ~ the first JHĀNA is to be directly known ~ 2nd ~ 3rd ~ 4th
22. The 4 measureless states ~ the mind-deliverance of METTĀ … KARUNĀ … MUDITĀ …UPEKKHĀ.
23. The 4 ARŪPA- JHĀNAS ~ infinity of space … consciousness … nothingness … neither percipient nor non -percipient…
24. The 12 links of dependent origination ~ ignorance is to be directly known …aging-and-death is to be directly known

~ VISUDDHI-MAGGA continued ~ p.762 ~ "Discerning formations as void by knowledge of re-observation"

v.53 ~ Having thus discerned by knowledge of re-observation that "All formations are NATTA" ~ the yogi again discerns ANATTA in the following ways: ~

1. Discerns voidness in the double logical relation (DVIKOTIKA) ~ 1 ~ This is void of self, 2 ~ Nor what belongs to a self
2. Next discerns voidness in the quadruple logical relation: ~ 1 ~ He sees the non-existence of a self of his own; 2 ~ He sees of his own

self too that it is not the property of another's self; 3 ~ There is no other self anywhere; 4 ~ That other is not the property of his own self. ~ "My owning of that other self does not exist" ~

3. (v.55) Next ~ the yogi discerns voidness in six modes. ~ (Each mode is systematically applied to each and every component of the list on the preceding page ~ "24 categories of what is to be directly known") ~ eye ~ dependent origination ~ aging-and-death ~ 1 ~ is void of self; 2 ~ or of the property of a self; 3 ~ or of permanence; 4 ~ or of lastingness; 5 ~ or of eternalness; 6 ~ or of non-subjectiveness to change.

4. (v.56) ~ Next the yogi discerns voidness in eight modes: ~ (applies to all 24 categories ~ each mode) ~ eye-materiality ~ feeling ~ perception ~ etc…aging and death ~ has no core ~ is careless ~ without core ~ as far as concerns ~ 1 ~ any core of permanence; 2 ~ core of lastingness; 3 ~ core of pleasure; 4 ~ core of self, or as far as concerns; 5 ~ what is permanent; or 6 ~ what is lasting; or 7 ~ what is eternal; or 8 ~ what is subject to change.

5. (v.57) ~ Next ~ the yogi discerns voidness in ten modes: ~ (applies to all 24 categories ~ each mode) "He sees eye …materiality… etc. As 1 ~ empty; 2 ~ as vain; 3 ~ as not self; 4 ~ as having no overlord; 5 ~ as being incapable of being made into what one wants; 6 ~ as incapable as being as one wishes; 7 ~ as insusceptible to the exercise of mastery; 8 ~ as alien; 9 ~ as secluded from past; 10 ~ as secluded from future.

6. (v.58) ~ Next ~ he discerns voidness in twelve ways: ~ (applies to all 24 categories) ~ eye…materiality …etc.…is: ~ 1 ~ no living being; 2 ~ no soul; 3 ~ no human being; 4 ~ no man; 5 ~ no female; 6 ~ no male; 7 ~ no self; 8 ~ no property of a self; 9 ~ not I; 10 ~ not mine; 11 ~ not another; 12 ~ not anyone's.

7. Next ~ the yogi discerns voidness in 42 modes through full understanding as investigating: ~ (applies to each component of all 24 categories) ~ He sees eye…materiality…aging and death as: ~ 1 ~ impermanent; 2 ~ painful; 3 ~ a disease; 4 ~ a tumor; 5 ~ a dart; 6 ~ a calamity; 7 ~ an affliction; 8 ~ alien; 9 ~ disintegrating; 10 ~ a plague; 11 ~ a disaster; 12 ~ a terror; 13

~ a menace; 14 ~ fickle; 15 ~ perishable; 16 ~ unenduring; 17 ~ no protection; 18 ~ no shelter; 19 ~ no refuge; 20 ~ unfit to be a refuge; 21 ~ empty; 22 ~ vain; 23 ~ void; 24 ~ not self; 25 ~ a danger; 26 ~ subject to change; 27 ~ having no core; 28 ~ the root of calamity; 29 ~ murderous; 30 ~ due to be annihilated; 31 ~ subject to cankers; 32 ~ formed; 33 ~ MĀRA'S BAIT, 34 ~ subject to birth, 35 ~ subject to ageing, 36 ~ to illness, 37 ~ to death; 38 ~ to sorrow; 39 ~ lamentation; 40 ~ pain; 41 ~ grief; 42 ~ and despair as arising ~ as departing ~ what satisfaction ~ as escape.

Concluding with ~ (all 24 categories combined = the world) thus taking them as a whole. Thus, the yogi when he sees the eye-materiality ~ etc. ~ as impermanent ~ as painful etc. ~ all 42 aspects).

~ "He looks upon the world as void" ~ p.765, v.60 ~

11. Knowledge of Equanimity about Formations (SANKHĀRUPEKKHĀ – ÑĀNA)
(See VIS.MAG.CH, XXI ~ p.765, v.61 and 66)
"Knowledge of Equanimity about Formations"

(MAHASI- Progress of Insight, p.21) ~ "When this knowledge of re-observation is mature there will arise knowledge perceiving evident bodily and mental processes in continuous succession quite naturally ~ as if borne onward of itself. ~ The mind will be very clear and able to notice the formations very lucidly; ~ noticing runs smoothly as if no effort is required. Subtle formations too ~ are noticed without effort ~ Effort is no longer required for keeping formations before the mind or for understanding them (this is SANKHĀRUPEKKHĀ- ÑĀNA) ~ without special effort. ~ One object of attention after another appears spontaneously. The awareness of noting likewise arises spontaneously and continuously one after another. After completion of each single act of noticing, the object to be noticed will then appear of itself ~ and insight knowledge ~ too ~ will of itself notice and understand it. The TILAKKHANA are clear and evident without any reflection.

"When the PATISANKHĀ- ÑĀNA is mature ~ contemplation proceeds automatically like a click without special effort for perception and knowledge. ~ It proceeds contemplating an object with equanimity ~ (just to take notice of NĀMA- RŪPA without depressing into the pleasantness and or unpleasantness attraction ~ joy ~ aversion ~ sadness). This contemplation is peaceful and effortless and it proceeds knowing its objects so automatically that it may extend over one ~ two ~ or three hours: and even though it may last this long ~ there will not be tiredness or exhaustion. (MAHASI ~ "Noting with effort is made only for the initial 4 ~ 5 or 10 times ~ (after which effortless and spontaneous noting goes on continually for as long as an hour or two or more.) The yogi may even come to feel that he can go on noting thus for a whole day with ease and comfort and without changing his posture." ~ (Even if the yogi thinks about something fearful or sad ~ no mental disturbance will arise ~ be it in the form of fear or sorrow. ~ This firstly ~ is the "abandoning of fear" ~ at the stage of "equanimity about formations").

(Formerly ~ owing to seeing the dissolution of formations ~ there arose ~ in successive order ~ the aspect of fearfulness ~ the perception of misery ~ the aspect of disgust ~ the desire for deliverance ~ and the dissatisfaction with the knowledge so far acquired; ~ but now these mental states no longer arise ~ although also in the present state ~ the breaking up of formations which are dissolving more rapidly ~ is perceived closely. ~ Generally, there is an absence of pain and similar physical discomfort ~ even if painful feeling arises in the body ~ no mental disturbance arises ~ and there is no lack of fortitude in bearing it. (The awareness is exceptionally still ~ subtle and smooth ~ frictionless mind sailing) ~ "Attention is directed to a particular spot at any part of the body wherever a sensation occurs ~ but the feeling of touch is as smooth as that of cotton. ~ Sometimes, both body and mind appear to be pulling upwards; ~ the objects noticed become sparse and one can notice them easily and calmly. ~ Sometimes the bodily formations disappear altogether, leaving only the mental formations. Then the meditator will experience within himself a feeling of rapture (very subtle joy) as if enjoying a shower of tiny particles of water. (Every cell feels transparent and tranquil beyond comparison sometimes). He

14. THE PROGRESS OF INSIGHT THROUGH THE STAGES OF PURIFICATION

is also suffused with serenity. ~ He might also see brightness like a clear sky. (But Yogi is not so influenced by such experiences; ~ he will remain ~ calm ~ balanced ~ and in the middle.) ~ It is still possible to find enjoyment in such things but not excessive overjoy. ~ The yogi must notice this enjoyment. ~ He must also notice rapture ~ serenity and bright light ~ if they do not vanish when being noticed. ~ He should pay no heed to them and notice any other object that arises." ~ (From the SATIPATTHANA VIPASSANĀ orange book ~ published. Rangoon ~ p.40)

~ (From MAHASI ~ Progress of Insight, p.22 ~ "At the earlier stage, on attaining "knowledge of arising and passing away" ~ great joy had arisen on account of the clarity of insight. ~ But now this kind of (strong delight – rapture) joy does not arise, even though there is present the exceedingly peaceful and sublime clarity of mind belonging to "equanimity about formations". ~ Though he actually sees desirable objects conducive to joy, or though he thinks about various enjoyable things ~ no strong feeling of joy will arise. ~ This is "abandoning delight" at the stages of "equanimity about formations.")

"The yogi, having discarded fear and delight ~ is impartial and neutral towards all formations." ~ At this stage the yogi becomes satisfied with the knowledge that there is no 'I', 'mind', 'he' or 'his', and that only formations arise; ~ formations only, are cognizing formations. (The DHAMMA will see and do what is necessary to enlighten itself. ~ Only PARAMATTHA DHAMMAS observing themselves. ~ The practice at this level embeds ANATTA into one's understanding. ~ The fact remains clearly before your eyes; ~ bare attention is so sound and unwavering that one feels like an empty mechanism that knows objects.) ~ From this point on there is no need for the yogi to make further deliberate effort. (You have become the practice so to speak ~ just the power of SATI ~ + other INDRIYAS ~ highly mature acting according to its nature). ~ Though he does not make a deliberate effort ~ his noticing will proceed in a continuous and steady flow for a long time, (PATISAMBHIDA-MAGGA ~ "This is the stage of long-lasting practice" ~ "The wisdom lasting long" is the knowledge present in mental states of "Equanimity about Formations" (The yogi find satisfaction in noticing objects ~ without becoming tired ~ and generally free from DUKKHA-VEDANA ~ one after another ~ in whatever posture he chooses. He can retain it long ~ either sitting ~ lying ~ etc. The yogi goes on effortlessly and tirelessly practicing (for 2 or 3 hours) ~ contemplating without experiencing any discomfort. Even after that time his posture is as firm as before).

~ "Commentary to VIS.MAG" ~ Thus is said (with reference to knowledge/understanding/wisdom functioning in a continuous flow): ~ "Now when noticing formations spontaneously as if borne onward of itself ~ the mind ~ even if sent out towards a variety of objects ~ generally refuses to go. ~ And even if it does go ~ it will not stay long ~ but will soon return to the usual object to be noticed ~ and will resume continuous noticing. In this connection it was said: ~ "He shrinks recoils and retreats ~ he does not go forth to it." ~ (U PANDITA refers to this state as "the boomerang mind": ~ Throw it out and it comes right back!)

(MAHASI ~ SATIPATTHANA-VIP ~ Rangoon ~ p.41) ~ "At times formations arise swiftly and the yogi is noticing them well. ~ Then he may become anxious (or expectant) as to what might happen to him. (The yogi should notice such anxiety). He feels that he is doing well in the meditation. (He should notice such a thought). He looks forward to the progress of insight. ~ (He should notice this anticipation). ~ He should notice steadily (precisely) whatever arises. ~ He should not put forth a special effort not relax (balanced sensitivity). In some cases, because of the anxiety, joy, attachment or anticipation, noticing becomes lax and retrogressive. ~ Some who think that the goal is very near contemplate with great energy ~ and while doing so, noticing becomes lax and retrogression sets in. ~ This happens because a restless mind cannot concentrate properly on formations. ~ So, when noticing if it is flowing along smoothly, the meditator must go on steadily." That means that he should neither relax nor put forth special effort. ~ If he does go on steadily, he will rapidly gain insight into the end of all the formations and realize NIBBĀNA. In the case of some meditators ~ they may at this stage rise higher and again fall several times. (In such cases ~ maintain a smooth-continuous effort ~ allow for no gaps in the SATI ~ at any moment in any moment ~ remain determined ~ sensitive ~ a cool-relaxed-razor-sharp-focus, noticing whatever arises at the time it becomes evident at each of the 6-sense doors).

(If necessary ~ utilize the primary object if necessary. ~ Watch rising/falling abdomen until momentum is gained ~ then the noticing will go on of its own accord, smoothly and calmly including objects at the 6-sense doors). It will appear that one is observing with ease the ceasing and vanishing of the formations in a clear manner. At this point the mind is quite free from all the defilements; ~ However pleasant and inviting an object may be, it is no longer so to him. Again, however loathsome an object may be, it is no longer so to him. (Best description of this ÑĀNA – in general). "He simply sees ~ hears ~ smells ~ tastes ~ feels a touch ~ or cognizes ~ with the 6 kinds of equanimity that accompany each respective sense door experience he notices all the formations."

At this stage the yogi is not even aware of the length of time he is engaged in noticing (one knows distinctly the timeless quality of practice at this point) ~ but if he does not develop sufficient progress of insight to gain ~ MAGGA-PHALA ~ "within 2 or 3 hours" ~ concentration becomes slack and reflection sets in. ~ On the other hand, if he is making good progress, he may anticipate further advance. He will become so delighted with the result that he will experience a fall (bare attention); a steady contemplation will achieve smooth progress again; ~ but if sufficient strength of insight has not yet been achieved ~ concentration becomes slack again. ~ In this way ~ some yogis progress and fall back like this several times. ~ In spite of such fluctuations in one's progress the yogi must not allow himself to be overcome by disappointment or despair. ~ He is now ~ as it were ~ at the threshold of MAGGA and PHALA: ~ (As soon as the 5 INDRIYAS ~ faith ~ energy ~ mindfulness ~ concentration and wisdom are developed in an even-balanced manner ~ NIBBĀNA will follow).

~ VISUDDHI MAGGA ~ p.765, v.61 ~ "When he has discerned formations by attributing the three characteristics to them, and seeing them as void in this way ~ he abandons both terror and delight. ~ He neither takes them as 'I' nor as 'mine' ~ he becomes indifferent to them and neutral" ~ v.63 ~ "When he knows and sees thus ~ his heart retreats

~ retracts and recoils from formations ~ his heart no longer goes out to them…Equanimity is established."

~ v. 64 ~ "But if this (knowledge) sees NIBBĀNA ~ the state of peace ~ as peaceful ~ it rejects the occurrence of all formations and enters only into NIBBĀNA. ~ If it does not see NIBBĀNA as peaceful ~ it occurs again and again with formations as its object." ~ Like the sailor's crow, v.65 (described under "How NIBBĀNA is realized".)

~ VIS. MAG. p.771, v.79 ~ "The last three kinds of knowledge are one." ~ "This knowledge of equanimity about formations" is the same in meaning as the two kinds (of knowledges) that precede. it: Hence the ancients said: "This knowledge of equanimity about formations is one only, and has three names. At the onset it has the name of "Knowledge of Desire for Deliverance" ~ in the middle it has the name "Knowledge of Re-Observation" ~ at the end when it has reached its culmination it is called "Knowledge of Equanimity about Formations". (This is said in PATISAMBHIDĀMAGGA II.64)

~ v.81 ~ "So in the first stage ~ it is the desire to give up ~ the desire to be delivered from ~ arising, ~ etc. In one who has become dispassionate by "Knowledge of Disgust" ~ that is "Desire for Deliverance" ~ it is re-observation in the middle stage for the purpose of finding a means to deliverance; ~ that is Re-Observation. ~It is equanimous (calm), onlooking in the end stage on being delivered. ~ That is composure. ~ It has been said in reference to this: Arising is formations. He looks with equanimity on those formations: Thus, it is Equanimity about Formations. ~ This is only one kind of knowledge." ~

(Manual of Insight, Mahasi Sayadaw, ch. 6, pp.401-403)

How phenomena are observed from ten aspects:

One sees physical phenomena as: empty (of permanence, pleasure, beauty, and the ability to control) (RITTA); insubstantial (and therefore vain, empty of the above qualities) (TUCCHA); empty of a substantial self (that accomplishes things according to its will) (SUÑÑA); having no self (that accomplishes things according to its will) (ANATTĀ); not having control (ANISSARIYA); not subject to creation by will (AKĀMAKĀRIYA); not subject to control (by desire) (ALABBHANĪYA); not subject to anyone's wishes (AVASAVATTANA);

14. THE PROGRESS OF INSIGHT THROUGH THE STAGES OF PURIFICATION

strangers or outsiders (PARA); and secluded (because there is neither the effect within the cause nor the cause within the effect; cause and effect are empty of each other) (VIVITTA).

In order to understand the aspect of not being subject to creation by will, consider the example of a bubble. There is no way that a bubble can be fashioned into a durable cup that will hold liquid. In the same way, it is impossible to command physical phenomena to become permanent, pleasurable, beautiful ~ and identified with a self. In other words, only when the necessary conditions exist do physical activities occur (such as walking, standing, sitting, lying down, bending, stretching, feeling hot or cold, seeing clearly, and so on). It is impossible to cause a physical activity to occur simply by will.

The term "secluded" (VIVITTATO) means "secluded from cause and effect":

KAMMA does not exist in its result, and the KAMMIC result does not exist in KAMMA, either. They are secluded from each other, although there is no result without KAMMA.

The sub-commentary, consistent with this passage, explains: "Causal phenomena are not pregnant with resultant phenomena, nor vice versa."

(For a more detailed explanation, see the section on Insight Knowledge that Discerns Conditionality earlier in this chapter.)

It is interesting that only the first four of the ten aspects mentioned above are the same as those found in the NIDDESA, which says:

"Then one sees the world in terms of emptiness. One sees physical phenomena as: empty (of permanence, pleasure, beauty, and the ability to control) (RITTA); insubstantial (and therefore vain, empty of the above qualities) (TUCCHA); empty of a substantial self (that accomplishes things according to its will) (SUÑÑA); having no self (that accomplishes things according to its will) (ANATTĀ); without core or essence (ASĀRAKA); a murderer (VADHAKA); non-enduring (VIBHĀVA); the root of (a great array) of unwholesomeness (AGHAMŪLA); intoxicating, being associated with mental defilements (SĀSAVA); and conditioned (SANKHATĀ).

Thus, the commentary on this Pāḷi text lists ten aspects that are not all the same as those found in the original source material. Given this inconsistency, one should not consider it necessary to memorize these ten aspects, or to follow them in exact order when one practices. If one is able to experience only one or a few of these aspects of impermanence ~ unsatisfactoriness, and 'not-self'~ it will serve the purpose. However, one may experience all the aspects mentioned here, depending on one's perfections and disposition.

So, understand that these are possible manifestations of practice, rather than a procedure to follow."

How phenomena are observed from twelve aspects:

One sees that physical phenomena are not a being, not a soul, not a human, not a child, not a female, not a male, not a self, not 'I', not belonging to a 'self', not 'mine', not belonging to another, and not belonging to anyone.

This is how physical phenomena are observed. The same applies for feeling, perception, and so on.

The first eight of these twelve aspects reject the existence of an everlasting self in the body with the ability to perform actions according to its will; the last four show that physical phenomena do not belong to a self. But these are not meant to reject the conventional understanding that people apply in their daily lives, such as saying 'a person', 'his property', 'my property', 'his limbs', 'my limbs', 'her children', 'my children', and so on.

Some are critical of this commentary because it mentions different aspects than the original Pāḷi text, and they claim that the commentary written by Venerable BUDDHAGHOSA rejects not only the notion of a self, as did the BUDDHA, but rejects also the conventional truth that is applied in everyday life. This is just a misinterpretation. There are many commentarial descriptions of 'not-self', as was the case with insight knowledge by comprehension, wherein some of the aspects mentioned in the commentary differ from those found in the original text. But their purpose is certainly not to refute the validity of conventional truth, but rather to refute the validity of 'an everlasting self'.

This is why the VISUDDHIMAGGA-MAHĀṬĪKĀ says:

In statements such as, "The body is not a being," and so on, the word 'being' is not used in the everyday sense because it is already implicitly understood that the body is not a 'being' in that conventional sense. No one would ever call the body alone a 'being'. Instead, it refers to the 'self' that others imagine to be a 'being'. They consider the self to be an entity that is attached (to the body) or attaches (the body) to itself. However, the body is not associated with such a self. Thus, seeing that the body is not a being refers to knowing that the body is empty of any self. The same applies for the statements, "The body is not a soul," and so on.

(SANKHĀRUPEKKHĀ- ÑĀNA) – continued
(From "To NIBBĀNA via the noble-8-fold path" ~ MAHASI ~ pp.47-50)

~ The six characteristics of SANKHĀRUPEKKHĀ- ÑĀNA ~

~ Knowledge of Equanimity towards Conditioned Things has six characteristics ~

1. The first relates to neutrality where the mind is unmoved by fear or delight induced by objects of sense. Before reaching this stage of knowledge, a yogi is apprehensive of the dangers thrown in his way by conditioned things. ~ As BHAYA- ÑĀNA is invoked he realizes with anxiety and fear that things have gone wrong. He then develops weariness in his mind. He longs to be free from this undesirable phenomenon, so he makes a great effort in meditation (PATISANKHA- ÑĀNA). Thereby he develops further SANKHĀRUPEKKHĀ- ÑĀNA, which is knowledge about equanimity of mind unaffected by fear or anxiety. ~ Tranquility is thus established.
2. The second characteristic is mental ~ equilibrium where he neither feels glad for things pleasant ~ nor sad for things that bring about pain and distress. He can now note joy as joy and pain or sorrow can be noted as such. He is able to view things impartially with neither attachment nor aversion towards the sense-objects.
3. The third characteristic ~ related to the yogi's balance of mind: While observing formations he establishes a fine balance of mind that remains right in the middle ~ neutral towards all formations. ~ The yogi is effortless in focusing his mind on sense-door phenomena as well as on the very act of noticing. ~ The 2 processes of noting

and knowing objects will become spontaneous ~ running together in their own (natural) sequence. Concentration is rendered easy.

4. The fourth characteristic is the firm establishment of knowledge. It means ~ the knowledge achieved is retained for a long time in all its sequences. Formerly the knowledge attained lasted for 4 or 5 minutes to get dissipated or forgotten thereafter for various reasons. But when SANKHĀRUPEKKHĀ- ÑĀNA is mature, the stream of knowledge will flow without losing momentum after the yogi has initially repeated his efforts to notice 4 or 5 ~ or at most 10 times. When this momentum is achieved the yogi will be noting and knowing formations for 2 or 3 hours. At a stretch, this is how knowledge is established firmly.

5. The fifth characteristic of this ÑĀNA is refinement: ~ When grounded or pondered rice is sifted again and again in a sieve, all the chaff will be discarded and only the finest grain will remain. In much the same way refinement is achieved when this ÑĀNA is exercised, time and again.

6. The last characteristic of this ÑĀNA is the ability of the observing mind to remain fixed only on the object it has set itself to work ~ without wavering. The texts (PATISAMBHIDĀMAGGA) say that at this stage the mind withdraws from the many enjoyable sensations it encounters, and refuses to flicker. It might direct its attention to those pleasurable sensations for a fleeting moment, but it does not dwell on them for long. It reverts to its task of noting and knowing formations impartially as it has done before. ~ The yogi may be noting and knowing various sense-objects within himself, but his mind will not be hopping about to get dispersed. ~ In fact, he will recoil or withdraw from them, and finally fix his mind on only a few selected prominent ones among them.

Summary: ~ The last 3 characteristics should be known as relating to "Firm establishment of knowledge" ~ "5 – Achievement of refinement" ~ #6 as "Building up an unwavering mind."

Yogis in meditation should examine themselves about whether they are qualified for this insight with its six aspects. ~ If found lacking in any one of them they may not be considered as proficient, and therefore they may regard themselves as having not attained the stage of ARIYA MAGGA (MAGGA-PHALA).

12. Insight Leading to Emergence (VUTTHĀNAGĀMINĪ - VIPASSANĀ - ÑĀNA)
(See VIS.MAG p.772, v.83 ~p.781, v.127)
"Insight leading to Emergence of the Faith"

(This ÑĀNA comprehends ANICCA ~ DUKKHA ~ or ANATTA ~ lucidly, ~ emerging thus: ~ I am delivered ~ by 1 of these 3 doorways. ~ (See chart p.165)

MAHASI: ~ "So through SANKHĀRUPEKKHĀ- ÑĀNA ~ which is endowed with many virtues and powers ~ the yogi notices the formations as they occur. ~ When this knowledge is mature ~ on having become keen, strong and lucid, and on having reached its culmination point ~ it will understand any of the formations as being ANICCA, or DUKKHA or ANATTA ~ just by seeing their dissolution.

"Now that act of noticing any one characteristic out of the 3 ~ which is still, even more lucid in its perfect understanding, manifests itself 2 or 3 times, or more, in rapid succession: This is called "Insight, Leading to Emergence." (Thereupon ~ immediately after the last consciousness in the series of acts of noticing, belonging to this "Insight Leading to Emergence" ~ the yogi's consciousness leaps forth into (taking as its object) NIBBĀNA, which is "the Cessation of All Formations". Then there appears to him the stilling (subsidence) of all formations called "Cessation".

MAHASI: ~ "With the maturing of SANKHĀRUPEKKHĀ - ÑĀNA ~ noting becomes fast ~ occurring 2 or 3 times rapidly, and without any special effort. The knowledge that occurs two or three times is VUTTHĀNAGĀMINĪ. ~ Of the knowledge that thus occurs 2 or 3 times ~ the one that occurs last is ANULOMA- ÑĀNA (Adaptation Knowledge). ~ VUTTHĀNA means the ARIYA MAGGA that ascends to and glimpses ~ NIBBĀNA. ~ GĀMINĪ means the special insight -knowledge that proceeds to that ARIYA-MAGGA. ~ ANULOMA- ÑĀNA is the last of the VIPASSANĀ-ÑĀNAS that, with realization of ANICCA ~ DUKKHA ~ or ANATTA ~ occurs comfortably to the preceding VIPASSANĀ-ÑĀNAS, and to the ARIYA-MAGGA (concerned). ANULOMA-ÑĀNA is the last of the 2 or 3 VUTTHĀNAGĀMINĪ-ÑĀNAS that occur rapidly (as if racing).

"The yogi who wishes to realize NIBBĀNA should repeatedly bring to mind, through the practice of noticing ~ every bodily and mental process that appears at any of the 6-sense doors. When he brings it to mind thus ~ how consciousness engaged in noticing ~ (here called "bringing to mind") ~ will until ANULOMA-ÑĀNA is reached ~ fall at every moment until the conditioned NĀMA-RŪPA formations called here "continuous occurrence" (because they are going on occurring over and over again in and unbroken flow ~ like a river's current.) ~~ But in the last phase ~ instead of falling upon that "continuous occurrence" ~ consciousness passes beyond it and alights upon "non- occurrence" (which is the very opposite of the bodily and mental formations called here "occurrence". In other words, it arrives at "non-occurrence"; that is to say, it reaches, as if it "alights upon" ~ cessation, which is the stilling of the conditioned phenomenal formations. (When the yogi having already practiced correctly and without deviation by way of the "Knowledge of Arising and Passing Away" and the other knowledges – or by way of the purification of conduct, of mind, of view, etc – has in this manner arrived at "non-occurrence" (by the supra-mundane consciousness taking non-occurrence or NIBBĀNA as an object) ~ he is said to have "realized NIBBĀNA". ~ (From questions of King MILINDA: ~ "His consciousness while carrying on the practice of noticing (bringing to mind) passes beyond the continuous occurrence of phenomena and alights upon non-occurrence. One who, having practiced in correct manner, has alighted upon non-occurrence ~ the King ~ is said to have realized NIBBĀNA.")

VIS. MAG.p.772, v.83 ~ "Now when the yogi has reached equanimity about formations ~ his insight has reached its culmination and leads to emergence. ~ "Insight that has Reached Culmination" or "Insight Leading to Emergence" are names for the three kinds of knowledge beginning with "Equanimity about Formations" 2 ~, 3~, 4~. It has reached its culmination, because it has reached its culminating

14. THE PROGRESS OF INSIGHT THROUGH THE STAGES OF PURIFICATION

(final) stage. ~ It is called "Leading to Emergence" because it goes towards emergence. ~ The path is called 'emergence' because it emerges externally from the objective bases interpreted as a sign (5 aggregates as object of insight) and also internally from occurrence (wrong view and defilement). It goes to that ~ thus it leads to emergence. ~ The meaning is that it joins with the path.

p.773, v.84 (Lists the 18 kinds of emergence ~ ex. #18 ~ After interpreting (gains insight into) as (formations) ANATTA. It emerges from the DUKKHA."

~ Insight Leading to Emergence ~ continued ~
~ The seven ways individuals attain to NIBBĀNA ~

(p.770, v.74-78) (p.770, v.76-78). (V.M.p.776, v.66-73)

7 Noble individuals	3 Emergences	3 Faculties	3 Deliverances	8 Positions
1 ~ The faith devotee (SADDHĀNUSĀRI) 2 ~ One liberated by faith (SADDHĀ-VIMUTTA)	ANICCA (impermanence) When insight discerns formations as impermanent; yogi leaves the sign of permanence and realizes NIBBĀNA as the state of sinlessness.	Faith (SADDHiNDRIYA)	Sign-less (ANIMITTA) Yogi sees NIBBĀNA as the state that has no sign ~ thus formations have the sign of NICCA.	First-path (1) (SOTAPANNA-MAGGA) The fruit of the first path and the remaining three paths and their fruits ~ (7)
3 ~ The body-witness (KĀYASAKKHI) 4 ~ The both-ways liberated (UBHATOBHĀGA-VIMUTTA)	DUKKHA (suffering) Insight discerns formations as DUKKHA; yogi realizes NIBBĀNA is the state of desirelessness.	Concentration (SAMADHINDRIYA)	Desireless (APPANIHITA) Yogi sees NIBBĀNA as the state free from desire ~ thus he is one delivered through the insight that discerns desirelessness.	The 4 paths & 4 fruits (8) ARAHANTSHIP (1)
5 ~ The DHAMMA devotee (DHAMMĀNUSĀRI) 6 ~ One attained to vision (DITTHIPPATTA) 7 ~ One liberated by understanding (PAÑÑĀVIMUTTA)	ANATTA (not-self) When insight discerns formations as not-self ~ the yogi is said to be delivered or released onto NIBBĀNA, by the realization that NIBBĀNA is the state "void of self"	Wisdom (PAÑÑINDRIYA)	The void (SUÑÑATA) ('This means 'void of self')	First-path (1) (SOTAPANNA-MAGGA) The fruit of the first path, the second and third paths, and their fruits and the ARAHANT path (6) ARAHANTSHIP (1)

14. THE PROGRESS OF INSIGHT THROUGH THE STAGES OF PURIFICATION

Notes to chart:

A. Seven noble individuals (VIS.MAG. p.770, v.74). (Also see KITĀGIRI SUTTA-MAJ.70).

There are these 7 classifications of ARIYA-PUGGALAS which derive from the circumstances of one's liberation. ~ For instance, #1 ~ When a yogi brings formations to mind as ANICCA ~ and acquires the faith faculty. ~ (Faith will be the predominant INDRIYA in this type of noble individual whose doorway to liberation is contemplation of ANICCA).

B. Three emergences ~ 1 and 2 ~ After the formations have been contemplated as ANICCA ~ 3 and 4 as DUKKHA ~ 5 ~ 6 ~ 7 ~ or ANATTA ~ and the yogi reaches the attainment of NIBBĀNA ~ by means of the predominance of one of these 3 characteristics (3 doorways) ~ he is then said to be predominant in:

C. Three faculties ~ one of the INDRIYAS at the time of attainment. (See chart).

D. At which moment depending on what LAKKHANA predominated in contemplating the formations ~ he is then said to be delivered (to NIBBĀNA) by the respective (1 of the 3) entrances to NIBBĀNA.

Summarized as follows (PATISAMBHIDĀMAGGA ii.58): ~ "He who contemplated ANICCA ~ being abundant in SADDHA ~ attains the deliverance of the signless (ANIMITTA-VIMOKKHA). ~ He who contemplates DUKKHA, being abundant in SAMĀDHI ~ attains the deliverance of the desireless liberation (APPANIHITTA-VIMOKKHA). He who contemplates ANATTA ~ being predominant in PAÑÑĀ attains the deliverance of the void ~ liberation. (For further clarification ~ the yogi enters upon NIBBĀNA via a door-way of liberation in 1 of 3 ways ~ ANICCA = signless, ~ DUKKHA = desireless, ~ ANATTA = void, with the predominance of an INDRIYA (in 1 of 3 ways ~ ANICCA = faith ~ DUKKHA = SAMĀDHI ~ ANATTA = PAÑÑĀ) as the contemplation occurs in one of three ways (ANICCA ~ DUKKHA ~ ANATTA) VIS.MAG. v.67 ~ "For it is the 3 contemplations that are called the gateways or doorways to liberation."

Insight Leading to Emergence (continued):
(VUTTHĀNAGĀMINĪ – VIPASSANĀ – ÑĀNA)

(MAHASI ~ p.43 ~ SATIPATTHANA-VIP ~ "How NIBBĀNA is realized")

"The ups and downs of Insight Knowledge occurring at the stage of ANKHĀRUPEKKHĀ- ÑĀNA because of anticipation/expectations, etc. (Reread 1st paragraph, p.162 ~ this text) are comparable to "a bird let loose from a sea-going ship" ~ (Simile from VIS.MAG. p.766, v.65). ~ In ancient times ~ the captain of a sea-going ship ~ finding it difficult to know whether the ship was approaching land ~ released a bird they had taken along for this purpose. ~ The bird flies in all four directions to look for a shore. ~ Whenever he cannot find any land ~ the bird comes back to the ship. ~ In a similar way ~ as soon as the yogi's insight knowledge is not mature enough to grow into path and fruition knowledge, and thereby attain to the realization of NIBBĀNA ~ it becomes lax and retarded ~ just as the bird returns to the ship. ~ When the bird sees land (when PAÑÑĀ is ripe enough) ~ it flies on in that direction without returning to the ship (and the consciousness will go to NIBBĀNA and forsake the ship of formations). ~ Similarly, when insight knowledge is mature ~ on having become sharp ~ strong ~ and lucid ~ it will understand one of the formations ~ observed at one of the six-sense doors ~ as being ANICCA ~ or DUKKHA ~ or ANATTA. The act of noticing any one characteristic out of the three has a higher degree of lucidity and strength in its perfect understanding ~ and becomes faster and manifests itself 3 or 4 times in rapid succession (this is "Insight Leading to Emergence" ~ the rapid series of noticings) ~ immediately after the last consciousness in this series of accelerated noticing. (This last lucid noticing in the series of 3 or 4 is ANULOMA-ÑĀNA) has ceased ~ MAGGA and PHALA arises ~ realizing NIBBĀNA, the Cessation of All Formations.)

13. Knowledge of Adaptation (ANULOMA – ÑĀNA)
(See VIS. MAG.CH. XXI ~ p. 782, v. 128 – v.136)

The Knowledge by way of Noticing that occurs last in the series constituting "Insight leading to Emergence" ~ is called ANULOMA-ÑĀNA.

ANULOMA- ÑĀNA is the last of the VIPASSANĀ- ÑĀNAS that ~ with the ludic realization of one of the TI-LAKKHANA ~ ANICCA ~ DUKKHA ~ or ANATTA ~ occurs conformably to the preceding ÑĀNAS and to the ARIYA MAGGA (concerned). ~ This is the last of the two or three VUTTHĀNAGĀMINĪ -ÑĀNAS that occur rapidly ~ as if it were racing.

VIS.MAG 782, v.128 ~ "As he repeats, develops and cultivates SANKHĀRUPEKKHĀ-ÑĀNA his faith becomes more resolute, ~ energy better exerted ~ mindfulness better established ~ and his mind better concentrated ~ while his equanimity about formations grows more refined." ~ (From this point ~ VIS.MAG. explains the mind-door thought process ~ through ANULOMA. ~ See description of same further on).

v.130 ~ ANULOMA = conformity (or adaptation). Conformity to what? ~ "To what precedes and to what follows ~ for it conforms to the function of truth both in the eight preceding kinds of insight knowledge, and in the thirty-seven factors of enlightenment that follow."

v. 131 ~ Since its occurrence is contingent upon formations through comprehending the characteristic of ANICCA ~ DUKKHA ~ and ANATTA it (so to speak) says: ~ "Knowledge of Rise and Fall indeed saw the rise and fall of precisely those states that possess rise and fall ~ and Contemplation of Dissolution indeed saw the dissolution of precisely those states that possess dissolution"; and "It was indeed precisely what was fearful that appeared as fearful to Knowledge of Fearfulness ~ and ~ Contemplation of Misery indeed saw misery in precisely what was miserable ~ and ~ Knowledge of Disgust indeed became disgusted towards precisely that which should be regarded with disgust"; ~ and "Knowledge of Desire for Deliverance indeed produced desire for deliverance from precisely what there should be deliverance from"; ~ and ~ "What was re-observed by Knowledge of Re-Observation was indeed precisely what should be re-observed"; ~ and ~ "What was looked on at with equanimity by Equanimity about Formations was indeed precisely what should be looked on at with equanimity". So, it conforms (or adapts) to the functions of truth, both in these 8 kinds of knowledge and in the 37 states partaking of enlightenment ~ which follow because they are to be reached by entering upon it."

14. Maturity Knowledge or "Change-of-Lineage" (GOTRABHŪ- ÑĀNA)

(See VIS.MAG. CH. XXII ~ p.785 v.1~ v.14) "Change-of-Lineage"

Immediately after the ANULOMA moment ~ a type of knowledge manifests itself that ~ as it were ~ falls for the first time into NIBBĀNA ~ which is void of formations (conditioned phenomena) since it is the cessation of them. ~ This knowledge is called "Maturity Knowledge" (GOTRABHŪ- ÑĀNA).

(MAHASI ~ "GOTRABHŪ-ÑĀNA" is literally ~ "The knowledge of one who has become one of the lineage (meaning GOTRA) ~ by attaining to that knowledge. One has left behind the designation and stage of an unliberated wording, and is entering the lineage and rank of the noble ones (IE. SOTAPANNA ~ etc.) Insight now has come to full maturity; ~ that is ~ it matures into the knowledge of the supra mundane paths and fruitions. ~ GOTRABHŪ- ÑĀNA occurs only as a single moment of consciousness. ~ It does not recur since it is immediately followed by the path-consciousness of stream-entry. ~ Etc."

VIS.MAG ~ Change of Lineage Knowledge comes next (after ANULOMA- ÑĀNA). ~ Its position is to advert to the path ~ and so it belongs neither to "Purification of Knowledge and Vision of the Way" nor to "Purification by Knowledge and Vision (4 paths and 4 fruits)"; ~ but being intermediate, it is unassignable. ~ Still, it is considered to be/included as insight because it falls in line with insight.

TIKA on VIS. MAG P.672 ~ "In its technical sense GOTRABHŪ may be rendered 'suggestive' ~ for its purpose is to suggest to the mind the abandonment of worldly objects and the adoption of NIBBĀNA as its object. The psychological value of GOTRABHŪ is that it "stands at the point of turning to the path" ~ forming as it were the dividing line between the world and NIBBĀNA. Hence it is neither a part of the Insight Knowledges ~ nor does it appertain to the Knowledge of the Path. ~ However, it is associated with the insight process as a psychic action ~ pointing out NIBBĀNA as the object to consciousness: It should therefore be regarded as Insight."

"GOTRABHŪ is the last KĀMAVACARA CITTA in a process ~ before (in this case) a CITTA of supra-mundane consciousness (LOKUTTARA) arises in that process. (MAGGA-CITTA follows immediately after GOTRABHŪ). GOTRABHŪ arising before the LOKUTTARA CITTA has NIBBĀNA as the object.

Q ~ Why is GOTRABHŪ not LOKUTTARA CITTA? It is the first CITTA which has NIBBĀNA as the object.

A ~ At the moment of GOTRABHŪ the person who is about to attain enlightenment is still a non-ARIYAN ~ GOTRABHŪ as he does not eradicate defilements. ~ GOTRABHŪ is succeeded by MAGGA-CITTA which eradicates the defilements that are to be eradicated at the stage of SOTĀPANNA, etc. ~ The MAGGA-CITTA is the first LOKUTTARA CITTA in that process of CITTAS. (p.706, v.6-14 ~ Explanation with simile explains this point very clearly.)

VIS.MAG ~ v.3 ~ Herein ~ nothing further needs to be done by one who wants to achieve: ~ Firstly ~ the knowledge of the first path ~ for what he needs to do has already been done by arousing insight that ends in ANULOMA-ÑĀNA. As soon as ANULOMA-ÑĀNA has arisen in him in this way ~ and the thick murk that hides the truths has been dispelled by the respective force peculiar to each of the 3 kinds of ANULOMA-ÑĀNA (1 ~ PARIKAMMA; ~ 2 ~UPACĀRA; ~ 3 ~ ANULOMA = all 3 can be classified as ANULOMA ~ see chart on the following page.) For clarification ~ each one is just a moment in the thought- process (see also V.M. p.782, v.125). Then his consciousness no longer enters or settles down on or resolves upon any field of formations at all ~ or clings ~ or cleaves ~ or clutches onto it ~ but retreats and recoils 'as water does from a lotus leaf'; and every sign as object, every occurrence as object, appears as impediment. ~ v.5 ~ Then while every sign and occurrence appears to him as an impediment ~ when ANULOMA's repetition has ended, GOTRABHŪ-ÑĀNA arises in him ~ which takes as its object the signless: ~ no-occurrence ~ no-formation ~ cessation. NIBBĀNA as object ~ GOTRABHŪ-ÑĀNA is the culminating peak of insight ~ which is irrevocable ~ of which is said:

~ "How is it that understanding of emergence and turning away from the field of formations is GOTRABHŪ-ÑANA?" It overcomes arising ~ it overcomes occurrence (accumulations ~ birth ~ aging ~ sorrow ~ death~ etc) ~ it overcomes despair ~ it overcomes the formations ~ it enters into non-arising ~ non-occurrence ~ non-despair ~ it enters into cessation ~ NIBBĀNA ~ thus it is change-of-lineage (GOTRABHŪ-ÑANA). "Having overcome arising it enters into non-arising."

MAHASI ~ "Out of this contemplation which proceeds automatically (mature SANKHĀRUPEKKHĀ- ÑANA) and by its own momentum realizing its objects ~ there arises knowledge which is exceptionally quick and lucid. ~ This knowledge which rises straight away towards a noble-path which is also known as VUTTHĀNA (elevation) is ~ VUTTHĀNAGĀMINĪ – VIPASSANĀ- ÑANA (Insight Leading to Emergence or Elevation). ~ That special knowledge that arises realized that physical and mental phenomena which appear at the six-sense doors at that very moment are ANICCA, DUKKHA and ANATTA. ~ The last of such knowledge is ANULOMA- ÑANA (Adaptation Knowledge) which consists of the three JAVANAS (impulse moments) called:

#1 ~ PARIKAMMA (preparation) ~ #2 ~ UPACĀRA (proximity) and ~ #3 ~ ANULOMA (adaptation). ~ This is the ÑANA which fits in both with the preceding eight Insight Knowledges (beginning with Arising and Passing Away) and subsequent MAGGA-ÑANA (Path Knowledge). ~ Insights from the mature UDAYABBAYA- ÑANA to the ANULOMA-ÑANA are collectively known as PATIPADĀ-ÑANA-DASSANA-VISUDDHI (Purification by Knowledge and Vision of the Course of Practice). ~ After ANULOMA- ÑANA there arises GOTRABHŪ-ÑANA (Maturity Knowledge or Change-of-Lineage Knowledge) which is the first CITTA that takes NIBBĀNA as an object. ~ This is knowledge which cuts the lineage of PUTHUJJANAS (unenlightened worldlings) and enters the lineage of ARIYAS (noble beings or enlightened individuals). ~ Then in the next CITTA (which is a LOKUTTARA-CITTA or supra-mundane consciousness) following GOTRABHŪ- ÑANA there arises the SOTĀPATTI- MAGGA and PHALA- ÑANA (Insight arising from the Noble Path of stream-entry and its fruition) which realize (CITTA takes as object) NIBBĀNA. ~ The MAGGA- ÑĀNA (Path Knowledge) is called ÑĀNA- DASSANA- VISUDDHI (Purification or Insight by Knowledge and Vision). ~ The MAGGA and PHALA- ÑĀNA mind moments or consciousness moments do not last in duration for even a second ~ then there arises reflection of the particular experiences of the MAGGA, PHALA and NIBBĀNA. ~ This is PACCAVAKKHANA-ÑĀNA (Knowledge of Reviewing or Insight of Retrospection). ~ One who has acquired this PACCAVAKKHANA-ÑĀNA, according to this procedure ~ is a SOTĀPANNA (stream winner).

G. Purification by Knowledge and Vision (ÑĀNADASSANA – VISUDDHI)

(See VIS.MAG. p.787. v.10-14 regarding MAGGA- ÑĀNA)

(See VIS.MAG. p.788. v.15-18 regarding PHALA- ÑĀNA)

(See VIS.MAG. p.789. v.19-21 regarding reviewing knowledge ~ ÑĀNA #17)

15. Path Knowledge (MAGGA – ÑĀNA)

16. Fruition Knowledge (PHALA – ÑĀNA)

After ANULOMA- ÑĀNA ~ follow in succession GOTRABHŪ- ÑĀNA ARIYA-MAGGA-ÑĀNA and PHALA-ÑĀNA ~ of these ÑĀNAS ~ ANULOMA-ÑĀNA notices the arising and vanishing of mind and body formations, and goes on to notice the same in the light of any of the three characteristics of ANICCA ~ DUKKHA and ANATTA. (MAHASI: "Mostly in the light of ANICCA") ~ GOTRABHŪ- ÑĀNA is that which inclines awards the cessation of the body-mind SANKHĀRAS (phenomenal processes) ~ MAGGA- ÑĀNA and PHALA-ÑĀNA are those supra- mundane consciousness moments that attain to and realize NIBBĀNA, the cessation and absence of mind and body formations (SANKHĀRAS). ~ This does not last long, ~ only for a fleeting moment ~ not even a second.

Path Knowledge is one supra-mundane (LOKUTTARA) conscious

moment that has NIBBĀNA as its object. A moment of NIBBĀNA is a moment void of formations ~ since it is the cessation of them. ~ This is MAGGA- ÑĀNA.

Fruition Knowledge is one supra-mundane conscious moment which has NIBBĀNA as its object that arises as the result of MAGGA-ÑĀNA that directly precedes it. (Note: Fruition Knowledge ~ PHALA ~ can last in some cases up to 3 moments ~ in most cases just 2 moments of consciousness ~ unlike the MAGGA CITTA, which is always one moment of consciousness.)

SAYADAW MAHASI ~ Those who have realized NIBBĀNA would say: "The objects noticed and the consciousness noticing them cease altogether." ~ Or ~ "The objects and the act of noticing are cut off as a vine is cut by a knife." ~ Or ~ "The objects and the act of noticing fall off as if one is relieved of a heavy load." ~ Or ~ "The objects and the acts of noticing are suddenly freed as if from a prison." ~ Or ~ "The objects and acts of noticing are blown off as if a candle is suddenly extinguished." ~ Or ~ "They disappear as if darkness is suddenly replaced by light." ~ Or ~ "They are released as if freed from an embroilment." ~ Or ~ "They sink as if in water." ~ Or ~ "They abruptly stop as if a person running was stopped by a violent rush." ~ Or ~ "They cease altogether."

MAGGA – ÑĀNA is the last of the seven stages of purification (VISUDDHI) ~ namely Purification by Knowledge and Vision. (Immediately after the rapid attainment of cessation by means of MAGGA and PHALA-ÑĀNA ~ there is Reviewing Knowledge that Arises (PACCAVAKKHANA- ÑĀNA). (See knowledge-insight #17 ~ the following page)

VIS.MAG. p.787, v. II ~ GOTRABHŪ-ÑANA has NIBBĀNA as an object but it cannot (at this point) dispel the defilements. Hence it is called "Adverting to the Path" ~ for although it is not adverting ~ it occupies the position of adverting. ~ And then ~ after as it were ~ giving a sign to the path to come into being ~ it ceases and without pausing after the sign given by that change-of-lineage knowledge the path follows upon it in uninterrupted continuity. And as it comes into being it pierces and explodes the mass of LOBHA ~ the mass of DOSA

~ and the mass of MOHA ~ never pierced and exploded before (and eradicates 3 lower KILESAS).

V.M. p.788, v.15 (The first fruition ~ second noble person) ~ Immediately next to that path-knowledge ~ there arises either 2 or 3 PHALA-CITTAS ~ which are its result (VIPAKA-CITTAS) ~ owing to that fact that LOKUTTARA consciousness results immediately, ~ and at this point this stream enterer is called the second noble person. ~ However negligent he may be ~ he is bound to make an end of DUKKHA within seven lives ~ thus he has entered the stream to final liberation."

When some meditators emerge from the attainment of path and fruition ~ great faith ~ happiness ~ rapture and tranquility proceed by the virtue of the attainment-and experience arises, flooding the whole body. ~ Owing to that they are unable to carry out the practice of noticing in a distinct manner. ~ Even if the yogi makes an ardent effort and attempts to proceed with the meditation, they fail to discern the phenomena clearly and separately ~ at the moment of their occurrence. They continue to experience only rapture ~ tranquility and happiness which occur with great force. ~ This state of mind ~ is extraordinarily serene through the upsurge of strong faith prevailing (due to the added strength ~ conviction ~ and confident truth in the 3 gems). However, ~ this intense and spontaneous upsurge of happiness and other ecstatic experiences will wane gradually after some hours or days, and the yogi will then be able to notice the formations as distinctly as they occur ~ distinguishing them clearly and separately ~ but at that time too ~ first the "Knowledge of Arising and Passing Away" will appear.

(Note: ~ MAHASI ~ "One who has attained to MAGGA-PHALA is aware of the distinct change of their temperament and mental attitude, and feels that their life has been changed. In some cases, ~ the yogi ~ having attained MAGGA-PHALA ~ feels relieved of a great burden ~ free and easy ~ and does not wish to go on contemplating. ~ Their object ~ the attainment of MAGGA-PHALA ~ has been achieved, and their heart's content is understandable. ~ Due (in some cases) to the waves of rapture tranquility and happiness ~ the yogi's mind becomes extraordinarily serene. ~ Because of this fact ~ yogis feel as if they were in some such place as a wide-open space suffused with radiance and most delightful ~ the rapture and happiness ~ of a serene character ~ that arise then ~ are praised by meditators thus: ~ "Surely, I have never before felt and experienced such happiness." ~ (In a few hours or so, such intensity of rapture etc. fade, and again noticing is clear ~ but still at the UDAYABBAYA stage.)

(See VIS.MAG. p.789, v.19-21)

17. Knowledge of Reviewing (PACCAVEKKHANĀ – ÑĀNA)

The duration of that 3-fold knowledge of GOTRABHŪ-ÑĀNA and PHALA-ÑĀNA is extremely short, and lasts for just an instant, like the duration of a single noticing. ~ Subsequently there arises "Knowledge of Reviewing." ~ Through that knowledge of reviewing the yogi discerns that the "Insight leading to Emergence" came along with the very rapid function of noting (noticing) and that immediately after the last phase of Noticing the Path Consciousness entered into the Cessation (of the Formations). ~ This is the "Knowledge of Reviewing the Path." ~ The yogi also discerns that the consciousness was abiding in that state of cessation at the intervening period between the path and reviewing ~ "This is the Knowledge of Reviewing the Fruition." ~ The yogi further discerns that the object just experienced is void of all formations. ~ "This is "Knowledge of Reviewing NIBBĀNA".

(Another way of stating the same): ~ The duration of Realizing the Cessation of Formations is so short it lasts just for an instant of noting ~ then the yogi reviews what has occurred. ~ He knows that the cessation of the material processes noticed and the mental processes noticing them is the realization of MAGGA-PHALA- NIBBĀNA ~ Those who are well informed know that the Cessation of Formations is NIBBĀNA. The yogi would say inwardly ~ "I have now realized NIBBĀNA and have attained SOTĀPANNA- MAGGA- PHALA." ~ Such a clear knowledge is evident to one who has studied the Canon or heard discourses on this subject.

Some yogis review defilements ~ those already abandoned and those remaining to be abandoned. (Note: ~ Not all yogis experience this aspect of reviewing. ~ It may occur or may not occur ~ at the stage of ARAHANTSHIP. ~ Reviewing of Defilements still remaining ~ obviously ~ will not occur).

After having reviewed in this way ~ they still continue the practice of noticing bodily and mental processes as they become evident. ~ While the yogi is thus engaged in noticing, the various NĀMA- RŪPA formations ~ however ~ appear to be coarse. Both the arising and passing away of the processes are clearly evident to the meditator ~ and yet the yogi now feels as if his noticing is lax and has regressed ~ not nearly as subtle and refined as before at the time of the "Knowledge of Equanimity about Formations." ~ The reason for this is that he has come back to the "Knowledge of Arising and Passing Away" ~ It is true his noticing has become lax and regressed, because the yogi has come back to this stage. ~ He is likely to see bright lights or shapes of objects. ~ In some cases, this reversion results in unbalanced contemplation in that the objects noticed and acts of noticing do not go together. ~ Some yogis experience slight pain for a while ~ and by and large ~ the meditators notice that their mental processes are clear and bright. ~ At this stage the yogi feels that his mind is absolutely free from any encumbrance. ~ He feels happily unhindered, ~ in such a frame of mind he cannot notice the mental processes; ~ and even if he does so ~ he cannot notice it distinctly. ~ He simply feels bright and blissful. ~ When this feeling loses its vigor or intensity, he can again notice the bodily and mental formations and know their arising and passing away distinctly. ~ After some time, the yogi reaches the stage where he can notice the formations smoothly and calmly. ~ Then if the insight knowledge is mature ~ he can again attain to the cessation of formations (PHALA). ~ If such is the power of a yogi's SAMĀDHI to be solid and firm ~ then such PHALA – cessations ~ can repeat itself frequently (refer to section on "Attainment of Fruition").

~ 1 ~ Sense door thought process
1. ATĪTA – BHAVANGA ~ BHAVANGA disturbed
2. BHAVANGA – CALANA ~ vibrating BHAVANGA
3. BHAVANGUPACCHEDA ~ arrest BHAVANGA
4. PAÑCADVĀRAVĀJJANA ~ 3 sense door adverting CITTA

5. PAÑCA- VIÑÑĀNA ~ 3 sense door cognition (object is known)
6. SAMPATICCHANA ~ receiving consciousness
7. SANTĪRANA ~ investigating consciousness
8. VOTTHAPANA ~ determining consciousness
9. JAVANA ~ impulse
10. JAVANA
11. JAVANA
12. JAVANA
13. JAVANA
14. JAVANA
15. JAVANA
16. TADĀLAMBANA ~ registering consciousness
17. TADĀLAMBANA

~ 2 ~ Mental process of attainment of MAGGA-PHALA
1. BHAVANGA
2. BHAVANGA
3. BHAVANGA disturbed
4. Vibrating BHAVANGA
5. Arrest BHAVANGA
6. MANO- DVĀRAVĀJJANA – CITTA ~ mind door adverting consciousness
7. PARIKAMMA-CITTA ~ predatory consciousness
8. UPACARA-CITTA ~ proximity -consciousness or access
9. ANULOMA-CITTA ~ adaptation (7 ~ 8 ~ 9 can all together be called ANULOMA)
10. GOTRABHU ~ change of lineage
11. MAGGA ~ path consciousness
12. PHALA ~ fruition
13. PHALA ~ fruition (10 to 13 has NIBBĀNA as object); (7 to 13 are JAVANA moments)
14. BHAVANGA
15. BHAVANGA
16. BHAVANGA
17. BHAVANGA

14. THE PROGRESS OF INSIGHT THROUGH THE STAGES OF PURIFICATION

~ 3 ~ Reviewing process of MAGGA-PHALA attainment
(8 to 14 ~ These 7 JAVANAS reflect on MAGGA-PHALA)

~ 4 ~ Mental process entering into PHALA- SAMĀPATTI

(~ 5 to 8 ~ Usually 4 ANULOMA moments); (~ 9 to 16 ~ Fruition Consciousness)

~ The yogi can continue in PHALA- SAMĀPATTI until resolved upon time expires.

~ The mind then comes out of that fruition consciousness and into BHAVANGA ~ then again into various mind-body formations.

~ 5 ~ Entering into PARINIBBĀNA

This is the general process of ARAHANT attaining to PARINIBBĀNA ~

There are three ways it can be proceeded: ~ 1 ~ JHĀNA process, 2 ~ NIRODHA process, 3 ~ PHALA- SAMĀPATTI process

(~ 5 to 9 ~) ~ The JAVANA CITTAS are KIRIYA-CITTAS
~ 10 ~ CUTI-CITTA ~ ... PARINIBBĀNA

Defilements of mind are classified in different ways: ~
1. Fetters (SAMYOJANA) ~ 10
2. Defilements (KILESAS) ~ 10
3. States of wrongness (MICCHATTA)
4. Ties (GANTHA)
5. Impurities (ĀSAVA)
6. Floods (OGHA)
7. Yoke (YOGA)
8. Hindrances (NIVARANA) ~ etc.

(MAHASI, p.44. ARIYAVAVA-SUTTA ~ "Some ignorant yogis are often deluded into a false sense of freedom, for they continue to do evil ~ thereby giving the lie to their claim. They say that it is not improper for a SOTĀPANNA to drink under certain circumstances. Their arguments are purely rationalizations for unwholesome desires.")

H. The Fetters and Their Eradication at the Various Stages of Enlightenment

The 10 fetters (SAMYOJANAS)
1. Wrong view (SAKKĀYA- DITTHI)
2. Doubt (VICIKKCHĀ)
3. Belief in mere rite and ritual (SILABBATA-PARĀMĀSA)
4. Sensuous craving (KĀMA- RĀGA)
5. Coarse ill-will (PATIGHA or VYĀPĀDA)
6. Craving for fine-material existence or desiring rebirth in the RŪPA worlds (RŪPA- RĀGA)
7. Craving for immaterial existence or desiring rebirth or experience in the ARŪPA worlds (ARŪPA- RĀGA)
8. Conceit – pride (MĀNA)
9. Restlessness (UDDHACCA)
10. Ignorance – delusion/all KILESAS (AVIJJĀ)

1. By the path of stream entry (SOTĀPATTI-MAGGA or a SOTĀPANNA) are abandoned:

1. Wrong views ~ (belief in self; ~ wrong view that the 5 aggregates of physical and mental phenomena are 'ego' ~ 'self' ~ or 'me'; ~ personality belief ~ DITTHI about the past ~ future ~ or present; ~ 62 kinds of wrong view ~ see p.61)

2. Doubt ~ (doubt about the BUDDHA ~ the DHAMMA; ~ i.e., ~ doubt about realities; ~ about NĀMA and RŪPA; ~ about KAMMA and VĪPAKA; ~ about dependent origination; ~ about ANICCA ~ ANATTA ~ DUKKHA ~ etc; ~ about the 4 noble truths; ~ doubts about the past ~ Who was I? ~ What was I? ~ about the future ~ Where will I go? etc; ~ and about the present: ~ Who am I? ~ Do I exist? ~ Do I not exist? ~ etc.)

3. Clinging to rites and rituals ~ (Belief that methods other than that of cultivating the qualities of the 8-fold noble path and developing insight into the 4 Noble Truths will bring true and ultimate peace: NIBBĀNA).

~ The SOTAPANNA also eradicates 6 other defiling factors of mind.

14. THE PROGRESS OF INSIGHT THROUGH THE STAGES OF PURIFICATION

1. MAKKO ~ inability to hear good spoken of others ~ seeking to wipe out the good of others or depreciation another's worth ~ denigration ~ contempt.

2. PHALĀSO ~ the weakness of comparing oneself with those more virtuous than oneself or malice or spite ~ not quite malice ~ domineering or presumption.

3. ISSĀ ~ jealousy ~ envy ~ jealous of another's success (DOSA-MULA-CITTA)

4. MACCHARIYA ~ selfishness or avarice ~ stinginess (regarding dwelling, families, gain, DHAMMA and practice ~ (V.M. p.799, v.52) Inability to share any of these 5 with others.

5. MĀYĀ ~ fraud ~ deceit ~ hypocrisy ~ pretending to be innocent when one is not.

6. SĀTEIYYA ~ cunning ~ or fraud.

Regarding doubts ~ yogi has first conviction in the 3-fold training of SILA- SAMĀDHI – PAÑÑĀ. Also, no doubts about the SANGHA. (MAHASI ~ SANGHA means one who practices SILA- SAMĀDHI – PAÑÑĀ)

A. A SOTĀPANNA is secure from being reborn in the 4 lower worlds.

B. He will lead a happy life in the world of humans and DEVAS for 7 existences at the most, and during this period he will attain ARAHANTSHIP.

C. Wrong livelihood ~ lying ~ wrong action is uprooted.

D. Views of ANICCA as NICCA ~ ANATTA as ATTA ~ and DUKKHA as SUKKHA are eliminated.

(MAHASI ~ "If one is truly a SOTĀPANNA, its experience leaves no doubt about the TI-LAKKHANA ~ the nature of NIBBĀNA, dependent origination, 4 Truths, etc. ~ He was unshakeable SADDHA in the BUDDHA, DHAMMA, and SANGHA (one who cultivates SILA- SAMĀDHI – PAÑÑĀ) ~ and he strictly avoids killing, stealing, involving in illicit sex, lying and drinking. These are the 4 attributes of a SOTĀPANNA: ~ a real SOTĀPANNA has no desire to do evil ~ his moral life does not need self-restraint, since it is spontaneous. ~ The false SOTĀPANNA'S morality is superficial and proves to be backsliding.)

2. By the path of a once-returner (SAKADĀGAMI-MAGGA) are weakened (not eradicated):

1. Is free from the coarse form of sensuous craving ~ KĀMA-RĀGA ~ which is rooted in LOBHA.

2. Is free from the coarse form of ill-will (PATIGHA or VYAPĀDA) ~ which is rooted in DOSA.

A SAKADĀGAMI will lead a happy life in the world of humans and DEVAS for 2 existences at the most and will attain ARAHANTSHIP during this period. (MAHASI ~ as SOTĀPANNA and SAKADĀGAMI are not fully clear of KĀMA- RĀGA and VYĀPĀDA (desire, lust, ill-will) or (anxiety) they will relapse into these feelings to a certain extent during off periods from meditation. Once into it again, they will regain their insight of the truth. ~ It is like going out of one's stately mansion to several places during the day for one reason or another and coming back to their homes for the night.)

3. By the attainment of the path of a non-returner (ANĀGAMI-MAGGA) are uprooted.

1. Is totally free from sensuous craving (KĀMA- RĀGA)

2. Is totally free from ill-will/ anger ~ all forms ~ fear ~ hostility ~ etc. worry

3. Slandering and harsh speech is uprooted (mental inclination towards)

4. The respondency involved in loss, misfortune, blame and suffering is uprooted.

5. The perception that regards impurity to be purity is eliminated.

4. By the path of complete liberation (ARAHATTA-MAGGA) all remaining impurities are eradicated. ~ (The ARAHANT will know that he is completely liberated.)

1. RŪPA- RĀGA ~ clinging to any form of rebirth/becoming is uprooted (no LOBHA)

2. ARŪPA- RĀGA ~ pursuit of life is uprooted.

3. MĀNA ~ all forms of conceit ~ of 'I am' ~ vanity ~ arrogance.

4. UDDHACCA

5. AVIJJĀ

- All forms of LOBHA ~ DOSA ~ and MOHA are completely vanquished from mind
- All of the UPAKKILESAS remaining are also eliminated
- Sloth (THĪNA) and torpor (MIDDHA) are eradicated
- AHIRIKA (shamelessness) and ANOTAPPA (fearlessness of blame) are eradicated
- Excitement ~ and frivolous talk are eliminated
- The servitude of fawning involved in seeking gain ~ fortune ~ praise and pleasure ~ uprooted
- Hallucinations of perception and thought that consider ill to be bliss are abandoned

~ Names given to NIBBĀNA in various SUTTAS by the BUDDHA ~
ACCANTA ~ the everlasting
APALOKITA ~ the indestructible
KHEMA ~ the safety
PARĀYANA ~ the goal
SACCA ~ the truth
ANĀSA ~ the freedom from longing
ASANKHĀTA ~ the uncreated
NIRODHA ~ the extinction
DHUVA ~ the permanent
VIVATTA ~ the standstill of the cycle of existence
ANĀLAYA ~ the detached
AKKHARA ~ the lasting
VIRĀGA ~ the dispassionate
VISUDDHI ~ the purity
NIBUTTA ~ the allayment
AKATA ~ the unmade
PANĪTA ~ the sublime
TĀNA ~ the shelter
SIVA ~ the bliss
DUKKHAKKHAYA ~ the cessation of misery
SUDUDDASA ~ that which is difficult to grasp
PARA ~ the further shore

ANIDASSANA ~ the imperceptible
JAPA ~ the quested for
KEVALA ~ the absolute
PADA ~ the law
VIMUTTA ~ the liberation
YOGA KKHEMA ~ the peace from bondage
ASANKHATA ~ the uncaused
ANANTA ~ the endless
SARANA ~ the refuge
LENA ~ the retreat
NIPUNA ~ the profound
PĀRA ~ the beyond
MOKKHA ~ the deliverance
NIBBĀNA ~ the extinction of craving
AVYĀPAJJA ~ the unoppressed
ANITIKA ~ the undistressed
ACCUTA ~ the deathless
APAVAGGA ~ the total completion
SANTI ~ the stillness
SUDDHI ~ the pure

(Adopted from "NIBBĀNA via the 8-fold path" ~ MAHASI p.95 – 122) from KOSAMBHIYA SUTTA of MŪLAPANNĀSA ~

I. Seven Principles of Self – Examination Regarding the SOTĀPANNA Attainment (MAHĀPACCAVEKKHANĀ)

1. First MAHĀPACCAVEKKHANĀ ~ BUDDHA: ~ "O, BHIKKHUS ~ a SOTĀPANNA ~ be he a monk or a laymen under the aegis of my teaching ~ retires to a forest ~ seeks shelter under a tree ~ or takes up his abode in a suitable place of solitude ~ and makes an appreciation (examination) of himself thus: ~ "Possessed by KILESĀ ~ my mind may be under their influence, in which case ~ I shall neither perceive nor know the nature of the phenomena of arising and passing away of NĀMA- RŪPA ~ so I must examine myself if KILESĀS of the mind still remain with me." ~ So saying, he makes a repeated self-examination. ~

A SOTĀPANNA removes doubt with the help of his path knowledge. ~ Care and anxiety are absent in him. ~ practicing VIPASSANĀ in solitude he is able to overcome all hindrances (5 NIVARANAS) from his mind. ~ His clear mind is able to notice every phenomenon of the arising and passing away of NĀMA and RŪPA. (ARIYAS have conquered the NĪVARANAS. ~ BUDDHA has said ~ "A SOTAPANNA ~ practicing VIPASSANĀ will come to the conclusion: ~ 'Formerly I might not have known correctly the nature of conditioned things because obstructions (NIVARANAS) lie in my way in all directions. ~ Now that I am able to remove them ~ I have established myself in the knowledge of the 4-noble truths.' " (MAHASI ~ "So, those who regard themselves as having reached the SOTĀPANNA stage should make a self-examination to ascertain whether they are freed from the clutches of the upsurging defilements (NIVARANAS) when they are noting in solitude all phenomena that become evident at the 6-sense doors. ~ When they find their minds cleared of all hindrances (5) they may feel certain that they have become a SOTĀPANNA ~ but if they find out that their minds are still hovering over so many imagined objects of their desires, they may regard themselves as having failed in the test.")

2. Second MAHĀPACCAVEKKHANĀ ~ In a SOTĀPANNA'S mind is a firmly established wisdom relating to NĀMA and RŪPA being subject to the laws of ANICCA ~ DUKKHA and ANATTA. ~ He is also in a position to examine himself if he has gained SAMĀDHI ~ by which all obstructions dying in the way of deliverance from defilements are to be extirpated (removed, destroyed). These defilements are of 2 kinds: ~ the coarse (NIVARANAS), and the subtle (ANUSAYA KILESA). ~ (BUDDHA ~ "A SOTĀPANNA who examines himself in that way will come to the conclusion thus: ~ I have practiced this knowledge ~ developed it and extended it many a time. I have mastered concentration, which has eliminated defilements in my mind. ~ I have now come to the stage of deliverance from defilements." ~ A SOTĀPANNA can establish concentration of mind by doing away with care and anxiety and restlessness with regard to sensual pleasures. ~ To a SOTĀPANNA life is but a manifestation of NĀMA and RŪPA. ~ With SOTĀPANNAS doubts never arise in their minds regarding

moralities compatible with BUDDHA ~ DHAMMA and SANGHA ~ and ~ wrong views ~ doubts ~ and belief in rites and rituals has been eradicated. ~ (He knows that NIBBĀNA is attained by 8-fold path). ~ SOTĀPANNA is also free from LOBHA ~ DOSA ~ and MOHA which lead to unwholesome deeds such as killing ~ stealing ~ lying ~ etc. which all belong to coarser types of defilements. ~ ANUSAYAS or subtle types occur when one fails to gain the truth of conviction that all is ANICCA ~ DUKKHA ~ ANATTA. ~ MAHASI. ~ The Second MAHĀPACCAVEKKHANĀ is therefore a self-examination as to whether coarse and subtle forms of defilements have been eradicated through repeated VIPASSANĀ practice, with a view to realize the knowledge of the path leading to NIBBĀNA.

3. Third PACCAVEKKHANĀ ~ "There is, O BHIKKHUS, another method of self-examination. A SOTĀPANNA thinks over thus: "I have accomplished myself in the knowledge relating to the phenomena of NĀMA and RŪPA that arise and pass away at the 6-sense doors ~ outside BUDDHASĀSANĀ. Is there any individual who is likewise accomplished in this knowledge?" ~ The yogi then comes to the conclusion that he has truly become accomplished in this knowledge ~ while outside BUDDHASĀSANĀ there have appeared no individuals who are so accomplished. ~ (How can a SOTĀPANNA arrive at this conclusion? ~ Other systems do not teach VIPASSANĀ ~ noting with SATI the 6-sense door experience. ~ Others do not enlighten the fact of ANATTA and what is taken as 'self' is verily 'not-self' ~ just a manifestation of the arising and passing away of NĀMA and RŪPA. ~ Others do not reveal the way to NIBBĀNA (8-fold path ~ DANĀ- SĪLA- BHĀVANĀ- SĪLA- SAMĀDHI- PAÑÑĀ ~ thus the SOTĀPANNA concludes that no others outside the BUDDHASĀSANĀ fold are so accomplished regarding truth (of NĀMA- RŪPA). The yogi also concludes that even within the DHAMMA-fold ~ if SATIPATTHĀNA, exercise in mindfulness, is not practiced methodically, no one can attain enlightenment about the conditioned things, the TI-LAKKHANA, etc. and so no one can attain the status of a SOTĀPANNA. (This knowledge came upon uprooted of belief in rites and rituals).

14. THE PROGRESS OF INSIGHT THROUGH THE STAGES OF PURIFICATION

4. Fourth PACCAVEKKHANĀ ~ "O BHIKKHUS ~ there is another method of self-examination. ~ A SOTĀPANNA examines himself thus: ~ "A noble one accomplished in the knowledge of the noble path possesses a nature characteristic of his nobility. ~ Have I possessed this nature?" As he considers this ~ he comes to the conclusion that he has basically what is meant. ~ With even the slightest technical ĀPATTI a monk (if he commits one) immediately atones for his guilt.

(VINAYA offense: There are ten types of offenses ~ PĀRĀJIKA, SANGHĀDISESA, ANIYATA (indefinite), NISSAGGIYA PĀCTITTIYA (forfeiture and confession), PĀCTITTIYA (confession only), PĀTIDESANĪYA (acknowledgement), SEKHIA (training), DUKKATA, DUBBHĀSITA (wrong speech) and THULLACCAYA (grave offense). When an infant accidentally touches fire, he withdraws his hand quickly. ~ Furthermore, the monk takes special care not to repeat the same transgression. This habit is in the nature of SOTĀPANNAS. ~ He never commits grave offenses: ~ killing, lying, stealing, adultery, cheating, "taking intoxicants" ~ etc. Yet he is not completely free from avarice and DOSA, so he might commit minor offenses. ~ He will openly confess guilt though ~ unlike ordinary folks. A common man rarely tries to restrain himself from committing grave offenses ~ and usually pretends that he is innocent if approached. ~ SOTĀPANNA might still enjoy himself in sensual pleasures, however he is fully aware that such enjoyments are unwholesome and should be abstained. ~ Ordinary individuals would not think of sensual restraint.

5. Fifth PACCAVEKKHANĀ ~ the 4th and 5th are almost identical. ~ The 4th relates to the habit of SOTĀPANNA in confessing their guilt and abstaining from repeating it. ~ The 5th ~ the SOTĀPANNA makes it a habit to observe 3 SIKKHĀS (rules of higher training) (or conduct) such as ADHISĪLA- higher morality, ADHICITTTA – higher meditation practice and ADHIPAÑÑĀ – higher knowledge. ~ (The SOTĀPANNA ~ monk or laity never relaxes in the cultivation of SĪLA- SAMĀDHI and PAÑÑĀ. ~ He never forgets to note phenomena in the exercise of VIPASSANĀ practice. ~ "The nature of an ARIYĀ is therefore, never to forget the practice of insight meditation. ~ When one makes an appraisal of himself and finds that he has acquired the

habit of meditation he can rest assured that he has reached the stage of SOTĀPANNA."

6. Sixth PACCAVEKKHANĀ~ and again, O BHIKKHUS, an ARIYĀ examines himself in this way ~ "One who is accomplished in the wisdom of the ATUVĀS is endowed with strength, am I so endowed with it? ~ What is the strength of the ARIYĀS?" ~ When listening to one DHAMMA the ARIYĀ treats the situation as if he is counting or guarding gold or involved in a delicate transition. He notes carefully each word and point discussed without diverting his attention. ~ Most worldlings grow tired of DHAMMA talks very quickly; ~ they feel like they have to be entertained ~ made to laugh, etc. If you are endowed with such sensitive attentiveness, you possess the "strength of ARIYĀS".

7. Seventh PACCAVEKKHANĀ ~ Eventually (close to #6) means ~ "Joy in listening to DHAMMA as the listener fully realizes the significance of the DHAMMA" ~ He is thrilled with joy that permeates through his body ~ feeling joyous as he gets the true meaning of what has been preached. He may be regarded as "possessing the strength of the ARIYĀS".

"A listener to DHAMMA and VINAYA must try to get at their meaning and purport. He must also try to understand how salient points in the DHAMMA are arranged or programmed. He must listen to DHAMMA discourses with joy: ~ If one takes up DHAMMA in this way, one may be regarded as having been endowed with the strength of the ARIYĀS."

A yogi well-experienced in VIPASSANĀ can appreciate the meaning of the texts better and assimilate the philosophy of NĀMA and RŪPA.

BUDDHA ~ "O BHIKKHUS ~ if you have qualified yourselves in these texts laid down under the 7 principles of self-appreciation ~ you are a SOTĀPANNA." ~ (These principles can be understood by SOTĀPANNAS. Anyone who thinks that they have reached the SOTĀPANNA stage may examine himself applying these tests.)"

And then there are certain respected SAMANAS and BRĀHMANS who, living on the food offered out of faith, are given to mutually disparaging disputes. And what are they? They are as follows: "You don't know this doctrine and discipline. I know this doctrine and discipline. How can you ever know this doctrine and discipline? Your practice is wrong. My practice is right. What I say is coherent and sensible. What you say is not coherent and sensible. What you say first you say last: and what you say last you should say first. What you have long practiced to say has been upset now. I have exposed the faults in your doctrine. You stand rebuked. Try to escape from this censure, or explain it if you can." A BHIKKHU abstains from such mutually disparaging disputes. This is one of the precepts of a BHIKKHUS morality.

~ DIGHA NIKAYA ~ SĪLAKKHANDA VAGGA ~ SĀMAÑÑA-PHALA SUTTA, para.202

15.
THE EIGHTEEN GREAT KNOWLEDGES OF INSIGHT

(Manual of Insight – Mahasi Sayadaw, Chapter 7)

The eighteen great Insight Knowledges (ATTHĀRASA MAHĀVIPASSANĀ) are:

1. One abandons the perception of permanence by developing contemplation of impermanence.
2. One abandons the perception of satisfaction by developing contemplation of unsatisfactoriness.
3. One abandons the perception of self by developing the contemplation of not-self.
4. One abandons delight by developing the contemplation of disenchantment.
5. One abandons passion by developing the contemplation of dispassion.
6. One abandons origination by developing contemplation of cessation.
7. One abandons grasping by developing contemplation of relinquishment.
8. One abandons the perception of solidity by developing contemplation of destruction.
9. One abandons the accumulation of KAMMA by developing contemplation of fall.
10. One abandons the perception of stability by developing contemplation of change.

11. One abandons the sign by developing contemplation of the signless.
12. One abandons desire by developing contemplation of the desireless.
13. One abandons adherence by developing contemplation of emptiness.
14. One abandons adherence to the grasping after substance by developing contemplation of "Insight into phenomena that is higher wisdom."
15. One abandons adherence to delusion by developing knowledge and vision of things as they really are.
16. One abandons adherence due to reliance by developing contemplation of danger.
17. One abandons non reflection by developing contemplation of reflection.
18. One abandons adherence due to bondage by developing contemplation of turning away.

A. The Seven Main Contemplations

1. Contemplation of Impermanence

Contemplation of impermanence (ANICCĀNUPASSANĀ) refers to seeing conditioned phenomena arise and pass away while observing their unique characteristics. According to the VISUDDHIMAGGA, one should understand three aspects of this contemplation: impermanence, the characteristic of impermanence, and contemplation of impermanence.

The five aggregates are impermanent. Why? Because they arise, pass away, and change, or because of their immediate disappearance after having arisen. Arising, passing away, and change are the characteristics of impermanence ~ or the mode of change. (i.e. nonexistence after having arisen.)

The characteristic of impermanence is arising, passing away, and change, or 'nonexistence after having arisen'. Phenomena that have arisen do not remain in their initial state due to change; they

15. THE EIGHTEEN GREAT KNOWLEDGES OF INSIGHT

disappear that very moment. Contemplation of impermanence is seeing phenomena to be impermanent.

For the characteristic of impermanence, two kinds of definitions are given (in the quotes above). The second one of these (nonexistence after having arisen) becomes especially apparent at the higher stages of knowledge, such as Knowledge of Dissolution, and so becomes an outstanding characteristic. When one clearly sees that characteristic, one's knowledge derived from contemplation of impermanence becomes sharp and keen. This is why the sub-commentary to the ABHIDHAMMA says: Because four kinds of definitions are included in this phrase and can be taken as a whole, the commentary mentions this phrase separately.

The SAMMOHAVINODANĪ ATTHAKATĀ, a commentary on ABHIDHAMMA, mentions four ways that one can see the characteristic of impermanence, all of which can be included in "impermanence — that is, nonexistence after having arisen." The four definitions from this commentary are: arising and passing away (UPPĀDAVAYAVANTATA), change (VIPARINĀMA), momentariness (TĀVAKĀLIKA), and denying permanence (NICCAPATIKKHEPA).

According to the VISUDDHIMAGGA-MAHĀTĪKĀ:

Appearance, presence, and disappearance characterize the impermanence of all conditioned phenomena. However, the first two are not as obviously characteristics of impermanence as is the last. Therefore, the commentary says that "disappearance is the outstanding portion of impermanence."

Phenomena that arise depending on many causes and conditions are called "conditioned phenomena". All these conditioned phenomena are marked by appearance, presence, and disappearance. These three phases can also be called birth, aging, and death, since they are noted as conditioned phenomena, they are called "conditioned characteristics" (SANKHATA- LAKKHANĀ). Impermanent phenomena are also conditioned. And because the conditioned characteristics of arising, presence, and disappearance are impermanent as well, they are also called "impermanent characteristics" (ANICCALAKKHANĀ).

However, one cannot yet clearly know impermanence by just

knowing the appearance and presence of conditioned phenomena. Where there is appearance and presence, there must always be disappearance too. Due to this, we can know their impermanent nature by reflecting about it. The impermanent nature of phenomena is not very obvious while they are appearing and being present. But when one knows the disappearance or end of phenomena, one can clearly know their impermanent nature. Thus, at the moment of disappearance their impermanent nature becomes easily apparent. Among the three phases of appearance, presence, and disappearance, the characteristic of impermanence is particularly obvious at the moment of disappearance. This is why the commentary says that disappearance is the outstanding portion of impermanence.

The five aggregates that are called "impermanent" are actually different from impermanence itself, which is called "the characteristic of impermanence". However, if one is only aware of impermanence itself, without observing the unique characteristics of the aggregates, then genuine knowledge derived from contemplation of impermanence cannot develop. This is because the impermanence that one is aware of is merely conceptual. In fact, one can only directly see the impermanence of the mental and physical aggregates (characterized by appearance, presence, and disappearance) while one is observing their unique characteristics. So only then can genuine contemplation of impermanence develop.

This is why the commentary on the ABHIDHAMMA says:

What is the object of the insight called "Knowledge that leads to Emergence"? It is the three universal characteristics (of impermanence, unsatisfactoriness, and not-self).

However, by themselves, these characteristics are merely concepts and cannot be described (as something that exists in the sensual, fine-material, or immaterial realms). But if a person sees these three universal characteristics, the five aggregates will seem "like a rotten carcass hung about his or her neck". Thus (by simultaneously seeing phenomena and their three universal characteristics) by means of knowledge that takes conditioned phenomena as its object, one emerges from those very phenomena.

15. THE EIGHTEEN GREAT KNOWLEDGES OF INSIGHT

Suppose a BHIKKHU wishes to buy an alms bowl. He will be initially pleased when he sees a bowl-seller bringing him a bowl. However, if he examines the bowl and finds that there are three holes in it, he will lose interest; not in the three holes, but in the bowl itself. In the same way, when one sees the three characteristics, one will lose interest in conditioned phenomena. Thus, one emerges from conditioned phenomena by means of the insight that takes those very phenomena as its object.

This passage addresses the question of whether the objects that "Knowledge that Leads to Emergence" takes are themselves conditioned phenomena, or the three universal characteristics of impermanence, unsatisfactoriness, and not-self. If the meditation only took the phenomena themselves as its objects, then it would not be able to see impermanence, and so on. On the other hand, if it only took impermanence and so on as its objects, then we could not say that knowledge of change-of-lineage, and the path knowledge and fruition knowledge that follow it, are an escape from conditioned phenomena.

Thus, the meaning of this passage is that "Knowledge that Leads to Emergence" sees phenomena in terms of their unique characteristics (such as hardness, mental contact, or knowing an object) and, by simultaneously seeing their disappearance, sees one of their three universal characteristics (impermanence, unsatisfactoriness, and not-self). This causes the meditator to feel thoroughly repulsed by phenomena connected with the observed characteristic, just as he or she would be disgusted by "a rotten carcass hung about his or her neck". It is obvious that just as that person wants to get rid of the carcass, so will meditators look at phenomena as something to be gotten rid of by means of their knowledge.

Not only does one observe characteristics, one also observes conditioned phenomena as a whole. This is why knowledge of change-of-lineage and path knowledge emerge from conditioned phenomena while knowledge of adaptation sees their impermanent nature, and so on. "To emerge" means that conditioned phenomena are no longer the mind's object and that the mind takes NIBBĀNA, the cessation of conditioned phenomena, as its object.

This is the example of how one wants to abandon conditioned phenomena that are connected with the characteristics by experiencing these very characteristics. The monk who decided to buy an alms bowl found out, after inspecting it, that it had three holes. So, he no longer had any desire for the alms bowl. The monk still wanted the alms bowl before he saw the three holes. When he saw the holes, it wasn't that he didn't want the holes, he did not want the bowl itself. Why? Because his previous desire was only for the bowl, and not for the holes.

Likewise, meditators are attached to conditioned phenomena before they see the three universal characteristics, but they have never been attached to the characteristics of impermanence, unsatisfactoriness, and not-self. So, when they see the three characteristics, their desire to abandon them or to be freed from attachment is connected only with the conditioned phenomena that are bound up with these characteristics. One wants only to abandon conditioned phenomena. Because one had no attachment to the characteristics, one has no desire to abandon them.

Conditioned phenomena along with their characteristics are something to be abandoned. So, the Knowledge of Change-of-Lineage and Path Knowledge that take NIBBĀNA as their object (which arise based on the highest Knowledges) do not emerge only from conditioned phenomena. A sub-commentary to the ABHIDHAMMA further explains the commentary's meaning as follows:

One knows the three universal characteristics by realizing that conditioned phenomena are impermanent and so on. When one sees phenomena in this way, it is said that knowledge that leads to emergence takes the three characteristics as its object. In this sense, insight is said to take the three characteristics as its object, even though it actually takes phenomena as its object.

Thus (the commentary says), "By themselves, these characteristics are merely concepts," and so on. If these characteristics are perceived independent (of phenomena) as impermanent, unsatisfactory, and not-self, they should be considered to be concepts and not something that truly exists in an ultimate sense. For this reason, they cannot be described (as anything belonging to the sensual, fine-material, or immaterial worlds). In an ultimate sense, it is impossible to find any characteristics that are separate from the actual phenomena.

So, it is only when one sees phenomena in terms of their unique characteristics (such as hardness and so on), that one can see their universal characteristics (impermanence, unsatisfactoriness, and not-self). Thus (the commentary says), "If a person sees these three universal characteristics," and so on. Because one sees conditioned phenomena themselves to be impermanent and so on, they are what should be discarded, as if they were "a rotten carcass hung about one's neck".

According to these texts contemplation of impermanence is insight into impermanence brought about by observing the unique characteristics of mental and physical phenomena. So, we cannot say that knowledge that discerns mental and physical phenomena and knowledge that discerns conditionality are contemplations of impermanence, because these insights only consider unique characteristics. It is the Higher Insight Knowledges, beginning from Insight Knowledge by Comprehension that one should consider contemplations of impermanence, because these Insight Knowledges see universal characteristics as well.

Moreover, if one sees impermanence, one is considered to be contemplating impermanence – but not unsatisfactoriness or not-self. Similarly, if one sees unsatisfactoriness, one is considered to be contemplating unsatisfactoriness – but not the other two contemplations. And if one sees not-self, one is considered to be contemplating not-self – but not the other two.

The MŪLATĪKĀ refers to this point:

"The universal characteristics of impermanence and so on are mentioned separately from the phenomena that are impermanent and so on, because understanding impermanence and so on is different from knowledge that discerns the unique characteristics of the phenomena. Therefore, "Knowledge that Discerns Mental and Physical Phenomena" cannot, by itself, bring about insight. Rather, one must see impermanence, unsatisfactoriness, and not-self by means of further insight. We cannot say that seeing impermanence is the same as seeing unsatisfactoriness or not-self. The same applies for the other two."

Developing contemplation of impermanence:

We begin to develop contemplation of impermanence from the

moment that insight becomes clear enough to break up the continuity of phenomena. To explain further, unless one notes the mental and physical phenomena involved in mental and physical movements or actions the moment they occur, it is impossible to see them as they really are, let alone to see them arising and passing away. Because of this one mistakes a series of successive phenomena for a single phenomenon. When one sees something repeatedly or over a prolonged period, for example, one thinks that what one is currently seeing is the same as what one saw before. This kind of delusion also occurs when one hears something and so on. The term 'continuity' (SANTATI) refers to the continuity of phenomena that causes one to think that the thing one is currently seeing is the same thing one saw before, and so on. Because this continuity obscures it, one is not able to see the impermanence of phenomena, and thinks that they exist forever.

Thus, continuity can only hide phenomena when one fails to observe their arising and passing away. But if one uninterruptedly observes phenomena, he or she will be able to see them occurring one by one, and to distinguish between successive phenomena. One will even be able to distinguish between the initial arising and final disappearance of a single object. As a result of seeing phenomena as separate entities that are not joined to the previous or following one, the continuity of phenomena is destroyed, and the characteristic of impermanence – including appearance, presence, and disappearance, or nonexistence after having arisen – becomes obvious of its own accord. In this way one begins to develop Contemplation of Impermanence.

When one clearly sees the characteristic of impermanence, one may begin to note phenomena in a different way, as simply "impermanent, impermanent." Similarly, if one sees phenomena as unsatisfactory or not-self, one may note, "unsatisfactory, unsatisfactory," or "not-self, not-self," respectively. However, simply reciting "impermanent," "unsatisfactory," or "not-self," does not accomplish anything at all. What is important is to accurately understand these characteristics. We can develop the contemplations of impermanence, unsatisfactoriness, and not-self without using this kind of labeling at all, if we understand the true characteristics of impermanence, unsatisfactoriness, and not-

15. THE EIGHTEEN GREAT KNOWLEDGES OF INSIGHT

self by observing phenomena the moment they occur.

Such labeling may give rise to assumed knowledge, without any actual understanding of impermanence, and so on. So I would advise meditators to observe the actual mental and physical phenomena involved in actions or movements the moment they occur, rather than reciting "impermanence," "unsatisfactoriness," and "not-self." I mention this other way of labeling only for general information.

Impermanence does not appear because continuity hides it, because one has not contemplated arising and passing away. If one sees arising and passing away and continuity is broken, the characteristic of impermanence appears in its true nature.

For one who does not pay attention, the characteristic of impermanence does not appear because continuity hides it. Continuity is able to hide it because one does not pay attention to arising and passing away. This means that the characteristic of impermanence does not appear while continuity is concealing it. For one who sees arising and passing away, arising does not go into passing away, and passing away does not go into the next arising: The moment of arising is one thing, and the moment of passing away is another thing. Separate moments of arising and passing away appear even for a single phenomenon, not to mention for past phenomena. This means that past and present phenomena, as well as present and future phenomena, are separate things. This is why the commentary says, "If one sees arising and passing away..." and so on. Here, "continuity is broken" means that observation that phenomena happen one after the other and in succession reveals that the continuity of mental and physical phenomena is false. Phenomena do not appear to be joined together to one who correctly observes arising and passing away. Actually, they appear to be separate, like iron bars that are not joined together. In this way, the characteristic of impermanence is exceedingly obvious.

In accordance with this text, the initial arising and the final passing away of a single phenomenon becomes apparent to a meditator who uninterruptedly observes phenomena at the moment they occur. So it becomes obvious that the previous phenomenon is one thing and the following phenomenon is another. They are seen as separate things, and not as one thing or two things joined together. This reveals and destroys the previously held concept of continuity. For one who has destroyed the concept of continuity, the characteristic of impermanence arises in its true nature and becomes obvious of its own accord. We can see the characteristic of impermanence in one of these two ways: as arising, presence, and passing away, or as nonexistence after having arisen. When we experience this genuine and real characteristic of impermanence, we call the knowledge that understands phenomena to be impermanent "contemplation of impermanence." Whenever this genuine knowledge occurs, the perception of permanence (NICCASAÑÑĀ) and resulting unsatisfactoriness are abandoned. The PATISAMBHIDĀMAGGA says:

"One who sees impermanence abandons the perception of permanence."

Here "One abandons the perception of permanence" refers explicitly to perversion of perception, and implicitly to perversion of consciousness and perversion of view. This method of implying the full meaning of a statement is called "figurative usage" (PADHĀNANAYA). The most important or obvious aspect is mentioned explicitly when using it, and the other aspects are implied. In the statement "The king is coming" for example, it is implied that not only the king but also his retinue of many attendants is coming. In the same way, this sentence explicitly mentions perversion of perception, which implicitly includes perversion of view and perversion of consciousness, and all of their mental constituents. According to the MAHĀTĪKĀ:

"The perception of permanence believes in permanence and is taken as the leader of the various kinds of perception for the purpose of this description. The same is true for the perception of pleasure (SUKHASAÑÑĀ) and the perception of self (ATTASAÑÑĀ)."

Abandoning latent defilements

Which perception of permanence must be abandoned – past, present, or future? Past defilements have already disappeared and no longer exist, so one does not need to abandon previous defilements. Future defilements will come into existence at some point, but they have not yet arisen at the moment of observation, so one does not need to abandon future defilements either. Whenever one is observing impermanence in the present moment, only wholesome insight awareness exists, and there are no defilements to be abandoned; so one doesn't need to abandon present defilements, either. When the mental and physical phenomena that arise at the six sense doors are not rightly observed and understood to be impermanent, while these mental and physical phenomena are being perceived to be permanent, conditions are actually right for defilements to be able to arise. So, you should understand that defilements that could arise when conditions are right are the defilements that must be abandoned. These defilements, which cannot be described as actually existing in the past, present, or future, are called "latent defilements."

There are two types of latent defilements: Those that dwell in a continuum (SANTĀNĀNUSAYA) and those that dwell in objects (ĀRAMMANĀNUSAYA). "Defilements that dwell in a continuum" are defilements that dwell in the mental continuum of ordinary people (PUTHUJJANA) and trainees, those noble ones who have not yet attained the fourth fruition knowledge, the fruit of ARAHANTSHIP (ARAHATTAPHALA). These may arise any time that conditions become favorable. "Defilements that dwell in objects" are defilements that dwell in objects when they are not observed. Whenever an object is not rightly understood to be 'impermanent', 'unsatisfactory', and 'not-self', defilements may arise in ordinary people and trainees because they take it to be 'permanent', 'satisfactory', and 'self' — and in accordance with conditions. This kind of defilement is also called "Defilements that arise when sense objects are not observed" (ĀRAMMANĀDHIGGATUPPANNA). It is only this defilement that dwells in the objects that is abandoned by means of insight.

Latent defilements are of seven kinds, namely: Desire for sensual objects (KĀMARĀGĀNUSAYA); aversion (PATIGHĀNUSAYA); conceit (MĀNĀNUSAYA); wrong view (DITTHĀNUSAYA); doubt (VICIKICCHĀNUSAYA); desire for existence (BHAVARĀG-ĀNUSAYA); and ignorance (AVIJJĀNUSAYA). In this world, attachment to sensual objects and to existence lies dormant in everything that is lovable and pleasant, while aversion lies dormant in everything that is unlovable and unpleasant. Delusion lies dormant in both of these.

Also, conceit, wrong view, and doubt, which go hand in hand with delusion, should be regarded to exist in that mind.

The "lovable and pleasant" sense objects (ITTHĀRAMMANA) mentioned here are of two types: Those that are inherently pleasing (SABHĀVA ITTHĀRAMMANA) and those that deceptively appear to be pleasing (PARIKAPPA ITTHĀRAMMANA). For example, those objects, beings, sounds, and so on that are truly beautiful are regarded as inherently pleasing. While human waste, rotting corpses, and so on may be pleasing to a dog, pig, or vulture, that appearance is deceptive. But both are considered to be pleasing objects *(piyarūpa, sātarūpa)* in which desire for sensual objects and existence lies dormant.

Likewise, there are two types of disagreeable objects: Those that are inherently unpleasant (SABHĀVA ANITTHĀRAMMANA) and those that deceptively appear to be unpleasant (PARIKAPPA ANITTHĀRAMMANA). Both of these, the inherently unpleasant one and the deceptively unpleasant one, are considered unpleasant objects (APPIYARŪPA, ASĀTARŪPA). Aversion lies latent in all of these unpleasant worldly phenomena.

Whenever desire or aversion lies latent in these "pleasant-pleasing" and "unpleasant-displeasing" objects, delusion also lies latent in them. And if delusion lies latent in them, it also means that conceit, wrong view, and doubt, which go hand in hand with delusion, lie latent in that mind. "To lie dormant" does not mean that they exist hiding somewhere but that they provide an opportunity for the mental defilements to arise when conditions are right, because either insight knowledge or path knowledge has yet to abandon the defilements.

According to the texts: Here, "Desire lies latent" means that it lies latent in pleasing objects, because it has not yet been abandoned.

Of the two types of potential defilements, attachment lies latent in pleasant objects by means of the defilements latent in objects.

Of the two types of potential defilement, desire, having not yet been completely abandoned by the paths, lies latent in one's mental continuum in such a way that it may arise when conditions are favorable. The same is true when it lies latent in pleasing and agreeable sense objects.

There exists the possibility that defilements will arise with respect to every object that Insight Knowledge or Path Knowledge has not yet rightly understood. This is obvious in the phrase "Defilements lie latent in these objects" mentioned above in the commentary and sub-commentary. Therefore, the BUDDHA said:

The underlying tendency to lust should be abandoned in regard to pleasant feeling. The underlying tendency to aversion should be abandoned in regard to painful feeling. The underlying tendency to ignorance should be abandoned in regard to neither-painful-nor-pleasant feeling.

Defilements that lie dormant in sense objects

The type of defilement that lies dormant in sense objects is also called "defilements that arise when sense objects are not observed" (ĀRAMMAṆĀDHIGGA- HITUPPANNA).

This term is defined by the commentaries as follows:

When with the arising of a visible form (and so on, at the eye door and so on) one apprehends the object first, defilements do not yet arise. Only after the object has been firmly grasped and in accordance with the conditions do they arise. That is why they are called "defilements that lie dormant in sense objects."

If one clearly experiences a pleasing or displeasing object (such as visible form, sound, smell, taste, touch, or mental object), then defilements (like greed, aversion, and so on) can arise either in that very moment or later. If they arise at that very moment, it is obvious that they are able to recur later on. Due to wise attention and other factors, the defilements may not yet arise at that very moment. However, for a person who has a distinct impression and keeps the object firmly in mind, the defilements can certainly arise later when one reflects on the object, when similar or dissimilar objects are encountered, or when somebody else gives a reminder.

The defilements arise because the object has left a lasting impression and is kept firmly in the mind. Thus, this kind of defilement that is ready to arise because the object has left a lasting impression and is kept firmly in the mind is called "a defilement that lies dormant in sense objects." Regarding this matter, one should pay special attention to the passage "…only after the object has been firmly grasped." It is only because the object has left a lasting impression and is kept firmly in the mind that the defilements connected with that object arise at a later time. One should understand that if this were not the case, the defilements would not be able to arise.

There is no doubt that a noble one is free from this kind of latent defilement, having completely abandoned them by means of Path Knowledge. How can one abandon it by means of Insight? If one observes objects (such as visible form, seeing consciousness, sound, hearing consciousness, and so on) the moment they arise at the six sense doors, and sees them to be impermanent, unsatisfactory, and not-self, then one does not perceive them as permanent, satisfactory, and self, either in that moment or later when one thinks about those objects. Thus, defilements do not arise, are not able to arise, or do not have an opportunity to arise based on an object that one has observed.

"Having no opportunity to arise" means that whenever an object is observed, defilements do not lie dormant in it, and that such firmly grasped objects are free from latent defilements. Being free from defilements that lie dormant in objects, one is also free from obsessive and transgressive defilements, as well as from wholesome and unwholesome KAMMA and their resultant mental and physical phenomena. Because right understanding emerges from insight, it becomes impossible for defilements, KAMMA, and its results to arise, since all of these are based on wrong perception. They are abandoned by means of knowledge.

The sub-commentary says:

First, contemplation of impermanence temporarily abandons the perception of permanence by means of substitution of opposites. Without this contemplation, defilements based on the perception of permanence and the volitional deeds resulting from these defilements will give rise to resultant phenomena later on. All of these are abandoned by not giving them an opportunity to arise. They are likewise abandoned by means of contemplation of unsatisfactoriness, and so on. This is why the commentary says that insight temporarily abandons defilements, together with their resultant phenomena.

If one fails to understand the characteristic of impermanence with respect to an object that occurs at the six sense doors, the defilements associated with the perception of permanence will have the opportunity to arise. These defilements are said to "lie dormant" in objects that are not understood to be impermanent, because due to this lack of understanding one will again think about these objects later when the necessary conditions are present. Such thought is actually an obsessive defilement. And again, after one has thought about this object, when the necessary conditions are present, because one still sees it to be permanent, one may act on it; either to obtain or enjoy it, or to destroy it. So, these defilements amount to the real volitional actions (ABHISANKHĀRĀ). Resultant phenomena arise in a new existence due to these wholesome and unwholesome volitional actions, in accordance with conditions.

In a new existence mental and physical phenomenon can only arise when there is KAMMA. They cannot arise without KAMMA. KAMMA cannot arise without the defilement that perceives things as permanent. Defilement cannot arise without the opportunity to perceive things as permanent. When an object is rightly understood to be impermanent the moment it arises at the six sense doors, there is also no longer any opportunity to perceive it to be permanent. Therefore, when we rightly understand an object that arises at the six sense doors to be impermanent and contemplation of impermanence arises, then the object is completely freed from the latent defilement that perceives it to be permanent. The object will also be completely freed from the obsessive defilement that thinks about it as being permanent, as well as from the transgressive defilement that commits (unwholesome acts) connected with that object.

When there are no volitional actions, a new existence that is the result of KAMMA can no longer arise; one has been completely freed from it. Because contemplation of impermanence is able to completely free one from even a new existence, it is said that it abandons the defilements, beginning with the latent defilements, KAMMA, and their resultant phenomena. "Abandon" means to cause to disappear, to not arise, or to give no opportunity to arise. The same is true with respect to contemplations of unsatisfactoriness and not-self: the defilements that will arise when perceiving things to be satisfactory or self are abandoned in the same way. This is why the commentary says that "insight temporarily abandons the defilements, together with their resultant phenomena."

Defilements latent in the mind-continuum

Some defilements lie dormant in the mind-continuum of ordinary people and noble ones at the three lower stages of enlightenment. Such defilements can arise any time, when conditions are right, because they have not yet been abandoned by means of the four paths. This is similar to the situation of a person with malaria: One is considered sick so long as one has not been completely cured of the disease, even though one may not currently be experiencing any of its symptoms. Likewise, if a person who has not given up eating meat is asked, "Do you eat meat?" then, although this person isn't eating meat at that very moment, he or she would have to answer, "I eat meat," because he or she has previously eaten meat and will eat it again in the future.

In the same way, the seven types of potential defilements lie dormant in the continuum of ordinary people. Five of these are also dormant in noble ones at the first and second stages of enlightenment, where wrong view and doubt have been abandoned. Three –desire for existence, conceit, and delusion – are dormant in noble ones at the third stage of enlightenment. Although these defilements may not be arising with the three phases of appearance, presence, and disappearance at this moment, they have arisen in the past and will arise in the future according to conditions. Because the possibility that they will arise has not yet been eliminated, they are ready to arise or lie dormant in each and every person's continuum.

This is why the ABHIDHAMMA says:

The latent defilement of delusion, the latent defilement of conceit, and the latent defilement of desire for existence lie dormant in the continuum of a non-returner (ANĀGĀMI). The latent defilement of delusion, the latent defilement of desire for sensual objects, the latent defilement of aversion, the latent defilement of conceit, and the latent defilement of desire for existence lie dormant in the continuum of noble beings at the first and second stages of enlightenment (stream enterer and once returner). But the latent defilement of wrong view and the latent defilement of doubt do not lie dormant in their continuum. The latent defilement of delusion, the latent defilement of desire for sensual objects, the latent defilement of aversion, the latent defilement of conceit, the latent defilement of wrong view, the latent defilement of doubt, and the latent defilement of desire for existence lie dormant in the continuum of an ordinary person.

However, all seven of these latent defilements cannot occur together at once. For example, desire for sensual objects cannot arise at the same time as desire for existence; desire cannot arise along with aversion and doubt; aversion cannot occur at the same time as conceit, wrong view, doubt, and desire; conceit cannot accompany wrong view, doubt, and aversion; wrong view cannot coexist with doubt, desire for existence, and conceit. However, they can all lie dormant together.

We also cannot say that latent defilements arise, exist, and pass away like the obsessive and transgressive defilements. Actually, because path knowledge has not yet abandoned them, they lie dormant in the continuum of beings, and have the potential to arise in accordance with their conditions. The following passages from the ABHIDHAMMA show how these latent defilements of desire for sensual objects and aversion lie dormant together, and how they arise:

The latent defilement of desire for sensual objects lies dormant in a person's continuum. Can the latent defilement of aversion lie dormant in that person's continuum as well? Yes.

The latent defilement of desire for sensual objects is arising in a person's continuum. Can the latent defilement of aversion arise in that person's continuum as well? Yes.

The latent defilements have not yet been abandoned in a person's continuum, nor are they prevented from arising when conditions are favorable. They arose in his or her continuum before and will do so again later, even though they are not arising at the moment. It is with reference to this that it was said, "The latent defilement of desire for sensual objects arises in a person's continuum, and the latent defilement of aversion arises in a person's continuum as well."

Based on the phrase "...nor are they prevented from arising," the MŪLATĪKĀ, a sub-commentary on the ABHIDHAMMA, says that only seven types of defilement, and not others, are strong enough to lie dormant in one's continuum. The commentary also explains that these are called "latent defilements" because if conditions are favorable, they will arise, not only because the paths have not yet abandoned them, but because tranquility and insight are not preventing them from arising.

According to the Pāḷi texts and commentaries, seven, five, or three types of latent defilement always lie dormant in the continuum of ordinary people and trainees. These latent defilements also lie dormant when wholesome states, resultant states, relinking consciousness, life-continuum, and death consciousness are occurring.

They even lie dormant in non-percipient beings, not to mention when unwholesome states are occurring. These latent defilements lie dormant in the continuum of ordinary people and trainees because they have yet to be abandoned and can arise when the necessary conditions are present. Only path knowledge can completely abandon these kinds of latent defilements. Insight, however, cannot completely abandon them, but it can only temporarily abandon them by means of suppression.

This is in accordance with this passage from the VISUDDHIMAGGA:

Even when suppressed by serenity or insight, they are still called "… arisen through non abolition."

Thus, as the phrase "contemplation of impermanence abandons the perception of permanence" illustrated before, we should understand that the latent defilements lying dormant in objects and the states that are connected to them (obsessive and transgressive defilements, KAMMA, resultant phenomena) are only temporarily abandoned. The VISUDDHIMAGGA says with this aim: "Contemplation of impermanence abandons the perception of permanence."

Impermanence reveals unsatisfactoriness and not-self

In this case it is obvious that if one has understood the object to be impermanent the perception of it as permanent can no longer arise. But one may wonder: "Although one has understood objects to be impermanent, can the defilements that perceive them to be satisfactory and self still arise?" We can conclude that they cannot.

If one has clearly experienced the characteristic of impermanence by seeing objects disappearing after they have arisen, then one cannot see these impermanent objects to be satisfactory, to be a self, or to be a being.

15. THE EIGHTEEN GREAT KNOWLEDGES OF INSIGHT

In fact, if one reflects on phenomena that disappear as soon as they have arisen according to one's empirical knowledge of impermanence, one can determine that because they constantly arise and pass away, these phenomena are unsatisfactory, unpleasant, not to be accepted, and undesirable. And because these phenomena do not obey one's wishes, they do not belong to anyone but arise and pass away of their own accord.

The following text from the ANGUTTARA NIKĀYA provides an irrefutable example:

The perception of impermanence should be developed to eradicate the conceit "I am." When one perceives impermanence, the perception of not-self is stabilized. One who perceives 'non-self' eradicates the conceit "I am," which is NIBBĀNA in this very life.

This passage makes the point that perception of impermanence establishes perception of not-self. In other words, perception of not-self develops of its own accord when one sees things to be impermanent. The phrase "the conceit 'I am'" (ASMIMĀNA) refers to the type of conceit that believes "I am'. This type of conceit of self-existence arises even in the continuum of life of a noble being of the first three stages. When they do something admirable, for example, they may think, "It is I who has done this thing"; this is also called "pride in what is worthy" (YĀTHĀVAMĀNA). Noble ones, of course, know that there is no such thing as what ordinary people identify in a conventional sense as a 'self', a 'being', or 'life'. However, when they do something praiseworthy, they may still act or speak with conceit, thinking, "It is I who thinks, speaks, or acts this way."

This type of conceit that occurs in noble ones should be called "conceit of view" (DITTHIMĀNA), because it is uprooted in a similar way to the way that the wrong view of personality is uprooted. When we say that the right view abandons the wrong view in the case of the higher paths, the wrong view (being referred to) is actually this kind of conceit, rather than the wrong view of personality that the first path abandons. Only the fourth and final path knowledge of Arahant-ship can completely abandon this kind of conceit. When one clearly sees impermanence, one can also see 'not-self'. When one clearly sees not-self, one can completely abandon the conceit "I am" by means of the path knowledge of ARAHANTSHIP.

Therefore, in order to abandon the conceit "I am" the BUDDHA said, "The perception of impermanence should be developed." The commentary gives this explanation:

The line "When one perceives impermanence, the perception of non-self is stabilized" means that if one sees the characteristic of impermanence, one also sees the characteristic of not-self. If one sees one of the three universal characteristics, one also sees the other two. This is why the BUDDHA says, "When one perceives impermanence, BHIKKHUS, the perception of 'non-self' is stabilized."

If one understands one among the three characteristics of impermanence, unsatisfactoriness, and not-self, then one also understands the remaining two. According to the two texts mentioned above, when one reflects on an object that one has seen to be impermanent, one only sees it as unsatisfactory and not-self by nature all the time; one does not see it as satisfactory and self by nature. So, understand that when one understands an object to be impermanent, one eliminates not only the defilements that would arise based on the perception of permanence, but the defilements that would arise based on the perception of satisfaction and self are also eliminated because one can also see that the object is by nature unsatisfactory and not-self.

Conceptual and absolute characteristics

I will now discuss the following passage from a commentary on the ABHIDHAMMA:

People tend to say, "It's impermanent," when for example, a pot or a cup breaks. The characteristic of impermanence appears to them in this way. They tend to say, "It's suffering," when they experience pain, such as from a boil or a thorn. The characteristic of unsatisfactoriness appears to them in this way. The characteristic of impersonality, however, does not appear. It is like darkness; it is not evident and is difficult to know. It is difficult to talk about and explain. Whether or not a BUDDHA has arisen, the characteristics of impermanence and unsatisfactoriness appear. But the characteristic of 'not-self' does not appear when a BUDDHA has not arisen, only when a BUDDHA has arisen.

Even the most powerful masters, like the BODHISATTA SARABHANGA and other hermits and ascetics, could only teach the characteristics of impermanence and unsatisfactoriness, but not 'not-self'. If they could have taught about the third characteristic, their disciples might have attained path knowledge and fruition knowledge. However, the characteristic of not-self is the domain of only an omniscient Buddha, and no one else. Thus, it is said that the BUDDHA had to teach about the characteristic of not-self from the basis of either the characteristic of impermanence, the characteristic of unsatisfactoriness, or both of them.

Actually, the characteristics of impermanence and unsatisfactoriness that non-Buddhist teachers are able to teach are not the real characteristics of impermanence and unsatisfactoriness that are objects of insight; they are only conventional ideas connected with the characteristics of impermanence and unsatisfactoriness. To elaborate, a pot or a cup is a conventional idea that does not really exist in the ultimate sense. So the breaking of a cup does not reflect the real characteristic of impermanence that one must experience with insight. The understanding of impermanence upon the death of a person is only a fake understanding of the characteristic of impermanence. For ordinary people, the characteristic of unsatisfactoriness that appears as unpleasantness resulting from a boil or a thorn is not the characteristic of unsatisfactoriness in its ultimate sense. This is because they identify it as something that belongs to a person, who doesn't really exist in the ultimate sense. They think, "I am suffering; I am in pain," and so on. Thus it has nothing to do with the ultimate mental and physical phenomena that one must understand with knowledge.

The three characteristics that are referred to in the passage from the commentary on the ANGUTTARA NIKĀYA explained above are the real ones that can only be understood by means of knowledge. If one understands one among those three characteristics, then one understands the other two. So, as the commentary to the SAMMOHAVINODANĪ says, in order to cause people to understand the characteristic of not-self, the BUDDHA taught it on the basis of the characteristics of impermanence and unsatisfactoriness.

Having said this, the characteristics of impermanence and

unsatisfactoriness (by means of which one can understand the characteristic of not-self) are the real characteristics that one must understand by means of insight. Like the characteristic of not-self, they are also difficult to understand, and persons other than the Buddha cannot teach them.

That is why the MŪLATĪKĀ says:

"Teaching the characteristic of not-self is not the domain of anyone other than the BUDDHA. The teaching of the characteristics of impermanence and unsatisfactoriness that reveal the characteristic of not-self is not the domain of anyone other than the BUDDHA. It is difficult to teach these because they are not obvious."

The commentary states that no one other than the BUDDHA can teach the characteristic of not-self, and that he had to teach it on the basis of the characteristics of impermanence and unsatisfactoriness. In light of this, it is shown that when one has not understood the real characteristics of impermanence and unsatisfactoriness, one has not understood the characteristic of not-self. Or in other words, if one understands the real characteristics of impermanence and unsatisfactoriness, one also understands the characteristic of not-self. Other than the BUDDHA, no other person can understand the characteristic of not-self, nor can they understand the characteristics of impermanence and unsatisfactoriness. Therefore, other than the BUDDHA, no other person can teach the characteristics of impermanence and unsatisfactoriness that reveal the characteristic of not-self; only the BUDDHA can do it. This means that it is difficult to teach the real characteristics of impermanence, unsatisfactoriness, and not-self, because they are not obvious.

The characteristics of impermanence and unsatisfactoriness that reveal the characteristic of not-self that are mentioned in this sub-commentary are the real characteristics of impermanence and unsatisfactoriness that one must understand with insight. They are not the fake characteristics of impermanence and unsatisfactoriness connected with a broken pot or a piercing thorn. The ANUTĪKĀ, a sub-commentary, distinguishes between these two types of knowledge as follows:

"The understanding of the characteristics of impermanence and unsatisfactoriness gained from seeing a broken pot or from feeling a piercing thorn is not a way that can lead beings to a definite understanding of the characteristic of not-self. The characteristic of not-self is only definitely understood when one understands the conditioned and oppressive nature of phenomena.

"To elaborate, one who has developed insight or cultivated insight *pāramī* and observes mental and physical phenomena is able to see that "The mental and physical phenomena that constitute the eye and so on are conditioned by KAMMA, the primary elements, and so on. Thus, they are impermanent, since they arise without having existed before and vanish after they have arisen; they are unsatisfactory, being constantly oppressed by arising and passing away; and they are not-self, occurring of their own accord without obeying anyone's will."

Summary

Contemplation of impermanence is to understand impermanence by observing the unique characteristics of mental and physical phenomena that arise at the six sense doors, and to see both their arising and passing away or only their disappearance. Knowledge that understands a presently-observed object to be impermanent is called "empirical contemplation of impermanence" (PACCAKKHA ANICCĀNUPASSANĀ).

After thoroughly empirically understanding this, one also understands that the mental and physical phenomena from the past, which one cannot directly know, were likewise impermanent. One also understands that whatever mental and physical phenomena there are in this world are also impermanent in the same way. This understanding that comes by way of reflection is called "inferential contemplation of impermanence" (ANUMĀNA ANICCĀNUPASSANĀ).

The contemplation of impermanence, either empirically or inferentially, begins to arise with insight knowledge of comprehension. It is fully developed with regard to its function of abandoning the defilements, beginning with insight knowledge of dissolution.

This is why in the PATISAMBHIDĀMAGGA of the KHUDDAKA NIKĀYA the BUDDHA said:

"One who sees impermanence abandons the perception of permanence."

I will now briefly explain contemplations of unsatisfactoriness and not-self. One can understand them in detail in the same way that contemplation of impermanence has been explained above.

2. Contemplation of Unsatisfactoriness

Contemplation of unsatisfactoriness (DUKKHĀNUPASSANĀ) is to understand unsatisfactoriness by observing the unique characteristics of mental and physical phenomena, and seeing that arising and passing away continuously oppress them.

The mental and physical phenomena that arise at the six sense doors are called "That which is unsatisfying" because continuous arising and passing away oppresses them. The condition of being oppressed by continuous arising and passing away is called "The characteristic of unsatisfactoriness" (DUKKHALAKKHANĀ). While observing mental and physical phenomena as they arise and pass away, one can also see the characteristic of unsatisfactoriness; the insight that understands them to be unsatisfactory is called "contemplation of unsatisfactoriness." It sees phenomena as fearful, dangerous, disenchanting, bad, or detestable.

In accord with the statement that "What is impermanent is unsatisfactory," the five aggregates of mental and physical phenomena themselves are called unsatisfactory. Why? Because they are constantly oppressed by arising and passing away. The condition of being constantly oppressed in this way is the characteristic of unsatisfactoriness.

There are three aspects of unsatisfactoriness: The occurrence of mental or physical pain (DUKKHADUKKHA), the impermanence of mental or physical pleasure (VIPARINĀMADUKKHA), and the condition of being subject to arising and passing away (SANKHĀRADUKKA).

Of these three aspects, we use the last one here because it is common to all conditioned phenomena.

As the MAHĀTĪKĀ says:

"Of the three types of unsatisfactoriness, being subject to arising and passing away is common to all conditioned phenomena.

"If one does not observe the mental and physical phenomena that constantly arise and pass away at the six sense doors, one cannot understand that arising and passing away oppresses them. If one adjusts the posture as soon as one experiences any kind of unpleasant feeling due to remaining in one position for a long time, then even the occurrence of mental and physical pain doesn't appear – let alone the impermanence of mental or physical pleasure or the condition of being subject to arising and passing away – because they are concealed by changing the posture. In the case of not even seeing the roughest form of unsatisfactoriness, contemplation of unsatisfactoriness cannot arise.

"On the other hand, if one observes mental and physical phenomena that arise and pass away at the six sense doors, one can see how arising and passing away continuously oppress them. Because one is aware of the continuous oppression by arising and passing away, one can also know the disappearance of a pleasant feeling that had appeared earlier while sitting in the same posture. Then one observes the unpleasant feelings (such as stiffness or heat) that have arisen. Because they are unpleasant, one wants to change the posture, or one actually changes the posture. After changing the posture, the unpleasant feeling disappears and is replaced by a pleasant feeling. One will see all of this while noting. Thus one uncovers how changing postures obscures the characteristic of unsatisfactoriness when one sees continuous oppression through arising and passing away, and observes the unpleasant feeling that comes from prolonged sitting, the desire to change the posture, and the act of actually changing it. Then real contemplation of unsatisfactoriness arises because the subtle characteristic of being subject to arising and passing away appears.

"The characteristic of unsatisfactoriness does not appear when continuous oppression is not given attention, because it is concealed by the postures. When one exposes the postures by paying attention to continuous oppression, the characteristic of unsatisfactoriness appears in its true nature.

"The phrase "When one exposes the postures, the characteristic of unsatisfactoriness appears" makes it seem that this passage only applies to the characteristic of the occurrence of mental or physical pain. But it also applies to the characteristics of "being subject to arising and passing away" and "the impermanence of mental or physical pleasure," which are referred to with the phrase "by paying attention to continuous oppression." So, this is how all the three types of characteristics of unsatisfactoriness appear.

"Whenever real contemplation of unsatisfactoriness arises due to seeing the characteristic of unsatisfactoriness, the perception of satisfaction and so on is abandoned. To explain further, if one does not rightly understand the object (mental and physical phenomena) to be unsatisfactory, then a perversion of perception that perceives the object to be satisfactory can arise. The perversions of view and consciousness can also arise. Based on that, defilements can also arise, and this in turn leads to wholesome and unwholesome volitional actions, the effects of which are resultant phenomena. However, if one rightly understands phenomena to be unsatisfactory, then the perversion of perception and so on can no longer arise. Thus, all the phenomena beginning with perversion of perception and ending with resultant phenomena cannot arise, because they are abandoned and cut off by contemplation of unsatisfactoriness."

Thus, the VISUDDHIMAGGA says:

"One who develops contemplation of unsatisfactoriness abandons the perception of satisfaction."

In the PATISAMBHIDĀMAGGA, the BUDDHA says:

"One who sees unsatisfactoriness abandons the perception of satisfaction."

Summary

Contemplation of unsatisfactoriness is to understand unsatisfactoriness by observing the unique characteristics of mental and physical phenomena that arise at the six sense doors, and seeing either oppression by arising and passing away, change and destruction, or unbearable torture. The knowledge that understands presently observed objects to be unsatisfactory is called "empirical contemplation of unsatisfactoriness" (PACCAKKHA DUKKHĀNUPASSANĀ).

After thoroughly empirically understanding unsatisfactoriness, one also understands that mental and physical phenomena from the past and future as well as all mental and physical phenomena there are in this world are also unsatisfactory in the same way. The understanding that comes by means of reflection is called "inferential contemplation of unsatisfactoriness" (ANUMĀNA DUKKHĀNUPASSANĀ).

Contemplation of unsatisfactoriness, whether empirical or inferential, begins to arise with insight knowledge of comprehension. Beginning from insight knowledge of dissolution it is fully developed with regard to its function of abandoning the defilements.

3. Contemplation of 'Not-Self'

Contemplation of 'not-self' (ANATTĀNUPASSANĀ) is to understand 'not-self' by observing the unique characteristics of mental and physical phenomena, and to see that they are unamenable to the exercise of control, and that they are phenomena that happen of their own accord.

The term 'self', which is the opposite of 'not-self', does not refer to groups of physical or mental phenomena, the body, or any visible forms. Actually, it only refers to what ordinary people think of as 'the soul' or 'self'. They mistakenly think that this 'self' is a master, an eternal resident, a doer, a feeler, a director, or a controller. But this so-called self is neither the five aggregates of mental and physical phenomena, nor is it inside the five aggregates of mental and physical phenomena, or anywhere else. It is merely a concept held by ordinary people who are not yet free from the wrong view.

Therefore, the five aggregates of mental and physical phenomena are called 'not-self'. This means that they do not possess a 'self'. Why? If there was a 'self', it could exercise control. But as there is no exercising of control over the five aggregates, they are 'not-self'. Being unamenable to the exercise of control is called "the characteristic of not-self" (ANATTĀLAKKHANA).

If one observes all mental and physical phenomena when they arise, one can only see phenomena that arise and pass away of their own accord. One cannot find anything in them that might be called a 'self' that could be identified as the master or the controller of the phenomena. Thus, one understands that the phenomena one observes are not a self that has mastery or control, but only natural phenomena. This understanding is the contemplation of 'not-self'.

In accord with the statement that "What is unsatisfying is not-self," these five aggregates are called 'not-self'. Why? Because there is no exercising of control over them. Being unamenable to the exercise of control is the characteristic of 'not-self'.

If one does not observe the phenomena that arise at the six sense doors, one will not see that they are of different types, characteristics, functions, and objects. Instead, one will see them appear as one single and solid entity. The moment one sees, for example, eye-consciousness does not appear as a separate entity. Rather, all phenomena such as the intention to see, eye-consciousness, and thoughts about what one sees appear as one single and solid entity. The concept of solidity conceals the characteristic of not- self. When the characteristic of not-self doesn't appear, real understanding regarding contemplation of not-self cannot arise.

On the other hand, when one's mindfulness, concentration, and insight are mature, and one observes phenomena at the six sense doors, each of these phenomena appear as separate entities in various ways: As objects, or in terms of their momentariness, characteristics, or functions. They do not appear as a single and solid entity. The moment we see, for example, eye-consciousness alone appears as a single and separate entity. Then the concept of solidity is broken and the characteristic of not-self appears in its true nature, of its own accord. Therefore, only when the characteristic of not-self appears can real understanding regarding contemplation of not-self arise.

The characteristic of not-self does not appear because when one does not pay attention to resolution into the various elements it is concealed by solidity. When the breaking up of the solid is affected by resolution into elements, the characteristic of not-self appears in its true nature.

There are four types of concepts of solidity that conceal the characteristic of not-self: those associated with the continuity of phenomena, called "solidity of continuity" (SANTATIGHANA), those associated with the mass of phenomena, called "solidity of mass" (SAMŪHAGHANA), those associated with the functions of

15. THE EIGHTEEN GREAT KNOWLEDGES OF INSIGHT

phenomena, called "solidity of function" (KICCAGHANA), and those associated with the objects of phenomena, called "solidity of object" (ĀRAMMANAGHANA).

The solidity of continuity

Solidity of continuity refers to all concepts of solidity that are based on the continuity of phenomena.

If one does not know that the visual process consists of separate phenomena such as the intention to see, the initial eye-consciousness, the recurring eye-consciousness, and thoughts about what has been seen, then all these phenomena are perceived as one single entity. Because of taking these phenomena to be continuous, one thinks that there is a self that exercises control, and that it is this self that can look, see, or think whenever it wants.

Understand this likewise with respect to a moment of hearing. This also applies to moments of bending, stretching, walking, standing, sitting, or lying down. If one does not understand the separate processes involved in these activities, such as the desire and the actual activity as well as the separate segments within one movement or activity, one thinks that there is a self that can do these activities whenever it wants. Solidity of continuity prevents us from distinguishing separate phenomena by means of their momentariness, and so conceals the characteristic of not-self. Not being able to differentiate between successive mental and physical phenomena, one takes them to be a self.

How can one break down the concept of solidity of continuity and make the characteristic of not-self appear? When one practices insight meditation, one understands that the desire to look and the actual act of looking are different or separate. One understands other phenomena likewise; one does not perceive any of them to be continuous or a self, and so the solidity of continuity is broken. When the solidity of continuity is broken, one understands: "The desire to look cannot accomplish looking or seeing. Looking cannot accomplish the desire to look or seeing. Seeing cannot accomplish the desire to look or looking." Therefore, there is no self that can do whatever it wants, but only natural phenomena that arise according to conditions. Understand the characteristics of not-self in this way.

Understand this, too, with regard to a moment of hearing. This also applies to moments of bending, stretching, walking, standing, sitting, or lying down. If one understands the separate processes involved in these activities, such as the desire and the actual activity as well as the separate segments within one movement or activity, one can understand that the desire to bend cannot accomplish bending. Bending cannot accomplish the desire to bend. Likewise, the desire to stretch cannot accomplish stretching, and stretching cannot accomplish the desire to stretch. Therefore, there is no self that can bend or stretch whenever it wants, but only natural phenomena that arise according to conditions. Understand the characteristics of not-self in this way. Understand walking and so on in the same way as well.

The solidity of mass

Solidity of mass refers to all concepts of solidity that are based on the apparent mass of phenomena.

If one has not already observed and distinguished between the mental and physical phenomena that arise at the six sense doors by means of insight, one will perceive mentality and physicality as a single entity. One cannot differentiate that mentality is one thing and that physicality is another. While bending the arm, for example, one will perceive the intention to bend (i.e., mentality) and the arm that is bending (i.e., physicality) as a single thing.

Further, one will also perceive the eye, the ear, and so on within the continuum of one's person as a single thing, and one will also perceive visible form, audible sound, and so on as a single thing. So when one sees the hand touching something, one will perceive the visible form (that is touched) and the sensation of touch as one thing. Moreover, one will perceive the physical basis of seeing and the physical basis of touch as one thing. This is just one example. There are too many cases to explain them all in detail. Perceiving the totality of mental and physical phenomena as one mass is the concept of solidity of mass. Because one cannot differentiate the phenomena by means of their different natures through insight meditation practice, their characteristic of not-self is concealed by the concept of solidity of mass.

How can one break down the concept of solidity of mass? When one continuously observes the mental and physical phenomena that arise at the six sense doors, at the very least mind and matter will appear as separate. While bending, for example, it will be obvious that the intention to bend is one thing, and the actual bending movement is another. Likewise, while stretching it will be obvious that the intention to stretch is one thing and the actual stretching movement is another. Or when observing the rising movement of the abdomen, it will be obvious that the rising movement is one thing and that the mind that notes it is another. Or else when one observes any other object, it will be obvious in the same way that they are separate. If this much is apparent, the concept of mental and physical phenomena being one mass will be broken.

Then one can understand: "The intention to bend or to stretch cannot carry out the movement of bending or stretching, and also the movement of bending or stretching cannot happen by itself without the intention to bend or to stretch. Moreover, the noting mind cannot arise by itself without something to note, such as the rise or fall of the abdomen." Thus, the characteristic of not-self appears in its true nature.

Furthermore, when one continuously observes seeing, hearing, touching, and so on, it becomes apparent that visible form is one thing, audible sound is another thing, and the sensation of touch is yet another. It also becomes apparent that the eye that is the base of seeing is one thing, the ear that is the base of hearing is another thing, and the body that is the basis of the touch is yet another. And moreover, it becomes apparent that eye-consciousness is one thing, the contact between the visible form and eye-consciousness is another thing, and pleasant or unpleasant feeling is yet another. When each and every phenomenon appears as separate, one has thoroughly broken the concept of solidity of mass.

Thus, one understands that none of the bodily, verbal, and mental actions can happen due to the exercise of control; they can only be accomplished in accordance with conditions. Then the true nature of the characteristic of not-self, namely the inability to exercise control, clearly appears.

The solidity of function

Solidity of function refers to all concepts of solidity that are related to the functions of phenomena.

Mental and physical phenomena are different from each other with regard to their functions. However, without having distinguished them by means of insight, one perceives these phenomena to be one single entity. At a moment of seeing, the eye is able to see the visible form, eye-consciousness is able to see, and the visible form is able to be seen. Although these functions are distinct, one perceives the eye, the visible form, and eye-consciousness that happen in a single continuum to be one entity. It is the same with hearing.

Eye-consciousness is able to see, ear-consciousness is able to hear, nose- consciousness is able to smell, tongue-consciousness is able to taste, body- consciousness is able to know touch, and mind-consciousness is able to think. Although these functions are different, one perceives these mental phenomena that happen in a single continuum to be one entity. One thinks that it is 'I' who sees and likewise that it is 'I' who hears, smells, tastes, touches, and thinks.

A pleasant feeling makes the mind happy, an unpleasant feeling withers the mind, and a 'neither-unpleasant- nor-pleasant' feeling, while neither making the mind happy nor withering it, puts it in a peaceful state. Although these functions are different, one perceives these three kinds of feeling that happen in a single continuum to be one entity. One thinks that it is 'I' who is happy and glad, it is 'I' who is unhappy and depressed, it is 'I' who is neither happy nor unhappy, but peaceful.

It is the intention to bend that is able to cause movement to happen. Although these functions are different, one perceives the mind (intention) and the movements (matter) to be one entity. One thinks that it is 'I' who has the intention to bend and it is 'I' who am bending; or that 'I' am the intention to bend and that 'I' am the bending. It is the same for stretching and walking. Because one does not understand by means of insight that the mental and physical phenomena that are distinct according to their functions are separate, one perceives them to be one entity. This is the concept of solidity of function.

How can one break down the concept of solidity of function?

While observing mental and physical phenomena at the time of their occurrence by means of insight, one can differentiate them as separate phenomena. It becomes apparent that these mental and physical phenomena have different functions and do not mix with each other, but happen separately. Thus, the previously held perception that saw them as one entity will be broken, and one will understand that phenomena that have one specific function cannot perform another. Then the true nature of the characteristic of 'not- self', namely the inability to exercise control, clearly appears.

The solidity of objects

Solidity of objects refers to all concepts of solidity related to objects taken by mental phenomena.

Mental phenomena are distinct with regard to their objects. However, without having distinguished them by means of insight, one perceives these different mental phenomena as a single entity. In reality, eye-consciousness takes visible forms as its object, ear-consciousness takes sounds as its objects, nose-consciousness takes odors as its objects, tongue-consciousness takes flavors as its objects, body-consciousness takes bodily sensations as its objects, and mind-consciousness takes the various kinds of mental phenomena as its objects.

The consciousness that sees visible forms as distinct from the consciousness that hears sounds or experiences any of the other objects; the consciousness that hears is distinct from the consciousness that sees or experiences any of the other objects. Eye-consciousness is distinct with respect to each different color it sees as well. The consciousness that sees white, for example, is distinct from the consciousness that sees black, blue, or yellow, and the consciousness that sees black, blue, or yellow is distinct from the consciousness that sees white. The same is true of the ear-consciousness that hears each different sound. Furthermore, when one sees the same color for some period of time, each successive moment of eye-consciousness is distinct from those before and after it. The same is true when one hears the same sound for some time.

Each different object is experienced by a different consciousness. But one perceives all these mental objects that happen in a single continuum to be one entity. One thinks: "It is I myself who is seeing and hearing";

or "I am the one who wants to look at something and then sees it"; or "I see white, black, blue, and yellow"; or "I have been seeing this same color for some time," and so on. In this way, one perceives these mental phenomena that are distinct with regard to their objects as one single entity. This is the concept of solidity of object. This concept is another reason why the characteristic of not-self does not appear to ordinary persons, but remains concealed.

How can the solidity of an object be broken? If one's concentration, mindfulness, and insight knowledge are strong and one observes seeing, hearing, and so on the moment they occur, one will thoroughly break through the concept of solidity of objects. At the time of seeing, it will become apparent that the intention to see is one thing and the noting mind that notes the intention is another; the seeing mind is one thing and the noting mind that notes the seeing mind is another, and likewise at the time of hearing. It also becomes apparent that the seeing mind is different from the hearing mind, the touching mind, or the thinking mind. Or when seeing colors, it will become apparent that the mind that sees white is different from the mind that notes it, and the mind that sees black is different from the mind that notes it. When hearing various sounds, it will become apparent that the first mind that hears is different from the first mind that notes it, and the second mind that hears is different from the second mind that notes it. When one hears a sound for a long time, it is the same.

If one can distinguish between these mental phenomena that take different objects, then the true nature of the characteristic of not-self, the inability to exercise control, clearly appears.

The VISUDDHIMAGGA-MAHĀTĪKĀ gives this summary of the different perceptions of solidity:

When mental and physical phenomena have arisen and are mutually steadying each other, then (owing to misinterpreting that as a unity) solidity of mass is assumed through failure to subject formations to examination by means of insight. And likewise, solidity of function is assumed when, although definite differences exist in the functions of such and such states, they are taken as one. And likewise, solidity of object is assumed when, although differences exist in the ways in

15. THE EIGHTEEN GREAT KNOWLEDGES OF INSIGHT

which states that take objects make them their objects, those objects are taken as one. But when they are seen after resolving them by means of Knowledge into these elements, they disintegrate like froth subjected to compression by the hand. They are mere states (DHAMMA) occurring due to conditions and are void. In this way the characteristic of not-self becomes more evident.

According to the commentary and sub-commentary, when the concept of solidity is broken and the object is observed in its true nature of having the characteristic of not-self, then the concept of self is abandoned whenever real contemplation of not-self arises. If objects (mental and physical phenomena) are not rightly understood to be 'not-self', then based on these objects that are not rightly understood perversion of perception that takes them for an 'I' or a 'self' can arise. The perversions of view and consciousness can also arise. Based on these perversions, defilements and volitional actions are able to arise as well. These, in turn, can turn into resultant phenomena. However, if one rightly understands these phenomena to be 'not-self', then the perversions of perception, view, and consciousness that arose in connection with the objects cannot arise anymore. Thus, all the suffering that starts with the perversion of perception and ends with the resultant phenomena cannot arise anymore because it has been abandoned by the contemplation of not-self. That is why the VISUDDHIMAGGA says: "One who sees not-self abandons the perception of self."

Summary

The contemplation of not-self is to understand not-self by observing the unique characteristics of mental and physical phenomena that arise at the six sense doors, and to see either that they do not happen according to one's wishes, are unable to exercise control, or are impermanent and unsatisfactory. Insight knowledge that understands presently observed objects to be not-self is called "empirical contemplation of not-self" (PACCAKKHA ANATTĀNUPASSANĀ).

After thoroughly empirically understanding not-self, one also understands in the same way that the mental and physical phenomena from the past and future, as well as all mental and physical phenomena that are in this world, are also 'not-self' and 'not a being', but just natural phenomena. The understanding that comes by means of such reflection is called "Inferential Contemplation of not-self" (ANUMĀNA ANATTĀNUPASSANĀ).

The contemplation of not-self, whether empirical or inferential, begins to arise with insight knowledge of comprehension. Beginning from insight knowledge of dissolution it is fully developed with regard to its function of abandoning the defilements.

Seeing three characteristics through disappearance

The momentary cessation of mental and physical phenomena, in particular, is impermanence. Thus, the commentary mentions the phrase "nonexistence after having arisen," and so on.

Disappearance is the culminating point for one who understands impermanence. Thus, contemplation of impermanence is suitable for one who observes disappearance.

According to these passages, the second of the two characteristics of impermanence — that is, "nonexistence after having arisen" — is the outstanding one. This refers to the momentary disappearance of present phenomena. Thus, one should understand that contemplation of impermanence is accomplished by just observing the disappearance, vanishing, or dissolution of mental and physical phenomena that are arising and passing away. This happens at the mature stage of Insight Knowledge of Dissolution. When one sees their disappearance, one no longer regards these phenomena as satisfactory or pleasant. Actually because of their continuous oppression by disappearance, one understands them to be phenomena that are unsatisfactory, bad, and devoid of pleasure. Then Contemplation of Unsatisfactoriness arises.

When one understands that one is not able to prevent these mental and physical phenomena from disappearing, or that one cannot make them pleasurable or last forever, then the contemplation of not-self arises. This is how each of the three contemplations arises by paying attention to observing the disappearance of present mental and physical phenomena.

The VISUDDHIMAGGA says:

Dissolution is the peak of impermanence. The meditator who observes it contemplates that all conditioned phenomena are impermanent and not permanent.

Then because what is impermanent is unsatisfactory, and unsatisfactoriness is not-self, the meditator can also see that these very phenomena are unsatisfactory – not satisfactory – and not-self – not related to a self.

Thus, one can accomplish these three contemplations at the peak of Insight Knowledge of Dissolution by seeing disappearance alone. This point will become clearer in the following sections.

4. Contemplation of Disenchantment

Contemplation of Disenchantment (NIBBIDĀNUPASSANĀ) refers to Insight Knowledge of Disenchantment that follows Insight Knowledge of Danger. With the momentum gained from Insight Knowledge of Dissolution, one only sees disappearance whenever one notes. After seeing Conditioned Phenomena to be Fearful and Full of Flaws, one becomes weary of and fed up with them, either by seeing their disappearance and dissolution while noting them, or by reflecting about conditioned phenomena. This is how Contemplation of Disenchantment arises.

Without this contemplation, one perceives conditioned phenomena as something to delight in, and so "Attachment accompanied by joy" (SAPPĪ – TIKATANHĀ) can arise. Based on this kind of delight, defilements and volitional actions can arise, and they in turn can lead to resultant phenomena. But due to this contemplation, such delight and attachment cannot arise with regard to conditioned phenomena that one usually perceives to be something to delight in. Thus, Contemplation of Disenchantment abandons delight and attachment. This is why the VISUDDHIMAGGA says:

"One who develops Contemplation of Disenchantment abandons delight."

This is further explained by the VISUDDHIMAGGA-MAHĀTĪKĀ, which says:

"Contemplation of Disenchantment refers to contemplation that manifests as a sense of feeling weary of conditioned phenomena. Delight refers to attachment accompanied by joy."

5. Dontemplation of Dispassion

The Contemplation of Dispassion (VIRĀGĀNUPASSANĀ) is contemplation that manifests as "detachment from conditioned phenomena".

According to this sub-commentary passage, one becomes weary of conditioned phenomena by means of Insight Knowledge of Disenchantment. Because one only sees the disappearance of conditioned phenomena whenever one observes them, one becomes detached from phenomena and inclines toward *nibbāna*, the cessation of conditioned phenomena. This contemplation is Contemplation of Dispassion.

According to the VISUDDHIMAGGA:

'Destructional dispassion (KHAYAVIRĀGA)' refers to the momentary disappearance of conditioned phenomena. 'Complete dispassion (ACCANTAVIRĀGA)' refers to NIBBĀNA. Seeing these two kinds of dispassion when Insight or Path Knowledge occurs is Contemplation of Dispassion.

Destructional dispassion is Insight Knowledge that arises due to Insight Practice by Understanding Disappearance, while taking conditioned phenomena as one's object.

Complete dispassion is being free and cut off from all conditioned phenomena, that is, it is NIBBĀNA. Insight cannot see NIBBĀNA, complete dispassion, as NIBBĀNA is not an object of insight. However, insight knowledge of desire for deliverance, which follows insight knowledge of disenchantment, wishes to become free from conditioned phenomena. The desire for deliverance is the inclination of the mind toward NIBBĀNA, freedom from conditioned phenomena. So, Insight in the form of the Desire for Deliverance sees NIBBĀNA by inclining the mind toward it. Thus, because it observes these two kinds of dispassion, insight knowledge of desire for deliverance is Contemplation of Dispassion.

The phrase from the MAHĀTĪKĀ "One becomes detached from the conditioned phenomena" is synonymous with the phrase "sees NIBBĀNA by inclining the mind toward it." The noble paths see NIBBĀNA (or the complete dispassion) since NIBBĀNA is taken as their object. They also see destructional dispassion because the function

15. THE EIGHTEEN GREAT KNOWLEDGES OF INSIGHT

of seeing is also accomplished. Therefore, it is the Contemplation of Dispassion. One should know that here we analyze the mundane knowledges, and so only Knowledge that results from Insight is Contemplation of Dispassion.

Contemplation of disenchantment and contemplation of dispassion only arise in a meditator whose insight knowledge of dissolution is sharp and mature. This is why the Paṭisambhidāmagga of the KHUDDAKA NIKĀYA says (regarding the insight knowledge of dissolution):

"One becomes weary rather than taking delight; one becomes detached rather than attached."

The VISUDDHIMAGGA says:

But what is impermanent, unsatisfactory, not-self, is not something to delight in; and what is not something to delight in is not something to become attached to; consequently, when that field of formations is seen as impermanent, unsatisfactory, not-self, in accordance with contemplation of dissolution, then one becomes weary, one does not delight; one becomes detached, one does not become attached.

As mentioned in the case of contemplations of impermanence and so on, it is suitable to note "impermanence, impermanence" in order to pay attention. However, in the case of contemplations of disenchantment and dispassion, it is obvious that it is not suitable to label "disenchantment, disenchantment" or "dispassion, dispassion." As shown above in the VISUDDHIMAGGA, after one understands that conditioned phenomena are impermanent, unsatisfactory, and not-self by means of Insight Knowledge of Dissolution, one progresses to understanding that these conditioned phenomena are not delightful but wearisome. This insight knowledge is Contemplation of Disenchantment. Then one becomes detached. This insight knowledge is Contemplation of Dispassion.

As was the case with Contemplation of Impermanence and so on, to label "impermanence, impermanence" is not the main point. One should bear in mind that the main point is to understand whatever mental and physical phenomena one happens to note or think about to be impermanent.

6. Contemplation of Cessation

Contemplation of cessation (NIRODHĀNUPASSANĀ) is contemplation of the cessation of conditioned phenomena, or contemplation that causes the cessation of conditioned phenomena so that they cannot arise again later. Contemplating in this way is contemplation of cessation. It is Insight Knowledge of Desire for Deliverance that has reached its full strength.

According to this passage, contemplation of cessation can be defined in two ways: as either "contemplation of cessation" or "contemplation for cessation." In the ultimate sense, however, these two are not different. Insight knowledge of desire for deliverance sees conditioned phenomena disappearing and also wants to become free of them. This insight knowledge of desire for deliverance, when sharp and keen, is "empirical contemplation of cessation (PACCAKKHANIRODHĀNUPASSANĀ).

The conditioned phenomena, from which one wants to become free (but whose cessation one has not seen), will lead to the arising of new existences and conditioned phenomena in the future. Conditioned phenomena that are observed with this contemplation of cessation cannot lead to the arising of new existences and conditioned phenomena. Thus, this contemplation that is undertaken in order that new existences and conditioned phenomena cannot arise anymore causes them to cease. Therefore, the MAHĀTĪKĀ defines the first way as "contemplation that contemplates the cessation of conditioned phenomena", and the second way as "contemplation that contemplates in order to cause new existences and conditioned phenomena to cease."

The commentaries on in- and out-breath define contemplation of cessation in the same way. While empirically experiencing the momentary cessation and destruction (KHAYANIRODHA) of conditioned phenomena that are observed in the present, the mind inclines toward the complete cessation (ACCANTANIRODHA) of conditioned phenomena, NIBBĀNA. Thus, Insight Knowledge of Desire for Deliverance, when sharp and keen, is Contemplation of Cessation. And the inclination to complete cessation is Desire for Deliverance from these Conditioned Phenomena.

The following line from the PATISAMBHIDĀMAGGA explains

Contemplation of Cessation as follows:

"He causes cessation, not origination. Having caused cessation, origination is abandoned."

According to the VISUDDHIMAGGA, we can interpret this in these two ways: "Thus one who is not attached causes the cessation of lust (RĀGA), not its origination. This happens firstly by means of mundane knowledge. The meaning is that one does not cause origination"; or alternatively, "One who has become detached and has caused the cessation of the seen (the presently experienced) field of conditioned phenomena also causes the cessation of the unseen (the past and the future) by means of inferential knowledge; one does not originate it. The meaning is that one gives attention only to its cessation. One sees only its cessation, not its origin."

But although the phrase "causes cessation" (NIRODHETI) can be formed and interpreted in these two ways, they mean the same thing. Both refer to Insight Knowledge of the Desire for Deliverance that has reached its full strength.

Contemplation of cessation is not differentiated into two ways of contemplation.

The first definition says, "one causes cessation of lust." But it does not say which phenomena have to be observed in which way, and which lust is caused to cease. However as said in the second definition, it is the cessation of the presently experienced conditioned phenomena and of those in the past and future. So one should adequately understand that one causes cessation of greed while perceiving those phenomena to exist.

The second definition shows which defilements have been caused to cease. But since the first definition says, "one causes cessation of lust," one should adequately understand this statement. How? If one contemplates the cessation of conditioned phenomena, one does not perceive them to exist forever, and so lust does not arise. Thus, the meaning of these two definitions is the same.

One should understand that the phrase "one causes cessation of lust" also refers to the cessation of other defilements, the volitional actions for which lust is the fundamental cause, and the resultant phenomena of these volitional actions. Thus, one should understand that the two explanations from the MAHĀTĪKĀ and this passage from the VISUDDHIMAGGA are actually the same.

The contemplation of cessation that observes the cessation of the present conditioned phenomena is called "Empirical Knowledge." When this empirical knowledge matures, there arises the contemplation of cessation that reflects that past and future conditioned phenomena are subject to cessation, just as the present ones are. This is called "Inferential Knowledge."

According to the VISUDDHIMAGGA-MAHĀTĪKĀ:

One is aware of the cessation of conditioned phenomena that have presently arisen and are seen. Likewise, one reflects by the power of inferential knowledge on past and future conditioned phenomena that are not seen: "Like these present conditioned phenomena, others cease in the same way." Thus, one is also aware of the cessation of those phenomena one has reflected on.

The sub-commentary says that this contemplation of cessation refers to insight knowledge of desire for deliverance that has reached its full strength. Thus, it should be understood that contemplation of dispassion refers to the tender stage of that same insight knowledge.

One is aware of conditioned phenomena that are able to give rise to greed and other defilements by means of Inferential Knowledge. The abandonment of these defilements is only temporary. Therefore, in the MAHĀTĪKĀ:

It is said: "He causes the temporary cessation of greed." He abandons the defilements, and so the temporary cessation of greed is accomplished. This is what is meant by 'to abandon'.

This is because the latent defilements lying dormant in conditioned phenomena from the past and future cannot be completely uprooted by mundane knowledge, but only by supramundane path knowledge.

7. Contemplation of Relinquishment

Contemplation of Relinquishment PATINISSAGGĀNUPASSANĀ) is the contemplation that occurs as a way of relinquishing conditioned phenomena (or the defilements that perceive conditioned phenomena to be permanent, satisfactory, and self.) It is Insight Knowledge of Re-observation and Insight Knowledge of Equanimity toward Phenomena.

The phrase "that occurs as a way of relinquishing conditioned phenomena" is used here in a figurative sense, since it is not actually phenomena themselves that should be relinquished, but the defilements associated with them. Therefore, I have translated this phrase more explicitly to include "the defilements that perceive conditioned phenomena as permanent, satisfactory, and self." This is similar to the BUDDHA'S teaching:

"BHIKKHUS…Material form is not yours. Abandon it."

The commentary explains that the term "abandon" in this case does not mean to abandon one's body, but to give up one's attachment to the body.

Suppose, for example, that one has a disobedient and very wicked child who frequently gives one much trouble and causes one to suffer. In that case one would want to disown this child, and would repeatedly reflect on the heavy and deplorable flaws he or she has. If one completely abandons the perception of him or her as one's son or daughter, then one not only abandons the mental and physical suffering connected with the wicked child but also the child him- or her- self. In this case when one is able to completely abandon the perception of the child as one's son or daughter, then one has truly abandoned one's child.

Likewise, when one re-observes conditioned phenomena and sees them to be impermanent, unsatisfactory, and not-self, then one's relinquishment of the defilements (that take conditioned phenomena to be permanent, satisfactory, and self) is also the relinquishment of conditioned phenomena. Therefore, the sub-commentary says that contemplation that is able to relinquish the defilements "occurs as a way of relinquishing conditioned phenomena."

The VISUDDHIMAGGA says:

This contemplation of impermanence and so on is also called both "relinquishment as giving up" and "relinquishment as entering into" because it temporarily abandons defilements along with volitional actions and resultant phenomena; and because, by seeing the unsatisfactoriness of conditioned phenomena, it inclines toward and enters into NIBBĀNA, which is the opposite of conditioned phenomena.

Therefore, the BHIKKHU who possesses this contemplation gives up defilements and enters into NIBBĀNA in the way stated; he does not grasp defilements by causing arising, nor does he grasp a conditioned object by failing to see its danger. Hence it was said, "He relinquishes, he does not grasp."

As explained in this passage, the term "relinquishment" can have the sense of either "giving up" (PARICCĀGAPATINISSAGGA) something one does not need any more or "entering into": I.e., "launching out into" (PAKKHANDANAPATINISSAGGA), the place to which one aspires. Being included in Insight Knowledges of Re-observation and Equanimity toward phenomena, it is able to temporarily relinquish the defilements that arise based on the perception of permanence, satisfactoriness, and self, the volitional actions caused by these defilements, and the resultant phenomena. Thus, it is "relinquishment".

Just as somebody, when seeing a place full of danger, wants to go to another place that is free of danger, so does insight knowledge, when seeing the danger of conditioned phenomena, incline toward NIBBĀNA, the opposite of conditioned phenomena. "To incline" only means to desire to become free of conditioned phenomena; it does not mean to take NIBBĀNA as one's object. By so inclining one is able to enter into NIBBĀNA and relinquish one's body. Thus, it is relinquishment. It is contemplation of relinquishment because it is able to observe giving up of the defilements by means of Insight Knowledge of Re-observation and Insight Knowledge of Equanimity toward Phenomena, and because it is able to observe entering into NIBBĀNA by inclining toward it.

If one does not contemplate phenomena as impermanent, unsatisfactory, and not-self, then defilements get an opportunity to arise depending on those objects that go unobserved. When we say that they get an opportunity, we actually mean "They are caused to arise" or "grasping." However, by clearly observing phenomena to be impermanent, unsatisfactory, and not-self, defilements do not get an opportunity to arise in dependence on objects that go unobserved. When we say that they do not get an opportunity, we mean they are not caused to arise" or "not grasping."

Therefore, it is said, "He does not grasp defilements by causing arising."

15. THE EIGHTEEN GREAT KNOWLEDGES OF INSIGHT

Failing to see the danger of impermanence and so on, whenever one is aware of (or reflects on) these conditioned phenomena, one grasps conditioned objects with defilements. However, if one sees the danger of impermanence and so on through awareness, then although one takes conditioned phenomena as one's object, one does not grasp them. And since defilements do not arise when one observes a conditioned object, one relinquishes it, not having grasped it. Therefore, it is said, "One does not grasp a conditioned object by failing to see its danger."

As the passage from the MAHĀTĪKĀ at the beginning of this section mentioned, Contemplation of Relinquishment is Insight Knowledge of Re-observation and Insight Knowledge of Equanimity toward Phenomena.

Summary

If one has fully established these first seven contemplations, from contemplation of impermanence through to contemplation of relinquishment, one also establishes the following eleven contemplations, which are included in them. For this reason, there are many places in the commentaries that say that meditators should practice these seven contemplations. The BUDDHA also spoke many times about these seven contemplations in the PATISAMBHIDĀMAGGA.

Furthermore, if one fully establishes the three contemplations of impermanence, unsatisfactoriness, and not-self, the four contemplations of disenchantment, dispassion, cessation, and relinquishment, which are included in them, will also be established. For this reason, the three baskets of the Pāli canon mostly mention only the contemplations of impermanence, unsatisfactoriness, and not-self.

The following example from the VISUDDHIMAGGA-MAHĀTĪKĀ is given in order to make the reader firmly believe this:

Although there are seven different kinds of contemplation and eighteen different kinds of insight that should be contemplated, they are all included in the three contemplations of impermanence, unsatisfactoriness, and not-self. Thus, due to their power, these three contemplations are the culminating point of insight.

Although these contemplations and insight knowledges are divided into seven contemplations, eighteen great insight knowledges, forty insight knowledges, and so on, they are all included in the three contemplations of impermanence, unsatisfactoriness, and not-self. If the three contemplations are fully established, all the remaining insight knowledges, which are included in them, are also established.

Therefore, when insight knowledge is sharp and fully developed and reaches its peak, it is well established even with only the three contemplations of impermanence, unsatisfactoriness, and not-self.

Contemplation of Impermanence and contemplation of the Signless are one in meaning and different only in the letter; as are Contemplation of Unsatisfactoriness and Contemplation of the Desireless; as are Contemplation of Not-self and Contemplation of Emptiness.

Thus, if one establishes Contemplation of Impermanence, Contemplation of the Signless is also established. If one establishes Contemplation of Unsatisfactoriness, Contemplation of the Desireless is also established. If one establishes Contemplation of Not-self, Contemplation of Emptiness is also established.

But insight into states that are higher understanding is all kinds of insight; and knowledge and vision of things as they really are is included in the purification by overcoming doubt.

Therefore, if one establishes the three contemplations of impermanence, unsatisfactoriness, and not-self, the states that are higher understanding are also established. Because of these three contemplations, Insight Knowledge and Vision of Things as they Really Are is established first of all. The MAHĀTĪKĀ illustrates how the remaining eleven contemplations are included and established:

When contemplation of impermanence is established, then the contemplations of cessation, destruction, fall, and change are partly established. When contemplation of unsatisfactoriness is established, then the contemplations of disenchantment, dis- passion, and danger are partly established. When contemplation of not-self is established, then the other contemplations are partly established.

This text says "are partly established" in reference to the stage of Insight Knowledge of Comprehension. One should bear in mind that contemplations of impermanence and so on, together with their corresponding insights, are established at the higher stages of insight

15. THE EIGHTEEN GREAT KNOWLEDGES OF INSIGHT

knowledge, beginning with Insight Knowledge of Dissolution.

The sub-commentaries do not mention contemplation of dispassion being included in contemplation of unsatisfactoriness. Why? The PATISAMBHIDĀMAGGA of the KHUDDAKA NIKĀYA says that contemplation of dispassion abandons attachment to sensual desire, but it does not say that contemplation of dispassion abandons attachment to view, rites and rituals, and self, as contemplation of not-self does.

Therefore, contemplation of dispassion should not be included in contemplation of not-self, since contemplation of not-self has a different function of abandoning. It should only be included in contemplation of unsatisfactoriness, since contemplation of unsatisfactoriness has the same function of abandoning. However, one should understand that this phrase has been dropped since one does not find it in those texts.

According to the text of the VISUDDHIMAGGA-MAHĀTĪKĀ, when one establishes contemplation of impermanence, the four contemplations of cessation, destruction, fall, and change are also established. When one establishes contemplation of unsatisfactoriness, the three contemplations of disenchantment, dispassion, and danger are also established. When one establishes contemplation of not-self, the three contemplations of relinquishment, reflection, and turning away are also established. So, this is how all the Insight Knowledges are included and established within the three Contemplations of Impermanence, Unsatisfactoriness, and Not-self.

The three contemplations of impermanence, unsatisfactoriness, and not-self are only established when one's Insight Knowledge into the Dissolution of Conditioned Phenomena becomes sharp.

According to the MAHĀTĪKĀ:

Some scholars say that at this stage of insight knowledge of dissolution, there is no need to see impermanence in various ways. Rather, by seeing just the disappearance of phenomena, one sees all of the characteristics of impermanence. But this is only true when contemplation of dissolution reaches its peak. Before that it is necessary to see impermanence in a variety of ways.

What "some scholars" say in this passage from the MAHĀTĪKĀ refers only to the tender stage of Insight Knowledge of Dissolution. The sub-commentator supports the view that the three contemplations are only established when insight knowledge of dissolution reaches its peak. This is why, in the PATISAMBHIDĀMAGGA of the KHUDDAKA NIKĀYA, the BUDDHA said:

The identity of the characteristic of fall is the single cause of the arising of the mind of insight (a meditator's mind, free of defilements).

B. The Remaining Contemplations

1. Contemplation of Destruction

According to the VISUDDHIMAGGA-MAHĀTĪKĀ, Contemplation of Destruction (KHAYĀNUPASSANĀ) is Insight Knowledge that sees the Momentary Dissolution of Conditioned Phenomena while Observing their Unique Characteristics, or Insight Knowledge that sees the Momentary Dissolution of the Noting Mind Itself. This contemplation is an insight knowledge of dissolution that understands the dissolution of both the object and the noting mind. Thus, this contemplation becomes fully developed when one breaks the concept of things as solid forms, and sees conditioned phenomena are merely dissolving processes.

Contemplation of Destruction is to see the dissolution of present aggregates immediately followed by seeing the dissolution of the very mind and mental factors that observed those aggregates.

Contemplation of Destruction, however, is the Insight Knowledge in one who breaks through the concept of solidity and so sees destruction as "impermanent in the sense of destruction."

I have explained above how to break through the four types of concepts of solidity. If one's insight knowledge of dissolution becomes sharp and keen so that the solidity is broken, then, while one is bending one's arm, only the little movements happening one after the other appear, and so these little movements are seen as dissolving or disappearing. One also sees the noting mind, which is different from the object, and successively follows it, as immediately dissolving or disappearing. Thus, the material form that is called "bending" does not appear as a solid form such as an "arm" or a "hand," as it does for ordinary people. Even the arm no longer appears to permanently exist.

Furthermore, the noting mind no longer appears as somebody who is aware, as it usually does for ordinary people.

With awareness it becomes apparent that the noting mind simply disappears moment by moment. One knows these mental and physical phenomena exactly the way they are, as "disappearing, disappearing." The same applies to stretching, seeing, and so on. Due to this understanding, the perversions of perception and so on can no longer arise. This is why it is said, "One who develops this contemplation abandons the perception of solidity."

Contemplation of destruction is fully established beginning with insight knowledge of dissolution. Thus, the perception of solidity is abandoned. Before that, the perception of solidity is not yet abandoned. The same is true for all the other contemplations. Thus, whether or not one's insight is fully established should be regarded in terms of full understanding by abandoning (PAHĀNAPARIÑÑĀ) and full understanding by investigating (TĪRANAPARIÑÑĀ).

Based on the first sentence of this passage, one should clearly understand that one cannot abandon the concept of solidity before Insight Knowledge of Dissolution has been attained. "Full understanding by investigating" refers to Insight Knowledge of Comprehension and Insight Knowledge of Arising and Passing Away. At that time insight knowledge is not yet powerful enough, so contemplations of impermanence and so on cannot yet completely abandon the perception of permanence and so on.

"Full understanding by abandoning" refers to the Insight Knowledges beginning with Insight Knowledge of Dissolution. At that time insight knowledge is fully established, so the contemplations of impermanence and so on can completely abandon the perceptions of permanence and so on.

2. Contemplation of Fall

Contemplation of fall (VAYĀNUPASSANĀ) is stated thus:
Defining both to be alike by interference from that same object. Inclination on Cessation—these are insights in the mark of fall.

It is inclination toward cessation, in other words, toward that same dissolution, after seeing dissolution of seen formations by means of personal experience and unseen formations by means of inference. The abandoning of accumulation occurs due to these contemplations. When one sees with insight that "I might accumulate KAMMA for the sake of things that are thus subject to fall," one's mind no longer inclines to accumulation.

After seeing the momentary dissolution of present mental and physical phenomena, one sees by means of inference that past and future phenomena also momentarily disappear. At that time, one understands: "All conditioned phenomena are momentarily and relentlessly disappearing. There are no states that last forever without ceasing." With this there arises insight knowledge that is inclined toward cessation. This insight knowledge is called "Contemplation of Fall." This contemplation causes the accumulation of sense pleasures to completely cease. When one does not yet fully understand that mental and physical phenomena are momentarily and relentlessly disappearing, one will think that one's body and the bodies of others are stable and firm. Because one wants to enjoy the conditioned phenomena that one perceives to be stable and firm (such as one's own or another person's body) one accumulates actions for both the present and future life.

When one thoroughly understands that all conditioned phenomena are momentarily and relentlessly disappearing by means of this contemplation of fall, one will see no need to expend any energy enjoying phenomena that one previously thought to be permanent. One has no further interest in accumulating actions. Suppose, for example, that there is a person who makes a huge effort and works hard to provide his beloved sons and daughters with beautiful and nice clothes. Upon hearing that his sons and daughters have passed away, that person would lose interest in making such efforts. Contemplation of Fall abandons the accumulation of actions for the sake of enjoying sense pleasures; one simply has no more interest in it.

3. Contemplation of Change

Contemplation of Change (VIPARINĀMĀNUPASSANĀ) is the act of seeing, according to the material septal (RŪPASATTAKA), etc., how momentary occurrences in continuity take place differently by gradually diverging from any definition; or, it is the act of seeing change in the two

15. THE EIGHTEEN GREAT KNOWLEDGES OF INSIGHT

aspects of the aging and the death of what has arisen.

The first way of seeing change by way of both observation and reflection is as follows: One sees that all the physical phenomena (i.e., one's body) that arise from the moment of relinking consciousness until the moment of death consciousness finally disappear, and are destroyed at the time of death. One sees that the physical phenomena of the first phase of one's life have changed in the second phase of life and that they are not the same anymore; one sees that the physical phenomena of the second phase of life have likewise changed in the third phase of life, and that they are not the same anymore; and finally, one sees that the physical phenomena at the time of death have changed, and that they are not the same anymore. One sees that the physical phenomena from the first ten years of one's life have changed in one's teens, and that they are not the same anymore; and one sees that the physical phenomena from one's teens have changed when one is over twenty, and that they are not the same anymore. One sees that the physical phenomena from the night have changed by day, and that they are not the same anymore; and one sees that the physical phenomena from the day have changed by night, and that they are not the same anymore. One sees that the physical phenomena from the morning have changed by midday and that they are not the same anymore; and one sees that they have changed by the afternoon, evening, first watch of the night, midnight, dawn, and morning, and that they are not the same anymore. This is the coarse way of seeing change.

This is how one can see change in more detail: One sees that the physical phenomena of going forward have changed when going backward, or one sees that they are not the same anymore. One sees that the physical phenomena of going backward, seeing, or bending have changed when going forward, and that they are not the same anymore. One sees that the physical phenomena while being still have changed when being active, and that they are not the same anymore; and vice versa. One sees that the physical phenomena of rising of the abdomen have changed when the abdomen is falling, and that they are not the same anymore; and vice versa. One sees that the physical phenomena of lifting, pushing, dropping, pressing, and the next lifting have changed in the next phase, and that they are not the same anymore. One sees that the physical phenomena while feeling cold have changed when feeling hot, and that they are not the same anymore; and vice versa. One sees that the physical phenomena while feeling hungry have changed when feeling full, and that they are not the same anymore; and vice versa. One sees that the physical phenomena while feeling glad have changed when feeling sad, and that they are not the same anymore; and vice versa.

Whenever one sees the physical phenomena in a different activity or state, one sees their change. Furthermore, whenever one sees successive mind-moments, one sees that the preceding and following mind-moments are not the same—that they have changed. This is how contemplation of change comes about by means of the first way of seeing change.

The second way of seeing change mentioned above in the quote from the **VISUDDHIMAGGA** is to see the way that aging and death change mental and physical phenomena. Using these two aspects one sees that phenomena do not remain in their original state, but change and deteriorate. This is the coarse way of seeing change.

This is how one can see change in more detail: When one constantly observes mental and physical phenomena when they occur and one's Insight Knowledge matures, then one sees that the middle phase of these phenomena, which we can also call aging, is not the same as the initial phase, since it has changed. One also sees that the final phase, which we can also call death, disappears or is destroyed. Thus, whenever one observes mental and physical phenomena, one personally sees that the middle phase and the final phase are not the same as the initial phase and that they have changed. When one thoroughly understands that present mental and physical phenomena do not remain in their original state but change, by means of inferential knowledge one understands that past and future mental and physical phenomena, as well as all mental and physical phenomena in the entire world, are the same: they, too, do not remain in their original state, but change. They change from the middle phase to the final phase, from presence to disappearance, or from aging to death. This is how the Contemplation of Change comes about by means of the second way of seeing change.

Both empirical and inferential insight knowledges that see that phenomena do not remain in their original state but change are called "Contemplation of Change." This contemplation removes the perception of stability that sees phenomena as unchanging and stable.

In reference to contemplation of destruction and "Insight into Phenomena that is Higher Wisdom" (ADHIPAÑÑĀDHAMMAVIPASSANĀ), the commentary to the PATISAMBHIDĀMAGGA says that inferential Insight Knowledge of Dissolution is contemplation of fall and that the knowledge that sees "All states are changing" due to the power of this contemplation of fall is called "contemplation of change." The commentary to the PATISAMBHIDĀMAGGA in the KHUDDAKA NIKĀYA says the following:

Contemplation of Fall is the inferential insight that sees the dissolution of past and future aggregates and immediately follows the empirical experience of seeing the dissolution of present aggregates. Contemplation of Change is the insight that sees, due to inclination toward cessation, that all past, future, and present aggregates are changing and thereby sees change in all states (DHAMMA).

Understand, based on this passage, that Contemplation of Change only arises with peak Insight Knowledge of Dissolution.

4. Contemplation of the Signless

Contemplation of the Signless (ANIMITTĀNUPASSANĀ) is actually the same as Contemplation of Impermanence, as I explained in the summary above. Nevertheless, this different term should be defined, so I will explain it in brief.

"Sign" (NIMITTA) means the sign of conditioned phenomena or formations.

"The sign of conditioned phenomena" (SANKHĀRANIMITTA) refers to phenomena that seem to be solid to a non-meditator due to the concepts of solidity of mass and so on. But the sign of conditioned phenomena appears to a meditator due to the discernment and separation of their individual functions and so on.

Bodily activities and movements that are conditioned physical phenomena—such as walking, standing, sitting, lying, bending, stretching, and so on—conditioned mental phenomena—such as seeing, hearing, smelling, tasting, touching, thinking, and so on—and the objects that appear at the six sense doors—such as visible form, sound, smell, taste, touch, and mental objects—do not appear to be mere activities and phenomena, or to be distinct from each other, or to only exist momentarily. Actually, they appear to have solid forms, to be one single entity, and to be permanent. This concept of solidity is also referred to as "The sign of permanence," "The sign of stability" (DHUVANIMITTA), or "The sign of eternity" (SASSATANIMITTA).

Contemplation of Impermanence, which sees conditioned phenomena as impermanent, is called "The signless" because it is opposite to the sign of permanence, the sign of stability, and the sign of eternity. It is called "Contemplation" because it observes impermanence. When we compound the two terms we have "Contemplation of the Signless," which means to observe the opposite of the signs of solidity in conditioned phenomena.

When one constantly observes mental and physical phenomena at the time of their occurrence, the conditioned phenomena that arise at the six sense doors do not appear to have solid forms, to be one single entity, to be permanent, or to be enduring and stable. Actually, they appear to be mere activities and phenomena, to be different from each other, to only exist momentarily, and to disappear a moment after they have arisen. Because they appear in this way when one attains Insight Knowledge of Dissolution, one sees conditioned phenomena as disappearing, ending, being destroyed, vanishing, or impermanent. When one sees conditioned phenomena this way, they cannot appear as permanent and solid entities, and the defilements that develop based on seeing things to be permanent and solid can no longer arise.

Because one can abandon the sign of solidity in conditioned phenomena, the VISUDDHIMAGGA says:

Thus, it is called the signless, because the sign of permanence, the sign of stability, and the sign of eternity are abandoned after breaking through the concept of solidity by means of contemplation of impermanence.

If one uninterruptedly observes the signs of conditioned phenomena, each of the different functions of these conditioned phenomena will become apparent. Not only this, but their unique characteristics, their momentariness, and their objects (in the case of mental conditioned phenomena), will become apparent. For a detailed description of how they appear see the section dealing with the four types of concepts of solidity under the heading "Contemplation of Not-self."

The way conditioned phenomena appear when one is distinguishing between their function, characteristic, momentariness, and object is the sign of conditioned phenomena. When one can distinguish them by means of their function, characteristic, momentariness, and object, one sees these signs of conditioned phenomena and takes them as one's object at the same time. Thus, contemplation of impermanence is neither the opposite of the signs of conditioned phenomena nor is it able to be free of them. This is why this contemplation is called contemplation of the signless: because it is the opposite of the signs of solidity (permanence, stability, and eternity) in conditioned phenomena and because its object is free from these signs of solidity in conditioned phenomena.

When Contemplation of the Signless, which is Contemplation of Impermanence, is well established, conditioned phenomena only appear by means of the nature of their dissolution. As a result, one will rightly understand the signs of conditioned phenomena that previously appeared to be solid and lasting entities.

How does this understanding happen? It is similar to finding that an unsophisticated and uncultured person that one imagined to be cultured and refined is not. Or it is similar to being unable to find any heartwood or core when one removes the different layers of a plantain tree. In the same way, with contemplation of impermanence one sees the conditioned phenomena that one previously perceived to be stable and permanent entities dissolving into separate entities, not lasting for even the duration of a flash of lightning. Thus, one rightly understands the signs of conditioned phenomena by seeing that there is no permanent entity but only momentarily and unceasingly disappearing phenomena. As a result, one abandons the sign of solidity and the sign of permanence in conditioned phenomena, along with the defilements, volitional actions, and resultant phenomena that spring from them.

The destruction of conditioned phenomena appears to one who pays attention to impermanence.

One who pays attention to impermanence knows and sees the signs as they really are.

5. Contemplation of the Desireless

People perceive the mental and physical phenomena that are involved in walking, standing, sitting, bending, stretching, seeing, hearing, touching, thinking, and so on to be something pleasing, good, and delightful. This is called desire (PANIDHI) or craving (PANIHITA).

Contemplation of Unsatisfactoriness understands that conditioned phenomena are constantly oppressed by arising and passing away and sees that they are unsatisfactory, not good, and nothing to delight in. This understanding, being the opposite of desire and craving, is called "Contemplation of the Desireless" (APPANIHITĀNUPASSANĀ). Therefore, it is said, "One who develops this contemplation abandons desire."

6. Contemplation of Emptiness

When one has not sufficiently developed one's contemplation of not-self, one thinks that there is a self or a being who is able to exercise complete control over mental and physical phenomena (such as sitting, standing up, bending, stretching, seeing, hearing, and so on). However, the power of one's Insight Knowledge of Dissolution, which breaks up the four types of concepts of solidity, causes Contemplation of Not-self to become well established, and thus one only sees objects swiftly arising and passing away whenever one observes them. When this happens, one cannot find any so-called "self" or "being" that is able to exercise complete control. Instead, one finds that when the necessary conditions are present, not only do states arise that one does not wish to arise, but also states disappear that one does not wish to disappear. One cannot find a self or being that has complete mastery over phenomena. Thus, one understands that objects and the mind that notes them are merely natural phenomena that rapidly disappear, and that there is no self or being who is either able to perform such activities as sitting, standing up, bending, stretching, seeing, hearing, and so on or who is able to observe or to be aware. One understands that there are merely natural phenomena that disappear and are empty of a self. Since Contemplation of Not-self understands that phenomena are empty of a self, it is called "Contemplation of Emptiness" (SUÑÑATĀNUPASSANĀ). This contemplation is able to abandon defilements and so on that develop based on adherence to the perception of self.

7. Insight into Phenomena that is Higher Wisdom

"Insight into phenomena that is higher wisdom" is insight into emptiness by means of dissolution. It occurs thusly: "Only conditioned phenomena disintegrate; it is the death of conditioned phenomena that takes place; there is nothing else." This insight occurs after knowing physical phenomena and so on as objects by seeing the dissolution of both the object and the mind that noted that object. This insight is higher wisdom and insight into phenomena and it should be called "Insight into Phenomena that is Higher Wisdom." With it one abandons adherence to grasping at a core, because one clearly sees that there is no core of permanence, and no core of self.

When Insight Knowledge of Dissolution grows sharp and keen and one is just aware of a given object occurring at the six sense doors, one knows its disappearance, and in turn one also knows the disappearance of the noting mind. In this way one sees that the object and the mind that notes it very swiftly, and unceasingly disappear one after the other in succession; and that the object and the mind that notes it are merely conditioned phenomena. Also, all the things that disappear one after another are merely conditioned phenomena; it is these conditioned phenomena that are disappearing and dying. Apart from these conditioned phenomena there is nothing else, no 'self', no 'I', and no 'being'. One thoroughly understands that these conditioned phenomena are empty of a permanent entity, empty of a self or a being. This insight knowledge is "Insight into Phenomena that is Higher Wisdom" (ADHIPAÑÑĀDHAMMAVIPASSANĀ).

8. Knowledge and Vision of Things as they Really Are

Knowledge and Vision of Things as they Really Are is the discernment of mental and physical phenomena, along with the discernment of their causes and conditions. With it one abandons adherence through confusion that occurs thusly: "Was I in the past?" and "Did God create living beings?"

The insight knowledge that discerns conditionality is "Knowledge and Vision of Things as they Really Are" (YATHĀBHŪTAÑĀNADASSANA). When this insight knowledge is sufficiently established, one sees that in the present there are only mental and physical phenomena related through cause and effect. Thus, one is able to conclude that the totality of mental and physical phenomena in this life has arisen due to ignorance, craving, clinging, and KAMMA from past lives. And there was also ignorance, craving, clinging, and KAMMA based on mental and physical phenomena in past lives. Due to ignorance, craving, clinging, and KAMMA in this life, mental and physical phenomena will arise in a new life. In this way one can conclude that in all the three periods— past, present, and future— merely the mental and physical phenomena of cause and effect exist. As a result, one no longer doubts that one has existed in the past and is no longer confused about whether God or another divine being has created living beings. This means that one has abandoned this doubt and confusion.

The MAHĀTĪKĀ says:

"Delusion (SAMMOHA) is deep confusion by means of doubt and misinterpretation."

9. Contemplation of Danger

Contemplation of danger (ĀDĪNAVĀNUPASSANĀ) is Knowledge that sees Danger in All Kinds of Becoming, and so on. It arises due to the appearance of phenomena as frightening. With it one abandons adherence based on reliance, because one does not see anything reliable.

When Insight Knowledge of Fear becomes sharp and keen, as one sees conditioned phenomena to be dangerous insight, knowledge of danger arises. This is also Contemplation of Danger. When this insight knowledge arises, one does not see even a single conditioned phenomenon to be something reliable: neither objects nor the mind that notes them; neither objects that are reflected upon nor the mind that reflects upon them. One used to think: "If only I were a human being in every life, that would be good. If only I were a millionaire, that would be good. If only I were a king, that would be good. If only I were a DEVĀ, that would be good. If only I were a BRAHMĀ, that would be good." Before Insight Knowledge of Danger arises, the meditator thought that there was something reliable, a reliable existence, or some reliable conditioned phenomena. But now he or she has not found anything reliable. Thus, this insight knowledge abandons adherence to the thought that there is anything reliable in conditioned phenomena connected with sense realm existence, fine-material realm existence, or immaterial realm existence. Here in an ultimate sense, adherence to conditioned phenomena as something reliable (ĀLAYĀBHINIVESA) is attachment to existence.

Adherence to conditioned phenomena as something reliable or as something that gives protection is, in the ultimate sense, attachment to existence.

When one's Insight Knowledge of Danger has not yet been well established, one is not able to relinquish existence along with conditioned phenomena, however miserable one may feel. One thinks that there must be something in existence that can make one happy, and so one only wishes to escape from present misery. If one feels sick or has a fever, for example, one wishes only for good health. If one is poor, one only wishes to be rich and affluent. If one's present life seems hopeless, one longs for a better life in the next existence. If one thinks that human life is miserable, one wishes for existence as DEVĀ or BRAHMĀ. But one does not desire to be completely free from all existences or conditioned phenomena. This attachment to, delight or entanglement in, existence and conditioned phenomena is Adherence due to Reliance. Contemplation of Danger abandons adherence due to reliance. Thus, when this insight knowledge is mature, Insight Knowledge of Disenchantment and so on arises.

10. Contemplation of Reflection

Contemplation of Reflection (PATISANKHĀNUPASSANĀ) is Knowledge of Reflection that affects the means to gain liberation. With it one abandons non reflection.

Insight Knowledge of Re-observation is the correct means for liberation from conditioned phenomena. It is Contemplation of

Reflection. With it one abandons the ignorance that is the non-reflection on impermanence and so on, which is the opposite of the reflection of impermanence and so on.

Insight Knowledge of Desire for Deliverance arises so that one is able to relinquish conditioned phenomena or to escape from conditioned phenomena. When this insight knowledge is well established, Insight Knowledge of Re-observation, which is Contemplation of Reflection, arises. In this case, one should note that the two expressions "so that one is able to relinquish conditioned phenomena" and "so that one is able to escape from conditioned phenomena" have the same meaning. Thus, it is said that the commentary uses these two expressions interchangeably with reference to Insight Knowledge of Desire for Deliverance.

This is how one can relinquish conditioned phenomena: If one does not yet thoroughly understand conditioned phenomena to be impermanent, unsatisfactory, and not-self whenever they arise, then desire and delight may arise regarding such conditioned phenomena. When unpleasant feelings arise or pleasant feelings change one sees the arising and passing away of all conditioned phenomena, and so distress, fear, or disenchantment may arise. Due to 'Adherence to conditioned phenomena' when this happens, one cannot yet relinquish conditioned phenomena, nor escape from them.

If one thoroughly understands conditioned phenomena to be impermanent, unsatisfactory, and not-self whenever they arise, one does not take any of these conditioned phenomena to be pleasurable or likable, nor does one take them to be a self or something related to a self. Thus, one does not hope or wish for the pleasure of these conditioned phenomena, nor does one hope or wish for their disappearance, should one not want them. One doesn't worry if they are not pleasant; one is not concerned about the arising of phenomena one does not want. It is like not having any hopes, wishes, worries, or concerns about things one does not care about, such as stones, sand, grass, leaves, or rubbish. Being free from such want and worry, one is able to simply be aware of each conditioned phenomenon as they arise. Since there are no obstacles with regard to these conditioned phenomena, one has already relinquished them. One has also escaped from these conditioned phenomena. One should also understand the meaning of the example of the disobedient and wicked child in the section on Contemplation of Relinquishment in the same way.

An ARAHANT, a fully enlightened being, completely accomplishes this escape from conditioned phenomena. In the case of insight meditation, at the stage of Equanimity toward Formations, which is endowed with the six-limbed equanimity, one has well escaped from conditioned phenomena. However, the function of escaping from conditioned phenomena is not yet accomplished by merely having the desire for deliverance, or by merely spending one's time without observing or being aware of these phenomena. It can only be accomplished when one thoroughly understands by means of insight that conditioned phenomena are impermanent, unsatisfactory, and not-self. This understanding can only be established when conditioned phenomena are again observed as usual and without any gaps. Thus, Insight Knowledge of Re-observation becomes the means to relinquish conditioned phenomena with respect to Insight Knowledge of Desire for Deliverance, since one wants to relinquish conditioned phenomena on its account. If one wants to relinquish them, one must actually re-observe each arising conditioned phenomenon. When one observes in this way, but is not yet able to be equanimous regarding conditioned phenomena, one's insight knowledge is considered to be Contemplation of Reflection.

At the beginning of their Insight Knowledge of Re-observation, some meditators want to give up conditioned phenomena because they are afraid of or disenchanted with them. They think that they could become free of them without observing them any further, assuming that they will have to continuously face these dreadful states if they continue to note. So, they may stop meditating and no longer think of being mindful. But then the latent defilement of delusion will creep in with regard to unobserved conditioned phenomena. This delusion only has the opportunity to arise because the meditator's noting was not continued as usual. But if noting continues uninterruptedly, delusion will not have an opportunity to arise. So, this delusion that does not understand phenomena to be impermanent, unsatisfactory, and not-self is called "non re-observation" (APPATISANKHĀNA), the opposite of Insight Knowledge of Re-observation. What this means is that Insight Knowledge of Re-observation abandons non re-observation or delusion, or does not allow it an opportunity to arise.

11. Contemplation of Turning Away

Contemplation of Turning Away (VIVAṬṬĀNUPASSANĀ) includes both Insight Knowledge of Equanimity toward Formations and Insight Knowledge of Adaptation. At this point, one's mind is said to turn away, shrink back, and withdraw from all conditioned phenomena, 'just as a water drop rolls off a slightly sloping lotus leaf'. With it one abandons adherence due to bondage.

With change-of-lineage, path, and fruition, the mind relinquishes conditioned phenomena and rushes into NIBBĀNA, which is the cessation of the round of conditioned phenomena. Considering this, it should be said that Insight Knowledge of Equanimity toward Formations and Insight Knowledge of Adaptation are Contemplation of Turning Away. The fetters and other defilements that are engrossed in and derived from conditioned phenomena are adhered to due to defilements (KILESĀBHINIVESA).

The two Insight Knowledges of Equanimity toward formations and adaptation are Contemplation of Turning Away. When these two insight knowledges arise, although one observes the disappearance of conditioned phenomena (the objects and the noting mind), on one hand, one has neither attachment nor liking as one has at the lower stages of knowledge; and on the other hand, one has no fear, disenchantment, weariness, or a desire to escape, as one does with insight knowledges starting with Insight Knowledge of Fear.

One needs no effort to make objects appear, and one does not worry or fear that unpleasant objects will appear. Actually, having an extremely clear and purified mind, one is just aware of the Dissolution of Conditioned Phenomena while uninterruptedly being aware of them. At this point, it is as if the mind is turning away from these conditioned phenomena. In the same way that a water drop runs down a lotus leaf that slopes a little, so the mind turns away from any conditioned phenomenon that it observes. Whether it is an extremely good object or a terribly distressing one, the mind does not engage in thinking about it, but is simply aware of it.

Due to this turning away from conditioned phenomena (and after the Insight Knowledge of Adaptation has arisen), the mind at the moment of change-of-lineage and path relinquishes all these conditioned phenomena, and is able to rush into NIBBĀNA, which is free from conditioned phenomena. This way of observing is done in order that the mind at the time of change-of-lineage and path can rush into the object of NIBBĀNA (or the cessation of the round). These two insight knowledges are called 'Contemplation of Turning Away'.

This Contemplation of Turning Away abandons all of the fetters, such as the fetter of lust for sensual desires that is fed by interest in pleasant sensual objects; the fetter of aversion that is fed by interest in unpleasant sensual objects; and so on. So, if one has reached the stage of Equanimity toward Formations, the mind neither relishes worldly objects nor becomes engrossed in them if thoughts arise about them. The mind shows no interest in such things, and there are long periods where the wish to think does not occur. Only when one stops practicing insight for some time is one able to think about or imagine worldly objects.

The commentary on the PATISAMBHIDĀMAGGA gives a different definition for Contemplation of Turning Away. It says that it is the Insight Knowledge of Change-of-Lineage that arises due to the power of Insight Knowledge of Adaptation. It also says that the definition given in the VISUDDHIMAGGA seems to contradict the PATISAMBHIDĀMAGGA. When the BUDDHA explained Contemplation of Turning Away, he did not mention adverting consciousness, the first mind-moment that adverts to a new object. Given this fact, the commentary states that Insight Knowledge of Change-of-lineage, which does not require adverting consciousness, is the most appropriate function for 'Contemplation of turning away'. One can take whichever view one finds most suitable on this issue.

16.
INSIGHT

(Mahasi Sayadaw, Manual of Insight, chapter 5, pp.275-292)

A. Mind and Body

When a meditator practice noting and their mindfulness, concentration, and insight mature, he or she will find that the noting mind and the noted objects occur in pairs. You will observe, for example, both the physical phenomena (body) involved in the rise of the abdomen and the mental phenomenon (mind) that notes it; the physical phenomena involved in the fall of the abdomen, and the mental phenomenon that notes it; the physical phenomena involved in lifting the foot, and the mental phenomenon that notes it; the physical phenomena involved in moving the foot forward, and the mental phenomenon that notes it; the physical phenomena involved in dropping the foot and the mental phenomenon that notes it; and so on.

When practice is going well, you will see the rise and fall of the abdomen and the mind that notes it separately in this way. Thus, you will be able to distinguish between mental and physical phenomena, or mind and body. It will seem like the noting mind rushes toward noted objects. This is awareness of the mind's characteristic of inclining toward its objects (NAMANA-LAKKHANĀ). The clearer your observation of physical objects becomes, the more obvious the noting mind will become.

The VISUDDHIMAGGA says: "Whenever physical phenomena

become clear, unambiguous, and obvious to a meditator, the mental phenomena associated with those physical sense objects will also become obvious to him or her of their own accord."

When ordinary people experience this realization of mind and body in meditation, they are pleased and tend to have thoughts such as: "Nothing exists but mind and body. There is only the rising of the abdomen and the mind noting it; only the falling of the abdomen and the mind noting it; only the sitting posture and the mind noting it; only the bending movement and the mind noting it. What we call a human being is nothing but these two kinds of phenomena. Except for these two phenomena there is nothing else. Also, what we call a woman or man is only these two phenomena. Except for these two phenomena there is no independent person or being."

When people with scriptural knowledge clearly experience physical sense objects, the sense bases, and the knowing mind, they are pleased and tend to reflect on it in this way: "It really is true that there are only mental and physical phenomena. In a moment of noting, what I really experience are the noted physical phenomena and the noting mind. The same is true at other times, too. There is no 'woman,' 'man,' or other living being that exists independent of these phenomena. The mental and physical phenomena of the present moment are all that really exists. These phenomena are commonly called a person, being, woman, or man, but those are just names. In reality, there is no independent 'person,' 'being,' 'woman,' or 'man,' only the mental and physical phenomena I experience while noting them."

When these kinds of reflections arise, note the mental state of reflection itself as "reflecting, reflecting," then return to the primary object and note it uninterruptedly.

B. Cause and Effect

As practice matures further, the intention to move becomes obvious by itself when you intend to move your body. As soon as an intention arises, you will easily be able to be aware of it. At the beginning of practice, for example, even if he or she notes "intending to bend," a meditator is not able to be clearly aware of the intention to bend his or her arm. However, when practice matures, you will be clearly aware of the intention to bend without confusing it with anything else. Any time you want to change your bodily posture, first note the intention and then note the actual movements involved.

When first beginning to practice, you change your bodily posture often without noticing it. Due to this, you tend to think, "The body is fast; the noting mind is slow." But as empirical knowledge matures, it will seem as if the noting mind welcomes objects in advance. You will be able to note the intentions to bend or stretch, sit, stand, or walk, and so on and notice the different movements involved in bending and so on, as well. Then you will realize: "The body is slow; the noting mind is quick." You will experience for yourself that only after the intention to move has arisen can the movement of bending, stretching, and so on take place.

When you feel hot or cold, note "hot, hot" or "cold, cold." As you note, you will be able to experience the heat or cold getting stronger. When you note while eating, you will be able to experience your strength being replenished. After you have noted an object, do not return to the primary object if another object arises. A meditator should stay with a newly arisen object and note it uninterruptedly. Moreover, while noting mental images (such as images of the BUDDHA or an ARAHANT) or physical sensations (like itchiness, heat, aching, or pain), another object may arise even before the object being presently noted has disappeared. In this case, you should change to the new object and continue to note it uninterruptedly.

By noting every object that occurs, you will experience that the noting mind arises whenever there is an object. Moreover, at times the rise and fall of the abdomen will become so subtle that you cannot note them. Then you will realize that the noting mind cannot arise if there is no object. In this case, you should switch to noting "sitting, touching" as the primary object if you are sitting, or "lying, touching" if you are lying down, rather than noting "rising, falling." You can also alternate between various touch points. For example, after noting "sitting" once, you can note the touch point of the right foot as "touching." Then note "sitting" again, followed by the touch point of the left foot. In this manner, you can alternate among four, five, or six touch points. Furthermore, when noting "seeing" or "hearing" you will clearly understand that when the eye and a visible form are present you experience seeing, and when the ear and a sound are present you experience hearing.

Thus, as you note various objects, you will clearly understand the different causes that give rise to different effects. For example: The intention to bend or stretch results in the movement of bending or stretching; a cold or hot environment results in cold or hot physical sensations; eating nutritious food results in the survival of the physical body; the presence of objects to note, such as the rise and fall of the abdomen, results in the noting mind; attention to mental objects results in the mental states of thought or imagination; the presence of visible objects of form or audible objects of sound results in eye-consciousness or ear-consciousness; and the presence of the physical phenomenon of the eye or ear also results in eye-consciousness or ear-consciousness. A meditator also comes to clearly understand that the volitional actions that he or she has performed in past lives give rise to pleasant or unpleasant feelings in the present. Mental and physical phenomena have happened throughout this present life since birth because of past volitional actions. These phenomena have no creator. They arise in accord with the law of cause and effect.

When these realizations happen, you needn't stop noting in order to intellectualize or reflect on them. These realizations will occur suddenly and of their own accord as you note. Note these realizations as "realizing, realizing" or "comprehending, comprehending" or "reflecting, reflecting," and then return to continuously noting the primary object.

After realizing how the law of cause and effect or the interaction of mind and body operates in this life, you will comprehend how it operated in past lives and how it will operate in future lives as well. You may reflect: "The mental and physical phenomena of past and future lives had, or will have, the same causes as these present phenomena. There is neither an independent person, a being, nor a 'creator' that exists in relation to them, but only the law of cause and effect."

These kinds of reflections tend to occur more often for people of high intelligence and less often for those of average intelligence. The more intelligent the person, the broader his or her comprehension tends to be. However, a meditator should simply note these reflections and return to the primary object. If you make continuing to note a higher priority than engaging in reflection, you will spend less time reflecting, and your practice will develop faster. Just a few moments of reflection will suffice.

C. Effects of Concentration

As concentration grows particularly strong, you may experience a variety of unpleasant feelings, such as itchiness, heat, aches and pains, a feeling of heaviness or tightness, and so on. These often disappear immediately if you stop noting and tend to reappear when noting is resumed. Such feelings are not a sign of any kind of disease. The practice itself is what causes them to appear. So a meditator shouldn't fear them but should focus exclusively on these feelings, noting them persistently, and they will gradually weaken and fade away.

A meditator may also see various kinds of images or visions. These can be as vivid as if you were actually seeing them with your eyes. You may see, for example, the radiant image of a graceful BUDDHA, a group of monks, or other noble people approaching you. You may feel as if you are actually in front of a BUDDHA statue, a pagoda, a panoramic vista of woods, hills, gardens, clouds, and so on. Or you may feel as if you are actually seeing a swollen corpse or skeleton lying nearby, or a huge building or giant person disintegrating. Or a meditator may see visions of his or her body swelling, bleeding, being torn into two or three pieces, or turning into a skeleton. You may see images of the internal parts of your body, such as the bones, flesh, sinews, intestines, liver, and so on. Or visions of the hell realms and its victims, the hungry ghosts, or the celestial world with its DEVAS and DEVĪS may appear. It is only concentration that gives rise to these unusual kinds of conceptual images and visions. So, you shouldn't be elated or frightened by them. Such images are just like dreams.

However, the mind-consciousness that experiences these mental images is an ultimate reality, so you must note it. But you shouldn't note it if it is not very obvious. You should only note an object when it is obvious. Therefore, focus your mind on whatever image you are seeing and note it as "seeing, seeing" until it disappears. You will find that the image or vision will undergo some changes and fades away or disintegrates. Initially, you will have to note three, four, or more times before it disappears. However, when your insight matures, you will find that it disappears after you note it just once or twice.

On the other hand, if you are curious about, afraid of, or attached to these images, they will tend to last for a long time. So, take extra care not to think about any of these unusual objects. If a meditator finds himself or herself thinking about them, he or she should immediately abandon that thought by closely noting it. Since some do not experience any of these unusual visions or feelings and only note the primary object, they grow lazy. Note this laziness as "lazy, lazy" until it disappears.

D. Seeing the Three Characteristics

Regardless of whether or not you have any unusual experiences at this level of insight, you will clearly see the beginning, middle, and end of an object each time you note it. Prior to this stage, you will have had to note new objects that arose before previous objects had disappeared, so you will not have been able to clearly see objects disappear. At this level, you will be able to see one object disappear before noting a new one, and you will thus clearly see the beginning, middle, and end of an object. Clearly seeing each object instantly arise and immediately disappear with each noting, you will understand the impermanence of objects as described in Pāli texts and commentaries: impermanent in the sense of destruction...impermanent in the sense of 'nonexistence after having come to be'.

You may reflect: "These objects are just disappearing! They are just vanishing. It is true that they are impermanent." Anything that is impermanent is unsatisfying. Because it is frightening, it is unsatisfactory. It is suffering to be constantly tormented by arising and passing away.

You may reflect: "We enjoy our lives because of delusion. In truth, there is nothing to enjoy in our lives. It is really frightening that everything arises and passes away. It is constant torment. Everything is miserable and unsatisfying because it arises and immediately passes away. We can die at any time." When you encounter unpleasant feelings, you will tend to comprehend the misery and suffering in things as described in the Pāḷi texts and commentaries: as suffering, as a disease, as a boil, as a dart ...

Or you may reflect: "All mental and physical phenomena are unsatisfying, and no one can make them otherwise. They do not obey anyone's will. They pass away immediately after arising, so they lack a solid core, are insubstantial and useless. There is no self that has control and can keep them from arising or passing away. In truth they arise and pass away of their own accord." This realization is in accordance with the Pāḷi texts and commentaries: "What is suffering is (not-self) ...is not-self in the sense of having no core...and does not obey anyone's will."

Immediately after you note these reflections, return to noting the primary object.

After seeing for yourself that every object that you directly note is impermanent, unsatisfying, and impersonal, you will reflect that all other phenomena you experience must also be impermanent, unsatisfying, and impersonal. This is called 'inferential knowledge' (ANUMĀNAÑĀNA). Those who are less analytical or knowledgeable and those who give priority to continuous noting rather than to analyzing will experience less reflection on this inferential knowledge. Those who give precedence to it will tend to reflect a lot. Some meditators, though, continue to analyze this realization, interspersed with their noting, and their practice stagnates. Even without such analysis, however, your understanding will become clearer at higher levels of insight; so prioritize noting, rather than analyzing. If you do analyze, note it without fail.

After you inferentially realize the arising and passing away of all phenomena, you will simply be aware of whatever arises without any further analysis. The five mental faculties—faith, energy, mindfulness, concentration, and wisdom—will then fall into harmony, and the noting mind will become quicker than ever before. Your object—that is, mental and physical phenomena—will also appear extremely quickly. Each time you breathe in, for example, you will clearly see that the rising movement of the abdomen consists of many segments. The same is true for other movements, such as the falling of the abdomen, bending, stretching, and so on. You will clearly experience subtle vibrations or sensations all over your body, which arise very quickly one after another. Some experience fine sensations of itchiness or prickling that arise very quickly and instantly one after another. Unpleasant sensations are rarely experienced during this period of practice.

You will be unable to keep up with objects by trying to label or name each of them when they arise so quickly. A meditator should simply be aware of them from moment to moment, without naming them, so that he or she can follow them. If a meditator wants to name them, he or she does not try to name them all. When one object is labeled, he or she may become aware of four, five, or ten other objects. This isn't a problem. You may tire if you attempt to name all the objects that occur. What matters most is being precisely and accurately aware of each object. In this case, note any objects that come in through the six sense doors, without following the normal procedure. Of course, if noting in this way does not go smoothly, you can always revert to the normal procedure.

Mental and physical phenomena arise and pass away much faster than the twinkling of an eye or a flash of lightning. But when your Insight Knowledge matures, you will be able to clearly perceive each fleeting phenomena (without missing a single one) by simply being aware of them from moment to moment. Your mindfulness will become so strong it will seem as if it rushes into the object that arises; it will seem as if objects fall into the noting mind. The knowing mind, too, will clearly and distinctly know each and every single object that arises. You might even think: "Phenomena are arising and passing away instantaneously; their appearance and disappearance are very fast, like a machine running at full speed. Yet I am able to perceive them all from moment to moment. I don't think I am missing anything or that there's anything else that I should be aware of."

This is the personally experienced insight knowledge that we cannot even dream of.

E. Distractions from the Path

Due to the momentum of this insight knowledge, you are likely to see a bright light or experience rapture as a result of being greatly delighted with both the noting mind and the noted objects. You may get goosebumps, feel a tear roll down your cheek, or find your body shaking. A meditator may experience a "springy" feeling, often mistaken for dizziness, or a "light, comfortable" feeling, as if swaying back and forth in a hammock, that creeps over his or her whole body. You may experience a "peaceful calm" that makes you feel comfortable whether sitting, reclining, standing, or in any other posture. Both the mind and body will become so light, supple, and flexible due to this quality of lightness that you will feel comfortable even during long periods of sitting or reclining, without any pain, heat, or stiffness.

At this point, the noting mind and the noted objects flow along concurrently and harmoniously. Your mental attitude becomes straightforward. Your mind avoids unwholesome activities and becomes extremely clear due to your strong faith and confidence. At times this mental clarity may last for a long period, even when there is no object to be noted. As your faith grows stronger, you may reflect: "It really is true that the BUDDHA knew everything", or "There really is nothing other than impermanent, unsatisfying, and impersonal mental and physical phenomena." While noting, you will often see, extremely clearly, the arising and passing away of mental and physical phenomena, as well as impermanence and unsatisfactoriness, and you will probably think about encouraging others to practice. Without too much strain and free from laziness, balanced effort will manifest. It will seem as if objects are known of their own accord and so Insight Equanimity (VIPASSANUPEKKHĀ) dawns. A meditator is likely to experience an unusual degree of very strong delight or happiness, and will be excited to tell others about it.

A meditator may like any of the pleasant experiences that occur – the bright light, good mindfulness, insight, rapture, and so on. This liking will cause him or her to think: "This practice is exceedingly enjoyable!" He or she may really enjoy the practice. But do not waste time enjoying the bright light and other pleasant experiences. Instead, whenever they arise, note them as "brightness, comfort, knowing, reflecting, venerating, happiness, liking, delight," and so on, according to whatever you experience.

If you notice brightness, note it as "bright, bright." If you think that you see it, note it as "seeing, seeing" until it disappears. You may often forget to note bright light and other pleasant experiences because you are so happy to experience them. Although you are noting, the light may not disappear very quickly because you are delighting in it. Only after experiencing it many times will you be able to note it skillfully enough that it disappears quickly. For some meditators, light is so powerful that even if they note it for a long time, it doesn't disappear; it remains. In this case, ignore the light completely and divert your attention to some other mental or physical object. Do not think about whether the light is still bright. If you do, you will find that it is. Any thoughts about the light should be noted so precisely that your awareness of them is very clear and firm.

Since your concentration will have become very powerful, other unusual objects besides bright light can arise if you incline your mind toward them. Do not let the mind incline in this way. If you do, quickly note it until it disappears. Some meditators see various kinds of faint shapes and forms arise one after another, like the linked carriages of a train. If this happens, note it as "seeing, seeing." With each noting, an object will disappear. If your insight weakens, the shapes and forms will tend to become more pronounced. But if you note them closely, each object will disappear on the spot as it is noted. Eventually they will stop coming.

To delight in bright light and other pleasant experiences is to be on the wrong path. The correct path of insight is to just continue noting. If you keep this in mind and carry on noting mental and physical phenomena that actually arise, your awareness will grow clearer and clearer. You will clearly see the sudden appearance and disappearance of phenomena. Every time you note, you will see each object arising and passing away on the spot. A meditator clearly sees that successive occurrences are distinct from one another, break up bit by bit, and cease. Thus, every object you note helps you to realize impermanence, unsatisfactoriness, and not-self.

After practicing for quite a while, a meditator may feel satisfied with his or her practice and take a break every now and again, thinking: "It can't get any better than this. There can't be anything else special to experience." But you should not just relax whenever you want. Instead, you should practice for longer and longer periods without taking a break.

F. Disappearance

When Insight Knowledge develops to the next stage, you will no longer see objects arising but only passing away. You will think that they are disappearing faster and faster. A meditator will also see that the noting minds disappear one after the other. When the rise of the abdomen is noted, for example, you will clearly see how the tiny movements of rising instantly disappear and how the noting mind, too, vanishes very quickly. So, you will see that moments of both the rising movement and your awareness of it disappear one after the other. You will clearly see this for all other objects, as well, such as the falling of the abdomen, sitting, bending, stretching, stiffness, and so on: Each object and your awareness of them disappears moment by moment, one after the other. Some meditators even find that there are three things arising and passing away in sequence: a sense object, their awareness of it, and their knowledge of that very awareness. But it is sufficient to observe that objects and the mind that notes them disappear in pairs.

When noting becomes clear enough that you can see both sense objects and your awareness of them disappearing in pairs, you will lose the illusory sense of conceptual forms or shapes, such as the form of your body, head, arms, legs, and so on. You will only experience instantly disappearing phenomena. As a result, you may feel like your practice has become superficial, is not as good as it had been before, or that there are many gaps in your noting. But that is not actually the case. It's only that the mind naturally delights in concepts of solid form, and so it cannot feel comfortable when those concepts are absent.

In any case this condition is an indication of progress in practice. When your meditation practice is immature, you first perceive concepts of solid form or shape when you note seeing, hearing, touching, and so on. But at this level of insight meditation, you perceive the instant disappearance of phenomena first. In other words, you experience Insight Knowledge of Dissolution first; the sense of solid form will only return when you deliberately evoke it. Otherwise, due simply to uninterruptedly noting, your awareness will remain attuned to the ultimate reality of the dissolution of phenomena.

Thus, you verify that the saying from sages of old is true: "When conventional reality emerges, absolute reality submerges; when absolute reality emerges, conventional reality submerges."

Although your awareness will have become extremely clear at this point, it may seem like there are gaps between successive moments of awareness. This is because you are starting to become aware of the life-continuum that occurs between cognitive processes (VĪTHI). For example, when you note an intention to bend or stretch the arm, you may find that the movement of bending or stretching seems to be delayed for some time. This means that your awareness has become sharp and powerful. In this case, you should also note any distinct objects that arise at the six sense doors.

After your practice gains momentum due to noting the main objects, such as the rise and fall of the abdomen, sitting, and so on, you should note any obvious objects that arise, such as any sensations in other parts of the body, seeing, hearing, and so on. If your awareness becomes less precise or accurate while noting in this way, or if thoughts begin to interfere, or if you feel exhausted, return to just noting the primary objects of rising, falling, sitting, and so on. When, after a while, your practice again gains momentum, return to noting whatever arises. A meditator should let his or her practice proceed in this way some of the time.

Once you are able to extend, without strain, the range of objects that you note and observe, you will clearly see that whatever you see or hear instantly disappears and that two consecutive moments are not connected but are separate units. This is "Understanding things as they really are." As a result of this, however, things may seem blurry or hazy when you look at them. A meditator is likely to worry: "I think something is wrong with my eyesight; it's getting dim." But nothing is actually wrong with your vision. It's just that your awareness is discerning each individual moment of seeing separately, which causes conceptual forms to blur.

At this point, as well, a meditator will continue to be aware of mental and physical phenomena even if he or she stops trying to practice. You may not even be able to fall asleep when trying to, but you will instead feel alert and awake day and night. There is no need to worry about this, as it will not harm your health in any way. A meditator should simply continue practicing energetically. When your insight becomes powerful enough, it will seem as if your awareness pierces objects.

G. Disillusionment

When you deeply understand that both objects and the mind that notes them instantly disappear, you will tend to reflect: "Nothing lasts for the twinkling of an eye or a flash of lightning. They are indeed impermanent. Previously I was simply ignorant of this fact. Everything that has happened in the past must have also disappeared in this way. Everything that happens in the future will disappear in this way, too." Note these reflections.

You may also occasionally reflect on how unstable and incessantly vanishing phenomena are, thinking: "Clearly, we are able to enjoy ourselves due to ignorance. To realize that phenomena instantly disappear is truly terrifying. Each time they disappear could be the moment of my death. To have come into existence and to have to continue existing endlessly is really horrible. How dreadful to make such great effort in order to be well off in a situation in which everything constantly vanishes. How appalling it is that these instantly disappearing phenomena continue to occur, now and in a new life. That we are all subject to aging, sickness, death, distress, worry, lamentation, and so on is truly frightening." Note this mental state of reflection without fail.

At this stage of practice, a meditator generally feels helpless, dejected, and languid, being frightened by mental and physical phenomena that disintegrate so quickly. You have no enthusiasm or joy, and you tend to feel sad. There is no need to worry. This indicates that your practice is improving according to the usual development of the meditation process. All you need to do is remain equanimous by noting any reflections and other objects that arise. If you do so, you will soon overcome this stage. Otherwise, being long caught up in these reflections while feeling displeasure, a meditator might become so afraid that he or she cannot stand it. This kind of fear based on displeasure is not Insight Knowledge. Therefore, note all these reflections without fail so that fear based on displeasure cannot arise.

In between instances of noting, you may have thoughts that find fault, such as: "These mental and physical phenomena are no good, because they constantly vanish and do not last. It is depressing to see how they have continuously arisen since the beginning of this life without ever coming to an end, and that they create all kinds of forms and shapes although they do not exist. Striving hard to gain happiness and well-being feels so miserable. A new existence is undesirable. It is depressing to be subject to aging, sickness, death, distress, worry, grief, and lamentation. This is all suffering and devoid of peace." You should not forget to note these kinds of reflections.

Sometimes, it will seem like every phenomenon that you note and the mind that notes them are terrible, harsh, useless, disgusting, rotten, decaying, and fragile. At such times, even though you note mental and physical phenomena as they arise, you will no longer feel pleased with them. You will clearly see them passing away every time they are noted, but you will not be as enthusiastic about this as before. Instead, you will feel weary of phenomena. As a result, you will become lazy about noting. But you will not be able to help being aware. It is like being forced to travel on a filthy road, wherein every step arouses disgust and disillusionment.

Thus, when you consider human life, you will understand that you cannot exist without these incessantly vanishing mental and physical phenomena. So, you won't see anything delightful in becoming a man, a woman, a king, a rich person, or a celestial being. These instead will inspire disenchantment and disillusionment.

H. Looking for Relief

Because you feel so weary of phenomena every time they are noted, it will seem as if the mind is struggling to escape from them. With the desire to be liberated from the conditioned phenomena, a meditator may think: "It would be so nice if there were no such thing as seeing, hearing, touching, thinking, sitting down, standing up, bending, stretching, and so on. I wish I could escape from those things or go somewhere where they don't exist." Do not fail to note such thoughts.

At other times, a meditator may wonder: "What can I do to escape from these phenomena? Continuing to note them seems like deliberately contemplating vile things. Everything I notice is disgusting. It would be nice not to have to notice them at all." Of course, you should note these mental states of wondering and thinking.

Based on such reflections, some meditators even try to avoid noting at this point and put off practice. But mental and physical phenomena such as seeing, hearing, knowing, the rise and fall of the abdomen, sitting, bending, stretching, thinking, and so on will not stop arising; they will continue to appear as always. They continue to be apparent to meditators as a result of their intensive insight practice. Awareness of phenomena simply continues of its own accord.

A meditator will be encouraged by this, considering: "Even though I'm not trying to note, I keep noticing phenomena that arise anyway; my awareness of them just keeps going. So just avoiding practice won't help me get away from them. It's only when I note these phenomena as they are, and realize their three characteristics, that I won't worry about them, and will be able to note with equanimity. That's what will lead me to the experience of NIBBĀNA, where none of these exist. Only then can I realize liberation." Once you are able to appreciate your own experience in this way, you will carry on with your practice. Some meditators do not come to this conclusion by themselves. However, once their teachers explain their experience to them, they can carry on with their practice.

Some meditators will experience unbearable pain when their practice gains this kind of momentum. Do not despair. The true characteristics of unpleasant sensation are actually becoming obvious to you as pain

(DUKKHATO), disease (ROGATO), an ulcer (GANDATO), a thorn (SALLATO), unprofitable (AGHATO), afflictions (ĀBĀDHATO), and so on. Note the pain until you can overcome it.

Those who do not encounter severe pain may experience one of the forty qualities of impermanence, unsatisfactoriness, or not-self whenever they note. Even though their practice is going well and their thoughts do not wander, they will tend to think that their practice is no good, or feel that objects and the mind that notes them are not concurrent. Actually, it is simply that you are so eager to realize the impermanent, unsatisfactory, and not-self nature of mental and physical phenomena that you cannot feel satisfied with your practice. As a result, you may often change your posture. For example, when you are sitting you feel like you want to walk; when you are walking, you want to sit down again. You feel agitated and want to rearrange your arms and legs, move to another place, or lie down. You cannot manage to stay in your place or posture for very long and keep changing. Do not feel frustrated!

A meditator lacks satisfaction because he or she rightly understands that there are no pleasurable conditioned mental and physical phenomena. At this point, you think that your noting is not good. You will not yet be able to note with equanimity, as you will be when you attain the next insight knowledge, knowledge of equanimity toward phenomena. Try your best to practice without constantly changing your posture and to remain in one posture for a long time. After a while, you will be able to practice calmly again. If you practice with patience and persistence, your mind will grow clearer and clearer, until all the agitation and dissatisfaction disappear.

I. Equanimity

Eventually, your insight meditation will strengthen enough that you will be effortlessly able to be equanimous with respect to conditioned mental and physical phenomena. The noting mind will become so clear and subtle that your awareness will seem to easily flow by itself. A meditator will even be able to perceive very subtle mental and physical activities without any effort, and will see their impermanence, unsatisfactoriness, and not-self natures without reflecting about it.

If a meditator notes touch points at different places on the body, he or she will be aware of just one sensation of touch after another, but not of any physical form or shape; and the sensations of touch will feel very subtle, like the touch of a cotton ball. Sometimes you may feel so many different sensations in the body that your awareness moves very quickly all around the body. Sometimes it will feel as if both the body and the mind are moving upward. At other times, only a few regular objects will be obvious, and you will be able to calmly and steadily note them.

Sometimes the rising, falling, touching, hearing, and so on, together with the whole body, may disappear, and you will only be aware of the mind arising and passing away. You may experience a rapture that feels like being bathed in a cool, soothing shower, a tranquility, or a crystal-clear light like a bright sky. Although a meditator may not take such extreme delight in such pleasant experiences as he or she would have before, he or she may still become attached to them. Note any attachment that arises, in addition to noting the rapture, tranquility, or clear light. If these experiences persist, ignore them and note other objects instead.

At this level of insight meditation, a meditator will clearly comprehend every object and the mind that notes them. You will know: "These phenomena are not me or mine, and they are also not anyone else or anyone else's. They are only conditioned mental and physical phenomena. Conditioned phenomena are noting conditioned phenomena." Observing objects becomes very pleasant at this point, like tasting a delicious flavor. No matter how long you practice, you will not be gratified and will not feel any unpleasant sensations, such as stiffness, numbness, pain, or itching. Thus, your meditation postures will become very stable. You will be able to easily maintain the positions of your head, body, arms, and legs, and will be able to practice for two or three hours in a single posture, whether sitting or reclining, without getting tired or feeling stiff. Time will pass so quickly that two or three hours of practice will seem like just a few moments.

Sometimes the noting mind will become very swift and your

noting will be especially good. If you begin to feel anxious about what is happening, note it as "anxious, anxious." If you begin to think that your practice is improving, note it as "evaluating, evaluating." And if you begin to anticipate further progress in insight knowledge, note it as "anticipating, anticipating." Afterward, return to steadily noting the usual objects.

You should neither increase nor decrease your energy at this stage. Because some meditators fail to note mental states such as anxiety, excitement, attachment, or anticipation, their awareness gets dispersed and decreases. Some meditators feel excited and increase their energy. Ironically, this leads to a decline in practice because the wandering minds of anxiety, excitement, attachment, or anticipation take them far away from insight. This is why, when your awareness becomes swift and your noting becomes especially good, you should keep your practice steady, without increasing or decreasing your energy. Using this approach, your practice will lead directly to *Nibbāna*, where all conditioned phenomena cease.

Nonetheless, a meditator may experience many fluctuations in his or her practice at this level of insight meditation. Do not be disappointed; be persistent. Priority should be given to noting any objects that arise at the six sense doors as they present themselves, and to widening your awareness to note whatever arises in any part of the body. But it is impossible to note this way once your practice becomes very subtle and continuous. So once your practice gains momentum, before it becomes too subtle, note objects without setting any limits. If a meditator notes objects carefully, whether it is "rising", "falling", "sitting", or other mental and physical activities, his or her practice will gain momentum before long. Then your awareness will flow smoothly, as if by itself, without much effort. A meditator clearly and calmly perceives conditioned phenomena that instantaneously disappear.

At this point, your mind will no longer be vulnerable to any kind of temptation or disturbance. However alluring an object might be, it will not be able to captivate your mind. Likewise, however disgusting an object might be, it will not affect your mind either. A meditator simply perceives seeing as seeing, hearing as hearing, smelling as smelling, tasting as tasting, touching as touching, and knowing as knowing. Thus "sixfold equanimity" or Equanimity Regarding the Six Senses will appear every time you note. Even thoughts or reflections like, "How long have I been sitting? What time is it?" will no longer arise; these thoughts, let alone the previous kinds of reflections, will have ceased.

However, if your Insight Knowledge is not yet mature enough to produce Noble Path Knowledge, after one, two, or three hours your concentration will weaken and the mind will begin to wander. Then your noting mind may slacken and have gaps in between. On the other hand, if your noting becomes swift and especially good, you may become excited and anticipate progress. This, too, can lead to slackening. If you note these mental states of evaluation, anticipation, or excitement without fail, then your practice will regain strength.

But if your Insight Knowledge is still not mature enough, your practice will eventually decline again. Thus, there can be a great deal of fluctuation in practice at this time. Those who know or have heard about the stages of Insight Knowledge may encounter even more fluctuations. This is why it is better not to learn how the insight knowledges progress in advance. In any event, do not be disappointed. These fluctuations indicate that your insight is coming very close to Path Knowledge and Fruition Knowledge. You could realize path, fruition, and NIBBĀNA at any time, once the mental faculties of faith, energy, mindfulness, concentration, and wisdom fall in harmony.

17.
NIBBĀNA

(MAHASI Sayadaw, Manual of Insight Chapter 5, pp.292-300 & chapter 6, pp. 454-466)

A. The Experience of NIBBĀNA

These fluctuations in Insight Knowledge are 'like the flights of a bird sent out from a ship at sea': In the old days when sailors didn't know where the nearest land was, they would send out a crow that they had brought along on the voyage. The bird would fly in every direction, looking for the nearest shore. As long as it couldn't find any nearby land, the bird would keep returning to the ship. But once it spied land, it would fly directly to it.

In the same way, as long as your insight is not strong enough to realize NIBBĀNA by attaining Path Knowledge, it keeps drawing back. That is, there will be gaps in your noting. But once your Insight Knowledge is mature enough and the five mental faculties are in harmony, for at least three or four moments you will see mental and physical phenomena arising and passing away with increasing swiftness and clarity. Then, immediately after noting an obvious object from among the six kinds of conditioned mental and physical phenomena, you will attain to Path and Fruition while experiencing NIBBĀNA as the cessation of both noted objects and the mind that notes them.

Those who reach that spiritual state clearly experience their awareness accelerating prior to their attainment. They also clearly experience how all conditioned objects are abandoned after a final moment of noting, and how the mind takes NIBBĀNA, the cessation of all those conditioned phenomena, as its object. These are some of the ways meditators describe the experience:

"Both the objects and the noting mind were abruptly cut off and stopped."

"The objects and the noting mind were cut off, like a creeping vine being hewn down."

"I saw the objects and the noting mind drop away, like a heavy burden being dumped."

"Objects and the mind noting them seemed to fall away, as if I had lost my hold on them."

"I got away from objects and the mind that notes them, as if suddenly escaping from confinement in prison."

"Objects and the mind that notes them suddenly disappeared, like the light of a candle being blown out."

"I escaped from objects and the mind that notes them, as if suddenly emerging from darkness into light."

"I emerged from objects and the mind that notes them, as if suddenly emerging from a mess into a clear space."

"I found that both objects and the mind that notes them submerged, as if sinking into water."

"Both objects and the mind that notes them suddenly stopped, like a running person thwarted by a blocked passage."

The experience of the Cessation of Conditioned Mental and Physical Phenomena does not last very long. It's as brief as a single moment of noting. Afterward one has a recollection of the event, such as: "The cessation of objects and the mind that notes them that I've just experienced must have been either something special, or Path, Fruition, and NIBBĀNA." Those with scriptural knowledge might reflect: "The Cessation of Conditioned Mental and Physical Phenomena is NIBBĀNA. What I have realized while experiencing the cessation is Path Knowledge and Fruition Knowledge. I have realized NIBBĀNA, and I have attained the path and fruition of the first stage of enlightenment."

These kinds of reflections tend to arise in a systematic and thorough way for those who have heard how it is to experience the cessation of conditioned mental and physical phenomena. Such people also tend to reflect on which mental defilements have been eliminated, and which have not.

After these recollections they return to noting mental and physical phenomena as usual. At that time the arising and disappearance of phenomena is quite coarse, and so is obvious. They are clearly aware of the beginning and end, or of the arising and passing away, of phenomena. Thus, they may think that there must be gaps in their noting again or that their practice must have declined. This is actually true. They have returned to Insight Knowledge of Arising and Passing Away. Accordingly, they may again experience bright light and images, as is usual at this stage. Some meditators may find that their noting mind is suddenly not concurrent with the objects it notes, as it was in the beginning stages of practice, or they encounter moments of various kinds of unpleasant sensation.

For the most part, however, their minds remain very clear from moment to moment. At this stage they will feel very peaceful, as if their minds were floating alone in space. But they will not be able to note that mental state. Even if they try to note it, they will not be able to be effectively aware of it. They will not want to contemplate anything else, and will not be able to note other objects. Their minds are simply clear and peaceful. Gradually this clear mental state will grow weaker and weaker. Then if they continue noting, they will be able to clearly see arising and passing away again. After some time, they will return to a state of very subtle noting, and if their insight is strong enough, they may fall into the Cessation of Phenomena again, as they did before. They might experience this repeatedly, depending on the strength of their concentration and Insight Knowledge. Nowadays many repeatedly attain the first Fruition Knowledge that they have already experienced, because their main aim is only to attain the first Path and Fruition. This is how the Fruition of the First Stage of Enlightenment is attained through successive insights.

The mental attitude of those who have achieved Path and Fruition is not the same as it was before; it is so special that they feel as if they have been reborn. Their faith becomes extremely strong and, as a result, they experience very powerful rapture and tranquility. Happiness also often spontaneously arises. Sometimes the mental factors of faith, rapture, tranquility, and happiness may be so strong that immediately after having attained Path and Fruition objects cannot be distinguished very well, even though meditators note them. However, after a few hours or days those mental factors will weaken, and they will be able to distinguish objects again, so the practice will improve once more.

Some meditators feel relieved, reluctant to note, or satisfied immediately after attaining the path and fruition. Such contentment probably arises because their initial motivation was only to achieve that Path Knowledge and Fruition Knowledge. If they wish to realize and experience the peace of NIBBĀNA again by means of the fruition that they have already attained, they should note present phenomena as usual.

B. Entering Fruition

The first Insight Knowledge that ordinary meditators encounter in the course of insight meditation is the Insight Knowledge that Discerns Mental and Physical Phenomena. But for meditators with Path Knowledge and Fruition Knowledge it will be the Insight Knowledge of Arising and Passing Away. So, if the Insight Knowledge of Arising and Passing Away is the first to occur while you are noting phenomena, it will soon be followed by successively higher Insight Knowledges, up through Equanimity toward Phenomena, which is the most subtle and best knowledge. When that Knowledge is strong enough, the mind will shift its attention to NIBBĀNA, The Cessation of all Conditioned Phenomena, just as before, and the mental process of Fruition will appear.

If you do not determine the period for this fruition absorption in advance, it may last for only a few moments or for quite a long time: Five, ten, or fifteen minutes, half an hour, or an hour. The commentaries say that it can even last for a whole day and night, or for whatever period you have predetermined. These days, too, we can find meditators with strong concentration and sharp insight who are able to become absorbed in fruition for long periods of time, such as one, two, or three hours, or a period that they have predetermined, as described in the commentaries. Even when there is no need to do so, if you predetermine that the fruition absorption should end, you will easily emerge. In the case of such long periods of absorption, however, there may be intervals of reflection. If you note such reflection four or five times, you will become absorbed in fruition again. In this way, you may experience fruition absorption for hours.

During Fruition Absorption, the mind is fully absorbed in its object, NIBBĀNA, the Cessation of all Conditioned Phenomena. It does not perceive anything else. NIBBĀNA is completely different from the conditioned mental and physical phenomena and conceptual objects that belong to this world or any other. So you cannot perceive or remember this world (i.e., your own body) or any other during fruition absorption, and you are free from all thoughts. Even if there are obvious objects around to see, hear, smell, touch, and so on, you will not be aware of any of them. Your bodily posture will also be firm and stable while you are absorbed, even if for long periods. For example, if you are sitting when you become absorbed in fruition, you will maintain that sitting posture without swaying, slouching, or changing it in any way. As the *Pāli* passage says:

"... the [impulsions] of absorption also uphold the bodily postures."

When the mental process of fruition ends, the first object that you experience might be the Recollection of Cessation or of Absorption in that Cessation, some kind of visual image, or simply a thought. Then the normal noting process, brightness, or reflections will accordingly appear. Initially you will only intermittently be able to be aware of obvious objects after you emerge from Absorption in Fruition. However, there may also be times when you will be continuously able to be aware of subtle objects immediately after the fruition process, if your insight is strong. Remember that the determination to enter fruition quickly or to be absorbed for a long time should be made before beginning to note. While you are noting, you should not think about it.

When your insight is not yet strong enough for you to become absorbed in fruition, you may experience goosebumps, yawning, shaking, and deep breaths, followed by intermittent noting. At other times, when your noting is improving, you may become excited, thinking that NIBBĀNA is near. But, as a result of this, your noting will then become discontinuous, so you should not entertain such thoughts. If they arise, note them precisely and accurately. Some meditators encounter these kinds of fluctuations many times before they are able to enter Fruition Absorption. Even then, if your concentration and Insight Knowledge are still weak, it may take some time to reach the state of fruition, or you may not be able to remain there for very long.

C. Clarifying the Insight Knowledges

Sometimes, the Insight Knowledges of Fear, Danger, Disenchantment, and Desire for Deliverance are not clear because you have not experienced them for a long time. If you want to experience them clearly and distinctly, you should determine a time period for the experience of each Insight Knowledge. For example, if you set a time limit when you practice by resolving, "May the knowledge of Arising and Passing Away last for half an hour," then that Insight Knowledge will occur within that time period, but not beyond. Afterward, the subsequent Insight Knowledge of Dissolution will occur spontaneously, since you only see phenomena passing away. But if that knowledge does not occur spontaneously, you should resolve that it will arise. Then it will be present for that period of time, and the next higher Insight Knowledge will spontaneously follow it. Proceed this way, in order, for all of the Knowledges.

If your practice does not automatically move to the next higher Insight Knowledge after achieving mastery of the current level of Knowledge, resolve that it will arise. And after attaining insight knowledge of dissolution, resolve: "May Insight Knowledge of Fear arise." That Knowledge will then occur. When you are satisfied with it, resolve: "May Insight Knowledge of Danger arise." Then you will realize that Knowledge by seeing the dangers of phenomena every time you note them. When you are satisfied with that Knowledge, resolve to attain Insight Knowledge of Disenchantment. That Knowledge will then occur, causing you to become weary and disenchanted. When you are satisfied with that Knowledge, resolve: "May Insight Knowledge of Desire for Deliverance arise." Then that Knowledge will arise, causing you to wish to escape from phenomena every time you note them. Then resolve to attain Insight Knowledge of Re-observation. That Knowledge will then occur, accompanied by unpleasant sensations, discontentment, and the desire to change posture. Finally, resolve to attain Insight Knowledge of Equanimity toward Phenomena. Then that very subtle knowledge will arise, during which the momentum of noting will flow as if by itself.

Thus, you will find that you can reach a particular level of Insight Knowledge within a specified time limit, according to your resolve. You will also find that your Knowledge shifts, in due time, 'like the needle of a compass', to the next higher level of knowledge once you are satisfied with the current level. If you have not yet experienced all of the Insight Knowledges distinctly, repeatedly practice in this way.

On the other hand, people with strong concentration and sharp insight may reach Insight Knowledge of Equanimity within a short time, like within about four, five, or ten notings when they note without resolve. They can often experience Fruition, too. If you become very proficient at the practice, you can even experience fruition while walking, eating, and so on.

D. Practicing for Higher Paths and Fruitions

When you are skilled enough in the practice that you can very quickly enter the fruition that you have attained, and remain in it for a long time, you should practice with the purpose of attaining higher paths and fruitions. To do this, you should first determine how many days you are going to practice, and then resolve: "May the fruition that I have already attained no longer arise during this period of time; may the next Higher Path Knowledge and Fruition Knowledge arise instead." After this, simply note present phenomena as usual.

The reason for making a resolution is so that your Insight Knowledge, if strong enough, can lead directly to a higher path and fruition within the specified time period, rather than returning to the previous one. Otherwise, you will often return to the fruition that you have already attained. The benefit of making a resolution in the form stated above is that if the Higher Path Knowledge and Fruition Knowledge do not arise, the previous Fruition Knowledge may be realized again after your period of practice. Otherwise, if you resolve, "From now on, may the next Higher Path Knowledge and Fruition Knowledge arise," you may find it difficult to return to the previous fruition. Then the meditator may feel upset if he or she can neither gain a Higher Path Knowledge and Fruition Knowledge nor return to one previously attained.

After determining a time period and wishing not to return to the previous fruition before the period ends, simply note phenomena as usual. Then the Insight Knowledges will arise in order, beginning with Insight Knowledge of Arising and Passing Away, and Insights will develop in a manner similar to that which led to the first Path, rather than that which led to the first Fruition. Before the Insight Knowledge of Arising and Passing Away matures, you may experience bright lights, images, and unpleasant sensations. The Arising and Passing Away of Mental and Physical Phenomena tend to be not very refined or distinct. Even if when you practice to reach Fruition it usually only takes a few moments to return to Knowledge of Equanimity toward Phenomena and the Absorption of Fruition, you may now spend a long time at lower levels of Insight Knowledge. But you will not experience as much difficulty or delay in attaining Knowledge of Equanimity toward Phenomena as you experienced in the immature stages of practice. You will be able to progress through the successive stages of Insight Knowledge to return to Knowledge of Equanimity toward Phenomena within a single day.

Your awareness will be much better than it was during the first stages of practice. It will be more precise and accurate. Your understanding will be broader and clearer. Sensual, worldly objects and the cycle of suffering will be more frightening, dangerous, and wearying to the meditator, and the desire to escape will be stronger than before. Even if you were formerly able to enter fruition three or four times an hour, your Insight Knowledge may now stagnate at the level of Equanimity toward Phenomena, because it is not strong enough to progress to the next Higher Path Knowledge. You may remain in that condition for a long time, anywhere from one or two days to months, or years.

When your Insight Knowledge eventually grows strong enough, your noting mind will become extremely clear and swift. Following this acceleration, your mind will shift its focus and take NIBBĀNA, the Cessation of all Conditioned Phenomena, as its object. Thus, you will attain the Second Stage of Path Knowledge and Fruition Knowledge, followed by recollection of this new Path and Fruition, and a review of remaining mental defilements. Afterward, as you note as usual, Knowledge of Arising and Passing Away will arise together with an extremely clear mind. This is how you should practice for, and experience, the Second Stage of Path Knowledge and Fruition Knowledge, and become a 'once returner'.

If you want to attain the Path Knowledge and Fruition Knowledge of the Third Stage of Enlightenment, you should determine a period of time to practice and stop wishing for the Absorption of the Fruition that you have already attained. Resolve: "May the Fruition already realized no longer arise during this period of time." Then note mental and physical phenomena in the usual way. Beginning with Insight Knowledge of Arising and Passing away, the Insight Knowledges will progress in sequence, until before long you reach Knowledge of Equanimity toward Phenomena. If your Insight Knowledge is not yet mature, it will stagnate at that level for some time. As it did previously, when it is powerful enough, it will shift its focus and take NIBBĀNA, the Cessation of Conditioned Phenomena, as its object. Thus, the Path Knowledge and Fruition Knowledge of the Third Stage of Enlightenment will arise, followed by the usual process of recollection. This is how you should practice for (and experience) the Third Path Knowledge and Fruition Knowledge and become a 'non-returner'.

To attain the Path Knowledge and Fruition Knowledge of the Fourth and Final stage of Enlightenment, simply follow the same procedure: After determining a time period, setting aside your desire for the current fruition absorption, and resolving to experience the peak of enlightenment, note present mental and physical phenomena. There is no other way to practice. This is why the Satipaṭṭhāna Sutta uses the term "the only way." Beginning with Insight Knowledge of Arising and Passing Away, the Knowledges will progress in sequence, until before long you will reach Insight Knowledge of Equanimity toward Phenomena. If this Knowledge is not yet powerful enough, you will stop and remain at this stage. When it is powerful enough, it will shift its focus and take NIBBĀNA, the Cessation of Conditioned Phenomena, as its object, just as it did previously. Thus, will the Path Knowledge and Fruition Knowledge of the Fourth Stage of Enlightenment Arise.

Immediately after you have attained the Path and Fruition Knowledge of ARAHANTSHIP, you will recollect the Path, Fruition, and NIBBĀNA that you have clearly comprehended. You might reflect: "All mental defilements have been eradicated; they will no longer arise. I have accomplished everything that needed to be done." This is how you should practice for and experience the attainment of ARAHANTSHIP.

E. A Note on PĀRAMĪ

The phrase "Thus will such-and-such Path Knowledge and Fruition Knowledge arise" is only intended for those whose PĀRAMĪ are mature. If your PĀRAMĪ is not yet mature enough, your insight will not move beyond Insight Knowledge of Equanimity toward Phenomena.

In addition, it is relatively easy to attain the Second Path Knowledge and Fruition Knowledge fairly soon after attaining the First, but it will probably take a long time to attain the Third Path Knowledge and Fruition Knowledge after the Second. The reason for this is that only training in morality needs be completely fulfilled in order to attain both the First and Second Path Knowledge and Fruition Knowledge, but you must also completely fulfill training in concentration (SAMĀDHISIKKHĀ) in order to attain the Third Path Knowledge and Fruition Knowledge. Therefore, someone who has already attained the First Path Knowledge and Fruition Knowledge can easily attain the Second, but it is not so easy to then attain the Third.

In any event, it is not possible to know in advance whether your

PĀRAMĪ are mature enough to reach a particular level of Path Knowledge and Fruition Knowledge. Moreover, different people may need days, months, or years to attain Enlightenment. If you have just been practicing for a few days or months without attaining Path Knowledge and Fruition Knowledge, you cannot yet decide that your PĀRAMĪ are not mature. Besides, your current practice itself naturally helps your PĀRAMĪ to mature, so you should not evaluate whether or not your PĀRAMĪ are mature.

One should never give up, but continue practicing with full energy, keeping this point in mind: "If I don't practice, then there is no way that my PĀRAMĪ can develop. And even if my *pāramī* were mature, I cannot attain Path and Fruition in this life without practice. On the other hand, if my PĀRAMĪ are mature and I also practice, then I can easily and quickly attain Path and Fruition. And if my PĀRAMĪ are fairly mature, then my current practice will help it to mature enough to attain Path and Fruition in this very life. At the very least, my current practice certainly develops my PĀRAMĪ and my potential to attain Path and Fruition in the life to come."

F. Definitions of NIBBĀNA

NIBBĀNA is not like a splendid palace, city, or country. It is not like a bright light or some kind of clear, calm element. All of these things are not unconditioned ultimate realities, but are concepts or conditioned realities.

In fact, NIBBĀNA, as an Unconditioned Reality, has simply the Nature of Cessation called "the Characteristic of Peacefulness" (SANTILAKKHAṆĀ). It is the Cessation of the Defilements and the Rounds of Suffering. Or, it is the Nonexistence of Conditioned Phenomena (VISANKHĀRA), the Cessation of Conditioned Phenomena, and the opposite of 'what is conditioned'. Thus, the PATISAMBHIDĀMAGGA defines it by contrasting it with conditioned phenomena in these ways:

Mental and physical arising is conditioned phenomena. Non-arising is NIBBĀNA.

Mental and physical occurrence is conditioned phenomena. Non-occurrence is NIBBĀNA.

Mental and physical sign is conditioned phenomena. Non-sign is NIBBĀNA.

Mental and physical accumulation of KAMMA is conditioned phenomena. Non-accumulation of KAMMA is NIBBĀNA.

Mental and physical rebirth is a conditioned phenomenon. Non-rebirth is NIBBĀNA.

This *Pali* quote shows that the nature of NIBBĀNA is the complete Cessation of Conditioned Phenomena, expressed in terms of the Cessation of Arising, Occurrence, Sign, Accumulation, and Rebirth.

Grammatically the word NIBBĀNA can be considered a 'verbal noun' and could be interpreted as having any of the following three senses:

NIBBĀNA: Where the cycle of suffering ceases. (loc., act.)
NIBBĀNA: Through which the cycle of suffering ceases. (instr., act.)
NIBBĀNA: The cessation of the cycle of suffering. (med.)

This definition of NIBBĀNA does not mean that it is simply some kind of empty state that can be understood through everyday ideas. NIBBĀNA is described as being beyond logic (ATAKKĀVACARO), too profound (GAMBHĪRO), and difficult to be understood (DUDDASO) through common knowledge, and experienced only by the wise (PANDITAVEDANĪYO) with empirical knowledge. Moreover, since it is beyond the reach of craving, it is also beyond Entanglement (VĀNA), which is another term for Craving. When NIBBĀNA is experienced by a meditator through Path Knowledge, that person's mind is freed from craving.

Thus, the commentaries also define it as follows: NIBBĀNA: Liberation from Entanglement. (med.) NIBBĀNA: Where there is no entanglement. (loc., act.) NIBBĀNA: through which entanglement is eradicated. (instr., act.)

NIBBĀNA is simply the Cessation of Mental and Physical Phenomena that becomes manifest as the Signless (ANIMITTAPACCUPATTHĀNAM) to a noble one. So, although one has experienced it, one cannot describe it in terms of color or form or say what it is like. It can only be experienced or described as the

Cessation or End of all Conditioned Mental and Physical Phenomena.

In the MILINDAPAÑHA of the KUDDHAKA NIKĀYA it is shown in this way: "O Great King (MILINDA), NIBBĀNA is incomparable. It cannot be described in its color, shape, size, dimension, likeness, remote cause, immediate cause, or any other logical way of thinking."

NIBBĀNA is said to be the Cessation, Liberation, Non-arising, or Non-existence of Conditioned Phenomena. It is also said that NIBBĀNA has no color, form, or size. It cannot be described by using a simile. Because of these points one might believe that NIBBĀNA is nothing and think that it is the same as the concept of nonexistence (ABHĀVAPAÑÑATTI). But it is absolutely not like the concept of Non-existence. It is obvious that it has the nature of Cessation, Liberation, Non-arising, or Non-existence of Conditioned Phenomena. And because this nature is obvious, the Phenomena of Path and Fruition can arise while directly experiencing the Cessation of Conditioned Phenomena. The mental and physical processes of an ARAHANT do not arise anymore after they have entered PARINIBBĀNA; they have completely ceased. The following texts from the KHUDDAKA NIKĀYA show how the nature of NIBBĀNA is obvious when directly experienced.

"There is, BHIKKHUS, a not-born, a not-brought-to-being, a not-made, a not-conditioned. If, with NIBBĀNA, there were no not-born, not-brought-to-being, not-made, not-conditioned, no escape would be discerned from what is born, brought-to-being, made, conditioned. But since there is a not-born, a not-brought-to-being, a not-made, a not-conditioned, therefore an escape is discerned from what is born, brought-to-being, made, conditioned.

"Because there is no arising in the NIBBĀNA element (which is the Cessation of Conditioned Phenomena through their Non-arising), it is called Not- born (AJĀTA) and Not-brought-to-being (ABHŪTA). Because it is not made by a cause it is called Not-made (AKATA). Because it is not made dependent on causes and conditions, it is called Not-conditioned. If the NIBBĀNA element does not exist, then the Cessation of the Mental and Physical Processes or the aggregates could not happen. Thus it is not true that the NIBBĀNA element is 'nothing', like the concept of Non-existence. "Being the object of path and fruition, it is obvious in an ultimate sense. And because it is so obvious, the constantly arising mental and physical processes or aggregates in a person who practices correctly do not arise anymore after that person's PARINIBBĀNA. Then they are able to cease forever. It means that the cessation is something that can be obvious. May you believe this!

"There is, BHIKKHUS, that base where there is no earth, no water, no fire, no air; no base consisting of the infinity of space, no base consisting of the infinity of consciousness, no base consisting of nothingness, no base consisting of neither-perception-nor-non-perception; neither this world nor another world nor both; neither sun nor moon. Here, BHIKKHUS, I say there is no coming, no going, no staying, no deceasing, no uprising. Not fixed, not movable, it has no support. Just this is the end of suffering.

"The Nonexistence of the four elements shows the Nonexistence of the derived material phenomena (UPĀDĀRŪPA) and the Nonexistence of the mental phenomena that arise in the sense desire and fine-material existences based on physical phenomena.

"There are no sense objects connected with the immaterial existence.

"'Neither this world nor another world' refers to the nonexistence of any phenomena concerning these worlds. Therefore, at the moment of path and fruition that take NIBBĀNA as its object, one knows no objects concerning this or another world.

"'Neither sun nor moon' means that because there are no material phenomena there is no darkness. Thus, no light is needed to dispel darkness. Thus, it is shown that the sun, moon, other planets, and stars do not exist.

"'There is no coming, no going, no staying, no deceasing, and no uprising' means that while one can come and go to another realm from the human or the celestial realm, one cannot come to NIBBĀNA; and from NIBBĀNA one cannot go somewhere else. Unlike the human and celestial realms, there are no persons or beings in NIBBĀNA.

"'Nothing new arises in NIBBĀNA' means that it can only be known and taken as an object by Path, Fruition, and Reviewing Knowledges.

"'It has no support' means that because it is not a material phenomenon, it is not located anywhere and it is not based on any other phenomena. Even though it is a mental phenomenon, it is not a result or an effect. This means that it is not based on any conditions.

"'Just this is the end of suffering' means that there is no occurrence in *Nibbāna*. NIBBĀNA is the opposite of the Constantly Arising Process of Mental and Physical Phenomena. Although it is a mental phenomenon, it does not have the characteristic of being aware of an object as consciousness, and the mental factors do. Because it is the Object of Path and Fruition, when one experiences NIBBĀNA there is no suffering at all – and so it is the end of suffering.

"Because NIBBĀNA is the opposite of all conditioned phenomena (such as fire and water, heat and cold, light and dark)], there is no NIBBĀNA in conditioned phenomena, and there are also no conditioned phenomena in NIBBĀNA. The conditioned and the unconditioned never coexist."

In accordance with this commentary from the UDĀNA, as long as there are still conditioned phenomena, NIBBĀNA cannot yet be reached. While experiencing NIBBĀNA, no conditioned phenomena arise. When entering PARINIBBĀNA, conditioned phenomena no longer arise; they cease to exist.

When NIBBĀNA is realized by means of the four Path Knowledges, there is no room left for any form of craving, either those that lead to lower rebirths, gross forms of sense desire, subtle forms of sense desire, or fine-material and immaterial forms; all these forms of craving are totally destroyed. All these forms of craving have been discarded, destroyed, their bondage has been severed, and the tangle has been untangled.

That is why the BUDDHA also spoke with these words about NIBBĀNA:

"And what, BHIKKHUS, is the noble truth of the cessation of suffering? It is the remainderless fading away and cessation of that same craving, the giving up and relinquishing of it, freedom from it, non-reliance on it. This is called the Noble Truth of the Cessation of Suffering.

"And it is hard to see this truth, namely, the stilling of all formations, the relinquishing of all acquisitions, the destruction of craving, dispassion, cessation, NIBBĀNA."

G. Two types of NIBBĀNA

There is only one kind of NIBBĀNA in terms of being the Cessation of all Mental and Physical Suffering that has the characteristic of peacefulness. However, in another sense, NIBBĀNA may be further divided into two types as follows: with residue remaining (SA-UPĀDISESA) – this is the NIBBĀNA of an ARAHANT, one who has completely extinguished all mental defilements but still experiences the 'residue' of the aggregates as a result of past craving, clinging, and volitional actions; and without residue remaining (ANUPĀDISESA) – this is the NIBBĀNA of an ARAHANT who has passed away; that is, after entering PARINIBBĀNA – and refers to the complete cessation of all conditioned phenomena.

The Buddha explained these two types of NIBBĀNA as follows:

"BHIKKHUS, there are these NIBBĀNA-elements. What are the two? The NIBBĀNA-element with residue left and the NIBBĀNA-element with no residue left."

What, Bhikkhus, is the NIBBĀNA-element with residue left? Here a BHIKKHU is an ARAHANT, one whose taints are destroyed, the Holy life fulfilled, who has done what had to be done, laid down the burden, attained the goal, destroyed the fetters of being, completely released through final knowledge. However, his five sense faculties remain unimpaired, by which he still experiences what is agreeable and disagreeable, and feels pleasure and pain. It is the extinction of attachment, hate, and delusion in him that is called the NIBBĀNA-element with residue left.

Now what, BHIKKHU, is the NIBBĀNA-element with no residue left? Here a BHIKKHU is an ARAHANT...completely released through final knowledge. For him, here in this very life, all that is experienced, not being delighted in, will be extinguished. That, BHIKKHU, is called the NIBBĀNA-element with no residue left.

Note that in the first section of this passage that describes NIBBĀNA with residue left, a living ARAHANT is said to have 'laid down the burden' of the five aggregates, even though one still possesses a mind and body. This is because they are one's last aggregates and no more will arise, so we can say that they have effectively 'set down the burden' of the five aggregates.

Note that in the second section of this passage that describes NIBBĀNA with no residue left, the feeling that is mentioned refers to the particular type of feeling that is experienced only by ARAHANTS. This is KAMMICALLY indeterminate (ABYĀKATA) feeling, that cannot be said to be wholesome or unwholesome, and produces no KAMMIC results. Also, although only feeling is mentioned explicitly, it should be taken to include all five aggregates. The arahant has no involvement with any of the aggregates that might lead to rebirth. None of the phenomena that one experiences while still alive are associated with desire, pride, or wrong view. Thus, they all arise and pass away completely, without leaving any KAMMIC residue that might create the potential for another life.

A fire that does not get any more fuel cannot continue to burn, but simply dies down and becomes extinguished. Likewise, an ARAHANT'S aggregates that have been caused through previous KAMMA do not arise as a new life or new aggregates but, after having arisen, simply cease and become extinguished. After the Cessation of the Aggregates the aggregates no longer arise. As a result, the aggregates that constantly arise in an Arahant due to the momentum of previous KAMMA do not continue to arise in a new life, but are extinguished in this very life.

NIBBĀNA without residue remaining is synonymous with the Cessation of the Aggregates (KHANDHAPARINIBBĀNA). Once the path has been attained and after having entered PARINIBBĀNA, there is no longer any opportunity for the arising of mental and physical phenomena that would come into existence if the Path were not attained. In addition, Cessation of the Five Aggregates is accomplished with the Realization of the Path Knowledge of ARAHANTSHIP.

However, this cessation is not something that actually arises, so it cannot be described in terms of time. Prior to the development of the path, the defilements and their resultant phenomena (new life, aggregates) may arise at any time when the conditions are favorable. However, such potential defilements and phenomena cannot be said to actually exist in the past, present, or future. Thus, they are considered to be 'independent of time' (KĀLAVIMUTTA). Thus, both kinds of NIBBĀNA, NIBBĀNA with residue (SA-UPĀDISESANIBBĀNA = KILESAPARINIBBĀNA) and NIBBĀNA without residue (ANUPĀDISESANIBBĀNA = KHANDHAPARINIBBĀNA), are independent of time. Thus, they cannot be said to exist in the past, present, or future.

Therefore, one should not ask questions such as, "Did the NIBBĀNA that was experienced at the moment of Knowledge of Change-of-Lineage occur in the past, present, or future?"

These two NIBBĀNA-elements were made known by the Seeing One, stable and unattached: One is the element seen here and now, with residue, but with the cord of being destroyed. The other, having no residue for the future, is that wherein all modes of being utterly cease. Having understood the unconditioned state, released in mind with the cord of being destroyed, they have attained to the DHAMMA-essence. Delighting in the destruction (of craving), those stable ones have abandoned all being.

In these verses, the Cessation of the Defilements or the Aggregates, that is NIBBĀNA either with or without residue remaining, is called the Unconditioned. Just as the opposites of fire and water, heat and cold, dark and light, or jungle and open space, so is it the opposite of conditioned phenomena, and therefore called the Unconditioned. NIBBĀNA is also called a 'state' (PADA) because it can be attained and experienced through the Path Knowledge and Fruition Knowledge. Based on this, it can be concluded that the NIBBĀNA that is experienced through Path and Fruition is the same as the two types of NIBBĀNA with and without residue remaining.

If this were not the case, then the ABHIDHAMMA would be incorrect in saying:

"Though NIBBĀNA is onefold according to its intrinsic nature, by reference to a basis (for distinction), it is twofold, namely, the element of

NIBBĀNA with the residue remaining, and the element of NIBBĀNA without the residue remaining"

The unique characteristic of NIBBĀNA is the peacefulness associated with the cessation (of conditioned phenomena). Or, in other words, this unique characteristic must necessarily belong to any type of NIBBĀNA. In this sense there is only one type of NIBBĀNA, even though it may be divided into two types, one with and one without residue remaining.

Even though it is clearly stated that NIBBĀNA is twofold, if NIBBĀNA either with or without residue remaining and NIBBĀNA that is experienced through path and fruition were divided, it would also contradict the ABHIDHAMMATTHA SANGAHA. If NIBBĀNA were divided in such a way, then we would have to say that the NIBBĀNA that is experienced through path and fruition is real, being an ultimate reality; while the NIBBĀNA that is with or without residue remaining is imaginary, being simply a concept. But if this were the case, then NIBBĀNA would have to be classified into three types, rather than two: one real NIBBĀNA, having its unique characteristic of peace, and two (other conceptual types of NIBBĀNA), one with and one without residue remaining.

Some even claim that NIBBĀNA is conceptual non-existence (ABHĀVA- PAÑÑATTI) and that in an ultimate sense it does not exist. Then one would also have to say that Cessation of the Defilements and Aggregates is just a concept like the concept of 'a self' (based on wrong view). This would mean that there is no cessation of potential defilements and aggregates. In that case the defilements would continue to arise in an ARAHANT'S mind continuum, and after having entered PARINIBBĀNA the aggregates would also continue to arise. There would be no possibility of escape from the round of suffering.

Therefore, we must conclude that the NIBBĀNA that is experienced by means of path and fruition is general NIBBĀNA (SĀMAÑÑANIBBĀNA). The two types of NIBBĀNA—with and without residue remaining—that are specific NIBBĀNA (VISESANIBBĀNA) are included within general NIBBĀNA. This is why the NIBBĀNA that is experienced by means of Path and Fruition is not identified as being with or without residue remaining, or as the cessation of desire, aversion, delusion, material phenomena, or feeling; or as present, past, or future; or as the cessation of defilements or phenomena. In reality NIBBĀNA is simply experienced and known as the cessation of conditioned phenomena that perceive or are perceived. Because all mental and physical phenomena are extinguished in NIBBĀNA, it also includes NIBBĀNA with residue remaining, and NIBBĀNA without residue remaining.

H. Experiencing NIBBĀNA

Because you do not yet rightly understand the Cessation of the Defilements and Aggregates, you may think that it is just the concept of non-existence, that it is not profound, or that it is so profound that you will be unable to rightly understand it. So if you are not yet satisfied, you should resolve to practice in order to forever extinguish not only the defilements, but also the arising of the aggregates in a new life. Only then will you be able to comprehend that the Cessation of the Defilements and Aggregates is not a concept of non-existence, but an ultimately and obviously existing unconditioned phenomenon: Profound, difficult to see, and beyond the reach of logical thought.

Before you have realized NIBBĀNA by means of the Four Paths, you must develop diligence and mindfulness in order to protect your mind from yielding to temptation.

Therefore, BHIKKHUS, that base should be understood, where the eye ceases and perception of forms fades away. That base should be understood, where the ear ceases and perception of sounds fades away. That base should be understood, where the nose ceases and perception of smells fades away. That base should be understood, where the tongue ceases and perception of tastes fades away. That base should be understood, where the body ceases and perception of touch fades away. That base should be understood, where the mind ceases and perception of mental phenomena fades away. That base should be understood.

A meditator may arrive at the realization of NIBBĀNA by primarily observing the eye and perception of forms, or any of the other pairs of phenomena mentioned above. If Cessation of the Eye and Perception of Forms is obvious, then Cessation and Awareness of their Physical and Mental Constituents will also be obvious. The same applies to the other pairs of phenomena. In fact, the Cessation of All Conditioned Phenomena is obvious when one experiences NIBBĀNA. This is why the perception of conditioned phenomena completely ceases the moment one experiences NIBBĀNA.

Thus, NIBBĀNA is described as the Cessation of any of these pairs of phenomena. Taken as a whole, NIBBĀNA is the cessation of all twelve of these sense bases.

Venerable Ānanda once explained this, saying: "This was stated by the Blessed One, Friends, with reference to the Cessation of the Six (internal and external) Sense Bases."

The commentary to the UDĀNA of the KHUDDAKA NIKĀYA also describes NIBBĀNA as "the cessation of all twelve sense bases" and refers to an explanation that the BUDDHA gave to BĀHIYA, which other scholars cite. According to those scholars, the passage "Then, BĀHIYA, you will neither be here nor beyond nor in between the two" can be explained as follows:

"(If one is no longer involved with defilements in what is seen, heard, experienced, or perceived, then, BĀHIYA,) one will no longer exist here in the internal (sense bases of the eye, ear, nose, tongue, body, and mind), nor there in the external (sense bases of visible form, sound, odor, flavor, touch and mental objects), nor anywhere else in the sense consciousnesses (of seeing, hearing, smelling, tasting, touching, and perceiving. This is the end of suffering)."

A meditator proceeds by observing the most obvious object from among these twelve sense bases, consciousnesses, and mental factors. But at the moment of path and fruition, the meditator stops perceiving the object, and instead experiences the total cessation of all of these objects. This experience of cessation is NIBBĀNA. It is very important to understand this.

The sense bases actually represent all conditioned phenomena, so the cessation of the sense bases refers to the Cessation of all Conditioned Phenomena. In the following discourse, NIBBĀNA is said to be that state that is the opposite of conditioned phenomena. According to the texts:

"Where water, earth, fire, and air do not gain a footing:

It is from here, that the streams (of phenomena) turn back,

Here that the round (of the defilements, KAMMA, and its result) no longer revolves. There, name-and-form ceases.

Where consciousness is sign-less, boundless, all-luminous,

That's where earth, water, fire, and air find no footing,

There both long and short, small and great, fair and foul,

There "name-and-form" (mental and physical phenomena) are wholly destroyed.

With the cessation of consciousness this is all destroyed."

The statement that NIBBĀNA is "all-luminous" in this passage means that it is completely cleansed of all defilements. Similar metaphors are used in such expressions as "the light of wisdom" (PAÑÑĀ-ĀLOKA), "the luster of wisdom" (PAÑÑĀ-OBHĀSA), and "the torch of wisdom" (PAÑÑĀPAJJOTA). It is in this same sense that the BUDDHA said, "BHIKKHUS, the mind is luminous." The sense here is that NIBBĀNA is always luminous. The mind and wisdom, which possess an innate luminosity, can be soiled by defiling phenomena. NIBBĀNA, however, which is the cessation of defilements or conditioned phenomena, can never be connected with defiling phenomena. Therefore, there is no way that any of these phenomena can soil or defile NIBBĀNA, 'just as the sky can never be painted'. As a result, it is said that "NIBBĀNA is all-luminous." To be straightforward, the meaning of the commentary and sub-commentary is only that NIBBĀNA is absolutely not connected to the defilements, or is completely cleansed of them.

So one should not misinterpret this statement to mean that NIBBĀNA is literally shining, like the sun, moon, or stars, and that one sees this luminosity by means of Path Knowledge and Fruition Knowledge. This kind of interpretation would negate previous statement that NIBBĀNA is sign-less, would be inconsistent with its unique "sign-less" manifestation (ANIMITTA-PACCUPATTHĀNA), and would contradict Venerable Nāgasena's answer to King Milinda's question about the nature of NIBBĀNA. In fact, this kind of literal interpretation would be in opposition to all the *Pāli* texts and commentaries that say that there is no materiality in NIBBĀNA. In any event the Cessation of potential Defilements and Aggregates is not something that is luminous and bright. If it were, the *Pāli* texts and commentaries could easily have said that "NIBBĀNA is luminous and bright." Otherwise, they would not explain it with difficult names, such as "destruction of lust" (RĀGAKKHAYO), "the peaceful ending of all conditioned phenomena" (SAB-BASANKHĀRASAMATHO), "non-arising" (ANUPPĀDO), and so on, which are taken to be opposites of conditioned phenomena. One should reflect deeply about this!

"That's where earth, water, fire, and air find no footing,

There both long and short, small and great, fair and foul—

There "name-and-form" (mental and physical phenomena) are wholly destroyed.

With the cessation of consciousness this is all destroyed."

These lines point out NIBBĀNA, or cessation. The last line points out the cause of this cessation. "Consciousness" here refers to both the death consciousness (CUTICITTA) and the volitional mind (ABHISANKHĀRAVIÑÑĀNA) at the time of PARINIBBĀNA. All presently existing conditioned phenomena come to an end due to the destruction of death consciousness at the time of PARINIBBĀNA; and because there is no volitional mind that can produce results, new phenomena do not arise but cease to exist. Thus, with the cessation of these two kinds of consciousness, all conditioned phenomena cease. This is like the cessation of the emission of light from an oil lamp whose oil and wick have been completely consumed.

In summary:

"Nissesa saṅkhāra vivekalakkhaṇaṃ

sabhala saṅkhata vidhura sabhāvaṃ

nibbāna metaṃ sugatana desitaṃ

jhāneyya saṅkhāranirodha mattakaṃ."

The BUDDHA described NIBBĀNA as having the characteristic of being secluded from conditioned phenomena and as being their complete opposite. To the wise, NIBBĀNA is simply known as the Utter Cessation of Conditioned Phenomena.

18.
MEDITATION TEACHER'S RECORD BOOK

A NOTE FROM THE TRANSLATOR

The yogi is represented as 'he' for the sake of convenience.

'A' represents an answer from a yogi.

Several 'A's mean answers from several yogis.

Very plain and simple words are used in the translation, so that the readers could see through the originality in the natural expressions of the Burmese yogis' report of their experiences.

"MEDITATION TEACHER'S DIARY (OR) RECORDS"

VENERABLE MAHASI SAYADAW'S Introduction.

NAMO TASSA, BHAGAVATO, ARAHATO, SAMMA SAMBUDDHASSA

"Homage to him, the exalted, the worthy, the fully Enlightened one."

It is usual for wealthy industrialists, millionaires, research workers or the administrative executives in the government to keep records about any special events they come across.

These records will be of great value for the future generation in order that they may fully accomplish their purposes without difficulty.

Our true refuge Lord BUDDHA had worked hard in search of Enlightenment. After finding out the true Path to NIBBĀNA himself, Lord BUDDHA left records of this ARIYA work by giving sermons on SUTTA, VINAYA, and ABHIDHAMMA. Those who have listened to or received these teachings either from BUDDHA himself or from his pupils had the chance to practice these DHAMMA. Out of those billions and billions of beings (worldly and celestial), some were liberated from SAMSĀRA and had reached NIBBĀNA through this Path. Therefore, these kinds of records concerning the Supra-mundane DHAMMA are invaluable, and beneficial for all beings.

In fact, the custom of keeping records of real practical events, either ordinary worldly ones or Supra-mundane ones, is undoubtedly beneficial. Therefore, in a deep and profound practice like the VIPASSANĀ Meditation such diaries or records of Meditation teachers can act as a directory for the future generation. These records can guide the teachers in interviews with their students or yogis. It will also be useful in judging the yogi's level of VIPASSANĀ (Insight) Knowledge attained.

SPECIAL NOTE: The words of yogis in this book were just a colloquial everyday language. This record of the Meditation Teacher's diary was not extracted from any Pali Scriptures, nor is it a proof to attract those who do not believe in VIPASSANĀ Meditation. Therefore, there is no need for the doubtful person to consider whether this book is in agreement with the Pali Scriptures or not. (This record is only for people who have complete trust in this practice.)

This book is meant to help the qualified VIPASSANĀ Teachers who had practiced according to the Venerable Mahasi Sayadaw's method, and had practiced long enough to appreciate the 16 levels of knowledge. Therefore, those who had not practiced the VIPASSANĀ Meditation or those who had not practiced long enough to attain the full 16 levels of knowledge, should not be allowed to look at this book. Because if they had known the contents of this book, they might form ideas or concepts on them, or they might not understand and begin to have doubts about the practice. Furthermore, they might make condescending remarks which could only cause harm for them. Even if one understands the points made out in this book, one may think about these while meditating. That person's mind would be vulnerable to complex ideas or thoughts. Then the knowledge will not be a pure one (but one with pre-existing knowledge gained by reading). Also, it can be a hindrance to improving the level of knowledge.

Therefore, those who possess the Teacher's Record Book should not let the students or those people who had not attained knowledge see it. Those who had not attained all the 16 levels of knowledge should avoid the book, even if they come across it. If for the worst they had read it and liked it, they should not bear the contents of this book in their minds.

But there is an exception, for one who truly and honestly believes in this method, who also wishes to practice systematically until a satisfactory stage is reached; and if there is nobody to guide him, this book can be used as a teacher or guide. But here the student should not think about this book while meditating. Since this book contains the teacher's guidance in relation to the Yogis reports, if used properly, it can take you to NIBBĀNA:

CAUTION: The presentations in this book are only individual accounts of their experiences. The yogis' statements and the examples should not be taken as an exemplary way to conduct interviews. The way the teacher helps his student in this book is just to give you an idea of how to correct them. This is not a complete manual or a guide book for the Meditation Teacher. Sometimes special attention is needed for a student upon whom the teacher could spend about an hour on that student alone. Such records could not be stated here fully. Therefore, care should be taken so as not to restrict the teaching according to the contents of this book only. If it is needed to be explained more elaborately, use your own intuition with the background knowledge gained from this book.

Sometimes the teacher may find it difficult to judge the yogi's level of knowledge, then you compare your own experiences (yogi's statement) and the ones in the book. Make careful comparisons, and when you are sure of your student's level of knowledge, keep it to yourself. Sometimes the yogi has really reached a certain level of knowledge, but he could not state clearly. In such cases, the teacher should drop hints concerning the level of knowledge the student had gained, so that the student can compare himself.

In the SAMMASANAÑĀNA level, the yogi's experience, his knowledge, and his way of thinking is very wide-ranging. The student's account of his experience may be similar to the states of mind in higher levels. The outspoken yogi's way of relating his experience is very similar to that of SANKHĀRUPEKKHĀ-ÑĀNA level. The quiet type may have reached higher levels, but he would express as if he is still in lower levels.

Sometimes the yogi may have reached a higher level and had made it known to the teacher. Later that yogi may not reach back to that level, so he goes back to explaining about his past experiences of the lower levels. Because of this, sometimes it is difficult to set a rule for judgment on hearing the yogi's statements.

Therefore, keep the judgment on yogi's level of knowledge to yourself. If and when it is needed for the teacher to tell someone about the student's achievement, speak out your opinion only if you are absolutely certain. Otherwise, do not declare your opinion, but just relate the yogi's expressions.

If you are not clear yourself when deciding on whether the yogi's level is higher or lower, you should decide to yourself that it is lower.

The teacher is responsible for his student's mistakes or right achievements. Therefore, in every aspect, weigh out your judgment of pupils carefully and use this book as a helping hand to guide your students in such a way that you could surely lead them to the True Path of NIBBĀNA.

NANO TASSA BHAGAVATO ARAHATO SAMA SAMBUDDHASA

BUDDHA THE INCOMPARABLE ONE WHO TAMED THOSE WHO WERE IN NEED OF TEACHING

Our true refuge BUDDHA, the Enlightened One who possessed the SĪLA (virtue, morality), SAMĀDHI (concentration) and PAÑÑĀ (wisdom) tamed the celestial and worldly beings. His instruction and guidance are the most skillful and the holiest of all. Therefore, He is recollected as BUDDHA, The Incomparable One Who Tamed Those Who Were in Need of Teaching.

Those who followed his teachings, worldly or celestial, could be fully liberated in one sitting. Because of this skill to give guidance until fully liberated, He is recollected as 'BUDDHA The Incomparable One Who Tamed Those Who Were in Need of Teaching'.

He could teach and guide the celestial and worldly beings to give benefit to their present and future well-being and the benefit of NIBBĀNA. Therefore, He is the only True and Holy Teacher the celestial and human beings could take refuge in.

Let us pay homage to the Buddha Who had the honor of 'BUDDHA: The Incomparable One Who Tamed Those Who Were in Need of Teaching'; 'BUDDHA Who should be honored and respected as the Enlightened One'; 'The DHAMMA which was taught by BUDDHA as MAGGA, PHALA, NIBBĀNA'; 'the ARIYA SANGHA who are the true sons of BUDDHA':

With the intention of helping the Meditation teachers in their VIPASSANĀ work, this book is written in such a way that the Meditation teachers would be able to guide their students easily by asking the right questions.

A. Three Types of Yogis

First Type: Out of the yogis we have interviewed there were three types. Some yogis could tell their experiences in contemplation very clearly, explaining step by step about what they themselves saw. With such yogis we did not need to emphasize the question, nor give leading questions. We only had to listen to what they say, giving instructions when necessary, correcting wrong concepts or wrong way of noting. Sometimes when the yogis are slackening in their practice, lectures or discourses should be given accordingly at an appropriate time. This book gives records of such yogis.

Second type: Some yogis could not tell clearly how they noted and what they saw, step by step. This may be so because of their shyness. In such cases, leading questions should be asked when necessary. When such questions are made, the yogi sometimes admitted that he could remember, or otherwise. The yogi honestly admitted about his experiences. To test whether the yogi was speaking the true experience or not we asked about the sort of experiences which could not be met as yet; and also, which do not relate to the condition of the yogi's experience, or when they sometimes said the wrong thing as if it was right. Sometimes we asked questions that could give two types of answers. From time to time the teacher could ask the honest and frank yogi about things, which could have been missed out in the yogi's description of his experiences.

Third Type: There are some types of yogis who cannot explain well, but when the teacher asked some leading questions, they give a reply which they had learnt from some other people.

Leading questions or hints should not be said to such yogis. Instead, the teacher should just listen to his account. If there were points that you would like to know from him, ask questions which could give two types of answers. Or ask for example, "When you were noting on the arising process, what did you know and how did you know it?" Ask in such a way that the yogi could not guess what you wish to know. Then only you can know the yogi's true level of concentration and knowledge. This gives you a general idea of interviewing the three types of yogis at each level of knowledge.

B. NĀMA-RŪPA-PARICCHEDA-ÑĀNA (The Knowledge That Distinguishes Between Mind and Matter)

For a beginner who had done one or two days of work:

QUESTION: How were you contemplating? How did you feel when noting?

A yogi with little effort would answer thus:

ANSWER: As instructed, I was noting on the rising and falling of the abdomen. It was quite easy to note, no problem.

COMMENT: The answer was quite flippant.

Q: What else could you note?
A: There was nothing else to note, so I did not note on other things. Some would say: When bending I noted bending, when stretching I noted stretching, I could note all events easily.

COMMENT: The yogi replied quite lightly.

Q: Could you note your mind wandering?
A: My mind did not wander anywhere; it was very still.
Q: Very well, then could you tell step by step how you noted when you were standing still, lying down, getting up, bending, stretching and so on?

COMMENT: The yogi could not answer specifically. Such a yogi might not have understood the procedure of meditation or his faith (*Saddha*), desire (*Sandha*), and effort (*Viriya*) were not strong enough. In other words, he is not working hard enough.

CORRECTION: Tell the student that in every noting, serious and energetic effort should be made. Tell him to put in more energy in noting. The yogi who was seriously contemplating would answer the above questions thus:

A: While noting the rising and falling process, it was difficult to note at first. I was quite tired with perspiration; now I am getting better and I am beginning to do well in my notings.
Q: When noting on the rising and falling, could you say that the occurrence of each rising and falling coincided with your mental noting?

A: Now they are fitting better.

A: Sometimes the rising falling and my noting coincided well but sometimes they did not. I made a mental note of rising before the abdomen had really risen. I made a note of falling before it had really fallen. Or sometimes I noted only after it had risen or fallen. Sometimes I noted rising when it was falling and vice versa. That was why I said "Sometimes my noting was accurate and sometimes it was not."

INSTRUCTION: Be careful to aim accurately, so that the noting and the happening will coincide. Very soon you will get to that coinciding stage. Everybody has to undergo that difficult stage in the beginning.

Some would answer thus: "Whenever I noted I always found the noting hit straight to the object (target)."

Q: Then, while you were noting on the rising and falling process, did your mind wander elsewhere?

A: While contemplating, my mind did not wander anywhere, it was always still.

COMMENT: At this stage the yogi said this only because he could not notice the wandering, running mind.

WARNING AND INSTRUCTION: Note energetically, so that you know very distinctly and precisely about the rising and falling process.

A: While noting on rising and falling, my mind was elsewhere. Only after a while I noticed that my mind was elsewhere. Even if I knew, I could note sometimes; at other times I could not note the wandering mind. Sometimes the wandering mind stopped after noting. Sometimes it did not stop wandering.

INSTRUCTION: While you are noting with energetic effort on the rising and falling process, your mind could not wander. Even if it wandered, you could note quickly. On the other hand, if you were enjoying your thoughts, they would not disappear. But if you did not like them and noted carefully, the wandering thoughts would disappear. In future when such thoughts occur, do not have a liking for them. Instead, have a complete faith in noting, and remember that if you note they will disappear.

Some would say thus: "While I could note the rising and falling very clearly, the mind did not wander. When the mind was wandering, the rising and falling was not evident. Only because I could not note well on the rising and falling, the mind went elsewhere." (Clear Knowledge)

Q: When you have noted the wandering mind and went back to rising and falling, could you say that you could contemplate easily and accurately?

A: Sometimes the aim was accurate, sometimes it was not. Sometimes I could not find the rising process. I had to wait for a moment, then I could see the "rising" began, and I went on noting as usual.

INSTRUCTION: Do not wait for rising, if you found falling first, note as "falling". If you had waited, just note "waited" and note whatever you notice first.

Some would say: "My mind was running off to different places."

INSTRUCTION: Note that mind which ran off repeatedly until it disappeared. As soon as each individual thought had disappeared, go back to the rising and falling. Note with special attention.

Some would say: "I kept on noting one thought after another, so I could not note well on the rising and falling."

INSTRUCTION: Note once or twice on each thought, then go back to note the rising and falling. Try to do that every time you notice any thought coming up. Do not be curious to find if any other thought would come up.

If you saw any visions of BUDDHA, temple, houses, human beings, note as "seeing" or "meeting" two or three times. If these visions did not disappear after noting two or three times, note very ardently and repeatedly as "seeing" "seeing" until they disappear. When those visions had disappeared, go back to the rising and falling, and if you found the rising, first note as "rising"; if you found the falling first note as "falling". If nothing appeared, do not wait for anything; if you had waited, note as "waiting". Then go on noting continuously on whatever comes up with great effort.

Q: Did you note on the nature of bodily sensations, e.g., irritation, pain, ache, heat, cold, etc.

A: There was no irritation, pain, ache, heat or cold.
(This was because the yogi's mindfulness, concentration and knowledge were not mature enough to be conscious about these feelings.)

A: Sometimes there was slight irritation, pain, ache, heat and cold, but I could rarely note them. Sometimes I could not note them at all.

Q: When there was irritation and you wanted to scratch, did you note them as "want to scratch", "wish to ease the irritation"? If so, when you raised your hand to scratch, did you note as "raising", "bending", "stretching", "moving" and so on.

A: I noted as "wanting to scratch, wishing to ease". Then I noted the moving of the hand as "raising", "bending" about 2 or 3 times in each action.

A: I could not remember the desire to bend or stretch, I just noted while scratching, bending or stretching. Sometimes I did not know the bending or stretching movements. I knew about it only after they occurred. It was only after scratching and the itchy feeling was gone that I became aware of it. Sometimes it took some time before I was aware.

INSTRUCTION: Try to be able to note the intentions. You must be able to know the original desire to bend, stretch, scratch, etc.

A: I could not note the bending, stretching or the other body actions as yet. I was just trying to note efficiently the rising and falling.

INSTRUCTION: You should not think that you would note the actions of the body only after you have done well with the rising and falling. Whatever is happening at the moment will not exist later. And later you might reflect on the thought that you missed noting. Then the dormant forms of defilement could come up. While noting on the rising and falling, if any bodily action, sensation or thoughts became dominant, do not miss out on anything, be continuous in noting. Then only, the yogi's knowledge would improve. The older people have a tendency to miss a lot in the notings. Pay attention to them; the teacher should take special care to improve such students.

A: I could note the pain, ache etc., only sometimes. At times I just knew that they were there, but I did not note them. Sometimes I had pain, ache, heat but it was only after quite a while that I remembered to note.

Q: When you remembered to note, did you note the desire or intention to bend, stretch, etc? (Ask the same question for 'itchy', 'the desire to scratch' etc.)

COMMENT: For the yogi who could not note well, tell him that changing the body posture, bending, stretching or any other actions were made because of some sort of pain. Therefore, the yogi should bear the pain patiently and note. There is a saying that "patience will get you to NIBBĀNA", which is most appropriate here. Try not to move or change position every time you feel restless. If the yogi could tolerate the pain and could note ardently without changing posture, yogi would be able to note the desire to change posture and the actual movements in changing the posture.

Q: Could you note when turning to either side when you were lying down?
A: I did not know how to note this, so I did not note on it.

INSTRUCTION: Tell yogi to note ardently in these actions.
A: I noted as "intending to lean" or "intending to shift, change etc." Sometimes I could not note the intention. It was only after I actually moved that I remembered to note.

COMMENT: The yogi did not tolerate the painful feeling and had failed to note firmly. That was why yogi did not know as much as he should know.

INSTRUCTION: Before one bends, stretches, moves, changes position, sensations occur first. First of all, be tolerant of the DUKKHA VEDANA and note, for example, as "itchy" for a little while. If you wanted to scratch or wanted to change posture, firstly you should note the desire to scratch. Do not scratch or move as yet, but go on noting the pain or itch. Only act when the pain or itch became unbearable; you should note the intention to scratch first, then note the lifting of the hand, bending, stretching, scratching so on – noting ardently and accurately all the time. The teacher should ask the yogis whether they were mindfully noting when walking, standing, sitting, sleeping, getting up, changing clothes, eating, looking, seeing, listening, hearing, etc. If the yogi's way of noting was not correct, instruct the yogi to note systematically step by step.

A: My head felt stiff and frozen, itchy in the face. My hand felt painful, my back ached, my thighs ached, my head was bending.

COMMENT: The yogi was describing the feeling and naming the place where the pain occurred.

INSTRUCTION: Do not label the name of the place from which the feeling originated. Just note the feeling, labeling as painful, itchy, aching, bending, stretching etc. Very often the yogi would note the wandering mind as "going to the house", "reaching at the place", "seeing the temple", "seeing the Buddha", "talking to someone" etc. Do not label the object. Just note with the name of the verb, e.g., "going", "going", "reaching", "reaching".

INSTRUCTION: Do not label the object, just note the feeling.

Some people would deliberately bend and stretch just to note the slow motion of the hand, noting as bending, stretching etc. The yogi should not make deliberate actions to have something to note. If you noted in this way, you would be expecting to find something to note. This would create greed in you. Sometimes the mind could over-react and extreme bending could happen by itself. Besides, there is nothing to be gained from this sort of contemplation.

Only when the wish to bend or stretch comes up naturally, one should note the intention to bend first and then note the actual bending process. This sort of noting is natural and can help you attain mature and concentrated knowledge.

Some yogis deliberately look at something and note it as "seeing", "seeing" for quite a long time. The yogi would also find some sort of sound or noise and would listen for some time, noting as "hearing", "hearing".

You should forbid such method of noting. Tell the yogi to note what is happening inside his or her own body, such as rising and falling. If a yogi heard or felt something while noting on rising and falling, he should note once or twice as "hearing" and then go back to the rising and falling. The yogi must be able to note more of the occurrences inside his body.

A: I could see things arising and passing away and I could see ANICCA (impermanence), DUKKHA (suffering), and ANATTA (selflessness).

Q: How could you see it?

A: The rising of the abdomen was the arising phenomena and the falling of the abdomen was the passing away phenomena. The rising and falling processes were changing all the time, thus it was impermanent. The noting effort was itself a kind of suffering. When the body form disappeared, I reflected on it as ANATTA.

INSTRUCTION: Try to make yogi understand that all these were just thoughts and imaginations.

The rising, falling, and the noting itself were all arising and passing away processes. All these were impermanent, miserable, and selfless entities. Do not think about all these, it would not bring you any benefit. Just go on noting as usual. There would come a time when you could know all about these very clearly just by noting. If you had been thinking, do not miss that thought.

If you have been thinking, you could note that thought without missing it, note as "noted", "noted". If you noticed that you had been thinking, simply note as "thinking", "thinking". If you recollected as "passing away", note as "passing away" or simply note as "recollecting", "recollecting". If you recollected as "impermanent", note as "impermanent", "impermanent" or simply note as "recollecting".

If you thought you knew automatically, then note as "knowing", "knowing". Then, force yourself to go back to the usual noting on rising and falling continuously.

Those who did not know how to note, should be guided carefully. Every day ask what objects he noted, and how he noted; give instruction where and when necessary.

Encouragement should be given to the yogis, so that their faith, desire, and the effort in meditation could be improved quickly. From this stage up to the stage where UPAKKILESA (hindrances) occur, if the teacher could give daily talks on DHAMMA that would improve the faith, desire, and effort; and the yogi's knowledge and concentration would progress more quickly. Give DHAMMA talks with full faith and compassion.

When the yogi is experiencing the UPAKKILESA very vividly, there is no need to give talks that would inject more faith. On the contrary, you should give the kind of talks that would calm down the over-enthusiasm in the yogi's statement. Warn them to note with strong effort every time something happens in their minds or bodies, never missing out on each event.

After quite a number of days, the yogi who had gained quite a strength in mindfulness, concentration, and knowledge would say:

A: Sometimes it was very good to contemplate. My mind did not go anywhere. Every time I contemplated, I could always note on rising, falling, sitting, touching very stably and very well. Sometimes while noting on the rising and falling, I was just saying (actually mentally noting) it, but my mind was elsewhere. I could not say exactly where it went, but I just knew it had wandered.

Q: When you found you were not able to note well, was it like that from the beginning of meditation, or was it a change from being good at noting to bad?

A: At first, it was good contemplation all the time, the mind always stayed with the rising, falling, sitting, touching, etc. The mindfulness was stable. But suddenly I did not know where the mind went; it did not stick to the object of noting. I tried very hard to be able to note well. But the longer I tried, the worse it became, and I got very disappointed.

ENCOURAGEMENT: When you could note well, there would be a feeling of joy, satisfaction, and the will to work harder in contemplation. If you could not note these feelings, the noting would not be good anymore. (Sometimes the yogi would be sluggish in his effort and contemplated in an easy-going manner. Because of this, the yogi's noting could not be good. Sometimes yogi would expect to reach to the stage where he could note well, but that could lead him to worse condition.

18. MEDITATION TEACHER'S RECORD BOOK

Give him some encouraging words like mentioned above, and warn him that in the future, in order to prevent feeling glad or liking the goodness in noting, tell him not to miss anything and to remember to note as soon as those feelings occur.)

If you could note instantly, they will disappear. Also, when you were able to contemplate well, just go on as usual. Do not slacken or become over-enthusiastic, just note regularly and you will not lose the goodness in noting.

A: At first the contemplation was very good, but the next time it was not good from the very beginning. Then I thought, "Why is it that I could not note well now, when it was alright before?" So then I tried very hard to note. But it got worse and I was disappointed.

ENCOURAGEMENT: The expectation for a good noting was because of greed, and it could make you feel worse. Sometimes if you are too eager and trying too hard you would be worse off. Yogi was practicing mindfulness in order to dispel greed or anger; therefore, yogi should not let greed and anger come in. Then only yogi could improve his practice. The good noting you experienced before had finished and gone, there is no need to expect the same thing to happen again. There is nothing you could expect to happen as you wish. Therefore, accept the fact that things happen in their own way, let it be; just go on noting on what appears.

Instruct the yogi to note calmly and regularly. Also tell the yogi about the NIYYA AVARANA, which are the dangers of SAMĀDHI, and mention the remedies to cure them. Once the yogi felt confident on such an advice, and if he practiced systematically, within an hour or half an hour the yogi's power to contemplate precisely on the present mind object would become accurate and stable. The noting process was found to be especially good in such cases.

When the power of contemplation was good like that, some people might see lights in their eyes, or some visions, forest or clouds, or BUDDHA or ARAHANT, or houses, temples or people, animals etc. Or sometimes visions of a dead body or skeleton or bloated corpses. Sometimes the yogi might feel as if his skin was torn out or as if his head, hands, legs, or other parts of the body were torn apart. Then yogi would tend to react to these with joy, happiness or with great fear. Some would see the most respectful image of Buddha, and went on worshiping. Because the yogi was experiencing these outstanding visions, he felt very respectful and grateful to the practice, and to the teacher.

INSTRUCTION: The yogi should not be glad when these objects appear. If yogi was feeling glad, greed would be formed and the noting process would be disrupted. One should not worship either, as it would interrupt your contemplation. If yogi was afraid of something, anger would come up and the noting would be disrupted. All these visions or mind objects were not special events. When the power of concentration was good, yogi had formed ideas or thoughts without being aware of it; in fact, they were not extraordinary occurrences. They were only PANNATTI (named concepts) of objects like those in the dreams. They were not real. These were so subtle that you would not notice that they were your own thoughts. But the mind object you had visualized was quite evident, as if you were actually seeing it. So, in such instances note as "seeing", "seeing" until it has disappeared.

Every time you come across such kinds of mind objects do not accept them, but note ardently as "seeing", "seeing" until it disappears. Have confidence in noting in this way, so that they would disappear quickly. If you still felt glad, liking it, worshiping or frightened, then just note accordingly, and discard the particular feeling with each noting. Afterwards, always go back to the usual way of noting.

Sometimes in such cases the DUKKHA VEDANA or the pain would become evident and some yogi had grumbled about it, saying it was unbearable. Some could not note because of the feeling of fear in them.

ENCOURAGEMENT: These sorts of VEDANAS had happened before accordingly, but they were so subtle that you would not be able to notice it. Now your power of mindfulness, concentration and knowledge is considerably strong, so you were able to feel the "submerged" VEDANAS. Do not be afraid, do not be disappointed. Later, if you still find these VEDANAS, note deliberately and ardently until they disappear. If you contemplate with the powerful energy of knowledge, these *vedanas* will not last long. They are also impermanent

SANKHARA objects. As your power of meditative knowledge gets stronger, these feelings will disappear.

The yogi who had contemplated as usual after the various objects and different thoughts had disappeared, could differentiate clearly between various objects (e.g., rising/falling) and noting/knowing mind. Each noting mind gave a very distinct and clear-cut awareness. The noting became exceptionally good. Then some yogi would say:

A: The objects such as rising, falling, sitting, touching, bending, stretching, and the noting mind were pairing off at each noting.
A: The noting mind and the object were separate events.
A: The mind and the object seemed very close to each other.
A: The noting mind and the object were fluttering together.
A: First, I thought the noting mind was from the mouth, but now I think it is from the abdomen.
A: First, I thought the noting mind was from inside the body, but now I think it is from above the body.

COMMENT: The yogi said this because the bending of the mind onto the object (NAMANA LEKHANA) was very prominent.

A: The noting mind fell precisely on the object, as if a beam of light fell on a particular object or place.
A: Previously, I had thought the rising and falling were one object because they occurred from the same abdomen. Now I know that the rising and the falling were two separate things, and the noting was yet another event. They did not mix with one another. We could not mix them either.
A: At first, I had thought that the rising and falling were from the same place (abdomen) and I thought they were a combined process. But now I see them as separate events and even the mental noting was a different thing.
A: Previously I said the rising and falling processes were clear to me, but then I was not quite sure: Now they are really separate, and the noting mind is separate by itself. All of them are individual phenomena, and they do not mix with each other, and we cannot mix them either.

A: Previously, I thought the mind which was noting was the same one throughout. But now I find individuality in each noting.

A: I often found the rising and falling seemed to move further and further away from me.

A: The falling stayed in its place, but the rising got larger and larger until it reached the ceiling.

COMMENT: This was because when the yogi was noting comfortably on the rising and falling, the power of concentration became very strong, yet the knowledge was still weak. Therefore, the mind bent back to the object. The yogi did not understand this, he just explained as he thought. The teacher should instruct him to put in extra notings (such as sitting, touching, lying, touching) in his notings.

A: When noting the hearing, I could see that the hearing and the noting mind were different.

A: The sound was different from the noting mind.

A: Hearing was a different thing; the sound was another.

A: Hearing, the sound itself and the noting mind were separate.

A: The sound came into the ear; the hearing was from inside the ear.

A: When noting on bending, the intention to bend was one thing and the actual bending was another. The noting itself was one thing and the act of bending another.

A: The noting on bending was separate from the actual bending.

A: When noting the stretching, the intention to stretch was one thing and actual process was another. The noting as stretching was one thing and the stretching act was another. The intention was a different thing from the actual stretching.

A: While noting on the rising falling, the rising was done by a person and the falling by another.

COMMENT: The yogi described the noting as being done by a person, but that did not mean that he had attachment on any person or being.

A: When noting on the rising and falling, the place of noting was one thing and the action of rising and falling was another.

A: I did not know from where the mind was noting. I did not know from where it was rising and falling, but the noting was good.

COMMENT: The posture of the body was lost. The noting itself and the rising and falling processes were clearly distinguished.

A: When noting as "sitting", "sitting", the mental noting was one thing and the actual sitting was another.

A: While sitting, I noted as "sitting". I knew I was sitting but I could not say from where I knew.

COMMENT: This was because the yogi knew the physical form of sitting and the mental state of knowing were different events.

A: While eating, chewing, the mental note as "chewing" was one thing and the actual chewing was another.

A: The body was eating because the mind wanted to eat.

COMMENT: This sort of remark was made by a person who was not intelligent.

A: When noting as "touching", "touching", each noting fell directly on a particular point of touch, as if it really touched it.

A: When I put one hand on top of another and focused my attention on the point of touch of the upper hand, I could not feel the lower hand. I could only see the touch of upper hand. I did not know about the touch of lower hand.

A: Whenever I shifted my noting on the points of touch, each individual point of touch was a separate thing. Wherever and whenever I noted the point of touch was one thing, the noting mind, which was noting as "touching", was another.

A: I was noting on the rising / falling, sitting / touching, or I was bending / stretching. Whenever I noted I could only see the object and the noting mind. There was only those two.

A: Every time I noted, the target and the noting mind were going in pairs.

COMMENT: Some yogis gave examples to what they had experienced:

A: When I noted on rising and falling, it was as if the dart was hitting the bulls-eye target.

A: The noting on rising and falling was as if I was throwing hard stone to hit the soft mud.

COMMENT: In the yogi's example the rising and falling were comparable to the soft mud and the hard stone was the noting mind.

A: The noting was like throwing stone or stick at the fruits on the tree. (Here the rising and falling were compared to the fruits and the stone was like the noting mind. The hitting was the knowing awareness.)

A: It was like playing drums which were surrounding me. (Here the drums would be the object/target and the hand playing on them was like the noting mind.)

A: When I was going to sleep, I noted as "sleeping", I felt as if a log was laid down and I did not know anything. I could not move. The mind which was noting as "sleeping" went on noting.

COMMENT: Here the yogi was clear that the physical form was not able to know and only the mind could know.

A: Whatever I noted, the way the noting mind ran into the target/object was like the pecking of a bird's beak.

A: The way the body did what the mind commanded was like the slave and its master, or like the bullock and the cart-driver.

SUMMARY: Only the objects noted and the noting mind were sticking together in pairs. Apart from the object and noting mind, there was nothing else, such as a being or a person. If the yogi could realize this clearly and distinctly while he was noting, the yogi would be pleased about his knowledge, which could be called as NĀMA- RŪPA-PARICCHEDA-ÑĀNA: (The Knowledge that Distinguishes between Mind and Matter.)

The yogi who had fully experienced this *nana* would be able to explain clearly in his own words to indicate his knowledge. Ask appropriate questions to test the yogis who could not explain what they knew.

END OF NĀMA-RŪPA-PARICCHEDA-ÑĀNA

C. PACCAYA PARIGGAHA ÑĀNA (The Knowledge That Distinguishes Between Cause and Effect)

The yogis at this level of knowledge would say:

A: While I was noting as rising/falling/sitting, I found that after noting rising or falling there was always something ready to note. I did not have to think deliberately of something to note. Objects or targets to note appeared one by one automatically, and I kept on noting them as they came up.

COMMENT: Here the existence of object to note was the cause, and the noting was the effect.

A: I saw visions of BUDDHA, ARAHANT and noted whenever they came up. Before I finished noting something, another came up, and I had to note one after another in succession.

COMMENT: This was because the mind object appeared as a cause and the noting on it was the effect. Later explain the cause-and-effect relationship of object and noting; explain how the yogi would come to enjoy that knowledge.

A: I was noting the internal *vedanas*, such as pain, itch, etc, and before I finished noting one, some other VEDANA came up from elsewhere inside my body. I kept on noting whenever anything appeared.
A: I thought to myself I was very unfortunate to have so many bad *vedanas*.

COMMENT: The teacher should recognize that the yogi knew that the VEDANA was formed according to KAMMA, which included delusion, craving, and attachment.

A: When I was noting on rising and falling, it was very good to find appearance of object and the noting in harmony. When I noted "rising", "rising", "falling", "falling", the noting hit the target object directly. Whatever I noted, it was very straight and very clear. The good noting, I had experienced before was not as good as it is now. Only now the object and the noting were in perfect harmony and well-paced too; it was really good.

A: I was thinking to myself how lucky I was to be able to appreciate such Dhamma and meet such good teachers. I was grateful to the people who urged me to come to this retreat, and also to the person who taught me about meditation.

COMMENT: The yogi gained BHĀVANĀ KUSALA (contemplation merit) by SUPA NISSAYA SADDHAMMA SAVANA (relying on worthy men and by listening to the true DHAMMA.)

WARNING: In your past experiences there were times when you had good contemplation. But you should not expect it to be good all the time like this. Sometimes the pace of noting would become slow. If you found yourself slackening, do not despair and give up noting. Just go on contemplating. You must note with energetic effort so that you would overcome the dull state. Do not forget to note that thought or feeling.

A: I could note quite quickly and very well. Then suddenly the rising and falling seemed smaller and smaller. I felt as if my notings were spaced farther and farther, then I felt my noting was not good anymore.

COMMENT: Here find out the reason for this and correct it.

A: The rising and falling disappeared completely, and there was nothing to note. I had to find for the rising and falling and noted.

COMMENT: If you had no object (cause), there would be no noting (effect). This explains the relationship of cause and effect.

CORRECTION AND ENCOURAGEMENT: When the rising and falling was not clear, or when they disappeared completely, do not search for them. Just note on "sitting, touching" or "lying, touching". When noting on touching, change the point of noting target from place to place.

For example, after noting as sitting, note "touching" on the right leg. Then note again on sitting and note "touching" on the left leg. In this way, change position of the "touching" noting to five or six places or even more. The diminishing condition of the rising and falling to the point of subtle state was in accordance with the nature of DHAMMA.

At the moment the yogi's knowledge was quite young, so yogi could not know this. "Do not despair, just go on noting ardently. Very soon, your knowledge will become matured. You will know very clearly and your contemplation will be very good." Encourage the yogi until he becomes refreshed and inspired.

A: When I heard something the noises got inside the ear automatically. It was only when the sound got inside the ear that I heard it. Only when I actually heard that, I noted "hearing", "hearing".

COMMENT: That yogi understood that he could hear because there was the physical form of the ear and the sound; it was only because there was an object of hearing that the noting was done.

A: At first, I only heard the sound. Since I was noting ardently on rising and falling, it seemed as if there was no sound. Because I did not pay any attention to the sound, I could not hear anything.

COMMENT: Here the yogi knew that only if there was MANASI KARA directing the attention of mind (cause), there was hearing (effect). Without MANASI KARA (cause), there would be no hearing (effect).

A: All sorts of objects appeared in front of me automatically and I noted "seeing", "seeing". When they first appeared, I forgot to note and I just watched, I did not note. Then I realized that I should note all of them, so I paid attention towards all the objects. Now as soon as they appeared, I could note "seeing"/, "seeing" without missing.

INSTRUCTION: Tell yogis that because of YONJSO MANASIKARA wisely paying attention (cause), noting was done (effect).

A: Almost all the time I had to note the various objects, like visions of BUDDHA or Arahant, in all sorts of shapes and forms.

A: I was noting BUDDHA and ARAHANT shaped objects. Alternatively, when they disappeared, I noted on rising, falling, sitting, touching, changing the targets accordingly.

A: I had to note all sorts of VEDANAS, such as irritation, heat, uneasiness, ache, pain, changing from one VEDANA to another very often.

A: I noted on the VEDANAS like the itchiness, heat, uneasiness and alternatively noted on the rising and falling. I had to change my noting target very often.

WARNING and ENCOURAGEMENT: While you were experiencing different objects, you should note them, so that you would not feel glad or feel attached to them. If you had been happy or liked the object, first note "happy", "happy" or "liking", "liking", discarding the feeling as you note. Also warn the yogi not to be afraid or be disappointed when all sorts of objects and Vedanas appear. Tell yogi to put more force into his effort of noting.

A: I was noting on rising and falling all the time. I could not see visions of clouds, BUDDHA, ARAHANT, or green, blue, yellow, light or multi colors like other yogis. I wonder whether it would happen to me.

Q: How did you find the noting? It was clear was it not? Did you like the fact that only if there was an object, there could be knowing mind?

A: It was very clear to note, only when the "rising" appeared, I could note as rising. Only when the "falling" appeared that I could note as "falling". The desire to bend, stretch, the actual stretching and the wandering mind were noted in succession, but only when they appeared dominant. I quite liked that experience, but I could not see any special objects like other people.

COMMENT: The yogi failed to recognize the good contemplation he had had. His morale was low and he was feeling bored, because he could not appreciate the good contemplation.

ENCOURAGEMENT: The visions of BUDDHA, ARAHANT, etc, that the other yogis saw, were to be noted. The rising and falling (which you had been noting) were also the object to be noted. Whatever came up were objects that were to be noted. There was nothing special about the objects, as they would not bring any special results. Explain that whatever object yogi noted in each noting, the three trainings were included.

EXAMPLE: Whenever you were noting, either on the extraordinary objects, the rising, falling, bending, stretching, seeing or hearing, you were observing precepts on SĪLA (virtue). Thus, your SĪLA training was fully accomplished and intact. Every time you could say the mind fell on the target, directly the SAMĀDHI training of concentration was included completely. The mind, which knew the true nature of objects being noted, would be recognized as the PAÑÑĀ training (wisdom). Every time you knew the rising/falling process had happened, you gained PAÑÑĀ. Because the rising/falling existed, you noted and knew about it – that was PAÑÑĀ.

Because of the desire to bend you actually bent; because of the desire to stretch you actually stretched, and had noted those individual actions. You might be pleased with yourself at each noting. With each noting the satisfaction you felt would be called PAÑÑĀ.

As you went on noting you came to know that because there was desire, you noted as "wanting-wanting", because there was object that you liked, you noted "liking-liking", because you were feeling disappointed, you noted as "disappointed-disappointed"; because the mind went elsewhere, you noted as "wandering-wandering". Each time you noted, your awareness was sharp and you felt satisfied with each noting. This was called PAÑÑĀ. Therefore, a yogi who could note precisely on each object would have had the Three Trainings of Mind (SĪLA, SAMĀDHI, PAÑÑĀ) completely. Each noting would accumulate virtue, concentration and wisdom; what more could you ask? Just go on noting with an energetic effort and accuracy. (Here the teacher should give words of encouragement as much as he could.)

A: Previously, when I noted on bending and stretching, I noted just "bending" or "stretching", but never really recognized the desire to bend or stretch. Now I could recognize the desire to bend from the moment it appeared. Now, it was only after I noted the intention to bend that I noted "bending", "bending". Previously, I had thought that I could bend whenever I wanted. Now I know that only because the mind wanted to bend that I actually bent.

A: If I was going to bend, the desire to bend was first formed, then only the bending process began. After I had noted the desire to bend, there appeared yet another desire to bend, so I noted again. After about three or four repeated notings on the desire to bend, it was gone. So I did not have to bend at all.

COMMENT: Such yogi would describe the same experience in noting the other actions like stretching, sitting, sleeping, getting up, walking, standing, moving, changing posture etc. Yogi would also say that the eating, drinking process was carried out because of the desire to eat or drink.

A: Sometimes I felt a chill running up from my legs to the thighs, I felt gooseflesh flashing in me. I felt vibrations of shock.

A: I felt very pleased with my contemplation. I felt very happy.

A: I was so frightened. I did not go on noting. I just stopped.

INSTRUCTION: The feeling of chill, thrill, gentle vibration and gooseflesh rippling in the body were psycho-physical phenomena, which were due to the force of PĪTI (Joy) related to the VIPASSANĀ meditation. So just note as you feel, for example: chilling, cooling, moving up, gooseflesh, happy, glad, liking. If you do not know what to label, note as "knowing–knowing", "fear–fear", etc.; note ardently until they disappear. When such feelings as gooseflesh appear, tell yogis not to be afraid, explain to them that they were just forces of joy, which were the nature of DHAMMA.

A: After having the gooseflesh, I often saw flashes of light, brightness, sparkling rays of light from the corner of the eyes, near the chin and on the chest. They seemed to be like fireworks.

A: When I was noting the various objects, whatever object I had to note, I noted because there appeared something to note. The noting mind was formed every time there was something to note.

A: If there was no mind the body would be useless, as though it was a log or a dead body. The actions of the body were made only because there was the desire to move, otherwise there would be no movement.

A: Previously, I did not know about those things, and I had thought they were good. Because I had thought they were good, I came into existence repeatedly again and again.

COMMENT: Here the yogi appreciated the knowledge because of

delusion (AVIJJA) the effect of mind and matter (NĀMA- RŪPA) was formed.

SUMMARY: Each time yogi noted, he found only the Cause and the Effect. Yogi knew and liked the fact that there were only those two and nothing else. Such knowledge is called "PACCAYA-PARIGGAHA-ÑĀNA": "The Knowledge that Distinguishes between Cause and Effect."

Furthermore, the yogi came to know that because of the desire to bend (Cause = mental phenomena) the bending (Effect = physical phenomena) was done. Because of the existence of objects, like the physical appearance and the sound (Cause), and the doors of the body, like the eye and the ear (Cause), the yogi experienced hearing, seeing etc, which were mental phenomenal (Effect). Also, the yogi knew that, because of the distinct appearance of various objects (Cause), there was mindful notings, which were mental phenomena (Effect). Because of previous KAMMA (Cause), the good or bad mental and physical phenomena (Effect) were formed.

A yogi with such knowledge gained from personal experience of noting (according to the degree of "PARAMITA, Perfection" he was gifted with) could clearly understand the "Cause and Effect" nature of phenomena. That yogi would appreciate his own knowledge and would say, "In the past lives, one existence of mind and body had caused the existence of another mind and body (Effect). In the future lives, the same thing will happen again; the mental and physical form which exists now, will be the Cause of another mental and physical form in another life Effect."

Thus, such yogi would come to know that in the" Three Time Periods (past, present, future)", there exist only Cause and Effect nature of mind and body, and there is not a substantial thing, such as a person or being, that you would name as "Self", "Soul" or "Ego".

This sort of appreciation brings the yogi to the highest degree of the PACCAYA-PARIGGAHA-ÑĀNA, "The Knowledge that Distinguishes between Cause and Effect."

(END OF PACCAYA-PARIGGAHA-ÑĀNA)

D. SAMMASANA ÑĀNA (Investigation Knowledge)

At this stage, the yogi would say that, when noting various objects like the rising, falling, sitting, touching etc., the noting was swift. In a way, it was even better than before.

A: While I was noting as "rising", I was conscious of the rising the moment, and it began to rise, gradually rising up until it stopped rising. It was the same with "falling". I knew from the moment it started to fall, slowly falling down until it stopped falling. So at each noting I was aware of the object from the beginning, the middle, and the end.

A: While noting on rising, I could see about two or three "risings" in sequence. While noting on falling, I could see about two or three "fallings" in sequence.

A: The "risings" came up abruptly and the "fallings" fell abruptly.

A: The risings and fallings appeared and disappeared abruptly in succession.

A: The rising and falling processes seemed liked rhythmic beatings.

A: The risings and fallings were forming one after another.

A: The risings and fallings came creeping up and faded off like shadows.

A: The risings came hopping up and the fallings fell step by step.

COMMENT: This sort of remark was made by an intelligent person.

A: When objects like BUDDHA, ARAHANT, human, clouds, etc., appeared, I noted "seeing", "seeing". Then those objects disappeared bit by bit in slow motion.

A: The objects appeared from the left and moved to the right or appeared from the right and moved towards the left.

A: The objects appeared from above and stepped down slowly.

A: The objects appeared from below and moved up gradually.

A: The objects appeared from a faraway distance, then moved towards me and popped off.

A: The objects appeared distinctly right in front of me, and slowly moved off farther away and disappeared completely.

A: The objects appeared clearly in front of me, and faded off gradually.

A: The objects became dim and disappeared.

A: The objects became smaller and smaller and disappeared.

COMMENT: The above expressions were made in the same sense.

Some yogis become very enthusiastic mentally and physically when their contemplation was very good. When they noted ardently with energetic effort, they found that the objects faded off, smaller and smaller. Then the yogis became dissatisfied and started guessing, planning, thinking until their minds went astray. At such times the yogis would say: "I was feeling like a vacuum while noting. The noting pace was slackened and I felt very bored."

INSTRUCTION: This was because you were contemplating greedily. In the future, try not to be too eager in contemplation. When the noting becomes good, just go on regularly. Do not be disappointed when it was not good, just go on noting accurately. The imaginations and the thought that the contemplation was not good should be noted. Also note the mind which was bored. When you note, hit the target with an accurate aim, so that each noting removes an object.

Some people, while noting on the rising, falling or other bodily sensations, found that their minds wandered elsewhere to the objects, such as BUDDHA, temple, places, house, human beings, forest, mountains, fields or their working places. But when suddenly the yogi remembered to note and noted as "reaching", "reaching", those thoughts disappeared. Then the noting mind fell back on objects inside the body, like the rising and falling.

After noting about nine or ten times, the mind slipped outside again. Then, after about four or five notings, the yogi remembered to note and noted "reaching", "reaching" three or four times. After that yogi went back to noting the objects inside the body, like rising and falling, as usual.

COMMENT: In this way the yogi noted on rising, falling, and alternatively on the wandering mind. The pattern of noting was changed from one to the other quite often.

Then the yogi said:

A: My mind was going from one place to the other, there were too many things on my mind. I could seldom note on the rising and falling most of the time I had to cope with the wandering mind. But it was not as good as noting on the rising and falling only.

ENCOURAGEMENT: The mind that thought it was not good to note and the mind that was bored should be noted again and again until they disappeared. The mind that wandered was also an object of DHAMMA, which must be noted with the practice of VIPASSANĀ.

The ability to note them should be appreciated as a good VIPASSANĀ achievement. If you had not realized that the mind had wandered, you would be led astray to endless wandering and it would be worse. Therefore, to lessen the "wanderings", you should put more effort in noting the rising, falling, sitting, touching, until the objects appear more clearly and distinctly than ever before. If you could do that, very soon your contemplation would be good. Sometimes the yogi could see clearly on the bodily sensations, like heat, cold, pain, ache, and itch.

A: Sometimes there was a bubble of air coming up.

A: Sometimes an acute pain shot up inside the abdomen and it was like being pricked by a fork or a spike or by a spear-head. It was extremely painful.

Sometimes the yogi said he was trembling and swaying. Some said they felt very heavy and very congested. It was a very tense feeling. The yogis who felt like this would talk about their experiences quite despairingly.

INSTRUCTION AND ENCOURAGEMENT: These sorts of pains or *vedanas* are not really serious. They had appeared before according to conditions, and they are ordinary ones. Before you started contemplating, you had no SAMĀDHI (concentration), so you were not aware of them. Since your concentration was good, you could clearly see the inner bodily sensations, which were always making you suffer. They were not easily detected before, only now they became clear to you. When you said you noted as "heavy", "heavy", you were able to know the true nature of the heavy body. You were practicing this meditation in order to know the true nature of these kinds of suffering. If you did not know this, you would think everything was nice and good. These *vedanas* stayed on long because your power of ÑĀNA (knowledge) was not as strong as your power of concentration. Whenever you become aware of these VEDANAS, note forcefully and ardently, so that your power of knowledge would become stronger and stronger until it could wash away those VEDANAS. Later with more practice, these would disappear completely.

Therefore, please try harder to put more effort in your noting. If you were scared of those pains and stopped noting altogether, you would have to face these VEDANAS again and again. Just force yourself deliberately to note the pain. You could overcome them. These are not serious enough to make you die. So do not be afraid. Just have full confidence that they would disappear if you could note well. Very soon you would be able to overcome them.

A: The VEDANAS would come up from different places all over the body. I could not cope with all of them. They would not disappear when I noted.

INSTRUCTION: You should not note in such a way. Instead of trying to note at random on a wide range of VEDANAS, focus on the most distinguishing pain, which was unbearable. While noting as "pain", "pain", be very arduous and note with strong will-power until the pain disappeared. Very soon it will go away.

NOTE: Here the pain due to a certain disease, and the pain occurring while meditating, are different. The pain from a disease is evident before meditation, and also evident when the noting is not good. Even if one noted the VEDANAS, it would not disappear, because the power of knowledge was still young. The pain could grow worse. On the other hand, if the yogi stopped noting, the pain was still persistent.

So, try to note the VEDANAS (due to disease or defect) if you could. If the pain was really unbearable and the yogi found it impossible to note, then do not pay attention to the pain. Ignore it altogether. Instead pay more attention to the other objects, like the rising and falling. If you could note like that you would forget about the pain, and you would feel very relieved.

For the yogi whose concentration was strong, while he was ignoring the pain, the pain due to disease would be gone completely. Even if that yogi stopped noting, the pain would not come back suddenly. There would be a pain-free period for quite some time. Only after a while the pain could come back.

Another type of VEDANA is the one which becomes dominant when the concentration is deep. It does not appear when one is not noting or before the noting is good. Even when the yogi tries to look for it, the VEDANAS would not appear. One would not know these sorts of VEDANAS exist in his body. But when the concentration is strong and the noting is good, the VEDANAS comes up. If the yogi would not note that VEDANAS and go on noting other objects, the VEDANAS would increase.

If you are afraid of something or if for any other reasons you stopped noting, the VEDANA would disappear completely. Once your noting becomes good again, the VEDANA would appear as before. If the yogi was able to note accurately on the increasing VEDANA, it would gradually decrease. And eventually it would disappear completely. If the VEDANA disappeared like that while noting on it, you would not be bothered by it again forever. This is the sign of VEDANA due to the nature of DHAMMA.

A: Even while I was resting and not noting, there was still a slight VEDANA.

COMMENT: Here the yogi said he was not noting but actually he was spontaneously aware of the VEDANA, without deliberately noting. That was why the yogi knew the VEDANA was still there. If the teacher wanted to test the yogi, try to talk on subjects, which are not connected with DHAMMA, just let him listen, or let him do some work. Then the yogi's VEDANA would vanish completely. Once the teacher had tested like this, the teacher could confidently decide that it was a VEDANA due to the nature of DHAMMA. Then tell yogi to note ardently until he could overcome the VEDANA.

The yogi who seriously followed the teacher's instructions would say thus:

A: When I felt itchy, it was not just a bit, it was all over my body. It was as if the whole body became swollen with unbearable itchiness. It was so itchy that my hands and body felt jerky. My face, my body, and my arms were so itchy, with lumps of swollen skin. I thought I might just be imagining it, so I even showed it to other people. They also said they could see the lumps of swollen skin. But I remembered my teacher's instruction to note the itchy feeling, so that it would go away. I had full faith in my teacher's instruction, so I noted without fear. I had to note for a long time, then suddenly something snapped and the swollen lumps were gone. All of the swollen points disappeared simultaneously.

A: My hands, legs and head jerked automatically. I was noting as "jerky", "jerky" and after a while my head swayed. I noted on it continuously until I felt dizzy, and the jerks disappeared.

WARNING: Yogi's head swayed a bit because of the force of PĪTI (Joy). But the yogi could not control (note) the mind which bent on the swaying action, and got carried away with the swaying. Yogi must note ardently on the swaying until it stopped. In the future, if it happened again yogi must note until he could overcome the swaying. Yogi should not ponder upon the thought that it might sway again in future.

If yogi had pondered, note as "pondering". If yogi had imagined how it would happen in future, note as "imagining". Note precisely and firmly on these mind objects.

A: My hands and legs were swaying violently as if they would fall off. It was frightful. But I remembered what my teacher said, that everything could disappear only if they are noted. So instead of getting frightened, I noted continuously and after a long time it stopped swaying.

Some said the swaying stopped after one or two hours.
Some said it went on for almost all night long and it stopped.
Some said it stopped after about one or two hours.
Some said it stayed the whole night and disappeared.

A: I could note on slight *vedanas* until they were gone. But I could not note the strong *vedanas*, so I gave up and stayed without noting.

INSTRUCTION: In future, if you felt like this, do not rest. The more often you rested, the more often you would encounter these VEDANA. Be determined to note forcefully until they disappear completely.

Actually, the VEDANA are also impermanent DHAMMA of SANKHARA: (All conditioned things which are subject to change.) The VIPASSANĀ noting/knowing bears the BODDHIPAKKAYA DHAMMA (Recollection of the 37 Factors of Enlightenment).

Our Lord BUDDHA was able to overcome deadly VEDANA by VIPASSANĀ, so the yogi should be able to fight off the meditative VEDANA very well by VIPASSANĀ. When the knowledge became fully strengthened, all these VEDANAS would disappear completely. Do not give up, just go on noting confidently.

The yogi who followed these instructions seriously would say:

A: I strictly followed my teacher's instructions and noted attentively. The *vedanas* appeared, but when I noted on them for a long time the *vedanas* decreased gradually and slowly, until finally they disappeared completely.

A: *Vedanas* such as pain or ache jerked up once or twice, but there were only a few. Sometimes I did not have to note: I just knew it was there and it disappeared. Sometimes I noted, but not for long. After noting two or three times, or sometimes four or five times, they always disappeared.

A: Sometimes I did not know why, but a vibration rippled up from my foot to the legs and shot out through my head. Sometimes the vibrations started from my head, and streamed down towards my leg. When this happened, I was frightened and gazed without remembering to note. Only afterwards I remembered to note, and those feelings were gone. Sometimes, before long the vibrations came back again with more intensity. Sometimes I had to note for quite a long time until they disappeared. But sometimes I only had to note a few times, and it was gone.

INSTRUCTION: The vibrations are the reactions of psycho-physical phenomenon due to the force of PĪTI (joy). The yogi should not be afraid of this feeling of joy, nor should they enjoy it, nor be glad about it. The yogi should note (as instructed).

A few yogis would say:

I could not find any specific VEDANA such as pain. I could not feel any vibrations. I just noted step by step as usual. After quite a long time nothing special was experienced, so I got bored and lazy.

INSTRUCTION: The yogi was thinking that the contemplation was considered to be good only if he could experience extraordinary things. He did not realize that his noting was good, so he was in despair. Therefore, ask the yogi whether they could notice the beginning and the end of each of all the objects every time they noted. Encourage them until they become enthusiastic.

ENCOURAGEMENT: The noting on the painful VEDANA was VIPASSANĀ. Knowing about the vibrations was also VIPASSANĀ. Noting and knowing about the rising and falling was also VIPASSANĀ. By noting the yogi knew that the pain and the vibrations came up, ended abruptly and disappeared; thus, they were all impermanent. (ANICCA NUPASSANA ÑĀNA).

While noting on the rising and falling, the yogi knew that they appeared, disappeared and ended. The Knowledge which knew about the impermanent nature of rising and falling would be called ANICCA NUPASSANA ÑĀNA. Whatever object yogi noted, the most important thing is to be able to note the objects from the beginning to the end, and to know each individual object distinctly. So long as the yogis discovered the same facts, their knowledge would be the same. There is no difference. All are DHAMMA leading to MAGGA PHALA NIBBĀNA:

COMMENT: If yogi was able to note while the objects were appearing, he would know that they disappeared, once they were noted. So, yogi came to know that all the objects were not good and worthy; the yogi who realized this fact knew the real sign of DUKKHA, and his knowledge would be called DUKKHA NUPASSANA ÑĀNA.

When the yogi realized that all the objects appeared and disappeared independently, that nothing happened as the yogi wished, that they were all uncontrollable phenomena, the yogi's knowledge would be the real sign of ANATTA NUPASSANA ÑĀNA.

Once the yogi had fully accomplished these three ÑĀNAS, he could reach NIBBĀNA: The yogis who noted on the outstanding VEDANA or the other feelings like vibrations had reached MAGGA PHALA NIBBĀNA, and were liberated from the conditioned suffering.

Thus, the yogi should not contemplate expecting to find special experiences. Those extraordinary objects or visions are not common for everybody. Therefore, yogi might not experience it. Very often yogi would not see it. The unbearable pains made noting even more difficult, so you should not expect anything. Just make a resolution to note whatever appeared, so that after each noting, you know about it very clearly. Note ardently and accurately on the rising and falling and the other bodily sensations which are dominant.

A: When I was bending, I knew the beginning, the moment while bending, and the end of bending. I could say that the bending process happened slowly, inch by inch. But I could not say that the whole process was a series of "bendings." It was the same with stretching.

COMMENT: This type of report usually comes from a yogi with little knowledge.

A: Each time I bent, I noted "bending", "bending"; then I found the bending process was a chain of four or five bends. It was the same with stretching.

A: I noted five or six times as "bending"; after each noting there was an abrupt end and bended about five or six times. It was the same with stretching.

COMMENT: This sort of remark was made by a yogi with an intelligent or matured knowledge.

Some yogi could describe their experiences of how distinctly they could note on the rising and falling, but they could not note accurately on the bending and stretching, thus they would say:

A: Most of the time I still could not note carefully on the bending and stretching. Even if I could note on these acts, I just knew it was one bending each time I bent. I could not differentiate each bending into parts.

INSTRUCTIONS: Pay special attention not to miss all the actions of the body and note ardently on them. If you noted ardently, you would know very clearly and distinctly, like you did in noting the rising and falling. If you had not noted ardently and noted flippantly, the progress of your knowledge would be slow.

ON WALKING MEDITATION:

A: While noting lifting, pushing, placing, I found that the lifting process was one thing, pushing another thing and placing yet another separate thing. One part did not combine with another part. They just fell off bit by bit, and ended one by one.

A: The lifting was one thing, the mind which knew about lifting was another. Pushing was one thing, and the mind that knew the leg had pushed was another. The placing was one thing, and the mind that knew about placing was another. Every time I noted I could discriminate between the objects.

A: I noted "lifting" when my heel was lifting. When I raised the foot from the floor, I noted "raising". When I was pushing the leg, I noted "pushing". When I was putting the foot down, before my leg actually touched the floor, I noted as "placing", "placing". When the foot touched the floor, I noted "touching", "touching". When I pressed the foot on the floor, I noted "pressing", "pressing".

NOTE: Those who could note in this way (6 part noting), could discriminate between lifting, raising, pushing, placing (putting), touching, pressing. Yogi knew them clearly as separate, individual events. Although this kind of 6-part noting is not shown in the (ATTHAKATHA) commentary, the main purpose of yogi is to know clearly about the object (the individuality of each action of the foot), and to know that each of them were segmented and finally disappeared. Thus, the yogi knew about their impermanence.

So it isn't wrong to note in such a way. It is in agreement with the 6-part noting shown in the commentary. The yogi who could note in such a way has reached the matured stage of SAMMASANA ÑĀNA.

A: Whenever I noted "lifting, pushing, placing", I could not say I knew each part clearly. Sometimes I could notice all the parts very clearly.

WARNING: If you were able to note accurately, you could discriminate parts of your noting very clearly; so, warn the yogi to note ardently.

As the yogi was noting on the various objects appearing, sometimes the yogi noticed that each time he noted, he saw the objects appeared and disappeared, thus he knew clearly that they were impermanent. Sometimes the yogi noticed clearly that the way the objects appeared and disappeared was an awful suffering. Sometimes the yogi noticed that nothing happened as he wished, that things happened and dissolved as they wished, thus uncontrollable and selfless. There is no being, but just the nature of phenomena.

A: Every time I noted I noticed The Knowledge on the Impermanence, Suffering and Uncontrollable Self-less Nature following closely.

TEST AND INSTRUCTION: When you knew/liked the fact that everything was impermanent, did it occur to you spontaneously while noting? Did you bend your mind on that fact and imagine it deliberately? If the yogi said it occurred to him naturally, the teacher should decide that the yogi's knowledge was PACCAKKHA ÑĀNA (evident knowledge). If a yogi had deliberately thought about it or imagined it, the teacher should forbid him. If yogi had recollected on the impermanence, he should note that too.

A: In the past similar conditions with the ANICCA (impermanence), DUKKHA (suffering) and ANATTA (uncontrollable), there was no substantial self or soul. It was just that I did not realize like I do now. Likewise in the future, things are going to be impermanent, prone to suffering and non-self-controllable. (Thus, the yogi was pleased with his knowledge while he was noting.)

TEST AND GUIDANCE: Find out from yogi whether he has noticed this (reflecting on ANICCA, DUKKHA and ANATTA in the past, present and future) after discovering about them (ANICCA, DUKKHA, ANATTA) spontaneously while he was noting. If it was so, his knowledge would be ANUMANA ÑĀNA (imaginative knowledge) which was the continuation of the present insight knowledge gained at the moment of noting. If the yogi had been pleased with his knowledge, tell him to note that too. If yogi had been thinking, reflecting deliberately without noting at all, tell him that he should never do it. He should never imagine or recollect deliberately without noting that imagination or recollection.

SUMMARY: While noting on the objects of NĀMA- RŪPA, which were clearly evident at the present moment, the yogi came to know that the objects were just arising and passing away, and thus, impermanent; the objects were not reliable but just sufferings; that there is no being, but just phenomena of nature.

The yogi saw things as they really were, and appreciated his knowledge thus:

All entities of NĀMA- RŪPA had the nature of ANICCA (impermanence).

All were arising and immediately passing away. They were not worthy enough to cling to, therefore they bear the nature of DUKKHA (suffering).

All were uncontrollable, happening against one's wish, so in these phenomena of NĀMA- RŪPA, there is no such thing as a being self, soul or ego (ANATTA).

The yogi who could appreciate or decide himself on the above-mentioned knowledge, had achieved the SAMMASANA ÑĀNA (the Knowledge that Investigates, Observes, Explores, Grasps or Determines).

(END OF SAMMASANA ÑĀNA)

E. UDAYABBAYA ÑĀNA (The Knowledge Aware of the Arising and Passing Away Phenomena)

The yogi who attained this level of knowledge usually described their feelings with much joy and excitement.

A: I was able to note all the objects that appeared. My noting was very light and swift. It was going quite fast and it was very nice to note.

WARNING:
Q: Can you describe what it was like to be nice?

A: I could note as usual on rising, falling, sitting, touching, accurately and rarely missed. I could also note the outstanding objects which appeared in between the noting on rising, falling, sitting, touching. There was continuity in my notings. My noting and the mindfulness were so good that I could not possibly describe it. The noting was very light and swift and very enjoyable. I did not forget to note, and there was nothing that I could not note.

A: Some objects appeared faint; they seemed like the carriages of a train moving rapidly. They were like shadows moving along the sides. Besides there were "flickering", "fluttering" sensations all over the body. I would experience those sensations quite often, and I had to note quite a long time on them. Sometimes there were some kinds of pain which emerged with jerks. The moment the pain appeared with a jerk I could note instantly. It was a well-aimed, straight hit on the target.

Sometimes when I missed noting, I could even note as "missing". I could note fast and my noting was very good. Now there is nothing that I could not note. I think I could note on everything. I think I could note even on the rain drops. When I moved my hands and legs or made any other bodily actions, I could note them all. If I moved a bit, I was mindful. If I wanted to change my posture, I could note the mind which wanted to change the moment it was formed. I could also note on the intending mind. Wherever my mind went I could follow it, noting accurately. I could even note on the intention to go, whatever happened, the noting mind automatically fell straight on to the object of happening. The object appeared very clearly in my mind.

COMMENT: The yogi would explain his good experience in noting like that. The yogi's explanation was in fact UPPATHANA UPPAKILASA, i.e., Impurity of mind due to attachment to fixed mindfulness.

A: Previously, when I felt good in my contemplation it was nothing like this. Now it is really good. I even thought if I had to note until these good notings disappear, I will not bother to note them.

(Yogi said this because he has a clinging on Craving.)

SOME YOGI WOULD TELL OTHERS:

A: I do not think there is anyone who could note as well as me. I do not even think the teachers themselves had this sort of enjoyable noting. (Yogi said this with a clinging to pride.)

A: I thought to myself my awareness was very sharp and my noting was very good. (Yogi said this with a clinging to false doctrine.)

A: Now that I am so good in my noting and mindfulness, I must be achieving a special DHAMMA. What people say about the DHAMMA being good or become expert in DHAMMA, must be referred to what I am experiencing now. I shall stop contemplating now. I shall try for higher levels later on. (Yogi said this with a clinging to the wrong MAGGA, not the Path.)

A: The noting and knowing mind was moving very quickly and very clearly. I was aware of everything that was to be noted. I could note the slightest sensations inside the body, I could note them individually.

A: The noting and the knowing mind were like a rotating fan, really quick. Whenever I changed my body posture or made any bodily actions, I could note all the movements step by step.

A: If I swung a ring of beads round my wrist, I could feel the touch of each bead on my skin. It was like that with my noting, I could note each and individual object.

A: Previously I thought the itch and the pain were linked. But now, when I noted "itchy", "painful" two or three times each, I noted that each noting was a separate thing.

A: The pain or VEDANA did not last long like before. If I noted once or twice the pain was gone altogether. But sometimes there were sudden shots of pain, like being pricked by a needle. It was quite uncomfortable, I felt jerky and slightly shocked. Sometimes, as soon as the pain was there I knew instantly that it was there; the pain and the noting hit each other with accurate timing. Then the pain disappeared instantly.

A: Previously when I was saying "ANICCA, DUKKHA, ANATTA", they were just words; only now I really understand. Nothing lasted long. Every time I noted, the objects disappeared. I noticed that objects were arising and passing away. They were all unstable, thus they were not worthy enough to cling to; they were all miserable sufferings. Previously I did not think there would be endless suffering inside my body.

A: Now I found suffering pain inside my body occurring continuously. Previously I thought there was a permanent being whose body could last forever. Now I found that whenever I noted I just found the nature of phenomena, nothing else. Only now I knew there were only nature of phenomena.

A: Before I meditated, I had heard other people say that just noting on "rising" "falling" "stretching" etc., would not lead to VIPASSANĀ insight, and ANICCA, DUKKHA and ANATTA would not be known. I had thought like that too. Now I understand about this practice, and I am able to appreciate it. Those people who said VIPASSANĀ insight could not be gained by just noting did not know anything about it. They were all totally wrong. This practice of noting is an excellent work. Each time one noted, one could discriminate each object clearly from the other. The way objects appeared and disappeared was clear, as if they were held out by hand. The impermanent, suffering and ego-less nature of objects were known every time I noted. I wanted to go and talk about my experiences to those people who said insight would not be gained by just noting.

A: Previously when I was noting on hearing, each time I noted, only the sound ended. (Yogi meant the sound stopped and disintegrated.) Later on, whenever I noted on hearing the various sounds, the moment the sound ended I found that I had finished noting. The timing was very exact (yogi meant the sound and the noting ended together). Whenever I noted ardently and accurately nothing lasted. All the objects I noted were thrust away, they always disappeared.

A: Whenever I noted rising, falling, sitting, touching, I knew very distinctly and clearly of their individual occurrences. When my noting was good like that, I gained knowledge thus: "What I knew from my notings were evidence of mental and physical phenomena. None of these were permanent. They were all impermanent. None of these happened as I wished; therefore, they were all uncontrollable.

Whatever happened were like this. There was nothing that lasted. (Yogi meant nothing was permanent, nothing existed as an enjoyable object, and that nothing lasted as an ultimate being.)

A: There is nothing ever-lasting in this human world, nor in the celestial world, nor in the BRAHMA world. Wherever I looked there was nothing left. I just knew that there was nothing. (Yogi knew and liked the fact that in human world, and celestial world and BRAHMA world, there existed only the mental/physical phenomena. There is only the nature of ANICCA, DUKKHA and ANATTA.) Therefore, what I thought before as a being who was NICCA (permanent), SUKKHA (pleasant) and ATTA (controllable self) was actually non-existent.

(This sort of remark was made by a yogi with little ÑĀNA)

A: What I knew before I contemplated was all wrong. Only now I came to know the truth completely. Previously I did not know anything, only now my knowledge has progressed.

A: When I noted "hot", "hot", as soon as I noted and knew the hotness both the noting mind and the hotness disappeared completely. I also knew that the "hotness" was due to TEJO, the element of heat. (All these descriptions were ÑĀNA UPAKKILESA, which in fact are 47 impurities of mind, which arose from the knowledge gained.)

DISCOVERING ABOUT THE NOTING AND KNOWING MIND

A: I was very pleased because my noting and knowing were quite extraordinary. I even wished that every time I contemplated, I could experience this sort of noting and knowing. I thought if I could experience this kind of knowledge, I would never be bored in contemplation. (The yogi spoke like this because he was clinging to TANHĀ, craving.)

A: I wonder if there would be anyone who had good experience in contemplation like me. I thought to myself that if I told this to others, they would not believe me. I wonder whether the teachers had this kind of experience or not. (Yogi was clinging to MĀNA pride.)

A: I have attained special knowledge quite wholesomely; I have the power to know everything. (Yogi was clinging to DITTHI, false doctrine.)

A: I thought to myself, what some people referred to as DHAMMA being good must be this, what I am experiencing now; this must be the special DHAMMA. I must have achieved an extraordinary DHAMMA, since I was experiencing good contemplation. I knew clearly of ANICCA, DUKKHA and ANATTA: I have attained an extraordinary DHAMMA. I have penetrated through DHAMMA. I am free of DITTHI, false doctrine and VICIKICCHA, doubt, uncertainty. Now I have become a SOTAPANNA. (Yogi was clinging to the wrong MAGGA, not the Path.)

A: Now I really know everything. Previously, I listened to discourses but I could not understand as well as this. Now everything was very clear, as if each of them was held out on my hand. There was nothing for me to worry about, and there was no need to worry about other people. Besides, I was not enjoying the goodness in contemplation. I did not want to do bad deeds and misconduct. I thought to myself "This sort of knowledge must be what people referred to as achieving special DHAMMA. What I know now must indeed be the special DHAMMA." (Yogi was clinging to the wrong MAGGA, not the Path.)

OBHASA UPAKKILESA:

A: While my noting was good, I saw bright colors and rays of light, so I noted "bright", "bright". I was noting like that because the teachers had said all the objects which appeared would have to be noted. But in my mind, I was liking it. The brightness would not go away in spite of my noting. It stayed on. When I sat in the meditation hall, it was all bright. I think, "If I contemplated now, I would see those bright lights again."

A: There were different kinds of light, I could even see myself. The meditation hall seemed as if there was no roof, nor walls. It was plain space and I could see through the hall. The places which I had lived before or had been before seemed to have appeared in front of me.

A: When I opened my eyes and looked, the brightness would not go away suddenly. I could see it for quite a long time.

A: Last night I saw lights so I held up my hand just to see whether it was

18. MEDITATION TEACHER'S RECORD BOOK

real. I could see the spaces in between the fingers. When I looked at the door, it was so bright I thought the doors were open. But when I went to the door, I found it was shut.

A: The brightness seemed like the beam of light from a torch held in front of me.

A: There was a flash of light like the front lights of a car.

A: The whole room was brilliant with lights.

A: It was very bright up to a distance of about a hundred to two hundred yards in front of my eyes. I could even see the dirt and the sand.

A: A ball of bright light came straight into my eyes.

A: The brightness which appeared in front of my eyes was like a whirling disc.

A: I saw brightness from the roof. It was as if the moon was shining.

A: Bright colors came out from my body.

A: Light came from above, below, at the sides from the front, from the back, etc.

(Yogis described the brightness, according to their individual experiences, which were signs of OBHASA UPPAKILESA: As a result of keen insight Aura radiated from yogi's body (OBHASA) and as yogi was enjoying it, the enjoying mind became an impediment to the progress of Insight Knowledge.)

A: When I saw the bright lights, I was so happy that I could not go on noting.

A: I noted but I was pleased with the brightness. It would not disappear in spite of my noting.

A: When I saw the bright lights, I was quite pleased. I was even enjoying it.

A: As instructed I was noting on whatever object appeared, but to be quite honest, I would not like the brightness to disappear. (Yogi was clinging to TANHA, craving).

A: Perhaps I was the only one to experience such brightness. I do not think the others had had such an extraordinary experience like mine. (Yogi was clinging to MĀNA, pride).

A: I am full of bright lights; these must be radiating from my body. (Yogi was clinging to DITTHI, false doctrine).

A: The brightness was NIBBĀNA, the mind that noted it was

MAGGA. There was brightness because I attained an outstanding DHAMMA. (Yogi was clinging to the wrong MAGGA, not the Path).

PĪTI (Joy)

A: While my noting was swift and the contemplation was good, I felt something seep down from my head through my body to my legs. It was a soothing sensation which flashed off and on. Sometimes when my noting was good, a soothing chill passed through my body, and I felt as if I was swung gently. (Yogi was experiencing KHUDDIKA PĪTI, minor joy).

A: Sometimes I felt continuous vibrations, cool thrills and as if being swung gently again and again. (Yogi was experiencing KHANIKA PĪTI, momentary joy).

A: Sometimes I felt the soothing coolness and vibrations coming up from the legs, and when they reached up to the chest, they disappeared. Sometimes it reached up to the throat, then head, and disappeared.

A: Sometimes I felt as if all of a sudden, I was showered by cold/coldness (or) heat/hotness, and then it disappeared.

A: Sometimes something fluttered up from inside until my whole body was full of flickering feelings, then everything cleared up (This was a description of OKKANTIKA PĪTI, showering joy).

A: Sometimes I felt my body was bloated, then I felt as if I was sleeping on waves, or swung on a hammock. It was nice.

A I felt as if my body was flying near the ceiling.

A: I felt as if I was riding in the air. It was nice.

A: While sitting, my body was moving up.

A: While I was walking, I noted lifting, placing. I felt like I was walking on a spring, it felt very light to walk.

A: When I was sitting and noting, I thought the whole meditation hall was swaying.

A: Sometimes when my contemplation was especially good, I felt as if I was unconscious. And then I was conscious again: It was like being emerged from under water. And I could still note very well, like before.

A: I felt I was asleep, but I was not actually asleep.

A: When I was lying down and noting I felt as if my body was not touching the bed. My body was moving back and forth. It was like being rocked gently. (All these descriptions meant OKKANTIKA PĪTI, showering joy.)

A: While I was lying down, I put both hands on my belly, and placed one foot on top of the other. I noted "rising" "falling" "lying" "touching". When my noting was very good, I felt gentle vibrations about 3 or 4 times. Then suddenly I felt as if both of my hands were pulled out and dropped on the floor. Also, my foot, which was lying on top of the other, was thrust down to the floor.

A: During my sitting meditation my body felt as if it was lifted up, and I think it moved upwards two or three times.

A: When I was sitting and noting I felt a soothing chill run through my body about three or four times, then still in my sitting posture I hopped forward to a distance of about four or five feet. The people near me were frightened. When my body in sitting posture jumped up like that, I did not feel pain.

A: When I was lying down on the right side of my body, suddenly it changed to the left side by itself. Sometimes I was lying down on my side, and the body changed position by itself to lie on the back.

A: Sometimes my hands or feet were stretched automatically from a bent position. Sometimes the stretched hands or feet were bent automatically. They happened so suddenly I could not note. I could only remember after they happened.

A: When I was sitting and noting, only my head felt jerky. Sometimes I felt pushed from behind so that my body leaned forward. Sometimes I felt as if someone felt my head and turned it left and right; my head seemed like it was being spun.

A: I only felt jerks in my mouth. Sometimes the closed mouth was swung open so that it was gaping by itself.

A: Sometimes my upper and lower set of teeth chattered; (The yogi's experience was UBBEGA PĪTI – uplifting happiness).

A: When I was noting very well, something heaved up inside my body and stayed still in the chest. Sometimes it went out through the mouth, my whole body felt as if some sort of soothing vibration was passing through me. That sensation was so pleasant I did not want to open my eyes, I did not even want a flicker of my eyelids to happen. In my whole life I had never experienced this sort of pleasant sensation. It was sheer luxury.

A: There were slight vibrations in my body, then the whole body felt as if it was receiving a soothing vibration.

A: After contemplating for a while, there were flashes of subtle vibrations inside my body. My whole body felt so nice with soothing and gentle thrill and rocking. I just could not describe it fully. It was really good. (The yogi had felt PHARANA PĪTI – pervading, rapturous joy).

A: I felt soothing thrills from my waist and above.

A: I felt a thrill running from my waist downwards.

A: Sometimes the upper and sometimes the lower part of the body felt a soothing thrill. (The yogi meant KHUDDIKA PĪTI – minor joy.)

A: The thrills I felt in my body and in my chest were very pleasant. I just felt so good. It was not just nice; it was really marvelous. If I were to note this until it disappeared, I would not like to go on noting.

A: I felt as if I was swaying gently, many times. It was really good. (The yogi was clinging to craving.)

A: The endless thrills rippling in my body was so good, I did not think the others felt as good as me. (The yogi was clinging to pride.)

A: The soothing thrills were from my own body. (The yogi was clinging to DITTHI – false doctrine).

A: What some people describe as 'the DHAMMA being good', 'discovering DHAMMA', 'attaining special DHAMMA' must be referring to these sorts of pleasant, thrilling sensations. (This yogi is clinging to the wrong MAGGA – not the Path).

PASSADHI (Tranquility)

A: Sometimes my whole body felt very peaceful and tranquil. It was very good to contemplate.

A: I felt pleasant thrills in my chest and my body, I felt very peaceful and content. It was very good like that.

A: Some said: I felt so peaceful and so tranquil that I stayed without noting for about one or two hours; I was just enjoying that peaceful feeling.

A: Sometimes I felt so peaceful and so rich with pleasant feelings that I could not note at all; I just gazed.

A: I was gazing quite often and I remembered to note only after some time. Then suddenly I got startled, and I went on noting as usual.

A: I felt really peaceful and tranquil in my mind and body.

A: I was feeling peaceful and pleasant in my mind and body. I stayed on like that for quite a while.

A: I did not have to note as ardently as before. My mind did not wander at all. I contemplated for a long time without moving and without losing continuity. My noting was very good, although I did not have to note with special care. My mind was very still, and stayed on as peaceful as ever. (This is the description of PASSADHI – tranquility).

LAHUTĀ (Lightness of Mind)

A: My mind was moving very swiftly and lightly.

A: My mind and my body were very light and swift; I was noting very peacefully and pleasantly.

A: Previously, the objects were coming fast and my noting was slow. Now my noting mind was very active and quick. My body felt very light. I thought to myself that if I were to travel now, I would be able to go a long way within a short time.

A: While I was walking and noting as lifting, pushing, placing, I felt very light. I felt so light I did not even think I had legs. My notings were very easy and light. My notings were so subtle that it seemed as if they were not there. And it seemed as if I could not note accurately. When I noted with more attentive effort, the notings were always accurate. The noting mind never missed the target object.

A: When I was noting while walking both my mind and body felt so light that I even wanted to run.

A: I felt like running, so I ran but I kept on noting. I could note all (This is a description of LAHUTĀ – lightness of mind which is associated with PASSADHI).

MUDUTA (Pliancy of Mind)

A: I felt so subtle in my mind and body, it was very nice to...

A: Previously, if I wanted my mind to stay in one place, it would not stay; the mind went out as it wished. Now my mind was automatically noting on each object that appeared. My mind stayed where I wanted it to stay, and it was very tamed and gentle.

A: My mind and body were very gentle in a sublime state. I did not want to meet anybody, I did not feel like talking, I did not want to hear other people talking. I did not want to see or hear anything. I just wanted to stay in the meditating hall and go on contemplating quietly. (The yogi was explaining about MUDUTA, which is parallel to Tranquility PASSADHI)

KAMMAÑÑATTĀ (Workableness or Serviceableness)

A: Now both my mind and body were very strong and consolidated. I could stay still for a long time without changing posture. My mind did not wander, I did not forget to note, nor had I slackened in noting. I could note in continuity for a long time. (The yogi's description was KAMMAÑÑATTĀ – Parallel to PASSADDHI)

PĀGUÑÑATĀ (Proficiency or Skillfulness)

A: It was very good to note. It was as if I was reciting the verses I had learnt very well. I could note easily and smoothly without being tired, mentally and physically. All my previous thoughts and ideas had vanished. (This is PĀGUÑÑATĀ – Parallel to PASSADHI).

UJJUKATA (Straightness or Rectitude)

COMMENT: Some people who had lived a rough life after reaching this level of knowledge would say: "Previously I had done bad deeds because I was ignorant of this knowledge. The Dhamma is very gentle. In future I would never commit bad unwholesome deeds (AKUSALAS) again." This sort of yogi would admit honestly to their teacher about their past actions. (This is comparable to PASSADHI).

COMMENT: If the yogi thought the peacefulness, swiftness and lightness of the body and mind were good and enjoyed it thoroughly, the yogi got a clinging to craving. If the yogi thought that only he was experiencing the extraordinary happenings, the yogi got a clinging to pride.

If the yogi thought he himself was feeling peaceful, the yogi got a clinging to DITTHI (False Doctrine). If the yogi thought "This peaceful condition is the DHAMMA, I must be achieving a special DHAMMA, that is why I am feeling light", he is clinging to the wrong MAGGA (i.e., Not the Path).

SUKHA

A: My mind and body felt so peaceful and I felt waves of satisfaction inside my chest. I felt so good. I had never had this sort of wealth before in my life. It was so good I could not really describe it in words.

A: While I was noting, my heart suddenly jumped up a bit and I felt a pleasant soothing thrill which enriched my pre-existing feeling of pleasantness. Sometimes there was a long chain of rhythmic beats, and there was a continuous flow of thrills. It was very nice to note. Sometimes the waves of thrills were so good I did not want to go on noting.

A: It was so good while noting, I felt very happy. Now I really enjoy my contemplation. Now every time I noted I felt really good. Now I do not want to let go of my noting. I never felt happy like this before. I was even afraid I would go crazy by being overjoyed. (The yogi's description was SUKHA UPPAKILASA – happiness causing impurity of mind).

A: It was good to note and I was enjoying the feeling of richness in my mind and body. They were very good. I never felt like this before.

I could enjoy it only now. I would not like to note until they disappear. I noted the feeling only because my teacher had told me to note. I felt really wonderful, it was great. I want to enjoy this feeling of peaceful richness for at least a day. (The yogi was clinging to craving).

A: I wonder if the teacher had an experience like this. (The yogi was clinging to pride.)

A: I am experiencing a rich and pleasant feeling like I had never felt before. I am full of rich feelings. I am enjoying all of them. I am very happy. (Yogi was clinging to false doctrine, DITTHI).

COMMENT: The yogi thought that the peaceful feeling he had felt was the special DHAMMA. He thought he was feeling very peaceful because he had achieved special DHAMMA. Yogi may not speak it out but he usually thinks like that. The teachers could find out by asking questions.

A: This must be the special DHAMMA. I do not think there is anything which is better or more peaceful than this feeling. (Yogi's description showed he was clinging to the wrong MAGGA, not the Path).

ADDHIMOKKHA SADDHA (Determined Faith)

A: Now every time I noted, there were no impurities in my mind; it was very fresh and clear, sometimes there was nothing dominant enough to note. There was just this clear, clean mind. So, I noted "knowing", "knowing" and "clear", "clear" for quite a long time.

A: I felt some kind of energy coming up like waves and I was noting it. While I was noting very well, I suddenly felt as if I was unconscious, and everything turned out to be an empty clear space. There was nothing special to note. My mind was very clean and tranquil. It went on about an hour, and stayed like that until and unless I wanted to scrape it off.

A: The object and the noting mind hit each other and got stuck in pairs. When I was aware of the arising and passing away of objects, I became extremely devoted to Buddha. I just wanted to bow down and pay respect to Buddha again and again.

A: Now I know the impermanence or the arising and passing away of the mental and physical phenomena. It was like what BUDDHA said. BUDDHA knew the truth about everything, I respected BUDDHA more than ever.

A: The DHAMMA I am experiencing now is the true DHAMMA. I should practice this continuously for many months and years; it would be better still if I could practice it my whole life. Even though I had practiced for a few days my contemplation was good. I now have more respect and faith in this practice of DHAMMA which produces immediate results. (SANDITTHIKA DHAMMA).

A: Now I can appreciate this DHAMMA very well. Now I truly respect and believe in DHAMMA. People who said that just noting on the rising, falling, bending, stretching would not make one understand about ANNICCA, DUKKHA and ANATTA were ignorant of the truth. Now I really like this DHAMMA. I am going to practice this throughout my life; even if I were to die, I would practice.

A: Those people who had been preaching to others that if one just recites the DHAMMA or know about DHAMMA is sufficient were the people who had not practiced themselves. They were all wrong. One would never understand the truth about ANICCA, DUKKHA and ANATTA, the nature of the mind and matter, if one had not practiced. With enough practice, one could know the truth, and the defilements would be extinguished completely.

A: Previously I did not respect the meditators like I do now. Now I fully respect the people who are practicing DHAMMA. I felt that even I could nearly overcome the boredom and had improved my knowledge; similarly, those people who had meditated must have contemplated well like me, until they knew about the arising and passing away of all phenomena. I believe they must have attained the ultimate MAGGA PHALA NIBBĀNA through such knowledge. I also admire and respect those people who had contemplated.

A: I have never known this kind of DHAMMA and yet I could understand the true nature of mind and matter, the arising and passing away phenomena; the ANICCA, DUKKHA AND ANATTA clearly. This is because I had the chance to practice according to the instructions given by Mahasi Sayadaw Payagyi. If I had not had this chance, I would never have experienced this kind of DHAMMA. Sayadaw Payagyi himself had practiced this difficult and profound DHAMMA, and had worked out instructions which could be understood by everyone. I was thinking of the enormous respect and gratitude I felt towards Sayadaw Payagyi for quite a long time, and quite often too.

A: I contemplated day and night, but when the time comes for discussion with my teacher, I could not relate all of my experiences in detail, and not in a systematic way. But the teacher seemed to know the facts which I had overlooked in the description of my experiences. The teacher seemed to know what I could note and what I had missed. The teacher must have practiced and accomplished the knowledge fully. That must be the reason why he could know all the stages I had been going through. Then I felt very respectful towards my teacher. I went on admiring my teacher for how much he knew; how well he could help me when I was wrong; how patient he was in explaining to me about the things that I did not understand; and how he was helping me to make progress in contemplation. I thought to myself that if it were not for the teacher, it would be impossible for me to go on with this practice. I felt forever indebted to the teacher. I wondered how I could repay the gratitude I owe to my teacher. I resolved to do this by all means. (Yogi felt very grateful to the meditation teacher, and expressed his feeling in the above way.)

A: I felt respectful and grateful to my teacher. I kept on seeing him, and I had to note "seeing", "seeing" for quite a long time. My mind often went to my teacher, so I had to note "respecting", "respecting" quite often.

A: Now I had practiced and had gained a fair amount of knowledge, but my parents and relatives had died without knowing anything about DHAMMA. If only they were alive today, they would practice like me. Now that they were dead, they had no chance. When I remembered how they had missed such valuable DHAMMA, I felt very sad; later there were tears rolling down, and I actually cried.

A: I was thinking of how I could persuade my relatives and friends to practice this meditation. If I explained it to them, I am sure they would agree to practice. I am sure they would really practice hard.

COMMENT: The yogi admitted to the teacher how often he planned to encourage other people to practice DHAMMA. This was because the yogi believed that this DHAMMA would surely take him to MAGGA PHALA NIBBĀNA. His faith in DHAMMA was reaching a zenith point. This is called ADDHIMOKKHA UPAKKILESA (Impurity of mind due to a well-established faith in DHAMMA).

A: Previously I did not know how to cultivate the respect for BUDDHA,

DHAMMA, SANGHA and the teachers. But now I really know how it is like to feel respectful. I feel happy just to be respectful. Actually, the feeling of respect is a good deed (KUSALA). It is appreciable. So, why should I note that feeling? Some people had to try hard to appreciate the feeling of respect. Why should the teachers tell us to note until this feeling is gone? Now every time I noted my mind was clear. I felt good. (Yogi was clinging to TANHĀ, craving).

A: I do not think the others felt as respectful as me. I think I have more faith than the others. (Yogi was clinging to MĀNA, pride.)

A: I have full faith in Dhamma, my mind is clear, I know how to appreciate the feeling of respect. (Yogi was clinging to DITTHI, false doctrine.)

A: When my mind was clear, I must be experiencing the real DHAMMA. I think the special DHAMMA must be able to make one's mind clear. The stable feeling of respect I am experiencing must be the special DHAMMA. (Yogi was clinging to the wrong MAGGA, not the Path).

PAGGAHA VIRIYA (Ascending, Increasing Effort)

A: Previously I was deliberately trying hard to note well, yet it was not good. Now I did not have to note hard; I just noted everything that appeared. Yet I could note them one by one and my contemplation did not become slackened. It was good all the time.

A: It was very good to contemplate on various objects. I was not lazy at all. I could not help noting continuously.

A: Now my effort in contemplation is not like before. I made more effort. I did not rest at all. I just wanted to make more and more effort. (Yogi had PAGGAHA UPAKKILESA, Impurity of mind due to over-energetic effort).

COMMENT: The yogi liked the ability to note easily and continuously without much effort, without being lazy and could note strongly. (Yogi was clinging to TANHĀ, craving.)

A: I could contemplate better than others, I do not think there would be others who could contemplate as well as me. (Yogi was clinging to MĀNA, pride).

A: I could contemplate continuously, I was not lazy, my effort in contemplation was perfect. (Yogi was clinging to DITTHI, false doctrine).

A: The fact that I could note in continuity must be the special DHAMMA. When one achieved that special DHAMMA, one would never be lazy and could note continuously. (Yogi was clinging to the wrong MAGGA, not the Path).

UPEKKHA (Equanimity)

A: In the beginning even though I tried hard in contemplation I could not note the objects accurately. Most of the time I missed the target in my notings. I did not know clearly and distinctly about each object. Now whatever object appeared I could note instantly and accurately without having to make a special effort. I did not miss anything. Each noting was a separate entity. When I was noting on various sounds, I notice that as soon as the sound ended, I had finished noting. It was a perfect timing. Previously I thought about the beginning and end of the arising and passing away of the objects; I also made a mental analysis of ANICCA, DUKKHA and ANATTA. But I never understood clearly. Now I did not even have to think; just by noting I came to know very clearly about the beginning and end, the arising and passing away, the appearances and disappearances, ANICCA, DUKKHA and ANATTA. (Yogi was reflecting on VIPASSANĀ with AVIJJA NUPEKHA).

A: I do not think that my contemplation at the moment is not as good as before. Nor could I say that it was better. There was no need to be lazy, nor happy. It was neither hateful nor sad. I could not say it was enjoyable or not enjoyable. It was just a neutral feeling. I was simply noting well. Each time I noted the object was clear and well-focused. I was contemplating very quietly and very still.

(Yogi was experiencing TATRA MIJJHATTATA UPPEKKHA, Impartial indifference or Equanimity of mind on objects.)

COMMENT: If the yogi felt pleased with such a good contemplation, there would be a clinging to Craving. If the yogi thought he was the only person who was experiencing like that, he had a clinging to Pride. If yogi thought he could contemplate well without making much effort and noting with indifferent feelings, he would be clinging to False Doctrine. If yogi thought the ability to note easily and calmly was the experience of special DHAMMA, he would be clinging to the wrong MAGGA.

NIKANTI

(Delicate form of craving or attachment arising from the satisfaction of one's own good experience in contemplation.)

A: Now I could note very swiftly and my notings were quick and good, I felt very happy to contemplate. I saw bright lights and I was very impressed and happy. Now I felt so happy in noting, I just want to go on noting forever.

A: Previously I did not understand when people said it was good to note; I just felt tired and bored. Now I know very well how it is like to be good in noting. Now I can really appreciate the DHAMMA and the BHĀVANĀ wonderfully.

A: I was very happy because I felt very good to note and I saw bright lights. I was experiencing the sort of happiness which I had never experienced before. No matter what the teacher said, I am afraid this feeling would disappear, and I would hate to part with this kind of happiness. I would not like to note this wonderful happiness until it disappeared. I just wanted to enjoy it fully, even if it was for a day.

A: After experiencing the bright lights it was very good to note on all the different objects. Suddenly I felt really peaceful and comfortable. It had a cooling and blissful effect on me. Then I felt happy, as I thought of noting that happy mind, there was nothing to note at all. Then I thought, "Oh, I had lost all my notings. Everything was gone, the good experience had finished, things have come to an end — and I did not have anything to do anymore." After thinking like that I suggested my fellow-yogis to work hard with more effort in contemplation. I told them to be determined, to contemplate hard day and night, even if they have to face death. (This is NIKANTI UPAKKILESA, Impurity of Mind due to the appreciation of a good contemplation).

COMMENT: In the above description the fact that the yogi was indulging in the happiness gained from the contemplation meant there was a clinging to Craving. If yogi thought there would not be anyone who was as happy as he was, he was clinging to Pride. If yogi thought he was enjoying the BHĀVANĀ and felt happy in noting, he was clinging to DITTHI, False Doctrine. If yogi thought the happiness, he had experienced was the special DHAMMA, he was clinging to Wrong MAGGA, not the Path.

TEN UPAKKILESAS

Ten kinds of impurities of mind formed during contemplation.

1. The ability to note on all the objects swiftly was the mindfulness DHAMMA (SATI).
2. The ability to note quickly and the ability to distinguish each object clearly was the DHAMMA of knowledge (ÑĀNA).
3. Vividly experiencing the bright lights was the DHAMMA of AURA, OBHASA.
4. The experience of vibrations, thrills and gentle rocking, etc, and the blissful feeling of a happy noting was PĪTI, DHAMMA of Rapturous Joy.
5. The cool, peaceful and tranquil effect on the mind and body devoid of worry, over-enthusiasm and stray thoughts was the DHAMMA of PASSADHI Tranquility.
6. The overjoyed feeling of the mind and the pleasant feeling in the body was the DHAMMA of SUKHA, Beautiful Happiness.
7. The noting mind being clear, the feeling of respect for BUDDHA, ARAHANTS or teachers was SADDHA, the DHAMMA of Faith.
8. Contemplation easily without being bored or slackened, noting with a regular pace was the DHAMMA of Effort (VIRIYA).
9. The ability to note accurately on the objects at the moment they appeared; knowing clearly about the arising and passing away of the phenomena, the ability to note firmly and clearly on the appearing objects without making special effort; the balanced feeling which was free of love or hate; these are called UPPEKHA, Equanimity.
10. Thinking that BHĀVANĀ practice made one happy and felt like clinging to BHĀVANĀ, appreciation of that happiness is NIKANTI DHAMMA: (When yogi was thinking that he was happy in the

BHĀVANĀ work, he would be inclined to breed an attachment or the enjoyment on his contemplation. This is called NIKANTI DHAMMA).

The above were the ten points of UPPAKILASA: They were shown in the order in which the yogis expressed their work. Some yogis explained in such a way that only later the teacher could see the knowledge and faith cultured in them. Out of the ten UPAKKILESA some yogis could relate clearly only about two or three types.

The yogi's experiences were found to be in varying degrees concerning the ten UPAKKILESAS. Some experienced all ten of them. Mostly the yogis could describe all the UPAKKILESAS. But some yogis could not describe clearly what they had experienced.

The yogi who experienced just a few of the Ten UPAKKILESAS would describe his experiences enthusiastically. The yogi who could clearly experience quite a lot of UPAKKILESAS without affecting the good noting, would be happy beyond control. The yogi would feel happy for a long time.

COMMENT: The teacher should listen carefully to the yogi's enthusiastic description of his UPAKKILESAS. Some yogi who experienced just a few UPAKKILESAS may describe the UPAKKILESAS unenthusiastically. Encourage those yogis so that they may have more faith, desire and effort in contemplation. The yogi who might or might not have experienced lots of UPAKKILESAS but nevertheless described the experiences enthusiastically, would have to be toned down. Give little encouragement and pressure down his enthusiasm.

HOW TO LECTURE: The yogis had worked hard in contemplation so that their power of concentration and knowledge became good. From now on the contemplation will remain as good as ever. There is no need to be overjoyed with just this experience. This is only the beginning of a good phase. There are more good turnovers to come. One should not be like a foolish man who picked up just a pebble when there were precious stones around. Such experiences are nothing. Some could even reach that stage within 3 or 4 days. The feeling of happiness, appreciation, etc., are only impurities of mind and one should not culture them. Yogi reached this stage of ÑĀNA only because yogi noted. In order to reach the higher levels of ÑĀNA the yogi must go on noting. (Explain to yogis until they understand the need to go on noting everything. Yogis should note all the feeling, including the feeling of extreme happiness with a very strong effort.)

For the over-enthusiastic yogi who did not need any encouragement, the teacher should tone him down and give instructions to note ardently on all objects with strong effort, and without missing any.

Give special warning to yogis who were experiencing the UPAKKILESAS to note continuously on all objects so that there would be no chance for any thoughts to come in. For the yogi who was overjoyed and found it impossible to note advise him to have sound sleep. Tell that yogi to start noting only after waking up.

For the yogi who thought he had achieved MAGGA PHALA stage and felt contented, ask him whether the noting process, being happy, being peaceful were SANKHARA DHAMMA (Conditioned Things Subject to Change), or not. If the yogi admitted they were indeed SANKHARA, then tell him that all SANKHARA have the nature of arising and passing away phenomena, and all are impermanent. Therefore, one should not be pleased with the experience of SANKHARA: One should contemplate continuously until NIBBĀNA is reached. NIBBĀNA is free of SANKHARA.

Some yogi said during good contemplation they were sort of unconscious, but later on the contemplation was good again. When that experience happened once (or many times) yogi began to think that the noting was VIPASSANĀ and the pause without any noting was the MAGGA PHALA NIBBĀNA. After deciding like that either through self-discovery or through general knowledge, the yogi felt contented and satisfied. The teacher should tell such yogi that sometimes the yogi may become unconscious due to the force of PĪTI (Joy) or the UPPEKHA (Indifference) or because of THINA MIDA (Sloth and Torpor) due to over-concentration); or it may be due to extreme tranquility. The yogi could be in that state of unconsciousness for a long time. Instruct the yogi to go on noting as before.

The yogis should be made to realize that this sort of experience was not the end, and further noting should be done continuously. Once the yogi realized this either through his own knowledge or by his teacher's prompting, yogi should go on contemplating as before. Then the yogi could overcome the UPAKKILESAS. After that yogi's noting would be a stable and clear process. When the noting became good like that some would say, "What I thought previously to be good notings were just rough ones. Only now I know a real good one. Each time I noted I could focus on each object separately. I knew very clearly and distinctly about each noting. My mind did not go anywhere. My mind just fell straight into the target and stayed there precisely and firmly. Previously what I had thought of as a good noting was nothing like this. At one time I even argued with my teacher after I had a very good contemplation. Now I know I was wrong (and feel very grateful to my teacher)."

After about one or two days later.

A: I could contemplate better day by day. My knowledge had progressed. Whenever I noted on appearing objects such as rising, falling bending, touching, pain or other bodily sensations, I could note accurately and clearly. As soon as the objects appeared I noted and they disappeared. Previously I had thought the objects came sliding in from somewhere else. But now I know the objects began and ended on the spot. Previously I thought objects moved to other places. Now each time I noted I know that as soon as I noted the appearing object, they disappeared on the spot. Each noting brought me a clear-cut knowledge.

COMMENT: When yogis reached the mature state of UDAYABBAYA ÑĀNA they gained such knowledge, and they often spoke like this. If they did not, ask them questions and find out.

A: It was good to note, my knowledge was clear, objects appeared and when I noted they disappeared. But after noting for a long time, I wanted to rest, so I often rested.

INSTRUCTION: Do not feel satisfied with your contemplation and do not rest often. Even if you wanted to rest, just be stubborn, do not give in to your desire. Instead of resting, go on noting longer than before. Be determined to contemplate longer and longer each time. If you rested often, you would not make any progress from this stage.

A: The arising and passing away of objects were like ripples formed by the raindrops falling on the surface of water, appearing and disappearing quickly. It was very quick, like lightning.

SUMMARY:
1. When the yogi was able to note continuously on the various objects that appeared.
2. When each time the yogi noted he knew clearly about:
   a) The object and the noting mind sticking together in pairs.
   b) Their appearance and disappearance.
   c) The beginning and the end.
   d) The arising and passing away phenomena.

The yogi is said to be free from UPAKKILESAS (Impurity of Mind) and had reached to UDAYABBAYA ÑĀNA level, with the knowledge which was aware of the ever-new phenomena (Conditioned Things) rapidly arising and passing away.

END OF UDAYABBAYA ÑĀNA

F. BHANGA ÑĀNA (The Knowledge That Was Aware of Dissolution)

A: I was noting very well on various objects like rising, falling sitting, touching etc., my noting was very swift and light. Then suddenly, I felt vibrations once or twice and I felt as if I was covered by a sheet. Sometimes the covering began from my head, sometimes it began from the legs. I also felt like I was being hypnotized, and I saw a transparent sheet. The objects came at wide intervals. I thought my noting was slackened.

A: I was able to note quite swiftly and quite fast until the noting was disconnected and became slackened; so, I could not note well.

A: I was noting quite well, then I found my noting pace became sparse. After that I could not find anything; my body just disappeared and I had to go on noting on the usual objects. The objects and the noting fitted very well but I felt as if my noting was not effective. I felt as if I was not satisfied with my slackened noting.

A: The objects appeared and disappeared when I noted. The object and my mind were pairing off nicely. It was very good to note. But I was able to see the appearance of objects only sometimes. Most of the time I saw only the disappearing objects. My noting seemed disconnected. I wondered why it became slackened like this (yogi heaved a sigh).

A: Whenever I noted it was like throwing one stone after another into the water. Each time an object appeared, I noted; it was as if my mind ran straight into the object like throwing a dart. I was aware of the appearance and disappearance of the objects. From such a good state, things began to become spoiled. It was as if I threw a tuft of grass onto the water surface, the noting was not precise and not penetrating anymore. It seemed like a lax and flippant noting.

COMMENT: When asked how it was like to be lax and flippant the yogi would say, "When I noted touching, I sent my mind towards the legs. I knew the mind focused on the legs but I could not visualize my legs. Similarly, when I focused the mind to my head, I could not visualize my head. When I noted sitting, I knew I was sitting but I could not visualize my body in sitting posture. When I was walking, I noted lifting, pushing, placing. I knew the lifting, pushing and placing processes but I could not find my legs. Whatever I noted on, it was like this. I could notice the objects but the shape or image of objects was not clear.

The objects did not appear to be clear-cut; it was a slippery noting. My noting was not as good as before; later I felt dissatisfied and bored so I often took rests. Then I got up, but I was restless. I would not stay long in noting. Although I was feeling like that I could not help noting as usual. But when I noted it was not satisfactorily good. Then I was disappointed. That sort of feeling left me bored and disheartened. So I gave up noting and I just gazed.

A: At first it was good to note, both the rising and falling were clearly noted. Then the falling seemed to fade off. After a while both the rising and falling were faint. When I noted on rising, it seemed there was no rising. When I noted on falling it seemed as if there was no falling. But I knew the rising and falling were there. It was just that they did not appear to be distinct. I thought I had bungled in my noting.

COMMENT: The yogi who reported like this was beginning to change from UDAYABBAYA ÑĀNA to BHANGA ÑĀNA level. Almost everyone felt despair at this stage. Therefore, the teacher must give encouragement.

ENCOURAGEMENT: Do not think that you could not note as well as before. Do not think your noting was spoiled, do not be disappointed. In fact, your noting was better than before. Now your knowledge has progressed. In the beginning of contemplation, the new yogis always felt disappointed like this. Everyone whose knowledge had progressed had to undergo this sort of feeling at this stage. Do not think you are the only one. It was like this: when your knowledge was still young, the knowledge was heavy and slow, so whatever you noted, you could not possibly know just the nature of objects. Your mind noted the objects with reference to the shape of the parts of body and the name given for each part, e.g., the shape of abdomen, hand, leg (labeled concept on material body).

Therefore, each time you noted, you were clear of the name and shape of the place of noting, plus the precision of the noting. And you thought your contemplating was excellent.

Your mind had been trained since childhood to recognize the PINNATTI, CONCEPTUAL OBJECT. (The name and shape of conceptual objects.) Therefore, you thought knowing the name and shape of objects was a better knowledge. Now that your knowledge had matured, your mind was light and swift. Each time you noted rising and falling, or on other objects, you just saw the nature of NĀMA- RŪPA. So, there was no chance for the slips of mind (which knew and which had the tendency to reflect upon the conceptual name given for the shape and condition of object) to occur between one noting and another. (After all these slips of mind are unnecessary, misused effort.) Now you know just the pure VIPASSANĀ, which enables you to recognize the intrinsic nature of objects.

A: Previously my awareness was slow and dull, the disappearance of objects was slow so I could see the beginning of the appearance of objects very well. (Now that the yogi's knowing mind was quick and accordingly the disappearance of the object was quick; yogi would not see the beginning of the appearance of objects. Instead, yogi sees only the ending and the dissolution of objects).

In the beginning, if yogi could not recognize the name and shape of the objects, a fixed stable concentration could not be established.

Therefore, at first the teachers instructed the yogis to visualize the name and shape of the objects when noting. It was not because knowing distinctly about the shape of objects was the best result. It was just to gather strength for the concentration.

Now that yogi could not see the conceptual name and shape of the objects, but knew just the natural phenomena, there is no need to imagine the name and shape deliberately. It is better if you could just know about the natural conditions of the object without any visions or shape. You might think your pace was getting slow and your noting was slackened. This was because it was only the beginning of this particular ÑĀNA (Knowledge).

Later on, you would find that there is no conceptual shape or form; there is no beginning but just the end of the disappearing objects. You would know the nature of dissolution of objects quite comfortably and casually, without having to make a special effort. You would be ever so pleased with this achievement.

Right now, you might not be able to appreciate my instructions. You might think that even though your noting was bad your teacher was giving you encouragement just to boost up your morale. Please do not think like that. What you are experiencing now is really a good DHAMMA. That is why I am telling you it is good. The nature of mind and matter has no shape, nor body. There is nothing but just the intrinsic nature, which is impermanent.

Now every time you noted the shapes were not distinct. You were just aware of the end of objects; you could only see the dissolving objects. You just knew about the impermanent nature of objects and nothing else. In fact, you were realizing the whole truth about the nature of

IMPERMANENCE. Therefore, do not expect the vague forms of concepts to become crystal-clear; nor search for the distinct objects among the faint ones. Have full confidence in your knowledge which has progressed according to the natural trend of DHAMMA. Just go on noting attentively and accurately as usual on the dominant object. If you thought your noting was slackened and flippant, note that thought. If you were disappointed, note and dispel that thought. The intrinsic nature of objects might appear faint to you but yogi should make a deliberate effort to note ardently on those faint objects. Very soon you would get to a satisfactory stage where your contemplation would be good in a unique way.

If the yogi followed the teacher's instruction with full faith and contemplation ardently, about a few hours or a day later some yogi would say:

A: My noting was very swift and good just like you (teacher) said.

A: Now whatever I noted appeared like moving shadows, it was a good contemplation.

A: Previously when the noting mind and the objects appeared and disappeared in pairs, I thought it was a good noting. Only now I realize they were only rough ones. Now my noting is very delicate and objects came up delicately and swiftly.

DESCRIPTION OF THE PASSING AWAY PHENOMENA:

A: Every time I noted, the objects were disappearing and then they vanished completely.

A: All the objects just ended when I noted.

A: I only saw the end.

A: I experienced a fluttering feeling.

A: The objects moved very serenely.

A: There was nothing to note. My noting was late.

A: As I noted on and on, the objects dissolved and disappeared.

COMMENT: The yogi's expressions were all similar. (Actually, they were seeing the passing away phenomena.)

A: When I noted as "rising" I knew the end of the rising process and I also knew the dissolution of the mind that knew about rising.

18. MEDITATION TEACHER'S RECORD BOOK

Whatever I noted it was like that. Each time I noted, I knew that things ended in pairs.

THE YOGI WITH A CLEAR KNOWLEDGE WOULD SAY:

A: I knew the end of rising. I also knew the end of the noting mind and I was aware of the passing away of the knowing mind. Each time I noted I was aware of the end of those three things.

A: There was quite a big gap between the notings.

A: It seemed as if there was a distance of about 4 or 5 inches between the notings.

A: When I was noting as "seeing", "seeing" on what I saw, it seemed as if the nature of seeing phenomena was broken off, and gradually diminished and disappeared completely. If I noted ardently for quite a long time, there was nothing but just a wide space.

A: When I looked at the trees. I only saw them rapidly passing away. Whatever I looked at, I just saw the dissolution of things.

A: When I looked it seemed as if my eyesight was not good.

A: When my eyes saw something I made a great effort to note as "seeing", "seeing". Then I noticed that the "seeing" mind disappeared one by one.

A: When I heard something in my ear I noted as "hearing", "hearing", then the buzzing sound became separated one by one. I could not fathom what sort of sound it was; I just heard something and I knew it disappeared.

A: When I heard the siren, a dog barking, birds chirping, cock crowing I noted as "hearing", "hearing". Then each sound was broken into bits.

A: When I listened, the right ear was listening separately from the left ear. Everything disappeared one by one. When I noted as "hearing", "hearing" on what I heard, each noting disappeared, one by one.

A: While I was noting on the eating process during a meal I noted as "chewing", "chewing", "sweetness", "sourness" "knowing" etc. Each time I focused my mind on the chewing, the movement of the tongue, the touching on the tongue and the awareness of the taste, all the phenomena were broken bit by bit and ended there and then.

A: I noted as "touching", "touching" on the points of touch, the places of touch were very distinct and their disappearances were noticed clearly.

A: When I noted ardently on the aches, itches and pain, each of those feelings were cut into pieces and ended one by one.

A: When I was noting while walking, each time my leg was lifted, pushed and placed, I just knew each action ended swiftly.

A: It seemed as if the ground and the trees were whirled away swiftly.

A: While walking, I felt hazy like the fumes from the exhaust pipe of a car.

A: I felt very dizzy during my walking meditation.

SOME DESCRIBED THE BENDING PROCESS THUS:

A: I knew the slow and gradual movement bit by bit, and they disappeared.

A: There were series of separate bendings, and they disappeared.

A: I noted the intention to bend as "intending", "intending", then I noticed the intending mind disappeared bit by bit. After noting about five or six times, the intending mind disappeared completely, and I did not have to bend at all. If and when I actually bent, the separate bendings disappeared swiftly. (The same description was made for the stretching process).

A: Whatever object it may be, each one disappeared distinctly. The noting mind and the object were always pairing off and disappearing together.

A: The objects disappeared from the front and the mind just knew about it. Later the mind that noted the passing away of objects disappeared too.

COMMENT: For the yogis who had reached a higher level of knowledge of BHANGA ÑĀNA, tell them to note the objects from all six doors of the body. At the same time yogis should be instructed to note on a wide range of objects occasionally.

SUMMARY: Each time the dominant objects were noted, the yogi clearly saw the swift ending and disappearance; the yogi was aware of the passing away phenomena and the nothingness which followed; the yogi also noticed the disappearance of the knowing mind too.

The yogi who clearly knew about the disappearance of objects had reached BHANGA ÑĀNA: Here the yogi knew about the disappearance of object and mind at each noting. The yogi could accomplish BHANGA ÑĀNA fully, only if he was able to know about the end and dissolution of the object and the noting mind (Knowledge of Dissolution of Things).

END OF BHANGA ÑĀNA

G. BHAYA ÑĀNA (The Knowledge of Awareness of Fearfulness)

The various objects and the noting mind paired off and disappeared. The yogi could note continuously and each note was swift and accurate. Then some yogi said:

A: Every time I note I just saw the ending and disappearance of the objects, so I felt frightened. (The trend of frightened thoughts was noticed.) But I was not frightened as if I saw a ghost, some wild animals or any weapons. I could not say I was frightened of any particular thing, but I knew there was fear in my mind.

A: I could not tell exactly what I am afraid of, but I was frightened.

A: I saw the disappearance of objects, and that made me frightened.

A: I was afraid the objects like "rising", "falling" might appear and I would have to note them.

A: Previously before contemplation I did not know about this. But now I realize that things to be noted would disappear in future. I knew that as long as I live the objects would disappear like this, and I got frightened.

A: Whatever I saw disappeared or passed away. So I thought everything that was rising up was frightful, and I got very frightened.

A: While contemplating I saw various objects inside my body passing away, and I got frightened. I remembered my parents and friends who had not practiced, then I felt lonely and sad. I wanted to cry and I was frightened.

A: I thought to myself that in real life things were arising and passing away just like what I saw when I was noting. It must be the same in the celestial life. I thought the whole LOKA would be disappearing like this. I also saw the frightening aspects only, and I felt frightened.

ENCOURAGEMENT: The frightened feeling and the depression were due to the progress of knowledge. These are the true experiences of DHAMMA. Everybody would feel like this on reaching a higher level of knowledge. Console the yogi and tell him/her there is no need to worry, but just go on noting the feeling of depression and sadness to the verge of crying. Also tell yogi to note the frightened mind in the usual way. If the yogi would go on noting on all the objects, very soon the yogi would get over this stage.

SUMMARY: The mind which noticed that all the SANKARA objects observed from the six-doors disappeared, the mind that thought this knowledge was frightful and the mind that was aware of the frightened feeling was the indication of BHAYA ÑĀNA:

All the SANKARA objects upon which the yogi contemplated were frightening, the yogi's awareness of this and the actual feeling of fear or fright were the sign of BAYATUPATANA OR BHAYA ÑĀNA:

END OF BHAYA ÑĀNA

H. ĀDĪNAVA ÑĀNA (Knowledge of Misery)

When yogi noted yogi only saw the end and the disappearance of objects, thus the yogi felt frightened. The yogi should note that frightened feeling as well as all the SANKARA objects appearing from the six doors. The noting must be continuous without intervals. Once the yogi gathered speed in noting, the yogi's noting power became very good and swift. The noting was continuous and the yogi was well aware of it. Such yogis would say:

A: All the objects I had been noting were all miserable. Whatever I noted, not a single object was good. I thought of all the objects as miserable.

A: I could not find any object which was good.

A: I found that the objects and the noting mind were well fitted and got fixed in pairs. But I did not think any of them were good.

A: Out of the various objects that were noted, nothing was good. The noting and knowing mind were also miserable. Now each time I noted everything was miserable. I could not find one good thing.

A: All the arising phenomena were not good, and they were arising continuously and there was no end of noting. Therefore, they were miserable.

A: As long as these phenomena existed, I noted and knew they were not good. It would be better if all of them had perished.

A: In the human world because of these things life was miserable. The same applies to the celestial world and the BRAHMA world. None of the worlds was good. It would be better if these miserable phenomena had not existed.

(Here the teacher should encourage the yogi that the mind which thought and knew that all was miserable should be noted.)

SUMMARY: All the phenomena of objects appearing from the six sense doors should be noted. Each noting brought yogi the knowledge that it was miserable, there was nothing good about it. This was the correct knowledge, which could see the defects of natural phenomena.

Similarly, the yogi would see the miserable aspect of life and SANKHARA. This level of knowledge is called ĀDĪNAVA ÑĀNA (The Knowledge of Misery).

END OF ĀDĪNAVA ÑĀNA

I. NIBBIDĀ ÑĀNA (The Knowledge of Wearisomeness or Disgust)

The yogis who thought whatever they noted was not good but miserable went on noting continuously. When their knowledge became strengthened; noting and knowing were very swift and active.

A: I got fed up with whatever I noted. I felt as if I was bored or lazy while noting.

A: noting was clear and precise, but I felt bored for no reason. I did not want to note. But I could not help noting, so as usual I noted continuously.

A: For no particular reason I was feeling weary and dull over the objects I noted.

A: Previously when I heard other people say they were weary of SAMSARA, I did not understand what they meant. Only now I fully understand. I felt really wearisome. I used to be very frightened of existing in the lower world hell, but I liked the idea of enjoying the pleasures in human life and celestial life. Now I do not look forward to live in either of them. I just want to reach NIBBĀNA.

A: I was not happy over the objects I noted, and I was not pleased with the noting mind. I would not be happy in the celestial world. I just could not correlate happiness with anything at all.

A: I felt disgusted with myself and when I looked at other people. I could not see anything good in them. I was disgusted with whatever I observed.

A: All the Sankhara conditions I saw, I noted. Whatever I noted on, nothing was good. I could not find the slightest pleasure in any of them. I just got bored, disgusted and weary.

A: Whenever I noted the various objects, I just knew them as disgusting things. I did not feel like talking to other people. I did not want to meet anybody. I just wanted to stay by myself in the meditation hall and go on contemplating.

COMMENT: The teacher should encourage such yogis and instruct them to go on noting the bored and weary mind.

SUMMARY: As the yogi noted the natural phenomena occurring from the six doors, the yogi felt disgusted, bored and weary.

At the same time the kind of knowledge called PACCAKA ÑANA (Present Knowledge) is formed. The yogi thus noted and reflected upon all these conditions in a correct sequential order.

Then he felt bored and. wearisome over all forms of conditioned objects in life. This knowledge is called ANWA-YA ÑANA (Deductive Knowledge).

After progressing from PACCAKA ÑANA TO ANWA-YA ÑANA the yogi is said to have attained the NIBBIDĀ ÑANA:

ATTENTION: Some yogis could describe their experiences clearly about the knowledge of BHAYA ĀDĪNAVA AND NIBBIDĀ ÑĀNA. Some yogis could describe only one or two of the above three ÑĀNAS. They could not describe the other one or two. Some yogi could not describe the distinguishing characters of the three levels of knowledge, but they would just say:

A: Every time I noted, I noticed that the object and the noting mind disappeared. Sometimes the noting was very swift and good, sometimes it was neither swift nor slow, it was just a good, regular noting. Sometimes the noting was good but a little bit heavy. But sometimes I felt as if I was bored, drained out, or some sort of neutral feeling.

A: My noting was like before, there was nothing new. The noting was good as usual, but not better; I have nothing special to report. I did not lose continuity in noting.

A: The noting was quick at one time and slow at another. Both were good notings. But I would not say the notings were as good as yesterday. But still I could say they were good.

A: The rising and falling were very dim and delicate. Whatever object I noted, they were like the rising and falling, very delicately happening.

A: The noting was very quick. The noting speed was so good, it was like running with high speed. It was as if the body would run too. (The yogi would describe the experience as being a good one).

COMMENT: The teacher may come across such yogis who could give only an ordinary description. Then the teacher should observe the following signs from the yogi. The yogi may speak softly due to depression. The yogi was not enthusiastic as before. The face looked feeble with less speech, and yogi liked to be isolated from other people. The yogi also wished to stay alone in a secluded place.

By judging these signs, the teacher could decide that this yogi who had strongly experienced the BHANGA ÑĀNA had progressed further to the BHAYA ĀDĪNAVA AND NIBIDDĀ ÑĀNA:

On the other hand, if the yogi had already described the experiences relating to higher levels of knowledge, the teacher could decide that the yogi had already reached those 3 levels of knowledge at that time. The teacher should not set a hard and fast rule about the attainment of higher ÑĀNAS. The experiences of the BHAYA ĀDĪNAVA AND NIBBIDĀ may not be clearly described by all the yogis.

END OF NIBBIDĀ ÑĀNA

J. MUÑCITU KAMYATĀ ÑĀNA (Knowledge of the Desire for Deliverance)

At this the yogi would say:

A: Every time I noted, object and the noting mind ended in pairs. I just saw the disappearance of the mental and physical phenomena of SANKHARA disappearing quickly. The knowing mind moved quickly too.

The yogi would describe the good contemplation:

A: I felt friable [breaking easily] as if some tiny insects were crawling all over my body.

A: It was like being crawled over by insects. I thought some ants were coming up my body, so I even got up and shook my clothes. But I could not find anything. So, I went back to noting as before. Again, I felt those friable sensations. Sometimes the sensations disappeared after noting. Sometimes they just decreased but not totally disappeared. Sometimes if I noted very ardently all of them disappeared.

A: I was confused with what I should note, and how I should note. I felt restless and I wanted to change position so I often changed. But it did not make any difference. I was lying on my right side and I changed to the left side without any reason. Also, I changed from the left to right. When I was lying on my back I turned to lie on my right side. I was restless so I got up and walked. But not for long, I sat down again. I just could not stay still. I was moving all the time. I bent and stretched very often; I could stay still in any position. Because of the restlessness and too much moving I had to change the objects of noting very often. I began to feel uncomfortable in the contemplation. I did not want to sit in the meditation hall. I did not even want to go near it. I did not think I could go on. I did not feel like noting, but I could not help noting. Then I was afraid of noting. I just wanted to be free from it soon.

A: As I was noting I just saw the passing away of the objects all the time. I thought it would even be better if I did not note at all, so I stopped noting and tried to sleep. But I did not sleep at all. I thought I would not note but the mind was automatically aware of the objects, and went on noting by itself.

A: I felt the friable sensations from the body, arms, thighs and the legs. There were scratchy sensations, irritations, and prickly feelings. Sometimes it was hurting like being pricked by a needle. Sometimes there was a burning in the chest, a bit painful too. Sometimes my abdomen seemed to be bloated.

A: The whole body was quiet and still, but my teeth were chattering quite often.

A: I noticed my head was swaying from one side to the other, and later on it was swaying quite rapidly. It was like that very often.

A: While I was noting, my whole body disappeared. There was just the knowing mind. Then I felt gentle vibrations in the body. The mind was in a sublime state. It was a very good experience.

A: I was not tired bodily; I found the objects and the noting mind appeared and disappeared all the time. I did not want to exist in the human world, nor in the celestial and the BRAHMA world; I did not want to live anywhere. I thought there was no real goodness in any form of life.

A: As I came to know all the SANKHARA objects arising up were bad and miserable I felt very fatigued in my mind. I just wanted to escape from the arising and passing away phenomena.

A: Each time I noted, I noticed that the objects and the noting mind disappeared all the time. So, I thought it would be nice if all of these had not existed. I wished I could discard all of them. I just wanted to be in a place where I would be free from all these sufferings.

A: Previously I wanted to be free forever from existence in the lower world, and I thought I would be content to live in the celestial world.

I did not want NIBBĀNA so much. Now I do not want to live in any of the worlds. I just want to reach NIBBĀNA. I wanted peace and tranquility as soon as possible.

ENCOURAGEMENT: When all the SANKHARA phenomena to be noted were gone, you would be peaceful and that is true NIBBĀNA.

Only then you would find true peace and tranquility. You are contemplating in order to achieve that goal. You have done very well indeed, now with the Imaginative Knowledge you have come to know the true nature of NIBBĀNA. If you tried harder very soon you would be able to know NIBBĀNA with the Evident Knowledge of MAGGA PHALA ÑĀNA.

SUMMARY: The yogi had come to realize:
1. The NĀMA- RŪPA and SANKHARA DHAMMA which were known through noting.
2. That the NĀMA- RŪPA SANKHARA, which were re-observed, were ending, disappearing and dissolving, therefore they were not reliable enough to cling to.

Each time yogi noted he knew these facts and reflected on them, and he liked his own knowledge. Then the yogi wanted to get rid of these SANKHARA DHAMMA, the yogi did not feel attached to these SANKHARA DHAMMA and the yogi was also aware of this knowledge gained.

This kind of knowledge is called MUÑCITU KAMYATĀ ÑĀNA.

END OF MUÑCITU KAMYATĀ ÑĀNA

K. PATISANKHĀ ÑĀNA (Knowledge of Re- observation)

The yogi who had attained the MUÑCITU KAMYATĀ ÑĀNA wanted to be free from SANKHARA and went on noting all the objects appearing from the six doors. Then the yogi noticed that after each noting, the object and the noting mind disappeared, the knowing mind became very swift and alert, the noting became very good again.

Then, some would say:

A: All the objects ended and disappeared very quickly. Nothing lasted long enough for one or two notings. There were no thoughts that lasted long. All the thoughts disappeared after one or two notings. I did not even have to note some of them; I was just aware of them and they disappeared. I found out that nothing stayed still for even a while. The arising and passing away phenomena would very easily disappear. So, I concluded that these were all impermanent nature of phenomena.

A: My noting was as usual. Sometimes it was swift and good. Sometimes it was not so good, but rather slow and dull. Sometimes it was a sparse noting. But most of the time the noting was good.

A: I noticed that all the phenomena I noted were appearing and disappearing, I could not see any goodness in them. I thought all of them were miserable sufferings.

A: While I was deep in contemplation, the whole body seemed to move upwards and I felt irritable. If I noted, sometimes those feelings decreased. At times they increased. It was like that for one or two days. I thought to myself that the irritations and the noting mind were all miserable, they were all sufferings.

A: I found slight irritations but I could say everything was bad and miserable.

A: It was good to note, but I felt tense in the body and hands. The noting mind was heavy. My hands and legs felt so heavy that I could not really move them. My noting was very heavy and dull. I thought to myself that all these experiences of Dhamma were miserable sufferings.

A: When I was noting very well, I heard a buzzing sound. At first, I thought it was good to note. It easily disappeared after I had noted. Later the sound became more distinct and grew louder and louder. I heard it very clearly and it was very difficult to note. The sound would not disappear after I noted.

COMMENT: Some yogi would hear the sound for one, two or three days. Such yogi would say:

A: I could still hear those sounds. They would not disappear after noting. I did not want to hear any sound; I did not want to note if at all. Hearing these sounds was sheer misery and suffering. Nothing was good. I just did not want these sounds. I noticed boredom, hatred and disgust felt over these. My mind wanted to be free from the sound quickly.

INSTRUCTION: Ignore the sound completely. Do not pay any attention to the sound. Just focus your mind on the other objects forcefully. Do not expect to hear them. Do not be curious to find out whether the sound was still coming or not. Just do not think about the sound and go on contemplating with great effort. Actually, there was no sound, it was due to an affiliation of mind to conceptual object, and it was just an imagination.

A: My contemplation was getting on very well but whenever I was aware of the object and the noting mind, I felt very hot and tired. It was as if I was sitting on burning coal with my body being burdened by hot pots. They were all unbearable sufferings. All the time I thought everything was miserable.

A: The object seemed very far apart and each object was clearly distinct from another. The noting mind did not stick to (stay with) the object. Sometimes I was gazing away without noting for quite a long time. But my concentration was intact. When I remembered I just noted on anything at random, and it was still good.

A: I felt burning in my abdomen. It was so bad I had to stop noting altogether. Sometimes when I noted on that burning feeling, it disappeared immediately but came back later. Then I noted again on burning, and again it disappeared. Later it was burning again. The repetition of that burning sensation was so often that I was not happy with my contemplation at all. It was so bad I wanted to be free from it.

A: I felt congested in my chest. Sometimes it was like a heartburn. It was painful too. Sometimes there was tension in the whole body, it was boring to note. My contemplation was awful; my mind was perplexed and I just wanted to be liberated quickly.

A: Whatever I noted I could not see any goodness in anything. Now I really find it boring to note. I felt miserable.

ENCOURAGEMENT: Yogi is now seeing the truth with insight knowledge like he had never known before. What yogi is experiencing now is the noble truth of suffering, which yogi has not known before. You cannot find goodness in the noble truth of suffering. Every time you noted, you gained knowledge which clarified the noble truth of suffering (DUKKHA).

At the same time, you were discarding the noble truth of attachment SAMUDAYA, which could be formed on the objects you had noted. Thus, you were experiencing the momentary peace, NIRODHA: You were also exercising the Noble Truth of MAGGA practically. With the ARIYA MAGGA TICCA very soon you would see NIBBĀNA. Very soon you would be free from all the sufferings you are experiencing now and your noting would become good.

You would see NIBBĀNA and you could be free from all the sufferings of the lower world. If you compared your present suffering with the miseries of the lower world, your suffering is nothing. If you want to be free from the enormous suffering you should be patient and bear the small suffering.

COMMENT: Here the teacher should give instructions to the yogi according to his knowledge level. Instruct the yogi to note the mind that felt miserable, until the yogi was free from it. The teacher should encourage the yogi until the yogi became inspired and enthusiastic.

THE DISTINGUISHING CHARACTERS:
In the level of MUÑCITU KAMYATĀ ÑĀNA, there were only slight DUKKHA VEDANĀS. If the yogi noted about three, four or five times the VEDANĀ might vanish. Sometimes the VEDANĀ just decreased a bit and stayed on to be just bearable.

In the level of PATISANKHA ÑĀNA usually there were lots of DUKKHA VEDANĀS. But they did not stay long. They disappeared after one or two notings. Sometimes the yogi was just aware of it, and it was gone without having to note. Even if it did not disappear completely, the yogi understood clearly that each note dispelled the VEDANĀ once. This is the special characteristic of PATISANKHA ÑĀNA.

The yogi who contemplated according to the teacher's instruction and has reached maturity of this nana would say after a few hours or a few days:

A: Each time I noted, the object and the noting mind stayed fixed together. It was a good noting. I was happy in contemplation. There were no rough vedanas. It was a very swift and pleasant noting.

A: The objects, the noting-knowing mind and the Sankhara Phenomena which was arising and passing away came to an end. I rapidly saw them passing away so I knew that there was no stable body, and there was nothing that I could do as I wished. Everything happened according to its wish. Therefore, I resolved to go on noting at random on whatever came up and my noting was good again.

A: The noting was good and swift. Even though I had stopped noting, the mind was noting still and knowing spontaneously. Sometimes I had stopped noting, but the noting was going on by itself, so I had to note up to about ten times.

COMMENT: Here the yogi could not note long without making a real effort and the objects noted were not extremely delicate.

SUMMARY: In PATISANKHA ÑĀNA, the yogi might see any one of the ten ANICCA LEKHANA, or any one of the twenty-five DUKKHA TEKHANA, or any one of the five ANATTA LEKHANA, according to the varying degrees of PARAMI (Perfections) they were gifted with. Whatever it may be at this level of PATISANKHA ÑĀNA, the yogi could see the above characteristics at each noting and appreciated the continuity and swiftness of the noting knowing mind.

END OF PATISANKHA ÑĀNA

L. SANKHĀRUPEKKHĀ ÑĀNA (The Knowledge that Can View Psycho-Physical Phenomena with Equanimity)

When the PATISANKHA ÑĀNA matured, the notings seemed to be like running with good speed; they were continuous and swift. Then the yogi would say:

A: (1) Now I do not think the objects were good to note as I did before. I do not think they are awful too. I was neither happy nor bored with my noting. The noting was very light, swift and good. Yogi was not afraid of SANKHARA objects, nor liked them. (Yogi had a middle-way, balanced outlook on SANKHARA.)

A: (2) When I was sitting or lying down, I noted I just had to sit or lie down and the noting was spontaneous. I did not have to make a special effort and still it was a very good noting. It was like driving a cart with two strong bullocks. I did not have to make an effort; the noting was done by itself. Now I only have to note five or ten times in the beginning, later the noting became automatic. I did not have to be careful; it was a very comfortable and good contemplation. (Yogi reflected on the mind that contemplated and analyzed the nature of SANKHARA and had an indifferent outlook).

A: (3) Now no matter how long I sat, there was no pain, ache, heat, etc. in my hands, legs and body. I stayed very still and I could contemplate nicely. Only after noting a long time, I rested for a while. When I went back to noting. I could note without difficulty. After about four, five or ten notings, the noting speed gathers momentum as before. I think now if I contemplated in either posture, I could stay on the whole day or night without moving or changing posture. There was no question of ache, pain, heat, etc; I could note in continuity, very still and with good speed. (Yogi was explaining about the characteristics of SANKHĀRUPEKKHĀ- ÑĀNA and the Stationary Nature of Mind.)

A: (4) I did not have to note with special effort. The noting knowing mind was waiting to catch the objects without missing any, the noting was spontaneous. The mind did not go anywhere, I could not send it anywhere. The notings were just happening by themselves continuously.

A: My teacher had instructed to note all the objects in spread dimension (watching objects form all six sense doors). I noted accordingly. Gradually, there were less objects and my mind closed in to the usual noting on the rising, falling, sitting, touching. I could not note on the other objects. The objects became smaller and appeared less and less in number. The noting boundary was getting narrower and narrower. Later on, there were only the rising and falling left to be noted.

COMMENT: The yogi was aware of his mind (SANKHĀRUPEKKHĀ-ÑĀNA) which was fixed on the object he contemplated. That fixedness of mind was firm and strong.

A: (5) Now I could not find anything dominant in my notings. Everything was delicate. Only the beginning five or ten notes were dominant and distinct. Later on, everything was very fine and delicate. The objects were very delicate and disappeared gently. The noting mind also disappeared gently and delicately. Everything was so gentle and delicate that it was really nice to note. It was the first time I felt so good like this.

COMMENT: The yogi's SANKHĀRUPEKKHĀ- ÑĀNA got more and more refined. Also, more and more delicate as the contemplation went on.

(1) Like the statements in No. 1, 2, 3, 4 & 5, the yogi was neither frightened nor pleased with the objects and the noting mind. Yogi had ignored them spontaneously.
(2) The yogi did not have to worry about making a special effort in noting. It was automatically good.
(3) The yogi could bear the unpleasant visions and the undesirable VEDANĀS and mostly free of DUKKHA VEDANĀS.
(4) The ability to contemplate in any posture for as long as 2 or 3 hours without changing posture.
(5) The yogi did not want to think of other independent objects for a long time. When the noting was good the yogi could not even send the mind elsewhere. The yogi could not note on the general objects. The yogi could note only a few usual objects, staying very still.
(6) The longer the contemplation, the gentler and more delicate the objects and the noting mind became.

Once the yogi had experienced the above characteristics, yogi had fully achieved the SANKHĀRUPEKKHĀ- ÑĀNA. If the yogi did not express those facts, the teacher should ask test questions.

A: The risings and fallings gradually became smaller and smaller. Later on, they disappeared completely and I felt like a vacuum, clean and clear. It was a very peaceful and pleasant feeling. There was only the ultra-clear mind left. I had nothing to note so I just noted "knowing", "knowing". At that time of contemplation, I felt wonderful.

COMMENT: The yogi's already determined faith became more consolidated. My awareness was very swift in knowing the various objects while my noting was very good. Then I felt gentle vibrations sweeping inside my body. It was a marvelous feeling. I was very satisfied and pleased about it. It was a happy and a good noting.

I was so pleased with my good noting that I rested and noted again. When the noting became good again, I was pleased and rested again. I wanted to rest often. I did not want to note long. I wanted to get up often and wanted to talk to the people around me.

COMMENT: The yogi was contented with the good noting and had slackened in effort. The teacher should warn and instruct in these ways:

WARNING: Yogi should not think highly of this much of a good noting. This is not satisfactory enough. Since this is not the real happiness of NIBBĀNA you should not be contented with it. The objects noted were SANKHARA, the good noting was SANKHARA and the feeling of contentment, happiness and joy were also SANKHARA. All were impermanent.

There is nothing satisfactory in all these DHAMMAS. If the good noting stayed good forever, you should be pleased and satisfied with it. But now the good notings were good only at the moment of noting. After noting and knowing they all disappeared instantly.

Nothing lasted long enough. You had found out about this through your own experience. Knowing all of them were impermanent, if you were to be pleased and satisfied with these impermanent DHAMMAS, would it be wise? If you know for sure that you could get an enormous amount of gold, would it be wise to be content with just a measly sum of money?

So do not stop before you reach your destination. Note with great effort. Note the liking mind, the happy mind and the satisfied mind as soon as they come up, and dispel them instantly. If you could not dispel them, they would obstruct your path to NIBBĀNA.

A: While my noting was good and swift, sometimes it was very subtle and then it became very delicate, and seemed as if the continuity was cut off gently. After that I went on noting, and it was still good. (The unconsciousness could be associated with indifference or sloth and torpor).

A: There was nothing special in my noting. Whenever I noted it was good. Nothing better, nothing worse. After noting for quite a long time, I was momentarily unconscious, then I went on noting. It was still good. Sometimes I really fell asleep. When I remembered to note, the noting was good as usual. Later on, I went back to sleep. It was alternating like that all the time. (Because of slackened aim and effort, sloth and torpor became dominant. So, warn yogi.)

WARNING: When the noting had gathered momentum, it was comfortable and nice to note. Then the precision of the effort became less accurate, so that gradually the objects became dim and unidentifiable. Then the sloth and torpor came in and made yogi fall asleep and became unconscious for just a moment, or for quite a long time. So, warn the yogi to be careful when the noting became good; warn them not to slacken in the accuracy of the effort. Warn yogis to pay special attention in noting when the objects became smaller and dimmer.

When the yogi contemplated ardently and continuously:

A: The noting knowing mind was very swift and good. It seemed as if the notings were flying off from my body, they were struggling to rise up. It also seemed like they were running with full speed. When the noting was extremely good like that, I thought, "This time it was really going to be good, my noting had improved". As soon as I thought like that, my noting became slackened and awful. But I went on noting as usual, and after a while it was good again like before. But as soon as I thought my noting was good again and felt happy, my noting became bad again. The noting was alternating between good and bad all the time.

WARNING: Try to note firmly and accurately on the mind which thought the noting had become good, the mind that was happy, the mind which was curious about what would happen next and what it was going to be like later.

A: My noting was an alternate pattern of good and bad experience. But when I was really determined to go on noting, after a while my contemplation became very still, gentle and delicate. I could happily contemplate for as long as I liked.

A: My noting was very good; my whole body felt the soothing vibration of cool thrills. At that moment, I saw sparkles of light twinkling at the corner of my eyes and I often felt as if I was unconscious. As soon as I became aware of it, I noted and it was as good and as gentle as before.

COMMENT: When the yogi's power of concentration is better than the power of knowledge, sparkling lights or visions could be experienced. Because of the force of PĪTI (Joy), the yogi could experience a black-out condition similar to unconsciousness. Tell yogi that his power of concentration and power of knowledge had matured considerably. So, encourage yogi to work harder with greater effort.

SPECIAL NOTES: At this level if the yogi did not note on a wide range of objects appearing from the six-doors, and if he just noted the usual trend of noting in a very comfortable way, the yogi's aim and effort of noting could be slackened, and it could be a hindrance to further progress.

Therefore, as soon as the teacher had noticed the yogi's momentum of noting had gathered speed (i.e., before reaching to the sublime and still stage of noting), instruct the yogi to note ardently and accurately on the general objects appearing from the six-doors. But do not instruct like that once the yogi has reached a still and sublime state of noting. Actually, at that time it would be impossible to note on a wide range of objects. For the yogi who was instructed to note on a wide range of objects, even if he did note on a wide range of objects from all six doors, there could be no progress if the accuracy of the effort was slackened. Therefore, instruct yogi to note accurately on every object.

Sometimes the yogi knew that he had reached the SANKHĀRU- PEKKHĀ- ÑĀNA. Every time yogi's noting became good, he would think "Very soon I will reach MAGGA. Very soon I shall be alright." Such yogis could feel happy, over enthusiastic and looking forward too much. Thereby his progress could be hindered.

Therefore, it is better to not tell the contemplating yogis about their level of knowledge.

Even if the yogis knew (themselves) about their level of knowledge, do not speak out your judgment even if what they thought was correct. The teacher should not make a firm decision. Instead encourage them to work hard. Warn the yogis to be able to note the happy mind etc.; warn them not to be expectant and anxious but to go on noting calmly and coolly. If the yogis were too enthusiastic, much effort was wasted and the SAMĀDHI could become less powerful. Therefore, there would not be as much progress as there should be.

So, tell yogi to be less enthusiastic and contemplate coolly and calmly. In spite of this kind of instruction, if the yogi was still overzealous and over-anxious, let him have a nice sound sleep. Tell yogi to contemplate only after waking up. Or else tell the yogi to rest for two to three hours, or for a whole day or a whole night. Let the yogi do some work if he wished. Let the yogi contemplate only after having a break.

SUMMARY: Each noting brought yogi the knowledge of any one of the Three Marks of ANICCA, DUKKHA and ANATTA LEKHANA. The yogi knew this without having to make a special effort in noting. The yogi was not afraid of anything being dissolved. There was no feeling of fear, disgust, boredom, weariness and the desire to be free from all, like in the BHAYA ÑĀNA: There was no need to make a special effort in noting.

There was no feeling of happiness or liking to anything that was fully accomplished. There was no pleasure and happiness in spite of a good noting. It was a very clean and clear knowledge which was achieved spontaneously. That consistent knowledge which was achieved systematically and automatically would be called "SANKHĀRUPEKKHĀ MARA" (The Knowledge that can View the Psycho- Physical Phenomena with Equanimity.)

END OF SANKHĀRUPEKKHĀ- ÑĀNA

M. ANULOMA ÑĀNA (The Linkage)

ANULOMA ÑĀNA, GOTRABHU ÑĀNA, MAGGA ÑĀNA and PHALA ÑĀNA all four belong to one MAGGA VITHI. Therefore, the yogi could not describe all of them like in the lower nanas. They could be recollected by the PACCAVEKKHANĀ ÑĀNA: Then the yogi would be able to describe all of them in one go. Therefore, the following excerpts are taken from the statements of yogis who had described their experiences after recollecting through the PACCAVEKKHANĀ ÑĀNA:

When the noting was going on fine with stillness and gentleness, the yogi would describe the outstanding noting/knowing mind as:
THE ASCENDING FORCE OF MIND REACHING TO A CRESCENDO

A: Each time I noted, only the ending and dissolution were seen, so automatically the noting mind noted as "impermanent", "impermanent". Then the notings became very swift.
A: The disappearances were getting quicker and quicker.
A: The notings were accelerating to a high speed.
A: The notings were fluttering and became very quick.
A: The notings were getting faster with a force.
A: The notings were whirling into a crescendo.
A: I could see very clearly about the arising and passing away phenomena inside my body.

COMMENT: The yogis knew about the ANICCA LEKHANA (sign of Impermanence) and explained about the height of Sankharupekkha Nana, which was the VUTTHĀNAGĀMINĪ VIPASSANĀ, a powerful insight which reached to a climax with an ascending force or energy of mind.

A: Whatever I noted, whichever came up all of them were bad. I note as "awful", "awful".
A: There was not a trace of peaceful happiness in all the arising phenomena. I just knew they were all miserable.
A: All the time I knew they were just miserable sufferings.

A: My body was so stiff I could not open my mouth. Both sides of my jaw were very tight and I was feeling very uncomfortable, so I noted it as "awful", "awful".

A: It was as if I saw flames from a raging fire. Whatever I noticed of my notings, I felt miserable and thought everything was awful.

COMMENT: The yogi knew the DUKKHA LEKHANA (Characteristic sign of Suffering) and explained the attainment of the height of SANKHĀRUPEKKHĀ-ÑĀNA, which was the VUTTHĀNAGĀMINĪ – VIPASSANĀ, a powerful insight which reached to a climax with an ascending force or energy of mind.

A: All the phenomena I noted were happening as they wished, nothing happened according to my wish.

A: I saw things happening by themselves, and I noted the awareness of them.

A: I came to know that there was nothing except the mind and matter (NĀMA- RŪPA).

A: There was only the nature of objects and the nature of noting itself. Apart from those, there was nothing else. I knew that, and noted accordingly.

A: I knew there was nothing other than this.

A: I was noting as "uncontrollable", "uncontrollable".

COMMENT: The yogi knew the ANATTA LEKHANA (The Characteristic sign of Egoless, Selfless Condition) and explained the formation of the highest level of SANKHĀRUPEKKHĀ- ÑĀNA, which was VUTTHĀNAGĀMINĪ – VIPASSANĀ, a powerful insight which reached to a climax with an ascending force or energy of mind.

In VUTTHĀNAGĀMINĪ condition almost all the yogis could describe their experiences from the good noting stage to a very swift and outstandingly clear condition. Only a few yogis could not describe the especially swift and the distinct condition.

A: It was good, swift and clear noting as usual. But I could not know the moment at which the noting became very fast and very evident.

COMMENT: The yogi became aware of the impermanence, the

ending, the disappearance and the dissolution of ANICCA LEKHANA (The Sign of Impermanence).

The yogi knew about the miserable, torturing, uncomfortable, unpleasant, awful conditions, which are the Sign of Suffering, DUKKHA LEKHANA:

The yogi came to know that nothing happened as one wished; conditions were uncontrollable, arising and passing away by themselves, devoid of self-entity – and nothing but just phenomena of DHAMMA.

The yogi would describe how he noted the above signs of ANATTA LEKHANA two or three times or more than that. The yogis' noting mind was very extraordinary and very quick.

THEN THE YOGIS WOULD SAY:
A: Suddenly the objects and the noting/knowing mind were extinguished.
A: And then suddenly the object and the mind were cut off completely.
A: Everything just perished.
A: Everything dropped off.
A: The noting came to an end.
A: The noting was freed.
A: There was a black-out.
A: It was as if I fainted or fell asleep. But I was not actually unconscious nor asleep.
A: Life wept out of me. The continuity of life was cut off.
A: It was as if I was sinking underwater.
A: The notings were cut off abruptly.
A: I knew something extraordinary had happened and I thought I was free of VICIKICCHA (Doubting Mind).
A: I knew the noting mind and the objects were extinguished. I thought this might be the Realization of NIBBĀNA.

SUMMARY: The yogis would describe their experiences, just as they understood them. In fact, all their descriptions indicate how their noting mind and the notable objects had come to an end, how all the SANKHARA reached a finale, and how that extinguishment of Sankhara led the yogis to a condition of peaceful bliss.

THE TEACHER SHOULD ASK THE YOGI THUS:
At that moment, "What did yogi know? How was the knowing mind? Where has it gone?" (Try to find out whether there was any knowing mind or thinking mind.)

SUMMARY: When the yogi's SANKHĀRUPEKKHĀ- ÑĀNA reached the highest point of maturity, noting became very energetic and fast two or three times. But the yogi was not making a special effort. The knowledge that occurs rapidly two or three times is called VUTTHĀNAGĀMINĪ. Out of those two or three times, the one that occurs last is called ANULOMA ÑĀNA (The Insight that Ascends towards NIBBĀNA).

END OF ANULOMA ÑĀNA

N. GOTRABHU ÑĀNA

When all the noting was cut off, the object, the Noting Mind and Sankhara were extinguished completely. At that moment, the Knowing Mind, which reached ahead to that Nana, was called the GOTRABHU ÑĀNA.

O. MAGGA ÑĀNA

The Knowing Mind that stayed still just for a while during that moment of peaceful bliss is called MAGGA ÑĀNA.

P. PHALA ÑĀNA

The Knowing Mind which caught a final glimpse of the Moment of Peaceful Bliss is called the PHALA ÑĀNA: When the GOTRABHU, MAGGA, PHALA were occurring, it was like entering a phase which was devoid of SANKHARA.

The NIBBĀNA, which could be clearly known, is the extinguished condition of all SANKHARA. It is the peaceful ending. It is the null phenomena.

Therefore, when the yogi was asked, "What did you know at that moment?" the yogi would answer just as they thought: "I did not know anything at that moment".

COMMENT: Here the yogi was likely to think he did not know anything because:
a) The subtle DHAMMA of NĀMA (mind) could become evident only if the corresponding object is evident.
b) If the object is not evident, the DHAMMA of noting, the Knowing Mind, will not be evident.

The NIBBĀNA object is the formless, body-less phenomena. It is the sort of peaceful bliss SANTI SUKKHA, which was the extinction of SANKHARA SUFFERING.

Therefore, the NIBBĀNA object, unlike the SANKHARA objects, has no clear distinction of mental image, form or body. It was not clearly evident like the SUKKHA VEDANĀ (pleasant sensation). Therefore, the GOTRABHU MAGGA and PHALA (NĀMA DHAMMA) whose knowledge were affiliated to the non-evident NIBBĀNA were not evident like the rough and evident objects like the Noting/Knowing and Analyzing Mind (NĀMA DHAMMA). Because it was not evident, the yogi was inclined to think and say thus: "At that moment when the noting was interrupted, there was no kind of mind; there was no mind at all."

But when the yogi went through a period of recollection, yogi could realize there really was a moment of peaceful bliss. Therefore, the yogi knew definitely that: "At that brief moment while the noting had ceased, there really existed some NĀMA DHAMMA (mental phenomena), which knew the nature of peaceful extinction." For example, while a person is awake, at the interspaces between the forerunner and the rear part of the knowing mind (VITHI-Stream of Consciousness) such as the spaces between the seeing, analyzing and hearing, analyzing, there arose many BHAVANGA CITTA (Life Continuum, Subconscious mind). But these BHAVANGA CITTAS are very subtle, so one was not aware of the BHAVANGA CITTA arising up. Nor does one know that while the BHAVANGA CITTA was formed the knowing mind was cut off at intervals. Even though the BHAVANGA CITTA had actually arisen, one did not know how and when they were formed. If at that brief moment when the noting was being interrupted there was no knowing mind at all, the yogi would not know anything about the way everything became extinguished completely.

But the moment the yogi recollected and analyzed how things became extinguished, yogi could know about it very clearly. Therefore, at that brief moment while the noting had ceased, there existed a kind of knowing mind which was more evident than the formation of BHAVANGA CITTA (Life Continuum, Subconscious Mind).

The NEVA SANNA semi-consciousness JHĀNA state is very subtle. Therefore, even the ARAHANT SARIPUTTA could not enter that JHĀNA state with ANUPADA immediate knowledge following closely after, noting/knowing mind. For the beginners, no yogi could contemplate from that JHĀNA State. But later on, that JHĀNA would be evident if contemplated by KALAPA VIPASSANĀ. (Unique contemplation is contemplating on understanding of defining past-present-future states of mind by summarization).

The MAGGA PHALA are Supra-Mundane, thus they are more holy and subtle than NEVASANNA JHĀNA. Therefore, no one could contemplate VIPASSANĀ on the MAGGA PHALA DHAMMA. It is only possible to know how the MAGGA PHALA was formed by recollecting with PACCAVEKKHANĀ ÑĀNA: The BHAVANGA, Life Continuum (Subconscious Mind), is only VIPEKKHA DHAMMA which is affiliated to the object attained in the past life, so it is even more subtle. Therefore, it is impossible to know how the BHAVANGA CITTA is formed.

Therefore, one can say that it is totally impossible to know how the ultra-subtle BHAVANGA is formed; that the NEVA SANNA JHĀNA sublime semi-consciousness is subtle enough, so that it is impossible to look at it immediately; but it is evident enough to look through KALAPA VIPASSANĀ (Unique Contemplation). By judging the above facts one can know that at that brief moment when the noting lost continuity, it was impossible to contemplate with VIPASSANĀ as to how it became extinguished. But it would be possible to know it really happened by recollecting on that moment. From that recollection, it could be concluded that during the brief black-out period there existed a kind of conscious NĀMA DHAMMA, such as GOTRABHU MAGGA PHALA, which is not so subtle as the BHAVANGA CITTA but not so evident as the NEVA SANNA. This is one theory.

After the noting had been extinguished peacefully, the yogi became conscious and reflected on that condition. The mind that reflected is called PACCA VEKKHANA ÑĀNA. The yogi could relate the experience of that moment because of the existence of PACCA VEKKHANA. In the period of PACCA VEKKHANA it was possible to remember how the noting had gathered speed at first; how later the noting/knowing became very swift, and how during that noting/knowing period, the noting became cut off. While the yogi is recollecting the above instances, it is called the Recollection of MAGGA. It is like looking back at the road you came.

Before the yogi remembered to contemplate again, there was a period when the yogi was recollecting about and viewing the way the noting had extinguished. That period is called the recollection of PHALA. The PHALA SAMĀPATTI is very evidently experienced. The yogi realized that these are the benefits of his contemplation.

While the noting was cut off, the yogi knew that both the object and noting had been extinguished completely; there was nothing but just a peaceful bliss. That moment of recollection is called the Recollection of NIBBĀNA. Here the objects and the noting mind reached to a point where everything was extinguished completely. That attainment is called MAGGA: The existence in that state is called PHALA. The extinguishment of all SANKHARA is NIBBĀNA. Thus, it is possible to recollect with definite names.

The recollection with the decision that one is free of the DITTHI, VICIKICCHA, is the recollection of the already discarded KILESA (Defilement).

The reflection that one is not yet free of LOBHA, DOSA and MOHA (Greed, Anger, Delusion), the determination that one must go on contemplating and that one must continue noting is actually reflecting the KILESA which are not discarded yet.

END OF ANULOMA ÑĀNA

END OF ALL SIXTEEN LEVELS OF KNOWLEDGE ÑĀNA

Q. ARIYA BHUMI

The yogi who had attained all the 16 levels of ÑĀNA from the NĀMA-RŪPA-PARICCHEDA ÑĀNA up to the PACCAVEKKHANĀ ÑĀNA, after reviewing how the notings became peacefully extinguished, went on noting as usual. At the beginning of contemplation, the rising and the falling could be found very distinctly and coarsely. It was not gentle and delicate like before the cessation of noting. It was quite rough and lax. Both the beginning of objects (Appearing) and the end of objects (Dissolution) could be found very clearly.

Therefore, a lot of yogis would say:

A: I reviewed about what had happened and went on noting as usual. But it was not like before, the risings and fallings were not delicate like before. They were quite big and rough. The noting was quite slackened too. I thought the noting had been spoiled.

A: The notings were not firm, they were stumbling and falling off to the sides. It was awful to note.

COMMENT: The yogi retrogressed towards the UDAYABBAYA ÑĀNA, so the objects appeared clear and coarse. Both the arising and passing away phenomena were seen clearly. The knowledge had gone back to a very young stage, therefore the noting was not quite accurate. But the teacher should not yet reveal the true stage of ÑĀNA and the real nature of phenomena at this stage.

ENCOURAGEMENT: What had happened could not be classified as a bad experience. The noting was not at all spoiled. Things happened according to the nature of DHAMMA. It is quite a good thing by itself. Previously you were able to note very gently and delicately, but there had been a sudden change of ÑĀNA, that was why you thought the noting was not good now. It is usual to feel like this at this particular stage. You are bound to think it is awful. But things were not as bad and dissolving as you thought. Actually, you had improved further. Do not be disappointed. Just go on noting as usual. Later you would get back to the stage where the noting was good as usual.

ENCOURAGE LIKE THIS AND TELL THEM TO GO ON NOTING:

A: It was very peaceful, blissful and very clear. There was nothing to note. It seemed as if the noting mind was searching for something to note. It was like that for quite a long time, about half an hour or about an hour. It was impossible to note and I did not note at all. But even if I had not noted, the mind was not led astray, there were no defilements. It was as if the noting mind was alone in the middle of a big field. It was very clear, empty and clean. I felt so good. It was extremely blissful.

COMMENT: The yogi had a very clean SADDHĀ (Faith) and a very strong SUKHA (Pleasant Sensation) for a long time due to the force of MAGGA PHALA. It is not possible to note those minds.

Even if the yogi had noted, the current ÑĀNA was only UDAYABBAYA ÑĀNA. Since it was not so strong, the yogi could not know each part clearly. Therefore, do not suggest the yogi to note that kind of mind. Tell them to note as usual in continuity only after the slackened (clean SADDHĀ and strong SUKHA bearing) mind had gone.

A: After the noting was interrupted, I did not know what was happening in my mind. It was as if I was floating. I felt sort of happy. I felt thrilled and flustered. It was impossible to note.

The yogi whose noting had been cut off and had reached the extinction of SANKHARA was bound to feel happy and excited like that. It was due to the force of SADDHĀ at that stage. It was impossible to identify distinctly what kind of mind had been formed.

If it was possible to identify the yogi's experiences by definite names of ÑĀNA, the force of this happy and excited feeling was even stronger. While the yogi's power of faith was very strong like that, it would be impossible to note. Therefore, do not suggest that yogi try hard in contemplation. If you did, it would be useless. It would only make the yogi tired. Therefore, tell yogi to note on whatever came up. If nothing happened and if the yogi wished to stop noting, let the yogi have a rest. After a few hours/days the force of SADDHĀ would be lessened. Only then only tell the yogi to note ardently.

Besides, the yogi who had just reached a state of extraordinary DHAMMA would be very full of SADDHĀ (Faith) and the noting would be spoiled, especially if the yogi knew definitively about the DHAMMA he had just accomplished. In that case it would be difficult for the teacher to decide whether the yogi had really accomplished or not.

Therefore, even if the teacher is definitely sure that what yogi had described was a true MAGGA, the teacher should not speak out. Do not give the slightest hint to the yogi that you are pleased with him. Just say that "What happened was in accordance with the true nature of DHAMMA. When one's ÑĀNA was fulfilled strongly, it was usual for the noting to be cut off like this. It would be better now to note ardently."

A: Now my noting was good and after a while it became very swift. It was especially good to note and I often felt as if I was unconscious. After that, my noting was slackened and spoiled.

TEACHER'S ENCOURAGEMENT: It is alright. Let the unconsciousness creep in often. Actually, you should contemplate with the aim to reach that state often. It is better to give you instructions only after periods of unconsciousness have occurred often. It is not difficult if you wish it to be otherwise. It is quite easy to change. Now let it occur often. Note with the aim to reach the state of unconsciousness often. I would help you change that condition when the time comes. One more instruction and you would be alright.

HOW TO CONTEMPLATE SO AS TO REACH QUICKLY TO THE STATE OF UNCONSCIOUSNESS:

Note as usual with a resolution that you would reach within an hour to the condition where the continuity of noting was cut off.

There is no need for you to make a wish again to reach that condition while you are actually contemplating. Do not think about anything concerning your wish to reach that condition. Just note attentively that once you reach within an hour, make a resolution to reach within half an hour, quarter of an hour, ten minutes, five minutes or one minute.

Thus, make the time shorter and shorter gradually, until finally you could resolve to reach with four or five notings. If the yogi who had those instructions reported that he reached that condition two or three times within an hour, tell the yogi to contemplate staying still in that cut-off condition for a very long time.

For the yogi whose power of concentration and ÑĀNA is weak, even if the yogi could reach that stage only three or four times within a day or night, instruct the yogi to try to preserve that condition by staying still for a long time.

HOW TO CONTEMPLATE IN THAT CONDITION FOR A LONG TIME:

When you reach the unconscious condition, make a resolution to stay still for five minutes, and then go on noting as usual. But while contemplating, do not expect, hope, or be anxious to be able to stay long in that condition. Only after you had stayed still and unconscious for five minutes should you make a wish to stay for ten, fifteen minutes, half an hour, an hour, gradually increasing the time accordingly. You could, if you wished, try to stay in that condition for three, four or five hours.

The ability to reach that stage within fifteen minutes or half an hour and the ability to stay still in that condition for a long time could be fully achieved by yogis with strong concentration and ÑĀNA. Those with weak concentration and ÑĀNA could not accomplish to a full extent. But it is possible for them if they practiced for months repeatedly. Therefore, the teacher should judge the yogi's power of concentration and ÑĀNA first, then only the teacher should give appropriate instructions.

After testing the yogi whether or not the yogi could often reach the unconscious condition within the required time, and if the teacher felt confident in the yogi, the teacher could give a discourse on the formation of the sixteen levels of ÑĀNA, step by step.

After hearing that discourse yogis could compare the contents of the discourse with their own experiences, and the yogis could decide on their level of ÑĀNAS by themselves.

If the yogi admitted that all sixteen levels of ÑĀNA were accomplished fully, his own experiences were in agreement with all the ÑĀNAS, yogi could appreciate and understand very well. Then that yogi should be given a discourse on DHAMMA DASA SUTTA concerning the KILESA misconduct which should be discarded, and the honor which should be accomplished. The yogi should also be warned about the possibility of KILESA building up in the yogi's mind and body; the misconduct still being carried out, or the honor not yet been achieved fully.

In that case, the yogi should know that his DHAMMA was not like what had been described, so the yogi had not reached the true MAGGA PHALA. Thus the teacher should instruct the yogi to contemplate further until true MAGGA PHALA is reached.

SPECIAL NOTE: If the yogi had originally been a person with a coarse manner of speech and action, the teacher should not give a discourse on Progress of Insight (16 levels of ÑĀNA) at this stage. Watch and investigate his manner, behavior for quite a long time. If the teacher was sure that the yogi had fully achieved all the ÑĀNA, the teacher could then give a discourse. Soon after the contemplation, if it was unavoidable and became necessary to give a discourse on Progress of Insight, the yogi should be told about the three types of SOTAPANNA.

Three Types of SOTAPANNA
Those who admitted as Sotapaasnna could be categorized as follows:
1. ADHIMANIKA SOTAPANNA (One who thinks that he/she has attained some supernatural knowledge when not actually being so)
2. ULLAPANA SOTAPANNA (False SOTAPANNA)
3. ARIYA SOTAPANNA (Real SOTAPANNA)

1. If the yogi who had listened to a discourse on the Progress of Insight with or without the teacher's recognition thought that he had reached ARIYA MAGGA, and if it was not true, that yogi could be termed as ADHIMANIKA SOTAPANNA.

2. Yogi knew that he had not reached the level of special DHAMMA. Yet yogi reported to the teacher as if he had personally experienced

it, from the knowledge he had learned from the other people. Here the teacher believed the yogi and gave a discourse on the Progress of Insight. Afterwards that sort of yogi would lie to the teacher, saying that he had gone through those stages of ÑANAS. Such a person is called ULLAPANA SOTAPANNA.

Those two types of SOTAPANNA are not true SOTAPANNA. Therefore, very soon after, they misbehaved and their true color was known.

3. ARIYA SOTAPANNA. The third type is the one who really reached the true MAGGA PHALA. This is a true SOTAPANNA and would never misbehave.

After explaining about the three types of SOTAPANNA, the teacher could only estimate the yogi's *nana* level by judging his speech, then judging the yogi. There could be some similarities which might appear to be identical to the characteristics of a Sotapanna, but are not actually so. Thus, it is impossible to make a definite decision.

When faced with KILESAS, one could see whether or not one is free from the *kilesas* which should not be there. If that person is sure that these KILESAS would never come up again, then that person could feel confident about being a SOTAPANNA. If the KILESA misconduct (which should be discarded) came up again, one can judge that one had not achieved the SOTAPANNA status as it was thought before. Then the yogi could contemplate further, so that true MAGGA PHALA would be achieved quickly.

If the yogi could contemplate many more days, do not give a discourse on Progress of Insight yet even if the yogi could attain the condition of MAGGA PHALA as long and as still as he wished. Let the yogi contemplate further to the second stage.

INSTRUCTION: The condition of discontinued noting was the effect of the KUSALA DHAMMA, which was accomplished by previous contemplation. If the yogi did not want this present effect, and if the yogi wants a kind of KUSALA DHAMMA, which was nobler than this effect, explain to the yogi that he should discard this present effect. Tell the yogi to contemplate with that resolution for one to seven or more days accordingly.

FOR EXAMPLE: THREE-DAY RESOLUTION PERIOD

First contemplate reaching the discontinued noting stage very often. If there were about 3 to 5 instances in one sitting, then one should make a resolution that: "From now on, within three days I do not wish to reach the effect of KUSALA DHAMMA already achieved. I wish to reach the higher KUSALA SPECIAL DHAMMA, which I had not attained before." Then go on noting as usual. During contemplation the yogi might think, "Previously I used to reach to the stage where the noting was cut off 4 to 10 times within an hour. But now I could not even reach it once."

COMMENT: If the power of nana was not strong enough, it might not be reached within one or two days. Previously, after noting about 4 to 10 times, the yogi had always reached the sublime state of SANKHĀRUPEKKHĀ-ÑĀNA. But now even after one or two hours, it is not possible to reach that stage. The yogi had to gather momentum starting from the UDAYABBAYA ÑĀNA level. The nana was maturing slowly step by step. Therefore, the yogi had to note in a quite relaxed manner and note roughly like in the early stages of contemplation. Some notings were not coinciding with the object. Sometimes the yogi's mind wandered. There could be VEDĀNA, such as pain. There could be bright lights and visions.

But some hours/days later the yogi would reach the SANKHĀR-UPEKKHĀ-ÑĀNA like before. If the ÑĀNA has not matured enough, the yogi's progress would be halted at that stage, and would never reach to the stage where the noting was cut off. Only when the ÑĀNA matured could the yogi experience the swift and extraordinary noting like before.

Then only the extraordinary notings would appear automatically, and yogi would reach to the condition of discontinued noting like before.

When the yogi was instructed to contemplate with resolution, the yogi might not reach back to the condition of discontinued noting. The objects might have appeared very distinct and coarse and the yogi might have had to note for a long time, but when the yogi made a resolution to reach back to that discontinued condition already achieved, yogi found that it was quite easy. Once the teacher had heard these facts the teacher could decide clearly on the yogi's condition. Only then should the yogi be allowed to listen to the Progress of Insight. Or else when the yogi had reached the second stage, give the discourse on Progress of Insight.

END OF ARIYA BHUMI

SPECIAL NOTE: The statements of yogis in this book were made by the first type of yogi out of the three types explained in the beginning. The first type of yogi could explain their own experiences very clearly. The contents of this book are not all of what the first type of yogi had said. Only some of them were shown just to give an idea. There were lots more descriptions left out because of the limited length of the book. Therefore, in each level of nana there were various ways of describing the extraordinary experiences of DHAMMA which had been left out. Thus, the teacher could guess the level of ÑĀNA of the yogis who could not explain clearly, and ask appropriate questions if necessary.

R. Summary

The yogi who reached the level of NĀMA- RŪPA-PARICCHEDA-ÑĀNA would describe that whenever yogi had noted, there were only the object and the noting mind. There were only those two.

At the PACCAYA- PARIGGAHA- ÑĀNA, each time the yogi noted, the yogi could know there was only cause and effect.

At the SAMMASANA ÑĀNA, each time the yogi noted, the yogi could see the beginning, middle, and the end of the object very clearly. Yogi could also reflect that all were impermanent, miserable, and ungovernable (uncontrollable).

At the UDAYABBAYA- ÑĀNA level, the yogi could see the beginning and the end, the appearance and disappearance, the arising and passing away of all the objects.

At the level of BHANGA-ÑĀNA, the yogi could see that every time yogi noted both the object and the noting mind ended, disappeared, and dissolved. It was the same at the higher levels.

For testing the second type of yogi who could not describe accurately, the teacher could refer to the statements of yogis who had reached the particular levels of ÑĀNA and ask relative questions.

For the third type of yogi who was lacking in the ability to explain clearly, the teacher should ask detailed questions on how yogi noted. But the teacher should not let the student know about the experiences likely to meet at that ÑĀNA. Let yogi describe by himself.

If the teacher felt that there were some facts left out, ask questions that could give two kinds of answers, reverse questions, or ordinary questions. The teacher should ask in such a way that the yogi could not guess what the teacher knew in his mind. When the teacher asked some leading questions, if the teacher thought that the yogi just copied what the teacher had said, ask the other way round without giving hints. Ask the wrong questions as if they were right. Ask the points which the yogi could not have known.

At the later part of any level of ÑĀNA, it is common that there could be a steady pace in contemplation, which was evident as equanimity of a balanced mind. At that time, the noting was easy because of the quality of equanimity. Then the precision of the effort could be slackened. Once the power of effort has become weak, the power of concentration would exceed the power of effort. Then the yogi went on noting for a long time, the objects would become gradually smaller and dimmer. There could be sloth and torpor. Because of that drowsiness, the yogi could experience fleeting moments of unconsciousness or hazy conditions of mind. From that hazy moment, suddenly the yogi remembered and noted, then the noting could be clear and as good as usual.

Apart from that, when the nine levels of VIPASSANĀ ÑĀNA, such as the SAMMASANA ÑĀNA had matured fully, especially at the UPAKKILESA part, the yogi could experience a condition similar to unconsciousness. This is true to the formation of a very forceful PĪTI (Joy).

From that condition, suddenly yogi remembered to note. The noting could be as good as usual. Sometimes it might even be better.

At the UPAKKILESA part, the yogi could be able to stay in the noting-free, peaceful condition for a long time due to the quality of PĪTI, PASSADHI (Tranquility), UPEKKHA (Equanimity). Then the yogi remembered to note, and the noting could be as good as usual.

Therefore, the teachers should be very careful not to make a rash decision on the noting-free, unconscious condition as MAGGA PHALA. Remember that there is always the possibility of unconscious conditions due to sleepiness, joy, tranquility and indifference (Equanimity), as mentioned above. This sort of unconsciousness could be categorized as the 2nd type of JHAYI person out of the four types.

4 TYPES OF JHAYI PERSONS:

There are four types of JHAYI persons. Some people who were at JHĀNA State, believed and decided that they had achieved fully and very well.

(1) The first type of JHAYI had attained or reached the SAMAPATTI but he did not think he had achieved so. That JHAYI'S meditation was correct and yet he thought it was not so. Such a JHAYI could be identified as a person who had attained JHĀNA but not accomplished fully yet, and was not very efficient.

The person who is not skillful at the JHĀNA state would mistake the attained JHĀNA as a sleepiness. It was not only at the beginning of entering the JHĀNA state: It was the same at the later experiences of JHĀNA.

(2) Some JHAYI thought that their JHĀNA was good when it was bad and not fully achieved yet.

This sort of person thought that he was enjoying the SAMAPATTI when actually he was not so. He thought his meditation was right when it was not right. Such a person is called the sleepy JHĀNA Person. While he was meditating wholeheartedly, he fell asleep and thought he had achieved the right JHĀNA on waking up.

(3) The Third type of JHAYI really reached a good JHĀNA State and he himself knew about it.

(4) Some JHAYI had an awful experience and he knew it as a bad

experience. Such a person had not reached the SAMAPATTI and knew about it.

The unconsciousness due to drowsiness, joy, tranquility and indifference were characters of the experience of the 2nd type of JHAYI. This is not the extra-ordinary (special) DHAMMA.

The unconsciousness of the True MAGGA PHALA is different from those mentioned. It could be reached by:

1. The systematic attainment of all VIPASSANĀ ÑĀNAS.
2. The extraordinary formation of the VUTTHĀNAGĀMINĪ VIPASSANĀ.
3. The PACCAVEKKHANĀ and the later UDAYABBAYA ÑĀNA:
4. The ultra-clear, clean stream of a later-formed mind.
5. The entering repeatedly into that stage.
6. The ability to reach quickly to that state through resolution.
7. The ability to stay long in that state as pre-determined.
8. The experience of extra-ordinary VIPASSANĀ achieved when resolved to discard the DHAMMA already achieved.

The teacher should refer to these characteristics and make comparisons repeatedly before reaching a firm decision.

May the noble meditation teachers help the yogis who really wanted to contemplate to reach the true MAGGA PHALA NIBBĀNA. May this book help the meditation teacher in giving guidance to the yogis until they reach the Supra-Mundane NIBBĀNA through the true MAGGA ÑĀNA and PHALA ÑĀNA.

Chapter Nineteen, *A Meditator's Guide to Intensive Practice*, my own extremely detailed and careful advice for undertaking practice based on my years of leading meditation retreats. Western yogis new to the practice will find this section particularly valuable as I introduce the new yogi to intensive vipassana practice and comportment, as well as outlining the potential pitfalls to be avoided. These are written in the form of 274 aphorisms, admonishments and encouragements for practice.

19.
A MEDITATOR'S GUIDE TO INTENSIVE PRACTICE

Alan Clements
December 1986 through February 1987

APPROACH SHOTS: Skillful means supportive of optimizing the successful deepening of one's intensive meditation practice.

1. Be watchful of thoughts that undermine or sabotage your entry into retreat, such as "I'm too tired," "I'm hungry," "I need better food," "This food is not suitable," "I'm not getting enough nutrition," etc. Note each such thought for what it is. Honest, courageous noting.

2. Be mindful of thoughts such as, "I'm not getting enough sleep," "This schedule doesn't work for me," "It's too hard," "It's too long," "It's too much," etc.

3. Be mindful of thoughts, "This isn't the right time to be here," "This isn't the proper time to practice," "I should have listened to my intuition before coming," etc.

4. Be mindful of thoughts: "It's too hot to practice," "It's too humid," "It's not agreeable to me," "My body just can't take it," "I'm not from an area with such an extreme climate," "I have to face it, this weather is just not suitable for me," "I've tried, given it my best, but it's counterproductive to my wellbeing," etc.

5. Be mindful of such thoughts, as: "The conditions here are not what I expected," "How can my practice deepen in a place like this?" "My practice cannot possibly be effective in a place like this," "This place is so loud, so busy, so not right for concentration to develop," etc.

6. Be mindful of 'other yogis' not behaving in the way they 'should' behave, such as, "He is disturbing me with such inconsiderate behavior," "He's always talking," "He always comes into the sitting late, and makes such an uproar when he gets into his posture," "I swear he's being annoying on purpose, even just trying to irritate me," or "Can't he even sit still even for one sitting?" or "Why does he always wait until he sits down to blow his nose or clear his throat? You would think he would do it outside the meditation hall. How rude and insensitive! He should be reported," and "He always moves around so quickly, his practice is going nowhere, I wish he would leave!" or "Goodness, he nods a lot and I bet he doesn't report it! What a hype, another fraud going nowhere fast."

7. Basically, there is no problem 'outside of oneself.' So called disturbances arise only out of the mind states of greed, anger and ignorance, LOBHA, DOSA, and MOHA. Self-deception tells you it is 'outside' of yourself. Be vigilant, be mindful of such projections. Study

the machinations of transference onto 'others' – making 'them' the issue. In retreat, there is no 'other,' no 'them', no 'outside of the mind'. Such reactions and projections come out of one's ignorance and lack of self-confidence. Along with being mindful, such opportunities give rise to cultivating wisdom of ANICCA, ANATTA and DUKKHA and KARUNĀ – compassion – for the struggling world.

8. On a discipline level, make a commitment not to look out. Keep one's eyes downcast about six feet ahead of yourself on the ground in front of yourself. Keep one's mindfulness inside one's body, inhabit the sensations of the body as basis of presence, nor investigate sounds 'outside of oneself' either by looking at 'the source of the sound' either by looking at "the so-called source of the sound" and or "thinking about the sound". Rather be mindful of the sound upon one's inner ear, feel the frequency of the sound, the vibrations, and any thoughts about the sound. Also, note 'wanting to look up,' etc. The outer world should be left outside. Re-commit each time to "being in retreat." If needed, re-inspire one's commitment to the importance of staying steadfast, and the rarity of being in retreat.

9. Make the vow, the commitment, not to speak with anyone other than one's teacher, ever, during the duration of the retreat. Kindly, shake one's head 'No', if one wishes to engage. Once is enough to move on. If you see someone approaching from a distance, you can politely wave them off, mindfully. You can also put a note on your door, as I did: "Please honor this request, do not knock on my door. If it is an emergency, please inform my teacher." Done. Others are not one's issue during the retreat, other than to behave according to the rules of the retreat, and one's own chosen degree of SĪLA. Of course, intensive retreat etiquette has its own Bible. As a general rule create optimal conditions and work upward from there, refining them higher and higher. It is easy to underestimate how subversive 'talking or interacting' is to one's retreat and the development of one's concentration: And essentially, how subversive it is to the progress of insight. Avoid the temptation. Remember, you have no obligation to 'engage with anyone' while in retreat, other than with one's teacher. Treat the retreat with the highest level of honor and protection possible, and increase the focus every day

throughout the full duration of the retreat, according to your teacher's guidance. And your own, of course.

10. Again, put a note on one's door that communicates in your own humble way that you are not available for speaking, or even notes being passed back and forth. Cut all communication. ALL. Gift yourself with this basic support/protection. It is also essential to have concluded all business before the retreat. Once in, dive deep and go deeper day by day. Function with what you have.

11. Eat sufficiently, but with mindful care and with moderation. Be mindful of preserving and protecting one's energy, mental and physical. Both too little food, or too much food, are to be avoided. Be mindful of what you eat. Be mindful of how you eat. Be grateful for the food that is provided. Overall, don't linger in the presence of food. Eat and be done with it. Also, clear the presence of food from one's room. Let one's room reflect nakedness, a clarity and cleanliness that supports moderation and in time, high balance. And even non-sleep and not eating. Reduce, reduce, reduce without severity. Food is medicine. It is one's responsibility to eat, but in time one will be surprised at how little food one can get by on, and not only feel healthy and cared for, but luminous and dynamically awake. DHAMMA is cognitive nutrition, for sure.

12. Keep your living space simple and tidy and ordered. Keep your sleeping materials ordered and if possible, tucked away. I like a cane mat and a monk's small lacquer neck cuff along with a simple blanket and mosquito net. Be mindful of the entire process of resting and sleeping. Make every minute of it an exercise in mindfulness, and not an activity for sleep. Try one's best to interrupt the conditioned patterns of "I need x number of hours to sleep or I'll be tired tomorrow," etc. Watch and mindfully feel the sensations associated with breathing until one falls asleep, and the same when one wakes throughout the night.

13. Overall, sleep moderately but cover your act. No heroics here. Balance. Cool. Calm. Don't think you eventually have to go without sleep. Or judge one's practice depth to be something that will occur "from only 4, 3, 2 or 1 hours of sleep." Or "Just once I will go a day or two (or three) without sleep." Overall, don't fuss over it too much. ARAHANTS

are said to sleep. The BUDDHA slept. Sleeping is obviously a biological necessity. Dedicate oneself to treating it like a sacred act, a devotion to mindfully interacting with a process that is normally relegated to going unconscious. When up and awake, really strive. Sleep and rest and napping patterns will evolve based on the quality of energy and awareness. Trust in the flow. Trust in the unfolding. Trust in the quality of one's wakefulness to dictate everything else: food, rest, sleep. Also, be watchful of thinking "One must be vigilant with reducing the amount of sleep." Be surprised by the unfolding and the changes that occur. Study everything and refine based upon one's empiricism. Generally, the progress of insight does not conform to one's expectations. There's only one duty: Be Mindful.

14. At times you will want to stay in bed until the defined limit of sleep is reached. Adopt an attitude of "no heroics" regarding the amount of sleep, except if you sleep more than four or four and a half hours, the maximum allowed at MTY. If you exceed the limit, step up the resolve and reduce until reached. There is power in the integrity of honoring the Center's guidelines, and not giving life to one's justified rebel. On the other hand, if one is awake after two or three hours, stay in bed until four hours, while being mindful of subversive or undermining thoughts, such as "Oh my, I will be tired throughout the day now," etc. Be mindfully poised and return to sleep by being aware of one's breathing, in the way you have chosen or been guided as a primary object. Continue to refine the sleeping process until it is effortless to get up after four hours of rest. Or if less is a natural occurrence, so be it. Make that your new normal, your new maximum number of hours of sleep, using the same principle.

15. Each night, before entering one's bed to meditatively go to sleep, make a final attempt to meditate sitting in a chair, (of course in a dignified and comfortable manner). Be alert to one's anticipation to sleep. Note the anticipation. Note all conceptual narratives as they arise. Stay in the chair for up to an hour or until you wake up from your first nodding over and sleeping episode, your first full slump. Then gracefully retire. This will become a source of power inspiration, and DHAMMA momentum capitalization.

16. Keep strictly to your agreed-upon practice schedule. No alterations. In other words, don't trust yourself other than in the most minor ways by adjusting here and there. In this way it eliminates having to think of what to do, and when. Or if what you do is appropriate. One tastes the sweetness of form and repetition.

17. Minimize room maintenance, as well as bodily maintenance. Do what one does: bathing, showering, yoga, washing clothes, fingernails and hair, and do each activity with care and mindful presence, more so than the activity itself.

18. Create a situation as a yogi, as if a factory worker on a 'seven-day, twenty hour a day' work week. Day after day, week after week. Two months only. If there's a need to extend, be blessed and extend: for a week, two, three or four. Three months is plenty. No deviation. You are in training. A most exact and intelligent training. Do it well. No do, no pay. No ÑĀNA, no NIBBĀNA.

19. No letters received. No letters written. Zero communication with others. Give oneself the gift of FULL IMMERSION. A complete mindful conscious cutting off of normal life as it is known. A complete shutting out of the outer world beyond the Center – and even outside of one's own body. Deep unremitting interiority. One must go beyond the world and not be reminded of it by laziness, habit, or allure. The world IS, it will be there when one re-enters it. Act is if you have died and everyone thinks you are dead. You have two months grace period to experience what dying is like, and at the end of the two months, you can return to the world; that is, if one hasn't really died. And I have known yogis who have died as yogis at MTY. Just like that, they fall over. Stay alert. Stay mindful: All the while, truly knowing one can die at any second. There are no exceptions to this truth. Empower the DHAMMA gift of the retreat to heighten all things needed to go as deeply as possible.

20. From Day One of the retreat, slow down and move more deliberately throughout the day. Always be looking for momentum bursts to inspire more sinking into the retreat space, slowing down more and more. Generally, walking quickly does not help in removing sleepiness or tiredness, as is so often instructed. Find one's own ways to

challenge sleepiness and tiredness, and soon you will find a beautiful source of dhamma vitality and joyful meditative stamina. Keep active in the pure knowledge of feeling (on a deeply felt level) the integrity and dignity of the practice itself. Feel the honor inherently in cultivating mindfulness, especially at this intensive level.

21. Of high importance: Follow your guide's instructions carefully and precisely. Cut through second guessing the appropriateness of an instruction. If there's doubt, ask for details of the wisdom of the instructions. Cultivate an elegant, highly respectful relationship with your KALYANAMITTA, the most precious of relationships. There is a freedom in carrying out the general instructions and more detailed guidance as precisely as possible. Be a model student.

22. Give your teachers the facts, only. Be likened to a great translator. Express the reality of your experience to the method of presentation presented by your guide, and within that framework take care and pride and precision to express or convey the "direct experience" as close to the actual experience as possible. Only share how NĀMA- RŪPA, mind and physical reality, was seen, felt, known and behaved. The more precisely one presents; the more precisely one's guide can offer more nuanced guidance. The yogi wants guidance. Give the guide the gift of your coordinates on the inner topography of your being. There's a book on understanding how a yogi conveys their experience in interviews, but best to keep it simple and not stress on 'getting it right', or "Am I doing it right, or am I giving the guide what they want?" They will ask when more is needed and help one to refine the process.

23. When sitting and walking do them for the specified amount of time. Not less. And until instructed differently, not more. More is not necessarily better. We are looking for momentum, a slow careful building of the dhamma faculties of consciousness, or the seven factors of enlightenment. As the retreat progresses and one's practice progresses, a natural effortless momentum will occur. And don't cut a sitting or walking short unless in an emergency or the absolute call of nature (such as a severe toilet need).

24. The retreat is a training-ground experience to come to understand the true nature of the mind-life. Stay mindfully focused on

one's interiority. Be an "in-dweller". Study one's interior consciousness, and the direct experience of inner phenomena as they are mindfully experienced at each of the six senses, the six sense bases. And not outside oneself. The world is always arising dependent on our willingness to conceptually create it. Note one's mental movements. Note the full dimensions of consciousness as they arise and are known. Become a student of consciousness, of the mind, and how to come into formation moment to moment. We see that the concepts of the world first originate in one's own mind. They are only in the mind. The world does not know itself as a human experiencing it. Through ideation and the proliferation of thought and conceptual narratives the world becomes what we attribute to it. One will either feel bored or provoked; allured or disappointed; excited or confused; frightened or desirous: And so on.

The world is interior born. It is not outside oneself. It's known through the lens of the senses. Study confluence and formations and ideation. "To know one's mind" (as Sayadaw is fond of saying) "is the most important task of one's life." The retreat is one of the rare and most precious arenas to cultivate wisdom about 'being', and refine our relationship to the world, to reality itself. In other words, keep the investigation inside oneself. Not misplaced, or outside one's self. And remember the retreat rules are for the retreat. The world is there for us when we return to it – perhaps with a new understanding, and a deeper more realistic relationship with it, and others close to us – even strangers and enemies. Give each its own integrity – the retreat and the world.

25. Be creative and skillful managing our approach to each day in retreat. Although we follow the schedule, employ DHAMMA artistry to all activities. We each have our own unique style as yogis. Keep evolving one's own. Be true to oneself while following the guidelines and the teacher's instructions. Find an elegant smooth authenticity to everything one does. Drop in, creatively. Let NIBBĀNA find us rather than chasing it. Cease forwards and backwards. Sit inwardly and timelessly, not with the attitude of duration. Extend the day by taking time out of consciousness. Drop into this rare gift of awakening to oneself, free of the constraints and challenges of others and the outer world.

26. During sitting and walking meditation sessions there are rules that are inflexible. Two of the most essential are: 1. No voluntary or volitional thinking about something/anything, no matter how compelling or necessary it may seem. 2. One's only task is to incessantly apply SATI to the predominant experience, at its respective sense door. These two basic rules should be considered golden during every activity of sitting and walking, as well as during transitions.

27. Abandon such thoughts with SATI, not thinking them through. Such thoughts as "I can't go on"; "I've got to talk this one issue out now (and if necessary, bring this issue to the attention of our teacher for evaluation and more refined guidance)"; "I'm on the verge of a breakthrough"; "I need to be my own psychotherapist here, just this one issue that has been plaguing me for years"; "If only I understood the real reason for this nagging compromising pattern," etc. No matter how compelling, just note it, be mindful of it. Trust in mindfulness to provide a greater resolution than thinking it through. Abandon problem-solving through conceptual reflection, as "emotionally compelling" as it may seem and feel. Greater resolution takes place through flashes of spontaneous intuition, and/or the insight-wisdom from seeing into *Anicca* and or *anatta*. Even on a purely content level, non-engagement is a higher reward, a higher freedom.

Cardinal rule, generally speaking: Good walking, good sitting. Do not neglect walking as a secondary activity. Abandon the thought that "The more I sit the deeper my practice will develop." Develop a systematic balanced approach of alternating sitting with walking throughout the day.

28. As cliched as it may seem, follow the dictum, "No pain, no gain." Essentially, take the pain out of pain. Facing pain there's gain. Gain comes through facing both pain and gain. Only true gain comes from going beyond both.

29. Be watchful and mindful of one's addiction to time. Be mindful of creating clocks, calendars or even sundials with branches or trees or with all things that can be calibrated or counted. Challenge and abandon the conditioned need to delineate and create time references, thinking that it supports one getting through something. Such as "Only

two weeks left", "Only 56 sittings remaining before I am back in the world", or "twenty meals", or "This is my last long retreat." Be in the steady flow of applying mindfulness to *nama* and *rupa*, and being mindful of any and all references to time and duration. Challenge the clock in consciousness. Take time out of being.

30. An insidious blind spot among some yogis is a type of insecurity syndrome, or "attainment trumpeting" or "boasting bugling." It's often masked in pseudo-humility, such as "Well, I can't really say, if you know what I mean. Only a BUDDHA can say or speak of another's attainment with certainty." Or, "But in my case, it sure seems likely." Or, "Sure I have had cessation experiences, but I don't know how to label them." Or, "All I know is I am not who I was before the retreat, nor do I have any doubt." Or, "It's not important for me to label my experience." — and there is that taint of false certainty. The machinations of this syndrome are nuanced and varied. Drop the past. If you are enlightened you want to be sure yourself. Go back in, and go deeper. Don't be tethered to a self-deceptive rip-off. One wants to be sure to hook up at the right dock!

31. Over-anxiousness is a form of impatience rooted in ATTA-MOHA – or ego-delusion-embellishment. This does not serve its imagined purpose. Like hope or worry is ANATTA: Anxiousness. Anticipation. Excitement. These states prevent going beyond. SAMĀDHI doesn't deepen from a restless mind. It's also reflective of non-ÑĀNA. It too must be noted. Get subtle. Get nuanced. Know the state of mind as it is for what it is. Know the most subtle expressions and textures of the KILESAS. Be watchful of the thoughts, like "I must be close" or "It's going to happen any second", "It will be during this sitting" etc., etc. Cool inner quiet silence. Then when the mind volutes on itself, one doesn't say "Now it's happening to me."

32. When sitting down to sit in meditation, allow a few seconds to get there. Arrive, then full go, noting according to instructions. NO loafing or half-hearted involvement. Drop in. Get right to DHAMMA work.

32. Accuracy and aim are the two pillars of ÑĀNA development. Elegantly applied intensely purposeful focused presence. Everything

good will come from such active noting, such as "Choiceless Awareness and, Subtlety beyond Description."

33. Develop a balanced posture, one good for an hour. Not a posture that is necessarily the most comfortable, but a posture that feels to be the most balanced, the most upright and dignified. Elegant poised dignity. Sit as if you were allowing your breathing to cease. Don't rush the breath. Don't anticipate it. Don't expect it. Each inhalation and exhalation has its own integrity, its own arising, duration and ending, and much more from there. Train the mindfulness to see and feel nuance. Go into an awareness of the changing sensation and not 'observe' (so to speak) the breath.

34. Your meditation center is your body. As it has been said, "The universe is inside one's own body." Looking for the DHAMMA, look within oneself. Keep our SATI within the boundaries of one's own body, SATI within the epidermis, in and through.

36. Cut the inner commentator on the day-to-day unfolding of the practice. We are not a Dharma sport announcing the "action" to a blind audience. Just open one's own mindful eye, and see what is to be seen, felt and known. Avoid something as humorously trite as, "Now, who in the hall will be the first to move, or the first to cough and/or fart?"

37. Don't entertain even a trace of voluntary thinking. Make this essential resolve at the start of each day, and/or the start of each section throughout the day.

38. Also resolve "Nothing I encounter is a problem." Just note that too. Even down to the last breath before sleeping and/or dying, as we may not wake up. All is lawfully unfolding. How simple: Just note it. Note everything.

39. No evaluation, no interpretation, just note it. Relinquish every attempt to determine, fixate, figure out, evaluate, access, reference, pigeonhole, etc. Every proliferation, just note it and allow it to do what it does, and just envelop it with mindfulness.

40. Imbue all events, each walking and sitting, and then each object noticed with its own singular integrity – a one-off event, a one-off experience of mindfulness and the object. Just that. Each has its own completeness: Straight, on-the-spot mindful presence.

41. Everything that arises does so from conditions and causes. Open the lens of mindfulness to include both clarity of the object and relational causality. ANATTA is a natural law. "Because of this, that arises." "Because of this, that ceases." Yet, it's all in the context of 'stringer pearls': There's an overall purpose to stringing moments of SATI together, and to reach the goal.

42. Trust in the lawfulness of the DHAMMA: When SAMĀDHI and ÑĀNA are strong and mature, PAÑÑĀ naturally arises; and when PAÑÑĀ matures, release from fixation occurs proportionally. Wisdom, not thinking, knows to follow the safest of all sanctuaries – the unconditioned. This is a natural law. This is when ANATTA-wisdom takes over and does its own bidding. If you find yourself still "doing", note it as such. Overall, just get yourself to the hall – to sit.

43. Struggle in your own elegant way with developing the supportive qualities of dignity and grace. As we enlighten the process, equally craft character and one's own unique DHAMMA style. Use meditative artistry – we will all do the day the same (schedule) and do each meditation differently. How we walk and move and bend and stand and stretch, all requires carefully applied mindfulness, and equally respect for the naturalness of one's own meditative style = DHAMMA artistry.

44. Meditation halls are like KILESA battlegrounds. We are elegant warriors on the battlefield of consciousness, fighting and finessing victory of the intrinsic forces of denigration, both to self and others. Fight with the knowing of how to vanquish KILESA power. ANICCA, ANATTA and seeing deeply into DUKKHA progressively undermines defilements. Win the war through wisdom, not will alone or by having a killer attitude. Take the life out of them. De-enthrall from the toxic charm of blame, judgment, worry, etc. etc. There are also DHAMMA education centers and platforms to go beyond. But as a spiritual battleground, clean off your KILESA wounds, gather your composure and carry on. Learn from the losses and struggles and scars. Conduct our war with as much grace and cool and potency as possible. This is your 'do or die' retreat. You may never have the opportunity to sit for this type of period ever again. Get into the game. And by God, don't blame your KILESA blood and wounds on fellow soldiers! Don't be

sloppy. Or careless or crass. Be mindful of projecting one's DUKKHA onto fellow yogis or your teacher. Learn the ancient honorable art of radical self-responsibility, at all times, with all postures, all contexts – everywhere and always. And conversely, be watchful of being seductive or a seductress, or an energetic poser with yogis and/or your teacher. Give up the game if and when you feel it. Tuck it in – then remove the tendency completely. Shape one's values, character and principles as one progresses towards wisdom, and NIBBĀNA.

45. Face up, brave up to painful sensations. Learn to face them with poise, ease, flow, balance, fortitude. Whatever is required (to keep on keeping) in facing them mindfully, be vigilant: Be on the watch for reactive patterns of dislike, cowering, upset, imbalance, anticipation etc. etc., on and on. Mindfully empower learning over outcome or vanquishing them. They will be in our experience for life. Learn from them, learn about their qualities and their true nature. They too are ANICCA and ANATTA. And there is no better time than now. There may not be a later.

46. Don't be careless with any moment. There is no activity too incidental not to be mindful. Always move with deliberate empty purpose. Leave as much of "yourself" out of it as you can. Do not try to be a yogi gymnast. Just don't be sloppy.

47. Become sensitive to your meditative vibrational glow. We are all fields of energy. This will become progressively more and more clear as one deepens in mindfulness and concentration. It too is ANICCA. It too is ANATTA. But learn the conditions for refined energy to arise. It's the feeling of a powerful confidence momentum. Know its textures and the conditions for its arising and enhancement – and its diminishment. Also, notice liking the state, notice hoping it continues, notice as much nuance as possible.

48. We are aware of the topography of consciousness, the landscape of inner-being-ness and moreover, the ecosystem of our interior environment. Meditation is the "eyes wide open" study of the nature of being, and removing obstacles to peace and freedom. I.e.: It's cleaning up our act. Developmental wisdom. Expanding freedom. A more sustainable balance and peace in the face of complexity and adversity,

while enjoying greater powers of character and morality.

49. Overall, learn what expands and what contracts. Look. See. Know. Learn and repeat patterns of sequences of activities that increase momentum, and what decreases it. This applies to everything: food, sleep, etc. Always be on the lookout for refinements, and develop an attitude of immediate integration or the etiquette of non-postponement.

50. Always be on the lookout for refinements; develop an attitude of high excellence, gathering meditative steam: Such a one gradually becomes unstoppable. One becomes enveloped in the spirit of DHAMMA. And as one builds in momentum again be watchful of anticipating. Also, one does not know where one is, on the path.

51. Just develop moment to moment mindfulness, as best as possible. As one progresses along the path of classical insight, only then can we look back to have a clearer sense of where we have been, and how we got to where we are. Go deeper and deeper. Carry on with diligence and poise.

52. Prepare in degrees of readiness and increased application. Develop one's mental attitude. Deepen our seriousness and commitment in degrees, while knowing it is a hard and arduous journey. Be willing to go head up with all that arises. Get psyched. Thus, the one-off two to three months 'do or die' intensive. Do not make a career of retreats. Approach just one skillfully (with a great guide) and go for it fully! Reflect how others have done this before, under much more challenging circumstances. Get willing to 'get one's hands dirty', so to speak. Keep on increasing the involvement and never let up: Other than with the wise reflection rooted in balancing the faculties. Otherwise just keep on noting the predominant object with cool and calm noting. Be willing to die for this retreat. Be willing to give up everything for this retreat. Nothing is more important or more urgent. Decide: "Nothing will stand in the way of my ascent into NIBBĀNA. The DUKKHA stakes are too high."

53. Be particularly mindful of thought whose content reflects doubt or lack of confidence. I.e., "I can't do it" or "I'm not able to", "I have to face it. I'm just not capable of this task" or "Another time will be more suitable." Note it and go on. Such thoughts are not true or truths. They

merely reflect the characteristics of the state itself. They cheat one. Why be hijacked by such undermining energies? These are kindergarten level card-mind-tricks. A magician within the mind tries to 'pull one over on' your integrity, and desire for truth.

54. It sounds simple and easy to remember: Take refuge in yourself by making DHAMMA one's refuge. Refuge through diligent SATI, seeking that danger-free place that eliminates the internal and the external APAYA world dangers.

55. Be educated by the process of awakening to the reality of the DHAMMA through the application of sustained SATI. Learn from the process. Good moment to moment awareness of eating; the entire process provides good digestion and nourishment. Live your DHAMMA in this same way. SATI-inspired DHAMMA is the source of rich growth. Insight liberates that which comes from full and ongoing association with the DHAMMA reality of seeing experience rightly. Take one's time. There's a joy and peace inherent within slowing down. Take the hurry (towards a desired outcome) out of consciousness, by noting it.

56. Be mindful of the specific characteristics of phenomena. Know the textures of each of the objects of the senses.

57. As a general rule: Always keep an aroused and actively present and moving mindfulness.

58. Don't try to overcome pain, but keep pressing to one's limits of observing it.

59. Be creative in problem-solving meditative issues.

60. Be watchful of passing a guilty verdict on one's illusory self as 'owner' or 'responsible for' the phenomena that arises. Phenomena is not yours. It arises according to the ANATTA conditions. Phenomena do not obey due to one's illusion command. Just note.

61. It's not necessary to piece up consciousness as 'good' and 'evil'. If invested in such dualities it is easy to activate pride and clinging and disappointment and anger/fear. NĀMA is ANATTA. While in intensive sustained silent practice, just note and let sustained noting be what delivers the truth of insight-wisdom.

62. There's no need to think one's way through something, no need to figure anything out nor trace something back (and back to its so-called

'origins.') Quieting the mind through the din of reflection habits will foster a clearer, more subtle sense of perception. Abandon agendas or curriculum and let the DHAMMA teach the class, not the presupposed 'I-identity' who thinks they are the one meditating.

63. Over and again one's only task is to be mindful and let everything else be. Mindfulness resolves what needs to be resolved on the terms of its maturity. This is synonymous with listening. It's also naive and/or presumptuous to think that "This life phenomena and conditions are purely the result of this life existence – behavior by us or towards us." There are other forces at play. That's like taking the color of the flower to be the integrity of the whole plant. Our roots go back a long way.

64. We are contextual creatures living in the illusion of a separate ATTA-based existence. Call the delusion "a surface circular unreliable conventional non-factual reality play": The illusion or relativity of psychotherapy. Rather than sand-play therapy it's "suburb-play therapy" or "white elite psycho-seduction pseudo therapy".

65. Premature involvement in cognitive content with an extremely repetitive KILESA theme most often comes from cultural pressure to belong, or full-on psycho-snake oil or improper guidance by "wanna-be-meditation teachers" looking for capitalizing on creating a cult of clients. It also comes from a quick fix LOBHA (fear-based mindset), and/or an impatience with a subtle form of DOSA.

66. If these doubts come up in practice (such as "What I really need is psychotherapy or MDMA therapy or psychedelic-oriented psychotherapy"), okay great: Do that after you leave, or before entering the retreat. But if one hankers back or longs for more after the retreat, note such thoughts with great mindful discipline.

67. Remember this is your ONE AND ONLY retreat to attain true Insight-Wisdom and NIBBĀNA. When in Rome, do as they do. When in Burma, do as they do. Intensive meditation is an art form. Be willing to learn it slowly, and quickly, and well.

68. Even if you grit your teeth to stay noting KILESA, it is not suppression in a negative sense. It is the Right DHAMMA effort, Right DHAMMA intention, Right DHAMMA concentration, Right DHAMMA mindfulness, Right DHAMMA suppression. Why

negotiate with tar when one can step out of it? Be persistent. You are reversing the habitual flow of the KILESAS. That force is a force worth developing. DHAMMA resistance force. Of course, be smart and learn navigational skills: Time to press, time to chill. But always note until the noting becomes effortless, arising on its own accord. Give yourself the 'wow moment' as the basis of a new future.

69. For gaining a sense of renewed slowing down and 'instant centering' STOP and stand absolutely still for a moment. Do the Mountain Pose (TADASANA), then lean over and hang forward. But standing is the best: Stand absolutely still and centered and present. And if it feels right, bend backwards with arms over head then back upright again. Or if you become lightheaded, bend forward with hands on knees to stabilize. Drop into being a yogi, more and more. Give over to being a full-time yogi.

70. A major key to success: Mindfully approach the retreat schedule in sections – meditative work shifts. In other words, take the 'day' out of the day. Small amounts of time are easy to manage. My approach: 4 am to 10 am – lunch. 12 noon to 5 pm. 5:30 pm to 9 pm. During these red alert – 'no excuse periods' give all one has, to continuity and the development of a forgetting, unrelenting SATI. No time off for any reason: You are at VIPASSANĀ work. You are in the operating theater of saving your own being from mental and existential suffering. At other times, less pressure: But also include and include, such as 2:30 am to 4 am; 10 am to 12 noon; 5:00 to 5:30 pm; and 9:00 pm to 10:30 pm. Be innovative during these times. Keep up the practice but equally be in flow mode, balancing intensity with some sense of chill and ease and carefree (but not lazy) mindfulness flow.

71. Be watchful not to reinforce a deeply held pattern: That of falsely empowering temporal time, which gives rise to (and can solidify) the sense of self – 'I am'. (I and other than I). Such a skilled meditator thus strengthening the world of illusion, through unrecognized immersion in 'thought.' All thought can and should be put through the lens of *sati*. Be watchful of splintering off into the 'meditator' versus objects that "I the meditator" observe.

72. On the other hand, allow for natural wisdom to arise and fortify

'the practice of DHAMMA.' In other words, allow for the natural processing of non-voluntary and/or involuntary thinking, of charged or seemingly unresolved mental and emotional constellations (i.e., issues on deeper and more subtle levels). Even so, if the issue seems to be progressively intensifying, keep applying mindfulness until it doesn't feel charged, becomes a non-issue, or is neutralized.

73. Regardless don't deny or disregard 'VIPASSANĀ lawful magic,' or the 'miracle of VIPASSANĀ,' or the 'lawful magic of mindfulness': It's the universal remedy for the overcoming of the DUKKHA of the KILESAS. The need to do or support 'in retreat self-psychotherapy' is a form of self-deception, not IT as such. No thought is worth thinking: Not in retreat, that is. Not in my one and only retreat. Give oneself this rare gift to see for oneself its value, as well as its DHAMMA power to transform thought like nothing else. This is the mindful evolution of thinking. So, in summary: 'Thinking about thinking,' reflecting on one's thoughts, may provide some sense of relief and satisfaction, but it's short lived, temporary. The other is more deeply placed, and a finer relief and self-confidence arises. This feel of 'DHAMMA confidence' gives rise to greater access to, and a more refined quality of vitality, energy and mindful effort.

74. Avoid as much as possible 'outside reliance' as the source of attempting to 'remedy inside issues' Temporary external resolutions are not resolutions at all. This is one's golden opportunity to see the true face of consciousness, and glimpse realities not yet seen. Keep gifting this to oneself, and allow for the momentum of self-respect to build. Once the retreat ends, one can then discuss what it means to integrate the retreat space into one's world.

75. Reference point free intensive practice. Be willing to become consciously unmoored from the familiar. Trust in the DHAMMA until the DHAMMA begins to feed the very best of one's being. DHAMMA dignity builds this way, freedom of mind itself. Keep unhitching and untethering.

76. Keep a mind free of conclusions. The practice of SATI is the practice of freedom, the practice of open-mindedness. Keep the experiment of intensive meditation actively building until the very last

minute of one's retreat.

77. Take full refuge in the fact that the deepening of practice is the direct result of one's "Right effort, right mindfulness and right concentration." EMC. The ANATTA of EMC will come later.

78. Be mindful of thoughts predicting how practice should or will unfold. Such as: "First this will happen, then that will be occurring." Even if you are sure of the progression of VIPASSANĀ insight from past practice, be open, as the unfolding of wisdom is a dynamic largely mysterious force (as it has the unprecedented power to cut through millenniums of *moha* involvement). Stay in a state of virginal readiness by being uninvested in one's most cherished thoughts of the past about wisdom. Just observe. Practice free of a programmed belief sequence of "It happened this way in the past, and I'll be on the lookout for it this time around." Unchain oneself as a prisoner of the past. A prisoner of the memory of Insight, a prisoner of previous so-called Realizations and/or Attainments. If you were previously enlightened, so be it. Verify it again this time out. Eliminate any hesitation or doubt. Take it higher. Go deeper, i.e.: No insight agenda. Open-mindedness. We are looking for a radical change in thinking. Be open to having your socks knocked off.

79. 'Accuracy and aim' should be written over one's doorway, both entering the room and leaving it. A and A applied with a cool and calm smooth balanced effort.

80. Relax and simply note the predominant object. Noting takes care of the DHAMMA. You did your part, so to speak. It's ANATTA the rest of the way. And with it ANATTA's complexities and nuances will be revealed.

81. Neither wish to live or long to die. Within each inhalation, neither wish for it to recur or fear its non-arising. Be way cool with the flow of arising and ending, as life and death, and life and death ...

82. No excitement or disappointment. Invest in the conditions that free one from ignorance.

83. Don't race off to bed, as in: "You made it! Work is over." Rather, if there is a reflection, consider something elegant and simple: "A good day spent in mindful awareness." Or... "It's a joyful time to be

developing my practice. Therefore, I'll kick back a tiny little bit and glide down into the prone, mindfully aware as Ananda did, of laying down, the entire process of lowering the body – as if one was enveloping the form with full spectrum presence." Not anticipating "sleep", presence over outcome, or forward projection of the activity underway. This is "the joy of remorseless effort."

84. There is nothing to rationally figure out. Figure out as much as possible BEFORE entering the retreat. Once in, engage the new approach with heart and fullness of engagement. In other words, trust the dhamma process as "a universal panacea for a universal malady".

85. Develop patience with the "KILESA predicament." Don't squeeze the pimple prematurely. It will only compound the pain and annoyance.

86. Be mindful of predicting outcomes and/or anticipating futuristic encounters, from the anticipation of painful sensations to a state of mind later in the afternoon. Note these machinations of the mind. Become so aware of these movements forward and backward that they are immediately known on the spot.

87. Situate mindfulness at the doorway for each sense. Be watchful of going outside the body with the experience. Hearing the barking coming out of the dog's mouth. Hear the sound on the ear door, and the thought of it being a dog as a thought on the mind, and the visual imprint of the color and form and context of where the dog is in relationship to you – the observer. Note these colors on the eye itself. Note thoughts of 'outside' and context as 'inner world experience'. In other words, with almost each sound heard, especially in the beginning, a mental image or a series of images appear in the mind. They are mind created; mind generated. Even with eyes closed it is easy to see and assume what one sees 'inside' as 'outside'. A bird chirping while you are sitting; a car passing by; a carpenter hammering or sawing. We see the image and we may feel annoyed. We may even be motivated to get up and look for "the source of our annoyance." It may happen towards another yogi. It is not uncommon to develop enemies based on perceived injustices or wrong doings of 'other yogis.' Or jealousies. Or comparisons that give rise to pride and or self-judgment. Notice everything as it is for

what it is, and keep learning about the nature of mind-generated suffering and mind-generated release from that suffering along the path of awakening. Of course, all of these occurrences – internal mental imagery or mind created — continue to change, "movie-like." A world of make believe. Just empty phenomena rolling on according to conditions. We are (figuratively speaking) prisoners of consciousness, prisoners of perception, prisoners of mental proliferation, prisoners of PAPAÑCA. Stay inside the mind during the retreat. Keep mindfulness inside the body. LOBHA and DOSA arise from the MOHA of "It is I who hears and sees and feels, and it is I who is wronged. It is I who am annoyed." Relationships don't end with the eyes closed. We carry our minds wherever we go. We carry our lives wherever we go. Note everything in the present as elements of NĀMA- RŪPA.

88. When required, reflect on how rare and wonderful it is to be in such a special environment where you can suspend the burdensome need to think about anything; like whether to decide something, or be expected to act or relate or communicate other than with one's teacher. Such a gift, such a rare freedom, such a relief from the world of ordinary. It's as if we have come in from "the storm of disconnection." We have found a home in the world of DHAMMA. The vocation of freedom – freeing consciousness of fear, anger, blame, greed, doubt, projection, denial, deception and so on. Regardless, you will not forget where the washroom is, or your toothbrush etc. Basic contextual intelligence remains in the absence of volitional thought.

89. You are enjoying the ancient practice of the uninterrupted application of awareness, knowing that true greatness arises from such an endeavor. All our lives we have heard about large telescopes that bring the vastness of mystery into focus. Now we are in the observatory with a master trained in the use of the telescope. This is our moment. Step up and see for yourself. Look through the lens of mindfulness. Don't turn away. Stay focused. Look. See. Know. Keep looking. Keep seeing. Keep knowing LSK, over and over again. With sustained application you will see the universe outside within one's own mind and body. It cannot be avoided if you keep 'LSK-ing'.

90. At times, especially during the transition periods or walking

you'll feel quite convinced, but with a little suspicion, that nothing is happening in your practice. Or that what you thought has been lost, but for no apparent reason you have been doing that same thing over and over. Be watchful not to mistake the feeling of intensity for depth (or the deepening of practice). Insight finds progress in practice, not the intensity of feeling from practicing: Not wondering or evaluating, etc. Just to observe the most seductive moments of the mind, regardless. Be mindful of becoming hooked by something. And when you notice to keep score or feel bad, develop a slow, sustained and evolving elegance, or an impassioned ease.

91. The simple, always-applicable VIPASSANĀ rule of thumb: Just keep including whatever is the most predominant within the mind, and/or in whatever activity you are doing, as continuously as possible. Keep it that clean, clear and simple. Let everything else stop. Let the process of awakening be the most natural occurrence possible.

92. Be watchful not to unconsciously set up a personal performance evaluation style report inside your (unmindful) head, of how well or poorly you think you are practicing, or remaining in some form of allegiance with a set of "achievement-failure standards". Remove corporate evaluation consciousness from your heart and mind. Be aware of such insidious narratives as "I failed now that I moved during the sitting." Or "I failed due to falling asleep during the sitting." Or "I'm nodding too much, this is bad, I'm not ever going to progress." Or even: "I ate too much." Watchful of how we scold ourselves through the primordial CETASIKA of MĀNA-infused DOSA. The self-comparing mind. Both evolve a more elegant attitude simultaneously to being more vigilant in noting, "comparison, judging, evaluating," etc. etc. HIRI and OTTAPPA are not DOSA-rooted judgment or guilt – weakness syndrome. Note such states of mind.

There's no time to dwell and linger. Keep the present. Keep it so simple. Note 'now', and not 'as it could have been', or 'should have been'. If those thoughts arise, note them in the now. Take refuge in mindfulness, not swimming in the thought stream. Keep relinquishing "reference buoys." Or stability, predictability and continuity concepts, like "Who am I?" Moments of consciousness arising with SATI observing the most predominant component of the primordial flow. "This is life, that's all." This is the role of the yogi.

93. It's important to know that a hard task is hard. In this way we'll approach it with seriousness and steadfastness. Meditation is a type of "open-mind surgery", without the anesthesia of denial, self-deception, avoidance, distractions, worldly pleasures, and all the LOKIYA games that most mortals call 'human existence'. A yogi truly embodies the life of the mind, in the truest sense. A yogi is a lover of freedom. A lover of self-honesty. A lover of integrity. A lover of dignity. A lover of self-responsibility. A lover of accountability. One who is doing their utmost to embody harmlessness and trust. How could they not with such a dedication to challenging the primordial forces of greed, anger and delusion with a vision of ARAHANTSHIP – uprooting them altogether from the very depths of the sub-stratum itself?

94. The ongoing question to be kept silently in mind during the retreat: "What appeared and how did it behave? Then what did I do? What appeared and how did it behave?"

95. Be mindful not to indulge thoughts that wish to sustain or avoid, to keep or remove. Simply be with what is, without preference. Prefer a 'mindful mind' over objects of mind or a desired state of mind.

96. Another rule of thumb: Always touching and rubbing NĀMA-RŪPA with SATI.

97. Be precise with all actions. Incline SATI towards the object.

98. Give yourself the gift of repetition. Follow the schedule precisely. Simply put in the time and the effort will reward you a thousandfold. And don't entertain even a glimmer of thinking. What a relief. Not even that one thought. Zero engagement. Enjoy the new way of allowing thought its own natural arising and passing. And all we do is 'see it as it is'. Touch, know, allow it to go.

99. Be watchful of "trying to make things happen, trying to rush the practice along, to hurry the journey." Digest fully, without the rush forward to the next, and the next.

100. Cultivate a heroic attitude of a heartfelt willingness to experience difficulty and unpleasantness, come what may; especially painful sensations. Again, challenging the attitude of "getting through

it," or "racing through it." It's empowering to engage complexity face to face. Stop equivocating and look at it, as it is. Once hardship passes keep the attitude available to re-engage it later, or whenever it may arise again. It's ANICCA and ANATTA.

101. Dignity and respect: Practice as if you were greeting a long procession of deep and meaningful guests, true soul allies, friends of the highest order, who have come a long way to pay their final respects to you before your death. You greet each one with the fullness of heart, the fullness of sincerity, with calm intimate eye contact. Face to face with changing phenomena – all guests you have known throughout countless lifetimes in SAMSARA. NĀMA- RŪPA knows you are exiting. Look mindfully into the specific characteristics of each face, each phenomenon, all phenomena. Allow for the grace of reactions to your exiting, and greet each one with honor, but no participation in their grief or attachment. You show up with high order DHAMMA beauty. DHAMMA dignity.

102. Careful not to race sittings and walking along, as if the more you do, the closer you will be to your goal. Occupy each sitting. Settle into each sitting. Take the time out of sittings and walking and each day. Get there for each sitting. Sometimes there's a symphony of objects in rapid unison. Other times, it is dull and boring. Get there. Truly arrive. Glide into the rhythm. Make each sitting a sacred act, the most genuine experience of being in one's life. Ultimately, the more silent, settled, and present (with increased SAMĀDHI and ÑANA) – the ultimate natural law dance of NĀMA- RŪPA that is always there at a particular speed will be seen and known. Yes, it's work in the beginning; but DHAMMA is the most honorable work in SAMSARA. Decoding ignorance from SAMSARA, from NĀMA- RŪPA. Each sitting will have its own relative rhythm, its unique musicality. Granted it will change. Change is our ever-present reminder of the wisdom of ANICCA and ANATTA. If we knew ANICCA and ANATTA and DUKKHA fully, we'd be ARAHANTS.

103. Be watchful of monitoring your practice, and progress according to conventional PUTHUJJANA worldly criteria, such as how happy you feel, or how contented or glad or psychically comfortable, or

the frequency of joy or SUKHA VEDANĀ. The unfolding of insight cannot be evaluated in this way. Furthermore, don't "believe" such evaluations: Note them each time they arise. Live, learn, allow, release; move on into the next now, and note it, onward in successive 'nows'. For clinging to cease requires "MOHA cleansing", which gradually exposes the stupidity of TANHĀ as a valid relationship with NĀMA-RŪPA. The mind is often devastated, frightened, worried, fearful, and disgusted by seeing the true antics of NĀMA- RŪPA. We gradually evolve and deepen our practice until all SANKHARAS are insight-awake. They are known by their 'true nature': all 'wanting' and all 'avoiding' is known as just that; suchness, joyless, unexcited naturalness.

104. Always be vigilant and on guard for comparing past with present (and vice versa) to establish evaluation of where you are, and if you are progressing. Such as: "Yesterday was all smooth and easy, and relatively free of pain." Or "I could so easily bear discomfort. Yet today I can hardly sit for ten minutes without pain and restlessness. I always want to move," etc. Or "I'm sure my practice is backsliding." Thoughts of returning to the world reassert themselves with a greater aura of seductiveness. Until one has arrived at a high degree of insight and development, all attempts at accurate evaluation must be seen as limited in scope and accuracy. Better to keep fortifying and empowering the 'here now' and the 'now here', giving each 'now' and 'here' its own integrity.

105. Again, be vigilant to note comparing and judging and evaluating and good and bad and all other dualities. Be watchful of thinking "I am being educated by mind conditioning." Yes, allow epiphanies and/or relative insights; but not to compromise the power of noting, the power of mindfulness. Challenge the need for a reference point to root a changing identity. Allow ATTA to recede and ANATTA to flower. Be vigilant and aware of the limiting self-deceptive antics of ego-fixation. Even "I'm a quality meditator." That may be true — as a political prisoner practicing poise and equanimity in solitary confinement under harsh conditions, like Uncle U Tin Oo did in prison!

106. Be watchful not to enter a sitting as if jumping into a pool and trying to hold your breath underwater for a while. Step up in dignity. A

cool refinement. A tender open-heartedness. Make each sitting the most sacred act of your life. You belong exactly where you are, as you are; foibles and weaknesses and all imperfections as well. So be it. 'Facing ourselves as we are' is one of the most powerful and honorable acts possible in a lifetime. Here in retreat, we are doing this noble activity on a micro every minute, every moment level. Of course, this is not easy a lot of the time: Don't be timid. Do not be a victim of existence. Sit down and make oneself at home. Show up. Get acquainted with the situation. It's your time. It's your home. It's your living room. No hurry to get home. You are there. You've arrived. And there IS no other place to be.

107. Be watchful of negative associations, subtle seductive ones, such as "Why is lunch late?" Be watchful of the insidious narrative of 'waiting.' Of course, 'waiting' is a concept. NĀMA-RŪPA is never 'waiting.' It's a lawful co-arising interrelated reality. Be watchful of the mind's oscillations from conventional and ultimate reality. Waiting has no truth in it. It's a precondition for LOBHA, DOSA and MOHA. Be watchful of being "inconvenienced from my attainment of enlightenment." Imagine the Prisoners of Conscience – and take it higher.

108. Learn to develop 'irritation management' and 'annoyance management' – each meal. Each sit. Each walking. Just eat what's on the plate. Renounce outer needs as much as possible.

109. Overall, be watchful not to evaluate practice in terms of quantity, intensity, location, frequency; or alterations of painful sensations, such as rate of pain subsiding or increasing. Do not keep score. Be watchful how one's story drama becomes progressively more real with increased intensity of pain subsiding or increasing. Keep dismantling and deconstructing the internal dialogue. With pain story-dialogue one easily goes from fiction to non-fiction. Be watchful of evaluating or considering how long it will last: "Will I have to move?" Or "This must be connected to that." Trying to figure it out. Or what it indicates. "Will I make it?" "I don't want to have to move." "I'm going to have to go to a chair, or God forbid – a bench."

110. Be exceptionally careful with highly sensitive, deep rooted emotional thought, issue themes, and narratives, such as "the search for meaning and/or greater security in your life" or "a deeper sense of

purpose." Or a need for reassurance.

111. Be mindful of the three forms of DUKKHA: 1) DUKKHA-DUKKHA – the suffering of physical suffering. This refers to the physical and emotional discomfort and pain all humans experience in their lives. 2) VIPARINAMA-DUKKHA – the mental sufferings. And 3) SANKHARA-DUKKHA – the suffering of existence. The suffering of change or ANICCA: In that ultimate control is not possible, unless one is fully enlightened.

112. When you become quiet you can feel the heart quivering – the existential KILESA tremble. Watch very carefully the mind grappling to find some idea of deeper meaning: "How can contentment, safety, security, happiness and peace be available as long as KILESAS are present in the heart?" DHAMMA practice slopes towards that one goal, a KILESSA free heart – NIBBĀNA. Keep dismantling. Allow for the NIBBĀNA motivation to gracefully emerge. The most beautiful of human endeavors and existential urges. Try to nurture the primary reason of focus of life – to end DUKKHA-oscillation by KILESA.

113. Be watchful of the subtleties of the unfolding not conforming to our personally preferred sequence of insight development, and within the unstated time-frame unconsciously held.

114. Remain watchful of deducing meditative results/semi-results/non-results and success/moderate success/failure in terms of form and outward in retreat appearances, such as sitting and walking, etc; and sacred concepts: Sitting a long time, walking slowly, these are also sacred concepts. NĀMA- RŪPA isn't slow or fast. It isn't affected by how slowly we walk, or how long we sit. We don't influence ANICCA, ANATTA and DUKKHA, whether we sit or walk. All forms are concepts. You are still in the concept role of 'meditator'. PAÑÑĀ arises from SAMĀDHI, SATI and VIRIYA – not from sitting and walking.

115. Mind states are what it is about. Train the mind in key liberating mind states. Know the states to develop. Know the states to abandon. The recognition of some; the realization of others. The Four Noble Truths are not concepts, they are states of consciousness. It is not posture-based, so be watchful of developing postural apartheid – "This posture is better than [another one]." See the entire day as a flow

of changing postures. Encased behind the skin are states of mind. Be aware of the sensations of the body, as well as the mind that knows them. See beyond postures, inner and outer. Be in the flow of energies. Don't take the mold for the donut. Always keep reforming back to the mind-states in development – enhancing some, abandoning others.

116. Allow yourself to become de-infatuated with everything you know. We are vessels of DHAMMA, driven by DHAMMA, awakened to DHAMMA. De-infatuated with everything you know, would want, every person you've known, would like to know, will come to know. All hopes, gains, successes, whether worldly or spiritually. All possessions. Your looks. Your knowledge. Your wisdom. Your future wisdom. All knowing. All future knowing. All your ideas of the spiritual assistance you can offer others. Relinquish it all. Relinquish the wish to live and the wish to die. Even relinquish the wish to breathe. Relinquish the desire for the next breath. But be so "there with it"— as if it were about to end any second. Be acute – aim and accuracy. Give up the wish to "go beyond." Let whatever arises, arise from deep naturalness. Just BE. Just NOW. And just keep doing this until YOU cease.

117. Be particularly watchful when unpleasant mind states and sensations arise of how real and serious the internal commentary becomes. How the solid 'you' emerges, the 'identifier' of the flow. 'Me'. 'Me'. 'I'. 'I'. Of course, keep a cool attitude about the awakening of this phenomenon. But this is serious business. Be careful. Be present. This is your one chance. Stay classy.

118. To avoid and/or challenge the self-deceptive tendency of backing oneself into a tight corner. If you ever feel yourself becoming compressed, tight, claustrophobic without exit, just say to yourself: "And that too", "and that too." In other words, "include", "include"— "and that too".

119. The power of self-reliance: It will become progressively clear that no one can truly help you emerge from your KILESAS. Yes, one's teacher is indispensable, but it is you who must face yourself day and night. There will be a lot of commenting over the years (from the sidelines) of how to do it better; but in the retreat of your life, be true to oneself: Man up, woman up. You on You. Face up with NĀMA- RŪPA

day and night. You've got to go it alone. Yes, "feed off of the group space as much as you can," but also join the energy of that group space by being a 'warrior yogi'. No one can hold your hand here. The war is on. It's you and the KILESAS. No other place of refuge. No whining. No wimping. Bold. Radical. Samurai DHAMMA.

120. Allow yourself to mindfully feel the poignancy of seeing your world fade and dissolve and the beauty of DHAMMA lawful reality emerge. Let the sand castle of concepts dissolve. That includes all that can be labeled. Person, place, time, things, events have no ultimate existence other than ideation – thoughts and sensations, textures of mind: Like a true-life substance-less hologram. This is existence. KILESA-consciousness (K-C) mixed with perception and proliferation give the appearance of "real." K-C keeps it tantalizing and titillating to the "mind-self-identity-illusion". PAÑÑĀ reveals reality rightly, "as it really is". It focuses the "inner eyes". We polish "the glasses of delusion" until the eyes are able to see without the need for the fake dependent foolish habit of MOHA-lens. Gracefully die and gracefully emerge – into the wisdom of rebirth; rebirthing into the now and the future, as it were, until the NĀMA- RŪPA momentum dissolves into NIBBĀNA. What a moment it will be to truly know that all KILESAS have been abandoned, even way down everywhere in the substratum of everything connected to one's self. There cannot be any real and lasting and trustworthy contentment until that time. The ARAHANT-urge.

121. If you consider the practice to be hard work, consider that you are knowing rightly. Indeed, to control the mind is very arduous work.

122. Keep an ever-present escalating effort. Always looking for nuanced ways to put effort on the increase, to turn up the heat, increase the fire: To burn more brightly. This is your time. Leave no room for regret. Give every opportunity for a life of celebration and self-honor.

123. Meditation in retreat like this is a human duty that means: "I wish to put an end to the harassment by the *kilesas* towards me – an illusioned self. And equally, put an end to the harassment by the *kilesas* towards me and them – an illusioned other than I." Allow the KILESA-issue to become your full blown (prime and only) concern in life. All – everything else – reflects back, roots back, to this issue. Which means:

Allow the familiar 'you' to fade away. Allow your familiar interests to fade away. Remember, DHAMMA is the remedy for the KILESA-issue. Here your mind will strive to embrace your DĀNA, SĪLA, BHĀVANĀ weapon, and to drink of SĪLA, SAMĀDHI and PAÑÑĀ medicine. In this way, we can affect the greatest change by fostering our "A-I – ARAHANT-urge" – one mindful moment at a time. In this way we do our part to keep the DHAMMA torch burning, in the darkness of SAMSARA.

124. What you perceive to be good noting or difficult noting is not important. What is important is to note what should be noted.

125. Note the mind that begins to be repulsed by the wandering mind. This is HIRI and OTTAPPA. In the stupor of the wandering mind, one is prey for the KILESAS. Frequenting such a state is a life of vulnerability to attack without guard. If coupled with concept-immersion, one thinks things are "being done to you". You become your reality.

126. In a retreat, normal conventions usually don't apply. Again, the only duty is to sit and walk and include all other postures throughout each day, and note the predominant object again in all postures, all states, all times — and all contexts and all degrees of complexity and challenge. Downplay everything other than this in retreat, until full abandonment is achieved. Full NEKKHAMMA. Bathing, cleaning, eating, naps, not to hold any retreat pattern as sacred, make the whole sacred. Primarily focus on sitting and walking as the basis of awakening. Keep the secondary activities flexible to alteration: i.e., Those little things you do after meals, when you bathe, wash your clothes, how much you eat, etc. As a general rule, relegate them to the background. Stick strictly to 8 one-hour sittings and 6 walkings, and fill in the blanks and fill in the gaps or lapses with mindfulness.

127. When working with painful sensations, you've got to get there for the intensification. Not partially. Got to roll up your sleeves and get on your back and look under the car. You just broke down on a back road. You are the one who has to check out the situation. Game on. You have to be willing to get dirty. Look all around the pain. Be bold. Courageous. See what is there.

128. Courage is a beautiful state of mind. Look around as if you were in the dark with a flashlight. Look closely. This is not a partial affair. Crawl through it. In it. Around and through it. Get to know the environment. Take your interior out of hiding, Take it out of the closet. Know what you are. Know what you are made of. Know yourself as you are and develop that 'as is' in the most steadfast, courageous and graceful way. Touch everything with *sati*, even things that are unfamiliar, such as your vulnerability, your hastiness, your over-estimation of your qualities, your under-estimation as well. Don't be afraid. Relax so attentively into it that it makes no difference whatsoever that it is pain or pleasure. I'm learning. Get down with that. I'm eating what's offered up, what's on the plate. That's enough for me.

129. With pain it's generally not the painful VEDANĀ that's so difficult; often the heat dial gets turned up by the unmindfulness of our thoughts that arise at the time. 'Struggle anxiety' is sourced here. They are the precursor to moving with agitation. Ultimately, since VEDANĀ is ANATTA you'll remain even and cool with whatever VEDANĀ arises. Such thoughts reflect ATTA. i.e.," It's an obstacle." "It should be there." "Wish it were not so hard." "I want to get rid of it." "It's preventing me from going deeper." "I just don't like it, no matter what the teacher says." "If it were not there, I'd progress so much faster."

130. The DHAMMA work we are engaged in is not to 'get rid of' the VEDANĀ, other than by removal of their dependent origins – consciousness. To affect this, we develop insight that removes the real obstacles that are without our reach to abandon. The anger, fear and unknowing… It's the "not knowing" the true nature of DUKKHA VEDANĀ and their constituent sensations that are the obstacle source, not DUKKHA VEDANĀ. This is tantamount to misdiagnosis, and consequently a wrong medicine, a wrong Rx prescription. It is not even a vaccine. We can't overcome delusion with delusion, no matter how seductive the replacement MOHA is.

131. I can't emphasize enough that when sitting and walking one must seriously and continuously note, according to the instructions. It's real work. Very hard work at times. The mind has been following its whims and rhythms from time immemorial. We are changing the

course of a well-developed river. It can be done. Progress is predicated upon the seriousness and skillfulness and continuity of the yogi. Draw upon any past training to inspire replication with training as a yogi. I remembered training at UVA football and Spring Ball. Hard ass training. It was the only way to compete at that level. The mind will wander unless it is influenced by SATI and PAÑÑĀ. It's all about cause and effect. This is a different domain than magical thinking or merely wishing or prayer for desired outcomes. No A. No B. No C. A + B = C. Thankfully, this simplicity points out to us that we have the resources and capacities to do it: The DHAMMA takes care of those who take care of the DHAMMA. When the mind wanders the hindrances easily arise. They grip the mind, influence thought, bear down on 'being'. Contort. Contract. Stupefy. Degrade. Dull. Etc. etc. Who wants that? Who needs that level of status-quo? We as yogis are cutting the addiction to KILESA-consciousness and displacing it with the NIBBĀNA-urge through the practical application of SATIPATTHANA VIPASSANĀ BHĀVANĀ. Make good on the N-U through the practice of S-V-B. KILESAS grip the mind, influence thoughts and speech, and KILESA actions and behaviors follow like a shadow. Shadows follow thoughts as much as they do actions. This means DUKKHA for you. DUKKHA for others. Again, A + B = C. It follows the cause-and-effect formula. We need to cut this KILESA habit as one would cease cigarettes, cocaine, Percodan [pain-reliever], free base, speed, alcohol, harmful actions to self and towards others. Cut the addiction to violating life. Cut the addiction to war, to cheating, to lying, to deception. Study the nature of KILESA: "Inhale enough of this bad smoke in one's lungs to become sickened by the tar of denial" and "cough out that black yellow sickening phlegm"— or run the risk of "KILESA emphysema" or "KILESA lung cancer". This is METTĀ and KARUNĀ rooted in PAÑÑĀ: The basis of dignity and self-respect.

132. With each new deepening – from the start of the retreat to two or three days in – etc., allow oneself to be awe-struck by how vast consciousness shifts are – and so close to each other. Juxtapose in retreat with just – what – 16 or so one-hour sittings, and 12 or so one-hour walkings — and the silence. Just mind-millimeters apart, yet we live

19. A MEDITATOR'S GUIDE TO INTENSIVE PRACTICE

side by side of this shift-awakening, pretty much blind to it being so close nearby. But isn't that the nature of empowering cultural normalcy, rather than risking the experiment of intensive yogi-immersion consciousness? Yes, volumes have been written about this topic. Just like the juxtaposition of a psychedelic for the first time, or even a year in between; and then you drop again. Wow. Same with yogi life. The most difficult thing is getting into the retreat. Once in, the hardest thing to do is leave. Since you will leave – to make room for others – go for it fully. Push beyond, WAY beyond into unfaltering levels of PAÑÑĀ through NIBBĀNA. Uproot KILESAS. Weaken others. Develop and nurture N-U. Allow the DHAMMA beauty of VIPASSANĀ momentum to arise and build. Become unstoppable.

133. Approach the retreat as if you are setting out on an essential journey to see someone who is the epicenter of your heart and life. You do not linger. You do not get distracted. You are focused. And what if this person were in their final days or hours? All the more focus. You must be there. You will be there. You remain steady, abide by the laws of the highway and may even push the limits just a bit. You may even cut back on food and sleep. The same with a yogi in retreat. This is a 'must do', 'must win' situation. And if not: well, you want to be sure you drove without regret. If you want to play a step below, that's your choice. Playing life and death may evoke stress or panic. If so, make the arrival of the utmost importance Your call. You are alert, regardless. Every minute is on the road. Every activity is on the road. Everything, no matter how arbitrary, is on the road. Yogis are on the road, not on the mat. Yogis are on life's highway to freedom from KILESAS, the NIBBĀNA Highway every mile of the way. Feel oneself gathering the effortless momentum of unconditional engagement with freedom. Level the craziness of the city behind. Do not anticipate returning. Leave 'the old you' behind; 'be reborn' into the new, the unknown – and follow the heart-signs of the N-U.

134. Focus and sharpness of focus. Increase, become more subtle and nuanced in our noting. Only then will details be seen, and new DHAMMA worlds emerge (that have always been there, mind you!) Nothing is being created. States of mind are being cultivated, and

through that cultivation hindrance and thought-stream-narratives are being abandoned. Evolution of the good. Displacement of the bad. Call the two sides of the DHAMMA what you will. Evolve and relax.

135. Sometimes you will reluctantly sit down, anticipating the impending predicted difficulties, and as soon as you sit down it's indeed not only difficult and uncomfortable — but it increases as the sitting unfolds. At other times you go into sit anticipating a repeat performance of the previous sitting's comfort and ease, and it's painful, and this only increases as the sitting goes on. Then smooth and easy like air or silk. You only get up because you are excited by the feeling. You develop a greater romance with meditation practice. Be vigilant to note "liking" and "anticipating." They too are ANATTA. They too are DUKKHA – changing, moment to moment. Freedom over feelings.

136. Summary: You've got to simply log in your hours of sitting and walking. Keep a good open inquisitive mind – empowering learning over all. The learning mind is informed by the emergence of wisdom. Follow your instructions with greater awareness. Eat with moderation. Sleep in moderation. Do not talk or write or read. Don't be careless with any action. Include, include, and that too. Keep one's eyes downcast. Follow the schedule carefully. Keep a high degree of focus and commitment – ever-evolving mindful intelligence. Ask questions of your guide when something isn't clear (another way of saying not to "think things through"). The gospel of accuracy and aim. And in two to three months, you will leave with a fair (if not a high) degree of knowing reality rightly. I.e., PAÑÑĀ. Truth cannot be avoided, if one engages the process of NĀMA- RŪPA rightly.

137. It's natural for thought-stream themes to surface and arise: And resurface, time and again. It's also natural for different emotions to arise with them. Many of these thoughts will be felt as reflective of deep concerns. They may well feel like they are essential to reflect upon, and try to resolve. You want to understand and gain clarity. You do not want a quick momentary fix. There's wisdom power in understanding thought formations through the wisdom lens of the DHAMMA, through wisdom-PAÑÑĀ. Remember, thoughts do not need your normal help: They need your DHAMMA help. Keep it simple. Noting gets you out

of the way and opens the fresh air of the DHAMMA door. Let these bubbles rise to the top, and pop. You do not need to reach in and squeeze them; that only creates more. In short, it's natural and don't be alarmed. Let them have their natural half-life through noting. Just note again and again. The dance of mindful presence.

138. Consider: Without SATI at the moment of sense-door occurrence, it's potentially a full-blown explosion of conceptual life-drama-creation. Each moment of non-mindfulness is potentially like entering a movie theater for a full-blown engagement. With SATI we cut off our personal "twilight zone" episode. We stop playing with psycho-puppets. We cut our fascination with light and dark shadow ghosts. Within the concept cave shadow creation proliferates.

KILESAS arise when they go from objective viewing to subjective participation, to a vital actor in the movie, to the main protagonist. We effect and affect others and vice versa. SATI wakes us out of living within dream bubbles. PAÑÑĀ bursts these bubbles. NIBBĀNA MAGGA-PHALA eradicates the delusion bubble. ARAHANT removes it completely and for good. What a vision! What a goal! What a beautiful vocation: The N-U as a way of life. This DHAMMA opportunity arises with each sense door experience. SATI guards and protects one from falling asleep, and ceases one from being among the walking dead, i.e.: Alive with eyes wide open, but blind and dead to the DHAMMA. SAMVEGA creates the inflection moment to snap awake, albeit briefly. Enough to see the light. That's all it takes. The retreat says, "I want to see reality, see life as it really is, and not my conditioned opinion of it."

139. This process of dismantling unrealistic ideas of life and being is an intimate type of wrong view suicide. Or ATTA suicide, without anyone who inflicts it. Observing all that is considered to be your "self" (and all that you cherish) die requires great courage — until the process of DITTHI-ATTA-death becomes exciting. This excitement-anxiousness-anticipation is reflective of incomplete ATTA-death. Then that will die too. The joy and happiness and sanctification will also die, until it's raw unsoiled lawful DHAMMA. Until then you will often feel that you are being pulled out to face a firing squad. At first you will feel that you are witnessing someone else's execution. Then it starts getting

progressively closer to home. You are forced to witness the murder of 'self'. Not one murder alone, but the many and manifold lives of ATTA refusing to die, and springing back up with new more insidious faces of self. Remember that all that is dying is DUKKHA. Not you. No, you to begin with. Just the ANATTA of ATTA. Therefore, die with grace. Die with dignity. And dignity is ATTA as well.

140. Sometimes, no matter how still and quiet it feels outside, you will feel internally as if you are at a busy crowded city intersection from the din and chaotic busyness of NĀMA- RŪPA.

141. Allow the potential shock to reverberate deeply: That the basic texture of the fabric of life is essentially DUKKHA – miserable, frightful, wearisome, disgusting, tiring, and dangerous. And no matter how good it feels, it's DUKKHA. No high drama. Just a basic level of fact-perception. And from this ÑĀNA-intelligence and SAMĀDHI … you will come to the wisdom of the UPEKKHA-solution to SANKHARAS that are ANICCA, ANATTA and DUKKHA related. All mental movement at that point will appear fruitless and foolish. Just clean and quiet smooth noticing. At this point it is out of your hands and in the hands of ANATTA-DHAMMA. Here the DHAMMA will do what it needs to do to refine itself. Just stay steady and keep eating; remain silent, stay in retreat, sit and walk, slow and steady.

142. To see that the world isn't particularly benevolent – to say the least – can come as quite a shock. Until you realize that cause and effect is much more adult-like, professional — in its weird sick crazy law-fullness. Yes, it exists. Why? Yes. A bad, brilliant design. Nonetheless, bad — as in 'really bad'. Unless you see it through the lens of lawful ANATTA DHAMMA. But still, the black hole of PARINIBBĀNA may offer a hyper-quantum new dimension without the nonsense of this 4D BS. Nonetheless, it doesn't become less dangerous, but only more workable. An exit is known. Extraction of ATTA-DUKKHA DHAMMA. Here you grow up fast. You mature way beyond your chronological age. This is known as PACCAYA PARAGIGHA ÑĀNA.

143. Eventually every movement of the mind – every like and dislike – will have to be included and noticed in order to pass through the eye of the needle. Begin now. Over and again. Eventually who you are,

where you are, what you are doing, and how it is occurring, will have to be okay. All the while you do not lose the fact that you are following a careful regime or course of medicine. You don't stop applying SATI and following the DHAMMA health care plan, until cured.

144. If you ever feel secure for any reason, note it carefully. Security conceived with KILESAS still dormant in the heart is self-deception. Let this serve to arouse greater urgency, greater SAMVEGA. Keep unhooking. You do not want to be prematurely satisfied. Blow the cover on this story. Don't buy it. MARA. Do everything to arrive at NIBBĀNA, and the real security.

145. In short: Thought and thinking in all manifestations brings close the possibility of a full blown KILESA ambush. There one then must face the consequences of being sucked back into thought-trance. Then you stop looking into the eyes of NĀMA- RŪPA and ANICCA, ANATTA and DUKKHA. The record gets stuck. Or you keep looping, unaware as it were of your mind looping. Here you are somewhat dead. The old. Stagnation can easily set in if one does not recover quickly. This condition is often the precursor to actually talking, or taking a break – as small as it may be perceived and/or necessary (note it). Or prioritizing "that" (something else) "over" the N-U. You may even feel like leaving the retreat. On and on proliferation grows and entanglements entwine, tighter and more convincingly, etc. Generally, it is yet another jaunt through the cemetery of selected memories; and occasionally compelled to dig up a grave and play with the skeleton, so to speak. Grave digging is alluring, the basis of much of western psychotherapy. The wisdom of back then, brought now – looking at the cognitive-psycho skeleton through so called "fresh eyes". Grave-dig DHAMMA. Future-dreaming DHAMMA. Present now possession-obsession. The wisdom of non-engagement – just NĀMA- RŪPA. The wisdom of noting, that's all. Of course, it is easier said than done. Skeleton (re-)dressing. The other side is LOBHA-fetishes, like window shopping: Either mannequins that are dressed up, or naked ones that you dress up. Seeing yourself as a manikin is tantamount to being a hungry ghost!

In short: Thinking of co-joining SATI with the stream is becoming one with the movie and the forgetfulness or MOHA of self-ATTA, and devoid of the wisdom of selflessness-ANATTA. Self-absorption is a hallucination bubble.

146. No matter how 'taken' 'exalted' or 'supreme' you feel yourself to have become, if needs, be reflect for a moment on the "humbler" truth – death comes to all. Death often comes without prior notice. "I am subject to this condition, death. It would be wise of me not to be content with mediocrity. I should do as the wise have done throughout time and re-engage mindfulness with zeal and with high regard for accuracy and simplicity. And get back to being a powerful yogi.

147. Pay attention to the deep underlying psychic tidal swings of mind, with energy levels, with inspiration levels, with wakefulness and tiredness, with strength and weaknesses. Also, be attentive to (and with) the very deep existential insistence at times to lean forward into the future. To move towards "the end of something." This often comes at the so-called "end of a sitting". Nothing ends here. This is just an idea overlaid onto NĀMA- RŪPA. The same with walking and eating and everything. Take the clock out of consciousness. Take the calendar out as well. Take above and below and forward and backward and up and down and around and here and there as well. Even the need to take another step. Another breath. Another sip. Another… another… another… Challenge the momentum-labeling of "another is now on the way." Chewing one bite of food to chew another bite, and so on. Drop every forming of "dropping". Drop into the primordial flow as it is, and notice it as it is. Cease wanting and anticipating the next segment. "Give me the next segment, damn it!" Same with rising and falling of the abdomen; the depth of restlessness and anticipation. Let's call it "the existential KILESA hum." The intrinsic electricity of DUKKHA running through existential consciousness. You practice as if you have 100 questions to complete with 'yes or no' answers. But here you only get one question at a time, because without answering it properly the other questions will not appear. There's more to a yes answer than simply 'Yes'. There's accuracy and aim, and the yes answers become more nuanced with deeper meaning as they relate to ANICCA ANATTA and DUKKHA and the progress of insight. Anxiety and depression do not support coming to the answer. It's quite a subtle dance. You can

feel that you spend days on the same old question, and there is never a sense of arriving at the right answer. Nothing is happening. Or take for example: "It's like one of those psychological illusion puzzles. You focus on the dark, it makes no sense. You keep looking and looking with greater awareness until the entire process becomes "right seeing." In a quick shift and a turn towards the light, all becomes embarrassingly clear and obvious — something like that. Keep it simple: Just fucking note; and keep on noting. And do as Sayadaw says: "Fill in the gaps."

148. During walkings, experiment at times with a very slight pause of each segment.

149. To be thankful. Thankful that you have the PARAMI to see the value of SATIPATTHANA. Be thankful that you are near a good KALYANAMITTA. Be thankful that your health is good enough to stand, walk, bathe, eat and move about without the assistance of others. Be thankful that you have the mental cognition to understand the system of practice well enough to practice correctly. Be thankful that you are in a setting where practice is honored and supported. Be thankful that you have the time and freedom from responsibilities. Be thankful that you have the inner conditions to attain favorable results from the practice. Be thankful just that you are here and able to begin the practice as you have. Dismiss other intrusive thoughts that only undermine these basic expressions of thankfulness. Give yourself over (fully) to being in retreat, and reflect on these expressions of gratitude when needed, to re-inspire your DHAMMA resolve. Give over all you can. Do it over and over. Don't stop doing it. Do it until it's 'doing you', and then a little bit more. This is your time. Do it well.

150. We must be progressively more available as the retreat unfolds to really give ourselves over to each and every aspect of every section, with no action being too incidental NOT to give more awareness to every aspect of it. Nuance DHAMMA; and without hope of anything remaining the same. PAÑÑĀ is the interior symmetry of thought and emotion with reality – with the true nature of NĀMA-RŪPA and the DHAMMA lawfulness of co-dependent arising. This DHAMMA symmetry becomes refined with MAGA-PHALA. And it only becomes fully realized upon ARAHANT.

151. There's no hurry to be with the next object. Let objects come to SATI, and greet each with accuracy and aim. A very fine dance of ATTA and ANATTA as well. Don't try to surgically remove DITTHI and ATTA, but learn the meditative art of seeing the distinction more and more clearly, and with respect to the dance of ATTA as revealing the wisdom of ANATTA. Grace along the journey is in itself a fine DHAMMA art. The gift of grace is a hard-earned elegance. Of course, it is very different to MĀNA or pride.

152. A less ambitious effort, at times. A plunging or sinking into objects rather than "skeet shooting" VIPASSANĀ. Going for a touchdown with each object, without the need to score as a setback.

153. Keep cutting through this near perpetual and unconsciously compelling momentum for the next ... for anything. i.e., "As soon as I hit the targets long enough then my SAMĀDHI will deepen." Keep coming back to full momentary integrity: No agenda. No progress itinerary. This is skillful means, not the end product. Be watchful of "attitudinal manifestation syndrome." Develop a greater sense of "breathing more freely and fully" into objects and events: Such as stretching the arm, bending forward,

turning around, lifting food to your mouth, turning over slowly while sleeping at night. Carry on the practice throughout the night, even in and out of sleep, going back to the breathing or the entire body. Momentum, day and night.

154. Let the world fall away. No place to return to. Let go. Let the world "before" fade away. No work to resume. Nothing back there. Untether from the familiar. Put the cup down. Then pick it back up again. Let go, fully. Back to only now. Let yourself forget that which can be forgotten. Don't bargain with cute narratives to make it all okay when you return. I mean, embrace becoming an ARAHANT. Why not? At the very least embrace N—U – the NIBBĀNA Urge. Remember, NIBBĀNA if available with such completeness and involvement and fullness of SATI-effort.

155. Conduct yourself on every level and in every way as if you were finely tuning an instrument: And then play with greater and greater precision now, attuning to your own inner sense of attunement to the

DHAMMA flow of sense objects and their DHAMMA frequencies of ANICCA ANATTA and DUKKHA, allowing the insights along the progress of insight to saturate your mind (as immersively as possible). Allow the mind to become overwhelmed with insight, and be vigilant to note expansive (even extraordinary) states of consciousness. Note, "mind being blown", "mind being blown", etc.

156. Or the simple smooth sound of a single chord. Or even a gong or a bell. Or the fragrance of a flower. The attunement of the eye and awareness (with the colors on the eye) of a sunset. The ripple of water on the pond. The thinning of the fog in the morning. Swallowing food with poise and smooth cool. Lifting the fork. On and on, everything is done well in service of our awakening from the delusions of the ordinary.

157. Be like a fine dancer moving with mindful elegance as we abandon the KILESAS, and harmonize the factors of enlightenment.

158. Generally, the unfolding process is happening at a much different pace than how we are holding it to be happening. One tends to believe their comments about the process, such as: "Now it's happening as it should be." "It's happening so nicely, now." "Oh, it must have stopped." "It's never going to happen." "Will I ever make it?" "I must be here." Etc. Correspondingly, we get anxious, excited, dejected, worried, disheartened, etc. As a result of "process-evaluation thoughts", increase vigilance and note "evaluation" etc. Invest in true conditions for true results. Right effort. Right effort. Right SAMĀDHI. With that, be patient. Watch the full spectrum of states – from mild stress to anxiety to dejection to sadness to self-abuse. Whether you think it is happening or not happening, it has no real bearing on whether it's happening or not happening. What should be happening is SATI of the flow of changing objects – a rider on the peace calm wave storm spectrum, and back down again. Results are more reliably tasted through life-attitudinal thinking heart shifts. How is the mind aligning with the right view?

If plagued by result- oriented thoughts, evolve a seasonal shift image metaphor and use it when needed. It will cut through the high drama that one brings to practice, all the while relating as if it's the last few yards of a 'neck and neck' Kentucky Derby. Before the KILESAS leaves drop from the branches of cognition after autumn, there is a whole gradual process of leaf alteration before they drop. It's a process, and often associated with great beauty. None of us are going to shed our leaves overnight unless a storm strips us, or a tornado of KILESAS rips branches, even entire trees. We must be patient. Patience leads to NIBBĀNA. In terms of gifts, patience seems to be the greatest gift within the DHAMMA we can give ourselves, outside or inside of the DHAMAMA itself. The gift of the retreat must often be coupled with active patience, and an entirely new order of KHANTI.

159. At times during the retreat you may reflect that the person in the retreat is no different – or identical to the person in the world. You just feel very ordinary. At other times you are so high on meditation you think it is "the only thing I ever want to do in life". You may even think you will extend your retreat by a year, or even two. You may even go so far as to think you will never leave. It's too precious to give this up. After all, it has taken so much to navigate to get here where I am, I'd be foolish to start this process over. "Now and in this life" is my new agenda.

Personally, I have seen this. I have met monks who have thought this. And you may even go so far as to think, "Well I'll go back only to teach, to tell the whole world what they are missing." Far reaching futuristic-projected MĀNA-MOHA-zeal. Maybe with a tad of SAMVEGA. Yet SAMVEGA recommits to this retreat being the one and only two-three-month period of intensive practice in this life. Two months for sure, and an additional week to week of the practice is mind-blowing. At other times you will feel meditation to be a simple "human duty." Other times you are not quite sure you will ever come back to normal. Indeed, you feel so far out there is no land in sight. No identity to the "Me" one remembered. No comparisons are readily available. You simply have an amnesia to the previous "you"; you try to know, but come up – "My God. Who was I out there?" You seem to have lost your mooring. At other times, you will feel repulsed by your previous pre-retreat life/lives. And still, at other times, you feel inspired by your new re-birth. Sometimes you feel powerful, then weak. Sometimes confident, other times unsure. Sometimes hopeful, other times hopeless. Time feels heavy and slow. At other moments, timeless and effortless. Sometimes you cannot bear to be around or even near people. Other times you love them beyond any previously known love. Sometimes all you want to be is an ARAHANT; the next day you wish to leave and be happy keeping the five precepts. One sit and it all makes sense, then the floor falls out and it's all totally unclear. Sometimes you hate your parents. Then you want to bow to them and serve them. Sometimes you laugh and sometimes you cry. Sometimes you sit still, and at other times you can't stop fidgeting. So many perspectives will arise and pass. Note them as best as you can, and just carry on fine-tuning the DHAMMA instrument of consciousness, or sculpting cognitive formations with the factors of enlightenment to reveal their true nature, ANICCA, ANATTA and DUKKHA. Let these characteristics sculpt DITTA and ATTA from consciousness.

160. Be watchful of overzealousness to succeed in practice. This can lead to the experience or feeling that SATI is sliding off the object. You feel like you can't hit objects face on. One needs to strike the proper balance. It's a combination of Baryshnikov and Rocky: At times ultra-finesse, and at other times sheer power where you put all of your mettle and muscle into it. Develop a graceful confrontation with objects.

161. If you ever feel yourself getting entangled with doubting type thoughts of the practice's relevance to your normal daily life, allow yourself, if need be, for a few minutes: And ask yourself, "Would my life be happier if I understood 1) ...exactly what the interior mental forces were that kept me unhappy at times, unclear and unsure and in conflict with myself and others? 2) ...how those mental factors arise? 3) ...and developed the means to weaken and overcome them when they arise in the future? 4) ...I could minimize their re-arising? 5) ...and could eventually abandon within myself the conditions for them to ever re-arise at any time in the future?" Reflect with cool calm absorption your deepest heart's feelings with regard to these basic questions. Inspire your DHAMMA. Nurture your N-U. Increase your love of activating SAMVEGA. These are some of the advantages born from SATIPATTHANA meditation.

162. You've pushed off from the conventional world of things known and familiar, and are heading towards the intruding mystery of the other shore – out beyond the world of concepts of and appearances. Let it go. Let it pass without fear, fright or condemnation; with jubilation

not trepidation for what lies beyond, not the anxiety of thinking you can't return to the other. Remind yourself that all that is being altered is your ability to free yourself from self-generated suffering; for suffering to be lessened, and perhaps the removal of certain classes and degrees of suffering permanently. Reality on all levels has always been (and will always remain) for those who have conditions present to perceive it. Weakening the KILESAS does not hinder one's ability to live: It lessens one's habit to suffer. As the shore of 'before' fades away from view, with it a lot of concerns also go. Eventually, it's just moments of life arising and the interest to see it "face up" – "as it truly is" – raw and naked and real – with SATI, mindful grace and mindful elegance. Just the present phenomenon and the alertness of mind to notice it with SAT. In relation to this all else will seem superfluous, and will be empty of purposeful significance. Give up and surrender to this basic yet sublime DHAMMA task – lessening one's DUKKHA-addiction, and perhaps overcoming it fully – in degrees, of course. And the DHAMMA joy, knowing you know this. This is the launching pad to the beyond. Ideas, hopes and imaginations are reality distortions. It's crystal ball play.

Let go in a trustful, safe and relaxed manner to the present; somewhat like the letting go I would imagine upon death. You are lying there, pierced by a projectile or last stage terminal illness, and death is imminent – a good time to be mindful. Give yourself wholly fully to the present. Your previously desired plans and the ideas you held of a long (er) life hopes and fears are over now. Unfinished business is over. Time to let go, fully. Be in, and abide in, the flow of a new-death-life-flow. The list of "could have", "would have", "wish I could", "wish I had", "if only" times 100, plus some: The 'death door' list is poignant, tragic, human, common. But who needs it now, when the 'rebirth door' is beckoning? Greet the "new now" with elegance. Each time you construct the world, the future or the past, on the spot, note it. Be with the present phenomena at their occurrence, and let this be your retreat life, your retreat world, your everything meaningful. This is our only work. Abide here and journey along the path of greatness.

163. Don't try to karate chop the KILESAS into smithereens, or constantly booby trap MARA. Use more finesse, like the Japanese game

'Go' – elegant conquest. Trust that you are going to win. KUSALA is smarter than AKUSALA; PAÑÑĀ is more powerful than MOHA; DHAMMA CETANA is stronger than the forces of darkness. Of course, KILESA-consciousness is a booby trap in itself, always lurking for a moment of forgetfulness. Doubt, fear, worry, tiredness, desire, grasping, on and on... So be it, keep right there: And develop a sufficient level of SAMĀDHI to rise above these antics of "Keep me down". When you fill a balloon with helium it only goes in one direction – up. When one's heart consistently gets filled with DHAMMA it will automatically find its way to NIBBĀNA, regardless of the circumstances of MARA'S attempt to "Keep me down".

163. If you have a good stretch of sits and walks and you begin to feel you're beginning to have the upper hand, you feel good; nothing fantastic but strong and powerful. You start planning your new stepped-up KILESA assault. You rewrite your schedule. Longer sits. Less sleep time is glibly an acknowledged given. Perhaps you consider that you won't even lie down from here on in. Try to remember, "No heroics." You are not an Olympian, yet. Bruce Jenner VIPASSANĀ hero still needs to eat his Wheaties. Remember: Slow and steady. Cool and calm. Be a "now" glamorous consistent yogi. Wear the KILESAS down from persistent continuity. Just keep putting in your scheduled time. Stay cool. "No heroics" is the best attitude. Almost force yourself to stay in a consistent, balanced rhythm: Unless you automatically begin to levitate, that is! Just keep increasing the frequency of noting within the chosen schedule. The more frequency of noting, the more momentum. It's a momentum game. When there's enough there's a tipping point, an inflection point; velocity lifts off and the noting occurs on its own. This is an important point to get to for a number of reasons: Cause and effect are clearly known. And the emergence of a more visceral experience of ANICCA and ANATTA are known. And all the more reason to keep cool and maintain "No heroics." Literally, work towards mastery of the one-hour sitting, and the same with the one-hour walking.

164. Sometimes you feel that you can do 360s around the schedule. You juggle your day like a professional. Or you feel like a bird flying and floating – effortlessly soaring – high above the earth in the transparent

wind currents. Other times you feel like you are looking up at Mt. Everest. Totally intimidating. The mere thought of your cushion (much less the sight of it) sends shivers of fear and loathing up your spine. You just do not feel 'up to it' yet again. And the bells keep ringing, and you feel plowed over and over like a tractor grating the land. It's all too much. But not so much that you feel hopeless. That would be too easy. You would just leave. But you can't. Your integrity and worth are fully on the line. If it makes it any easier, reflect: These feelings are natural, and moreover, they are ANATTA – empty. And furthermore, reflective of an underlying KILESA. Note the state of mind for what it is, and study its felt textures and characteristics. "To know your mind is the most important task of your life" is one of Sayadaw's favorites, and mine too. That "mind learning" motivates me. Call it the development of mindful intelligence: The greatest most important thing one can give oneself. This retreat is the opening to greatness. The N-U is being fully activated and realized. "Learning, learning, learning" all along the way. Keep a heart eager to learn, and from everything. When in doubt, say, "And that too." Include. Include. The state of mind – the SOM.

165. No matter what may arise as a "serious issue," pleasant or unpleasant, (and if it doesn't pass upon noting two or three times, it seems to become "really serious") – use a VIPASSANĀ mantra as your last resort: It will last no more than 12 hours. Keep noting. Don't panic. And if you do, note "Panicking, panicking" etc.

166. Sometimes you will feel justifiably critical or excessively judgmental towards your insight level (or lack thereof), a strong severity and inner-directed harshness not towards anything but your own lack of VIPASSANĀ wisdom. You simply feel "It's not enough, for God's sake. It's not clear enough." Etc. etc. This is a type of DOSA. Always good, of course, to note what is — according to "What is the S-O-M / State of Mind?" To know your mind is to know your CETASIKA as they arise, and the RŪPA and the VEDANĀ as well. Turn the objectified projection of "not enough" into the wisdom inspiration of "seeing" or "recognizing" the state for what it is. Always turn away from fusion with ideation into mindful awareness of the condition, and/or S—O—M: Awareness over reality rather than identification with dejection, or

sustained inclement leading to temporary paralysis. The converse to this "self-denigration insight negation syndrome" is the insistent yearning to improve and deepen. If frequent thoughts of this type arise it is a type of RAGA. Again, cool and steady SAMĀDHI and effort and SATI lead to ÑĀNA and wisdom. Cause and effect. "Do this, and that arises." Learn to live in causal reality until ultimate characteristics take precedence.

167. The unfolding of practice in the intensive retreat experience reveals many subtle flavors of life. It's a rare great beauty to watch the mind gradually come into greater and more refined focus, clarity and balance. Also, the quality of fullness. The power of SAMĀDHI and the significance of SATI – to both retrieve and save your life, and your sanity, and both safeguard and elevate your precious sense of freedom and inner freedom at that, the best 'You.' Watch yourself be willing and able to have the most trifling of worldly acts be the most profound action of your life. The movement of your wrist. Walking a few steps and simply bending down. A movement of the head one way or the other. Reaching for your napkin at a meal, or the lifting of a spoonful of soup to your mouth. Everything is a new-found wonder of subtlety, of deep interest and engagement. Allow this new-found ability to transform the mundane and trifling to become a profound and compelling source of DHAMMA power, practice power. Your cooking these little things becomes the aroma of insight. You are in the near vicinity of true transformation: Thus, the meaning of BHĀVANĀ – the beautification of the mind. But be aware not to be easily satisfied, or mistake this new-found practice ease for a signal of ultimate success or victory. Keep pushing the water apart; it's persistent in returning. Developing insight is like an internal parting of the sea. Continue to work your miracle of mindfulness. We are developing radical non-superficiality. No anxiousness or basic excitement of what is to come. Stay clear and on purpose and keep parting your inner sea until the entire process inverts, and you are walking on water, and then above it. Leave this earth behind. DHAMMA is our home.

168. Practice requires a consistent dying into the present, to the familiar, to hope and fears, to all considerations; to becoming and not becoming; to your idea of yourself, to the idea of the self you still

don't know; to non-self, to ambition, to success, to gains; to reputation, achievements; to ideas of happiness, and freedom; to your souvenirs in samsara; to your crusade against ignorance. To develop insight and attain NIBBĀNA is a death process. The strongly rooted belief in self and all of its subtle roots are cut off. In its struggle to survive it exposes its deepest and most powerfully-held territory and forces. The yogi becomes the VIPASSANĀ kamikaze, always willing to die for the sake of the truth. To enter, there are well established entry requirements. All SANKHĀRAS are an affliction. There's no joy to be found in knowing ANICCA SANKHĀRA, then the mind will truly "kamikaze in" on itself. The KILESAS are abandoned – and displaced through positive mind-filling PAÑÑĀ.

169. Be willing to consciously feel embarrassed and humiliated and humbled by (and through) your internal mindful discoveries. It's a rather sweet reaction. Be touched by it. Be inspired. Before, through MOHA, there was not knowing at all; then wrong knowing; then denial of not knowing, and wrong knowing; then anger towards both. Then guilt towards both. Then embarrassment and humiliation. Then thankfulness. Then SAMVEGA. Then UPEKKHA. With ongoing SATI then PAÑÑĀ. This is the MOHA displacement process.

170. Develop an attitude that takes noble pride in exposing shadow pride. Develop respect for the process of exposing ourselves. Train the mind to delight in seeing the layers of denial and self-deception. What a waste of psychic time to be so stingy with our dignity and true power! Give it up. Develop an interest in "fact finding", not shadow enhancement. You can meditate your way into greater entanglements and tightness and shrewdness. I have seen it, especially among teacher-types and/ or highly ambitious commercially-oriented 'snake oil' types looking for a hustle; i.e., the commodification of consciousness; spiritual shysters. Challenge "opinion-oriented" pseudo-insight. As the practice unfolds, you will see how intimately connected you are to 'your' thoughts. And to some degree your emotions. And to some extent one's body. Yogis often consider these different "intimacy-strata" as sacred dimensions. They are felt as personal property. They are cherished as "me, I, mine." They are interior "belongings." And with it comes degrees of identity-clinging

and grasping and ownership-attachment. One imbues them with values and even feeling bodies: "Harm my beliefs and you harm me." The Church of Me – XYZ onward. (Sometimes it does not even make sense what people identify with as "I – me."

TASHA and LOBHA are the basis of attachment, and MOHA – blindness to reality; we fear and/or cling. There is no wisdom-rooted reason for skillful clinging. The wisdom of clinging? Let it go and hold it closer to your heart, and freely. Thoughts are intimate to this self-confining process. The thoughts that we think are us. And we pick and choose at times which ones to respond to and to act out their message. At other times they take us along quite uninvited. To know whether a mind source is LOBHA, DOSA, MOHA or ALOBHA, ADOSA, or AMOHA requires PAÑÑĀ. Otherwise, life is a roulette wheel style experience. At times Russian roulette. Practice is likened to the reveler, the physician, the investigator: Make sure of premature diagnosis and or misdiagnosis, this would be MOHA. As a general attitude, challenge any level of perceived wisdom and accomplishment. Let it stand the test of repeated insight-scrutiny. It must be straight up and honest, to be sure. To be absolutely sure is a must. And then check it again over time and in critical circumstances. Be particularly careful not to confuse "insight" for "ideas that appeal". We have all heard the language of the DHAMMA, NĀMA, RŪPA, cause and effect' ANATTA, ANICCA and DUKKHA and SATIPATTHANA etc, etc, blah, blah; and even 'cessation', more blah blah. All the right answers have been heard and woven somewhat seamlessly into more elaborate garments of denial and self-deception; even high doses of acid are often immune to seeing through these forms of self-trance. Try not to FIT YOURSELF INTO INSIGHTS. Let the insights replace MOHA stories. Be swept away by genuine insight. And then still fight for your life until you drown in wisdom. But get back up and keep swimming. More SATI. One more stroke of SATI until MOHA drowns and wisdom breathes freely.

171. Remember that the practice is designed by function to put all aspects of oneself under the highest level of mindful scrutiny. There is so much more to the process than one can imagine. Focus on continuity and see the nuance of what's possible. Here continuity means "filling in

the gaps" of unawareness with mindfulness. Look closer, more carefully, at the flow of everything one does. Go from a general sense of awareness to a minute level, and then a microscopic level. If one does fill in the gaps – if the senses are not guarded – KILESAS easily squeak through. Your challenge is to come out of the cold. In order to do that one must eliminate "hiding spots" or "safe-havens of arrogance." One must play high stakes with the process. Take risks to "include, and include that too". There is nothing too sacred to not include. Do not dance with the devil. Do not be seduced by MARA. Support your teacher by knowing and exposing your "MOHA nests" – those places of neurotic, self-deceptive pseudo comfort. Cut through your cunning. Throw it back into the sea as unnecessary baggage. And in turn your teacher will support you in your own self-exposure process, supporting you in the DHAMMA art of seeing through the MOHA antics of seductive reduction of the seven factors of enlightenment. MOHA havens are seen as mind-mines. Indeed, most have entire MOHA-DITTHI subdivisions. Others entire counties, states, nations, galaxies. For some, who knows? Their MOHA may be universal and permanent. Who knows if all turn towards DHAMMA? Maybe some are MOHA-junkies for eternity. How frightening to think that may be possible! How rare it is to come to the DHAMMA. It stands to reason with the simile of the blind turtle that the turtle "never" hooks the yoke. In this way increase the passion for SAMVEGA and seize the rare opportunity to make the most of this one long intensive "do or die" retreat. Remember, SATI is the ultimate psychotherapist, friend, and consultant. It exposes how to conduct our life's business with grace, courage and wisdom. It alters and interrupts fully denigrating patterns of being, and aligns with a life of dynamic creative wisdom.

172. You don't need to assume that to interrupt with SATI safety and security that it is synonymous with becoming vulnerable. Vulnerability is a shrunken pseudo receptive state of mind, born from having shortcomings and weaknesses exposed – real or imagined – and the aftermath of the crush being a differentially outwardly directed weakness. This is very different than the true DHAMMA receptivity. "Empowered openness" is our direction. In retreat, we must remain wide

open to admonishment, constructive criticism and correction both from within – HIRI and OTTAPPA – and from outside, by one's teacher. In this way we refine purpose, clarity and self-confidence. And we strengthen our capacity for self-refugee and refuge in the DHAMMA.

172. DHAMMA practice-beauty arises and inspires in many ways. Allow yourself to quench your DHAMMA thirst all along the way. Allow yourself to be nurtured, empowered, and beautified by the littlest of things. Drink the nectar of awakening. Smell the fragrance of tiny DHAMMA flowers. Feel your edginess to be practicing in this timeless rare gorgeous lineage of greatness. Learn to know the attributes of DHAMMA beauty. The various fragrances of the SATI and its application in such a rare manner as intensive practice. This precious SATI guards you, protects and guides you, clarifies and resolves issues for you, induces radiance and peace, develops, strengthens and quiets KILESAS; it exposes and refines one. It shapes and crafts the mind, and it composes great mind states into even higher frequencies. One becomes graceful and caring. Generous by nature. Dignified. Polished. It makes one noble. It's the forerunner of PAÑÑĀ and NIBBĀNA. It becomes one's best friend, one's true refuge, one's lifelong companion. Treat it well, and it will reciprocate, plus some.

173. Be watchful of developing and reinforcing the dual you: the foolish you, the wise you, the lustful you. The celibate you. The 'in retreat' you. The 'out of retreat' you. The celibate nun you and the sex worker you. The "I want to do it" you. The "No, I must not do it" you. The "I like practice" you. And the "I don't like it" you. The "taker" and the "giver". The "contented" you and the "discontented" you. The "clear" you and the "confused" you. The "student" you. The "teacher" you. The hidden, secretive you. The gregarious and charismatic you. The cunning and slippery you. The poser and the transparent you. The one with all the words and the one who hides behind them. The one who hides beneath a facade of vulnerability and shame. The one who is all bravado and "puffed out like a dumb alpha ape". On and on. "This you" and "that you". I AM both of the "you's – "you are" and "you are not". Dueling duels. Forever dueling. Forever deadbeat.

Be SATI of anything and relax self-referencing from there. You do not have to feel that you are the owner of your thoughts. They come uninvited. Note them all. You are not the author of them. ANATTA. No blame. No guilt. No additional comment needed. Be mindful and cut the dialogue in oneself and cut the "truth" of the dueling duels. Be watchful of the falsely perceived need to counterbalance a thought-sequence with another thought-sequence. Do not think you need to get the last word in. You are not a jury of your own being in practice. And be watchful of the one who wants to resolve the dueling with a false sense of escape, who can't wait to go to bed. Correction of all things good comes from SATI, not on thinking about the thinking. Just rely on increasing the frequency and quality of SATI. Rely on the SAMVEGA urge and the fire of the N – U.

174. Allow this part of yourself that doesn't quite feel "into it" or "fully here" or "fully arrived" yet, to be a natural aspect of the 'getting into' process or the 'having' process. That part of you that still considers your life where you came from, and why you will be doing; that part of you that is still very conscious of time, that still considers "how much longer to go", etc. This is natural. Try not to compound it by value judgments. Or self-condemnation. Or "I shouldn't have them" types of thoughts. Just note them.

Soon just the breath will be enough. Indeed, more than enough to handle or consider. Just an in-breath. Just an out-breath. A rising. A falling. A sitting. A touching. A lifting. Etc., etc. Relaxed precise nothing at the moment of occurrence leads to super-refined noting. SATI is the nexus. The bridge. The raft.

175. Remember that this process of "waking up" isn't a progressive increase in what you might conventionally call "a progressive feeling better" or "a progressive sense of feeling lighter or happier". Indeed, one cannot calibrate or "expect" the process or progress in such terms. Nor can it be evaluated in terms of contentment levels. Nor in strength levels. Or how long you can sit. At times you will surely feel lost at sea while previously you felt clear. Destination-arrival thoughts are captivating in one moment – they are strong and clear. The next sitting, as we know, (but not really know) is everything we can do to keep it together! Weak. Aching. Dejected. Burdened. Heavy. Easily irradiated. Devoid even of

kindness. Why? Why? ANATTA lesson 101. "These are not I. These are not me. These are not anything to rely on. Note. Note. Note. So simple. Keep it so simple. Note. Note."

176. Allow yourself to be surprised, an innocent wonderment open to the mystery of being. Cut through – just 'drop', as in "get over it" – the tired worn-out predictability of what the universe of you will look like, feel like, its reality. Such "excessing forward" de-freshens, even deadens, or perhaps even petrifies, openness. It dulls sharp investigation. Be willing to be surprised. This attitude is crucial. Approach each sitting as a gifted opportunity to refine the telescopic lens of your own mind to peer into the deeper recesses of one's inner universe. Time travel with the lineage of the greats. Mind refinements are the vocation of the greats. Within seconds into a sitting the entire process can accelerate, and the next thing you know you are off into an entirely new trajectory – far from the gravity of predictability. Like Alice down the hole. You are blown away: "Right. Finally, I'm really cooking. Almost thought what I have been doing these past four weeks – 20 hours a day of SATI every day – is a powerful force." When you infuse consciousness with so much "power clarity" the greatest fruits known to life and mind become available. Keep yourself in a relaxed state of readiness, as if you were going to greet the BUDDHA at any moment: And in that inner exchange a personal SUTTA cognitively sculpted just for you to awaken to your highest potential. How cool would that be! Keep that level of "joyful openness to the miracle of consciousness" and "the higher miracle of freedom from suffering". That is my own highest aspiration.

177. Be prepared to become an authority of pain and meditative pain management. You'll also slowly, very slowly, begin to appreciate the experience. You'll see how one normally lives their life just on the border, the fringe of deep near-constant pain. It is barely masked. Always there above, below, inside – every moment of ANICCA is an out of control – lawfully conditioned – ANATTA event; – and therefore anything and everything could happen, along with the ANICCA event. Every nano second – screaming in its "You cannot control me, I am DUKKHA". And you do not know it, but you will if you have the courage to look at the flow of events – called me, NĀMA- RŪPA – that is A – A – & D.

A MEDITATOR'S REFUGE

Or A – D – A (ANICCA, DUKKHA and ANATTA). ADA. Ask, if in doubt, "Why do you always need to change your posture? Why the need to eat and sleep and drink and answer the call of nature, and bathe and brush the teeth, and diseases all around ready to be swallowed or injected by a mosquito or a bed bug or a centipede, or the vipers all around ready to take you out without even seeing them, as they do the dogs?" On and on, a disease-ridden violent context of crazy maddening behaviors: human, insect, reptiles, mammals, birds, all waiting to eat you alive if you are unable to move, and then reduce you to white bones.

We need to breathe oxygen. No air, dead. Compromise the quality of the air, faint, cough, cancers, etc. On and on DUKKHA is unrelenting. Just stop moving outside at sunset for five minutes and you become a McDonald's drive-through — for mosquitoes. If in doubt, just sit for as long as you can, and see what it feels like. Life works because of the ability to change posture and secure safety/comforts etc. Without such access it's a living hell. We have to work hard each day to keep pain at bay, and even so it's like a storm all around all the time. Just do one thing unconsciously and the whole thing can come tumbling down.

Again: sleep, food, clothing, transportation, electricity, blankets, pillows, sitting cushion, medicines etc. Raw life by itself isn't particularly an easy thing to handle. Sleep one night without your blanket or without your mosquito net or your mattress. Consider what you need to keep your retreat alive, and what others provide for you to allow and support the undertaking. From there, develop high gratitude to support the refinement of attitude to make haste, be as conscious as possible. Use the time wisely. What a rare opportunity when you reflect on all the various elements required to configure – for you to practice this one and only time – to achieve the highest levels of insight possible. SADHU those who are supporting you! And SADHU yourself for knowing that it was essential to undertake this sacred action. And moreover, use the time wisely.

Recommit to this process as frequently as it feels helpful. Developing a sacred reverence for DHAMMA and your own undertaking is a beautiful act of grace and self-honor. And remember the little things: no cushion, no meditation. No chair, no meditation. No food, no meditation. No teacher, serious handicap. No nutrition, no life. Become an expert on "dependency." Simple things: No breath, no life. No air, no breath. No TANHĀ, no DUKKHA. No VIJÑĀNA, no NĀMA-RŪPA, and so on. Be prepared for life-altering, heart-shaking insights, observing pain. DHAMMA disrupts MOHA patterns of denial. Although you may think of it as "only knee pain" the entire world of DUKKHA may flash before your mindful eye, and in a lightning flash of inferential reflective epiphany you see DUKKHA-addiction-denial like never before. Overall, treat pain as a gift of the DHAMMA; it could get far worse. Pain can be one of our greatest teachers.

178. Learn to catch your breath on the run. At times you feel the need to relax. Do so. But with legs still moving, somewhat. Don't stop noting, once started.

179. Not to think "Why the way [you are] feeling?" will be obvious. Indeed, it's not always clear. Just keep noting. As you drop into the practice more and more, especially, towards the end of a sitting or walking, there's the often unnoticed "anxiety of fluctuation." The slight sigh of wearisomeness of unrelentingly being forced to be "on call for change"- fluctuation or alternation or a perception will be recognized as "the DUKKHA of not being able to relax your noting." Why? An object, its conscious perception, thoughts if not noted: they continue. VEDANĀ perception expands in consciousness and KILESAS arise. Then more thought. Increased CETANĀ arises, more intensely we feel the need for something, and with it arises increased intensity of KILESAS. AKUSALA speech. And/or AKUSALA action. i.e., KILESA VATTA. VIPAKA VATTA = SAMSARA proliferating because of no SATI upon sense objects arising. No HIRI and OTTAPPA. No SAMVEGA. A whirlpool of KILESA-driven SAMSARA.

180. Allow for the obscene and sorrowful and grotesque to arise. It's natural. Visions. Images. Smells. Perceptions of all kinds. Of you. Of loved ones. Of others. Of existence at large. Of all of humanity. Of totality itself. Sometimes you will look upon beings and yourself, while mindfully observing "this breathing, fluid-oozing, matter-consuming, waste-producing air, water, heat, light-dependent, flesh and blood-stuffed skin-draped skeleton", "imprisoned by" and the "imprisoner of"

(and in "knowing and perceiving" and "feeling", the prisoner of sensing, and tortured) KILESAS. DHAMMA practice is crafting this bag of mental aggregates into a rarefied and purified mechanism, reflective of truth and dynamically skilled in expression through mind and speech and action, "the wisdom-reality of how things are." Truth attainment of view and mind state with NĀMA- RŪPA characteristics = PAÑÑĀ. All in order to "Be DHAMMA" until PARANIBBĀNA. Allowing the twofold KARUNĀ-PAÑÑĀ combination to express its ANATTA skill in any way. No way to uplift other NĀMA- RŪPAS to realize DHAMMA SADHA than with wise consideration of those processes following the timeless pathway to KILESA vanquishing.

181. There is a quality and frequency of effort that can be made that will be different for each, and will change as the retreat unfolds for each. Try not to determine it according to the precision of "telling time", and not so loosely that you can't at times feel you could be making much more realistic effort – as in "this time in retreat" effort. Not to compare what quality of effort you are making now with the TIPITAKA ARAHANT 'life on the line' effort. Keep it relative. You want to end your day in practice free of remorse – as in "no feelings of remorse or misgivings" – over things "left undone" or "not done well" or "thorough enough" or "things that shouldn't have been done". Of course, there is wisdom in the "conscious use of reflecting mindfully back or over one's day looking for ways to improve". There is a distinction between "negative self-recollection-reflection" and positive "mindful-recollection-reflection". One inspired positive change. One judges – often unknowing – how you did not do it well enough. "I'm not enough" versus "I'm learning the tricks of the retreat trade as I go along." Essentially, always be on the lookout for refinements. Keep a notebook handy, and get in the habit of noting key phrases – attitudinal practice enhancements, uniquely your own. Empower your climb up Everest – your ascent up Mount NIBBĀNA. Although there's the Eightfold Path, each of us will do it differently. No two of us will do it the same.

Keep pushing. Improve systems of engagement. Overall, it is important to take rest at night – retire – with a sense of gladness. Joy. Upliftment, no matter what is happening. Be your best friend. Foster an inner atmosphere of "remorseless effort." And be on the lookout for pride-driven shame, a "less than I should be" sense of denigration. This comparative state of mind is also MĀNA – comparison as 'better', 'less than', or 'equal with' and the 1000 shades of gray with each. It's not an ideal. Rather it is a great source of further effort, inspired DHAMMA-informed effort. Call it DHAMMA power, an inner N – U that is building a little bit more each and every day. We have been wandering in SAMSARA for a long time and in such a short time, look at the strides we are making. Remember: Proportions. When you find the chord, you will know the sound. Keep on DHAMMA fine-chording and the PAÑÑĀ refinement sound will be found.

182. Once into the retreat, you are well enough out to sea to keep in mind to practice with "a day without misses." Keep that as the direction of the practice.

183. "Does life have meaning?" "What is life's purpose?" Be watchful not to insist on premature answers to these timeless questions. Rather let the conditions for PAÑÑĀ be fulfilled. "Who am I? What was I? Where am I? What is this all about? Where am I going?" Such questions need answers. Invest in the conditions of resolution. One day, from one perspective, this SAMSARA will appear "breathtakingly absurd." You think the pain and suffering is way too real, surreal-like in its grip on you. Yet on another day during another sitting, its subtitles and lawful exquisiteness shine with a type of "brilliance of operational synchronicity at its best." You might think that SAMSARA is fundamentally flawed, or that it has natural laws that are insanely perfect – that these laws lawfully sting any NĀMA-RŪPA formation that has not abandoned KILESA completely. There's no "partial SAMSARA existential-national park, optimal beauty-viewing spot" that one can observe from in complete safety. Anywhere from an existential snake-bite to a complete forest-extinction event can happen at any time. Safety in SAMSARA is an illusion.

The ARAHANT ideal offers existential extraction of MOHA from the deal. The absolute abandonment of suffering conditions is the only logical-wise response. If you want to know and comment on SAMSARA facets, you have to be willing to be stung, both conventionally through

DUKKHA-DUKKHA and SANKHARA-DUKKHA recognition. Of course, knowing NIBBĀNA is the most exquisite viewing. Or a "KILESA free KARUNĀ-PAÑÑĀ natural 'no I-involved' form of service to uplift the lives of others." But NĀMA- RŪPA marbles hitting NĀMA- RŪPA marbles in unalterable ultimate patterns of pain-knowing according to CETANĀ duration-intensity and AKUSALA filters present at time plus PATTHANA involvement. In a short exact note: This SAMSARA is fundamentally flawed or it has natural laws that are 'pain-perfect' in that they are universally consistent and indiscriminate. The 'perfect flaw' or 'perfect mistake' is that the three types of DUKKHA must be experienced if there is consciousness – VIÑÑĀNA. This SAMSARA is a 'perfect DUKKHA machine' or a 'perfect pain wheel' or a 'perfect mistake' or flipped over a perfect generator of MOHA to be rubbed away, if Dharmically involved.

SAMSARA is. Therefore, you do DHAMMA as a matter of course. There is no other option other than die over and again suffering this way, then suffering that way, endlessly suffering. Thus, SAMSARA is a perfect suffering apparatus. DHAMMA is not your blowtorch to burn a NIBBĀNA hole from SAMSARA. Well, it may be if you are on fire with epic SAMVEGA. DHAMMA is rare to hear and even more rare to practice. SAMSARA is unrelenting in its demand for "living" regardless of "sleeping". In this sense it is wise to reflect on the true nature of SAMSARA to motivate wise action, and be heedful as much as possible. And how much more skillful, here, during your one and only intensive retreat. Burn!

184. No matter what you may think or perceive, to the contrary more than likely you'll resume a fairly normal life, somewhat like your life before the retreat, after you leave the retreat and re-enter the world. There's "retreat-SAMSARA" and "world-life-SAMSARA". They do not easily blend or work together, despite what spin is said about "integration". You'll return and still plan and have to make big and small decisions. And talk and relate and drive and sign checks, pay bills, take flights, etc., etc.: Endless 'etcetera's'. All of 'it' will reappear. Concepts will make sense; others will be seen as outdated; still others are absurd. Of course, you will remember your name and your friends' faces and phone

numbers too. Slowly, in most cases, you'll 'shed' – go from the familiar to the losing and fading of the familiar – to the 'learning' of the new, to – at times – being in a state of being totally okay with unfamiliarity. And then coming back into the old familiar. And you will have both expanded from your exploration a broader area of familiarity, and with it have a greater clarity of the previously familiar. As you launch out and concepts fade and NĀMA-RŪPA begins to dissolve rapidly, it does not do much for future planning. Just stay in your seat and proceed. No matter how "out there" you go from the familiar, the new territory feels 'saner' and 'safer'. If anything, the fear arises often from the falsity and dumbness of having taken the familiar of before to be so 'real', 'satisfying' and 'safe'. A lot of practice will be the revealing of false areas of safety, behaviors, familiar concepts, people and/or certain characteristics of others; so many nuances of awareness into the old and the new. We see how frail life is, and others too. We see how flawed the mind is, and our own as well. Humans are flawed creatures making good on a flawed system or flawed context: SAMSARA, urban SAMSARA, barren SAMSARA. So many textures and conditions of what we now see and know. We see how inherently vulnerable the human condition is, and for animals and all species as well. We begin to appreciate the range of SANKHARA, and in seeing them our fragile "green pastures ideas to be exposed" and we see the ruthlessness of quicksand pastures that are the deeper reality within all other realities. Keep stepping out of the dream, and take firm steps with PAÑÑĀ-informed wisdom of groundlessness. Keep stepping out of the dream – and the hoax of happiness. And move towards that place of" "no" safety – no stand" happiness. ANICCA-awake dream creatures dancing on a canvas of ANATTA particles, 'unshaping' them into NIBBĀNA-peace. Keep it simple: SATI makes good on the N – U.

185. You might find (yourself) seriously asking (yourself) challenging and provocative questions, along with radical realizations that may very well shake you deeply. Such as: Having come to know through your own direct experience that through SATI the mind can be refined and purified, and that by relaxing one effort to bring SATI to the ongoing moment of occurrence, thoughts, CETASIKA, VEDANĀ and AKUSALA/ KILESAS can and will arise. The mind is then

forcibly hijacked, influenced by "KILESA-grip" or "KILESA-siege-consciousness." As such thoughts, speech and actions occur, three VATAS are experientially tasted. This is normal life for the vast majority of people. One thinks, "This is me." One may think, "How could I ever end my practice knowing this? This is my opportunity to cultivate SATI until I truly arrive at that safe, KILESA-ridding, danger-free refuge of NIBBĀNA. Anything other than this would be stupid, dumb, to my demise and that of others." Or, "Think if Stalin practiced and decided to carry on with this practice rather than be allured back into the world by unseen KILESA?" On and on. "This would be foolish of me to leave the retreat, to end my practice and settle for the status quo of a far less level of SATI, even with a firm commitment to keep the precepts and practice every day, and practice DĀNA and BHĀVANĀ and the PARAMIS." You have your finest hands and touch on the sculpting of consciousness here in the retreat, the mind is pliable and supple and moist with qualities of awakening. Why let the mind become dry again and become like moistureless clay – harder and harder to mold or sculpt into NIBBĀNA? This is a very interesting edge of inquiry which brings up many subtleties. "How well do we keep the PAÑÑĀ lens clear and bright in the world and see ANICCA and ANATTA rather than ideation enthrallment?" Etc. etc. This can be a frightful realization during one's retreat. But one ponders, "Can I realistically spend the rest of my life in a retreat, or as a nun or monk? Perhaps that is the best avenue to take". Or "Maybe I should extend my retreat to one year and not two or three months. Just do it!" one thinks. "Have the office contact my family and responsibilities, and just do it." Then you wobble and ask yourself, "If I leave, does this really mean I must believe in an 'AVIJA compromise' to get back without any sense of SAMVEGA? Is it ever possible to stop practice, once started and tasted? Is stopping always a type of existential Russian roulette? Even if you do attain SOTĀPANNA (and as the theory goes, only 7 more lifetimes, maximum) that's a long time and lots of DUKKHA. Why not make a vow to be with the next BUDDHA and join his SANGHA in TUSITA and rejoin the best minds in SAMSARA and take only two more births; one in TUSITA and then rebirth with MAITREYA and the SANGHA as humans (and there attain ARAHANTSHIP in a flash, listening to a DHAMMA SUTTA)? How beautiful is that? But here I am in retreat now, so why not go for the highest outcome while the fire is burning? Why take wood out of the fire? Is it possible to ever stop the practice once one has started? What does stopping even mean?"

Not to panic. Allow the recognition to translate into "Here, and in retreat, Now". Let this flow of inferential insight with its own integrity to be recognized – but channel its power back to the present – here and now. The retreat will end later. Forget about that point. At that point it will be very clear what to do and how to go about doing it. Or reflect that you will be in the best position at that time to take care of that "then and now" when it occurs. Cross that hurdle, in other words, when it is real. Not now. Take care of the "here and now" or the "now here", or the "now, now" or the "here, here now." This will take optimal care of that "then now" ad infinitum all the way to NIBBĀNA, ARAHANTSHIP and PARINIBBĀNA. DHAMMA faith to the max, fortified by right DHAMMA action in the moment.

Allow for the variety of previously-held antics of joy to (gradually) be exposed, seen through, and to fall away gradually, until one reaches the joy of 'non-occurrence' and the happiness born from that 'trans-experience' or 'non-experience' or 'unconditioned experience'.

186. No matter how much you appreciate ANATTA, up until a certain point you are going to swear that they're "NĀMA-RŪPA-and-me." Even "NĀMA-RŪPA-ANATTA -and-me" – the hoax or illusion loves subtlety, and it's inherently a trickster. ATTA is like a mirror – it sees me as a function of its own reflection.

187. Allow for your scope of consideration of "life and inhabitants of life" to expand exponentially, to the point of bewilderment, awe, mystery, fascination, disgust, radical imaginative possibility. That means both a "birthing into broader humanity beyond your birthing into you," and conversely at times it might feel like a 'dying' or 'fading away' of pre-retreat friends, family and associates. It's natural to take on life with your considerations. Yet with that expansiveness all the extremes of normal relationship trappings will be missing. You can't be responsible for their lives, but you can serve where you can serve.

Ultimately, you see the wisdom and compassion of removing (from within oneself) LOBHA, DOSA and MOHA as the ultimate act of kindness to suffering humanity, suffering life – in all dimensions of thisness – this SAMSARA. As long as there is suffering anywhere you might consider how would it be possible for me to celebrate life and feel joyous about life when there are people everywhere (and indeed even if it were only one) that are suffering. These people are my kinsman, my family. If not DUKKHA-DUKKHA, you consider the other types of DUKKHA. Ultimately how can I celebrate life when humanity is gripped by MOHA? A world of life – teeming with life – dancing as if it were in a fire pit (SANKHARA DUKKHA). Would it not be like having a party for life, where all life is invited? And you start asking others when certain people don't show up, since they are all family and kin, and have been both invited and eagerly anticipated partying with them: Catching up on their lives, having a toast and celebration with them, dancing with them, maybe even doing acid together to bring in the new year, a new life, a rebirthing of all things beautiful about such SAMSARIC family members. And you ask, after a while, as the hours tick by and it's now 8 pm, only four hours to midnight and the New Year: "Oh well, they must have stopped for some wine and or gifts for the party" – and you go on partying without them – still anticipating seeing them – and then it's 9 pm and 10:30 pm and a chill fills the part: "Where is sister Carol and her kids? Where is Uncle Bob? Where is Aunt Khema-gyi?" On and on and on... "Where are they?" And the music stops because you are the one having the party. Is this compassion? Is this SAMVEGA? Is this conscience? Is this basic empathy? Where do these qualities stop and start? Why do they have boundaries and limits and bases? Why do the PARAMIS engage in apartheid? In discrimination. In downright racism and sexism and ageism, and '-isms' of all kinds, that serve only to divide up the world into "Who I love" and "Who is in, and who isn't"? Of course, take this further: "Who to kill and who do I protect?" On and on...And with each you are told, "Well we have heard [so and so] is in Kabul prison." "[So and so] was tortured to death." And "Frank was assassinated." And "Dorje self-immolated in Tibet in protest of the ongoing genocide". "Jane had to stay home because she lost her baby girl, and had a gun to her head." And "Helen was wrongly accused and sentenced to life in a maximum-security prison". And on and on and on... "And all of our brothers and sisters in [such and such country] are starving". And every form of DUKKHA was explained according to how the modern world knows it on the front page of every newspaper and TV news hour. How many billions of us are family on the planet? How many of our own children are being born into our "family" this very hour, and we do not give a shit whether they live or die? "Of course, we care, Alan. Of course, you do Joe." The entire swell of the party chants as one. "Of course, we do Alan, but we are helpless to do anything." And then they chant, "Alan, you are depressed. Take Prozac. Too much Buddhism in your blood. Too much meditation. Come on, it's a minute before midnight. A toast to freedom, love, prosperity and most of all, compassion for the greater global family."

How do we celebrate life when humanity is crippled by MOHA? It's not that you live righteously, perceiving suffering and declare "See, I recognize suffering, damn you." Or you live with your head hung low, mumbling your mantra of morbid, morose, gross, disgusting, vile, putrid, repeat nausea. And they call you "the Vomit Saint" or "Sir Angry". Or "The Poet Laureate of condemnation" for seeing the world as it truly is. Nobel Peace Prize in "Justified Rage Against the World of Stupidity of Others for Not Giving a Shit and Having Their Heads Up Their Ass in Arrogant Display of Narcissism and Satanism."

You can't fight suffering. Nor do you resign yourself to the fact of suffering. You simply endeavor to remove it to the very best of your ability, and do your bit. There are leaders and followers. Be a leader if moved to be a leader. Expand your reach and skill to motivate self and others. But in retreat, be careful not to become an activist yogi while being a "DHAMMA transformation of the KILESAS NIBBĀNA directed" yogi. The less DUKKHA we have, the more skillfully we can act with others. Basic causal reflection. Of course, let's not celebrate forgetfulness in the name of personal happiness. But celebrate – take time for collective prayer and action-oriented gatherings, to unify the efforts of those who wish to look, see and know — and respond or act, both to the removal of inner dangers, and outer dangers as well. And even so, while the celebration is going on, the VIPAKA VATTA keeps spinning, and off the living room floor in mid-dance step another family member is plucked out and removed to suffering. "Where did Mother go?" one asks. "She's having her throat slit in the bedroom by a fan of Charles Manson who hates us spiritual types who care about the future of life." And you shout to the party goers, "This denial is getting too close to home. Turn off the music." And you say, "Something is seriously amiss here. Let's reconsider our priorities. The house is on fire, and we need to act!" With such authentic DHAMMA alignment on purpose with urgency the gathering elevates and refines and becomes satisfied with the new priority. "Yes," they say, "we can smell the smoke of denial. We must act and act now. Time to activate the N – U and get out the compassion door before it is too late. We must save ourselves and grab the hands of others still dancing and get out. Once out, we can alert the village, that our house was burnt to the ground."

Do you have sparks on your roof? Probably so, as all our homes are interwoven. The multiple dilemmas of SAMSARA.

188. Allow with as much balance as possible a variety of life-practice perspectives to arise and of course, pass on in flow. At times you might feel the onslaught of recurring objects to be persistent, and as painfully fatiguing as a swarm of bees around you. Practice is like that. Often (especially in the 'world mind' and 'sense door' phenomena) it is for the most part liked, wanted and appreciated, if of a certain class of experience. As SATI is increased, the speed of NĀMA-RŪPA sense objects become revealed, and you feel like you are constantly being stung, assaulted, attacked, withered, oppressed; you understand the guarding or protecting function of SATI. Plus, you begin to acknowledge the moment from sense door experience as SUKHA to it, as the DUKKHA of SUKHA. Due to more clearly seeing the characteristics of ANICCA and ANATTA, at other times objects will appear as tenacious as black flies swarming around your head, trying to sting-bite and escape, again and again. Other times, it is felt as mosquitoes on the attack at sunset. So many world-life associations based upon our own unique conditioning and embedded memory associations. Rather than insects, associations can be human, such as 'childhood', 'teenage' or 'adult' sufferings,

transgressions, assaults, wounds and traumas. The more real and clear the insight associations in the moment, often the more triggered and real the mental imaging associations with events – real or dreamt or imagined – in the past, or even projected into the future. The mind will do just about anything and everything to create interior SAMSARIC MANDALAS to haunt, scare, bewilder (etc. etc.) the yogi. "Note, note, note" the moment as it occurs, and is seen with SATI. Know, touch with SATI, go – freely flow.

At other times – with the realistic arising of a phenomenon – you will swear you are being knifed by an attacker. It is so real. At other times, seduced by a celestial dodges-DEVA, allured as it were as the BUDDHA was said to have been allured by MARA under the Bodhi Tree. Dancing with SATI with the illusion of 'It' – MARA – as real. Empty phenomena roll on. You can literally 'feel' as if you are being beaten down and crushed. Then at times, you are being caressed like soft velvet, then delicate wisps of a celestial feather or the silken like fabric of pure light. The spectrum from coarse to refined seems to be endless.

I only once heard celestial music in my inner ear, when living as a monk in Sri Lanka at the Island Hermitage. It was hypnotic and enchanting and continuously novel and unpredictable in its poetic brilliance and musical symmetry beyond anything I had ever remotely heard: Never could I have imagined such music. But there it was, continually for many weeks, day and night in my inner ear, while I was living in silence and seclusion without electricity and running water.

The purity of the environment clearly has a lot to do with accessing deeper frequencies of innate existence. The same in meditation. The more inner refinement, the greater the access to nuanced, often suppressed (or spectrum) phenomena. The variety of experiences will be manifold. This is a challenge: Keep on noting and releasing regardless of whether the phenomena ignite reaction-states – of interest, fatigue, boredom, contempt, anger, sadness, excitement, liking, craving or needing to hold. Weariness, disgust, misery, fear, terror, recoiling, balance, more balance, clarity, quietness, ease, softness, delicateness, luminosity, misery, whispery smooth, frightful, coarse, jagged, transparent, immaculate steadiness... Until one grows progressively weary, downright PAÑÑĀ-activated frightened, and "sees SANKHARAS as an affliction". Always ANICCA, always ANATTA, always DUKKHA – in that they cannot be truly controlled, embedded as it were in an infinite net of forced experience, governed by laws that inherently force DUKKHA upon perception and the idea of "one – self – experience". This incessant flow of mind-existence generated psycho-psychical shrapnel: no matter how sweet it "feels," it is still DUKKHA. This is not a nihilistic pessimistic perspective. It is mature and wise.

Seek refuge in NIBBĀNA and pray that when we reach ARAHANT and go into PARINIBBĀNA it is a wormhole, a white hole to a parallel universe beyond the bad tortuous design of this universe. "If this exists, that must exist." Exit One to know release from suffering, and let's see what death (along with extinction of the KILESAS) brings "thisness – beingness" into the next. Who do we know who has ever returned to this realm after PARINIBBĀNA? There are clearly no words for that, so it seems, from the BUDDHA. Note now, and keep on noting no matter what life-practice perspectives appear. Just keep on maturing in the insight of incessant flux, unpredictability, and the uncontrollable nature of the mind. Stay in intimate proximity to one's true DHAMMA-heart, and seek the N–U NIBBĀNA refuge in transcending DUKKHA through SATI of phenomena as it occurs "now "and "now" and "here now."

189. At times in practice you might feel the waning and loss of that driving edge to accomplish, as if aim and goal have either become 'non-issue' concerns, or that you fully feel you will arrive "when conditions are ripe". Therefore, you don't invest thought energy into their potential future arising. The practice politics of "energy economics" are understood on a more subtle level. Note the relations of mind to the "driving edge to accomplish mind-state loss." Not to mistake this inner deepening quietness and contentment as "having arrived" or entertain notions that you are now "in the neighborhood of arriving". Just another interior environment shift; the "extraneous" shedded as practice deepens and matures. The shedding of the unessential occurs by DHAMMA nature. Remember it too is not permanent, not 'self'. It

will likely re-occur later in the practice with more ferocity.

These practice 'drop-ins' are significant. At times of their happening note the feeling. At other times you will feel the mind sink (or plunge more acutely completely directly) into changing phenomena. With these 'drop ins', you notice the SATI doesn't flit so superficially as before. Also, there's a greater sense of 'making contact,' as if someone you have been wanting to speak with stops, and looks at you, face on. With drop ins there will be an increase in energy and uplifting joy – for treading the path of purification-perfection. One's task is to keep noting interior environment shifts that become so much more interesting than the actual mental psychical topographical shifts. This is also another indicator of drop ins. You see 'practice truths' as truths on so many nuanced levels. Each new depth reveals a broader, deeper, more expansive meaning: More pithy, more profound – so much so that one in its expanded meaning is somewhat unimaginable prior to your arrival to it. You see and appreciate how subtle the mind veils are: 1/10,000th of a mind-second away is another dimension of unknown powers and benefits, revealing an understanding that is directly transformative to all previously-held opinions of life. Support this by attitudinally being unwilling to insist, or inflict yourself with opinions and ideas contrary to radical innocence and openness. One has a tendency to fill in the space quickly, not being able to bear having puzzle pieces still not in place. Let the insight of 'being unfinished' touch you deeply. This will further bring 'drop in.' Or "D – D – I = DHAMMA drop in." A further alignment of how to, with "arriving = drop in = how to arrive, drop in," etc. Until ANATTA wisdom docks the DHAMMA. This is when you step up meditating to peak engagement. Your ATTA dies before death occurs. Deathless is born from ATTA death. ANATTA birth gives rise to PAÑÑĀ rebirthing, until dauntlessness from ATTA dying again and again, an illusion evaporating away from the light of PAÑÑĀ.

190. As practice deepens, thinking often becomes much more interesting, as it reflects greater clarity, direction, reasoning, analyzing – extracting essence qualities more than before, at an earlier stage of the practice. Issues are bursting with energetic newfound clarity. You feel like the world is coming together as it dissolves. Things are felt to

be falling into place, but not a previously predicted place. It's fresh – a new powerful clarity is born. And of course, keeping on noting joy, and enthusiasm – and be especially careful not to relax the exact energetic noting. Nothing results in spontaneous issue-resolution clarity. Intuition is highlighted. Keep clearing the brush of "refined thinking" and "alluring narratives of fine design" or "glistening cognitive mosaics," like cherished SAMSARA souvenirs you wish to bag – and take to NIBBĀNA with you. Invest in "true nature thinking as behavior insights" reflective of ANICCA, ANATTA and DUKKHA, and of course, at times, BUDDHA, DHAMMA and SANGHA. Five portals to energetically embody their finest frequency as portals to the deathless, PAÑÑĀ, ANICCA, ANATTA, DUKKHA and NIBBĀNA, and guided and aligned and refined by SATI intelligence.

191. As practice unfolds (due to the nature of practice to be likened to a "righting process" an "aligning process" a "steering clear process" a "correction process" a "synchronizing process" and so on) one often feels compelled to reflect over their life while engaged in it. "Past before retreat" life events are often seen and understood in greatly clarity, as if your life were written on an empty balloon, then 20 times blown up, the clarity in full view. You might recognize clearly the "spiritual turning point, points" and "the event, events" that led to this "involution of direction interest", where and when you gave the experiential study of the mind (a high, nay the highest priority), and all the rest of it seemed as inhibitual (restrictive) to the fulfillment of that quest. You might recognize the inner wrenching in questing for clarity on the proper course of right practice and lifestyle engagement that would optimize fulfillment of this inner journey. You might reflect on what appears to have been a lot of wasted effort involved – one's accumulation of stuff including experiences, travels, rapidness, etc. etc. – as if you've had to lawfully cut your way through a jungle of traps. All that you know is that it felt hollow, insubstantial — but the voice of "not enough" was still very quiet at that time. And you might reflect: "And now is this too another 'subtle jungle trap'?" and then allow yourself to develop "right caution" and allow it to skillfully translate into "right investigation" and not "cynical righteousness" (which is really a foul-smelling stench for

insecurity, unclarity; it's a "confidence issue.") You might have reflective thoughts of appreciation towards the BUDDHA, the pathfinder and encouragement of following it; also, towards the DHAMMA, the straight lawfulness of SATIPATTHANA, of the 8-fold path, of just SATI alone. With the 3 trainings, SILA SEKKHA, etc., you feel "noble" for the first time in a sense, as you regard the 3 trainings as "the 3 converging inroads to purify the heart" using the "environment of our life" as the "grounds for enlightenment". Yet without mistaking the efficacy of one training for another, SILA SEKKHA is not mistaken as the way into NIBBĀNA, etc. etc. An indispensable component yes, but its spiritual link quality is appropriately regarded – but not over elevated. The pitfall of this is not to fully appreciate the power of intensive practice PAÑÑĀ development. You see practice as the way to emerge out of "the prisons of self-concern", and the mirage of "appearance into the true reality of what concept" involvement as" the face of death one can't forget".

192. PAÑÑĀ is regarded as an "aligning process". The alignment of 'right thinking', of 'right viewing', of 'right seeing', 'right knowing'. The alignment of the 'right mind' states that effortlessly cooperate with uninvited sense door objects, and VEDANĀS to keep them in clear perspective as to their true face of ANICCA, ANATTA and DUKKHA. You will not think of this effortless wisdom as silent recognition of phenomena to be something special, nor is it like constant mental gymnastics meet, or a karate demonstration; it is not even a chewing process. It's the natural realization this is the way the mind now functions, and relates. This is PAÑÑĀ in manifestation. The mind, heart, thoughts are living aligned with the way things are. This is when you might feel more "in tune".

Remember life synchronicity ease can often be misplaced, because of the carefully cushioned-out live arena that has been cleverly spiritually constructed unknowingly in your quest to become spiritual, and conversely you don't need to constantly "test" your DHAMMA life synchronicity ease level by stepping into or seeking out "DHAMMA test traps": "Let me see if I can freebase consciously, or if I'm really done with it." Or, "It won't make much difference if I wear 500 suits, I'll experiment for this year, charge it up," etc.etc. Keep it simple: You cook dinner for the week instead of starting to tithe your money. You sit for two hours a day, etc. etc. Your heart feels less driven, more at ease, more able to act, less necessary to move. Heart feels quieter, far fewer questions, far less issues to be resolved. You might feel that you could easily lie down, and if you didn't awaken you wouldn't feel like so much was outstanding. You feel protected not by unknown forces, but by the "power of PAÑÑĀ resilience."

193. A lot of practice recognition is feeling like you're waking from a long sleep, coming out of a trance, stepping out energy from the oppression of MOHA, the cult of MOHA. Having eyes when previously blind, but assuming I was seeing; born when dead; gaining health when sick. You look around internally and see the world drunk and intoxicated by the artistry of MOHA DITTHI, dressing up the world in concepts, dancing in delusion. Allow yourself to quiver, note it. SAMVEGA, move on.

194. When the mind, life, and heart are without wisdom, you might notice that you are eager for experiences to occur, and quite ill at ease and concerned about the possibility of the unpleasant to arise. This is "ordinary life mind". As SATI infiltrates the process and exposes this "ordinary behavior" it begins to see. Wisdom arises in a manner in which you thought life should be related to. Rather than treating certain SANKHARAS as 'special' and others as 'devilish', PAÑÑĀ begins the process known as the "delicious souring of the sweet "; standing on SANKHARAS as one's nutrition is treacherous nonsense. It's as preponderous as the wish to be airborne, so rather than getting a seat in an airplane you jump off a cliff! As PAÑÑĀ deepens and becomes a more significant mind force, there will be an increasing ability to both know and to "let-go-be" any single doubt phenomena. Experience will somehow never be sweet enough or satisfying enough to dislodge this ever-increasing sense of "simply being exquisitely quiet and very repulsed by phenomena." This wisdom speaks so continuously and immediately to every SANKHARA face, at any of your 6 sense doors, with exquisite skill of balance and silence. The objects that knock for inner recognition wouldn't know that someone was even home; the mind is so quiet, still, composed and equanimous, yet each and every moment

"no phenomena thing" can perturb. With wisdom like this, to this degree of maturity and beyond, one feels "the purposeless burden pinch of aggregate knowing, bearing". One tires of being mixed up with the 5 aggregates: their weight is heavy; their nature is burdensome. One tires of the forced and perpetual involvement with perception, with thoughts, sensations, VEDANĀS, with SANKHARAS, with concepts, with the toil of body, slaved to its needs, slaved to be on call constantly to avoid dangers within and outside. Tired of being so wrapped up tight with "anything could happen at any time". These perception truths grow, and living with the aggregates becomes like trying to find pleasure in eating a good apple. At first it is good, then another one, then another and so on. Eventually the apples are seen and taste rotten, then putrid, then poisonous, on and on — until the mind can't bite them anymore. Even the jewels become lusterless, and wanting ceases, and then there is "just balanced relationship". The process of tantalization is over, the game's up. It's a 'show close' time. This is "right cleansing," the way for KILESAS to be abandoned.

195. As you further train the control of your mind, you'll begin to appreciate the truly beautiful, a well-controlled trained purified mind — even if it's of a temporary level, PUTTHUJHANA side of ARIYA. You will see SATI run perfectly in step with phenomena, the perfect shadow dancing. You'll feel like a SATI machine. It's so ANATTA, "not missing – auto – pick- up". It becomes so "empty obvious" that the mind is a conditionally concerned, effected, transiently-arising lawful phenomena spewing non-entity, that has become DHAMMA faith confident to have empty right views launch appropriately placed on impartial phenomena arising, resulting in "things as they are", knowing "rightly true nature." A SATI trained mind mechanism to see clearly arising predominant phenomena, until so much "right viewing" sees nothing — which is NIBBĀNA.

196. Be willing when you engage in retreat to consider going to battle, to war, front line placement, a tour of combat duty: Put your warrior clothes on, consider dying for the cause. You need to employ the aggressive active force of non-compliance with KILESA activity: you must be a perfect pacifist, not 'passivity' but active use of the skillfully

passive force which is born from looking squarely and directly into the eyes of each appearing phenomena. Let struggle be a part of your retreat life!

197. Remember that practice isn't trying to get rid of thoughts, trying to clean them from the slate because they are hazardous. It is just to know them, according to their true, transient, empty, unsatisfactory nature.

198. In a long-term practice you will be confronted to skillfully manage (both physically and psychologically) the variety of expressions/depths/levels/meanings of "repetition", over and over again. Practice, perhaps as if you were sewing, stitch by stitch: each one important, each one repeated over and over, each one essential, indispensable, each put forth with its own challenge of perfection and completion. Quality is of utmost concern, as well as completing the project. Partially sewn is fair — but not really in our realm of acceptability. You sew something to repair it, so the quality and completion of the task is important. One stitch is contingently inter-sewn with the preceding one; same with sittings, walkings, moments of SATI, days of a retreat, etc. etc. The simile is applicable on many DHAMMA levels – keep putting each stitch, each sit, correctly and evenly. Apply the practice smoothly and gently, even when you feel deeply motivated and extremely energetic; like painting with smooth even strokes, or applying "just right butter" on a slice of toast. Just so smoothly, remember a balanced and graceful mode of operation.

199. Always keep observing your condition neutrally, as if you were constantly asking someone how they were. Your investment in observing the observed condition is the DHAMMA weather for the moment. Uninvited events moment after moment; with PAÑÑĀ you come out of the elements, you gain shelter and refuge.

200. Allow yourself the ongoing opportunity to have all your visions and opinions experientially contradicted. Allow your notions of happiness, joy, contentment, satisfaction, bliss, freedom and enlightenment to be experimentally contradicted. In other words, allow yourself to be experientially humiliated. If not this, at least be willing to be surprised. If not, let and allow for unknown things to be known. If

you can't do this, you should speak with a therapist before sitting.

201. Allow insight to slip into consciousness any way it wants, not to relegate the real stuff to deep sitting only. Let your views be crafted. "DHAMMA insight thoughts" are like the tremors of an insight quake, or the echo of the original sound; recognize it and move on.

202. Watchful of thinking you should 'feel something', 'feel something a certain way' or 'experience something more deeply or clearly'. Let the way it's happening be the way it's happening. For example: "I feel at times that I should feel more satisfied and balanced, but all these recurring DHAMMAS are so miserable."

203. The notion of "VIPASSANĀ repetition" on different levels of significance and understanding is important to understand. On one level you repeat the schedule over and over again, you repeat the exercise of sitting and walking over and over again, and you repeat the exercise of arousing mindfulness over ... and you repeat the exercise of directing SATI to the rising and falling over .... Yet more accurately, nothing remains the same. The idea of repetition even changes. In VIPASSANĀ you may read the same line over and over again. Yet in this DHAMMA world you'll see greater and greater meaning – each time. For others to read a line in this repetitious manner, it would be easy to become bored.

204. A simple summary of practice reminders: Be mindful as continuously as possible. Approach the practice in a calm, smooth and gentle manner, ever on guard for thoughts, especially ones of "wanting this experience to occur", or "Why isn't [this] happening?" Liking anything should be carefully noted. Any expectation, evaluation, hope also should be noted. Any sense of "being not enough" or frustrated should also be noted, likewise any 'towards or away' preference. Just observe any movement of mind at all, including SUKKHA-SADDHA or contentment from a present idea of practice or notion of past accomplishment— and let the DHAMMA do that which it needs to do to free itself.

205. Remember not to 'take a dime' when for a few seconds more you can 'have a dollar'. Be firm in wanting to know everything there is to know of this NIBBĀNA. Not to rest short of this, nor to relegate prior stages as "nothing special". "When you're wet all the way through

your coat and clothes, only then you can feel it on your skin". The whole path is very intricately connected. Don't disregard your mother for a preference for your father, or your grandmother for your brother, etc.

206. Remember that whatever good condition you experience, it can be refined and further refined. Insights can be placed up through resolve, and more polished, clearer. Fully glue them up, go back up the scale again. With NIBBĀNA as well, with the stage of SANKHARA UPPEKHA, it can be finely-tuned: 14 hour sits, no sleep, etc. At times the practice is 2 steps back, 3 steps forward.

207. At times, especially with feeling restless, 'force' yourself to sit and walk according to schedule, and even if you "hate it", carry on.

208. Let things be. It really doesn't matter when (or where) going deeper happens. When ÑĀNA and SAMĀDHI are sufficiently mature, you will automatically find yourself in the place where you only thought about 'being'. Keep putting yourself 'in the car and off the tracing of the map in the living room.' Just apply constantly ardent, cool, calm (no special) effort: It's all up to the DHAMMA from then on. ÑĀNA is a perfect unfolding, there is no 'premature' ÑĀNA or 'overdue' ÑĀNA. ÑĀNA arises according to conditions. ÑĀNA is also seen in degrees. Indisposition after the same

ÑĀNA of ANICCA-ANATTA and DUKKHA will ultimately need to be tasted fully enough to fully abandon all the cravings, MOHA.

209. Once practice is well developed, be "ultra-cool and calm", just 'be' with things without any special 'this' or 'that'. Just 'is.'

210. Ultimately make a "movement by movement" all-out effort, but be sensitive to it, making a fine balanced hum, not at all aggressive.

211. Be prepared to say "This is the clearest my mind has ever been", or "This is the best sitting I've ever had" (etc. etc.) – perhaps once or twice a week. Likewise, "This is the most balanced my mind has ever been", or "This is the most automatic noting that has ever been." Be watchful of drawing conclusions, of hitting the top of balance levels, clarity, insights, joy (etc. etc.). Conclusions often restrict the power flow of "urgently applied SATI".

212. Remember that we all have a long, long way to go. No matter what place of advantage one comes to, this sense of "urgent gladness"

is not the end.

213. If you feel 'pressed' in retreat, anxious, expectant of 'any moment' results, and if the noting is difficult, consider something you've done previously that has required time and patience. Give yourself 3 weeks to 'make the soup': Just stir occasionally, be patient.

214. Once reached to UDIYA BHAYA-ÑANA consider the image: "If this state is likened to just conceiving a child, if all conditions stay nourished a child will be born. A birth will occur, it can't be avoided. Therefore, sit, walk, accuracy, aim, note all activities – and in 9 months a child will emerge (like it or not)." Same with SANKHARUPEKKHA ÑANA into NIBBĀNA. Just an issue of impersonally maturing impersonal PAÑÑĀ and SAMĀDHI conditions. Then "non-occurrence" is automatic. Like it or not, it cannot be avoided.

215. Allow for the transparency of your previous "pleasure deriving involvements" to be clarified under "light scrutiny of PAÑÑĀ". Especially in seeing the MOHA of enjoying sense pleasures. To enjoy one needs to momentarily forget ANICCA-ANATTA-DUKKHA. If experienced with SATI – PAÑÑĀ the phenomena will be a source of affliction. Mind will either recoil, or if seen with enough PAÑÑĀ – UPPEKHA will be there to note the phenomena is a higher, more satisfactory and reliable source of happiness. The SUKHA of PAÑÑĀ, friendships, relationships will often be determined (whether easy, difficult, successful, etc.) based on one's ability to understand or not understand this switch in focus from "pleasure seeking, pain avoiding" in all its nuances, to "phenomena watching" with the range of PAÑÑĀ depths; and these two domains as they overlap, ultimately refining according to ÑANA depth, eradicating certain views, doubts, etc. "Wisdom confluence between people will dictate their depth of connection and subsidiary qualities, similarity of interests, etc."

216. When SANKHARAS are seen as dangerous, the mind will automatically relate to SANKHARAS in the wisest, most prudent manner known to the mind. It will be interested in reaching "the internal danger-free zone."

217. When thinking you're sleeping, and it blocks reality, note it. It's like telling reality to "Shut up!" Note "thinking" and resume "listening"

to NĀMA- RŪPA. Silently expose their true behavioral nature.

218. To maintain SANKHĀRUPEKKHĀ ÑĀNA, you need immaculate ÑĀNA credentials. No amount of hoping, waiting or cleverness can get you there. Entrance requirements are spontaneously recognized by instantaneous arrival in the SANKHĀRUPEKKHĀ state. Every quadrant, every millimeter of SANKHARAS must be realized as "ANATTA DUKKHA" and "ANICCA DUKKHA". SANKHARAS must be felt as a hopeless involvement, a tasteless joyless source. With each fall, consider it a positive step. You chip a little bit more MOHA away, a little less infatuation with a consideration, reaction. At this point the DHAMMA is demanding subtlety. If not, you return to "DUKKHA 101", PATISANKHARA ÑĀNA.

219. Practice is a "VIPASSANĀ ÑĀNA education". Learn all you can about the unfolding of PAÑÑĀ; this too is PAÑÑĀ as it sharpens clear comprehension.

220. Remember that your thoughts do not always accurately assess the situation. Every comment, feeling, speculation, conclusion, inclination, desire, dislike, fluctuating moment of mind: Just note. Let noting be the guide. Take complete refuge in the "silence of SATI mind" and its adorning qualities of VIRIYA and concentration. These states are the comrades of PAÑÑĀ; not thoughts, perceptions or VEDANĀS.

221. Be watchful of referring intensive practice back to daily life, let daily life 'be'. Each domain has its own rules, each has its own integrity, some overlap. Daily life will resume after intensive practice. All we are doing is developing or deepening the depth of right views in our life. 'Retreat life' or 'daily life', it doesn't matter. Living with the right view is the priority; whatever lifestyle involvement changes that consequently result, so be it. Right view development enhancement is the goal, the priority. Invest in conditions for it to arise. We want to be willing to revamp everything we know and do, should the right view direct it thus. Who cares? Who is reluctant, craving, attachment, MOHA? PAÑÑĀ results in right living, right action, right speech, right SAMĀDHI. What one wants and doesn't want is quite unessential. Let PAÑÑĀ dictate it, try not to complicate the work. Attitudes support the metamorphosis from MOHA life to PAÑÑĀ life. Be wise enough to assume that right

knowing reality will know how to optimally manifest your KHANDAS to most efficiently purify itself, or to serve the process of right view development continuation, or ultimately serving to free NĀMA-RŪPA from AKUSALA DHAMMAS i.e., DUKKHA.

221. Rather than noting at times, such as "thinking, thinking" or "hearing, hearing ", "planning, planning", "wanting, wanting" (which as practice deepens and quickens in pace might seem ancient or ineffective), use the phrase "refuge in silence" or "silence" or "refuge", whatever feels most appropriate. It reduces all arising of pleasant SANKHARAS to a "non-buy into them". It reminds the mind of silence as refuge. In silence, same as while walking, be generally mindful of the "six-sense door application" without labeling. When necessary, use the label "silence", "refuge" or "refuge in silence".

222. The question of "How long will it take?" might arise at one time or another. The practice's end is not simply "Be here now". That's the fundamental lesson in VIPASSANĀ. Here is the only place to spiritually work, and when to work is now, on and on. And in terms of where you are, on one level you're here and in terms of when you arrived or will arrive is "now". But the realization of revealing how long it will take (for enough to be truly revealed, according to the lawful truth in order to be enlightened) cannot accurately be said. If one practices correctly and follows the instructions diligently, approximately two months will be enough. But who can say about fully arriving to ARHANTA? We have no ARAHANTS who are talking, and the safest place for people (but not necessarily the wisest) is to go to "here" and "arrive". Work "now" – over and over. When you drink a glass of water, the drinking, swallowing does the work of emptying the glass. Same in practice: Emptying the mind of LOBHA, DOSA and MOHA are of utmost concern, as is the continual performing of "right efforts" in doing that. When they are completely emptied it is only valuable if it somehow supports the inspiration and effectiveness of one's continued "right effort to keep emptying".

223. Remember that if pain arises or not, it is not your domain of concern or control. You're not trying to sit free of pain, but to put an end to craving and aversion.

224. The bottom line of VIPASSANĀ is to note whatever is there. Your duty is just to note: it's ANATTA. If you are noting and don't feel satisfied, this is DOSA. If you are noting and you want more to note or more clarity, this is LOBHA. Just note, also, if you want something to reoccur or something not to repeat to happen, it is also LOBHA and DOSA: just note. Wanting to avoid something, just note it. Feeling satisfied or dissatisfied, note these swings. Wanting it different, note it. Wanting to be free or get rid of something, just note it. Note any nuance of mind swings, silence towards formations, and deep or dead inner cool quietude towards formations.

225. Noting will take care of the business of the DHAMMA. Not any form or thought or feeling. It's ANATTA: Do nothing special – just "cool carrying on." If feeling out of sync with the moment, anxious, etc., simply remember "Be here now". It's the only place one can be.

226. Great serenity, composure, processing mind stream with great cleanliness; very quiet and still, ultra-subtle, smooth and delicate noting. No trace of inner movement; large ultra-placid mind. Not just "balanced", but "wisely balanced": You know why it's balanced – it's because of having wearied of formations.

227. As one's retreat ends, emerge gracefully and re-enter softly. Be educated through the transition. Taper off this intensity gradually, with dignity. Also watch the mind swing carefully: "I'm losing it" or a gross commentary on "how radically different the mind is out of retreat:" This too is ANATTA, conditions are ANICCA. Just watch the mind in its various movements come out of the intensity, with no clinging, hope or concern. Re-empower your SILA commitment training with a special commitment to speech. You'll feel concepts forming again, becoming more real. ANICCA, ANATTA, DUKKHA will not be followed like before. The aftermath of insight will linger, dependent on your PAÑÑĀ depth. You become a person again, rather than an "insight perception machine". It's a time to be gentle; a lot has been seen and a lot more needs to be done. 'Be', not holding off the intensity: 'Let go, let go, let go.' You will be seeing the changes that have occurred.

228. The practice is a contracting process: First from the world, then from sense involvement, then into the body no further than some

doors, then from concepts, then just NĀMA- RŪPA, then just mind, then ÑĀNA deepens, then just stillness… and then contraction into NIBBĀNA.

229. One should never rest satisfied with KUSALAS attained. Reflect: Is there more work for me to do in training to be perfect DHAMMA dawn. Yes, do it!

230. Before one realizes their greatness to be a functioning human being, it's as if you're still a "yet to be found and polished large diamond" still buried deep in the earth, in thick SAMSARA, covered over by MOHA. Then one begins to recognize their potential to be a noble human, as if the diamond (through struggle) was discovered, yet still coated with carbon. And a bit of carbon is scraped off and the diamond glistens just a little, and one has a deep recognition of "the intrinsic specialness of human existence" and how workable it is. One is captivated and intrigued. Questions of all sorts arise: "How, why, how much carbon covers me? What lies underneath? Who has cleared their carbon away? By what method? Can I do it too? How? When can I begin?" Enthusiasm leads one to try to scrape it, and sooner or later one tires, enthusiasm wanes. You want the 'sure' technique; you seek to entrust your carbon removal to an expert. "Time is of essence". We enter the SATIPATTHANA world. We are eager to get down to the business of cutting, shaping, faceting ourselves and actually wearing our jewel. A big gem is good only for display. We want something functional. We cut it up, we enter a retreat, slice up the day by sitting and walking. Each sit, each walk is like a piece of that diamond. We're shaping, cutting, polishing and refining. After a lot of careful refinement, the diamond string is something we seek to wear. To wear it, we must make a necklace out of the diamonds. They must be strung together in order to wear it safely. Once at SANKHĀRA UPEKKHĀ ÑĀNA we realize how delicate the final finishing is, and the stringing together of each diamond. At PATISANKHARA ÑĀNA one wasn't satisfied; felt as if one tried to string the diamonds, all could fall if not careful. At SANKHARĀ UPEKKHĀ ÑĀNA the string is tied. Final polishing, and only a question of getting it around your head and being able to release your hands and thoughts about it. MAGGA PHALA puts it on.

It stays on effortlessly and it becomes your only real adornment. One's visible adornment – wearing your DHAMMA diamonds.

231. Summary – some short notes: Make the first day of a short retreat a day of adjusting. Much less strenuous, allowing for movement to be made. If it is a longer retreat, allow 2 or 3 days.

232. Think of everything you might need, including cushion, foam – or anticipate needing (and so bring) it.

233. Put away all familiarity in the room. Set a daily life-like setting. Keep stark, clean and vacant of stuff as possible, just the essence.

234. Firm resolve right off: "No thought deserving of consideration." Resolve not to entertain even a glimmer of thinking.

235. Keep your head down as much as possible; no investigating of sounds or other people's movements.

236. Keep SATI within your body, no further than your sense doors.

237. There is no-one's affairs or business you should involve or concern yourself with. Let all people and things be. Be with yourself.

238. Take several minutes every night or morning to reflect over the previous day's practice to consider ways improvement can be made. I.e.: slower walking, more care while eating, after lunch walk, no nap or sitting down for 20 minutes, stronger resolve to observe thoughts. No lag time upon sitting to get into it, for others. Resolve to stop talking, to come to the hall, etc.

239. Relax more into the space more often than not that "It's happening" rather than "It's not happening". Of course, there will be times where you can change your ways in practice to allow/facilitate going deeper.

240. Be watchful of "serious thoughts" i.e., "The timing is off, or inappropriate", "This place is too distracting", "I'm not able or capable", "This place has unsuitable weather for me", "The food is not right". These thoughts lead to the wrong kind of abandoning — that of ending the retreat.

241. SATIPATTHANA has the unique function of both cooling and composing the mind and heart. It also has the nature to refine the mind, resulting in a life of subtlety and nuance because it directs SATI in subtle ways to observe detail. SATI deals with nuance and subtlety

to degrees which are impossible to comprehend thought, thinking or description. It is the path that can replace wrong views with current ones, and with this, freeing the mind of all KILESAS. What other thing do we come across in life with such potency?

242. You can relax more, not hold on so tight. (E.g, When I found myself gripping tightly to my opposite hand while walking: "Soft touch everything.")

243. To appreciate the notion of NIBBĀNA being a "sensationless non-experience"; one will have to experience "tired and weary of sensing". That is to give up all notions of sense enjoyment, service, ideation, relating, life, further becoming as a human, DEVA or BRAHMA. Therefore, one must be attitudinally allowing to be "DHAMMA-cally frightened". SAMSARA is in fact a perfectly lawful DUKKHA as one awakens to NĀMA – RŪPA true nature. The multiplicity of DHAMMA frights will begin, both by seeing NĀMA – RŪPA according to SABHALA LACHANAS and the conceptual proliferation coupled with DUKKHA VEDANĀ, experiencing DUKKHA considered in terms of its "beginningless-ness," its present affecting and its potential to arise and inflict. The various ways to inflict are manifold. You wake up to SAMSARA'S behavior and you realize you're in its camp. You're available as a candidate. The heart quakes: Such insights and depth definition to insecurity. Not DOSA, fear but SAMVEGA – "DHAMMA reality insecurity fright". Once tasted, one lives cautiously, refining their actions to reach NIBBĀNA as soon as possible.

244. One also might have the consideration that "To be born again is an agonizing thought"; and "To be without SATI is ignoble and disgusting"; and "If there is no SATI, I'm blind." The "true nature is lost", "thoughts arise", "mind drifts over concepts", "liking-disliking-KILESA activity arises", "still no SATI". The "impulse to do" arises strongly. "One's mind becomes seized by impending KILESA surfacing". Speech, action occur, then VIPAKA, KILEASAS, KAMMA, on and on. "How can I ever stop intensive practice and relax my application of SATI" – or to live safely? "I should ordain and live mindfully with perfect SĪLA."

245. Through the practice one will learn of the valuableness of the vehicle. SATIPATTHANA is learning experientially through wisdom why KILESAS arise, and how those "arising tendencies", KILESA streams, are cut off temporarily and permanently.

246. The initial "practice delights" are nice. They indicate that the mind can be shaped and noble/crafted/purified. It is an indication that "SATI works." These initial samples are sweet, but it's the joy of being behind the wheel for the first time. Don't be deceived, as best as possible note 'delight' etc. Keep your VIPASSANĀ bootstraps buckled and tight. You just got ignition; it is time to take off, not land.

247. Remember that no matter how sluggish, boring or listless and repetitively dry the practice appears, this is only because there are sluggishness, boredom, listlessness and dryness mind-states arising. There is good news ahead. In time with SATI, the practice reveals so many succulent truth perspectives. A world you've always heard about, speculated on and imagined. The domain of understanding is higher up along the staircase you're walking, like sparkling gemstones that glisten in a multi-faceted manner. Continue, stay composed. With each new gem you must give away, and stand utterly impoverished before the next appears; no hype possible. Eventually all things known must be relinquished.

248. How important it is to handle psychologically the near paradox of practicing "repetition" along with "be here now" with the notions of "strive" and the attainment of "insight, NIBBĀNA and/or results". Day after day: Sit, walk, eat, sit, walk. etc. with the spirit of trust doing it. Being "fully present", putting the whole of you into it. Quality involvement without expectation of gain, result, etc. Just being "mindful moment" after "mindful moment". Yet all the while keeping your intelligence alert to increase "forward moving effort," and to look for ways to improve and refine. To increase forward movement and to avoid backsliding.

249. While sitting, do not "breathe the breath": That is, let the breath breathe itself. There's nothing one has to do to breathe and certainly nothing extra above nothing is needed. "Just sit and observe the resultant sensations of breath breathing".

250. One doesn't need to do anything for the objects to arise or vanish. They are ANATTA. That they arise and vanish is a natural law. Just observe objects and only arouse SATI at objects' moment of occurrence. Don't sit back and let them come to you, nor go after them "Rambo style." Meet them head-face-eyes on, straight on.

251. VIPASSANĀ practice is at first seeing "the appearance of things", like looking at the outside appearance of the body. Then one enters the interior in one way or another. In time to understand the heart fully you need to enter the stomach, colon, intestines and rectum. VIPASSANĀ practice is like walking into the colon of SAMSARA.

252. SATIPATTHANA brings one a mind filled with purposeful thought, yet as practice deepens "thoughts are reality segments" rather than "messages". Thoughts are seen as no more or less. They become uninteresting, like looking at a picture of a tropical beach and being there, or as if you had an ice cream cone in hand. Each investment in the "message" equals to licking the paper ice cream and not the real one.

253. In retreat it's important to continually reduce your presence and increase your invisibility, especially when eating, and with your basic meditation hall etiquette. In the other areas too. While in the bathroom, be conscientious about the length of time using it (especially when others are waiting), and cleanliness of the way you leave it, before leaving. When eating, eat quietly. Avoid clanking utensils or scraping, a tinging sound on plate, or gulping, chewing, even swallowing loudly. Also, same while in the meditation hall.

I've always wanted to tape people's "meditative fore-play" before they sit. The variety of activities from entering the hall to the point of sitting still. Some need a shower. There's so much activity and presence. You would think you're getting into the cockpit of an F-16 jet or trans-Pacific flight! Noise comes from "no SATI". Be mindful especially when it affects others; do things quietly. This also applies for "post-sit after-play": There's no need to write a novel, shake out your shawl, etc. Do it all quietly.

Also, while in the room, keep the SATI; be tidy, responsible, be silently polite and respectful. Be orderly in placing your shoes when entering the hall. The way you dress, your work – do it properly with attention to details. Leave no residue of yourself; edit yourself out of things; move out. Eat, bathe purposefully, bring dignity, purposefulness and gratefulness to the way you move.

254. Be watchful of thinking an experience is "special" and "badging" it.

255. At the end game of VIPASSANĀ, there cannot be even the slightest hint of wanting, not anything. "Just is what's there" after "Just is what's there"; "is-ness after is-ness," refuge in silence.

256. 3 period or 3 section walking: 1. Noting first for 15-30 minutes, 2. Noting next 15 minutes, 3. Noting very slowly for the final period before sitting.

257. It is important to consider how to manage a walking period, in order to carry as much SAMĀDHI momentum into the sitting. Educate yourself on how to do this. It will not always work to think that you can walk slowly the last 5-20 minutes, and creep into the hall to sit. This is ideal, of course, but not meant to pin failure on yourself if you stumble in exhaustion.

258. Realistically, develop an attitude of practicing one day at a time, and each day in segments. Before breakfast, up till lunch, up till tea and bed. Ideally it would be an attitude of moment after moment, but combine both. During each day's segment, keep the later attitude.

259. You will have to make peace with your thoughts, otherwise they stir you endlessly.

260. You'll think of 101 things you need to do, or become, or things to be remembered; this is natural. Just note, and each day make a firm resolve: "May I not volitionally entertain any discursive thinking."

261. Remain tidy and clean in all areas. It adds precision, brightness and energy to the mind.

262. Use labeling completely on a discretionary level, just on the primary object and then occasionally. Other objects just SATI, unless a wish arises to use more frequently.

263. Practice except for specialized phrases is hard work. The dignity and purpose of it renders the "hard" as necessary work and "compassionate work", and the "only work" or "real work".

264. While walking, do not take the next step before mindfully completing the preceding one, which doesn't mean non-movement of the next while the preceding step is still in motion. The shifting phase of walking usually requires simultaneous movement. One's new step volitional, preceding step just follows through. Yet to minimize and support both balance and SATI, take short steps.

265. Be willing to be disappointed before you learn the self-deceptive quality of disappointment. (Same with all AKUSALA variations.)

266. Develop an attitude of "non-specialness" and "non-surprise" towards all phenomena. "Oh, just that" is too much, "just that " and then "this only" not necessary. Don't build onto it; don't construct something with it; don't examine the phenomena. "This" after "this" is enough.

267. Cultivate a gradually increasing "simplicity level". Don't expect to manifest or achieve your ideal immediately. Use the gradual reduction approach: Eat less gradually, sleep less, use fewer and less elaborate sitting props and reduce sleeping luxury. Simplicity in appearance, clothing, hair, face; abandon more and more. Then keep the "middle path" in mind, to support the transcending of attachment.

268. The minimum sitting and walking hours per day are 14: Eight one hour sits or portions thereof, and six hours walking. This is the formula for "results" in retreats.

269. Whenever necessary, early before usual rising up or before sleep, use "the 30/30 sit/walk method" to practice and stay awake. Often the thought of an hour sitting or walking at 1 or 2 am puts you back to sleep. 30/30 is workable.

270. Sometimes sitting directly after meals is helpful, and cuts through it being a break in the schedule – even a short sit. It also allows for easy, good digestion. It often cuts through the need for a nap even if you nod while sitting. Also feel food intake precisely; the amount and type of food suitability and also nutritional energy is easily perceived. Cause, effect and good practice ensure no "momentum loss".

271. Limit the proximity of where you practice. Keep it small and compact, but not too tight. Avoid excessive walks and stray activities.

272. Take notes during DHAMMA talks, it helps to absorb material.

It is also useful for the future availability of SASANA. You never know when it will be of use to you and/or others.

273. Follow the practice method given by the teacher. If not clear, ask for clarity until clear.

274. Don't expect any aspect of the practice to remain the same: Food quantity, "your aura", body weight, energy level, sitting posture, cushion comfort, sleep quantity, length of sits, attitude, opinions about life, ideas about truth, your life, everything. ANICCA, ANATTA, DUKKHA – seek NIBBĀNA safety!

20.
KAMMA

(CETANĀ-Action-Volition) and related subjects

Definition of KAMMA/CETANĀ ~ Action ~ Volition

1. KAMMA literally means or denotes 'action' or 'doing'.
2. KAMMA is the law of moral causation (Pali-KAMMA) ~ (Sanskrit-KARMA).
3. Any kind of intentional action whether mental (thought), verbal (speech) or physical (deed) is regarded as KAMMA.
4. KAMMA means all moral/skillful/wholesome and immoral/unskillful/unwholesome volition (KUSALA-AKUSALA CETANA).
5. Involuntary, unintentional or unconscious actions do not constitute KAMMA, because volition is absent. (For example, rolling over in one's sleep and thus killing the mosquito that had landed on your arm.)
4. KAMMA is the law of cause and effect or "action-influence."
5. In the working of KAMMA, its most important feature is the mind. Words and deeds are colored by the mind.
6. KAMMA embraces both past and present deeds/volitions.
7. There is no KAMMA where there is no NĀMA or mentality/consciousness.
8. Nor is any action a KAMMA which is unintentional. KAMMA depends on volition. No volition – no KAMMA.
9. Every volition action, except that of a BUDDHA or ARAHANT

is called KAMMA. BUDDHAS and ARAHANTS do not accumulate fresh KAMMA as they have eradicated ignorance and craving, the roots of KAMMA.

10. The law of KAMMA is ANATTA: No independent ruling agency, other than causes and conditions.
11. As those properties which beings possess do not accompany them to their non-existences, they cannot be claimed as properties belonging to those beings; only the mental, verbal and physical volitional actions of beings always accompany them in this as well as in future existences. They are not liable to destruction by fire, water, thieves, robbers, etc. All beings (except BUDDHA and ARAHANTS) perform these 3 KAMMAS at all waking hours. All their work in all degrees is performed by means of these 3 KAMMAS.
12. CETANĀ according to ABHIDHAMMA is one of the 7 common universal mental factors which arise with every CITTA.
13. There is no CITTA without CETANĀ (ex. B. ARA)
14. From VIS. MAGGA XIV. 135 – CETANĀ wills (CETAYATI), thus it is volition. "It collects/coordinates" is the meaning; its characteristic is the state of 'willing'; its function is to 'accumulate' (AYJHĀNA). It's manifested as 'coordinating'.
15. CETANĀ sees to it that the other DHAMMAS it accompanies fulfill their tasks with regard to the objects which they all share.
16. CETANĀ arises with KUSALA CITTA, AKUSALA, VIPĀKA and KIRIYA CITTA.
17. CETANĀ which accompanies KUSALA and AKUSALA CITTA has in addition another task to perform – the function of "conation": Striving, exertion, karmic activity or accumulation. In other words, the CETANĀ which accompanies moral and immoral activities is "exceedingly energetic". And the accompanying CETASIKAS only play a restricted part, like a landowner who directs the work of his laborers, looks after them and also shares the work with them.
18. When we hear the word KAMMA in the most common meaning, we only think of volition accompanying KUSALA or AKUSALA CITTA or a deed motivated function of CETANĀ or AKUSALA CETANĀ. Through the door of body, speech or mind.

19. However, there are different functions of CETANĀ. The CETANĀ that accompanies VIPĀKA CITTA and KIRIYA CITTA merely coordinates the tasks of the other DHAMMAS it accompanies. It does not will KUSALA or AKUSALA, and does not motivate wholesome or unwholesome deeds.
20. CETANĀ sees to it that the appropriate result is produced later on, when there is an opportunity for it.
21. Volition is conventionally called "the doer" (KAMMA).
22. KAMMA is a natural law, which sees to it that acts bring their own rewards and punishments to the individual doer, whether human justice finds him or not. KAMMA is always just.
23. KAMMA neither loves nor hates, neither rewards nor punishes. Never angry, never pleased: Simply the law of KAMMA and VIPĀKA.
24. Wholesome and unwholesome KAMMA are distinguished by the roots of the actions. The motivating force of the deed, speech or thought. Greed, hatred and delusion or non-greed, generosity; non-hate/METTĀ or KARUNĀ and non-delusion/wisdom.
25. Only I receive the fruits of KAMMA made by me. Others cannot receive my fruits, or I the fruit of others. Thus, the law of KAMMA allows full moral responsibility.
26. We ourselves are responsible for our own happiness and misery. We create our own heaven and our own hell. We are the architects of our own fate.
27. There is no actor apart from action.

A. VIPĀKA – Fruit or Result

1. KAMMA is action. VIPĀKA is the fruit or result; its reaction. Just as an energy object is accompanied by a shadow, every volitional activity is inevitably accompanied by its due effect. Like: Potential seed is KAMMA. Fruit arising from the tree is the VIPĀKA, effect or result. As KAMMA may be wholesome or unwholesome, so may VIPĀKA. As KAMMA is mental, so is the VIPĀKA. It is experienced as happiness in its varying degrees, and unhappiness

or misery in all its shades, according to the nature of the KAMMA seed.

2. Inherent in KAMMA is the potentiality of producing its due effect. The cause produces the effect, the effect explains the cause; the seed produces the fruit, the fruit explains the seed; such is their relationship. So too are KAMMA and its effect. The Effect VIPĀKA, already blooms in the action. The Cause is KAMMA.
3. VIPĀKA is ANATTA. Not an all-pervasive, permanent ruling, judge; just a natural cosmic law.
4. VIPĀKA is one's own doing, KAMMA, reacting on oneself. One has the power to divert the cause of KAMMA. However, how far one diverts it depends on oneself.
5. The effects of our actions come back to us. Every action produces an effect, and it's a cause first, and effect afterwards.
6. Everything that comes to us is right. Nothing is random or ill-lawful.
7. VIPĀKA is not predestination; it is just the lawful effect of a cause free of any other agency.
8. VIPĀKA knows nothing about us. Does the fire know us when it burns us? No, it is the nature of the fire to burn, to give out heat.

Some people firmly hold the view that KAMMA is the main factor in regulating the destinies of men, that held that the day, hour of death and the manner of death is pre-ordained by his past KAMMA from the moment of his conception in his mother's womb. They hold that DĀNA (insight) and effort merely follow the promptness of past KAMMA. (Other laws are also in effect ~ NIYAMAS ~ see section "H". They ignore the role that present KAMMA – in this life, right now, as distinguished from past KAMMA – which plays in the creation of future destiny):

(In the Millinda PAÑHĀ, 8 causes of VEDANĀ are given. In the SAM. NIK and ANG. NIK, these same 8 causes are given as cause of death:

1. Hurt or ailment or death caused by the upset of the wind element.
2. Hurt or ailment or death caused by the upset of the bile element.
3. Hurt or ailment or death caused by the upset of the phlegm element.

4. Hurt or ailment or death caused by the upset of a combination of the 3 above causes.
5. Hurt or ailment or death caused by the upset of climatic conditions of temperature.
6. Hurt or ailment or death caused by one's own disagreeable acts.
7. Hurt or ailment or death caused by one's specifically directed acts of oneself or of others.
8. Hurt or ailment or death caused by counter-active or destructive KAMMA.

Cause #7 may be due to either past or present KAMMA. #8 is wholly due to past KAMMA. The remaining 6 causes are the VIPĀKA of present KAMMA.

For complete discussion of these 6 VEDANAS see SUTTAS or the light of DHAMMA vol, VII #3 – July 1960, p.49-52.)

B. KAMMA/VIPĀKA (ABHIDHAMMA Classification)

(See CETASIKAS – Ch.5 – The Universals – Nina van Gorkham, for detailed explanation of CETANĀ- VIPĀKA)

1. KAMMA constitutes the 12 types of immoral consciousness, 8 types of moral consciousness pertaining to the sentient realm (KĀMĀVACARA), 5 types of moral consciousness pertaining to the realms of form (RŪPĀVACARA) and 4 types of moral consciousness pertaining to the form-less (ARŪPĀVACARA)

The 8 types of supra-mundane (LOKUTTARA) consciousness are not regarded as KAMMA, because they eradicate the roots of KAMMA. In from the predominant factor is wisdom (PAÑÑĀ), while in the mundane it is volition (CETANĀ).

The 9 types of moral consciousness pertaining to the realms of form and formless are the 4 RŪPĀ and 4 ARŪPĀ JHĀNAS, which are purely mental.

Words and deeds are caused by the first 20 types of mundane consciousness; verbal actions are done by the mind by means of speech;

bodily actions are done by the mind (all movements of such parts of the body as hands and legs, etc.) through the instrument of the body. Of course, purely mental volitions have no other instrument than the mind.

These 29 types of consciousness are called KAMMA because they have the power to produce their due effects quite automatically, independent of any external agency.

These types of consciousness which one experiences as inevitable consciousness of one's moral and immoral thoughts are the 20 resultant (VIPĀKA) consciousness of the sentient realm, 5 of form (or 4), and 4 of formless.

C. The Cause of KAMMA

(See detailed study of dependent origination)

1. Ignorance (VAVIJJĀ), not knowing things as they truly are, is the root of KAMMA. Dependent on ignorance (of 4 Noble Truths) arise KAMMIC activities (AVIJJĀ PACCAYĀ SANKHĀRA). Associated with AVIJJĀ is its other root – TANHĀ or craving; unskillful actions and skillful actions are conditioned by these 2 causes.

D. The Doer of KAMMA/ Who Reaps the Result

1. ANATTA
2. Volition (CETANĀ) is the mental factor (doer)
3. Feeling (VEDANA) is the mental factor (fruit reaper)

E. Where is KAMMA?

1. "Where, Ven. Sir., is KAMMA?" King Milinda questioned the Ven. NĀGASENA.

    "O, King," replied the Ven. NĀGASENA. "KAMMA is not said to be stored somewhere in this fleeting consciousness origin or any other part of the body, but dependent on mind and matter. It rests, manifesting itself at the opportune moment, just as mangoes are not said to be stored somewhere in the mango tree, but dependent on the mango tree in which they lie, springing up in due season."

2. Neither wind nor fire is stored in any particular place, nor is KAMMA stored anywhere within or without the body.

F. The Results of KAMMA are Unthinkable

(Complete explanation see Manuals of Bud. Ledi. Sat., p.111-125)

1. BHIKKHUS, there are these four "Unthinkables" not to be thought of, as thinking of these would lead one to madness and frustration. What are these four?
    - ~ The realm of BUDDHAS is unthinkable, not to be thought of, thinking of which...
    - ~ The range of JHĀNA attained by one who has practiced JHĀNAS...
    - ~ The resultant of KAMMA is not thinkable...
    - ~ The evolution of the world (LOKA-CIÑTA)

(ANG.NIK. CATUKKA-NIPATA. APANNAKA-VAGGA. ACĪNTEYYA SUTTA)

1. Actions and interactions of the innumerable KAMMAS of a person, as also their inter-factions with the other forces of nature (called NIYAMA DHAMMAS – consciousness universal laws – 5 #- KAMMA just one) are so diverse and so infinite that no intellect – except that of a BUDDHA – can cover the entire domain of KAMMA and understand completely all the incidents and manifestations of KAMMA resultants (VIPĀKA).
2. KAMMA VIPĀKA in its entirety is imponderable, futile, impenetrable, and incomprehensible.

G. Is Everything Due to KAMMA?

1. Although Buddhism attributes many differences and variations to KAMMA, it does not assert that everything is due to KAMMA. If all were KAMMA one need not consult a physician to be cured of a

disease. For if one's KAMMA is such, one will be cured.

2. KAMMA is just one of the 5 cosmic orders operating in this universe.
3. Also, the law of KAMMA is only one of the 24 causal conditions (PACCAYĀ) – (PATTHĀNA of ABHIDHAMMA).
4. Refuting the erroneous view that whatsoever weal or woe (or neutral feeling) is experienced is all due to some previous action (PUBBEKATAHETU), the BUDDHA states: "So then owing to previous action, men will become murderers, thieves, unchaste, liars, slanderers, babblers, covetous, malicious and perverse in view. Thus, for those who fall back on their formed deeds as the essential reasons, there is neither the desire to do, nor effect to do this deed or abstain from that deed." (ANG. NIK – Grad. sayings, 1. p.157)
5. If the present life is totally conditioned or wholly controlled by our past actions, then KAMMA is tantamount to fatalism, predetermination or predestination. One would not be free to mold one's present and future. If this were true, free will would be an absurdity. Life would be purely mechanical, like a machine.
6. The absurdity also, that there is an almighty God who controls our destinies and fore-ordains our future, and who responds by purifying individuals who pray for such, is equally untenable. "O, BHIKKHUS, if beings experience pain and happiness as the result of God's creation, then certainly these naked ascetics must have been created by a wicked God, since they are at present experiencing such terrible pain." (MAJ. NIK. II, 222 – DEVADAHA SUTTA #101).

H. The Five-fold Cosmic Order (NIYĀMA-DIPANI)

(For detailed analysis see Manuals of BUDDHA by Ledi Say. pp. 103-108)

1. As discussed under 'G' Buddhism teaches that KAMMA is the chief cause of the inequalities in the world. Yet it does not teach fatalism or the doctrine of predestination, for it does not hold the view that everything is due to past actions. KAMMA-VIPĀKA is

only 1 of 24 PACCAYAS, or 1 of the 5 orders or laws that operate in the universe.

I. UTU NIYĀMA – physical inorganic order. Example: Seasonal phenomena of winds and rains. The unerring order of seasons, characteristic seasonal changes and events, causes of winds and rains, nature of heat, etc. belong to the UTU order.

UTU is the specific quality we know as heat: the bare primary quality of fire. Thus, with regard to this, the four great essential primary elements of all matter come into play.

All these elements (PATHAUĪ, ĀPO, TEJO, VĀYO) while persisting under the stated conditions, increase in magnitude when there is an efficient cause for increase and decrease. How may such a cause arise? In the case of solids, the cohesive element may obtain fluidity, and the solid substance begins to melt. In the case of water, heat may grow a flaming fire, while the cohesive element can merely arise the property of cohesion. It is on account of their intensity and magnitude that they are called the great elements (MAHĀBHUTĀNI). Their intensity and magnitude reach the climax on the eve of the destruction and disintegration of the world systems.

Heat is the primal form, or in its primal form is the germination of all material phenomena. Heat – UTU.

Therefore, this UTU NIYĀMA is the fixed process that determines the ordered succession of the 3 seasons: Winter, summer and rains. Also, the same process that determines the specific season in which trees, creepers, shrubs and grasses bring forth flowers and bear fruit. (Of course, just as ANATTA cosmic order, with no supreme agency responsible whether human, celestial, or divine: Just a natural order known as UTU NIYĀMA.)

II. BĪJA NIYĀMA – Physical organic order – of germs and seeds. (I.e., Rice produced from rice seed; sugary taste from sugarcane or honey; peculiar characteristics of certain fruits, etc.). The scientific theory of cells and genes and physical similarity of twins may be ascribed to this order.

The germinal order is that from which trees, etc. spring and grow in varying forms. This order signifies the sprouts, shoots, trunks, branches, twigs, leaves, flowers and fruits which spring from (say) the 'rose-apple-seed' do not cease to be of the rose apple species, type or family. This also applies to all forms of tree, plant, grass, etc. The BUDDHA stated (SAM. NIK, III p. 54- Pali): "There are, BHIKKHUS, 5 classes of seeds: Namely those which are propagated from roots, from stems, from joints, from shoots and from the seed itself." (A detailed account of this: Commentary to VINAYA – Behavior to plants)

III. KAMMA NIYĀMA – Order of cause and effect, of act and result. (E.g. Skillful and unskillful acts produce corresponding wholesome and unwholesome results.) As water seeks its own level, so does KAMMA, given opportunity, produce its inevitable result, not in the form of reward or punishment. So too KAMMA, given volition, is KAMMA: "It is though having 'willed' that a man does something in the form of deed, speech or thought." 'Willing' is carrying something meritorious or unmeritorious into effect. It deliberates and decides upon the steps to be taken, as leader of all the mental functions involved in doing so. It provides the tensions of those functions towards the desired object.

IV. DHAMMA NIYĀMA – Order of the norm. (E.g., The natural phenomena occurring at the birth of a BODHISATTVA in his last birth.) Gravitating and other similar laws of nature are included in this order. Natural phenomena sequence: a DHAMMA is that which bears its own nature. (E.g., Its own hardness to the touch, its specific individual mark as well as its universal characteristic, namely growth, decay and dissolution.) ANICCA, ANATTA and DUKKHA are natural fixed orders. Because of ignorance arises KAMMA – a fixed law. And so on with the other links in dependent origination (DHAMMATĀ – the rule or order). Also included is when a BODHISATTA, having fallen from the TUSITA heaven enters into a mother's womb, a splendid radiance appears throughout the world, including the DEVA and BRAHMĀ abodes. "And the

10,000-world systems tremble, shudder and quake."

(DIGHA-NIK. ii, 12- dialogues, ii.9). It is certain that someone with a sound view would consider a conditioned thing as something 'unchanging', and 'self'. This is impossible. (ANG. NIK. i.76). The overall characteristic of DHAMMA- NIYĀMA is best summarized by: "When that exists, this comes to rise; from the arising of that, this arises; when that does not exist, this does not come to be; when that ceases, then this cease." (VĀSETTHA SUTTA).

It is the DHAMMA of birth that is born, the DHAMMA of decay that grows old, the DHAMMA of dying that dies. Birth is a DHAMMA NIYĀMA. The state of BUDDHAHOOD is completely achieved and brought to pass by this order. They bring about the 10 perfections, 5 great renunciations, the grappling under the Bodhi tree. The utter perfection of BUDDHAS comes about by this cosmic natural empty law. (Complete dis. p.137-140 – Manuals of Bud. Ledi Say)

V. CITTA NIYĀMA – Order of mind or psychic law. (e.g., Processes of consciousness, arising and passing of consciousness, constituents of consciousness, power of the mind, etc.) Telepathy, telaesthesia, retro-cognition, clairvoyance, clairaudience, thought reading, all the idols, ABIÑÑAS, all psychic phenomena.

The act of thinking, the cognition of an object, exploration and investigation of an object. "I see, BHIKKHUS, no other thing which is so varied. As thought (mind), I see no other group (NIKAYA) which is so varied as beings of a lower order (animals, birds, insects, fish, etc.) But thought is said to be still more varied than these beings. By CITTA NIYĀMA, what is meant by the fixity or law of the consequences of thoughts or consciousness varying in function and on occasion? It is treated in the PATTHĀNA in the chapter on "The relation of succession of sequence."

The arising of the world, conditioned by the eye and objects. Visual consciousness arises, the triad is known as 'Contact' because of contact, feeling and so on, the 'Cessation of'. Through the cessation of craving, grasping ceases, etc. Thus, the cessation of all DUKKHA.

Conclusion – NIYĀMAS

1. These five orders embrace everything in the world, and all mental and physical phenomena can be explained by them. They are natural universal laws that extend infinitely in all directions, including all universes and the 31 planes of existence. They are all ANATTA, laws without a lawgiver.

    KAMMA is only one order among the five.

I. The Six Roots of KAMMA

(For detailed study refer to BPS. wheel No. 251-253 – NYANAPONIKA).

1. Three roots of all wholesome activity, speech and thought have been taught by the BUDDHA to be the basic causes of all suffering, for all beings, on all levels of existence.
   1) Greed (LOBHA)
   2) Hatred (DOSA)
   3) Delusion (MOHA) (AKUSALA)

   These 3 mental states comprise the entire range of evil. In all its intensities, subtle or coarse, speech or action.

2. Three roots of all wholesome activity, speech and thought.
   1) Non-greed ~ unselfishness, liberality, renunciation
   2) Non-hatred ~ loving kindness, compassion
   3) Non-delusion ~ knowledge, wisdom (KUSALA)

3. These 6 mental states are the roots from which everything harmful or beneficial sprouts.

4. These roots are the motivating force that prompt all action, words and thoughts, for all except ARAHANTS and BUDDHAS.

5. They fuel KAMMA which causes rebirth indefinitely.

6. All wholesome actions, etc. of those individuals who haven't uprooted ignorance, even though these actions, etc. are associated with the 3 wholesome roots of non-greed (ALOBHA), non-hatred (ADOSA)

and wisdom (AMOHA) are nevertheless regarded as KAMMA – because the 2 roots of ignorance and craving are dormant in him.

7. KUSALA ~ the wholesome. A healthy state of mind, morally faultless, has a favorable or happy result (SUKHA -VIPĀKA). Dexterous, skillful in the sense that karmically wholesome actions lead on to happiness in the present and future, and to progress on the path to liberation. The wholesome is free from affliction and harm.

   AKUSALA ~ the unwholesome, unhealthy or sickly state of mind (GELAÑÑA), morally faulty, blameworthy, has unhappy KAMMA results, (DUKHA- VIPĀKA)- unwholesome actions, speech and thoughts can be said to be unskillful responses to life. The unwholesome brings affliction and harm. (Commentary explanation from BAHITIKA SUTTA, MAJ. NIK. 86).

8. Greed ~ liking, wishing, longing, fondness, craving, infatuated, thrusting, wanting, needing, affliction, attachment, lust, cupidity, holding, self-indulgence, possessiveness, avarice, desire for 6 sense objects, desire for wealth, praise, fame, friends, children, a relationship. Any subtle 'wanting' at all, continued existence. 'Wanting' the JHĀNAS, the liberation, etc.

   Hatred ~ dislike, disgust, revulsion, ill-humor, vexation, irritability, antagonism, aversion, anger, frustration, wrath, vengefulness.

   Delusion ~ stupidity, dullness, confusion, ignorance (of KAMMA, 4 Noble Truths), prejudice, ideological dogmatism, fanaticism, wrong views, restlessness, conceit, pride.

   The wholesome ~ is not only the negative formation of the 3 terms, but also their positive aspects.

   Non-greed ~ unselfishness, liberality, generosity, sacrifice, sharing, dispassion, renunciation.

   Non-hatred ~ loving kindness, compassion, friendliness, forgiveness, forbearance.

   Non-delusion ~ wisdom, insight, knowledge, understanding,

intelligence of DHAMMA, sagacity, discrimination, equanimity, impartiality.

9. Greed = grasping, sticking, glued to an object. Proximate cause is 'seeing enjoyment in things that lead to bondage'.
    Hatred = intense dislike or subtle aversion ~ like a provoked snake, savageness. Spreads like poison. Proximate cause is 'annoyance'.
    Delusion = blindness, unknowing, no right view. Proximate cause is 'unwise attention'.
    Non-greed = mind that lacks for the object. A man who has fallen into filth will not cling to it.
    Non-hatred = non-opposing agreeableness, like the full moon.
    Non-delusion = characteristic of penetrating things according to their true nature. Functions to illuminate the objective field.

10. Causes of arising and non-arising of the roots.
    ~ unrisen greed arises, arisen greed becomes stronger cause ~ unwise attention to an attractive object.
    ~ unrisen hatred arises, arisen hatred becomes stronger cause ~ unwise attention to a repulsive object.
    ~ unrisen delusion arises, arisen delusion becomes stronger cause ~ in him who gives unwise attention.
    ~ unrisen greed not to arise, and for the abandoning of greed that has arisen ~ wise attention to an object of impurity.
    ~ unrisen hatred not to arise, and for the abandoning of hatred that has arisen ~ loving kindness.
    ~ unrisen delusion not to arise, and for the abandoning of delusion that has arisen ~ wise attention.

Objects of sight, sound, etc. are not intrinsically good or bad. It is our relationship to the accompanying pleasant or unpleasant VEDANA that conditions aversion, greed or the opposite.

Right mindfulness = wise attention.

11. "Greed, hatred, delusion ~ what is their distinction, their diversity, their difference?" If thus questioned, explain: "Greed is a lesser fault

and fades away slowly. Hatred is a great fault and fades away quickly. Delusion is a great fault and fades away slowly" (ANG. NIK. 3s, No. 68) (Full explanation WH. 251, p.27)

J. The Cause of Inequality, Variation and Diversity Among Beings

1. The apparent differences in the world of beings:
   - ~ One with luxury, another with poverty
   - ~ One with excellent mental, moral and physical qualities; one without, but with harmful tendencies and ugly appearance
   - ~ One with mental prodigy; another a dull idiot
   - ~ One with saintly characteristics; other with deformities, deaf or blind
   - ~ Born into a rich family or a poor family
   - ~ Why does a virtuous person face untold difficulties and hardships?
   - ~ A cruel dishonest individual appears happy and burden free; all comes so easily.
   - ~ Why are some generous, others are miserly?
   - ~ Why do some die at childbirth, others aged 10, 60 or 120?
   - ~ Why do some have good friends, while others are always being cursed and accused unjustly at times?
   - ~ Why are some born in comfort in one country, while others are born into starving families in poor countries?
   - ~ Why so many mental differences and physical differences?

2. What accounts for the manifold differences that can be seen among beings?

    ~ Accidental? ~ Supreme being-God? ~ The Creator's will? ~ Chemico-physical causes? ~ Heredity? ~ Environment? ~ Genetic?

    Can the theory of heredity account satisfactorily for the birth of a criminal in a long line of honorable ancestors, for the birth of a saint in a family of evil repute, child prodigies, etc. ~ Differences in identical twins. (For details of this subject see "Reincarnations" Dr. Th. Pascal, The Inequality of Mankind by J.B.S. Haldane)

3. According to Buddhism this inequality is due not only to heredity and environment, but also the KAMMA and VIPAKKA, as each shape our own future.

4. BUDDHA'S reply to this query. (MAJ.NIK. ~ CULLAKAMMA-VIBHANGA SUTTA, No. 135)

   SUBHA approached the BUDDHA and asked "What is the reason, what is the cause, O Lord, that we find among mankind the short-lived and the long-lived; the diseased and the healthy; the ugly and the beautiful; the powerless and the powerful; the poor and the rich; the low born and the high born; the ignorant and the wise?"

The BUDDHA replied: "Every living being has KAMMA of its own; its inheritance, its cause, its relative, its refuge. It is KAMMA that differentiates all living beings into low and high states."

5. The BUDDHA enumerates the causes of inequality ~ CULAKAMMA VIBHANGA SUTTA M.N. 135, only partial excerpt.

   "If a person destroys life, is a hunter, besmears his hands with blood, is engaged in killing and wounding, and is not merciful towards living beings, he – as the result of his own killing when born amongst mankind – will have a brief life, will be short-lived.

   If a person avoids killing, leaves aside cudgel and weapon, and is merciful and compassionate towards all living beings, he – as a result of his non-killing when born amongst mankind – will enjoy a long life.

   If a person is in the habit of harming others, with fist or clod, with a cudgel or sword, he – as the result of his harmfulness when born amongst mankind – will suffer from various diseases.

   If a person is not in the habit of harming others, he – as a result of his harmlessness when born amongst mankind – will enjoy good health.

   If a person is wrathful and turbulent, is irritated by a trivial word, gives vent to anger, ill-will and resentment, he – as the result of his irritability when born amongst mankind – will become ugly.

   If a person is not wrathful and turbulent, is not irritated even by a torrent of abuse, does not give vent to anger, ill-will and resentment, he – as the result of his amiability, when born amongst mankind – will become beautiful.

If a person is jealous, envies the gains of others, marks of respect and honor shown to others, stores jealousy in his heart, he – as a result of his jealousy, when born amongst mankind – will be powerless.

If a person is not jealous, does not envy the gains of others, marks of respect and honor shown to others, does not store jealousy in his heart, he – as a result of his absence of jealousy, when born amongst mankind – will be powerful.

If a person does not give anything for charity, he – as a result of his greediness, when born amongst mankind – will be poor.

If a person is bent on charitable giving, he – as a result of his generosity, when born amongst mankind – will be rich.

If a person is stubborn, haughty, honors not those who are worthy of honor, he – as a result of his arrogance and irreverence, when born amongst mankind – will be of low-birth.

If a person is not stubborn, not haughty, honors those who are worthy of honor, he – as a result of his humility and deference, when born amongst mankind – will be of high-birth.

If a person does not approach the learned and the virtuous and inquire what is good and what is evil, what is right and what is wrong, what should be practiced and what should not be practiced, what should be done and what should not be done, what conduces to one's welfare and what one's ruin, he – as a result of his non-inquiring spirit, when born amongst mankind – will be ignorant.

If a person does approach the learned and the virtuous, and makes inquiries in the foregoing manner, he – as a result of his inquiring spirit, when born amongst mankind – will be intelligent."

Conclusion ~ In addition to all unwholesome acts in the above quotation: After the explanation of his deed, this should be included, "…due to having performed such KAMMAS, on the dissolution of the body, after death, he reappears in one of the hell realms, if not there if born among humankind once often suffers a lot.

Thus, from a Buddhist standpoint, our present mental, moral, intellectual and temperamental differences are significant, due to our own past and present volitions, actions, words and thoughts.

However, everything is not due to KAMMA. (For complete

explanation refer to sections 'G' and 'H'.)

~ KAMMA is just 1 of 24 PACCAYAS of the ABHIDHAMMA PATTHANA

~ or just 1 of the 5 cosmic orders or laws – NIYĀMAS.

Note to #5 ~ Due to KAMMA being performed from an infinite past, even though a being might kill, steal, etc. upon death he can be reborn in a heaven world. And conversely, a person who has been generous, keeping the precepts, may upon death be reborn in hell worlds. However, KAMMA is never lost. Save complete enlightenment, (so the BUDDHA said), we are heirs to our volitions. They are our only personal property. (Full details in the MAHĀ KAMMA VIBHANGA SUTTA).

1. Example: A public executioner for 50 years upon death gained a heavenly world, because he was taught by SARIPUTTA.
2. Example: Queen Mallika, wife of King Pasenadi, who led a very virtuous life, keeping the 8 precepts, and doing DĀNA. However, at the time of death she recalled having sexual relations with a dog; unconfessed it weighed heavy on her mind, thus a 7-day rebirth in hell.

K. The Ten Ways of Action (10 AKUSALA, 10 KUSALA)

(Fine details and precise/complete explanations of each deed can be found in SAMANTAPĀSADIKĀ/ also commentary to VINAYA and expositor Pt. 1, p.126 for a complete description.)

1. Immoral actions (AKUSALA)

1. PĀNĀTIPĀTA ~ Injuring and killing living beings, the striking down, slaughtering, destruction of a breathing thing, the extinction of the life force of any living being.

Killing is unskillful and blamable. With killing beings without moral qualities. (i.e., animal kingdom) blame is less severe when the being killed is small bodied and heavy.

When it is big bodied, why more severe? Because of the greatness of the act of killing a big-bodied one, with the act of killing being the same, the blame of killing the large bodied is grave because of the magnitude of the property. In killing beings with moral qualities, humans and so forth, less severe consequences to the destruction of life in one with little good, and severe consequences to the taking of one of high moral behavior. If size and moral qualities are equal, severity is light or heavy according to the respective mildness or sharpness of the mental states involved, as well as the act. Severity is light or heavy, according to the respective mildness or sharpness of the mental states involved, as well as the act.

~ To complete the offense of killing, five conditions must be met:
1. A living being, 2. acknowledgement that it is living, 3. intention to take its life, 4. effort to kill it, 5. it dies

~ The consequences of killing are:
1. Lower birth/APAYA, 2. short life if human, 3. Disease-fulness, 4. fearful, 5. constant grief caused by separation from the loved

~ The various modes involved in taking life:
1. By one's own hands, 2. ordering of another to do so, 3. a weapon, 4. traps, 5. sorcery, 6. psychic power

2. ADINNĀDĀNA ~ Taking or destroying goods, items, things that belong to another and are not given to you. Theft, robbery, stealing, the taking away of what is not given. When what is taken from another is low in value, the severity is of a lighter degree. When value is high, heavy degree. Why? Because of the excellence of the property, there being equality of value in the property stolen, the blame is grave when the property belongs to the more virtuous, and lighter when it belongs to the less virtuous.

~ To complete the offense of stealing, five conditions are necessary:
1. Property of other people, 2. acknowledgement that this is so, 3. the intention to steal it, 4 efforts to do so, 5. removal

~ The various modes of stealing (same as under killing – one's own hands, etc.)

~ Types of kinds of stealing: Thievish stealing, 2. violent taking away, 3. secretly taking, 4. planned taking, 5. fraudulent taking away

~ Effects of stealing are: 1. APAYA birth, 2. If human-poverty, wretchedness, unfulfilled desires, dependent livelihood.

3. KAMESUMICCHĀCĀRA ~ Sexual misconduct, the volition with sexual intent, transgressing bounds, expressing itself in bodily action. Sexual misconduct is heavy of blame when what is out of bounds is endowed with good morals, and less of severity if lacking in high morality.

~ To complete the offense of sexual transgression/misconduct, four conditions are necessary: 1. Object which is not within bounds, 2.the intention of resorting to, 3. the act of resorting, 4. union physically

~ The consequences of sexual misconduct: 1. APAYA, 2. If born having many enemies, 3. getting undesirable wives, 4. birth as a woman or eunuch.

~ There are 20 types of women mentioned in the SUTTAs who should be considered out of bounds: 1. One who is protected by a mother, 2. by father, 3. by parents, 4. by brother, 5. by sister, 6. by relatives, 7. by lineage, 8. by clan, 9. by co-religionists, 10. by method of protection (marriage or claimed in any degree).

~ The next 10 relate to a woman already living with a man: 11. If living together because of desire to do so, 12. man provides for her, 13. in receipt of a cloth only, 14. one given in marriage by the parents by method of mutual hand dipping, 15. no longer considered a worker, 16. a slave wife, 17. servant wife, 18. a regular courtesan, 19. women held as security for debt (combined with no.10), 20. one purchased. 21. one gotten

4. MUSĀVADA ~ Lying, telling things which are not true. The welfare-destroying vocal or bodily act of him who is bent on deceiving others. Utter intentionally. That which is false, untrue to the fact of actuality as you know it. Wanting and expressing that which is fiction, false, as real or true with the intention, subtle or gross, to mislead or deceive.

~ To complete the offense of lying: four conditions are necessary: 1. Untrue things, 2. an intention to falsify or deceive, 3. the effort to do so, 4.

communication of the matter to others.

~ The effects of lying: 1. Lower rebirth, 2. if human again one is constantly confronted by abusive speech, 3. considered incredible, 4. foul smelling mouth

~ The means of conveyance is by oneself.

5. PISUNAVĀCĀ ~ Slandering, back-biting, the words spoken to someone else, and by which word one makes void the affection in the heart of the one spoken to, towards a third party; and creates friendship, in the heart of the one spoken to, towards oneself, the speaker. This is the offense of slandering.

~ To complete the offense of slandering, four conditions are necessary: 1. Divisions or separations of persons, 2. intention to separate them, 3.the effect, 4. communication = thus separated.

~ The effects of slandering are: 1. Lower rebirth, 2. if human, the dissolution of friendship without apparent cause.

6. PHARUSAVĀCĀ ~ Abusive or harsh language, that speech or word that by the fact of it being spoken makes oneself (and another) harsh. Words not pleasant and not heart-easing to the ear. By reason only of the harshness of the mind is there harshness of speech. The words are not in and of themselves harsh or gentle. A teacher or parent may speak harshly to a student or child, but be motivated by love and compassion. Talk does not become gentle by gentleness of speech. / Vocal action that cuts into the vital spots of another's mind is harsh language.

~ To complete the offense of harsh talk, three conditions are necessary: 1. Another individual or group to be abused, 2.the angry mind state, 3. speaking abusively

~ The effects of slander (harsh language) are: 1. Lower unhappy realm, 2. being detested by others although blameless, 3. a harsh voice if human.

7. SAMPHAPPALĀPA ~ Frivolous, superfluous, gossip. Excessive useless indulgence of speech that is profitless, an idle babbler, speaking of the irrelevant, of the unrighteous and unrestrained. One who utters speech not worth treasuring. Out of place, without discrimination, and not concerned with real human profit.

~ To complete the offense of frivolous talk, 2 conditions are necessary: 1. The inclination of such talk, 2. its communication

~ The effects of frivolous talk are: 1. Disorderliness of the physical bodily organs, 2. unacceptable speech (Traditionally frivolous talk includes ~ talk about rulers, robbers or political leaders, armies or fears, tale of fights, talk about food, drink, clothes, beds, lodging, flower-garlands, scents, kinfolk and transporting vehicles, about village suburbs, towns, provinces, women and soldiers, gossip of the streets and wells, and tales of ghosts, talk about the world and the ocean, of things existent and non-existent (Fr. DIGHA NIKAYA, iii, 36-7)

8. ABHIJJHĀ ~ Covetousness, a longing to possess. The yearning for something. It is the state of mind which is turned towards another's property with the thought, "Ah, if this were mine". The severity of covetousness is computed light or heavy in the same way stealing is. #2.
~ To commit the offense of covetousness, two conditions are necessary: 1. Another's property, 2. and subjective desire for it (though there may be the arising of covetous in regard to another's goods, yet so long as the desire does not occur to divert it to one's own use with the thought, "Ah, if this were mine", a thought/complete act of covetousness is not completed.)

~ The effect of covetousness: 1. Unfulfillment of one's wishes.

9. BYĀPĀDA ~ Anger, ill-will, that which injures welfare and well-being.

~ To commit the offense of ill-will or male violence two conditions are necessary: 1. Another being, 2. intention of doing harm or injury (though anger may arise in regard to another yet so long as one does not wish the destruction of that other being, saying "If only harm or destruction would befall..." A thorough/complete act of ill-will does not take place).

~ The effects of ill-will are: 1. Ugliness, 2. various diseases, 3. detestable nature

10. MICCĀDITTHI ~ Wrong views, false views, seeing things wrongly without understanding their true nature. Taking ANICCA, ANATTA and DUKKHA for their opposites, not understanding KAMMA and VIPĀKA.

~ To commit the offense of wrong view, two conditions are necessary: 1. An object that is wrongly viewed and understood to be correct (there is no benefit in giving)

~ The effects of wrong view are: 1. Base attachments, 2. lack of wisdom, 3. dull-witted, 4. chronic diseases, 5. blame worthy ideas.

The 10 immoral actions are rooted in 1. Greed, 2. hatred, 3. delusion.

1, 2 and 3 are committed by physical action/ 4, 5, 6 and 7 are committed by verbal action/ 8, 9 and 10 by mind ~ with all 10 rooted in LOBHA, DOSA and MOHA.

Note to 'immorals': These 10 courses of immoral action do not exhaust the range of the term 'unwholesome.' The range goes beyond the moral sphere. It is, for instance, not restricted to a violation of the 5 moral precepts, but compromises all deeds, words and thoughts which are motivated by any degree of greed, hatred and delusion. (E.g., An attraction for your favorite food, rooted in greed and delusion. Thoughts of lust, craving for one's wife, socially not immoral, but karmically unwholesome (AKUSALA) leads to DUKKA VIPĀKA, etc.

(A very detailed exposition of the 10 KUSALA and 10 AKUSALA actions from ethical and ABHIDHAMMA perspective can be found in "An exposition of KAMMA and rebirth" by Rastrapal BHIKKHU, published in India, 1965 by author, pp. 10-52)

L. Ten Ways of Moral Action (KUSALA KAMMA)

1. Moral actions (KUSALA)
1. DĀNA ~ Generosity: The effect is yielding wealth; human or DEVA rebirth.
2. SĪLA ~ Morality: Not killing, not stealing, no sexual misconduct; right speech, abstaining from intoxicants. Effects ~ being born into a noble family; human or heavenly DEVA rebirth.

3. BHĀVANĀ ~ Meditation/VIPASSANĀ: Wisdom/NIBBĀNA, SAMATHA= JHĀNAS ~ birth in BRAHMA realms.
4. APACĀYANA ~ Reverence" The effect is one of having noble parentage; human or DEVA rebirth.
5. VEYYĀVACCA ~ Service: The effect is one of developing a large following; human or DEVA rebirth.
6. PATTIDĀNA ~ Transference of merit: One is able to give in abundance in future births; human or DEVA rebirth.
7. PATTĀNUMODANA ~ Rejoicing in others' merit: One is able to give in abundance in future births; human or DEVA rebirth.
8. DHAMMASAVANA ~ Hearing the doctrine: Conducive to wisdom.
9. DHAMMADESANĀ ~ Expounding the doctrine: Conducive to wisdom.
10. DITTHIJUKAMMA ~ Forming correct views: Conducive to wisdom.

These 10 moral actions are prompted by the 3 wholesome roots of KUSALA KAMMA: non-greed (ALOBHA), non-hatred (ADOSA), non-delusion (AMOHA or PAÑÑĀ).

"Due to actions born of non-greed, non-hatred and non-delusion, neither the hells will appear, nor the animal kingdom, the realm of ghosts, nor any other kinds of woeful existence. Rather the rebirth will be of divine beings: Humans of any other kind of happy existence will appear due to an individual's actions born of non-greed, non-hatred and non-delusion. These, too, O monks, are three causes for the origin of actions." (BUDDHA – ANG. NIK. Sixed, no.39)

These 10 actions give rebirth in the sense-sphere (human and DEVA realms).

The four kinds of RŪPA-JHĀNA give rebirth in the realms of form.

The four kinds of ARŪPA-JHĀNA give rebirth in the formless realms.

(See The BUDDHA and His Teachings for details, pp.378-379)

M. The Sense-Door Thought Process (CITTAVĪTHI)

The working of KAMMA according to ABHIDHAMMA

A normal thought process that occurs during the course of one's lifetime (PAVATTI)

1. Past BHAVANGA (ATĪTA BHAVANGA)
2. Vibrating BHAVANGA (BHAVANGA CALANA)
3. Arrest BHAVANGA (BHAVANGA UPACCHEDA)
4. Sense-door consciousness (ĀVAJJANA)
5. Sense-consciousness (PAÑCA VIÑÑĀNA)
6. Receiving consciousness (SAMPATICCHANA)
7. Investigating consciousness (SANTĪRANA)
8. Determining consciousness (VOTTHAPANA)
9. JAVANA consciousness (9-15 JAVANA ~ KUSALA CITTAS or AKUSALA CITTAS (in the case of non-ARAHATS) running through the object
10. JAVANA consciousness
11. JAVANA consciousness
12. JAVANA consciousness
13. JAVANA consciousness
14. JAVANA consciousness
15. JAVANA consciousness
16. Registering consciousness (TADĀRAMMANA)
17. Registering consciousness (TADĀRAMMANA)

Immediately after this '5-Sense Door Thought-Process', the stream of consciousness subsides into BHAVANGA. Then there arises a mind-door through process perceiving the aforementioned visible object mentally as follows:

~ MANODVĀRIKA VĪTHI ~

1. MANODVĀRAVAJJANA
2. JAVANA
3. JAVANA

4. JAVANA
5. JAVANA
6. JAVANA
7. JAVANA
8. JAVANA
9. TADĀRAMMANA
10. TADĀRAMMANA

1. The thought process and its moment-to-moment explanation:

According to the Buddhist ABHIDHAMMICAL point of view, ordinarily there is no moment when we do not experience a particular type of consciousness associated with some object, whether physical or mental. The time limit of such a consciousness is termed "one thought-moment". The rapidity of the succession of such thought-moments, as stated in Buddhist canonical literature, is that within the brief duration of a flash of lightning, or in the blinking of an eye, several trillion of these thought-moments arise and perish.

Each thought-moment consists of three minor instants (KHANAS). They are arising or genesis (UPPĀDA), static or development (THITI) and cessation or dissolution (BHAÑGA). Birth, decay and death correspond to these three stages. The interval between birth and death is regarded as decay. Immediately after the cessation stage of a thought moment, there results the genesis stage of the subsequent thought-moment. Thus, each unit of consciousness perishes, conditioning another, transmitting at the same time all its potentialities to its successor. (Of course, each thought moment is ANATTA, just an intricate transference process. Like the seal pressed in wax. Not the same nor completely different: A series of candles each lit then extinguished by the proceeding one.) There is, therefore, a continuous flow of consciousness, like a stream without any interruption.

When a material object is presented to the mind through one of the five sense-doors, a thought-process occurs (VĪTHI- derived from VI=1, to go; here used in the sense of process), consisting of a series of separate thought moments, leading one to the other in particular uniform order. This order is known as "the psychic order" (CITTA-NIYĀMA – see section 'H'). As the rule for a complete perception of a physical object

20. KAMMA

through one of the sense doors, precisely 17 thought-moments must pass; as such the time duration of matter is fixed at 17 thought moments. After the expiration of that time limit, one fundamental unit of matter perishes, giving birth to another unit. The first moment is regarded as the 'genesis' (UPPĀDA). The last as 'dissolution' (BHAÑGA) and the interval 15 moments as 'decay' or 'development' (THITI or JARĀ).

(Note: In the compendium of thought-processes, 6 kinds of 6 classes are mentioned (see ABHIDHAMMATTA – SANGAHA – p. 196)

1. 6 bases
2. 6 doors
3. 6 objects
4. 6-fold consciousness
5. 6 processes
6. 6-fold presentation of objects

Explanation (only) of the six-fold presentation of objects:
1. At the 5-sense doors – very great, great, slight or very slight
2. At the mind-door – clear or obscure

As a rule, when an object enters the consciousness through any of the doors, one moment of the life continuum elapses. This is ATĪTA BHAVANGA. Then the corresponding thought-process runs uninterruptedly for 16-thought moments. The object thus presented is regarded as "very great".

If the thought-process ceases at the expiration of JAVANAS, without giving rise to two retentive moments (TADĀLAMBANA), thus completing only 14 moments, then the object is called "great".

Sometimes, the thought-process ceases at the moment of determining (VOTTHAPANA) without giving rise to the JAVANAS, completing only 7 thought moments. Then the object is termed "slight".

At times when an object enters the consciousness there is merely a vibration of the life-continuum. Then the object is termed "very slight".

When a so-called, "very great" or "great" object perceived through the 5-sense doors is subsequently conceived by the mind-door, or when a thought-process arising through the mind-door extends up to the retentive stage, then the object is regarded as "clear".

When a thought-process arising through the mind-door ceases at the JAVANA stage, the object is termed "obscure".

For instance, when a person looks at the radiant moon on a cloudless night, he gets a faint glimpse of the surrounding stars as well. He focuses his attention on the moon, but he cannot avoid the sight of stars around. The moon is regarded as a great object, while the stars are regarded as minor objects. Both moon and stars are perceived by the mind at different moments. (There is no place in ABHIDHAMMA to say that the stars are perceived by a subconsciousness and the moon by the consciousness).

(For the various thought-processes that occur at death, rebirth consciousness, JHĀNA attainments, NIBBĀNA – i.e., all supramundane consciousness processes – refer to ABHIDHAMMA for complete explanation.)

M.1. A thought-process continued ~ moment to moment explanation of KAMMA process

A. The 17 thought-moments explained in brief:

BHAVANGA ~ When a person is fast asleep in a dreamless state, he experiences a type of consciousness which is more or less passive than active. This type of consciousness according to ABHIDHAMMA is known as BHAVANGA. Like all other thought moments of consciousness, it also consists of 3 aspects: genesis, static and cessation. Arising and perishing in every moment, it flows on like a stream, not remaining the same for 2 consecutive moments. (This applies to consciousness as a vehicle, BHAVANGA isn't the only type of consciousness). Remembering that no two thought moments can co-exist; when an object enters this stream through any of the 6-sense doors, the BHAVANGA consciousness is arrested, and another type of consciousness appropriate to the object perceived arises. Not only in a dreamless state but also in our waking state we experience BHAVANGA thought-moments more than any other type of consciousness. Hence BHAVANGA is an indispensable condition of life. BHAVANGA is not what western psychologists think of as sub-consciousness, intimating that sub-consciousness is a separate compartment of the mind alleged by some to exist between the thresholds of consciousness. (According to ABHIDHAMMA, as mentioned before, no two types of consciousness co-exist, nor is BHAVANGA a 'sub-plane'.)

(BHAVANGA = BHAVA + ANGA = factor of life, or indispensable condition of existence). Whenever the mind does not receive a fresh external object, we experience BHAVANGA consciousness. Immediately after the occurrence of a thought process BHAVANGA arises. Sometimes it acts as a buffer between two thought-processes. Life continuum is perhaps the closest English equivalent. BHAVANGA-CITTA is KAMMA-resultant state of consciousness (VIPĀKA) and that, in birth as human or in a lower? form of existence, is always the result of wholesome KAMMA, though to be experienced in varying degrees or strength. (Refer to Bud. Dkt. NYANATILOKA, pp.38-39).

1., 2., 3. When an object (sight, odor, sound, etc.) enters the BHAVANGA stream of consciousness (ATĪTA BHAVANGA – past BHAVANGA), the thought-moment that immediately follows is called BHAVANGA CALANA: Vibrating BHAVANGA. That is because the object that has entered the field of presentation has produced a reverberation or perturbation in the stream of being (consciousness), causing this as it were to vibrate (just as a lamp flicker before it goes out) for two moments. This second moment is called BHAVANGA UPACCHEDA: arrest BHAVANGA. Owing to the rapidity of the flow of BHAVANGA, an external object does not immediately give rise to a thought-process. The original BHAVANGA thought moment perishes. Then the flow is checked. Before the actual transition to the BHAVANGA it vibrates for two moments. When the BHAVANGA is arrested, a thought-moment arises adverting the consciousness towards the object.

BHAVANGA continued (from ABHIDHAMMA in Daily Life, p.110-117, Gorham)

There are moments when there are no sense impressions, no thought, no AKUSALA or KUSALA CITTAS. However there still must be consciousness, otherwise there would be no life. At these moments, the BHAVANGA CITTA arises and passes away. The BHAVANGA CITTA is the same type of CITTA as the first CITTA in life (past ISANDHI-

CITTA or rebirth-consciousness). When the rebirth-consciousness falls away it conditions the next CITTA to arise, which is the second CITTA in that life. This second CITTA is the first BHAVANGA-CITTA in life. The BHAVANGA-CITTA is a VIPĀKA CITTA. It is the result of the same KAMMA which produced the PATISANDHI-CITTA. There is only one rebirth-CITTA in a life, but there are countless BHAVANGA-CITTAS. Not only the first BHAVANGA-CITTA, but all BHAVANGA- CITTAS arising during a lifespan are the result of the KAMMA which produced the PATISANDHI-CITTA. (There are 19 types of PATISANDHI-CITTA, thus 19 types of BHAVANGA-CITTA.) All BHAVANGA-CITTAS during a lifespan are of the same type as the PATISANDHI-CITTA of that life. (It could be of AKUSALA VIPĀKA, thus all BHAVANGA-CITTAS of that life term will be AKUSALA VIPĀKA as well. And so on with KUSALA-VIPĀKA and with the various unwholesome roots ~ wholesome roots.

With SOMANASSA – happy feelings, or its opposite. All BHAVANGA-CITTAS of that life are accompanied by SOMANASSA.

Every CITTA must have an object, and thus the BHAVANGA-CITTA too has an object. Seeing has color as an object, hearing has sound; but the BHAVANGA-CITTA has an object which is different from the objects presenting themselves through the senses and through the mind door. The BHAVANGA-CITTA has the same object as the PATISANDHI-CITTA, which has again the same object as the CITTAS which arose in the preceding life shortly before dying. The CITTAS arising shortly before the last CITTA in life, dying consciousness (CUTI-CITTA), are decisive for the next birth. (If AKUSALA CITTA = unhappy rebirth, KUSALA = happy). These CITTAS can experience an object through any of the 6 doors. The PATISANDHI-CITTA of any particular life (and all BHAVANGA-CITTAS of that life) experience the same object as the CITTAS arising shortly before the dying consciousness of the previous life. (VIS. MAG ~ as long as there is no other kind of arising consciousness to interrupt the continuity, they also go on occurring endlessly in periods of dreamless sleep, etc., like the current of a river.) BHAVANGA becomes interrupted when there is an object presenting itself through one of the five senses, or

20. KAMMA

through the mind-door (as explained above – as 1, 2, 3).

Now before going further, look more closely at this vibrating BHAVANGA. The vibrating BHAVANGA-CITTA arising at that moment is affected by an object from outside. It is vibrated or disturbed. How can a BHAVANGA-CITTA be affected from (or by) an object from the outside? Does the BHAVANGA-CITTA not have its own object, which is the same as the object of the PATISANDHI-CITTA? A CITTA can have only one object at a time. The BHAVANGA-CITTA can be affected by an object from the outside, and still have its own object. (Ex. from VIS. MAGGA ~ When sugar grains are put on a drum's surface and one of the grains of sugar are tapped, a fly sitting on another grain moves. – Chapter XIV, v.115m, Footnote 46).

However, these 3 BHAVANGA-CITTAS that are disturbed by the object, do not have the function of adverting to the new object which contacts one of the senses, nor of experiencing that object. They have their own function, which is to keep a person alive so that objects can be experienced during that life. Remembering that each BHAVANGA-CITTA maintains the same object that was of the PATISANDHI-CITTA.

When the sense-door process of CITTAS is over, the stream of BHAVANGA-CITTAS is resumed, so that the series of CITTAS succeeding one another in our life is not interrupted.

4. After the three BHAVANGA-CITTAS pass away, then the (PAÑCA-DVĀRĀVAJJANA-CITTA) five-sense-door adverting consciousness arises. The PAÑCA-DVĀRĀVAJJANA-CITTA is the first CITTA of the process of CITTAS experiencing the object which impinged on that sense door. The PAÑCA-DVĀRĀVAJJANA-CITTA performs the function of adverting (ĀVAJJANA) to the object which has impinged on one of the five-sense doors. It adverts to the object through that sense door (the PAÑCA-DVĀRĀVAJJANA-CITTA is an AHETUKA-KIRIYA-CITTA). The PAÑCA-DVĀRĀVAJJANA-CITTA is named after the sense door which the object impinged on. When this process is over, the object is experienced through the 'mind-door'. Thus, there are 2 kinds of CITTA which perform the function of adverting: (the PAÑCA-DVĀRĀVAJJANA-CITTA

adverts to the object through one of the 5-sense doors, and the MANO-DVĀRĀVAJJANA-CITTA adverts to the object through the mind-door.) After the advertence to the object, it is followed by KUSALA or AKUSALA CITTAS. (From Compendium of Philosophy) ~ At this stage the subject merely turns for one thought-moment to something that arouses its attention, after having produced a disturbance in the stream of being – but however, knows no more about it.

5. When color contacts the eye-sense (for example), the eye-door adverting consciousness (CAKKHU-DVĀRĀVAJJANA-CITTA) adverts to color through the 'eye-door'. When the CAKKHU-DVĀRĀVAJJANA-CITTA has fallen away, it is succeeded by 'seeing consciousness' (CAKKHU-VIÑÑĀNA). The function of seeing (DASSANA-KICCA) is performed by 'seeing consciousness' (or 'hearing consciousness', etc.; any one of the 5 senses thus named PAÑCA-VIÑÑĀNA). The object now is seen, but nothing more is known at this stage. The subject is merely aware of the fact that a certain object is seen, heard, smelled, tasted or felt. All of which are VIPĀKA; the result of KUSALA and AKUSALA KAMMA. We are born in order to receive the result of our volitions (actions, etc.) and therefore the current of the BHAVANGA-CITTAS is interrupted and VIPĀKA-CITTAS arise after the PAÑCA-DVĀRĀVAJJANA-CITTA. (Remembering that in every moment of consciousness, the minimum 7 universal CETASIKAS arise along with the CITTA~ thus VEDANĀ with every CITTA). The CITTA which performs the function of seeing only perceived color does not like or dislike. It is an AHETUKA-VIPĀKA-CITTA. The CITTAS which know what the object is, arise later on. (DASSANA= seeing, SAVANA = hearing, SHAYANA = smelling, SAYANA = tasting, PHUSANA = touching).

6. In the process of CITTAS, the PAÑCA-VIÑÑĀNA is succeeded by SAMPATICCHANA-CITTA or "receiving consciousness". Thus, the conscious moment performs the function of receiving the object after the "sense-consciousness" (PAÑCA-VIÑÑĀNA) has fallen away. (SAMPATICCHANA-CITTA is AHETUKA-VIPĀKA ~ 2 kinds of CITTA can perform this function: AKUSALA VIPĀKA and KUSALA-VIPĀKA).

(SAMPATICCHANA-CITTA is the marking of the object which has been received by the eye, ear, etc. From this receiving process, the mind finds the object as "something existing in the world of reality".)

7. Next arises "the investigating thought-moment" (SANTĪRANA) or "investigating consciousness", which has the function of momentarily examining the object so sensed. Investigating is another characteristic function of CITTA different from seeing, hearing, etc. and receiving. This CITTA is also an AHETUKA-VIPĀKA-CITTA.

(Note): There are 3 kinds of SANTĪRANA-CITTA which can perform the function of investigating depending on the nature of the object (ĀKAMMANA) which can be:

1. An unpleasant object (ANIDDHĀRAMMANA): If such, the CITTA performing the function of SANTĪRANA is AKUSALA VIPĀKA, accompanied by UPEKKHĀ (neutral feeling).
2. A pleasant object (IDDHĀRAMMANA): If such, the SANTĪRANA-CITTA is KUSALA VIPĀKA accompanied by UPEKKHĀ.
3. Or an extraordinarily pleasant object (ADHI-IDDHĀRAMMANA): If such, the SANTĪRANA-CITTA is KUSALA VIPĀKA accompanied by SOMANASSA (pleasant feeling).

SANTĪRANA-CITTA is knowing the object on the basis of previous experience.

8. This is followed by the determining thought-moment (VOTTHAPANA) when discrimination is exercised, and conscious volition may play its part. (VOTTHAPANA= VI=AVA=THĀ, 'to stand', 'to fix', 'to rest', through settling down). It is at this moment that the nature of the object is fully determined. This is the gateway to a moral or immoral thought-process. Discrimination, though wise or unwise attention employed at this stage determined the thought-process either for KUSALA or AKUSALA. VOTTHAPANA (according to Compendium of Philosophy): This is the arranging of the investigated material in such a manner as to constitute it into a definite object. This is done by differentiation and limitation, by discrimination and definition. For instance, a mango fruit, to be discerned as such and as nothing else,

must have certain definitive and constitutive features and attributes of its own. Up to this stage the subject is not yet intelligently aware of the nature and characteristic of the object.

From ABHIDHAMMA in Daily Life: VOTTHAPANA-CITTA determined the object in the sense-door process. It determines whether it is an object for KUSALA or for AKUSALA CITTAS, and according as it determines, it is succeeded by KUSALA CITTAS or AKUSALA CITTAS. VOTTHAPANA-CITTA is not a VIPĀKA and it is not KUSALA or AKUSALA, but it is an AHETUKA-KIRIYĀ-CITTA. The VOTTHAPANA- CITTA is actually the MANO-DVĀRĀVAJJANA-CITTA which performs in the sense door process the function of determining, and is then called VOTTHAPANA-CITTA. The MANO-DVĀRĀVAJJANA-CITTA or "the mind-door adverting consciousness" can perform more than one function. In the mind-door process it performs the function of adverting to an object though the mind-door: If the MANO-DVĀRĀVAJJANA-CITTA is succeeded by KUSALA CITTAS, there is "wise attention" and if it is succeeded by AKUSALA-CITTAS, there is "unwise attention".

9, 10, 11, 12, 13, 14, 15 ~ JAVANA-CITTA: Explained next.

16, 17 ~ TADĀLAMBANA (registering consciousness): Explained after that.

~ After this completed thought-process of the 17 mind moments, the stream of consciousness subsides into BHAVANGA. Then there arises a mind-door thought-process perceiving the aforementioned visible object mentally, as shown in the diagram on page 10. After which, the stream of consciousness subsides into BHAVANGA, and two more similar thought-processes will arise before an object is actually known. The BHAVANGA-CITTAS will resume until another object is received.

Mind-moments 9-15

9, 10, 11, 12, 13, 14, 15 ~ JAVANA-CITTA: (Refer to Compendium of Philosophy pp. 245-250: Complete explanation of JAVANA)

(For details see ABHIDHAMMATTHA-SANGHA, by NAKADA, pp.210-216.

Also, ABHIDHAMMA in daily life – Nina van Gorkom ~ Chapter 14, Function of JAVANA, p.130)

~ Now at this point in the movement of the thought-process or flow of consciousness, after the determining consciousness (VOTTHAPANA) passes, next arises the apperceptive stage for JAVANA. (JAVANA derived from UJU, to run swiftly.) It is so called because in the course of a thought-process, it runs consecutively for seven thought-moments, or five hanging on to an identical object. The mental states occurring in all these thought-moments are similar, but the potential factors differ. JAVANA is the act of utilization of the object in a positive or negative way. In most cases, habituated conditioned tendencies (if the object received is agreeable-pleasant, the mind is attracted or accepts it; OR if the object is disagreeable or unpleasant, the mind will be adverse, or not accept it). It is at this stage in the stream of consciousness that one's volition (action or KAMMA) is evaluated and classified, whether it be moral (KUSALA) or immoral (AKUSALA). This is the all-important stage where KAMMA is performed. If viewed rightly (YONISOMANASIKARA), it becomes moral; if wrongly (AYONISOMANASIKARA), immoral. Irrespective of the desirability or the undesirability of the object presented to the mind, it is possible for one to make the JAVANA process moral or immoral. (For instance, when one meets an enemy, anger will in most cases arise to varying degrees. A person with some wisdom, on the contrary, with wise attention (thus self-control), radiates a thought of love (METTĀ), compassion (KARUNĀ), mindfulness or equanimity towards him. As the BUDDHA has stated: "By self is the unskillful done: By self is the one defiled. By self is not skillful done: By self is one purified. Both defilement and purity depend on oneself. No one is purified by another." (DHP, v.165)

(From ABHIDHAMMA in Daily Life – pp.130-137) The VOTTHAPANA-CITTA determines the object and is then succeeded by KUSALA CITTAS or AKUSALA CITTAS. If one is not an ARAHANT, there will inevitably arise KUSALA or AKUSALA CITTAS in the sense door process after the VOTTHAPANA-CITTA. The KUSALA or AKUSALA CITTAS which arise perform the function of JAVANA or "running through the object". (In the 'sense-door' process the VOTTHAPANA-CITTA has determined the object already when the JAVANA-CITTA arise, and in the 'mind-door' process the MANO-DVĀRĀVAJJANA-CITTA has adverted to the object already when the JAVANA-CITTA arise. Thus, the KUSALA or AKUSALA CITTAS which follow have as their only function to "run through the object"). There are usually 7 CITTAS in succession which perform this function (the number of JAVANA moments can vary): If the first JAVANA-CITTA is KUSALA so the succeeding six CITTAS are also KUSALA CITTAS. If the first one is AKUSALA, so the following 6 CITTAS will be AKUSALA.

Procedure of JAVANA ~ Amongst the JAVANAS: In a minor JAVANA, the sense-sphere JAVANA runs only for six or seven times. In the case of a feeble process or at death-moment, only five JAVANA moments will arise. In the case of a BUDDHA performing the twin miracle, it is said only four or five moments arise. (JHĀNAS, fruitions, paths, etc. are also dealt with. For details see p.215 ABHIDHAMMATTHA-SANGHA, by NAKADA).

There are 55 kinds of CITTA which can perform the function of JAVANA:

8 LOBHA-MŪLA-CITTAS (rooted in attachment)
2 DOSA-MŪLA-CITTAS (rooted in aversion) ~ 12 AKUSALA CITTAS
2 MOHA-MŪLA-CITTAS (rooted in delusion)
8 MAHA-KUSALA-CITTAs (moral CITTAS of the sensuous plane of existence)
8 MAHA-KIRIYĀ-CITTAS
1 NASITUPPĀDA-CITTA (AHETUKA KIRIYA-CITTA which may arise when the ARAHAT smiles)
5 RŪPAVACARA KUSALA CITTAS (RŪPA-JHĀNA-CITTAS)
5 RŪPAVACARA KIRIYĀ CITTAS (RŪPA-JHĀNA-CITTAS of the ARAHAT)
4 ARŪPA KUSALA CITTAS (ARŪPA-JHĀNA-CITTAS)
4 ARŪPAVACARA KIRIYĀ CITTAS (ARŪPA-JHĀNA-CITTAS of the ARAHAT)
4 MAGGA-CITTAS
4 PHALA CITTAS (LOKUTTARA-VIPĀKA-CITTAS) ~ 8 LOKUTTARA CITTAS

~ (For detailed explanation of each CITTA group, refer to pages 132-137 ~ ABHIDHAMMA in Daily Life)

It is useful to know that when AKUSALA CITTAS arise on account of an object, there arise not just one, but seven AKUSALA CITTAS in one process; and of course, this possess of CITTA can be succeeded by innumerable other AKUSALA-JAVANA-CITTA processes. When AKUSALA CITTAS arise in the sense door process the VOTTHAPANA-CITTA has determined the object already, and when they arise in the mind-door process the mind-DVĀKĀVAJJANA-CITTA has adverted to the object already. When the first JAVANA-CITTA has arisen, it has to be followed by the other JAVANA-CITTAS. The first JAVANA-CITTA conditions the next, (second) one, and each JAVANA-CITTA is conditioned by the preceding one. It is during the time of the JAVANA-CITTAS that we accumulate wholesomeness or unwholesomeness. Thus, one does those things through body, speech and thought that give rise to KUSALA conditions. One abandons that which conditions AKUSALA to arise, thus removing "unwise attention" (wrong view – no SATI) with "wise attention" (right view with SATI). One develops KUSALA for the overcoming of volitional actions altogether. One treads the path towards greater wisdom, purity and freedom, thus enabling one to experience progressively the stages of liberation, until ARAHATTA. Then no more KUSALA or AKUSALA is possible, only volition-less actions, speech, etc.

(JAVANA pertains to the active side of the present existence, and determines the passive side of the future existence. The other stages of the cognitive processes pertain to the passive side of the present existence, and have already been unalterably determined at the active-volitional-kammic-side of the past existence.) JAVANA can be distinguished as a determining, free, casual act, and the rest, opposed to a fixed result or VIPAKĀ (Compendium. of Phil.)

16, 17. After the JAVANA stage, there follows TADĀRAMMANA, registering or identifying consciousness; it lasts for 2 'mind-moments', registering the object thus perceived.

In this sense-door thought-process, if the sense-object has not fallen away yet, KAMMA can produce two more moments of VIPĀLA after the JAVANA-CITTAS have fallen away. These 2 retention-moments are known as TADĀRAMMANA-CITTAS. It literally means "that object": the CITTA "hangs on" to that object, the object is experienced for 2 more moments. Only in the sensuous place of existence- KAMA LOKA can KAMMA, after the JAVANA-CITTAS, produce two more VIPĀKA-CITTAS which "hang on" to the object. Those born in RŪPA and ARŪPA-BRAHMA worlds have no VIPĀKA-CITTAS.

TADĀRAMMANA-CITTAS can also experience an object through the mind door. This is a CITTA (VIPĀKA-CITTA) which can experience an object through all 6 doors. If the object which contacts the sense-door is unpleasant or pleasant, all VIPĀKAS of that process (including the TADĀRAMMANA-CITTAS if they arise) will also be unpleasant ~ AKUSALA VIPĀKA, or pleasant ~ KUSALA VIPĀKA. Also, the TADĀRAMMANA-CITTAS of the mind-door process succeeding that sense-door process are also AKUSALA-VIPĀKA or KUSALA-VIPĀKA accordingly. (There are many other details regarding the function of this CITTA, for a more comprehensive examination refer to ABHIDHAMMA in Daily Life, pp.136-143).

Conclusion/Explanation of the sense-door thought-process in short with clarifying simile:

An object which impinges on one of the sense-doors can be color, sound, smell, taste or an impression through the body sense. Each one of these objects is RŪPA. When we see, hear, smell, taste or touch something pleasant or unpleasant, the CITTA is VIPĀKA, the result is a skillful or unskillful action (volition). Objects of RŪPA do not fall away as rapidly as NĀMA, RŪPAS last 17 moments of CITTA.

When an object impinges on one of the sense-doors, the PAÑCA-DVĀRĀVAJJANA- CITTA, or "five- sense- door- adverting consciousness", does not arise immediately. First there are three more BHAVANGA-CITTAS: BHAVANGA-CALĀNA, or vibrating BHAVANGA, then the BHAVANGA UPACCHEDA, or the arrest BHAVANGA, the last BHAVANGA-CITTA to arise before the stream of BHAVANGA-CITTAS are arrested. These two BHAVANGA-CITTAS are the second and third mind-CITTA movements to arise in a sense-door thought-process. They are preceded by the first BHAVANGA-CITTA to be disturbed, so to speak, in the process; thus called ATĪTA BHAVANGA. This is the first CITTA to arise once an object enters the BHAVANGA stream. However, none of these 3 CITTAS experience the new object which is impinging on one of the sense-doors. Now, when the impinging sense object (color, sound, etc.) contacts the eye-sense, ear-sense, etc., the "five sense-door adverting consciousness" (PAÑCA-DVĀRĀVAJJANA- CITTA) which is a KIRIYA-CITTA, arises and falls away. It is succeeded by "seeing, -consciousness", "hearing-consciousness", (depending on the object), collectively referred to as PAÑCA-VIÑÑĀNA. Seeing-consciousness, or "sense-consciousness" is the first VIPĀKA-CITTA of that process. Then there are two more VIPĀKA-CITTAS: SAMPATICCHANA-CITTA which receives the object; or the act of reception and SANTĪRANA-CITTA, which investigates the object. This CITTA is succeeded by the VOTTHAPANA-CITTA or "determining-consciousness". The object is actually known at this point, investigated and consequently defined or determined. A mango is known as such, this CITTA is a KIRIYĀ-CITTA. The VOTTHAPANA- CITTA functions in such a way as to determine whether the object will be an object for AKUSALA CITTAS or KUSALA-CITTAS. Discrimination is exercised and free-will plays its part at this point, however conditioned it might be. This CITTA is succeeded by seven JAVANA-CITTAS, which are, if one is not fully enlightened (ARAHAT), AKUSALA or KUSALA CITTAS. If the sense-object has not fallen away yet, 2 additional moments of VIPĀKA arise after the JAVANA- CITTAS have passed. These two CITTAs are known as TADĀRAMMANA- CITTAS, or registering or retention. The CITTA "hangs on" for two more moments of the same but changing object, only if the experience is in the sense realm (KAMA LOKA); TADĀRAMMANA does not arise in BRAHMA LOKAS.

~ This completes one complete sense-door thought-process ~

Clarifying simile of sense-door thought- process:

The mango tree simile to illustrate this thought-process.

A man, fast asleep, is lying at the foot of a mango tree with his head covered. A wind stirs the branches, and a fruit falls beside the head of the sleeping man. He removes his head covering and turns towards the object. He sees it, then picks it up. He examines it and ascertains that it is a ripe mango fruit, He eats it, and swallowing the remnants with saliva, once more resigns himself to sleep.

The dreamless sleep corresponds to the unperturbed current of BHAVANGA, the striking of the wind against the tree corresponds to the past BHAVANGA (ATĪTA BHAVANGA) and the swaying of the branches to vibrating BHAVANGA (BHAVANGA-CALĀNA). The falling of the fruit represents the arrest BHAVANGA (BHAVANGA-UPACCHEDA). Turning towards the object corresponds to "sense -door adverting- consciousness" (PAÑCA-DVĀRĀVAJJANA- CITTA); sight of the object, to "seeing consciousness" (or collectively PAÑCA-VIÑÑĀNA); picking up to "receiving consciousness" (SAMPATICCHANA-CITTA); examination to "investigating consciousness" (SANTĪRANA-CITTA); and ascertaining that it is a ripe mango fruit to "determining consciousness" (VOTTHAPANA- CITTA). The actual eating resembles the JAVANA process, and the swallowing of the fruit corresponds to "registering consciousness" or retention (TADĀRAMMANA-CITTA). His resigning to sleep resembles the subsidence of the mind into BHAVANGA again.

~ End of the sense-door thought- process section ~

N. Classification of KAMMA

1. Classification of KAMMA with reference to its time of operation
    1. Immediately effective KAMMA ~ DITTHADHAMMAVEDANIYA KAMMA
    2. Subsequently effective KAMMA ~ UPAPAJJAVEDANITA KAMMA
    3. Indefinitely effective KAMMA ~ APARĀPARIYAVEDANIYA KAMMA
    4. Ineffective effective KAMMA ~ AHOSI KAMMA

2. Classification of KAMMA according to function (KICCA)
   1. Reproductive KAMMA ~ JANAKA KAMMA
   2. Supportive KAMMA ~ UPATTHAMBHAKA KAMMA
   3. Counteractive KAMMA ~ UPAPIDAKA KAMMA
   4. Destructive KAMMA ~ UPAGHĀTAKA KAMMA

3. Classification of KAMMA according to the order in which the KAMMA takes place (VIPĀKADĀNAVASENA)
   1. Weighty KAMMA ~ GARUKA KAMMA
   2. Proximate KAMMA ~ ĀSANNA KAMMA
   3. Habitual KAMMA ~ ĀCINNA KAMMA
   4. Random KAMMA ~ KATATTĀ KAMMA

4. Classification of KAMMA with respect to the place in which the effect takes place (PAKATTHANAVASENA)
   1. Immoral KAMMA ~ AKUSALA KAMMA (KAMAVACARA)
   2. Moral KAMMA pertaining to the sense-sphere (KAMAVACARA KUSALA KAMMA)
   3. Habitual KAMMA pertaining to the RŪPA plane (RŪPAVACARA KUSALA KAMMA)
   4. Random KAMMA pertaining to the ARŪPA plane (ARŪPAVACARA KUSALA KAMMA)

A. Immoral KAMMA is 3-fold according to the doors of action:
   1. Bodily action ~ killing, stealing, sexual misconduct
   2. Verbal action ~ lying, slandering, harsh words, idle talk
   3. Mental action ~ covetousness, ill-will, wrong views.

B. Moral KAMMA pertaining to the sense-sphere is 3-fold:
   1. Bodily
   2. Verbal
   3. Mental

(Moral KAMMA is 10-fold according to 10 moral actions – see section 'L')

C. Moral KAMMA-RŪPA plane is only done though the mind door ~ 4 RŪPA JHĀNAS

D. Moral KAMMA-ARŪPA plane is only done though the mind door
~ 4 ARŪPA JHĀNAS

O. Classification of KAMMA with Reference to its Time of Operation

1. According to ABHIDHAMMA one does either KUSALA or AKUSALA during the JAVANA process, which usually lasts for 7 thought-moments. The effect of the first JAVANA thought-moment, being the weakest, is that one may reap or experience it in this life itself. This is known as immediately effective KAMMA (DITTHADHAMMAVEDANIYAM- KAMMA).

Examples: KAKAVALLI became a millionaire in this life, giving DĀNA to ARAHANT MAHAKASSAPA. MALLIKA became a queen by giving alms to the BUDDHA.

Examples of AKUSALA-KAMMA with immediately effective results: A hunter who went hunting to the forest, followed by his dogs, met a BHIKKHU who was on his alms-round. The hunter thought that the reason he couldn't procure any game was due to the unfortunate meeting of the BHIKKHU. When the hunter was returning home, he met the BHIKKHU a second time and became deeply enraged. In spite of the BHIKKHU'S innocence (entreating this to the hunter), the hunter nonetheless set the dogs on him. Finding no escape, the BHIKKHU climbed a tree. The wicked hunter followed him up the tree and pierced the BHIKKHU'S feet with the point of an arrow. The pain was so severe that the BHIKKHU'S robe fell off and onto the hunter below him, completely covering him. The vicious dogs, thinking that the BHIKKHU had fallen from the tree, devoured their own master. (Fr. Buddhist Legends, p.262).

~ If immediately effective KAMMA doesn't operate in this life, it becomes ineffective KAMMA #4.

2. The next weakest moment in the 7 JAVANA thought-moments is the seventh. The effect of this karmic moment one may experience in their next birth or subsequent birth after this present life term ceases. This is known as subsequently-effective-KAMMA (UPAPAJJAVEDANĪYA-

KAMMA). No fruit of such actions will be experienced in this life. This type of KAMMA too, becomes ineffective if it does not operate in the next rebirth.

Examples:

~ A millionaire's servant returned home in the evening after his laborious work in the field, to see that all were observing the eight precepts, since it was the full moon day. Learning that he also could observe them for half a day, he took the precepts and fasted at night. He just so happened to die on the following morning, and as a result of his KUSALA action was born as a DEVA. (Bud. Leg. p.282).

~ AJĀTASATTU, son of King BIMBISĀRA, who was a SAMANA-SOTAPANNA, was born immediately after his death in a state of misery (APĀYA) as the result of killing his father.

3. The effects of the intermediate fine JAVANA thought-moments may take place at any time, in any life. No being is exempt from this class of KAMMA, even the BUDDHAS and ARAHATS are subject to reap the effects of their past KAMMAS. This type of KAMMA is known as indefinitely-effective-KAMMA (APARĀPARĪYAVEDAĪYA-KAMMA).

Examples:

~ The MAHA-ARAHAT MOGGALLĀNA, in the remote past, instigated by his wicked wife, killed his mother and father. As a result of this action, he suffered for many thousands of years in a hell world, and in his last birth as one of the two chief disciples of the BUDDHA, was viciously clubbed to death by bandits.

~ The BUDDHA was falsely accused of the murder of a female devotee of a band of naked ascetics. This was the result of his having insulted a PACCEKA BUDDHA in one of his previous births.

~ The BUDDHA'S foot was injured when DEVADATTA made a futile attempt to kill him by pushing a large rock down a slope towards him. This was the result of his killing a step-brother in a previous birth with the motivation of appropriating his property.

4. There is no special class of KAMMA known as ineffective-KAMMA (AHOSI-KAMMA), but when such actions that should produce their

effects in this life or in a subsequent life do not operate, they are termed 'ineffective'.

P. Classification of KAMMA According to its Function (KICCA)

1. Every subsequent birth is conditioned by the KUSALA or AKUSALA KAMMA which predominated at the moment of death. This kind of KAMMA is known as reproductive KAMMA (JANAKA KAMMA). Therefore, reproductive KAMMA conditions the future birth. It is the KUSALA or AKUSALA JAVANA moments, only 5 in this thought-process. In this thought-process that conditions the next birth, of course, no one is reborn; only empty phenomena alone roll on. As a general rule, this last thought-process depends on the general behavior of a person. In some cases, however due to favorable or unfavorable circumstances, at the time of death a good person may experience AKUSALA or a bad person KUSALA. The future birth will be determined by this last thought-process, irrespective of the general conduct.

Examples:

~ Queen MALLIKA – even though she lived a very virtuous existence, giving DĀNA, observing the 5 and 8 precepts – on account of having remorse (AKUSALA) on her death moment for the unconfessed act of having sex with a dog was born for 7 days in a hell-realm, before dying there and taking a heavenly birth.

~ A public executioner for 50 years reflected on giving alms to Ven. SARIPUTTA at a previous time. Upon his death moment thought-process thus reflecting, giving rise to a KUSALA wholesome mind state, he died and took a heavenly birth.

However, the effects of an individual's past KAMMA are not obliterated (see 'O'), they will come to fruition at the appropriate moment. Reproductive-KAMMA determines in which plane of existence one will take rebirth.

2. Now to assist and maintain or to weaken and obstruct the fruition of reproductive KAMMA, another past KAMMA may intervene. This KAMMA is known as supportive KAMMA (UPATTHAMBHAKA-

KAMMA). It comes near the reproductive KAMMA and supports it. It is either KUSALA or AKUSALA and it assists or maintains the action of the reproductive-KAMMA during the course of one's lifetime. Immediately after the conception (rebirth-consciousness-PATISANDHI-VIÑÑĀNA) till the death moment, this KAMMA steps forward to support the reproductive KAMMA. A "moral supportive" KAMMA assists in giving health, wealth, happiness, etc. to the individual concerned. An "immoral supportive" KAMMA assists in giving pain, sorrow, grief, etc. to a person. This KAMMA is a type of action which helps the other types of moral and immoral actions in maintaining their existences, but they are not by themselves so powerful as to provide rebirth.

3. "Obstructive" or "counteractive" KAMMA (UPAPĪDAKA-KAMMA), unlike supportive-KAMMA tends to weaken, interrupt and retard the fruition of the reproductive-KAMMA. For instance, a person born with a good reproductive-KAMMA may be subject to various ailments, etc., thus preventing him from enjoying the results of his good actions. An animal, on the other hand, who is born with AKUSALA reproductive-KAMMA may lead a comfortable life by getting good food, lodging, etc., as a result of his good counteractive KAMMA, preventing the fruition of the unwholesome obstructive-KAMMA.

Example:

~ In the remote past, at the time of KASSAPA BUDDHA, a son of a BRAHMIN names JOTIPAL, who later became GAUTAMA BUDDHA, showed disrespect to KASSAPA BUDDHA, saying: "Shaven-headed recluse, where is BODHI or enlightenment? To attain enlightenment is a very difficult task." Thus, this act of irreverence compelled the BODHISATTA SIDDHATTHA to practice severe self-mortifying austerities for six long years. This is the obstructive KAMMA of SIDDHATTHA.

4. According to the law of KAMMA, the potential energy of the reproductive-KAMMA could be nullified by a more powerful opposing KAMMA of the past, which seeking an opportunity may quite unexpectedly operate — just as a counteractive powerful force

can obstruct the path of a flying arrow, and bring it suddenly down to the ground. The type of KAMMA that has this type of potential power is known as "destructive" KAMMA (UPAGHĀTAKA-KAMMA). Destructive-KAMMA is more effective than supportive and counteractive-KAMMA in that it not only obstructs but also destroys the whole force. Destructive KAMMA also may be either KUSALA or AKUSALA.

An example illustrating all four KAMMAS:

~ In the case of DEVADATTA who attempted to kill the BUDDHA and who caused a schism in the SANGHA, his good reproductive KAMMA conditioned him to a human birth in a royal family. (A human birth is very rare and considered the most precious, a happy plane of existence.) His continued comforts, prosperity and generally pleasant experiences were due to the action of the supportive KAMMA. The counteractive KAMMA came into operation when he was subject to a great humiliation (and subsequent unpleasant experiences) as a result of being excommunicated from the SANGHA. Finally, the destructive KAMMA brought his life to a miserable end.

Q. Classification of KAMMA According to the Order that KAMMA Takes to Come to Fruition

Or: At the moment of "death-proximate consciousness" there are 4 kinds of rebirth-KAMMA that may arise:

1. The first is called weighty-KAMMA (GARUKA-KAMMA), which can be either wholesome or unwholesome. Unwholesome weighty KAMMA is five-fold:
    1. Creating a schism in the SANGHA
    2. The wounding of a BUDDHA
    3. The killing (murder) of an ARAHANT – fully enlightened being
    4. Killing one's mother- matricide
    5. Killing one's father – patricide.

Any of these 5 weighty actions will take complete precedence over any other KAMMAS at the time of the final thought-process which will determine the next birth. They must bear their fruit at this time. (They all lead to a next birth in a hell realm for a long, long time.)

The wholesome weighty-KAMMA is if someone has cultivated the power of his concentration and reached the levels of absorption-JHĀNAS and maintained them until the time of death. The result will be purely mental with rebirth in the BRAHMA-LOKAS based on the strength and level of the JHĀNAS cultivated. This KUSALA-KAMMA will take predominance over other actions at the time of death, if one of the AKUSALA weighty KAMMAS has not been committed. The other wholesome weighty-KAMMA is the experience of the different stages of enlightenment. The first two stages of enlightenment do not determine precisely where one is reborn, but it assures one of never taking a lower rebirth again. One is destined for a complete liberation at this point. If the third stage has been reached, one will be reborn in the highest BRAHMA form realms (SUDDHADASA). Of course, if at the fourth stage, ARAHATTA, no rebirth is possible ~ PARINIBBĀNA.

Examples:

~ For instance, if any person were to develop the JHĀNAS and later to commit one of the unwholesome-weighty-KAMMAS (ĀNANTARIYA-KAMMA), his KUSALA KAMMA would be obliterated by the powerful unwholesome-weighty-KAMMA, his subsequent birth will be conditioned by the weight of that act, and override the KAMMA of his having gained the absorption-concentration earlier.

~ DEVADATTA lost his psychic powers and was subsequently reborn in his next life in a lower hell realm, because he wounded the BUDDHA and caused a schism in the SANGHA.

~ The king AJĀSATTU, as the BUDDHA remarked, would have attained the first stage of sainthood if he had not committed parricide. In this case the power of the weighty-KAMMA obstructed his spiritual attainment.

2. When there is no weighty-KAMMA to operate in the last moments of life, to condition the next rebirth, the proximate KAMMA or death-proximate KAMMA (ĀSANNA-KAMMA) will operate. This is the action one does immediately before dying. In other words, if in your dying moments you should remember something good you have done,

i.e., giving DĀNA, meditation, SATI, etc. or somebody reminds you of wholesome acts, or near the death moment you perform a good act, it is that KAMMA which determines rebirth. Sometimes a bad person may die happily and receive a good rebirth, if fortunately, he remembers or does a good act at those dying moments.

Examples:
~ The executioner (bad life ~ good birth)
~ Queen MALLIKA (good life ~ bad rebirth)
(Both examples explained see section 'O')

3. Consciousness can often become exceedingly weak at the time of proximate death, and there may not be the ability to redirect the mind or purposely recall certain events. If there is no proximate-KAMMA, a KAMMA known as habitual KAMMA (ĀCINNA-KAMMA) will then operate. This KAMMA is next in priority of effect. It is a KAMMA that can be wholesome or unwholesome, and one that has been repeatedly done. In other words, the constantly performed habitually, repeatedly done, actions during one's lifetime will then come to mind at these final moments before death. Habits, whether good or bad, skillful or unskillful become rather second nature to individuals, then tend to shape, mold or condition one by creating habituated tendencies. (If someone has done a lot of killing, that type of thought will arise at that dying thought-process. Or if someone has done many good deeds, has been generous or has done a lot of meditation practice or a lot of sexual activity, these habitual acts will condition the next rebirth.)

Examples:
~ Cunda, a butcher, who was living in the vicinity of the BUDDHA, died yelling like an animal as he was earning his living by slaughtering pigs.
~ King DUTTHAGĀMANI of Ceylon often gave alms to the BHIKKHUS before he took his own meal. It was his habitual KAMMA that gladdened him at the dying moment, and gave him birth in TUSITA realm.

4. If there is no weighty, proximate or habitual KAMMA, the fourth type of KAMMA which determines rebirth is known as cumulative or

random-KAMMA (KATATTĀ-KAMMA). This KAMMA embraces all KAMMAS which cannot be included in the forgoing there. We are all trailing an infinite reserve (so to speak) of wholesome and unwholesome KAMMA, and if there is no strong habitual KAMMA at the dying moments, then any deed we've done at any time (from a beginningless past) in the past may arise in those dying (JAVANA) moments.

Examples that illustrate the operation of these four KAMMAS:

~ There is a herd of cattle living in a barn. When the door is opened in the morning, the first one out will be the strongest bull. He will push his way out first due to his power and force, pushing aside all the others (weighty-KAMMA). Suppose there is no strong bull. The next one out the door will be the cow that is the nearest to the door. Due to its location or proximity to the door, it will pass quite easily out the door (proximate-KAMMA). Suppose there is no cow particularly near the door. Then the cow who is in the habit of leading the others will go out first (habitual-KAMMA). And if there is no cow in the habit of going out first, then any one of the cattle in the barn might be the first out the door (random-KAMMA).

~ Classification of KAMMA according to where its effect takes place (PAKATTHANA VASENA) ~ for details of this classification refer to section 'K' ~ the 10 ways of immoral action and section 'L' ~ the 10 ways of moral action. ~

~ Conclusion of classification of KAMMA ~

R. The Nature of KAMMA

1. Is an individual bound to reap all that one has sown in just proportion? No.

(BUDDHA ~ ANG. NIK. part 1, p.249) ~ "If anyone says that a man must reap according to his deeds, in that case there is no religious life nor is an opportunity afforded for the entire extinction of sorrow. But if anyone says that what a man reaps accords with his deeds, in that case there is a religious life, and an opportunity is afforded for the entire extinction of suffering.

(BUDDHA ~ DHAMMAPADA, v.127) ~ "Not in the sky, nor in mid-ocean, nor entering a mountain cave, is found that place on Earth where by abiding, one may escape from the consequence of an evil deed."

Yet one is not bound to reap all the effects of one's past KAMMAS. If such were the case, liberation would not be possible, eternal suffering would prevail.

~ We are always becoming something, and that becoming something depends on our actions.

~ The most vicious person can become a morally virtuous person.

~ One can shape and mold one's future by present actions.

~ How foolish it is to condemn the wicked or immoral. They can change. Have compassion, judgements and adverse condemnations only come from the ignorant. (Example of ANGULIMĀLA becoming ARAHAT, DEVADATTA – PACCEKA BUDDHA, AMBAPĀLI the courtesan becoming ARAHAT, ASOKA the wicked becoming ASOKA the Great King, also SOTAPANNA.)

2. How to modify of alter the severity of VIPĀKA, effects of one's KAMMA

(BUDDHA ~ ANG. NIK. part 1, p.249) ~ "Here, O BHIKKHUS, a certain person is not disciplined in body, in morality, in mind, in wisdom, has little good and less virtue, and lives painfully in consequence of trifling misdeeds. Even a trivial act committed by such a person will lead him to a state of misery.

"Here, O BHIKKHUS, a certain person is disciplined in body, in morality, in mind, in wisdom. He does much good, is of high character and lives with boundless compassion towards all.

"A similar evil committed by such a person ripens in this life itself and not even a small effect manifests itself after death, not to say of a great one (with reference to an ARAHANT).

"It is as if a man were to put a lump of salt into a small cup of water. What do you think, O BHIKKHUS? Would now the small amount of water in this cup become saltish and undrinkable?

"Yes, lord. And why? Because, lord, there was very little water in the cup and so it became saltish and undrinkable by this lump of salt.

"Suppose a man were to put a lump of salt into the river Ganges. What do you think, O BHIKKHUS? Would now the river Ganges become saltish and undrinkable by the lump of salt?"

"Not so, indeed, lord. And why not? Because, lord, the mass of water in the river Ganges is great, and so it would not become saltish and undrinkable.

"In exactly the same way we may have the case of a person who does some slight evil deed which brings him to a state of misery. Or again, we may have the case of another person who does the same trivial misdeed, yet he expiates it in his present life. Not even a small effect manifests after death, not to say a great one."

3. How KAMMA works ~ Cause of a mixed effect ~ How regret effects a wholesome deed. ~

(BUDDHA ~ SAMYUTTA NIKĀYA ~ part 1, p. 91)

"Lord, here in SĀVATTHI a millionaire householder has died. He has left no son behind him, and now I come here after having conveyed his property to the palace. Lord, I bring 100 LAKHS in gold, to say nothing of the silver; but this millionaire householder used to eat broken scraps of food and sour gruel and for dress he wore a robe of coarse hemp. And as to his coach, we drove in a broken cart rigged up with a leaf-awning."

The BUDDHA then replied, "Even so, O king, in a formed life this millionaire gave alms to a PACCEKA BUDDHA called TACARASIKHI. And after, had said to himself, "It would have been better if my servants and workmen ate the food I gave for alms." And besides this, he deprived his brother's only son of his life, for the sake of his property.

The effect of having given alms to the PACCEKA BUDDHA [meant] the millionaire was 7 times in a heavenly blissful state, and by the residual result of that same deed of giving alms, he was reborn 7 times a millionaire in SĀVATTHI.

The effect of having repented after the act of DĀNA, he had no appreciation of good food, no appreciation of fine dress, no appreciation of an elegant vehicle, no appreciation of the enjoyment of various senses of the 5-doors.

The effect of murdering his brother's son [meant] he was reborn and had to suffer many 100s or 1000s of years in pain, in states of misery. And by the residual effect of that same action, he is without a son for the 7th time, and in consequence of that he had to leave his property to the royal treasury."

4. Beneficent and maleficent forces that can counteract and support KAMMA

   A. Favorable birth and unfavorable birth (GATI SAMPATTI)- (GATI VIPATTI)

If, for instance, an individual is born into a noble or wealthy family or in a state of happiness, man, DEVA, etc. his fortunate birth will sometimes hinder the fruition of his unwholesome KAMMA.

Just the opposite, if of low family or lower birth, AKUSALA has given an easy opportunity to operate. An intelligent or unintelligent person, if beautiful or ugly-deformed, can easily influence situations. One an asset, another a burden. A person obtains a good birth but is hindered by the problem of deformity; a beautiful person even if of low family, opportunity and recognition prevail.

   B. Favorable appearance or unfavorable appearance (UPADHI SAMPATTI) – (UPADHI VIPATTI).

   C. Favorable time and occasion and opposite (KĀLA SAMPATTI)- (KĀLA- VIPATTI)

One aids and the other impedes the operation of KAMMA. In the case of famine all without exception will be compelled to suffer. The unfavorable conditions provide the opportunity for unwholesome KAMMAS to operate. Favorable conditions will prevent it.

   D. Effort

By present effort one can shade the future. If there is no effort or wrongly applied effort, opportunity can be missed. One can make the effort to cure themselves of a disease.

Example:

~ When a ship was wrecked in a deep sea, the BODHISATTVA

MAHA-JANAKA made a great effort to save himself, while the others prayed to the Gods and left their fate in their hands. The BODHISATTVA escaped, and the others drowned.

S. Concluding Points About KAMMA

Lessons taught by KAMMA:
1. Patience ~ Knowing the law, we understand DUKKHA-SUKKHA, as to our deeds. Impatience brings more DUKKHA. There's no one issuing the pain and pleasure, only cause and effects.
2. Confidence/ trust ~ an impersonal law. Live in accord/ harmony or otherwise. Light is shed in a dark room. Fear lessens. We must take responsibility for ourselves and our life. We gain strength. The law is our protector.
3. Self-reliance ~ External help is limited. We shape our futures. Purity and impurity belong to oneself. Make an effort.
4. Restraint ~ Why do that which will lead to more DUKKHA? We remain guarded, we know KAMMA.
5. Compassion ~ All are heirs to their actions. Why react to anything? People suffer because of their MOHA. Once the law is understood, it deflates the situation: no 'you', no 'me'; laws at work. Have compassion.

Mindfulness is all important as it leads one to freedom from the law, all the while sowing KUSALA and guarding against AKUSALA. SATI at dying moments, a powerful force. SATI all the time becomes a powerful tendency, it protects us. KAMMA is an incentive to do good and avoid evil. Effort is kindled, an individual responsibility. We must be careful of actions, speech and thoughts. Everything we do is our own baggage. One understands inequality in the world, and becomes accepting and loving. We don't know what we carry around, so do good: SATI; become ARAHATTA, and go beyond.

KAMMA is the only property inherited by individuals. They are never destroyed. Small acts of good or evil can produce long lasting and numerous effects. One mango seed can produce thousands of fruits. Giving DĀNA or killing an animal can yield manifold wholesome or unwholesome effects. Be careful and watchful, guarded.

KAMMA is one's constant companion, either great friend or the worst enemy. Learn your friends' ways of operating. No one else should be relied upon. Take refuge in KUSALA KAMMA. Prosperity or DUKKHA is up to us, certainly not up to God or the Almighty. Save your prayers: You are the creator or destroyer. Do good, and avoid evil.

Z. KAMMA Quotations, Examples, Illustrating Points

1. BUDDHA ~ ANG. NIK. iii, 415 ~ "I declare, O BHIKKHUS, that volition (CETANĀ) is KAMMA. Having willed one acts by body, speech and thought."
2. "When the mind is unguarded, bodily action is unguarded, speech also is unguarded, thought also is unguarded. When the mind is guarded, bodily action is guarded, speech also is guarded, and thought also is guarded." (ATTHASĀLINI p.68. The Expositor Part 1, p. 91)
3. According to the seed that's sown, so is the fruit ye reap there from. A doer of good will gather good; doer of evil, reaps evil. Sown is the seed, and thou shalt taste the fruit thereof" (SAM. NIK -1).
4. BUDDHA SABBE SATTĀ KAMMASSAKĀ ~ "The only property of all beings that accompanies them is their own volitional action."
5. "No doer is there who does the deed, nor is there one who feels the fruit, constituent parts alone roll on. This indeed is the right understanding." (VIS. MAGGA, 728).
6. "Throw a piece of wood or a small log into a pond and watch the effect. There is a splash and a number of rings appear around the place where it strikes. The rings grow wider and wider till they become too wide and too tiny for our eyes to follow. The initial splash of the log disturbs the entire surface of the pond. But its work is not finished yet. When the tiny waves reach the pond's edges, the water inevitably moves back until those very ripples disturb and ruffle the log that caused them." (Editorial- Light of DHAMMA Mag. Vol. X, No.1, 1963)

7. "I am owner of my KAMMA, heir of my KAMMA, born of my KAMMA, related to my KAMMA and abide supported by my KAMMA. Whatever KAMMA I have done, skillful or unskillful, of that shall I be heir." (MAJ. NIK. ~ CŪLAKAMMAVIBHANGA SUTTA)
8. "By oneself indeed is the unskillful done. By oneself is one defiled. By oneself is the unskillful left undone. By oneself indeed is one purified: purity, impurity depends upon oneself – no one is there who can purify another." (DHP, v.165)
9. "By mind the world is led, by mind is drawn. All men own the sovereignty of mind."
10. "Depending on this difference in KAMMA appears the differences in the birth of beings; high and low, base and exalted, happy and miserable. Depending on the difference in KAMMA appears the difference in the individual features of beings; as beautiful and ugly, high-born and low-born, well-built or deformed. Depending on the difference in KAMMA appears the difference in the worldly conditions of beings; as gain and loss, fame and disgrace, blame and praise, happiness and misery. "(The Expositor Part 1, p.128)

21.
DEATH AND REBIRTH

A. Definition of Death

Death is the cessation of the psycho-physical life of any one individual existence. It is the passing away of vitality (ĀYU). I.e., psychic and physical life (JĪVITINDRIYA), heat (USMA) and consciousness (VIÑÑĀNA). It is by understanding death that we understand life, for death is the part of the process of life in a larger sense. Life and death are two ends of the same process, and if we understand one end of the process, we also understand the other end. By understanding death, we understand life.

(VIS. MAGGA ~ "Death is the interruption of the life faculty included within the limits of a single existence.")

Of course, death is not the annihilation of a being. Only empty phenomena alone roll on ~ nothing but the 5 aggregates exist and dissolve, moment after conscious moment. No one is reborn, only a transformation takes place; for though a particular life-span ends, the force that propels it is not destroyed. Example: Just as an electric light is the outward visible manifestation of invisible electric energy, in the same way the so-called existing human individual is the outward manifestation of invisible KAMMIC energy. The bulb may break and the light may be extinguished but the current remains and the light may manifest again in another bulb. The KAMMIC force remains undisturbed by the disintegration of the physical body. And the passing away of the last moment of consciousness in this life leads to the conditioned arising of a rebirth moment of consciousness in the next existence. Nothing unchangeable or permanent passes from the present to the future. (See Research of Dependent Origination for detailed explanation).

Just as a wheel touches the ground at only one point only, so strictly speaking, we live only for one thought moment. We are always in the present, and that present is ever slipping, with incredible rapidity, into the irrevocable past. Each momentary consciousness of this ever-changing life process, on passing away, transmits its entire energy, all the indelibly recorded impressions on it, to its successor, like an echo or a stamp placed into wax, like light. ~ Momentary life and death ~ like pool balls lined in a straight row, one struck and so on, then stops; and the energy continues the process of hit, strike, stop. Or like dominoes, lined up and tipped over by an ongoing process from having knocked over the first one. Every new moment of consciousness consists of the potentialities of its predecessors, together with something more. At death, the consciousness passes away, only to give birth to another consciousness. In a rebirth, this rebirth consciousness inherits all past KARMIC activities.

For no two moments are we identically the same.

~ Of course, no being is changing, living or dying, only the 5 aggregates ~ ANATTA.

~ Life of living beings lasts only for a single conscious moment. When that consciousness has ceased, the being is said to have ceased. Every moment of our lives, we are dying and being reborn. This being so, why should one dread just one particular moment of death, that moment that marks the end of this existence? When there are innumerable moments of death, why fear the occurrence of one particular moment? Ignorance of the momentary nature of death makes one fearful of the particular death that occurs at the last moment of this one existence, especially since the next moment of living is not seen or understood.

~ Death is the temporary end of a temporary process.

"When we say in conventional language that a person has died, the CUTI-CITTA ("death consciousness") which is the last CITTA of that existence, has fallen away This CUTI-CITTA is immediately followed by the PATISANDHI-CITTA ("rebirth consciousness") of the following life.

~ Death is unavoidable ~

In the books it is mentioned birth, old age, sickness and death. Old age is mentioned immediately after birth, before sickness is mentioned. As soon as we are born, we are already aging, we are already on our way to death.

B. Causes of Death According to Dependent Origination

1. Exhaustion of the reproductive-KAMMIC energy (KAMMAKKHAYA).
2. The expiration of the life-term (ĀYUKKHAYA)
3. The combination of the above two (UBHAYAKKHAYA)
4. The opposing force of a stronger KAMMA unexpectedly obstructing the flow of the reproductive-KAMMA before the life-term expires. (UPPOCHEDAKA-KAMMA)

The first 3 causes are collectively called "timely deaths" (KĀLA-MARANA) and the fourth cause is known as "ultimately death" (AKĀLAMARANA).

~ Explanation of each cause ~

1. Exhaustion of the reproductive-KAMMIC energy

As a rule, the thoughts, volitional tendencies or desires, which are extremely strong during an individual's lifetime, become predominant at the time of death, and therefore conditions the dying moments which condition the subjsequent birth. This dying thought-process is of great potentiality. When the potential energy of this reproductive-KAMMA (JANAKA) is exhausted, the organic activities of the material form in which is embodied the life-force in that particular end. This often happens in the case of beings who are born in states of misery (APĀYA), but it can happen in other planes too.

2. The expiration of the life-term

Natural deaths, due to old-age, are classified under this category. Age limits vary according to the different planes of existence (see chart), respective of the KAMMIC-force that has yet to run. One must, however, succumb to death when the maximum age limit is reached.

3. The simultaneous exhaustion of the reproductive-KAMMIC energy and the expiration of the life-term.

4. The opposing force of a stronger KAMMA unexpectedly obstructing the flow of the reproductive-KAMMA before the life-term expires.

Sudden untimely death of persons and deaths of children are due to this cause. (See explanation of destructive KAMMA, part 1 ~ section P ~ p.18)

The destructive KAMMA can be a cause. Basically, a powerful KAMMA performed in the past is capable of nullifying the potential energy of the last thought-process, and may thus destroy the vital force (psychic-force) of an individual.

Example of all four causes of death ~

An oil lamp may get extinguished owing to any of the following four causes: The exhaustion of the wick, the exhaustion of the oil, simultaneous exhaustion of both wick and oil, or some extraneous cause like a gust of wind.

Example ~ Questions of King MILLINDA. ~

"Venerable NĀGASENA, when beings die, do they all die in fullness of time, or do some die out of season?" ~ "There is such a thing, O king, as death at the due time, and such a thing as premature death." ~ "Then who are they, whose decease is at the due time? And who are they whose decease is premature?"

"Have you ever noticed, O king, in the case of mango trees, or *jambu* trees, or other fruit bearing trees, that their fruits fall both when they are ripe and when they are not ripe?"

"Yes, I have."

"Well, those fallen fruits: Do they all fall at the due time, or do some fall prematurely?"

"Such fruits, Ven. NĀGASENA, are ripe and mature when they fall, fall in fullness of time. But of the rest, some fall because they are bored into by worms, some because they are knocked down by a long stick, some because they are blown by the wind, some because they have become rotten — and all these fall out of season."

"Just like this, O king, those men who die of the effect of old age, they die in fullness of time; but of the rest, some die of the inevitable effect of the KAMMA (of unwholesome actions), some because of excessive journeying, some from excessive activity."

"Ven. NĀGASENA, those who die of KAMMA, or of journeying, or of activity, or of old age, they all die in fullness of time. And even he who dies in the womb, that is his appointed time; and so too of him who dies in the birth chamber, or when he is a month old or at any age up to a hundred years. It is always his appointed time, and it is in the fullness of time that he dies. So, Ven NĀGASENA, there is no such thing as death out of due season, for all who die, die at the appointed time."

"There are seven kinds of persons, O king, who, there being still a portion of their appointed age to run, die out of time. And which are the seven? The starving man, O king, who can get no food, who can get no water, whose heart is dried up. ~ And the man bitten by a snake, who when consumed by the fierce energy of poison, can find no cure. ~ And he who has taken poison, and when all his limbs are burning, is unable to procure medicine. ~ And one fallen into fire, who when he is aflame, can find no means of putting out the fire. ~ And he who having fallen into water can find no firm ground to stand on. ~ And the man wounded by a dart, who in his illness can find no surgeon. All these seven, there being still a portion of their appointed time to run, die "out of due season". And herein, in all the seven cases, I declare that they are all of one nature.

"In 8 ways, O king, does the death of mortals take place. (See also The 8 ways of Causing VEDANA, section A, page 2).

1. Upset of the wind element
2. Upset of the bile element
3. Upset of the phlegm element
4. By the combination of these three.
5. Upset of the climate or variation in temperature.
6. Through inequality in direction.
7. By specifically directed acts (i.e., medical treatment)
8. By counteractive or destructive KAMMA (i.e., The working of KAMMA)

And of these, O King, it is only death by the workings of KAMMA that is death at the due season. All the rest are causes of death out of the proper season. (Cause #7 may be due to past or present (this life) KAMMA. #8 is wholly due to past life KAMMA. The remaining 6 causes are the result of present life KAMMA)."

C. Death Signs Appearing at the Dying Moments

1. KAMMA
2. KAMMA-NIMITTA
3. GATI-NIMITTA

Explanation of each ~

1. KAMMA
To the dying individual at the critical stage of his last dying thought-process, according to ABHIDHAMMA, is presented with one of the above three.

By KAMMA is meant some wholesome or unwholesome act during one's lifetime or immediately before his dying moment. It will be a wholesome or unwholesome thought if the dying person has committed one of the five heinous actions. (GARUKA-KAMMA), such as parricide, etc. or developed the JHĀNAS; he would experience such a KAMMA before his death. These acts are weighty enough that they totally eclipse all other actions, and appear very vividly before the mind. If there is no such weighty action, the object of the dying thought – process would be a KAMMA done immediately before death (ĀSANNA-KAMMA), or death-proximate KAMMA. In the absence of death- proximate-KAMMA, a habitual wholesome or unwholesome action (ĀCINNA-KAMMA) is presented: Such as the healing of the sick by a good physician, or the teaching of the DHAMMA (if a DHAMMA teacher), or stealing in the case of a thief. If nothing habitual has been developed, any trivial action, KUSALA or AKUSALA, KATATTĀ-KAMMA) becomes the object of the dying-thought-process.

2. KAMMA-NIMITTA ~ or symbol, or sign
This means a mental reproduction of any sight, sound, smell, taste, touch or idea which was predominant at the time of some influential wholesome or unwholesome activity, such as the mental image or vision

of knives, dying animals, smell of meat (in the case of a butcher), the BUDDHA in the case of a devoted monk, etc.

These various NIMITTAS will be something symbolic of the KAMMA performed by the individual – e.g. The empty whisky bottle of an alcoholic. All is experienced through the avenue of the mind-eye, not the physical eye base.

3. GATI-NIMITTA ~ or symbol of destiny ~ is meant by some symbol of the place of the next rebirth.

Fire may present itself to the mind's eye of a person destined to be reborn in a lower world, or golden luminescent flowers, jeweled mansions if reborn in a heavenly realm. These symbols might be indicated in the facial expressions of the dying individual. This is a time of influential weight if at the side of a dying individual ~ reminding them of wholesome acts: Chanting ~ a picture of the BUDDHA, etc.

D. How the Thought-Process at Death Functions

Man is a psycho-physical unit, a mind-body (NĀMA- RŪPA) combination. The body and mind co-exist in an intricate and intimately close association with each other. Like the flower and its scent: the body is like the flower, and the mind like the scent. Death is merely (this existence death) the radical transformation of the NĀMA-RŪPA process. Death is no interruption of the process of consciousness, nor is the RŪPA separated – unless reborn in ARŪPA-BRAHMA realms. Otherwise, the next consciousness moment will always have with it RŪPA in a transformed way. (See Rebirth Consciousness for details, under 'Study of dependent origination'.)

When an individual is on the point of dying, his body and mind are generally very weak. It may be that right up to the point of death, he was strong in every way; but at the point of death (dying thought-process), he is weak. This is because from the 17th thought-moment reckoned backwards from the actual dying moment, no renewed physical functioning occurs – just like a motorist releasing the accelerator before stopping, so no more pulling power is given to the engine. Similarly, no more material qualities born of KAMMA (KAMMAJA-RŪPA) arise while those which have already come into being before the stage of that thought moment will persist till the time of death consciousness (CUTI-CITTA), and then they will cease. As there is no more renewal of material qualities, the whole process becomes weaker and weaker. It is like the fading light of an oil lamp when the fuel has been expended. When the mind-body combination ceases temporarily to exist in its normally apparent way as a combination, neither the body nor the mind is destroyed or annihilated (nor is any essence or soul released). The changes continue conditioning each succeeding moment. The more fully developed RŪPA, or body, continues on in its decay process, and resumes its more invisible reality as just the 4 great elements: The mind, death consciousness conditions, rebirth consciousness which gives rise to NĀMA- RŪPA and so on in the next birth. This process of birth, decay and death will continue for eternity unless the driving forces of delusion and craving are completely uprooted from the mind. (As long as one wants ~ birth continues ~ until ARAHANT).

However weak or unconscious a dying person may appear to be, this last mental thought-process will unfailingly operate with every individual on every plane of existence. It cannot be avoided; whatever the circumstances of death don't matter. In the commentaries ~ whether someone is cast into water and immediately drowns ~ or a fly that is crushed by the stroke of a hammer on an anvil ~ there is always time for the dying thought process to operate. Death isn't occurring chaotically, or at random without cause.

1. Past BHAVANGA ~ BHAVANGA ATITA ~ this is the BHAVANGA before the process begins.
2. Vibrating BHAVANGA ~ BHAVANGA CALANA ~ consciousness is interrupted and vibrates due to the distraction.
3. Arresting BHAVANGA ~ BHAVANGA UPACCEDA ~ BHAVANGA is arrested ~ Disturbing stimulus is one of the 3 dying signs ~ Section C, no recognition yet.
4. Adverting through mind-door ~ MANODVĀRAVAJJANA ~ mind door consciousness arises and passes.
5. JAVANA (MARANASANNA JAVANA CITTA) ~ death proximate JAVANA ~ Since death is imminent, the JAVANA process runs for

only 5 moments rather than 7, everything else applies the same. The dying man is weak at this point, cannot originate a thought of his own. One of the 3 death signs is recognized: It induces the mind consciousness to arise, thus the mind is fully able to comprehend the stimulus that awakened it. Again, if the consciousness here is KUSALA, rebirth consciousness and death consciousness will be KUSALA, and vice-versa. By reason of the weakness these JHĀNA moments lack all reproductive power; they are only regulative of the new existence. (See section C.)

6. ~ the same ~
7. ~ the same ~
8. ~ the same ~
9. ~ the same ~
10. Registering consciousness ~ TADĀLAMBANA ~ Identification of the object ~ in the death process this CITTA (2) may or may not arise.
11. ~ the same ~
12. Death consciousness ~ CUTI-CITTA ~ the last thought moment in this present life.
13. Relinking/rebirth consciousness ~ PATISADHI-VIÑÑĀNA.

~ Death and rebirth consciousness are explained on the next page ~

1. CUTI-CITTA (Death consciousness) ~ PATISANDHI-CITTA (Rebirth consciousness)

The last function of consciousness in life is the function of CUTI (dying). Conventionally what is called death occurs after the CUTI-CITTA has fallen away. This CUTI-CITTA will inevitably be followed by the PATISANDHI-CITTA of the following life, unless one is an ARAHANT (then PARINIBBĀNA). Death is unavoidable if there is birth in all planes of existence.

The PATISANDHI-CITTA of the next life will be AKUSALA VIPĀKA, depending on the KAMMA which produces it. (The 5 death-thought-process JAVANA moments condition one's rebirth: If the JAVANA are AKUSALA, the PATISANDHI-CITTA will be

AKUSALA-VIPAKA and vice versa. The CUTI-CITTA is VIPAKA, the same type of CITTA as the PATISANDHI-CITTA and the BHAVANGA-CITTA of the life that is just ending, produced by the KAMMA which produced the PATISANDHI-CITTA and that life. There are 19 types of CITTA which can perform the function of PATISANDHI-CITTA and the function of BHAVANGA, thus there are 19 types of CITTA which can perform the function of CUTI.)

(See death and rebirth – dependent origination – for more complete details).

It is not the CUTI-CITTA but the proceeding MARANASANNA JAVANA CITTA that give rise to rebirth-consciousness. The CUTI-CITTA is an unconscious thought of the BHAVANGA-CITTA, whereas the terminal death – proximate JAVANA CITTA is a thought of the conscious VITTHI-CITTA. The CUTI-CITTA does not rise one to the PATISANDHI-VIÑÑĀNA. The CUTI-CITTA merely registers the awareness of death. (For complete details of PATISANDHI-CITTA or rebirth consciousness refer to chapter 11, p.98-110 ~ ABHIDHAMMA in Daily Life).

~ Rebirth-thought process ~
1. Rebirth consciousness (PATISANDHI-CITTA)
2. BHAVANGA (for 16 moments)
3. Mind-door-advertence (MANODVĀRĀVOJJANA) ~ desire (grasping) for the new existence. From this thought a CITTA arises. Grasping continues.
4. JĀVANA for 7 moments
5. BHAVANGA CITTA

~ Four modes of birth ~
1. Egg-born beings (ANDAJA) ~ birds, etc.
2. Womb-born beings (JALĀBUJA) ~ some animals, human birth.
3. Moisture-born beings (SAMSEDAJA) ~ certain lowly forms of animal life.
4. Spontaneous-born beings (OPAPĀTIKA) ~ these beings comprise the DEVA & BRAHMA realms. Also, PETAS belong to this class.

Rebirth takes place immediately irrespective of how and where; consciousness remains unbroken.

(Questions – King MILLINDA and Ven. NĀGASENA ~ "If someone dies here and is reborn in the world of BRAHMA and another dies here and is reborn in Kashmir, which of them would arrive first?" ~ "All the same.")

E. Planes of Existence

General grouping		Nr.	Specific plane of existence	Life-span	Birth cause of each plane
Formless realm ARŪPALOKA 28-31		31.	Sphere of neither perception nor non-perception NEVA-SAÑÑĀ-NĀSAÑÑĀYATANUPA-GA DEVĀ	84 000 M.K.	8th JHĀNA
		30.	Sphere of the knowledge of nothingness ĀKIÑ-CAÑÑĀYATANŪPAGA DEVĀ	60 000 M.K.	7th JHĀNA
		29.	Sphere of the infinity of consciousness VIÑÑĀNAÑ-CAYATANŪPAGA DEVĀ	40 000 M.K.	6th JHĀNA
		28.	Sphere of the infinity of space ĀKĀSĀÑCĀYA-TANŪPAGA DEVĀ	20 000 M.K.	5th JHĀNA
Fine material sphere RŪPALOKA 12-27	SUDDHĀYĀSA Pure abodes for ANAGAMIS and ARAH-ANTS 23-27	27.	World of supreme BRAHMAS AKANITTHĀ BRAHMĀ	16 000 M.K.	ANAGAMI with 4th JHĀNA
		26.	World of clear-sighted BRAHMAS SUDASI BRAHMĀ	8 000 M.K.	ANAGAMI with 4th JHĀNA
		25.	World of beautiful BRAHMAS SUDASSA BRAHMĀ	4 000 M.K.	ANAGAMI with 4th JHĀNA
		24.	World of serene BRAHMAS ATĀPPA BRAHMĀ	2 000 M.K.	ANAGAMI with 4th JHĀNA
		23.	World of immobile BRAHMAS AVIHĀ BRAHMĀ	1 000 M.K.	ANAGAMI with 4th JHĀNA

General grouping		Nr.	Specific plane of existence	Life-span	Birth cause of each plane
		22.	World of perceptionless BRAHMAS ASAÑÑĀ-SATTA BRAHMĀ	500 M.K.	4th JHĀNA moderately developed
		21.	World of greatly rewarded BRAHMAS VEHAPPHALA BRAHMĀ	500 M.K.	4th JHĀNA weakly developed
		20.	World of BRAHMAS of steady aura SUBHAKINHA BRAHMĀ	64 M.K.	3rd JHĀNA fully developed
		19.	World of BRAHMAS of infinite aura APPAMĀNA SUBHA BRAHMĀ	32 M.K.	3rd JHĀNA moderately developed
		18.	World of BRAHMAS of minor aura PARITTA SUBHA BRAHMĀ	16 M.K.	3rd JHĀNA weakly developed
		17.	World of radiant BRAHMAS ĀBHASSARA BRAHMĀ	8 M.K.	2nd JHĀNA fully developed
		16.	World of BRAHMAS of infinite luster APPAMĀNĀBHA BRAHMĀ	4 M.K.	2nd JHĀNA moderately developed
		15.	World of BRAHMAS of minor luster PARITTĀBHA BRAHMĀ	2 M.K.	2nd JHĀNA weakly developed
		14.	World of great BRAHMAS MAHĀ BRAHMĀ	1 A.K.	1st JHĀNA fully developed
		13.	Ministers of BRAHMA BRAHMA-PUROHITA BRAHMĀ	1/2 A.K.	1st JHĀNA moderately developed
		12.	Retinue of BRAHMA BRAHMA-PĀRISAJJA	1/3 A.K.	1st JHĀNA weakly developed
Sense desire sphere KĀMA-LOKA 1-11	SUGATI abodes Happy states	11.	DEVAS enjoying the creations of others PARANIMMITAVASA-VATTI DEVĀ	16 000 C.Y. 288 000 000 H.Y.	KUSALA KAMMA

21. DEATH AND REBIRTH

General grouping		Nr.	Specific plane of existence	Life-span	Birth cause of each plane
		10.	DEVAS enjoying their own creations NIMMĀNARATI DEVĀ	8 000 C.Y. 144 000 000 H.Y.	KUSALA KAMMA
		9.	DEVAS enjoying pleasure TUSITA DEVĀ	4 000 C.Y. 72 000 000 H.Y.	KUSALA KAMMA
		8.	YĀMA DEVAS YĀMA DEVAS	2 000 C.Y. 36 000 000 H.Y.	KUSALA KAMMA
		7.	Realm of the thirty-three DEVAS TĀVATIMSA	1 000 C.Y. 18 000 000 H.Y.	KUSALA KAMMA
		6.	Realm of the four great kings (of the 4 quarters) CĀTUMMAHĀRĀJIKA	500 C.Y. 9 000 000 H.Y.	KUSALA KAMMA
		5.	The human world MANUSSA LOKA	Limit varies	Mixed KAMMA both wholesome and unwholesome, predominantly KUSALA
	DUGGATI abodes Unhappy states	4.	The animal world TIRACCHĀNA YONI	Limit varies	AKUSALA KAMMA
		3.	The world of unhappy spirits PETA LOKA	Limit varies	AKUSALA KAMMA
		2.	The world of demons (titans) ASURA YONI	Limit varies	AKUSALA KAMMA
		1.	The realms of constant misery NIRAYA LOKA	Limit varies	AKUSALA KAMMA

M.K. = MĀHĀ KAPPA

A.K. = ASANKHEYYA KAPPA

C.Y. = Celestial years

(50 human years equals one celestial day. Thirty such days amounts to one month and 12 such months constitute one year.)

1500 H.YRS. = 1 Celestial month
18 000 H.YRS = 1 Celestial year
1 800 000 H.YRS = 100 Celestial years

F. Explanation of the Various Planes of Existence

1. NIRAYA ~ (NI+AYA) = Devoid of happiness ~ Woeful states (8 sub-divisions of this one reality) where beings are reborn due to the severity of unwholesome KAMMAS they have committed. AKUSALA weighty KAMMA has its effect in this realm. Misery as it's said is constantly experienced within the various divisions of NIRAYA. However, due to KAMMA and ANICCA, these realms are not eternal situations as long as they might be, and upon exhaustion of the unwholesome KAMMA there is a possibility of beings reborn in blissful states of existence as the result of their past KUSALA KAMMA. DEVADATTA resides in this plane but the BUDDHA foresaw that after a great period of time he would eventually become a PACEKKA BUDDHA.

2. TIRACCHĀNA YONI ~ (TIRO = across: ACCHĀNA = going). The animal world, i.e., insects, birds, fish, mammals, etc. Beings are reborn with animal forms due to AKUSALA KAMMA. The BODHISATTVA was reborn as an animal a number of times. At certain times, and mostly dogs and cats, they live more comfortable and happy lives than some humans. This of course is due to their past KAMMA. It's one's KAMMA that determines the nature of one's material form which will vary tremendously in this rebirth, according to the skillfulness or unskillfulness of one's actions.

3. PETA-LOKA ~ (PA+ITA = departed beings) or those absolutely of happiness, they are not disembodied spirits or ghosts. They possess deformed and disgusting physical forms of varying magnitude, generally invisible to the naked eye. They have no planes of their own, but live within forests, dirty surroundings, etc. (See PETAVATTHU or stories of the PETAS). Beings are reborn here as the result of AKUSALA offenses of cruelty, killing, torture, etc.

(Questions of Millinda: ~ 4 kinds of PETAS ~
1. VANTĀSIKAS ~ who feed on vomit.
2. KHUPPIPĀSINO ~ who are continually hungry and thirsty.
3. NIJJHĀMATANHIKĀ ~ who are consumed by thirst.
4. PARADATTŪPAJIVINO ~ who live on the gifts of others. (Merit that is spared if specifically intended for departed relatives in this realm will reap the benefits immediately.) They can therefore pass onto a better state of existence ~ See TIROKUDDA SUTTA of KINDDAKA PĀTHA).

4. ASURA-YONI ~ The abode of ASURA demons (ASURA= those who do not shine or who do not sport). They are similar to the PETAS. These ASURAS are of a different class than the ASURAS of the TAVATIMSA realm.

The four unhappy states ~ DUGGATI ↑

The seven happy states ~ SUGATI ↑

5. MANUSSA ~ (Literally = "Those who have an uplifted or developed mind.") The human realm is a unique mixture of both pleasure and pain. BODHISATTVAS use the human realm as it is the best field to serve the world and perfect the PARAMIS or requisites of BUDDHAHOOD. All BUDDHAS become such from the human realm. They are always born as humans. KUSALA KAMMA can be cultivated on this plane. It is difficult to do so in other realms due to the strong aversions that so frequently arise in the 4 lower worlds, and the levels of greed that are present due to the continuity of intense sensual pleasure of the 6 DEVA realms. The best of rebirths of all 30 other planes of existence for one to gain VIPASSANĀ insight. The human realm is considered a happy realm. A rebirth due to unwholesome KAMMA of the past. It is due to one's KAMMA that one experiences pleasant and unpleasant things through the eye, ear, nose, tongue, body and mind. Gain, loss, praise, blame, fame, shame, happiness and pain are KUSALA or AKUSALA VIPĀKA. Each person is born into the family and situation which is the right condition for them to experience the results of their deeds.

6. CĀTUMMAHĀRĀJIKA ~The lowest of the heavenly realms where the guardian deities of the 4 quarters of the firmament reside with their followers. In these heavenly DEVA realms, there is more KUSALA VIPĀKA than in the human plane and less AKUSALA VIPĀKA. The boundaries between the human realm and these DEVA realities immediately above it are not also clearly distinct. And therefore, communication or sight of such beings by certain individuals happens on occasion. For the most part DEVAS are passively enjoying the pleasurable results of good KAMMA performed in previous human lives, and are not confronted with the necessity for moral choice that devolves upon human beings. Of course, these are not eternal realms; the immensely long-life span of the DEVA encourages and could easily strengthen his wrong views, the belief in self and permanence. They might think they attained the eternal heaven they longed for as a human. In the higher BRAHMA realms, some mistake themselves as the eternal God himself (see AGGAÑÑA SUTTA – DIGHA NIKAYA #27). These beings are born spontaneously as either a male or female at age 15 or 16, fully developed. Aging will not occur, except for 7 days prior to their death; then they begin to show signs of the approaching death. They will perspire, an unpleasant odor manifest, etc. DEVA bodies are of a very superfine form ~ their food, ambrosia like, soft and delicate. Keeping good SĪLA, giving DĀNA and other meritorious acts will take one after human death to these realms.

7. TĀVATIMSA ~ literally means 'Thirty-three'. The celestial realm of the 33 DEVAS, where the DEVA SAKKA ("a stream winner") is the king. The origin of the name is attributed to a story which states that 33 selfless volunteers led by MAGHA (another name for SAKKA), having performed charitable deeds, were born in this heavenly realm. It was in this DEVA realm that the BUDDHA taught the ABHIDHAMMA to his mother for 5 months. (He then returned and explained all to SARIPUTTA).

8. YĀMA ~ the realm that literally means "That which destroys pain".

9. TUSITA ~ literally = "Happy dwellers, the return of delight".

The BODHISATTVAS who have perfected the requisites of BUDDHAHOOD reside in this plane until the opportune moment comes for them to appear in the human realm to attain BUDDHAHOOD, and establish the SASANA. (BODHISATTVA MAITREYA is said to be there now.) This is where the BUDDHA'S mother took birth after her death when he was 7 days old. She then went to TĀVATIMSA to hear the ABHIDHAMMA.

10. NIMMĀNARATI ~ The realm of the DEVAS who delight in created mansions.

11. PARANIMMITAVASAVATTI ~ The realm of the DEVAS who make others' creations serve their own ends. The MĀRA who hassled the BUDDHA so often is said to be the one who reigns over this realm (and is also destined to become a PACCEKA BUDDHA in the distant future).

These 11 planes of existence end the spheres of sense desires and sensual delight: The 4 unhappy realms, 1 human realm and 6 DEVA realms = KĀMA-LOKA ~ sense sphere.

All are attainable through KUSALA and AKUSALA actions ~ meditational attainments are not necessary.

~ Explanation of the various realms of existence (continued):

BRAHMA-LOKAS

The beings reborn in any of these remaining 20 BRAHMA realms of existence, 16 of which are fine material planes, 4 are formless realms. All 20 have consciousness except 22 ~ ASAÑÑĀ-SATTA BRAHMĀ LOKA. Here only a material flux exists, only motionless bodies of light in this realm. Mind is temporarily suspended due to the force of the power of cessation of consciousness; one has a realization for the knowing faculty. BODHISATTVAS are never reborn on this plane. By the power of meditation, NĀMA-RŪPA become separated – like a body immersed fully under the water. The shadow disappears also. (See Planes of Existence chart for correlation between realms, and the meditating attainments necessary to be reborn in each of them.)

The SUDDHĀVASAS or pure abodes are the exclusive realm of ANAGAMIS ("never-returners"), those who attain this 3rd stage of enlightenment are reborn in one of these 5 SUDDHĀVASA realms. From there they attain ARAHANT and eventually attain to PARINIBBĀNA from these abodes. (BODHISATTVAS never inhabit these planes). These realms are the only other realms besides the human world that one is able to pass directly into PARINIBBĀNA from, or in other words attain ARAHATTA in.

The 4 ARŪPALOKAS ~ immaterial or formless realities ~ correspond directly to the 4 ARŪPA JHĀNAS. Those who see the disadvantages of RŪPA cultivate ARŪPA JHĀNA. Only NĀMA exists in these planes. Still subject to KAMMA and VIPĀKA, one can fall from these realms and be reborn as DEVAS, then humans, then even as animals and PETAS, etc., (as each of us are trailing an infinite amount of AKUSALA KAMMA from the past). Thus, the necessity to liberate oneself from the unending wheel of birth and death. Every plane of existence is ANICCA, ANATTA and DUKKHA.

("Plane of existence" is the place where one is born. ~ "Plane of CITTA" is not the same as plane of existence. What plane of CITTA a CITTA belongs to, depends on the object (ĀRAMMANA) the CITTA experiences.)

(KĀMĀVACARA CITTA ~ RŪPAVACARA CITTA ~ ARŪPAVACARA CITTA ~ LOKUTTARA CITTAS) (For details ch.20, p.192 ABHIDDHARMA in Daily Life)

It is of great danger to be subject to birth. Total and complete freedom from birth, full enlightenment, is the highest aim. All existence is subject to the TILĀKKHANA, even the highest planes of bliss and mental absorption are temporary. The 4 Noble Truths are essential to comprehend. Realizing these leads to the cessation of suffering, and rebirth.

The Noble Truth about DUKKHA, the Noble Truth about the cause of DUKKHA, the Noble Truth about the cessation of DUKKHA, and the Noble Truth about the path that leads to that cessation of DUKKHA: When these Noble Truths are grasped and known, the craving for future life is rooted out. That which leads to

21. DEATH AND REBIRTH

"renewed becoming" is destroyed, and then there is no more birth. (MAHA PARINIBBĀNA SUTTA, D.N.)

We are born and we die. And when we go, we know not. The fact that we must go, we know for certain. Our cherished possessions, dear and loved relatives and friends, even those base bodies of matter some call their own, from elements they came, to elements they return empty: Fame, praise, happiness and gains, all vanish upon death. Each of us wander alone in this sea of SAMSARA, tossed from plane to plane by our various AKAMMA, appearing here as an animal, or human, DEVA, or BRAHMA; then again, here and there meeting and parting from an infinite past. For seldom do we find a being who in the course of our SAMSARIC wanderings, had not at one time been a mother, a father, a sister, son or daughter.

"If a man was to prone out the grasses, sticks, boughs and twigs in all of India and collect them together, he should make a pile laying them in a four-inch stack, saying for each: "This is my mother, this is my mother's mother... The grasses, sticks, boughs, and twigs in all of India would be used up, ended. But not the mother of that man's mother." (BUDDHA ~ Gradual Sayings ~ 1, pp.31-34)

~ So closely bound are we in our journeyings in SAMSARA.

BUDDHA ~ "The bones of a single person wandering in SAMSARA would be a cairn, a pile or heap as tall as Mount Vepulla, were there a collector of these bones, and were the collections not destroyed.

"Long time have you suffered the death of father and mother, of sons, daughters, brothers and sisters, and while you were thus suffering, you have verily shed tears upon this long way, more than there is water in the four oceans.

"Long time did your blood flow by this loss of your heads when you were born as oxen, buffaloes, rams, goats, etc.

"Long time have you been caught as dacoits or highwaymen or adulterers, and through your being beheaded verily more blood has flowed upon this long way than there is water in the four oceans.

"And thus, have you for a long-time undergone suffering, undergone torment, undergone misfortune and filled the graveyards full, verily long enough to be dissatisfied with every form of existence, long enough to turn away and free yourselves from them all."

(Gradual Sayings ~ 1, pp.31-34)

1. Time in relationship to existence

A KAPPA corresponds to the idea of eternity rather than a time.

1. MAHA KAPPA ~ "Is the measurement of cosmic time (or is an eon). Its duration is incalculable. Imagine a mountain consisting of a solid cube of rock, 1 league (or YOJANA) = 7 miles in length, breadth and height. If with a piece of Benares silk one were to rub it once at the end of every 100 years, the time that it would take to wear away such a mountain would not be so long as the duration of a great KAPPA. Thus long, BHIKKHUS, is the great KAPPA; of KAPPAS thus long many a KAPPA has passed away, many a 100 M.K, many a 1000 M.K., many a 100, 000 M.K." (S.N.11-178)

"Suppose there was a city of iron walls, 1 YOJANA in length, width and height, filled with mustard seeds. From there if a man was to take out 1 seed at the end of every 100 years, that pile of mustard seeds would in this way be sooner done away with and ended than an M.K." (S.N. 182)

A great KAPPA is divided into 4 periods called middle KAPAS or ASANKEYYA KAPPA. ~ 20 small KAPPAS or ANTARA KAPPA = 1 middle KAPPA ~ thus 80 small KAPPAS = 1 MAHA (great) KAPPA. During the time of one MAHA KAPPA is the cyclical period of a world system, during which the entirety of coming into being, existence, decay and destruction is completed. After destruction (by fire, water or wind), the process begins over again. It is repeated ceaselessly, without beginning or end. (Full details ~ VIS. MAGGA p. 454-464 ~ also Manual of Bud. Ledi Sayadaw, pp.111-126).

The 4 periods of great KAPPA are:
1. The enveloping KAPPA,
2. The enveloped KAPPA,
3. The developing KAPPA,
4. The developed KAPPA.

21. DEATH AND REBIRTH

Each is an incalculable period. (Additional explanatory reading ~ WH.#180 Gods and the Universe ~ WH 162 ~ Facets of Buddhist thoughts).

22.
THE PASSING AWAY OF THE VENERABLE MAHASI SAYADAW OF BURMA

By Bhikkhu U Aggacara
(Alan Clements)

At approximately 7.30 in the evening of Friday, August 13th, 1982, I went up to speak with my teacher Sayadaw U Pandita, at his residence located within the compound of the Mahasi Thathana Yeiktha, here in Rangoon, Burma. Immediately on arrival U Pandita's attendant, Maung Khin Hlaing, and the Malaysian Bhikkhu, U Aggacitta, informed me that U Pandita had been urgently summoned to Mahasi Sayadaw's Lodge just a few moments before by Mahasi Sayadaw's personal bhikkhu attendant, U Sobhana. They explained that the only reason given for the sudden request was that Mahasi Sayadaw was feeling a very unusual type of physical pain in the head, accompanied with a sense of giddiness. (We later found out that Mahasi Sayadaw had been seated in the chair behind his desk, engaged in a conversation with his attendant when, all of a sudden, the Ven. Sayadaw reached out for and began rubbing the top and back areas of the head. When the attendant asked him what was happening, the Ven. Sayadaw told him that he was experiencing very severe head pains. When the attendant asked him what he wished him to do, he remained silent and did not answer, while still holding his head; yet at this point not moving any bodily part. The Ven. Sayadaw was then helped to his bed, and while another lay attendant remained at his bedside, U Sobhana rushed over to inform Sayadaw U Pandita. Someone then informed U Thein Han, the Yeiktha's treasurer living in our building a few hundred yards away, to call and request Mahasi's doctors to come to his residence immediately). Soon after my arrival at U Pandita's cottage, his lay attendant left us and went over to the Mahasi Lodge to investigate the situation. At 9 pm Sayadaw U Pandita's attendant returned and explained that Mahasi Sayadaw was lying motionless on his bed, in what appeared to be an unconscious state, and that all of the monastery's 15 or so resident monks were gathered in silence around his bedside. He said that several doctors and nurses were attending to the Sayadaw. He continued by saying that the initial diagnosis was that the Ven. Sayadaw had undergone a stroke. At one point the Sayadaw's blood pressure reached approximately 260 over 160, and an injection had immediately been administered, bringing it down to a near normal level. Shortly afterwards the doctors performed a few simple sensitivity tests. The Sayadaw showed a very subtle response

22. THE PASSING AWAY OF THE VENERABLE MAHASI SAYADAW OF BURMA

on his right side only. Then they lifted up each of Mahasi's eyelids and, with a rolled piece of tissue paper, gently touched each of his eyes. Neither of the eyes showed any signs of response.

At 9.30 pm U Aggacitta and myself walked over to the Mahasi Lodge, observing the steadily growing number of cars and people who were gathered outside his building and on the downstairs floor of his residence. We walked over to the ambulance which was parked by the side entrance. The air was perfectly still and most of everyone I could see sat quietly awaiting the Ven. Sayadaw's departure to the Rangoon General Hospital. I sensed the critical nature of the situation, and the same was reflected in the faces of so many familiar people that I knew. Upstairs in Mahasi's room we began to hear people talking, and a few minutes later, at around 10 pm, a group of monks and laymen came slowly down the stairs, carrying on a stretcher the Ven. Sayadaw, who was lying motionless on his left side. He was carefully put into the ambulance, and along with a number of monastery attendants and resident monks, he was taken to the intensive care unit of the hospital 15 minutes away. We then accompanied Sayadaw U Pandita back to his residence, and he explained to us some of the events that took place while he was with the Mahasi Sayadaw in his room, as well as offering his own personal interpretation of the Mahasi Sayadaw's condition. U Pandita expressed his optimism and felt that the Ven. Sayadaw would recover in due time. But I sensed that we all know the criticalness of the Venerable Sayadaw's condition.

The next morning at 9 o'clock Sayadaw U Pandita, accompanied by a couple of his close lay disciples, and along with U Aggacitta and myself, went to the hospital to check on the Mahasi Sayadaw's condition. From an early morning report by one of the attendants who stayed by him throughout the night, it was said that the Ven. Sayadaw's condition was stable, but he was still in an unconscious state. Upon our arrival at the hospital, many resident monks and close lay disciples were gathered, awaiting news of the Ven. Sayadaw's condition. We were immediately ushered into a small glass viewing receptacle that looked in upon the intensive care unit where Mahasi Sayadaw was lying motionless. Doctors, nurses and attendants were busily administering care to the

Sayadaw in what appeared to be an urgently critical manner. A variety of very sophisticated machines were hooked up to him; one showing the rhythm of his heartbeat and another that appeared to be an artificial breathing mechanism. Oxygen was being given along with a bottle of intravenous liquid. We were told that Rangoon's foremost neuro-surgeon had earlier that morning given a preliminary diagnosis of Mahasi Sayadaw's condition, stating that he had undergone a massive cerebral stroke, and that there was at least a 75% likelihood of extensive cerebral hemorrhage. While we were there the neuro-surgeon again entered the intensive care unit, and we were informed that he was going to do a spinal inspection to determine more accurately the Ven. Sayadaw's condition, thus enabling him to determine more precisely the options available: Basically, either to enter the skull through surgery, locate and tie the ruptured artery while removing the clot, or to simply allow for a possible natural bodily recovery. Everyone felt that surgery was far too risky, and in the light of that, natural recovery was almost impossible. Sayadaw U Pandita remarked that the situation may appear hopeless from the medical viewpoint, but he still remained optimistic, reminding everyone that Mahasi Sayadaw was a man of extraordinarily powerful KAMMIC virtues and that this may be a far more potent force than anything else; stressing that however obvious or logical the outcome of a situation might appear to be, it didn't necessarily mean that it would happen in that way.

All of us went directly back to the monastery, placing the decision-making process with the senior attending doctor who was caring for the Ven. Sayadaw. Shortly after our return, several of us were gathered at U Pandita's residence, and at 11.30 the President of the Organization that manages the monastery, U Pwint Gaung, and several senior members of that committee, along with approximately 30 others, including resident monks, nuns and close lay disciples, came into the cottage and after paying their respects, announced to Sayadaw U Pandita that the Ven. Mahasi Sayadaw was only being kept alive by the use of machines. For the next few minutes everyone in the room remained still and quiet. There were no signs of sorrow or anguish, as a very obvious composure permeated the air. The President then proceeded to announce the urgent need to discuss the necessary arrangements that would have to be immediately agreed upon and made, should the Ven. Sayadaw pass away — which seemed a certainty at this point — to ensure the smooth functioning of the monastery and to accommodate the thousands of Mahasi devotees who would begin pouring into the monastery upon hearing of his death. (Up till this point the second most senior monk of the monastery, the Ven. Sayadaw U Sujata, had been kept purposely uninformed of what had happened the night before to Mahasi Sayadaw, because of the possible exacerbation of his own intensive heart condition. The same information was also being withheld from another senior Nayaka Sayadaw at the monastery, the Ven. U Javana, who is also dealing with a similar intensive ailment. (It was agreed that they both be carefully informed of the situation in a very skillful manner). U Pandita suggested that an urgent meeting be held at 12.30 in the downstairs area of the Mahasi Lodge with all Nayaka Sayadaws, resident monks, nuns and representative members of the various governing bodies that maintain the monastery present. Both U Aggacitta and myself attended the gathering, and it was translated to me that the President said that due to Mahasi Sayadaw's present condition, he felt that it was necessary to systematically outline and discuss all of the immediate relevant details involved in preparing for the Ven. Mahasi Sayadaw's funeral arrangements. The people present agreed to the suggestion. Sayadaw U Pandita then addressed the assembly, explaining that over the many years of his association with the Ven. Mahasi Sayadaw, it was very obvious that the Ven. Sayadaw's continual Dhamma instruction and presentation were always delivered in a very clear, straight and non-frivolous way — making the point that his funeral ceremony should also be conducted in the same manner: In essence, conducting the entire occasion with all of its accompanying details in a straight-to-the-point, concise and simple manner, completely free of pageantry and the extraneous. Nearly everyone present consented in complete agreement. Mahasi Sayadaw's long-time friend and disciple. Mingala U Aung Myint, recalled to everyone an experience he once shared with the Ven. Sayadaw, which occurred while they were both attending a funeral and cremation ceremony of a monk who had passed away. He explained that Mahasi had told him that a true Kammatthanacariya (Meditation Teacher) should only have his body lie in state for a maximum of seven days, and that all aspects of a meditation teacher's funeral ceremony and cremation should be very simple and short. He continued by stressing how the Ven. Sayadaw had explained how unnecessary and unbecoming it was for the teacher's students and devotees to make expensive ceremonial or decorative offerings, but should rather use the money to feed the Sangha and the meditating yogis. Everyone thus agreed that they should follow Mahasi Sayadaw's personal preference, allowing his body to lie in state for a seven-day period, and that the consequent funeral and cremation ceremony should be very low-key, short and simple.

At this point someone came in and made it known that the Ven. Mahasi Sayadaw had stopped breathing, and that his bodily processes were only being kept active by the use of a machine. It was then decided to have his body immediately transferred to the monastery. The Hospital was notified and while the Ven. Sayadaw was being brought by ambulance to the monastery, several lay attendants brought a bed from the guest room downstairs and assembled it in the far corner of the ground floor meditation hall where we were all gathered. In a few minutes, at approximately 1.15 pm, the ambulance arrived, and with it the crowd hastily made way for the Ven. Sayadaw, as he was being carried on a stretcher and carefully placed on the bed. A soft whispering could be heard throughout the crowd of over 200 people who were now gathered around his bedside. A few people could be seen softly crying, and a few others with facial expressions of disbelief and sorrow. However, most of the disciples assembled seemed to be in an expressionless state of composed stillness, observing the doctors, nurses and attendants trying as best as they could to keep the Ven. Sayadaw alive for as long as possible.

The room gradually settled and became silent and still, anticipating that which seemed to be the final moments of the Ven. Sayadaw's life. A doctor then began to check his blood pressure and pulse while the room took on an even greater sense of stillness. During the next few seconds, while the doctor stood leaning over the Ven. Sayadaw's body, the world seemed to stop, and the scene became like a timeless tableau of stillness, as everyone present must have known that the Ven. Sayadaw's existence had come to an end. The doctor removed the stethoscope from his ears and motioned to the other medical assistants who were attending to the Sayadaw to stop what they were doing. The Ven. Sayadaw was declared to have passed away at 1.36 pm, on Saturday, August 14th, 1982, at the age of 78 years old, having just celebrated his birthday a week ago and begun his 59th Vassa as a member of the SANGHA. Mingala U Aung Myint, with hands clapped in salutation, announced to the assembly of SANGHA members and lay disciples that the Ven. Sayadaw had just died. He prefaced that by reminding everyone that the Ven. Sayadaw continually spoke about the way that would take one beyond sorrow, grief and anguish. And through one's own personal effort one could come to know directly that all conditioned phenomena in this universe are impermanent, thereby developing a mind that abided by that fact, and living in a balanced and composed way. He concluded by saying that if we really considered ourselves true disciples of Mahasi Sayadaw and his teachings, we will remember this universal law of transformation and restrain ourselves through this wisdom, which will be a profound example for all who come to pay their final respects to the Ven. Sayadaw, as a visible demonstration of the profundity of the Dhamma.

He then asked Ven. Sayadaw U Pandita to lead the group in chanting a final tribute to the Ven. Sayadaw. We ended the session with recitation of "SADHU, SADHU, SADHU" and for the next few minutes everyone in the room remained quiet, acknowledging in silent homage the passing of the Great DHAMMA Master.

One of the Nayaka Sayadaws of the monastery then asked everyone to leave except for the resident SANGHA and the members of the monastery's governing body, and while everyone was departing a group of us carried the Ven. Sayadaw's body into a small adjacent room. A couple of laymen disciples washed the Ven. Sayadaw's body and a new set of robes was brought and placed on him. Later that evening the Ven. Sayadaw was brought back into the large hall where he now lies in state. A double robe covers his body, leaving just his face and head visible.

News of the Ven. Mahasi Sayadaw's demise rapidly spread

throughout the country, as witnessed by the increasing number of devotees that began streaming into the monastery to offer their final gestures of respect. From early morning until late into the night huge crowds gathered in and around the monastery, often swelling into the thousands, patiently waiting under the nearly constant torrential monsoon rains, each one eventually filing past the Ven. Sayadaw's body in an awesome display of devotion. The large hall where the Ven. Sayadaw's body was placed for viewing was usually filled with people. Many of them sat silently with eyes closed, others chanted softly in a pose of salutation, while the throngs of other devotees continued flowing past the bedside to gain their final glimpse of the late Ven. Sayadaw. Encircling the area where the Ven. Sayadaw's body was lying were a large variety of flower arrangements donated by various disciples, groups and organizations. The entire scene had a pristine quality to it, while retaining an obvious air of solemnity, austerity and simplicity. All duly in accord with how the late Ven. Sayadaw had said such a ceremony should be, some time before his passing away.

Along with the masses of lay disciples who had passed through the monastery this week, so too with members of the Sangha. Almost always large and small groups of **BHIKKHUS**, **SAMANERAS** and nuns could be seen walking slowly around the Ven. Sayadaw's body, showing signs of great reverence and honor. In addition, nearly all of the senior **BHIKKHU** disciples who head the numerous Mahasi branch monasteries throughout the country, an estimated 400 monks in all, traveled to Rangoon to show their respects and to participate in the ceremony. At times during the week when all the **SANGHA** members were gathered, various senior members of the Order would exhort them to be very conscientious of their behavior out of reverence and respect for the reason they were gathered; explaining that whenever they spoke and moved, to try to do so in a composed and tranquil manner; concluding that all of us should continually reflect on the transiency of conditioned existence, and to develop an increasing sense of meditative urgency, using this opportunity of the death of the Ven. Mahasi Sayadaw as a motivating impetus.

At 3 pm on Friday, August 20th, the funeral procession left the

22. THE PASSING AWAY OF THE VENERABLE MAHASI SAYADAW OF BURMA

monastery grounds en route to the indoor crematorium at the Kyandaw Cemetery, approximately four miles away, for the performance of the Ven. Sayadaw's last rites. The motorcade consisted of numerous cars and buses filled with several thousands of the Ven. Sayadaw's Sangha and lay disciples. Mahasi Sayadaw's body was placed in a glass casket surrounded by arrangements of red and white anthuriums and covered above by a canopy of white cloth, while in each corner was elected a large, traditional Burmese fringed white linen umbrella. As the procession slowly moved along the scheduled route to the cemetery under the suddenly cleared skies, tens of thousands of people (a top official from the monastery's governing body gave an estimate of 300 thousand) amassed along the streets; in windows, on balconies and on rooftops, most of them reverentially saluting in final respect to the Ven. Sayadaw as his body passed by. Nearly two hours later, at 5 pm, the procession reached the cemetery grounds, where a massive sea of people had gathered, engulfing graves and tombstones and the otherwise luxuriant green foliage. The vehicle carrying the Ven. Sayadaw's body halted in front of the platform where the hundreds of bhikkhus were seated. The air was extremely tense as the many thousands of devoted onlookers were tightly packed, surrounding the raised platform where the Ven. Sayadaw's body was lying. Everyone's attention appeared to be unified on that one central point. Then in a culminating group acknowledgement of final homage to the late Ven. Sayadaw, the Ven. Sayadaw U Pandita, with the aid of the microphone system, led the massive assembly in a short Pali chant:

"Anicca vata sankhara upada vaya dhammino;
Upajjitva nirujjhanti — tesam vupasamo sukho."
("All conditioned phenomena are impermanent; they have the nature to arise and pass away. Having arisen, they cease — their stilling is (indeed) happiness.")

This was chanted three times and immediately afterwards a group of laymen disciples removed the coffin from the platform and at once it was carried in through the doors of the crematorium a few yards away. The Ven. Mahasi Sayadaw's body was then cremated, and later the ashes and bone relics were collected, to be distributed and enshrined at the end of the rains retreat in November.

Thus, the conclusion of a most solemn and awe-inspiring week left the memory of the late Ven. Mahasi Sayadaw embedded in our minds as one of the greatest masters of the BUDDHA DHAMMA to have lived in modern times. A man who, nearly all of his life, impressed upon those who came to listen the magnitude and nobility of living fully and completely a life that is in accord with the BUDDHA'S Noble Eightfold Path that leads to the overcoming of all suffering.

May all beings live with (in) compassion and wisdom!

Bhikkhu U Aggacara
Mahasi Thathana Yeiktha Rangoon, Burma.
August 22nd, 1982.

And as if such a heavy blow to the Mahasi Empire was not enough, Death claimed another victim on Sunday night, 22nd August, 1982, just two days after the majestic funeral procession of the Grand Master. Only about 3 hours following the Buddha Sasananuggaha Organization's (BSO) appointment of the joint-successors to the throne at MTY, Rangoon, 73-year-old Sayadaw U Sujata, with 53 Vassa, was seized by heart failure at about 8.45 pm. Frantic attempts at resuscitation proved futile, and by 9 pm no signs of life could be detected. The body lay in state for 3 nights, after which funeral rites – simple yet dignified – were performed before cremation took place on 24th August, 1982. News of this latest death was deliberately kept from the ailing Ven. Sayadaw U Javana, who is also afflicted with this treacherous disease of the heart.

On 23rd August, 1982, the BSO ex-co-members invited the Sangha at MTY for a meeting to formally announce the appointment of two Spiritual Advisers over the Rangoon Yeiktha. With the untimely demise of Sayadaw U Sujata, the full burden of MTY's Ovadacariyaship falls upon the firm shoulders of Sayadaw U Panditabhivamsa, who ironically had just celebrated his 61st birthday on Friday, 13th August, 1982.

Bhikkhu Aggacitta
Mahasi Thathana Yeiktha Rangoon, Burma.
27th August, 1982.

22. THE PASSING AWAY OF THE VENERABLE MAHASI SAYADAW OF BURMA

TO NIBBĀNA VIA
THE NOBLE EIGHTFOLD PATH

"In your travels a vehicle takes you to your destination, while those who stand by it are left behind. Knowledge about the Noble Path is like that vehicle. If you ride in it, you will be conveyed to your destination; and if you merely stand by it, you will be left behind. Those who desire to be liberated from all sufferings should use that vehicle. That is to say, they should use knowledge they gained for practical purposes. The most important task for you while you are born into this Buddhasasana is to practice *DHAMMA* so that you get to *NIBBĀNA* where all sufferings cease. The least that you should do is to try to attain the stage of *SOTAPANNA*, the basic step in the liberation from sufferings attending the four nether worlds. To be worthy of this *SASANA* into which you are born, you should strive for liberation from suffering."

VENERABLE MAHASI SAYADAW

AUTHOR PAGE, ALAN CLEMENTS

BOSTON BORN ALAN CLEMENTS, after dropping out of the University of Virginia in his second year, went to the East and become one of the first Westerners to ordain as a Buddhist monk in Myanmar (formerly known as Burma), where he lived at the Mahasi Sasana Yeiktha (MSY) Mindfulness Meditation Centre Yangon (formerly Rangoon) for nearly four years, training in both the practice and teaching of Satipatthana Vipassana (insight) meditation and Buddhist psychology (Abhidhamma), under the guidance of his preceptor the Venerable Mahasi Sayadaw, and his successor Sayadaw U Pandita.

In 1984, forced to leave the monastery by Burma's military authorities, with no reason given, Clements returned to the West and through invitation, lectured widely on the "wisdom of mindfulness," in addition to leading numerous mindfulness-based meditation retreats and trainings throughout the US, Australia, and Canada, including assisting a three month mindfulness teacher training with Sayadaw U Pandita, at the Insight Meditation Society (IMS), in Massachusetts.

In 1988, Alan integrated into his classical Buddhist training a social and political awareness that included global human rights, environmental sanity, and the preciousness of everyday freedom. His efforts working on behalf of oppressed peoples led a former director of Amnesty International to call Alan "one of the most important and compelling voices of our times."

As an investigative journalist Alan has lived in some of the most highly volatile areas of the world. In the jungles of Burma, in 1990, he was one of the first eye-witnesses to document the mass oppression of ethnic minorities by Burma's military dictatorship, which resulted in his first book, *"Burma: The Next Killing Fields?"* (with a foreword by the Dalai Lama).

Shortly thereafter, Alan was invited to the former-Yugoslavia by a senior officer for the United Nations, where, based in Zagreb during the final year of the war, wrote the film *"Burning"* while consulting with NGO's and the United Nation's on the "vital role of consciousness in understanding human rights, freedom, and peace."

In 1995, a French publisher asked Alan to attempt reentering Burma for the purpose of meeting Aung San Suu Kyi, the leader of her country's pro-democracy movement and the recipient of 1991's Nobel Peace Prize. Just released after six years of incarceration, Alan invited Aung San Suu Kyi to share her story with the world, for the purpose of illuminating the philosophical and spiritual underpinnings of her country's courageous nonviolent struggle for freedom, known as a "revolution of the spirit."

The transcripts of their six months of conversations were smuggled out of the country and became the book *"The Voice of Hope."* Translated into numerous languages, *The Voice of Hope* offers insight into the nature totalitarianism, freedom and nonviolent revolution. Said the London Observer: "Clements is the perfect interlocutor....whatever the future of Burma, a possible future for politics itself is illuminated by these conversations."

Clements is also the co-author with Leslie Kean and a contributing photographer to *"Burma's Revolution of the Spirit"* (Aperture, NY) - a large format photographic tribute to Burma's nonviolent struggle for democracy, with a foreword by the Dalai Lama and essays by eight Nobel Peace laureates.

In addition, Clements was the script revisionist and principle adviser for *Beyond Rangoon* (Castle Rock Entertainment), a feature film depicting Burma's struggle for freedom, directed by John Boorman.

In 1999, Alan founded *World Dharma*, a nonsectarian, multicultural, trans-traditional organization of self-styled seekers, artists, writers, scholars, journalists, and activists dedicated to a trans-religious, trans-spiritual independent approach to personal and planetary transformation through the integration of radical authenticity, global human rights, mindful intelligence, and the experiential study of consciousness, with one's life expression through the arts, activism, and service.

In 2002 Alan wrote *"Instinct for Freedom—Finding Liberation Through Living"* (World Dharma Publications), as a spiritual/political memoir it chronicles his life-long pursuit of truth and freedom, while illuminating the framework of the World Dharma vision that forms the basis of the World Dharma Online Institute (WDOI) that he co-founded with his colleague, Jeannine Davies Ph.D., and Vice-President of the Buddha Sasana Foundation.

Instinct for Freedom was nominated for the best spiritual teaching/memoir by the National Spiritual Booksellers Association in 2003 and has been translated into a numerous languages.

Alan's most recent book, *"A Future to Believe In—108 Reflections on the Art and Activism of Freedom"* (World Dharma Publications, 2012), inspired by and dedicated to his daughter Bella, has received distinguished praise from numerous leaders and activists, including Dr. Helen Caldicott, Dr. Joanna Macy, Dr. Vandana Shiva, Bill McKibben, Paul Hawkin, and Derrick Jensen (the environmental poet laureate) who wrote:

"This culture is killing the planet. If we are to have any future at all, we must unlearn everything the culture has taught us and begin to listen to the planet, to listen to life – the core intelligence of nature and the human heart. This book not only helps us with the unlearning process – the greatest challenge humankind has ever faced – it provides the essential wisdom, the spiritual intelligence, to open ourselves to finally start to hear."

Alan is also a political and spiritual satirist, and performs his one person show "Spiritually Incorrect: In Defense of Being, Human," to audiences around the world, as benefits to raise awareness of global human rights, Burma's ongoing struggle for democracy, as well as to highlight the plight of prisoners of conscience, worldwide.

Clements has been interviewed on ABC's Nightline, CBS Evening News, Talk to America, CBC Canada, ABC National Australia, VOA,

BBC, and by the New York Times, London Times, Time and Newsweek magazines, Yoga Journal, Conscious Living, Utne, and scores of other media worldwide.

In addition, Alan has presented to such organizations as Mikhail Gorbachev's State of The World Forum, The Soros Foundation, United Nations Association of San Francisco, the universities of California, Toronto, Sydney, and many others, including a keynote address at the John Ford Theater in Los Angeles for Amnesty International's 30th year anniversary.

Additional books, films and albums by Alan Clements
- A Meditator's Refuge – A Vipassana Insight Reference Guide to Awaken Consciousness and Exit Samsara
- Burma's Voices of Freedom – a four volume set co-authored with Fergus Harlow
- Aung San Suu Kyi From Prison and A Letter to A Dictator, co-authored with Fergus Harlow
- Burma: The Next Killing Fields foreword by the Dalai Lama
- Freedom: Acts of Conscience – A Spoken Word Album
- The Dharma Art of Mindful Intelligence – a 10-hour, 37-chapter video book
- Extinction X-rated – An Auto Fictional Dark Satire About Good and Evil
- Wisdom for the World: Requisites of Reconciliation: Alan Clements in Conversation with Sayadaw U Pandita
- A Deva Appeared Tonight, An Angel of Love (for young people, also with a foreword by the Dalai Lama)
- Facing Death: Alan Clements In Conversation with Reverend Bodhi Be
- Spiritually Incorrect: The Rebel Wisdom of Alan Clements (a feature documentary directed by Peter Downey)
- Spiritually Incorrect: In Defense of Being Human (produced and edited by Ian McKenzie)
- Burning – Love in the Time of Genocide (a screenplay for a feature film, Chartoff Productions)

In 2022, Alan was acknowledged for his "devotion to the service of humanity" and presented with the Visionaries Award as a Hero of Humanity."

Visit Alan Clements website, www.AlanClements.com

"Alan's life is material for a legend. An intellectual artist, freedom fighter, former Buddhist monk, he shares his insights and experience with a passion rarely seen and even more rarely lived. He'll make you think and feel in ways that challenge your entire way of being."
—**CATHERINE INGRAM**, *In the Footsteps of Gandhi and Passionate Presence*

"One of the most important and compelling voices of our times . . . Alan Clements is a riveting communicator – challenging and inspiring. He articulates the essentials of courage and leadership in a way that can stir people from all sectors of society into action; his voice is not only a great contribution during these changeful times, it is a needed one."
—**JACK HEALY**, *former director of Amnesty International, founder, Human Rights Action Center*

"How to describe Alan's presentations? A tall order. Love poems/riffs/odes/chants to the goddesses of compassion, deeply inscribed with the blood of Burmese slaves, soldiers in Iraq, Palestinian children, freedom fighters anywhere. A momentary entry into an internal tête-à-tête, ad infinitum; a glimpse at all that inner discursive dialog which marks us unequivocally as members of the human race. Just in case we get too spiritual, let's not forget that we are required to, by nature, include everything. To paraphrase the Vietnamese monk Thich Nhat Hahn's poem, "Please Call Me by My True Names," I am both the 12-year-old raped girl and the pirate who raped her. It is difficult to reconcile seeming opposites, and it takes the heart of a poet. Thich Nhat Hahn is a poet; Alan is one as well."
—**MARCIA JACOBS**, *a psychotherapist specializing in victims of war, rape, and trauma; a senior U.N. representative for refugees in Bosnia and Croatia, 1993–1997; and a former officer of the International War Crimes Tribunal*

www.ingramcontent.com/pod-product-compliance
Lightning Source LLC
Chambersburg PA
CBHW020245010526
44107CB00002B/114